The Grammenos Library

Commodity Trade and Finance, Second Edition
Michael Tamvakis
(2014)

Port Infrastructure Finance
Hilde Meersman, Eddy Van de Voorde and Thierry Vanelslander
(2014)

Modelling and Shipping in Dry Bulk Forecasting
Shun Chen, Hilde Meersman, Eddy Van de Voorde and Koos Frouws
(2014)

The Handbook of Maritime Economics and Business, Second Edition
Costas Th. Grammenos
(2010)

Future Challenges for the Port and Shipping Sector
Hilde Meersman, Eddy Van de Voorde and Thierry Vanelslander
(2009)

Maritime Safety, Security and Piracy
Wayne Talley
(2008)

Commodity Trade and Finance
Michael Tamvakis
(2007)

The Handbook of Maritime Economics and Business, Second Edition
Costas Th. Grammenos
(2002)

Commodity Trade and Finance

What affects the supply of oil? How important is the weather in determining grain prices? Why has the price of copper skyrocketed?

This unique book analyses the economics of key commodity groups, including energy, agriculture and metals. It examines the supply/demand fundamentals of several major and minor commodities, physical characteristics, production and consumption patterns, trade flows and pricing mechanisms. It also explains the main tools used to hedge price risk, such as futures, options and swaps.

This second edition has been fully revised and restructured, and contains four new chapters, including oil refining, electricity and price risk management for energy, metals and agricultural commodities.

This book is an indispensable reference text for students, academics and those working in the commodity business.

Michael Tamvakis is Professor of Commodity Economics and Finance at Cass Business School, where he lectures in international commodity trade, commodity derivatives and trading, energy economics and shipping economics.

Commodity Trade and Finance

Second Edition

Michael Tamvakis

informa law
from Routledge

Second Edition published 2015
by Informa Law
2 Park Square, Milton Park, Abingdon, Oxon OX14 4RN

and by Informa Law from Routledge
711 Third Avenue, New York, NY 10017

*Informa Law is an imprint of the Taylor & Francis Group,
an informa business*

First Edition published by Informa 2007

Trademark notice: Product or corporate names may be trademarks or
registered trademarks, and are used only for identification and
explanation without intent to infringe.

British Library Cataloguing in Publication Data
A catalogue record for this book is available from the British Library

Library of Congress Cataloging in Publication Data
Tamvakis, Michael N.
Commodity trade and finance/by Michael Tamvakis. – Second
edition.
pages cm. – (The Grammenos library)
Summary: "This second edition has been fully revised and
restructured, and contains four new chapters, including oil refining,
electricity and price risk management for energy, metals and
agricultural commodities"– Provided by publisher.
Includes bibliographical references and index.
ISBN 978-0-415-73245-1 (hardback) – ISBN 978-1-315-76741-3
(ebook) 1. Primary commodities. 2. Primary commodities – Prices.
3. International trade. 4. Commodity exchanges. I. Title.
HF1040.7T36 2015
332.63′28 – dc23
2014033291

ISBN: 978-0-415-73245-1 (hbk)
ISBN: 978-1-315-76741-3 (ebk)

Typeset in Plantin
by Florence Production Ltd, Stoodleigh, Devon, UK

Printed by Bell & Bain Ltd, Glasgow

To Rebecca, Nicholas and Artemis

Contents

List of exhibits

Chapter 1

Chapter 2

Chapter 3

Chapter 4

Chapter 5

Chapter 6

Chapter 7

Chapter 8

Chapter 9

Chapter 10

Chapter 11

Chapter 12

Chapter 13

Chapter 14

Chapter 15

Chapter 16

1 Fundamental energy economics

Although all main groups of commodities are of paramount importance to our everyday lives, energy is the one that manages to capture our immediate attention, particularly in times of crises. Both by value and volume, energy constitutes the largest of the key commodity groups (the other two being metals and agriculture).

We start by looking at the fundamental economics of energy, before focusing on the key commodities making up this group. We elaborate on the economics of demand for, and supply of, exhaustible energy resources. The role and cross-substitutability of alternative energy resources will also be discussed, and subsequent chapters will elaborate on the three main commodities in this group: crude oil and refined products, natural gas, and coal. Finally, we will also take a brief look at the electricity industry. Although less thought of as a commodity, electricity is important, not only because it absorbs substantial amounts of primary energy commodities for its generation, but also because, in the last few decades, it has become a tradable commodity itself.

Definition and measurement of energy

First of all, it is worth taking a moment to consider two seemingly simple questions: 'What is energy?' and 'How do we measure it?' To answer the first question, the OED helps us by providing a formal definition:

> energy / ˈɛnədʒi / noun
>
> [French énergie or late Latin energia from Greek energeia (ἐνέργεια), formed as EN- (ἐν) ergon (ἔργον) work]
>
> . . . . . .
>
> 6 SCIENCE The ability to do work, i.e. move a body. Orig., that possessed by a body by virtue of its motion b→ This ability provided in a readily utilized form, such as electric current or piped gas; resources that can be drawn on for this purpose.

This definition immediately highlights that energy can appear in different forms. Boyle (2004, pp. 4–6) gives a brief but comprehensive review of energy forms and summarises four basic ones: *kinetic, gravitational, electrical* and *nuclear*. Obvious examples of *kinetic* energy would be the wind spinning a turbine, human and animal power, or a wound spring. *Gravitational* is the energy stored in an object that is lifted against the gravitational pull of the earth. Water stored in a dam is an example of stored (or potential) gravitational energy, and when the water is released it can transfer its energy to spinning a generator that produces electricity. *Electrical* energy, at its most fundamental level, is what keeps charged subatomic particles together into atoms and atoms into molecules. At this level, chemical energy can also be considered as electrical energy, which is then turned into heat (via kinetic energy) once a chemical reaction is in progress. Electrical energy is, of course, associated with electric currents, or the much more familiar electricity, which is an intermediary energy form that is generated using a number of different methods (burning a fuel, spinning a wind turbine, using a photovoltaic cell and so on), travels from a generator to a consumption point and is eventually transformed into another form of energy (light, heat, kinetic energy) that is required by the final consumer. Finally, *nuclear* is the basic energy form embodied in atomic nuclei. Changing of these atomic nuclei, either by fission (splitting) of heavier elements, such as uranium, or fusion of lighter elements, such as hydrogen, releases large amounts of heat. A common example of the former reaction is what happens in a nuclear reactor, while the latter is what produces the energy emitted by the sun.

It is already evident from the above that the various types of energy do not work in isolation. On the contrary, what we observe continuously are various types of energy transforming from one form to another. This is then a good point to mention the first law of thermodynamics, which has to do with energy conservation. This states that the energy in an isolated system is constant. Energy can be transformed from one form to another but cannot be created or destroyed. This leads on to the second law of thermodynamics, that of entropy. In a commercial context, this is quite an important property, because it leads to the issue of energy efficiency (i.e. how much of the energy that is transformed can be channelled to useful applications, rather than waste heat). For example, the amount of kinetic energy that can be created from the chemical reaction of burning a fuel determines how efficient a car engine is – this is most commonly expressed in terms of mileage per gallon or litres per 100 kilometres. In a similar fashion, the amount of electricity generated by burning a metric ton of coal or a cubic metre of methane (natural gas) determines the efficiency of the respective power station.

Having established the very basic definition of energy, it is now time to move to another fundamental aspect: measurement. From a physicist's point of view, energy is measured in standard units, irrespective of the source from which it originates. Several such units are in use, including BTUs (British thermal units), therms, calories and joules. Unfortunately, these units are not sufficient for covering all the various aspects of the business of producing, trading and consuming energy, so it is important to be familiar with at a least a few conversions between various units, depending on the context.

The world's scientific community came together in 1960 to establish the International System of Units, which is commonly abbreviated to SI, from the French Système International d'Unités. The system has several standard units, starting from seven base units that are based on the metre-kilogram-second system. In this system, the *joule* (J) is the base unit of energy. It is the energy expended in applying a force of one *newton* over a distance of one metre (also known as one N•m or newton-metre); or in passing an electric current of one *ampere* through a resistance of one *ohm* for one second. The SI also devised a system of prefixes that act as decimal-based multipliers. Exhibit 1.1 shows a list of these prefixes with their associated multipliers.

The joule is a very useful unit, but it is not very often that we see it used in the everyday parlance of the energy business. Depending on one's viewpoint, business is conducted in a number of different units. For an oil trader buying or selling a cargo of crude oil, a barrel is relevant for quoting the price and a ton is relevant for agreeing the freight rate. For a procurement manager of a coal-fired power station, a ton is relevant for buying coal, but the calorific content (in kcal/ton) is also very important in order to assess the quality of the particular coal in generating heat, which will eventually generate the electricity, which will be sold by the kilowatt-hour. Thus, it is still very important to have a good grasp of a number of different units and indeed to be able to perform basic energy conversions. So what does one need to measure? There are four main categories of measurements that are relevant in the energy business: heat, work/electric energy, mass/weight and volume. One or more of these types of measurement are necessary for nearly every economic and commercial aspect of energy, including production, consumption, trading, transportation, storage, pricing and conversion between different types of energy. Following are definitions for key energy units, with conversions between these units given in Exhibit 1.2. We start with heat units first.

Joule: Reprised from above, a joule is the energy expended in applying a force of one *newton* over a distance of one metre (also known as one N•m or

Name	deca-	hecto-	kilo-	mega-	giga-	terra-	peta-	exa-	zetta-	yotta-
Symbol	da	h	k	M	G	T	P	E	Z	Y
Factor	$\times 10^1$	$\times 10^2$	$\times 10^3$	$\times 10^6$	$\times 10^9$	$\times 10^{12}$	$\times 10^{15}$	$\times 10^{18}$	$\times 10^{21}$	$\times 10^{24}$

Name	deci-	centi-	milli-	micro-	nano-	pico-	femto-	atto-	zepto-	yocto-
Symbol	d	c	m	μ	n	p	f	a	z	y
Factor	$\times 10^{-1}$	$\times 10^{-2}$	$\times 10^{-3}$	$\times 10^{-6}$	$\times 10^{-9}$	$\times 10^{-12}$	$\times 10^{-15}$	$\times 10^{-18}$	$\times 10^{-21}$	$\times 10^{-24}$

Exhibit 1.1 SI prefixes and corresponding multipliers
Source: Author

newton-metre); or in passing an electric current of one *ampere* through a resistance of one *ohm* for one second.

BTU or *Btu*: A British thermal unit is equivalent to about 1,055 J or 1.055 kJ. It is the amount of energy approximately needed to heat one pound (1 lb = 0.454 kg) of water from 39 to 40° F (3.88 to 4.44° C) at a constant pressure of one atmosphere (1 atm or 1 bar or 100,000 pascal). It is common for Btu to be quoted in thousands or million. However, the prefixes used are non-SI. So MBtu is used for a thousand Btu (M is taken from the roman numeral for 1,000) and MMBtu us used for a million Btu. An MMBtu is very commonly used for natural gas, and indeed natural gas prices in the US market are quoted in $/MMBtu.

Therm: A therm is simply 100,000 Btu, so that 10 therms (a decatherm) are 1 MMBtu. A therm is commonly used in the UK natural gas market, whereby prices are quoted in pence/therm.

Calorie or *cal*: A calorie is the amount of energy approximately needed to heat one gram of air-free water by 1° C at standard atmospheric pressure. It is about 4.2 J, with 1 kcal = 1,000 cal = 4.2 kJ.

We now move on to work and electric energy units.

Watt or *W*: A watt is the power equal to the work done at the rate of one joule per second or to the power produced by a current of one ampere across a potential difference of one volt. It is most commonly used in the electricity industry or anything related to electrical applications, although it can also be found in automotive applications, for example when measuring the power generated by a car engine. Its multiples, especially kW, MW and GW, are often used to measure the generating capacity of power stations, or the load of an electrical system.

Watt-hour or *Wh*: Extending the concept of the watt over time, a watt-hour is simply the amount of energy generated or used at the rate of 1 W (1 J/s) over one hour. From this definition, it is quite easy to calculate that 1 Wh is equivalent to 3,600 J and, in a similar fashion, 1 kWh is equal to 3,600 kJ or 3.6 MJ. Panel A of Exhibit 1.2 shows the equivalence of the various units we have discussed so far.

From the point of view of production, consumption, transportation and trading of energy commodities, it is mass and weight units that are mostly used. Some of the most common units are described below.

Barrel or *bbl* (*bbls* in the plural form): Historically, there have been a lot of goods shipped into barrels, both dry and liquid. Indeed, barrels, casks, tuns and kegs are but a few of the terms used to describe the various versions of cylindrical (or quasi-cylindrical) containers, which come in lots of different specifications. The definition of a barrel in the energy industry is closely associated with crude oil and its refined products, and also other derived products such as lubricants. A barrel of oil is a unit of volume and is defined as 42 US gallons or 35 imperial gallons, which is equivalent to approximately 158.987 litres. This has been the standard in the US market since the very beginning of the oil industry in the second half of the nineteenth century and is now commonly used to measure crude oil production, consumption and trade.

As the number of barrels produced, consumed or traded in a year is quite staggering, it has become commonplace to refer to oil production, consumption or trade in terms of *barrels per day*, abbreviated to *bpd* or *b/d*. The quotation in *bpd* is quite useful because oil flow at the well head is usually measured in this unit, so that short-term (less than a year) supply changes become easier to comprehend in the market. In fact, this unit of measure is so popular that other energy commodities are often expressed in terms of *barrels of oil equivalent* or *boe*. Last, but not least, the price of oil itself, which is one of the most important energy benchmarks for the world economy, is expressed in $/bbl.

A final note on this unit is the rather odd abbreviation *bbl*. For some time, this was thought to be an abbreviation of 'blue barrel', named after the practice of oil companies (essentially Standard Oil in the US) to paint oil barrels blue, in order to distinguish them from other barrels used in trade. More recently, this version is being contested, as there seem to be cargo manifests where the abbreviation *bbl* predates the existence of the oil industry itself. It is now thought that *bbl* was used to differentiate a barrel from a *bale*, another unit of measurement, whose abbreviation was *bl*. Whatever the explanation is, the fact remains that the barrel is right at the centre of the oil business in particular, and the energy business at large.

Tonne or *metric ton*: A tonne is an SI unit of mass equal to 1,000 kg. It is probably the most widely used unit in international commodity trade and, of course, in energy. It is quite common for production, consumption and trade data to be recorded in tonnes per year (or *per annum*, abbreviated to *tpa*). It can also be referred to as a *metric ton*, to distinguish it from the two other types of ton: the *imperial* or *long ton* (2,240 lb) and the *US* or *short ton* (2,000 lb). The metric ton, by contrast, equals 2,204.6 lb. Another interesting relationship is that of the metric ton with the barrel. Strictly speaking, there is no exact equivalence of the two, as a barrel is a unit of volume, whereas a metric ton is a unit of mass. What links the two is the specific gravity of whatever is the commodity in question. As crude oil is commonly measured in both units, it is useful to know how to translate from one to the other. Crude oils come in many different quality specifications, with specific gravities varying from 0.75 to sometimes over 1 (for very heavy crude oils), and the number of barrels in a metric tonne vary as well. A rough approximation would be 6.5 to 7.5 barrels per metric ton, although it is common to use a convention when aggregating data on a worldwide basis. One such convention, used by the BP Statistical Review of Energy, is 7.33 barrels per metric ton, and is given in Panel B of Exhibit 1.2. In the same panel, there is also a conversion between the two most popular ways of summarising oil production and consumption: million barrels per day (mbpd) and million tonnes per annum (mtpa). This is simply calculated by using the simple formula: 1 mbpd × 365 (days) ÷ 7.33 (barrels per tonne) = 49.8 mtpa. For the same reason, the barrel/tonne equivalence for oil products also varies according to the specific gravity of the products. Lighter products, such as gasoline, have more barrels to the metric ton, when compared to heavier products, such as fuel oil.

Panel D in Exhibit 1.2 records some of these conversions. Finally, the importance of oil as a source of primary energy has meant that agents both within and outside the industry are very interested in measuring overall energy metrics (in particular, consumption) using a common base. This base is the *tonne of oil equivalent (toe)*. Panel C in Exhibit 1.2 shows a few indicative conversions of some of the most popular energy units into tonnes of oil equivalent.

Cubic metre or *cu m* or *cbm*: A cubic metre is a unit of volume derived from the SI system and represents the volume of a cube with sides one metre long. It is equal to 1,000 litres and is, therefore, also known as a kilolitre. The mass of a cubic metre of a particular cargo depends on its specific gravity. A cubic metre of water, for example, at a temperature of $4°$ C and at atmospheric pressure, weighs one metric tonne. In energy, the cubic metre is used for commodities that are relatively light and voluminous, such as natural gas and other liquid petroleum gases.

Cubic foot or *CF* or *cu ft* or *cbf*: Similar to the cubic metre, a cubic foot represents the volume of a cube with sides one foot (0.3048 metres) long. This is a non-SI unit, used extensively in the US and the UK, particularly in relation to natural gas. Like in the case of Btu, multiples of cubic feet are denoted with roman numerals; hence, MCF stands for one thousand cubic feet and MMCF stands for one million cubic feet. Both cubic metres and cubic feet emphasise the measurement of volume for natural gas, but the energy equivalence is also

Panel A: Energy units

	kJ	kcal	Btu	kWh
kJ	1	0.239	0.948	0.278×10^{-3}
kcal	4.187	1	3.968	1.162×10^{-3}
Btu	1.055	0.252	1	0.293×10^{-3}
kWh	3,600	860	3,412	1

Panel B: Crude oil

1 metric ton	7.33 barrels
1 barrel	42 US gallons
1 mbpd	49.8 mtpa

Panel C: One tonne oil equivalent (toe)

10 Gcal (10^6 kcal)	42 GJ	40 MMBtu
1.5 mt bituminous coal (on average)	3 mt lignite (on average)	7.33 boe
12 MWh	1,111 cu.m. NG	0.82 mt LNG

Panel D: Oil products

1 metric ton	Barrels
LPG	11.6
Gasoline	8.5
Kerosene	7.8
Gas oil/Diesel	7.5
Residual fuel oil	6.7

Panel E: Natural gas and LNG

1,000 cu.ft NG	28.3 cu.m	1.011 MMBtu	0.025 toe	0.19 boe
1,000 cu.m NG	35,300 cu.ft	35.7 MMBtu	0.9 toe	6.6 boe
1 mt LNG	1,360 cu.m	48,000 cu.ft	48.6 MMBtu	1.22 toe

Exhibit 1.2 Common energy conversion units

Source: Author

important. Panel E in Exhibit 1.2 shows typical conversions between various units of natural gas, as well as liquefied natural gas (LNG).

Although there may be more units in use in the energy business, the units defined above are probably the most widely used, and a good grasp of them will aid the reader when going through this and subsequent chapters, in our discussion of the economics of the energy industry and its key commodities.

Supply of energy

Like other minerals, energy commodities fall in the category of exhaustible resources. Available reserves, rates of extraction and economic rents are some of the parameters governing the usage of exhaustible resources. The theory behind this was explored early in the twentieth century. In his seminal paper, Hotelling (1931) built the basic economic framework for the exploitation of non-renewable natural resources. However, Hotelling's ideas lay dormant for the next 40 or so years, until economic thinking around the optimal rate of exhaustible resources came to the fore owing to the rapid depletion of oil in the United States and its increasing reliance on imports. In 1973, the first oil crisis focused the world's attention even more on questions about resource depletion, optimal extraction paths and ownership. Interest in Hotelling's theory gained momentum, so much so that the Ely lecture at the American Economic Association delivered by Robert Solow in 1974 focused solely on the economics of resources (Solow 1974b). In his seminal paper, Hotelling is looking at the question of producing exhaustible resources (he refers to oil and mining in particular) as an inter-temporal decision that depends on the price of resource now and in the future, which are linked with the interest rate. His formula assumes the simple form $p_t = p_0 e^{rt}$, whereby p_t is the price of the resource at a future time t (after deducting extraction and other costs) in the future, p is the price in the current period and r is the rate of interest. Assuming free competition (Hotelling also discusses the monopoly case later in the same paper), the resource producer is indifferent between receiving p now or p_t in the future, and hence the price of the resource must grow at a rate equal to the rate of interest.[1] This implies that, sooner or later, the various producers will make their resource available to the market, starting from the cheapest producer and moving on to the most expensive one, until the price becomes so high and either demand is killed off, or the resource is depleted. So the production path for a particular exhaustible resource becomes a problem of choosing whether to derive utility from the resource now or defer it for the future. A practical discussion of this issue is provided by Nordhaus (1973), who discusses the case of the United States as an energy producer and consumer, with the ability to trade freely. He (interestingly) concludes that:

---

1   For a further discussion of Hotelling's work, see Devarajan and Fisher (1981). A more expansive discussion of the economics of non-renewable resources is also given in Bhattacharyya (2011).

as a long-run policy it would be unwise to jack up the prices of energy products in the interests of artificially preserving energy resources. Nor does a more drastic policy of permanently rationing resources make sense. As long as investment yields around 10 percent, it seems best to use the cheap resources now and to put the real resources thereby saved to work on producing synthetic fuels later.

What is also implied from the above is that the problem is not just one of inter-temporal choice for one generation, but becomes one of resource allocation across generations. This poses the even bigger question of intergenerational equity: should the current generation save resources for future generations, or derive utility from the resource (and deplete it) now and invest some of this utility in capital goods for the following generations? I do not attempt to answer this question, as it is beyond the scope of this text, but the interested reader is directed to Solow (1974a), Hartwick (1977) and Solow (1986). For a broader discussion on how the discussion of exhaustible resource allocation by the previous authors fits in the context of political philosophy, a good starting point is Rawls (1999).

Returning now to a more microeconomic context, basic economic theory anticipates that each additional unit (the 'marginal' unit) of a natural resource will be extracted as long as the economic cost of extraction – which includes marginal cost[2] and user cost[3] – is lower or equal to the price[4] paid for the resource plus the marginal utility[5] of present consumption. Like in most production processes, extractive firms benefit initially from increasing returns to scale, then their average total cost curve stays flat for some time after reaching the minimum efficient scale, and if they decide to increase output further they are usually faced with decreasing returns to scale. In the long run, production tends to stabilise along the bottom of their long-run average total cost curve. Exhibit 1.3 shows the relationship between short-run and long-run average cost curves.

The theory, as it stands, implies that high-cost producers – which may also have limited reserves – should be the first to be squeezed out of the market when energy prices fall and operating costs are not covered. It also implies that large low-cost producers should be relatively immune to price downswings, and continue to produce under all – but the most extreme – market conditions. Alas, real life is not as clear-cut as this model suggests. To take

---

2   Marginal cost is the cost of extracting one additional unit of the commodity. This often includes the operating cost, a fixed cost element and possibly an allowance for the cost of capital investment required to achieve extra production.

3   User cost is usually defined as 'the present value of the resource foregone when a unit of the commodity is produced today rather than tomorrow'. Although a more 'academic' concept of cost, it becomes quite relevant when environmental concerns become of substance.

4   The price may also include a 'normal' rate of return on the investment undertaken.

5   The utility/satisfaction gained by bringing production forward (i.e. producing an additional unit today rather than tomorrow).

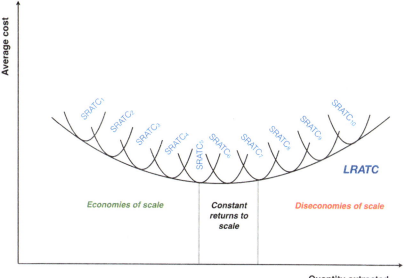

Average cost

SRATC₁ SRATC₂ SRATC₃ SRATC₄ SRATC₅ SRATC₆ SRATC₇ SRATC₈ SRATC₉ SRATC₁₀

LRATC

Economies of scale

Constant returns to scale

Diseconomies of scale

Quantity extracted

SRATC = short-run average total cost
LRATC = long-run average total cost

Exhibit 1.3 Long-run average total cost curve

Source: Author

an example from the oil industry: although Middle East countries are indisputably among the lowest-cost producers, it is high-cost producers that seem to be operating at full capacity, while low-cost competitors seem to play the role of 'swing' producer, balancing demand and supply. Why is that the case, then? There are quite a lot of other factors that make the up the 'puzzle' that is energy supply. Technology is one such factor, in fact a very important one. It is the relentless technological innovation, particularly in oil and gas exploration, which has brought on stream reserves that would have been economically unviable in the past. These are the so-called *unconventional* reserves, which we discuss later.

The puzzle becomes even more complicated when government policies are taken into account. Just as a brief example, let us look at energy policies first and then fiscal regimes. Energy supplies are of strategic importance to every government worldwide. If they are in abundance, they will be used to cover domestic needs and the balance will probably be exported; if they are in short supply, the government will resort to imports and a certain amount of stockpiling for security. In the case of a net importer of the energy resource, if security of supply is a major issue, then import demand may be directed towards more 'secure' (perhaps high-cost) suppliers, who can ensure continuous flow of the commodity, with a very low probability of supply disruption, whether for operational or geopolitical reasons. A net exporter of an energy resource, on the other hand, seeks to maximise financial flows from exports.

To do so, the exporter will probably put in place fiscal regulations, which try to optimise financial gain (through taxation, production sharing agreements and so forth) from energy production and exports, while trying to maintain the momentum for exploration and production activity in the country.

Energy projects use capital quite intensively and embody a substantial amount of risk. Even when adequate reserves are found, the high rate of discount applied to such projects makes the extraction of the commodity more desirable sooner rather than later. In any project for the extraction of mineral resources, there are three main stages: exploration, development and production. Exploration may last a few years, until proper geological surveys point with high probability to the existence of reserves. Several exploratory wells/shafts may have to be drilled in order to assess the quality and extent of the deposits. Costs at this stage can be substantial and are sunk. The development stage involves extensive drilling in the case of oil and gas, and construction of an open pit or underground mine in the case of coal. Again, costs at this stage are sunk, and further costs might have to be incurred at later stages of a project, in order to improve and/or extend capacity. One more point: the costs incurred at the exploration and development stage are often known by a number of different names. Depending on the source, the terms *capital costs*, *development costs*, *investment costs* and *finding costs* have all been used to the same effect.

The prevalent fiscal regime in a particular reserve-holding country is extremely important for all stages of the extraction and trading of the mineral resource. Earlier, we looked at the concepts of marginal cost and user cost. In doing so, we neglected momentarily the fiscal cost imposed by the government of the country where production takes place. For an energy producer (especially for mineral hydrocarbons such as oil, gas and coal) to be allowed to operate, the government, via its nominated agency (typically a ministry or other administrative body) must grant its permission, in exchange for an economic rent. This economic rent is normally extracted using a variety of instruments that fall into two broad categories of fiscal regimes: tax and royalty, and production share agreements or contracts (PSA or PSC). We will have a brief look at both regimes in later chapters, but the keen reader is directed to Johnston (2013) and Kasriel and Wood (2013), who provide a very detailed and practical account of such regimes in the oil industry. For now, it is worth mentioning that the financial implications of such regimes can make all the difference to the viability of the extraction of particular energy resources, either by increasing the overall production cost of a relatively easy-to-extract resource or by providing incentives to extract a relatively 'difficult' resource.

If we again ignore taxes, royalties and other government levies, at the production stage most of the costs are operating costs (also known as *lifting costs*), which tend to increase as reserves are being depleted and more effort is required to extract them. As a result, another important characteristic of the energy sector (and the mineral sector at large) is the large extent of heterogeneity in production costs. Depending on the geomorphology of the field and local climatic conditions, costs can vary considerably from one region

Region	Lifting (production) costs & production taxes	Finding (exploration) costs	Total upstream costs
United States			
On-shore	$10.69	$18.65	$29.34
Off-shore	$8.83	$41.51	$50.34
Average	$10.28	$21.58	$31.86
Other World			
Canada	$14.82	$12.07	$26.89
Europe	$10.75	$42.32	$53.07
Former Soviet Union	$8.59	$13.92	$22.51
Africa	$9.93	$35.01	$44.94
Middle East	$8.92	$6.99	$15.91
Other Eastern Hemisphere	$7.87	$7.64	$15.51
Other Western Hemisphere	$5.69	$20.43	$26.12

Exhibit 1.4 Comparative costs for producing oil and gas, 2007–2009

Source: Author, compiled with data from EIA (2011, Tables 10 and 11)

to the next. In the oil sector, for instance, capital expenditure for field development may range from 'low-cost' to 'frontier areas'. Exhibit 1.4 shows a range of average production costs in various parts of the world. These are reported by US companies that operate around the world and report back to the Energy Intelligence Agency of the US Department of Energy. They do not reflect the full range of costs incurred across all oil and gas fields, but give a good idea of how broad this range can be. A similar situation is evident in the coal industry, with Indonesia being at the low-cost end of production and Russia at the high-cost end (see Exhibit 1.5).

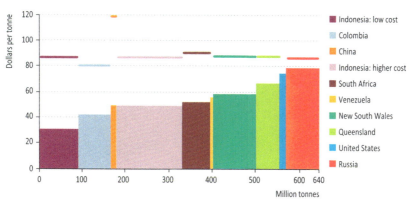

Notes: Prices, costs and volumes are adjusted to 6 000 kcal/kg. Boxes represent FOB costs and bars show FOB prices.

Sources: IEA Clean Coal Centre analysis partly based on Marston, IHS Global Insight and Wood Mackenzie.

Exhibit 1.5 Indicative supply costs and prices for internationally traded steam coal, 2010

Source: IEA (2012c, Figure 11.5, p. 406)

We will revisit the supply-side economics of the individual energy commodities in their respective chapter, but having covered some of the common fundamentals, it is now time to move to the demand side.

Demand for energy

In 2012, the world consumed nearly 12.5 billion *toe* of primary energy. The vast majority, some 87 per cent, came from hydrocarbons, with oil still at the top, coal firmly established in second place and natural gas in third (see Exhibit 1.6). The remaining primary energy was produced as primary electricity produced by water or nuclear fission, with only a meagre 2 per cent produced by all other forms of renewable generation. Each one of us, on average, consumed ca. 1,900 kilograms of oil equivalent (*kgoe*), but the inequality in the consumption patterns could not be wider. At the top of the list, Iceland and Qatar consumed more than 17,000 kgoe per capita and, at the bottom, Eritrea was at ca 130 kgoe.

The need for energy commodities is relatively recent, compared to the need for other commodities such as food and metals. In older societies, such a need was satisfied with readily available natural resources (such as fuelwood), natural forces (such as wind) and sheer manpower. With the widespread use of hydrocarbons in all aspects of economic activity, however, consumption of energy commodities has been closely linked with a nation's development and its transition from a traditional, agriculture-based economy, to a developed, industrialised one. On an aggregate basis, it is reasonable to assume that energy consumption is directly related to the level of gross domestic product (GDP).

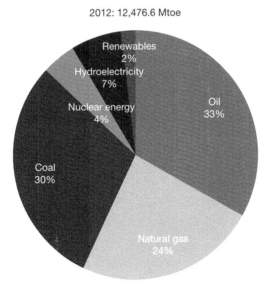

2012: 12,476.6 Mtoe

Exhibit 1.6 World primary energy consumption by fuel source

Source: Author, compiled with data from BP (2013)

Exhibit 1.7 shows the development of world GDP, expressed as an annual percentage change, and primary energy consumption since 1965. As can be seen, over the course of the last half-century the world has consumed increasing amounts of energy. With relatively few interruptions, world primary energy consumption increased from under 4 billion toe in 1965 to over 12 billion toe in 2012. A recent poignant example is that of China, which has transformed itself into the world's industrial powerhouse from the beginning of the new millennium onwards. In the process, China climbed up the ranks to become the world's largest energy consumer, with over one-fifth of the global primary energy consumption, as much as the whole of North America, and only slightly less than the whole of Europe and the former Soviet republics put together. Exhibit 1.8 shows the shares of primary energy consumed in key geographical regions in 2012.

The notion of a straightforward relationship between energy consumption and GDP is quite appealing, but rather simplistic. One has to look at the disaggregated picture of energy consumption to get a more accurate idea of the underlying demand parameters. Primary energy consumption is usually classified into four broad categories: industrial, transport, other (including residential and agriculture) and a fourth residual category encompassing all non-energy uses. Exhibit 1.9 shows an example of energy usage in OECD countries, by fuel, in 2011.

Given the diversity of sectors that require energy in large amounts and the choices of fuels available to generate this energy, it often makes sense to look

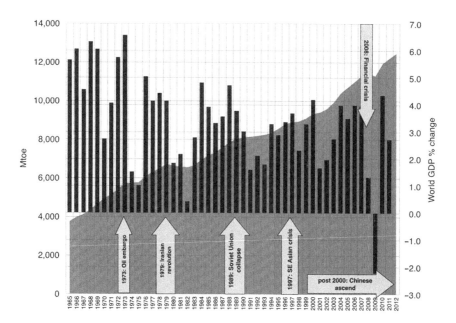

Exhibit 1.7 Changes in world GDP and energy consumption

Source: Author, compiled with data from BP (2013) and World Bank (2013)

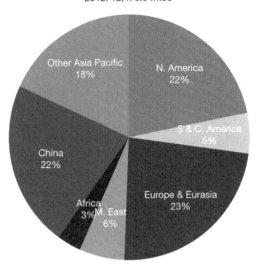

Exhibit 1.8 World primary energy consumption by major region
Source: Author, compiled with data from BP (2013)

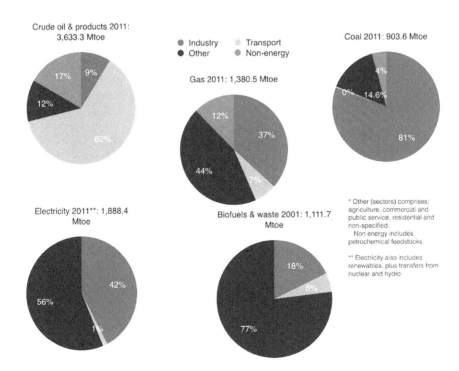

Exhibit 1.9 OECD energy consumption by fuel and sector
Source: Author, compiled with data from IEA (2012a)

at demand within each individual sector and for each individual fuel. This approach is otherwise known as *disaggregated* or *decomposed* demand analysis. This is the approach taken, for example, by various research and policy organisations when building their energy forecast models. This consists of demand from a number of sub-sectors for finished energy 'products' (electricity, natural gas, refined petroleum products, biofuels and so on), which then filter up the energy chain to generate demand for the fuels that produce these energy 'products' (coal, oil, gas and so on). An illustrative example of this is given in Exhibit 1.10, which shows the basic structure of the IEA's forecasting model.

Another example of actual energy flows this time is given in Exhibit 1.11, a typical energy flow chart showing the fuels (indigenous and imported) used to generate energy in the UK and how this energy flows to final consumer groups, either in their raw form (e.g. natural gas) or after they have been transformed to secondary products (e.g. electricity or refined petroleum products).

Another issue worth discussing is that of energy intensity, which is also closely associated with energy efficiency. In its most abstract form, energy intensity simply apportions the amount of energy consumed over whichever metric is relevant to the individual analyst. If, for example, the focus is usage of energy per person per year, then a relevant energy intensity metric would be energy consumed in, say, tonnes of oil equivalent per capita per year (see Exhibit 1.12). If, on the other hand, the focus is on energy consumption as

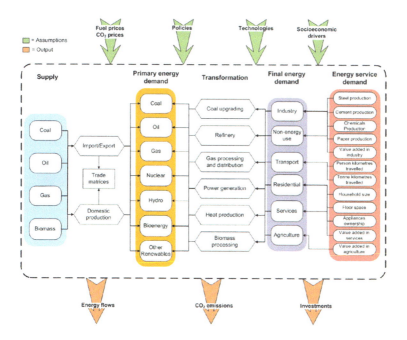

Exhibit 1.10 IEA world energy model overview
Source: IEA (2012b, p. 7)

Energy Flow Chart 2012
(million tonnes of oil equivalent)

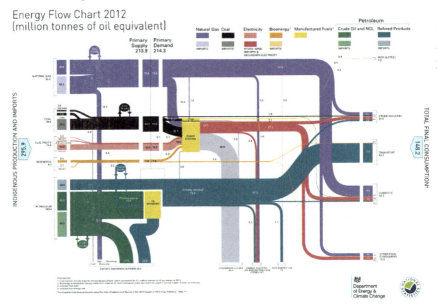

Exhibit 1.11 UK energy flow chart, 2012

Source: DECC (2013)

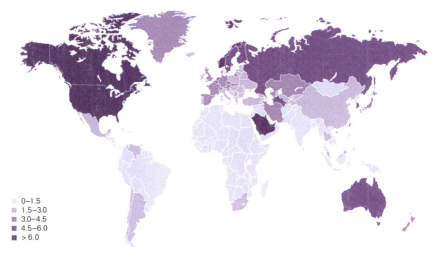

- 0–1.5
- 1.5–3.0
- 3.0–4.5
- 4.5–6.0
- > 6.0

Per capita energy consumption per annum in toe

Exhibit 1.12 Energy consumption per capita per annum

Source: BP (2013)

part of the income generated in an economy, a more appropriate metric is consumption, say in toe again, but this time per unit or income, typically $1,000 of GDP. Exhibit 1.13 shows the development path for a number of economies over the last 30 years, using this particular metric.

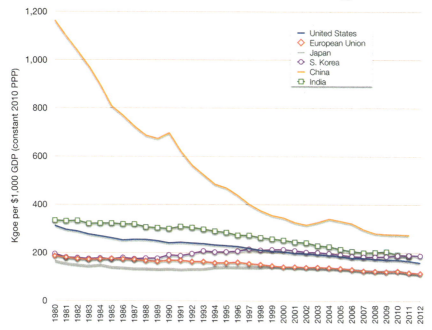

Exhibit 1.13 Development of energy consumption per unit of income around the world

Source: Author, compiled with data from World Bank (2013)

Given the development path for energy consumption so far, what does the future hold? Although the scope of this text does not cover forecasting for any of the commodities discussed, it is interesting to have a quick look at what two of the most eminent energy organisations have to say: the IEA and the EIA. Using its well-documented World Energy Model (WEM), the IEA produces a number of demand forecasts, short-, medium- and long-term, for individual fuels, as well as overall regional and world demand. As is common practice in economic modelling, the WEM produces a number of forecasts, based on a number of scenarios. For its long-term forecasts, the IEA has been using three main scenarios: Current Policies,[6] New Policies[7] and 450 Scenario[8]

6 Government policies that had been enacted or adopted by mid-2012 continue unchanged. The objective is to provide a baseline that shows how energy markets would evolve if underlying trends in energy demand and supply are not changed.

7 Existing policies are maintained and recently announced commitments and plans, including those yet to be formally adopted, are implemented in a cautious manner. The objective is to provide a benchmark to assess the potential achievements (and limitations) of recent developments in energy and climate policy.

8 Policies are adopted that put the world on a pathway that is consistent with having around a 50 per cent chance of limiting the global increase in average temperature to 2° C in the long term, compared with pre-industrial levels. The objective is to demonstrate a plausible path to achieve the climate target.

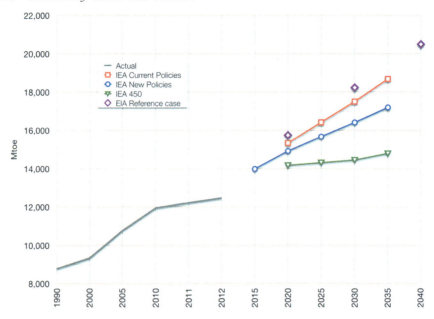

Exhibit 1.14 IEA and EIA forecasts for total primary energy demand to 2040

Source: Author, compiled with data from IEA (2012c) and EIA (2013b)

(IEA 2012b). Exhibit 1.14 shows the three scenarios and also incorporates the reference (base case) scenario of the demand forecast produced by the EIA. One can immediately observe that, under all scenarios, demand is set to rise and, if demand continues at the current pace, it is set to rise by another 50 per cent by 2030, and even more beyond that. Both agencies also break down their forecasts into a number of regions, which can then be aggregated again into OECD and non-OECD countries. Using this categorisation, Exhibit 1.15 reports the EIA reference case forecast, which clearly shows the increased importance of the non-OECD bloc in energy consumption and how this trend is to become even stronger in years to come. Let us now turn to the individual sectors that generate this demand.

Industrial consumption

Industry is, of course, one of the heaviest energy users. Each industrial sector uses a number of different production factors, including capital, labour, raw materials and, of course, energy. For example, to produce steel (in a basic oxygen converter), we need iron ore, steel scrap, limestone and other alloying metals (such as manganese), in addition to coking coal, which is our energy input. This is, of course, on the assumption that capital (in the form of the steel mill) and skilled labour are already in place. The combination of these production factors yields different levels of production of the particular good, depending always on the technical characteristics of each industrial process.

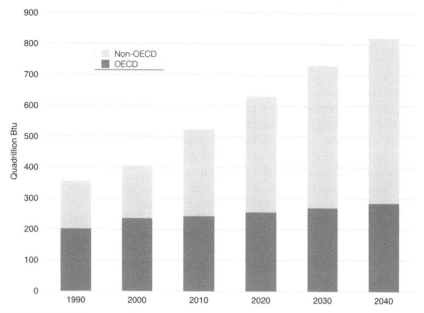

Exhibit 1.15 EIA forecast for total primary energy demand to 2040 by major country group

Source: Author, compiled with data from EIA (2013b)

The production cost of an industrial process depends – in the short to medium term – on the cost of its inputs and a set of fixed costs; in the long term, of course, all costs are variable. The production cost function can be formally written as $C = f(X_1, X_2, \ldots X_n, E, FC)$, where $X_1, X_2, \ldots X_n$ are production inputs, E is energy and FC is fixed cost. This function represents a slight deviation from the usual norm of depicting production costs as a function of capital and labour, and is more suitable for our purposes. The objective of each producer is to minimise costs, and this may be done by a number of combinations of production factors, which give him the same minimum cost for each level of production. In economic parlance, these various combinations can be plotted in an *isoquant* curve. Exhibit 1.16 shows a number of these curves, plotted for several levels of production, from $Q_1 = 10$ units, to $Q_4 = 40$ units. To simplify the graph, we assume just inputs: energy (E), which is plotted on the vertical axis and all other inputs (K), which are plotted on the horizontal axis. Note how all curves are plotted in the non-negative quadrant, are convex to the origin, do not cross, and reflect the principle of the diminishing marginal rate of technical substitution, this being the rate at which one input of production can be replaced by another, in order to achieve the same cost. The further up and to the right a curve lies, the higher the level of production, for which input costs are minimised.

However, not all inputs are readily available and some inputs may be prohibitively expensive as they become scarcer. This imposed a cost constraint and the producers can only produce at the minimum cost, subject to these constraints. In Exhibit 1.16, these constraints are depicted as the downward-sloping lines *A*, *B* and *C*, known as *isocost* lines. Assuming that our initial input cost constraint is depicted by line *A*, we will produce at the tangential point of this line with the Q_2 isoquant. If, for some reason, there is a decrease in the price of energy, *ceteris paribus* the constraint line will tilt from *A* to *B* to reflect that now more units of energy can be purchased. The result of this is that we move to the higher Q_3 isoquant line. A further (proportional) decrease in the prices of energy and other production inputs will move the isocost line further out to *C* and the new level of production will be along the Q_4 isoquant, at the point which the isocost and the isoquant touch.

The total demand for industrial energy can be viewed as an aggregation of all production cost functions, as described above. The effects of price changes on energy demand will depend on the rate of technical substitution. In practical terms, the rate of technical substitution shows how easily energy can be replaced by other input factors, and how easily different sources of energy can substitute one another in the same production process. This process is facilitated by technology, including innovations and increased efficiency in energy usage. A suitable example can be taken from the two oil price shocks, which we discuss later on. The first price shock in 1973 took industry by surprise, as no cost-effective alternatives to oil were available. As a result, many industrial processes continued using heavy oil products for power generation.

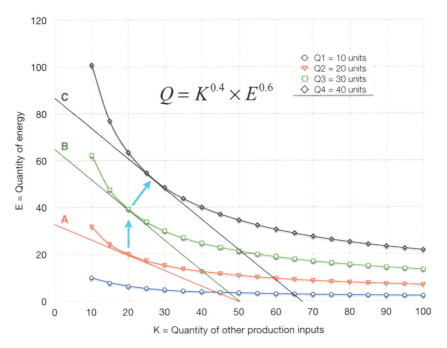

Exhibit 1.16 Isoquant map and isocost constraints

Source: Author

The second shock in 1979, however, came after considerable restructuring in energy usage and efficiency had been implemented, with the result that total energy requirements were reduced and alternative sources of energy – predominantly coal, but also natural gas and nuclear power – replaced oil.

All technical factors taken into consideration, it is now a matter of drilling down to the individual industries that require this energy. Major industries, such as power generation, mining, construction, base metals, cement, chemicals and paper, typically appear in the list of the key sectors contributing to energy demand. The list can extend further, of course, with sectors such as mining, machinery, food processing, transport equipment, non-ferrous metals and so forth, depending on the level of disaggregation sought.

Residential consumption

In practical terms, the residential sector generates demand for energy, which goes towards the building (the house) and its residents. Energy is required for heating or cooling the space, providing hot water, cooking, powering appliances and lighting. As a result, any factor that can affect the extent of these activities will have a bearing on the demand generated by households. At an aggregate level, factors such as population, degree of urbanisation, floor space occupied by each person or household, and weather (especially extreme cold and hot spells) are all important in determining demand.

In addition, like for any other good, demand for residential energy depends on the price of energy itself, prices of other goods and the total disposable income of households. How these three basic variables interact to form consumer choices is covered in most standard economics textbooks – see, for example, Lipsey and Chrystal (2007, Chapter 5). With a minor amendment for our purposes, each household has a choice between two goods: energy (E) and all other goods (X). Combinations of E and X, which maximise the utility for the household, are plotted on a curve, known as the consumer's *indifference curve*. Similar to a producer's isoquant, a consumer's indifference curve is plotted in the non-negative quadrant, is convex to the origin and reflects the principle of diminishing marginal substitution. A number of these indifference curves form an indifference map, such as the one depicted in Exhibit 1.17. Note that the four curves do not cross, and the further up and to the right they are, the higher the utility level, so that U4 represents a higher level of utility than U3, and so forth.

Consumption is, of course, subject to the household's budget. Disposable income and the prices of the various goods will affect the household's consumption choices. In Exhibit 1.17, the budget constraints are represented by the downward-sloping lines C, D and F. Starting with an initial budget depicted by line C, the household's optimal consumption is at the point where the budget line touches indifference curve U2. If, for some reason, the price of energy decreases, line D will tilt to a new position, line F, which means that the overall level of utility now improves, as the new consumption choice is at the tangential point between line F and curve U3. Following on from that, a

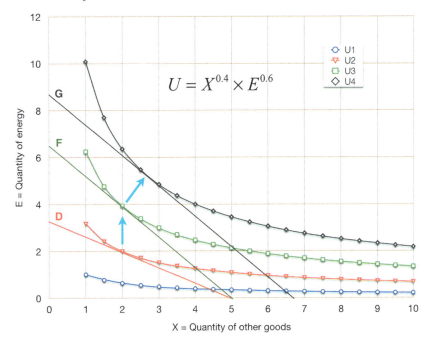

Exhibit 1.17 Indifference map and budget constraints

Source: Author

further proportional decrease for all goods would be interpreted as a further outward shift of the budget constraint to line *G* and the new level of consumption would now be tangential to curve U4, indicating yet again a higher level of utility.

Although there is the general principle that any change in the price of the commodity will affect the quantity purchased by consumers *ceteris paribus*, the change in consumption is not necessarily proportional. The total change in consumption is usually split between the income and the substitution effects. The first is attributed to the fact that with the new, lower price, the same amount of income will buy more units of the commodity; the second effect is due to the switch from other, more expensive substitutes to the lower-priced commodity.

When analysing the demand for specific energy commodities, it is always useful to know their responsiveness to changes in their own price, changes in disposable income and changes in the price of substitutes. This responsiveness is measured by the own price – or demand – elasticity, the income elasticity and the cross-price elasticity, respectively. The usefulness of these three parameters was eminently demonstrated during the two oil price shocks in 1973 and 1979. While the first shock put pressure on household incomes, which had to accommodate a larger expenditure for energy, it did not tamper demand for oil substantially. This was not the case with the second oil price shock, however, when income and price elasticity of oil experienced a structural change and led to a dramatically reduced demand for oil. In yet another demonstration of the change in these fundamental relationships, demand for energy in the 2000s seemed to grow unabated despite the persistent ascent of oil prices consistently above $100 per barrel on average and hitting an all-time high of $147 in the summer of 2008.

Transport consumption

Energy consumption in transport is dominated by oil, or rather oil products, which displaced coal earlier or later in the history of different transport means. In the car industry, for example, gasoline was used since the very beginning, as it was the most appropriate fuel for the internal combustion engine. At sea, coal was dominant until after the end of the First World War, but was rapidly replaced by diesel and heavy fuel oil (bunkers) afterwards. On land, coal persisted slightly more as a source of energy for locomotives, but eventually had to give in to oil's undisputed superiority.

Today, oil is used in transport almost exclusively, although in more recent years there is increased experimentation with other fuels. One such fuel is bioethanol, which is usually derived either from sugar (especially in Brazil) or corn (especially in the US). In the US and the majority of European countries, ethanol is used as a fuel additive, whereby a certain percentage of bioethanol (say 10 or 15 per cent) is mixed with unleaded gasoline (petrol) before it reaches motorists at the fuel pump. In Brazil, on the other hand, the advent of flex-fuel cars means that ethanol and gasoline compete on price at the pump and can either be mixed or completely substitute each other. Setting aside the current and possible future use of biofuels, very few other oil substitutes have been used in transport. Natural gas in liquid form has been used, particularly in public transport (buses) and, at the time of writing, is being promoted in the US as a cleaner and price-competitive fuel for trucks and other heavy-duty vehicles. The other alternative is liquid petroleum gas (LPG, a mix of propane and butane), which is used extensively in some countries, particularly for public service vehicles, such as taxis and buses.

Because oil has virtually no – commercially viable – substitutes in transport for the time being, demand for it depends very much on income and efficiency of use. The latter is probably more important, as is shown in Exhibit 1.18, which graphs the development of passenger car efficiency in the United States, expressed as the rate of fuel consumption in miles per gallon (mpg). Before 1980, there was a period of rapid increase in car fuel efficiency, assisted by the mass introduction of Japanese cars in the American market, which helped sustain the great love affair of US consumers with the automotive industry and provide endless material for 'road movies' to Hollywood scriptwriters. Over the last three decades or so, progress has been rather slow, however. The average fuel consumption for new cars remained stubbornly around the 25 mpg mark and it was only around 2010 that this rose to over 30 mpg. The data for this exhibit are sourced from the EIA, who also produce a forecast to 2040. This shows that fuel efficiency is expected to increase (with the help of

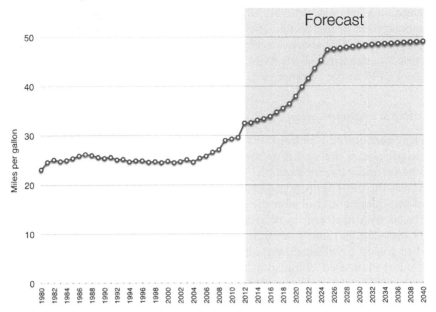

Exhibit 1.18 Average fuel economy for new light-duty vehicles (LDVs) in the US

Source: Author, compiled with data from EIA (2013a, Figure 71)

new federal regulations that make this compulsory for car manufacturers) and is predicted to almost double to about 50 mpg in the next 30 years. Although the data only pertain to one country, the importance of the US market cannot be overestimated. As Exhibit 1.19 shows, the US has some 240 million vehicles in use, nearly one-quarter of the estimated 1 billion vehicles used around the world. China climbed very quickly to become the second largest car owner, and with ownership rates at about 70 vehicles per 1,000 people (compared to ca. 800 in the US), it still has quite a way to go.

The next chapter in the story of the car is the advent of the electric vehicle or EV. The history of the EV began in the mid-nineteenth century, and for some time electric, steam and gasoline-powered cars competed against each other. The wider availability of cheap petroleum products, however, meant that gasoline-powered cars dominated the industry and the EV remained mostly a hobby and research pursuit. It was not until the mid to late 1990s that car manufacturers started contemplating the launch of an electric vehicle. In 1997, Toyota launched the Prius, probably the most successful hybrid electric car to date. Fifteen years later, there is still hesitation about the future prospects of EVs and, although more and more major companies either launch, or announce their intention to produce, such vehicles, there is still little consensus as to how this will be done: plug-in electric, hybrid or fuel cell vehicle? Until electric car technology progresses to the next stage, however, the gasoline-based car rules the roost and it will be the main driver of demand for transportation fuels.

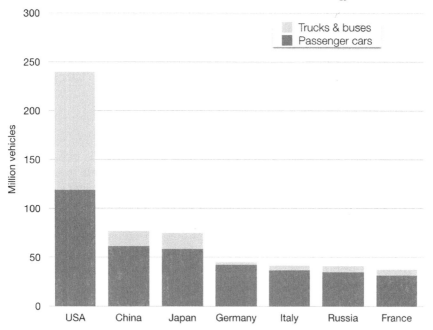

Exhibit 1.19 Major car-owning countries

Source: Author, compiled with data from JAMA (2012)

Transportation is not, of course, limited to road only. The other two major consumers are air and seaborne transportation. The former has risen to prominence, due to the general increase in passenger and cargo air miles travelled and due to the fact that the fuel used (aviation turbine fuel or jet kerosene) is one of the most valuable refined petroleum products. However, the importance of shipping fuel consumption (in the form of either heavy fuel oil or marine diesel) cannot be ignored either, given that an estimated 90 per cent of the world merchandise trade is seaborne.

Other consumption

This category encompasses all the remaining sectors of the economy, primarily energy consumption in commercial and public service buildings and agricultural use. The factors affecting demand generated by buildings are very similar to the ones discussed for residential consumption. In recent years, building design, technology and energy efficiency have attracted a lot more attention, as buildings often waste energy, either because of their design, use of building materials, continuous and unnecessary lighting, poor use of daylight, low adaptability of heating and cooling to weather conditions, and underutilisation of the building itself. There is still some way to go in making buildings more energy efficient, and hence reducing the total energy demand generated by this sector, so it will be interesting to see the developments in this area over the next few decades.

With regard to agricultural use, the demand generated by this sub-sector is affected by fuel efficiency for the various pieces of farm equipment, machinery, tractors, combine harvesters and other heavy vehicles, as well as the degree of mechanisation, which can vary widely from one country to the next. We will revisit this topic when we discuss the economics of agriculture later in the text.

Conclusion

In this chapter, we have looked at the principles of consumption and production in the energy sector. On the demand side, it is wise to distinguish among the different types of energy consumption, in order to be able to understand their effects on market equilibrium. On the supply side, an implicit – but crucial – assumption of classical microeconomic theory is that firms always seek to maximise their profits. Many theorists argue, however, that firms often have other prime targets (revenue maximisation, foreign exchange earnings, social contribution, survival and so on), which pushes profit maximisation lower down the list of priorities. This results in biased supply patterns, which may be further distorted by governmental policies, especially because energy commodities often are of strategic importance.

In the next few chapters, we are going to focus on the key hydrocarbon sources of primary energy: oil, natural gas and coal. In addition to their historical development and current trade patterns, we will also concentrate on the all-important pricing mechanisms and the role of modern markets, both physical and derivative, for each commodity.

References

Bhattacharyya, S.C. (2011) *Energy Economics: Concepts, Issues, Markets and Governance*, London: Springer.

Boyle, G. (ed.) (2004) *Renewable Energy: Power for a Sustainable Future*, 2nd edn, Oxford: Oxford University Press.

BP (2013) *Statistical Review of the World Energy 2013*, British Petroleum, accessed online at: www.bp.com/statisticalreview.

DECC (2013) *Energy Flow Chart 2012*, Department of Energy and Climate Change, accessed online at: www.gov.uk/government/publications/energy-flow-chart-2012.

Devarajan, S. and Fisher, A.C. (1981) 'Hotelling's "Economics of exhaustible resources": fifty years later', *Journal of Economic Literature*, 19: 65–73.

EIA (2011) *Performance Profiles of Major Energy Producers 2009*, Energy Intelligence Agency, DOE/EIA-0206(09), accessed online at www.eia.gov/finance/performance profiles/pdf/020609.pdf.

—— (2013a) *Annual Energy Outlook 2013*, Energy Information Administration, accessed online at: www.eia.gov/forecasts/aeo/pdf/0383(2013).pdf.

—— (2013b) *International Energy Outlook 2013*, Energy Information Administration, accessed online at: www.eia.gov/forecasts/ieo/pdf/0484(2013).pdf.

Hartwick, J.M. (1977) 'Intergenerational equity and the investing of rents from exhaustible resources', *The American Economic Review*, 67: 972–974.

Hotelling, H. (1931) 'The economics of exhaustible resources', *Journal of Political Economy*, 39: 137–175.

IEA (2012a) *Key World Energy Statistics 2012*, International Energy Agency, accessed online at: www.iea.org/publications/freepublications/publication/kwes.pdf.

—— (2012b) *World Energy Model Documentation: 2012 Version*, International Energy Agency, accessed online at: www.worldenergyoutlook.org/media/weowebsite/energy model/documentation/WEM_Documentation_WEO2012.pdf.

—— (2012c) *World Energy Outlook 2012*, International Energy Agency, accessed online at: www.worldenergyoutlook.org/publications/weo-2012/.

JAMA (2012) *Annual World Motor Vehicle Statistics 2012*, Japan Automobile Manufacturers Association, accessed online at: www.toyota-global.com/company/history_of_toyota/75years/data/conditions/automobile_data/vehicle_ownership.html.

Johnston, D. (2013) 'International petroleum fiscal system design and analysis', in B. Simkins and R. Simkins (eds), *Energy Finance and Economics: Analysis and Valuation, Risk Management and the Future of Energy*, Hoboken, NJ: Wiley, pp. 269–311.

Kasriel, K. and Wood, D. (2013) *Upstream Petroleum: Fiscal and Valuation Modeling in Excel; A Worked Examples Approach*, Chichester: Wiley.

Lipsey, R. and Chrystal, A. (2007) *Economics*, 7th edn, Oxford: Oxford University Press.

Nordhaus, W.D. (1973) 'The allocation of energy resources', *Brookings Papers on Economic Activity*, 3: 529–570.

Rawls, J. (1999) *A Theory of Justice*, rev. edn, Cambridge, MA: Harvard University Press.

Solow, R.M. (1974a) 'Intergenerational equity and exhaustible resources', *The Review of Economic Studies*, 41: 29–45.

—— (1974b) 'The Economics of Resources or the Resources of Economics', *American Economic Review*, 64: 1–4.

—— (1986) 'On the intergenerational allocation of natural resources', *The Scandinavian Journal of Economics*, 88: 141–149.

World Bank (2013) *World Development Indicators*, World Bank, accessed online at: http://databank.worldbank.org/data/views/variableSelection/selectvariables.aspx?source=world-development-indicators.

2   Crude oil

Having set the framework for the discussion of energy commodities, it is now time to turn to the commodities themselves and concentrate on their physical and economic characteristics, their trade patterns, and the distinctive procedures for their exchange and pricing.

Oil is probably the most important – and definitely the most written about – commodity, having provided energy for a host of human activities, from kerosene lamps, to motor cars and electricity generation. Fuelwood and wind were the main inanimate sources of power, until the discovery of steam power, which led to the use of coal for a vast number of applications. From heating, to steam locomotives, to textile factories and steamships, coal was the cornerstone of European and American industrialisation, which started from Great Britain. It was oil, however, which caught the imagination of consumers, dethroned 'King Coal' and sent shock waves through the entire world with three massive price crises in the 1970s and 1980s, deflated prices in the 1990s, a meteoric rise in the 2000s and a persistence around the $100-per-barrel mark so far in the 2010s.

We will first go on a brief tour of the history of oil and how the oil industry is organised, before discussing the physical characteristics of the commodity, how it is produced, who the main suppliers are, where it is consumed and how it is priced and traded. The refining end of the business is also very important, as it is refined products that are desired by the final consumers. However, we will take a closer look at refining in the next chapter.

A brief history

The history of oil is probably the most fascinating segment of modern industrial and commercial history. The oil sector is a relatively young industrial sector, just over 150 years old. Oil has been known to humanity since antiquity, but it was never used extensively, and then only for lighting. The little oil that was used was collected from oil seepages, since no one explored for, or extracted, oil systematically.

The birth of the oil industry in the USA is credited to one Edwin L. Drake, who was also known as the 'Colonel', although he was never actually a military man. After a long, expensive and desperate search, he eventually struck oil on 27 August 1859, in Titusville, Pennsylvania.

The new fuel was thick, murky and difficult to burn. It had already been demonstrated by a Yale professor,[1] however, that it could be boiled and refined to several products that were adequate for consumption. Refined to kerosene, the rock oil of Pennsylvania soon found its way to the market, where it was used in lamps for illumination.

The new discovery quickly captured the imagination of the people who flooded the Oil Creek area in their thousands in pursuit of oil. Like in a gold rush, fortunes were made and disappeared in a matter of a few months. The slightest suspicion of oil existence in an area would send land prices sky-high. New towns were built in a matter of weeks, and were deserted as quickly, when local wells dried up and news of fresh discoveries reached the drillers. There were few rules regarding ownership of reserves and rates of production. The ownership of any underground resources remained with the owner of the land above it. Anyone that managed to acquire a piece of land, drill a well and strike oil would start pumping it out as fast as possible, before his neighbour could do the same. Abundant discoveries and uncontrolled production soon brought oil prices down, however.

> Production in western Pennsylvania rose rapidly – from about 450,000 barrels in 1860 to 3 million barrels in 1862. The market could not develop quickly enough to match the swelling volume of oil. Prices, which had been $10 a barrel in January 1861, fell to 50 cents by June and, by the end of 1861, were down to 10 cents. But those cheap prices gave Pennsylvania oil a quick and decisive victory in the marketplace, swiftly capturing consumers and driving out coal-oils and other illuminants.[2]

The technology required to distil oil was not that complicated, and, in the meantime, oil refineries had also started to mushroom in the region. A large number of producers and refiners made the marketplace extremely competitive, suffering from a series of 'boom' and 'bust' periods, and giving the impression that it was run by a motley crew of speculators and soldiers of fortune – a picture not very different from that of the ship-owning community several decades later!

Standard Oil

It was that disorder in the new industry, from production to final consumption, that was scorned by John D. Rockefeller, who set out to implement his strategy – 'Our Plan', as he called it – of 'tidying up' the oil business through unification and control.

He understood quite early that the new fuel was useless unless it was refined and then properly marketed. His plan, therefore, was to acquire and control

---

1 Professor Benjamin Silliman, who was recruited by George Bisell; the latter was the leader of a group of investors, who also financed Colonel Drake's expedition.
2 Yergin (1993, p. 30).

as many oil refineries as possible. This was done very discreetly, often through representatives, and some of his shrewdest competitors joined the board of Standard Oil after being bought out. The name of the company itself was part of his strategy. Until then, oil products – essentially kerosene – were coming from all sorts of different suppliers, with great variations in quality, often with the intent to cheat customers. Standard Oil established reliability for its products and created brand loyalty. At the same time, Rockefeller built a massive organisation, which controlled over three-quarters of the US oil industry, although, through the Standard Oil Trust, it never actually looked that big on paper.

Standard Oil expanded its domination across the Atlantic and into Europe. The resistance it found there was a lot stronger than at home, as will be discussed in the next section. At home, the company staved off criticisms about its corporate power. From the turn of the century, however, public opinion started turning against Standard Oil, helped by Ida Tarbell's revelations regarding the company's predatory methods, and the eagerness of the Roosevelt administration to control corporate power. In November 1906, the US government brought a suit against Standard Oil, charging it under the Sherman Antitrust Act of 1890 with conspiring to restrain trade. The lawsuit became a battle for the survival of the company. In 1909, the federal court found in favour of the government and ordered the dissolution of Standard Oil.

> But how exactly was this vast, interconnected empire to be broken up? The scale was simply enormous. The company transported more than four-fifths of all oil produced in Pennsylvania, Ohio, and Indiana. It refined more than three-fourths of all United States crude oil; it owned more than half of all tank cars; it marketed more than four-fifths of all kerosene exported; it sold to the railroads more than nine-tenths of all their lubricating oils. It also sold a vast array of by-products – including 300 million candles of seven hundred different types. It even deployed its own navy – seventy-eight steamers and nineteen sailing vessels. How was all this to be dismembered?[3]

Eventually, Standard Oil was broken up into several companies, each with a different degree of vertical integration in oil. The biggest was Standard Oil of New Jersey, which eventually became Exxon; Standard Oil of New York became Mobil and then merged with Exxon to become modern-day ExxonMobil; Standard Oil (California), or Socal for short, eventually became Chevron; Standard Oil of Ohio became Sohio and was later taken over by BP; Standard Oil of Indiana became Amoco and was later also taken over by BP; Continental Oil is now ConocoPhillips; and Atlantic became part of ARCO, which was taken over by BP and has recently been sold to Tesoro, a downstream refiner.

3 Yergin (1993, p. 110).

The Europeans

The development of the oil industry in Europe was quite different from that in the United States. At the time, Western Europe did not have any oil reserves of its own. Coal was abundant in Britain and had captured the entire energy market. Due to lack of domestic reserves, European oil companies had to venture abroad from the very beginning. Oil had been discovered in Russia before 1800, in Baku, and it was soon developed with European capital; the Rothschilds and the Nobels were the most prominent investors in Russian oil.

The search for oil also led European companies to the Far East, where oil was discovered on the islands of Borneo and Sumatra. In this race to secure crude oil supplies and capture markets, two companies emerged as the strongest contenders: Shell and Royal Dutch. The former was founded and run by Marcus Samuel, the son of an immigrant Jewish merchant from London's East End. His company was originally set up to control the transportation and retail trading of the commodity; in fact, the full name of the company was 'Shell Transport and Trading'.

Royal Dutch was a rather small enterprise, which often struggled for survival. In December 1900, Henri Deterding was appointed 'interim manager' after his former boss suffered a heart attack. He went on to lead his company for over three decades, making Royal Dutch a leading international oil company. He managed to avoid being taken over by Standard Oil, which was monitoring Royal Dutch's rise very closely, and eventually succeeded in merging his company with Shell, on his own terms and conditions.

Royal Dutch Shell was the most prominent European oil company, but not the only one. Burmah Oil had been set up to exploit oil deposits discovered in Burma; and a new company, Anglo-Persian, was founded to take advantage of what seemed to be substantial oil reserves under the barren desert of Persia. Anglo-Persian was the culmination of the efforts of one William Knox D'Arcy to find oil in the area. The company was officially set up in 1909 and its main shareholder was Burmah Oil. The operations did not run as smoothly as it had been hoped. Anglo-Persian was far from an integrated oil company. It was a crude oil producer, and it had to strike a deal with Royal Dutch Shell to gain access to consumption markets. It was a political decision, however, that turned Anglo-Persian's fortunes around. Increasing friction between Germany and Britain created a need to develop a swift and powerful British Navy. Coal-powered warships were difficult to manoeuvre; oil, on the other hand, offered increased manoeuvrability, but was also riskier to acquire and control. It was the enthusiastic First Lord of the Admiralty, one Winston Churchill, who believed in the merits of using oil and succeeded in convincing the British Parliament to switch the entire Royal Navy to the new fuel. Churchill also believed that the government should have closer control over energy resources for defence purposes. After looking at both Royal Dutch Shell and Anglo-Persian, the British government decided to choose the latter – to Samuel and Deterding's intense discomfort and protest – and strengthened the company by acquiring a majority stake in it. It was the first demonstration of direct political involvement in the oil industry, and only the beginning of a history of political struggle to gain access to, and control over, the valuable commodity.

The Great War

The First World War was very much a war of attrition that dragged on for more than was initially anticipated. All the efforts put into technological developments during the late nineteenth and twentieth centuries were deployed during the conflict. Although the war was very much planned on the use of men and horses, it was the use of the oil-powered internal combustion engine that made the difference. Oil-powered aeroplanes and warships were used extensively, and vindicated Churchill's foresight to switch to oil.

The end of the Great War also signalled the break up of the Ottoman Empire, and the Allies scrummed in to get a share of the remains. The obvious target was the potentially oil-rich lands of modern Iraq and Saudi Arabia. The agreement took a few years to complete, and included Anglo-Persian, Royal Dutch, Compagnie Française des Pétroles (CFP – the French state oil company), a consortium of American companies, and the architect of the deal, Calouste Gulbenkian. The so-called 'Red Line Agreement' (sketched in Exhibit 2.1) established the framework for the orderly exploitation of an area stretching from Bosporus, and covering Turkey, Syria, Palestine, the Sinai Peninsula, Iraq, Saudi Arabia, Yemen and the Arab Emirates of Muscat and Oman, but not Persia or Kuwait.

At the beginning of the twentieth century, the oil industry received a massive boost, in terms of both supply and demand. The advent of the motor car had created the main market for oil products almost overnight, replacing the fast-disappearing market for illumination kerosene. It was the expansion of the car industry that provided the impetus in oil demand during the interwar years.

During the Great War, Europe witnessed the Bolshevik Revolution, which struck right at the heart of European oil companies that depended on Russian crude oil production. On the other side of the Atlantic, however, supply gained momentum, with the discovery of large oil reserves in Texas, and the entry into the market of countries such as Mexico and Venezuela with substantial oil reserves, but also troublesome relationships with the oil companies that produced their oil. At the same time, interest in Middle Eastern oil by American companies was revived. Gulf – the oil company of the Mellon family – struck oil in Kuwait, together with Anglo-Persian. At the same time, oil was found in Bahrain by Caltex, a joint venture between Socal and Texaco. With all the new discoveries, the world was definitely not short of crude, despite the surge in demand. But oil's central role in the world economy would be amply demonstrated during the Second World War.

World War II

If oil revolutionised tactics during the First World War, it definitely dominated the logistics of both sides during the Second World War. From beginning to

Exhibit 2.1 The Red Line Agreement

Source: Author, with Middle East map from www.cia.gov/library/publications/the-world-factbook/docs/refmaps.html

end, the struggle was on for control over valuable oil reserves. Among the first places Hitler set his eyes on, when he started his Russian invasion, were the oilfields of Baku. From the south, Rommel had a similar target: to advance and capture the plentiful oil resources of the Middle East. On the Pacific front, Japan followed exactly the same strategy, and moved swiftly to capture the oil-producing islands of the region.

The Allies' efforts were concentrated on stopping the Axis from gaining access to oil reserves, which they were controlling. The final stages of the Allies' push towards Berlin are eloquently described by Daniel Yergin:

> Toward the end of August 1944, however, fuel was becoming a very serious constraint on the Allied advance. There was no physical shortage of gasoline in France. The supplies were simply in the wrong place – back in Normandy, far behind the lines – and there was an immense logistical problem in getting the fuel to the front . . . In consequence of their logistical problems, the fast-moving Allied armies simply outran their gasoline

supplies. The same thing had happened to Rommel when his forces had raced across North Africa in 1942. Patton fumed about the situation. 'At the present time', he wrote to his son on August 28, 'my chief difficulty is not the Germans but gasoline. If they would give me enough gas, I could go anywhere I want' . . . At that moment, Eisenhower, as overall commander of the Allied forces, faced a critical decision: whether to direct the bulk of available supplies to Patton's Third Army or give the fuel to the United States First Army, to the north of the Third Army, in support of the British Twenty-first Army Group, under General Montgomery, which was closest to the coast. Was this the moment, Eisenhower had to ask himself, to forsake his own 'broad front' strategy – all flanks protected – and instead go for broke and let Patton and the Third Army try to punch through the Siegfried Line, the Nazis' West Wall, into Germany itself?[4]

In the end, Eisenhower chose his first alternative, to the utter frustration of Patton. His dilemmas on the battlefront, though, would make him extremely conscious to matters related to energy during his presidency of the United States.

Post-war growth

The massive reconstruction programme undertaken in Europe and Japan after the end of the Second World War would be impossible to sustain without a large influx of energy resources. In Europe, there was the obvious option to use coal. The coal industry was labour-intensive, and hence expensive. In Japan, on the other hand, the situation was more clear-cut: the country was simply devoid of any natural resources, save for some small coal reserves.

The result of that large appetite for energy gave oil the perfect chance to penetrate – and eventually dominate – primary energy consumption. By the early 1960s, oil had become the non-communist world's largest single source of commercial energy (having attained the same position in the United States at the beginning of the 1950s), although fuel demand patterns varied considerably from country to country. In 1965, the degree of dependence on oil in the main importing countries ranged from 57 per cent in Japan to 39 per cent in the United Kingdom, where coal was to remain the dominant energy source until 1970.

In the communist bloc, the two big powers, the USSR and China, remained dependent on coal throughout the 1950s and 1960s. In the former, oil became the main contributor in 1974, but China remained – and still is – very much dependent on coal.

During the war, oil from the Middle East became increasingly popular, both to the Europeans and the Japanese, which resulted in the region becoming a prominent oil producer and an equally important exporter. Interest in the

---

4 Yergin (1993, p. 384).

Middle East was not newly found, however. The Europeans had led the exploration of the lucrative oil reserves of the region, initially with Anglo-Persian (BP) in Iran, and IPC (Iraq Petroleum Company), which was the 'child' of the Red Line Agreement. American companies were only minority participants so far, and were quite keen to erase the Red Line and take advantage of the massive oil reserves in the Arabian Peninsula. In the meantime, those companies that were not part of the agreement had already made moves to strike concession agreements with the local sheikhs.

As Europe became increasingly oil-hungry during and after the Second World War, the importance of the Middle East as a cheap, short-haul supplier became evident. The Americans also noticed both the increasing importance of oil as a source of energy and the penetration of their domestic market by Middle East crude. Demand was rising rapidly, but supply could keep up the pace more than comfortably, exerting a downward pressure on prices. 'Prices' was exactly the point of friction between host oil-producing nations and oil companies, and in the 1970s the debate on oil prices would take centre stage in international economics and politics.

The struggle for power

The 1970s began with the best possible prospects to be a decade of prosperity and unprecedented growth. Oil had by now become the driving force of the world economy. Its abundance, however, meant that prices had to be curtailed throughout the 1960s, much to the discomfort of host countries, most of which relied largely on proceeds from their oil exports.

For many years, the most hotly contended issue in the industry had been the share of ownership and control over oil reserves, among host governments and oil companies. The dispute dated as far back as the nationalisation of the Mexican oil industry in the early 1940s, which left oil companies with bitter memories. Nationalistic sentiment gained strength again after the 1960s. The desire of host governments to control and exploit their own resources, coupled with the unfair deal they seemed to be getting from the oil companies – reflected in the low oil revenues they received – led to the formation of an international body with the mandate to rectify the situation: OPEC. The organisation was faced with contempt, or even plain indifference, by the boards of most oil companies. After all, it could not achieve much more than clamouring for higher prices all the time.

The first oil price shock

From the beginning of the 1970s, however, the first signs appeared, indicating an excessive dependence on imported crude oil, even in the United States. In fact, the situation in the US was encouraging oil imports, particularly from the Middle East, in two ways: demand was growing rapidly, and domestic oil production was faltering dramatically at the same time. It took the OPEC countries a few years before assuming their role as setters of world oil prices.

In fact, the first rehearsal of what was going to ensue took place in Libya in the early 1970s. The nationalisation of Armand Hammer's Occidental by the Qadaffi regime, and the 'Tripoli Agreement', took oil companies by surprise and raised the aspirations of host governments. It was the Yom Kippur War, however, that provided the excuse to oil producers to test their apparent favourable position. The Arab oil embargo – although abandoned soon after its imposition – also brought about two back-to-back increases in the price of crude, in October 1973 and January 1974.

The world was taken by surprise, but there was not much they could do. Oil was the lifeblood of most economies and higher prices would just have to be accommodated. Despite the price shock, both oil production and exports continued unabated throughout the 1970s.

The second oil price shock

Throughout the 1970s, OPEC countries had managed to keep some kind of agreement with regard to production shares and oil prices. Agreements were quite cumbersome to conclude, since different countries had different plans about the use and remuneration of their oil resources. Countries such as Persia were pushing for a larger share and higher oil prices. At the other end, Saudi Arabia was trying to moderate extreme demands by OPEC members.

It was politics, once more, that brought turmoil in the international oil industry. In 1979, the Iranian Revolution, led by the spiritual leader of many Iranian Islamic fundamentalists, Ayatollah Khomeini, dethroned the shah and sent him into exile. Persia had caused trouble to Western oil companies before. This time, it was going to be terminal. The new regime's hostility towards any kind of Western influence meant the dissolution of the oil companies and the repatriation of their staff. The new state of affairs shell-shocked the world and sent oil prices to unprecedented heights. The price for a barrel of crude reached the region of $35. Many talked of an equilibrium price of $40 and a steady rise with inflation thereafter.

This time around, the reaction to the new crisis was markedly different from that in 1973. The first oil crisis proved right many advocates of the need for political security of oil and less dependence on it. The second oil crisis needed not only a political response, but an economic and technological response. Conservation programmes were introduced in many countries with the aim to discourage the inefficient use of oil. One of the first victims of these policies in the US was the demise of the big cars of the 1950s onwards, which were beautiful to look at, but truly fuel-inefficient, the famous gas guzzlers. As a result, many American consumers turned to the much smaller, but also much more economical, Japanese imports, which gave a huge boost to the Japanese car industry and made it one of the biggest in the world.

Alongside the obvious demand destruction, high oil prices instigated oil exploration and production in politically safe areas – such as Alaska and the North Sea – and made other sources of energy competitive again. The net effect of those developments was the notable reduction of the share of oil in world primary energy consumption (PEC), as can be seen in Exhibit 2.2, combined with an overall reduction in PEC between 1980 and 1983, before it started rising again from 1984 onwards. The second, more acute, effect was the immediate reduction of oil consumed internationally and also oil imported from the Middle East. In 1980 alone, oil demand fell by more than 2.5 mbpd. The pattern would be repeated throughout the mid-1980s, and it took until 1988, almost 10 years, to restore oil consumption to its 1979 level.

The third oil price shock

Within the span of just one decade, the oil industry experienced two immense shocks whose effects rippled around the globe. With the price of oil sky-rocketing after the second oil crisis, oil consumers had to reduce their total primary energy demand, and at the same time move away from oil and into other sources of energy. In the meantime, OPEC members welcomed the new windfall of increased revenues, but mostly failed to recognise the deep structural changes in the world economy. Most of them were absorbed in their own plans of economic development, drafted on the back of strong oil revenues. When demand fell sharply, many OPEC countries felt threatened and struggled to gain market share, in order to keep their oil revenue intact. That, of course, meant anarchy within OPEC, as no country could be

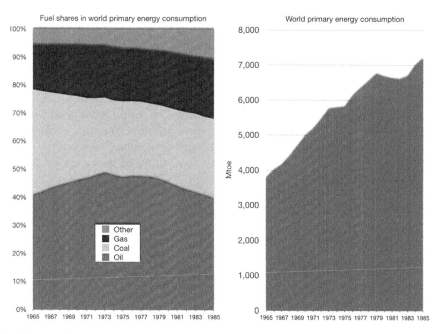

Exhibit 2.2 Fuel shares in world primary energy consumption and PEC development, 1965–1985

Source: Author, compiled with data from BP (2013a)

persuaded to curtail production to a pre-specified quota that would keep prices stable.

The first country to oppose any quota recommendation by OPEC was Nigeria. Its crude was very similar to that produced by the UK in the North Sea, and both countries were competing in the same market – the United States. Nigeria offered its crude at a discount of OPEC's official selling price, in a desperate attempt to retain its share of the American market. Other OPEC countries followed suit, as a high oil price was worthless without any sales! The country that refused to be dragged into the downfall was Saudi Arabia, continuing to play the role of the *swing producer*, and lowering its production in order to accommodate quota violations by other members. In the end, even Saudi Arabia gave in, and started quoting netback prices to refineries importing its crude. That sent the market down a roller coaster, with the price of oil hitting a low of just below $10/barrel.

The price collapse caused a shock not only for OPEC members, but also for non-OPEC oil producers. Among the hardest hit was the UK, which saw a very profitable business being threatened overnight. Both OPEC and non-OPEC producers recognised the need for restraint in order to re-establish market equilibrium. Analysts started arguing about the need for the price of oil to remain at levels manageable for both producers and consumers. Many people started quoting $18–20/barrel as the 'natural' price of oil, which would make production in high-cost areas viable, and would also provide some economic scope for further research in alternative sources of energy.

After the debacle of 1986, OPEC members had to resort to production allocation (quota) cuts in order to arrest the fall of oil prices. For the rest of the 1980s, oil prices fluctuated around $15–20/barrel in nominal terms. Throughout the 1990s, the price of oil remained almost uninterruptedly stable, with the exception of panic buying just after Iraq's invasion of Kuwait and before the successful military interference of Western countries. Once more, it was profoundly demonstrated how security of supplies was, and would continue to be, a major issue in the dynamics of the international oil industry. In the case of Iraq, confidence in the security of supplies was restored when Saudi Arabia stepped in as swing producer, in order to make up the loss of the Kuwaiti oil output.

At the end of the 1990s, the world economy experienced another major shock in the form of the Asian financial crisis, which started in the second half of 1997. The crisis brought with it devaluation of a number of currencies in the region, collapse of highly inflated asset prices, withdrawal of credit by panicking lenders, bankruptcies, and the resulting lack of confidence by consumers, producers and investors. The repercussions of a seemingly regional problem rippled through the world economy and did affect energy demand and demand for oil in particular. At the early stages of what became the crisis, OPEC members went to their November 1997 meeting in Jakarta with great optimism given by the growth of the Asian tiger and the great promise of the Chinese economy. Persuaded by Saudi Arabia, they decided to raise their production quotas from 25 to 27.5 mbpd (a 10 per cent increase), and this decision could not have come at a worst time. What followed was another collapse of the oil price, which dwindled to an anaemic $10/barrel on average throughout 1998, before starting to rise again from the second quarter of 1999 and end the year at an average of $25.

The new millennium

The new millennium was welcomed with great enthusiasm and celebrations around the globe. It brought with it a new dawn in the world economy, the rapid ascent of several emerging economies and even a new term, BRIC, used to summarise the four most promising of these developing economies – Brazil, Russia, India and China. The modest recovery of oil prices at the end of 1999 did not give any hints as to the spectacular way in which they would keep rising, particularly from 2003 onwards. From a 'reasonably firm' $28/barrel, prices moved to over $40 in 2004, continuing unabated to $55 the following year and closing 2006 with several occasions when they surpassed the psychological barrier of $70. That price would not be a barrier in 2007, when the annual average price for Brent crude oil was above $70, and towards the end of the year it was already above $90. The events of 2008 did not only affect the oil markets, but the world economy as a whole. During the year, oil prices kept rising, as exuberance about the current and future growth of emerging economies took over the markets. The oil price hit a historical $147 in the summer of 2008, but soon afterwards the collapse of Lehman Brothers set off a chain reaction leading to the collapse of the world financial system, increased uncertainty about the state of health of financial institutions, strong pessimism about the fate of the world economy and future growth, and an immediate slump in economic activity. Oil prices are frequently thought of as the barometer of the world economy, and this was demonstrated in the strongest possible way. Oil prices collapsed from the meteoric highs of the summer months to a measly $35/barrel, ending the year with an average of just over $40 for the month of December 2008.

The effects of the financial crisis were felt almost immediately in the last quarter of 2008 and throughout 2009. Oil production fell, albeit marginally from 86 to 85 mbpd, and so did oil trade. In the end, the demand destruction that was feared was narrowly missed. The world's appetite for oil continues – in 2012, we consumed almost 90 mbpd. This growth, however, is structurally different to that in the twentieth century. According to BP (2013b), oil consumption growth is forecast to slow down to 0.8 per cent p.a. from 2013 to 2030, compared to 1.4 per cent p.a. between 1990 and 2010 and 1.9 per cent p.a. between 1970 and 1990. OECD consumption is expected to fall, while non-OECD consumption is forecast to grow faster as population and changing consumer tastes exert more pressure. The overall effect is an anticipated growth in the demand for crude oil and associated natural gas liquids of 14 mbpd, taking total demand to nearly 105 mbpd by 2030.

Concluding this section, the history of oil has been characterised by rapid expansion, and dramatic up- and downswings. This pattern has continued in the new millennium, and challenges are still abound. Demand growth in emerging economies, the Arab Spring and its aftermath, shale oil, the continued supply disruptions in the Nigerian Delta, Arctic oil exploration, the embargo on Iranian oil exports, and carbon emissions from the production refining and use of oil and its products are but a few of the issues facing the oil industry at the time of writing. The only certainty in the oil industry is that it will continue to fascinate and surprise for years to come. Now, though, it is time to take a brief look at how this industry is organised.

Industry organisation

The oil industry is divided into three principal tiers, which cover all the stages from exploration to final consumption. The first tier is called *upstream* or *E&P*, and deals with oil exploration, drilling and crude oil production. The second tier is called *midstream*, and is concerned with the trading and transportation of the crude, which involves collection of crude oil cargoes from the production site and delivery to the final recipient's destination, which could be a storage depot or a refinery. Finally, the third tier – *downstream* – deals with the refining of crude, and the marketing and distribution of oil products. Related to the downstream tier is the petrochemicals sector, which uses high-end petroleum products for the production of plastics, organic chemicals, pharmaceuticals, fertilisers and fibres.

There is a host of different parties involved in the various sectors of the oil industry. Big oil companies – or 'oil majors', as they are most commonly known – came into existence very early in the history of the industry, and are involved in all three tiers of production, transportation and refining. Until the 1970s, the history of the industry was, to a great extent, the history of the oil majors. Despite the predominance of those corporations, however, independent producers, refiners and traders always remained active. Most of these companies survive to date, albeit having gone through mergers, or having acquired other smaller oil producers to consolidate their position. Companies such as ExxonMobil, Shell, BP, Chevron, Total and Lukoil are some of the best known ones on this list. They are now collectively known as IOCs (International Oil Companies), although the old collective 'oil majors' is still used extensively.

At the other end of the ownership spectrum stand the state trading corporations of oil-producing nations, collectively known as NOCs (National Oil Companies). They came to prominence at the beginning of the 1970s, when oil-producing nations flexed their muscle and succeeded in gaining far better remuneration for their natural resources. Since then, their decisions about production and prices have caught the immediate attention of the media, governments, producers and consumers worldwide. They top the list of the world's largest reserve holders, far exceeding the booked reserves of IOCs, and among them they control probably 80 per cent of world oil reserves. They are 'oil majors' in their own right, although their names are mostly known within their national boundaries and the oil industry, but are not household names per se. Such companies include Saudi Aramco, Venezuela's PdVSA, Iran's

NIOC, Iraq's NOC, Mexico's PEMEX, the UAE's ADNOC and ENOC, Kuwait's KPC, Nigeria's NNPC, Angola's Sonangol, Algeria's Sonatrach, Russia's Rosneft and Gazprom, Kazakhstan's KazMunayGas, Azerbaijan's SOCAR, and several more. Being state-owned corporations, they were initially set up as political instruments to ensure continuous production and income generation, which can then be used in government policies. This role included, for example, the collusion to control production and dictate prices, as was the case with the member NOCs of the Organisation of Petroleum Exporting Countries (OPEC). In more recent years, the role of these companies is evolving, as they try to balance the political demands of their governments with the need to be commercially competitive. Marcel (2006) gives a very detailed and eloquent account of NOCs in the Middle East and how they strive to cope with the challenges of the industry.

Somewhere between shareholder-owned IOCs and fully state-owned NOCs, the space is filled by corporatised national oil companies. The state still owns a big part of them, but they are also listed on one or more stock exchanges, they have strategic and operational autonomy, and function fully as corporate entities. Companies such as Brazil's Petrobras, Italy's ENI and Norway's Statoil are typical examples.

The examples given above refer to companies spanning all three tiers of the industry, or at least upstream and downstream. There is a host of companies that specialise at either end (i.e. E&P or refining). Several oil (and gas) exploration companies operate around the world, both in well-established and frontier exploration areas, such as deep offshore or the Arctic regions. Examples include Anadarko, BG Group, Cairn Energy, Dana Petroleum, Hess, Noble Energy, Perenco, and several more. Joining that list are ConocoPhillips and Marathon Oil, who used to be integrated oil companies, often referred to as 'mini-majors'. In 2012, both companies decided to split their upstream and downstream operations into separate entities. As a result, Phillips66 and Marathon Petroleum Corporation became the new refining entities out of ConocoPhillips and Marathon Oil, respectively.

There are also several downstream-only companies, concentrating on refining and distribution (via pipeline, trucks, tank railcars and so on) of petroleum products and petrochemicals. Examples include Valero, which holds the largest refining capacity in the US, Tesoro, Flint Hills Resources (part of Koch Industries), Phillips66 and Marathon Petroleum Corporation (mentioned above), as well as several smaller independent refiners, all of which buy their crude oil from the open market, domestic or international, and specialise in extracting the best possible value out of refining it and selling the finished products.

Since the mid-1970s, and especially since the 1980s, when spot crude oil trade became more widespread, independent trading companies started being formed and gradually gained in importance. Following on from the pioneering (and rather notorious) March Rich & Co., independent commodity trading companies have become more widely known. Names such as Glencore, Vitol, Trafigura, Gunvor, Mercuria and several more are now quoted in the financial press, and some of them even make it to the political dailies from time to time. Initially set up to take advantage of the few lucrative trading opportunities not pursued by international and national oil companies, commodity trading houses grew in terms of number and size of transactions, and geographical reach. More recently, they have also expanded their involvement in the supply chain of the specific commodities they deal with. They are not mere intermediaries, only engaging in sale, purchase and transportation of cargoes, with perhaps cargo blending added as well. They may own storage facilities, they may have stakes in the upstream side of the business (for example, oil and gas production licences, or stakes in mines if they also trade in mineral commodities), or the downstream side (with stakes in refineries or metal smelting), and they will generally try to extract value from all stages of the supply chain of the commodity.

In parallel to these companies, a number of financial institutions increased substantially their involvement in the business of trading oil derivative products, including forward, futures and option contracts, as well as physical crude oil and products. Their initial dominance in the oil derivatives (or paper) market was followed by increased activity in spot trading of the physical commodity, and even acquisition of storage facilities, shares in refineries and involvement in the transportation of the commodities. Financial houses such as Goldman Sachs (who acquired commodity trader J. Aron), Morgan Stanley, Barclays Capital, JP Morgan (until 2013, when it decided to start winding down some of its commodity activities), Macquarie and others came to be known as the 'Wall Street refiners'.

There are, of course, a myriad other companies involved in this industry. From suppliers of equipment to operators of storage depots, to oil tanker companies, to pipeline companies and so forth. Perhaps one important subgroup is that of oil (and gas) services firms. These are the companies that provide the technical equipment and the knowhow during the exploration and production phase. Names such as Schlumberger, Halliburton, Baker Hughes, GE Oil & Gas, Aker Solutions and Acteon are familiar to industry participants, although their expertise is mostly technical, albeit with substantial commercial significance. But now it is time to turn our attention to the commodity itself – oil.

Physical characteristics

Oil is one of a number of hydrocarbon compounds that can be found in the earth's crust. In fact, four-fifths of the world's sedimentary basins provide suitable geological conditions for the formation of crude oil. On several occasions, parts of the earth's crust move against each other to form an anticline, which creates a reservoir of impervious rock, where organic material is trapped and broken down by enzymes over a period of several million years. A reservoir usually contains several oil fields, some of them grouped together in provinces. The organic material contained in the fields is a mixture of oil, water and gas. Oil floats on top of the water, while gas provides pressure in the field, which is invaluable for the extraction of the precious fuel.

What comes out of the oil well is a mixture of hydrocarbons and, hopefully, small quantities of nitrogen, oxygen and sulphur, as well as traces of iron, nickel, copper, vanadium and other elements. The hydrocarbons are usually a mix of various different types, broadly classified in paraffins, napthenes, aromatics and asphaltics. Paraffins can be a mixture of short-chain molecules, such as methane, ethane, propane and butane, which are gaseous,[5] and longer-chain modules, such as pentanes and above, which are heavier and occur as liquids. Napthenes typically include cycloalkanes, which consist of one or more carbon rings to which hydrogen atoms are attached. Aromatics are more complicated molecules with alternating single and double bonds between carbon atoms. A typical example is benzene, which is an important component of gasoline because of its high octane number. Asphaltics are very heavy hydrocarbons, which occur as highly viscous liquids or solids, such as bitumen and asphalt.

Different geologic conditions affect the hydrocarbon formation in each and every reservoir. As a result, there is little standardisation in the composition of the various crude oils that are produced around the world. In fact, each oil needs to be analysed (or *assayed*) in a lab in order to determine its chemical composition. This *assay* typically includes characteristics such as density, specific gravity, viscosity, and content of sulphur and other metals. These are all important physical characteristics, which have commercial importance.

Of these physical characteristics, three are more widely know, especially when it comes to trading and pricing crude oil. The first one is specific gravity. Crude oils are classified as: light, or paraffinic; medium, or mixed-base; and heavy, or asphaltic. Light crudes have lower specific gravity and are easier to refine. Specific gravity is measured in 'degrees API', which were introduced by the American Petroleum Institute. The formula used to calculate this metric is

$$API = \frac{141.5}{specific\ gravity} - 131.5.$$

The baseline is the specific gravity of water, which is 10° API and can be derived from the previous formula by simply using 1, the specific gravity of water, in the denominator. The lighter the oil, the more degrees API attributed to it. Crude oils below 20° API are considered heavy, while those above 35° API are considered light, although the boundaries of this classification are not that strict.

The second characteristic is viscosity, which, in layman's terms, measures a fluid's resistance to flow. When density is also taken into account, this is called kinematic viscosity and is sometimes measured in mm²/s or centistokes.

---

5 Ethane, propane and butane are often in liquid form due to the pressure in the reservoir. They are collectively known as natural gas liquids or NGLs and belong to the category of associated gases, just like methane.

The more centistokes, the more viscous (thick) the crude, the more difficult it is to burn and the more energy needs to be spent to preheat it before it gets fed to the distillation tower to be refined. Two common grades of heavy oil products, typically used for vessel bunkers, have viscosities of 180 CST (intermediate fuel oil – IFO) and 380 CST (heavy fuel oil – HFO). One more detail: the centistoke value of a crude oil changes with temperature. Hence, a typical assay will contain viscosity measurements at several temperatures. For comparison, the kinematic viscosity of water at 20° C is approximately 1.

Finally, a crude's quality also depends on its content in sulphur. Crude oils with high sulphur content, above 0.5 per cent by volume, are known as 'sour' crudes, while the rest are known as 'sweet'.

Exploration and extraction

Oil exploration is the part of the oil industry that has always caught the imagination of the masses, as it contained a huge element of risk, but offering the possibility of extremely good returns. Modern oil exploration does not rely that much on luck any more. A number of scientific methods are used for the location of possible oil reservoirs and the estimation of their reserves. These are usually grouped in three main categories: geological analysis, geophysical surveys, and drilling and well logging.

Geological analysis includes a number of alternative – and often comple-mentary – methods, ranging from traditional field geology (examining surface rocks), to the use of orbiting satellites. Geochemical analysis is also used, in order to establish the presence of suitable material for the formation of oil deposits. The aim of all the above techniques is to understand the geological structure and history of an area, and decide whether it is worthwhile to spend more money on exploring it.

The main geophysical technique used for some time now is the seismic survey, although gravimetric and magnetic surveys can also be used to identify underlying structures that are possibly oil-bearing. Seismic surveys involve the artificial generation of shock waves, using a variety of techniques, such as controlled explosions, dropping of weights and vibration generators. The aim is to record the reflections of those waves by the various geological strata. The data are recorded by geophones, which are similar to seismographs, and then transmitted and recorded.

The recording stage is followed by the processing of the data collected, which involves their enhancement by computers. Finally, the results are interpreted by experts, who build an image of the underground formations and the likely location of deposits. All three stages (recording, processing and interpretation) have been immensely improved by the use of enhanced computer technology. The latter has allowed the advance from 2D to 3D seismic surveys, which use a lot more signal recorders and provide a far more accurate picture of underground formations. Initially, a traditional 2D seismic survey was shot along individual lines, at varying distances, producing 'pictures' of vertical sections of the underground formations. A 3D seismic survey, on the other hand, is shot in a closely spaced grid pattern and gives a complete, more accurate, picture of the subsurface.

The next stage in oil exploration is well drilling. To collect more accurate survey data, boreholes are drilled on top of the area suspected to contain oil reserves. Drilling is done by means of rotary drills, which create a borehole with the help of *mud*. The mud is used to lubricate and cool the drill bit, contain the pressure, remove the cuttings and prevent the borehole from collapsing on itself. It typically consists of water, bentonite clay, barite and several chemical additives.

Many of these *wildcat* drills end up as dry holes. The purpose of the boreholes is not only to extract the oil. For the purposes of *well* (or *mud*) *logging*, rock cuttings, core samples and geophysical data are extracted from boreholes, giving scientists a more accurate picture of the local geological structure and, if any oil does exist, the history, nature and extent of the reservoir. Drilling itself can be quite challenging due to the location and the structure of the reservoir. When exploration is on land, the drilling platform can be assembled reasonably quickly and efficiently and occupies a relatively small space. When the reservoir is offshore, then a number of solutions exist, depending on water depth and weather conditions. One such solution is a fixed drilling platform, however this can be quite limiting as it cannot be moved easily and relies on the fact that the field is large enough that production will last for a few decades, so that the platform can be used to the end of its life. A fixed platform also presumes that a subsea pipeline system is in place, which will take the oil production from platform and transfer it on shore.

As large reservoirs become more and more difficult to find, quite a lot of the new reservoirs are expected to last only for a few years, and drilling equipment has adapted to become a lot more versatile and mobile. A typical example of such a production facility is a floating production, storage and offloading (FPSO) unit. This is a floating unit, effectively a vessel, which is designed to receive the oil from a subsea production system, do the initial processing of the oil to remove mud and any water, as well as associated gas, store the oil temporarily, until it can be offloaded to a short-range tanker (also known as a shuttle tanker), which transfers the oil to onshore facilities for further processing. The number of techniques used to recover oil (and gas) are numerous and beyond the scope of this book. The interested reader is referred to Raymond and Leffler (2005), who provide a comprehensive and non-technical discussion of a wide range of oil and gas production techniques.

The boreholes that are successful eventually become oil wells. Neighbouring wells are normally grouped together to define an oilfield. To date, there are over 30,000 known oil wells. Of these, 330 produce just over 50 per cent of the world's oil output, while just 17 of them produce over 30 per cent of the same. Some of the wells are classified as giants – each holding over 0.5 billion barrels of reserves – while the biggest of wells and/or fields are also known as elephants. The largest of all oil fields, Ghawar, is located in Saudi Arabia, and is estimated to hold approximately 70 billion barrels of oil reserves. To put this in perspective, the Ghawar field accounts for more than one-quarter of Saudi reserves (estimated at 266 billion barrels in 2012).

The discovery of oil deposits and the drilling of oil producing wells is not, of course, the end of the story. The entire production process has to be organised properly. This involves a detailed reservoir management plan; the well layout and design; design of production and evacuation facilities; and an implementation schedule covering the drilling of wells and construction and installation of facilities, including oil treatment equipment to remove salt, water, sediment and other contaminants, local storage and transportation arrangements. The latter is typically a smaller, *gathering* pipeline that is connected to a larger, *trunk* pipeline, although transportation could mean the building of an offshore vessel terminal to load the oil on to tankers for export. In some cases, transportation can be by mode of tank railcars, as is the case with some of the oil lifted from Canadian oil sands production sites.

The next step is to ensure that oil can be extracted in the most efficient way. The reservoir's own pressure is usually sufficient to drive the oil or gas to the surface. In new oilfields, this pressure may last for years or even decades, when the oil recovery reaches a plateau. Ultimately, however, the removal of deposited oil will have a detrimental effect on the recovery level. When recovery levels are low, secondary recovery enhancements can be used, whereby the reservoir's natural drive is supplemented with the injection of water or gas. Finally, where both natural drive and secondary recovery are not producing the desired production levels, tertiary or *enhanced oil recovery* (EOR) methods can be used. These techniques are considerably more expensive and must be justified by oil market conditions. EOR methods include: the heating of oil by injecting hot water and/or steam and/or CO_2, in order to increase its viscosity and flow; mixture of oil with a suitable gas or liquid solvent to reduce or eliminate residual oil trapped in the displacement process; and use of chemical additives, which modify the properties of the water that displaces the oil and which change the way water and oil flow through the reservoir rock. Ultimately, no EOR technique can prevent the inevitable, which is the drying up of the well. However, with investment in improved technology, provided this is justified by the market price for oil, EOR can delay the decline of a field for a few more years, as shown in Exhibit 2.3.

In the last few years, there has been a lot more talk and excitement about considerable new sources of so-called *unconventional* oil. Not all experts agree on a definition and, indeed, any available definitions do change with time and new discoveries. Some industry experts focus on the method and economics of extraction; others are more interested in the specific gravity and viscosity of these oil resources. The IEA classifies unconventional oil resources in a number of categories. These include: bitumen and extra heavy oil, with specific gravity of less than 10° API, such as the Canadian oil sands; heavy and extra heavy oil, with specific gravity of less than 20° API, such as the resources in the Venezuelan Orinoco basin; oil obtained from kerogen contained in oil shales, like the ones abundant in the United States and in the process of being extracted at the time of writing; and synthetic oil obtained by using the Fischer-

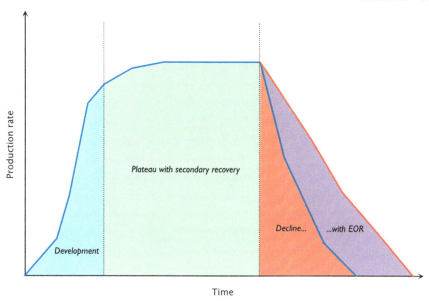

Exhibit 2.3 Typical life cycle of an oilfield
Source: Author

Tropsch process either directly on natural gas (gas-to-liquids or GTL), or on synthetic gas obtained from coal (coal-to-liquids or CTL). All of these oil resources are far from inexpensive. However, as the price of oil continued rising throughout the 2000s and stabilised around $100 per barrel, it has provided the economic incentive to continue developing these unconventional resources in order to satisfy the ever-growing demand for oil and its products.

Reserves

As with any non-renewable natural resource, it is important to be able to establish the stock of reserves available for future extraction. But what are *reserves* and how are they different to *resources*? Exhibit 2.4 gives a good idea of how to proceed. Potential resources are those quantities of oil that are estimated, as of a given date, to be potentially recoverable from undiscovered accumulations. Contingent resources are those quantities of oil estimated, as of a given date, to be potentially recoverable from known accumulations by application of development projects, but which are not currently considered to be commercially recoverable due to one or more contingencies, for example lack of access to the resource due to political issues. In contrast, reserves are those quantities of oil anticipated to be commercially recoverable from known accumulations from a given date forward under certain conditions, which are defined as follows. *Proven*, or *1P*, reserves are those quantities of oil that are estimated with reasonable certainty to be commercially recoverable from known reservoirs and under current economic conditions, technology and

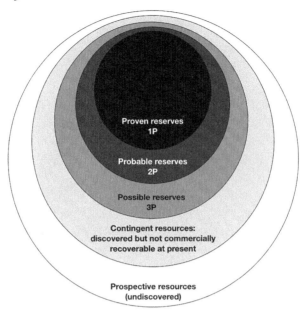

Exhibit 2.4 Definitions of resources and reserves
Source: Author

government regulations. *Probable*, or *2P*, reserves are those additional reserves that are deemed less likely to be recovered than proved reserves, but more certain to be recovered than possible reserves. Finally, *possible*, or *3P*, reserves are those additional reserves that are less likely to be recoverable than probable reserves. So, in essence, it comes down to economic conditions (e.g. oil prices, available demand and the state of the world economy), technology (e.g. the use of conventional or enhanced recovery methods and the cost of doing so), the operating environment (e.g. the willingness of a government to grant concessions for oil exploration and production) and the probability with which the above conditions will combine favourably to allow the extraction of a particular oil accumulation.

The figure in which we are normally interested is proven reserves, as well as the rate at which these reserves are depleted, given how much is produced every year. This is known as the reserves-to-production, or *R:P ratio*. Frequently, the ratio is used as an indicator of the future life of existing reserves. The ratio shows the number of years that reserves will last, if production continues at the current rate. The R:P ratio, however, only offers a view of the future, extrapolated from the present, and assuming that technology and prices remain unchanged. As of 2012, the world R:P ratio stood at just over 50 years, but it is interesting how this ratio differs among regions and how it has developed over time (see Exhibit 2.5).

As one can see from Exhibit 2.6, total proven oil reserves stand at ca. 1.67 trillion barrels, with Saudi Arabia, Iran and Iraq the biggest Middle East reserve

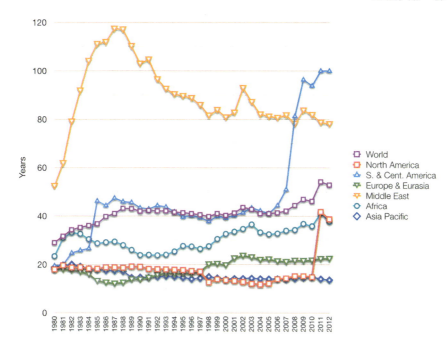

Exhibit 2.5 Reserves-to-production ratios in selected regions
Source: Author, compiled with data from BP (2013a)

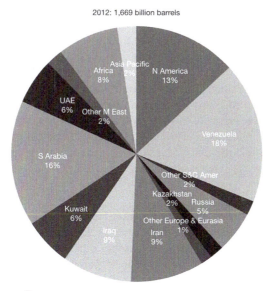

Exhibit 2.6 Proven oil reserves
Source: Author, compiled with data from BP (2013a)

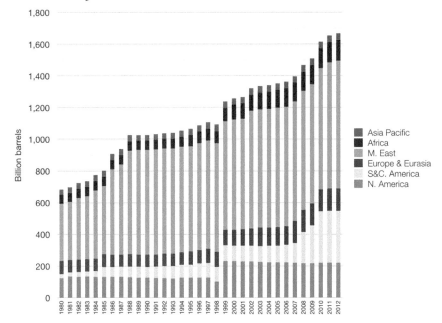

Exhibit 2.7 Development of proven oil reserves

Source: Author, compiled with data from BP (2013a)

holders, while in the rest of the world Venezuela is now listed as the biggest holder by virtue of its heavy oils in the Orinoco Basin, while North America has also increased with the inclusion of the Canadian oil sands in the proven reserves of the region.

Despite much talk in the 1990s and 2000s about the imminent end of oil reserves, this did not materialise, as reserves continued increasing through that time, as can be seen in Exhibit 2.7. However, this does not mean that reserves are abundant or that they can keep up with increasing demand. It is common knowledge that the addition of new reserves occurs at a decreasing rate and that they are often reserves of 'difficult oil' (i.e. technologically challenging and costly to extract), such as oil sands, extra heavy oil, shale oil and oil located deep offshore or in difficult-to-access areas such as the Arctic.

Oil ownership

When we talk about reserves and production of crude oil, we often do this with reference to the various countries where production takes place. However, it is individual companies, whether national or international, which extract the oil and also have title to at least part of this production. So how does ownership of the reserves work? In the United States and Canada, the law grants the owner of the land the rights to any mineral reserves, including hydrocarbons, of course, which are below the land. This rule has allowed intense oil prospecting, particularly in the United States, by private individuals and small entrepreneurs who may either produce their own oil or lease/sell their land to an oil company who can produce it on their behalf and pay them a proportion of the proceeds. Alternatively, oil companies can purchase and accumulate land where they feel there are good chances of discovering economically recoverable oil, and then proceed with production and sale of the crude oil found. The government still has the overall control over how the industry is allowed to develop and can indeed influence this through fiscal measures, such as tax incentives, import or export restrictions, and so forth.

In the rest of the world, national laws typically grant the state title to all hydrocarbons and general mineral rights, both within the land mass of the country and, where relevant, offshore and within the country's exclusive economic zone (EEZ). With this as the starting point, international oil companies (IOCs) can obtain title to a least a portion of the hydrocarbon production with the help of the particular contracts that each country decides to offer, in order to develop and exploit its hydrocarbon resources. These agreements can vary in their detail, but typically fall into two categories: concessions, licences or royalty/tax systems, and production sharing contracts or agreements (PSCs or PSAs).

In countries such as the United States, Norway, the United Kingdom, Australia and several others, the state invites IOCs to bid for concessions of licences, which grant the right to explore a specific area (known as a bloc) within a set period of time and produce the oil and/or gas contained therein, if indeed there is any. If exploration is unsuccessful, the IOC will have simply lost its licence fee and any investment that has gone in the oil exploration itself, all of which are sunk costs. If the exploration is successful and the company starts producing hydrocarbons, then the host government stands to earn additional income in the form of royalties and tax payments. A royalty is a percentage of the oil produced, which the oil company who has bought the lease (the *lessee*) has to give to the government that has granted the lease (the *lessor*). The royalty can be paid in kind (i.e. oil) if the government feels it has the right skills to sell this oil on its own to the international market, or simply needs the oil for domestic consumption. In practice, however, most governments prefer to collect the royalties in cash as a proportion of the value of production. For the IOCs, this means that they take title to the gross oil production at the well head, but they have to pay the royalty either in kind or in cash to the government.

Once the royalty has been deducted, the IOC is allowed to recover costs or take tax deductions. There are two main cost components here: investments, or capital, costs and operating costs. Governments will typically offer investment allowances and tax credits or deductions, in order to allow the oil company to recover its costs. In many cases, both methods do this by simply assuming that costs are a percentage of the gross revenue from production.

Having deducted the royalty and recovered costs, what now remains is known as *profit oil*. At this point, governments typically also require tax payments. Although the taxation principle may be quite straightforward, the details can vary considerably from country to country. For example, there may be a number of different layers of tax, as well as different tax rates. It is not uncommon for countries to impose a corporation tax on the companies' profits, after deducting investment/capital expenditure allowances as described above, and then to also impose a special petroleum tax. In Norway, for example, the government charges a normal corporate tax of 28 per cent and a special petroleum tax of 50 per cent, so that the marginal tax rate is 78 per cent. The way this works is as follows:[6]

> Sales income (calculated at a *norm* price that reflects arm's-length sale and purchase agreements)
>
>> *minus* Operating costs (inclusive of exploration costs and indirect taxes)
>>
>> *minus* Depreciation (calculated by rules particular to the petroleum sector)
>>
>> *minus* Net financial costs (based on the ratio between the tax value of operating assets on the shelf and the average interest-bearing debt over the tax year)
>>
>> *minus* Losses carried forward from previous years
>
> = Ordinary tax base taxed at 28 per cent
>
>> *minus* Uplift (investment-based 'supplementary depreciation')
>>
>> *minus* Unused uplift carried forward from previous years
>
> = Special tax base taxed at 50 per cent

From the mid-1960s onwards, an increasing number of governments, particularly in oil-rich developing nations, sought tighter control of their natural resources, in order to use the revenue from this resources to promote their own economic development programmes. This involved a large share of the oil production being taken over by the government, who then sold it to raise revenue for the country's needs. In order to formalise the way in which oil production would be shared between IOCs and the government (or in many cases the national oil company acting as a government agency), a number of production sharing contracts or agreements were devised. The PSC is for the host country both a means of raising revenue as well as developing its expertise in exploration, production and commercial exploitation of its resources. To this effect, a PSC normally stipulates that the national oil company (NOC) has the option to participate in the commercialisation of a discovery, at the point that it is evident that the discovery has been made and there is oil to extract and sell. This option may or may not be exercised, but if it does then

6 Sourced from Norwegian Ministry of Finance (2013).

it provides the NOC with an excellent opportunity to increase its knowhow, technical ability and commercial awareness, particularly if the NOC is a novice in the industry. The systems used in a PSC to share the production and costs are not dissimilar to Royalty/Tax regimes, although the terminology may vary somewhat. Many PSCs now also include an element of royalty as a percentage of the gross oil production. Once this is deducted, the IOC is allowed to recover its costs, or what is known as *cost oil*. Often, PSCs impose limits on how much of the cost can be recovered, so they make sure that not all oil becomes cost oil and they are left with nothing to share. Once the royalty and cost oil have been deducted, what is left is *profit oil*. It is this oil that is then shared between the government (or NOC) and the IOC. In addition to this, the government may also charge an additional income tax, although the way this is applied often varies from one country to the next and may burden the NOC, rather than the profit oil of the IOC.

A third way for an IOC to be involved in oil exploration with a host government is via a service contract or agreement. In this case, the IOC acts merely as a contractor, who is paid in cash and has no rights on the oil produced. There are cases, however, where the payment is in kind, so that the IOC is paid in oil or is given the right to purchase the oil from the host government at a preferential (lower than the market) price. Such service agreements, however, are rare between IOCs and governments, although the are common-place between IOC and oil services firms, such as Schlumberger, Baker Hughes, Halliburton and so forth.

Production

In 2012, the world was producing oil at the rate of 86 mbpd, the highest ever over the long history of oil. Looking back over the last half century of data in Exhibit 2.8, we can see how oil production kept on rising, despite temporary setbacks due to several political and economic interruptions. In the 1960s and early 1970s, production doubled. Even the first oil crisis only managed to reverse that trend for just one year, 1975. The second oil crisis, however, brought about year after year of negative or very low growth, until production eventually started picking up from the second half of the 1980s, but at a much slower pace than before.

The continued growth of oil production, however, does come with a number of challenges: decreasing rate of oil reserve growth, which many simply call *peak oil*, location of lower-cost reserves in politically challenging regions, and resorting to production of increasingly more 'difficult', and hence more costly, oil are just a few of these challenges. So which regions contributed to world oil production in 2012? Exhibit 2.9 shows the key oil-producing regions. The leading role that the Middle East has is no surprise at all – the region holds ca. two-thirds of the world's oil reserves. Europe and Eurasia come second, and in this slice the biggest part is taken by Eurasia, essentially Russia and Kazakhstan. Third comes North America, boosted by Canada's oil sands and the continued activity of the United States in exploiting old marginal wells

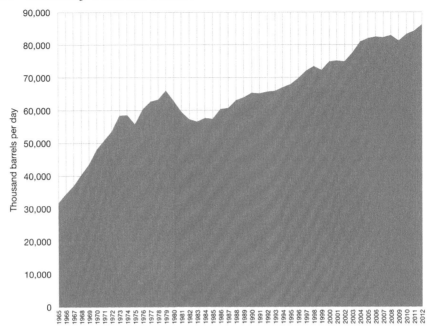

Exhibit 2.8 Oil production development, 1965–2012

Source: Author, compiled with data from BP (2013a)

and bringing shale oil into production. Next comes Africa, with countries in the West, such as Nigeria and Angola, taking the lead, but also supply disruptions in the North, such as those in Libya and Egypt. Asia Pacific is next, with China producing half of the region's output. Finally, South and Central America are led by Venezuela and Brazil, with the remaining countries making smaller contributions.

Also interesting to note in this exhibit is the relative contribution of the major oil-producing blocs, on the right-hand side, where the role of OPEC members can be clearly seen. For a more detailed look of the top producing countries, Exhibit 2.10 offers the relevant information. Worth noting is the fact that in the top 20 producers are all of the 11 OPEC members (marked with asterisk).

As it is already evident, OPEC's share of world production is important. OPEC members continue to meet frequently during the year, in order to discuss the demand and supply situation in the international oil market. Unlike earlier days, however, nowadays they do not set prices. Instead, they focus on setting (or leave unchanged) production allocations among members, the famous OPEC *quotas*. Official announcements coming from OPEC meetings still seem to exert some influence, although various academics who have studied this question do not seem to find one consistent answer. Adelman (2002) has studied one of the longest time series of oil prices, from 1947 to 2000. He observes that OPEC exerted more power and had a bigger impact on oil prices during this period of price setting, particularly in the late 1970s and all the

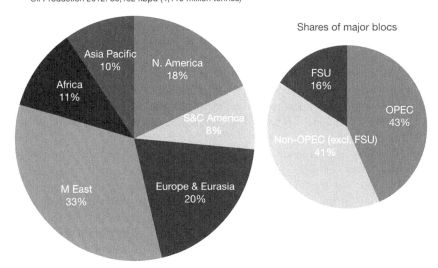

Oil Production 2012: 86,152 kbpd (4,119 million tonnes)

Shares of major blocs

Exhibit 2.9 Oil production shares
Source: Author, compiled with data from BP (2013a)

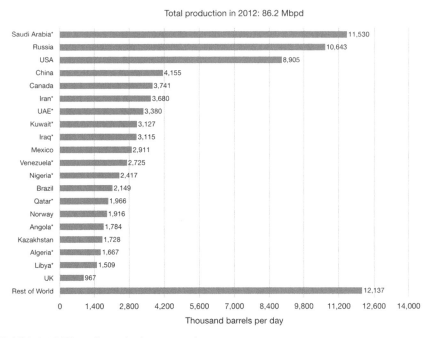

Total production in 2012: 86.2 Mbpd

Exhibit 2.10 Top oil-producing countries
Source: Author, compiled with data from BP (2013a)

way up to the mid-1980s. For the period post-1986, he notes the political problem of getting members to agree quotas, in the face of international competition and while trying to retain their share of the oil export market. Several authors have also tried to determine the market power of OPEC, as well as the possible impact of quota decisions at OPEC meetings on world oil prices. An extensive discussion of this topic is beyond the scope of this text, but the interested reader is advised to look at the work of Loderer (1985), Gülen (1996), Alhajji and Huettner (2000), Kohl (2002), Horan *et al.* (2004), Kaufmann *et al.* (2004), Wirl and Kujundzic (2004), Bentzen (2007), and Lin and Tamvakis (2010).

We will leave the reader with two more exhibits that demonstrate the relationship between OPEC-related figures and oil prices. Exhibit 2.11 shows data from the last two decades on OPEC official quotas (red line) plotted against actual OPEC production and world oil prices, using Brent crude as the benchmark. Although OPEC quotas are set, it is interesting to see that they are not always strictly adhered to and, in fact, actual production can vary considerably. The exhibit depicts a number of different levels of production coming out of OPEC members. At the lowest level is production excluding natural gas petroleum liquids (NGPLs or NGLs) and Iraqi production, which is excluded from the production allocation to allow for the reconstruction of the country. This level of production reflects the quota set by OPEC members and should be very close to it, but as is evident it does divert and runs at a higher level almost consistently. If we also add NGPLs and Iraqi production,

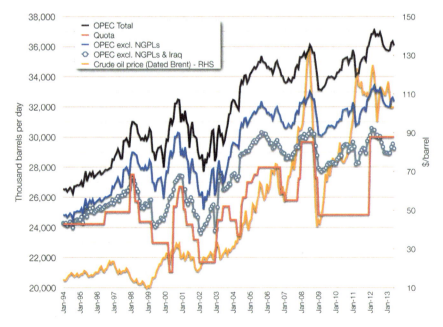

Exhibit 2.11 OPEC quotas and crude oil prices

Source: Author, compiled with data from EIA, OPEC and www.indexmundi.com

we end up with a much higher figure. For example, in June 2013, official OPEC quotas were stable at 30 mbpd, whereas actual total OPEC production ran at just over 36 mbpd.

Another interesting aspect of OPEC's role in the market is shown in Exhibit 2.12. This is the relationship between estimated OPEC spare production capacity, plotted against world oil prices, using West Texas Intermediate (WTI) as the benchmark this time. Although we do not formally quantify the relationship of the two series, a quick graphical inspection shows how low levels of spare production capacity puts a strain on oil prices. This relationship was evident during the period 2003–2008, when oil prices kept rising against a background of relatively low spare capacity, which ran between 1 and 2 mbpd, culminating in the oil price peaking in Q3 2008 while spare capacity remained at a measly 1 mpbd. This situation was reversed immediately after the 2008 financial crisis. By Q1 2009, spare capacity had tripled and oil prices had collapsed to an average of just over $40/bbl for that quarter.

Consumption

The world consumption of crude oil almost reached 90 mbpd in 2012, and is set to keep rising and exceed 100 mbpd some time before 2030. This is driven by the changing consumer tastes of emerging economies, but moderated by much slower growth in developed economies and increased energy efficiency

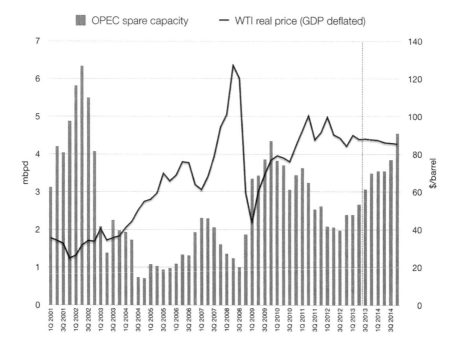

Exhibit 2.12 OPEC spare capacity and crude oil prices

Source: Author, compiled with data from EIA

brought about by improved technology. Historically, the growth of oil consumption has continued unabated for nearly 50 years, with the notable exceptions of 1974–1975, 1980–1983 and 2008–2009 (i.e. the two oil price shocks and the world financial crisis). Although the rate of growth from 1984 onwards is notably less steep than that of 1965–1973, and the share of oil in world primary energy consumption has fallen to 33 per cent, from a high of 48 per cent in 1973, oil remains the world's biggest commodity, both in terms of its value and its volume. Despite continued talk of oil's demise in the near future, there are several prime uses for it, which will find it very difficult to continue, unless an equally efficient technology comes along. Two sectors in particular rely on oil extensively: transportation and petrochemicals. The latter is obvious – petrochemicals are derivatives of oil and require refined oil products (primarily naphtha but also petroleum gases), which are then processed into plastics, chemicals, organic fertilisers and a whole range of products consumed by other industries and final consumers. For transportation, oil has been the most efficient way to move a vehicle between two points, particularly cars, trucks and aeroplanes. It is true that there is a lot of research and development going into oil substitutes for transportation, including EVs, use of biofuels, hybrid cars and so forth. All, however, also have disadvantages, and it will take some time until new technologies mature, work alongside existing oil-based technology and eventually take over.

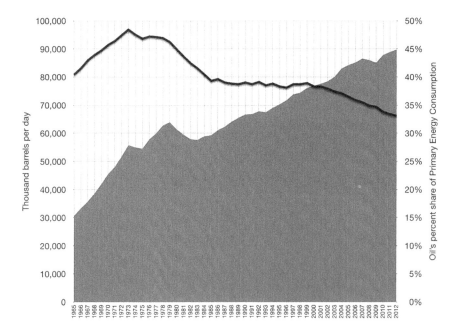

Exhibit 2.13 World oil consumption and share of oil in world primary energy consumption

Source: Author, compiled with data from BP (2013a)

With this as a background, let us now look at the world's major oil consumers. While North America and the EU have historically been the main hubs of oil consumption, it is Asia Pacific, led by China, which now dominates this field. North America consumes just over one-quarter of oil production, while Europe follows on with about one-fifth, although this grouping does include Russia and other former Soviet Union (FSU) countries. However, Asia Pacific dwarfs both of them, generating one-third of world oil demand. Exhibit 2.14 shows details for all major regions and their share of oil consumption.

On a country level, the United States continues being the world's foremost oil consumer, although their share of total consumption has fallen from over one-third about 50 years ago, to about one-quarter until the mid-2000s, and eventually to just under one-fifth in the last five years or so. As one can easily deduce, China has been the country with the most rapid growth for oil demand over the last 20 years. From 1991 to 2001, China's consumption doubled from around 2.5 mbpd to 5 mbpd. In another 10 years, from 2002 to 2012, it doubled again to just over 10 mbpd, and China is now the world's second largest consumer. One, of course, needs to put this into perspective with regard to the population of the two largest consumers – ca. 314 million for the US and ca. 1,350 million for China. This uncovers the big gap in per capita oil consumption in the two countries – 0.36 tonnes of oil per capita per year for China and 2.6 tonnes for the US, about seven times as much.

Exhibit 2.15 shows the world's 20 largest consumers of oil in 2012. In this list, worth noting is Japan, a country that is totally dependent on imports for its energy requirements. Since the first oil crisis, Japan has been striving to reduce its dependence on oil, first by increasing its oil efficiency (exemplified

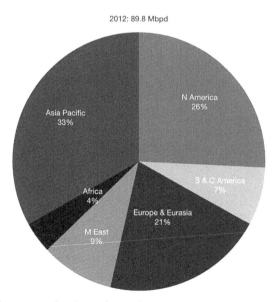

Exhibit 2.14 Oil consumption by major region

Source: Author, compiled with data from BP (2013a)

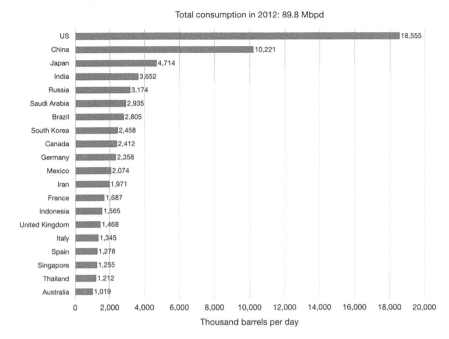

Total consumption in 2012: 89.8 Mbpd

Exhibit 2.15 Top oil consumers

Source: Author, compiled with data from BP (2013a)

by its car technology) and second by moving away from heavy industry and into more knowledge-based industry, such as consumer electronics. Japan's oil consumption peaked in 1999 at 5.7 mbpd and has been slowly but steadily declining since then, having shrunk to 4.7 mbpd in 2012.

The fourth country in the table, India, also registered an impressive ascent to a leading oil consumer, overtaking South Korea in 2001 and eventually Russia in 2007, although it still remains a very low per capita consumer, given its population of ca. 1,237 million.

The increasing role of emerging economies in the last decade or so is also confirmed in Exhibit 2.16, which shows how the balance of oil consumption has moved away from OECD towards non-OECD countries, and how each of these major groupings now consume about half of the world's oil production.

Trade in crude oil

From a total of ca. 4,119 million tons (or 86 mbpd) of crude oil produced in 2012, some 1,927 million tons (38.6 mbpd) were traded internationally (i.e. nearly 47 per cent of total production). Approximately 90 per cent of these exports were carried by sea, with the balance carried by pipelines, especially between the United States and Canada and between Russia and the rest of Europe.

Exhibit 2.16 OECD versus non-OECD oil consumption

Source: Author, compiled with data from BP (2013a)

Throughout oil's turbulent history, international trade has played an important role. In fact, one of the biggest integrated oil companies – Royal Dutch Shell – started life as a trade and transport company. The fortunes of the tanker market have been driven by the economics and politics of the oil market. It makes sense, therefore, to understand the development and current situation of international trade in crude oil and its products.

A brief history of oil trade

Trade in oil was initiated from the early days of the industry, near the end of the nineteenth century. Before the First World War, international trade was almost exclusively in products. Carrying crude was quite uneconomical, due to its low value in comparison with its transport cost. Refineries were also located at the production sites, so that the final products only were shipped to the end users. Most of the world trade in oil products was structured around the United States, which was the leading producer and exporter of oil. Standard Oil had a strong foothold in Europe and controlled most of the fleet carrying its oil from the United States. In Europe, in the meantime, Russian production became exportable with the completion of the Transcaucasian Railway. Subsequently, Russia dominated the markets of the Near East and a small share of the European market. The Bolshevik Revolution in 1917 disrupted Russian output, but both production and exports were resumed in 1920.

At about the same time, crude oil started being traded internationally, even though it was carried on short-haul routes. The main crude oil exporters were Mexico and later Venezuela, with the United States being the recipient. With the gradual expansion of Middle East and South-East Asian oil production, crude oil trade increased in importance; there was little scope for local refining, and the majority of refining capacity was now located in the consuming markets.

World oil production and exports from 1939 to 1945 reflected very much the energy needs of the Second World War. Oil for the Allied Forces was flowing in from the United States with increasing difficulty, due to the submarine war. On the other hand, the Allies managed to secure control over the oil reserves of the Middle East, whose contribution in oil production increased substantially during the war. The military importance of the area was highlighted towards the end of the war, with the construction of the big oil refinery and terminal in Ras Tanura.

After the end of the Second World War, Europe had increased needs for energy resources in order to proceed with its reconstruction. A large part of those needs were covered by the Middle East, which became the world's leading oil-exporting region, especially after production of the large Kuwaiti fields came on stream. During the same period, the United States turned into a net oil importer, with most of its imports coming from Venezuela, although some crude imports had already originated from the Middle East in the late 1940s. The old adversary of the US in the European market, the Soviet Union, resumed exports in the late 1940s, with most of them being directed to other countries in the communist bloc.

At the same time as Europe, Japan also embarked on its reconstruction programme. With energy resources virtually non-existent domestically, Japan had to turn to oil imports, in order to fuel its rapidly growing economy. In its quest to secure crude oil supplies, Japan turned initially to Indonesia (the former Netherlands East Indies), and even the Soviet Union. As the Middle East continued its rally to world domination of oil production, the Japanese eventually entered agreements with both Saudi Arabia and Kuwait, in the late 1950s. The Japanese involvement in the Middle East was very low profile from the beginning; even their exploration company was discreetly named 'Arabian Oil Company'. Their venture in the Middle East provided the Japanese with an independent (i.e. non-oil major) source of oil, supplying about 15 per cent of their needs.[7]

The major characteristic of this period (roughly between 1945 and 1960) was the substantial increase of international movements of oil, and the rising in importance of the trade in crude oil. The period, however, was not devoid of turmoil. In 1956, the Suez Canal was closed, causing a major disruption in the trade and distribution of crude oil from the Middle East, and sending the

---

7   Yergin (1993, p. 507).

tanker market sky-high overnight. Although the effects were not lasting, the whole incident amply demonstrated the role politics were going to play in the post-war order in the oil industry.

The 1960s was an era of growth: of oil trade, and crude oil in particular; of the export expansion of the Middle East; and of the size of tankers used to carry oil internationally. Western Europe, Japan and the United States experienced high levels of growth during the decade, with a resultant augmentation of their energy requirements. At the same time, refinery capacity and throughputs increased immensely in all the major importing regions. Within the span of 10 years, world refining throughputs increased from 21 mbpd to almost 45 mbpd. Most were accounted for by Western Europe and Japan. Within a decade, from 1960 to 1970, the volume of crude oil exports almost tripled, from just over 9 mbpd to just over 25 mbpd. In both cases, the Middle East accounted for about half of the world's crude oil exports, half of which were directed to Western Europe.

At the same time, Venezuela also became a prominent crude oil supplier, with total exports in 1970 amounting to just under 3.5 mbpd, two-thirds of which were exported to the United States. The vision of Pérez Alfonso, the Venezuelan Minister of Mines and Hydrocarbons back in the late 1950s, of oil-producing countries being able to command higher rents for their natural resources could now become a reality; the economic fundamentals were in place at the end of the decade. The three first years of the 1970s, however, were anything but ominous: GDP growth rates were buoyant, industrial production and energy production had strong forecasts attached to them, and the future of crude oil trade looked better than ever. The rush of shipowners to order new tanker tonnage could only be compared to the oil rush of the 1860s in Pennsylvania; the anticlimax would be equally harsh.

While world economic growth had been providing the necessary impetus for an upward movement of oil prices, increasing supply from old and new producers prevented the possibility of any demand squeeze. In fact, during the 1960s, prices had been rather slack and oil companies had repeatedly readjusted their posted prices downwards, much to the frustration of host governments, who saw their oil revenues being undercut.

The beginning of the 1970s, however, witnessed a demand rally, particularly in the United States, with a combined fall in domestic production and a surge in demand. As a result, crude oil import requirements had to be revised upwards and had to be covered mostly by the Middle East.

Despite the tight demand/supply balance, the oil price regime did not look particularly threatened. It was a political event once again – the Yom Kippur War, and the subsequent Arab oil embargo on exports to the US – that created a tremendous price rally, and gave oil producers the chance to test their strength. The result was an approximately fivefold increase of the price of crude oil, which jumped from about $2/bbl to over $15/bbl, with some extreme cases of bids over $20.

The new developments took everyone by surprise, including oil producers themselves, but there was no question of curtailing oil consumption. Even the embargo itself did not last for long. The blacklisted countries soon started procuring their crude oil requirements from other countries importing from the Middle East. It was now evident that the new price levels were there to stay. The interruption of world economic growth, because of the first oil price shock, was quite short-lived. Economic growth resumed in 1974, although at lower levels; so did oil consumption and the demand for oil imports. In fact, during the 1970s, dependence on the Middle East increased.

The Middle East, of course, was not the only OPEC producer. Venezuela had a substantial share of the American market, while Indonesia was an important oil supplier to the Japanese market. In the Western world, there were no substantial oil producers, or at least not large enough to substitute the Middle East as a prime source of oil imports. The USSR was a substantial producer and exporter, although not to the American market.

The increase in oil prices, however, was not detrimental to the Western world only. Awareness about the security of oil supplies became widespread, resulting in the foundation of the International Energy Agency by the country members of the OECD. At the same time, oil's high price provided the incentive for oil exploration in 'politically safe' regions, the most notable being the North Sea.

Although the existence of oil reserves in the North Sea was known since the 1960s, their exploitation was uneconomical. But with an international oil price high enough to cover the increased costs of offshore oil exploration, crude production in the North Sea covered a substantial part of the consumption requirements of the producing countries (the UK, Norway, Netherlands and Denmark) and allowed modest exports.

In the United States, oil companies had been exploring in Alaska since the late 1960s, following the Suez Canal crisis in 1956. Their attempts had been largely unsuccessful, until Boxing Day 1967, when the ARCO-Humble venture struck a massive oilfield at Prudhoe Bay. A few more drills confirmed that the deposit was of world class; in fact, it ranked third, behind Saudi Arabia's Ghawar and Kuwait's Burgan. Despite the massive discovery, plans to extract the crude and transport it to the mainland were delayed for the remainder of the 1960s. The cost of extracting the oil under Arctic weather conditions was not economically justifiable and, what was more, the whole plan stumbled on protests by environmental groups opposing any plans for the construction of a Trans-Alaskan pipeline, which would damage irreparably the Arctic flora and fauna. After the rude awakening of the first oil shock, most environmental considerations were brushed aside and the Alaskan project progressed at a much faster pace. Proposals for alternative pipeline routes through Canada had been considered but, in the end, the pipeline from Prudhoe Bay to Valdez was favoured.

During the 1970s, the new jigsaw of the world energy markets was being painstakingly put together. OPEC countries rose to prominence, with the Middle East at the forefront. Western producers sought new secure sources of oil and, at the same time, stability in their relationship with the Middle East. The USSR edged its way into the international oil market, taking advantage of the high prices to replenish its hard currency reserves. High energy consumption and broad dependence on oil, however, meant increased production costs and inevitable inflationary pressures. In fact, most of the oil producers' incomes were being severely eroded by the explosive world inflation of the late 1970s. The bubble was again ready to burst; the Iranian Revolution kindly obliged.

The reaction to the second oil price shock was markedly different from that to the first. A number of important adjustments changed the structure of energy consumption. More specifically:

- Renewed emphasis was put on energy conservation and oil substitution, with the result that the non-communist world's oil consumption went into steady decline after 1979.
- There was a switch to politically safer sources of oil, boosting the production of non-OPEC countries, while dependence on OPEC oil fell considerably during the first half of the 1980s.
- The switch to new supply sources resulted in higher utilisation of heavier and sourer crudes; this urged many refiners to upgrade an increasing proportion of their facilities in order to improve the yield of lighter products from heavier crudes.

The new price increase boosted immensely the fortunes of new, high-cost suppliers, such as the UK, Alaska and Canada. In the UK alone, a brand new industry was created almost overnight, giving a tremendous boost to the local and national economies.

The combination of changed demand and supply patterns resulted in a radical structural readjustment of the international oil trade. The share of OPEC in oil production fell by 45 per cent between 1979 and 1985, while that of non-OPEC producers increased by 26 per cent in the same period. The share of the Middle East in world oil trade fell from 58 per cent in 1978, to 42 per cent in 1983; the US alone decreased its imports from the Middle East and West Africa by almost 75 per cent, although its imports from Venezuela fell by less than 20 per cent.

Faced with decreasing world demand for oil, and increasing competition from non-OPEC producers, the OPEC countries attempted to redress market conditions by reducing official prices, and by introducing quotas with a view to establishing some order among member countries. Following the radical change of the fortunes of OPEC producers, many of them had to compete in order to secure market share, thus resorting to price undercutting all too often.

With tension among OPEC members increasing, due to poor market conditions, Saudi Arabia played the role of the 'swing' producer, decreasing its production to accommodate the needs of other members. In the end, however, even the Saudis could not restore order in OPEC circles, and resorted themselves to quoting netback prices, pulling world oil markets to prices around $10/bbl.

The new situation was not desirable for oil producers, OPEC and non-OPEC alike. Market prices eventually recovered in 1987, and the new level of about \$15–18/bbl made oil popular once more, and led to a steady growth of oil imports, from about 24.5 mbpd in 1985, to 40 mbpd in 1998. In terms of price fluctuations, of course, the situation remained as 'interesting' as ever. For most of the 1990s, the price fluctuated between \$15 and \$20 dollars per barrel (using Brent crude as a benchmark). Then, in 1998, prices collapsed at below \$15 to remain around \$12/bbl for most of the year. Although this was good news to consumers around the world, the protracted price squeeze far from pleased state oil producers and oil companies alike. As a result, 1999 witnessed major restructuring in the oil sector, with extensive M&A activity, which culminated in the creation of Exxon-Mobil and BPAmoco, the latter eventually reverting to its original name, simply BP. At the same time, a regenerated OPEC managed to instil some discipline among its members, which adhered to their quotas, forcing the oil price to above \$25/bbl in the space of a few weeks only.

Crude oil trade in the new millennium

As discussed earlier, the new millennium brought with it hope for world economic growth, after the debacle of the Asian financial crisis at the end of the 1990s. China spearheaded this economic growth, on the back of a spectacular increase in energy consumption and trade, including crude oil, although it is only in the last five years or so that Chinese growth in oil imports has gained momentum. Overall, crude oil trade increased between 2000 and 2012,

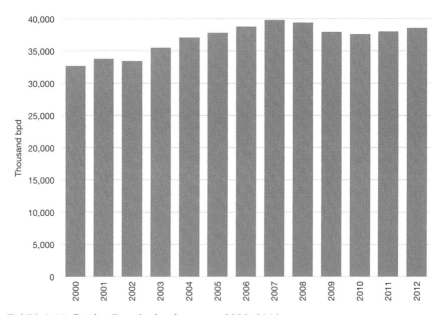

Exhibit 2.17 Crude oil trade development, 2000–2012

Source: Author, compiled with data from BP Statistical Review of World Energy issues, from 1999 to 2013

but only by a relatively modest 6 mbpd. Exhibit 2.17 shows this development, how it peaked in 2008, only to then contract in 2009 and 2010, before picking up again in the following two years.

Looking at the main oil-importing regions in Exhibit 2.18, it is evident that the United States and Europe remain the two largest ones, as they have done for several decades. However, it is also evident how much more prominent emerging economies have now become, with China now above Japan, and India following closely after. Asia Pacific now accounts for ca. 47 per cent of total crude oil imports, almost exactly the amount of imports generated by the United States and Europe put together.

Finally, Exhibit 2.19 shows an overview of world crude oil trade flows for 2012.

Looking at individual countries now in Exhibit 2.20, it is no surprise that the United States continues to top the league of oil importers, although recent increased activity in extracting domestic shale oil may result in the decline of its import requirements in coming years. China is now the world's second largest importer, with over 5 mbpd, followed by India, Japan and South Korea. The last five of the top 10 importers are all European countries, the largest of which is Germany.[8]

Before looking at exporters, it is worth looking in more detail at the provenance of imports for the two biggest importers: the United States and

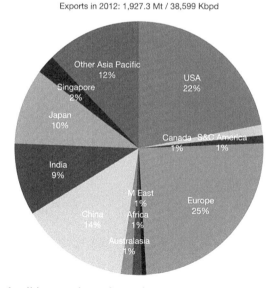

Exports in 2012: 1,927.3 Mt / 38,599 Kbpd

Exhibit 2.18 Crude oil imports by major region

Source: Author, compiled with data from BP (2013a)

---

8 There is a difference in the numbers included in Exhibits 2.19 and 2.20. This is because they originate from different sources.

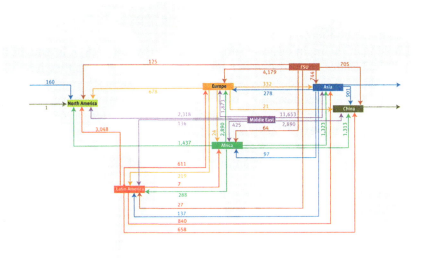

Exhibit 2.19 World crude oil trade flows
Source: OPEC (2013, p. 50)

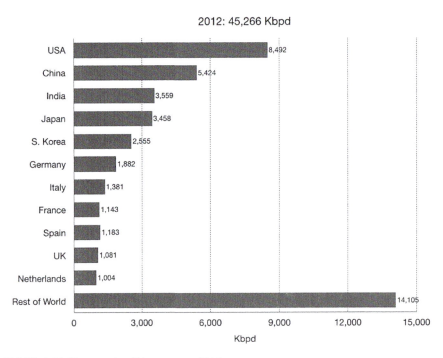

Exhibit 2.20 Top crude oil importers, 2012
Source: Author, compiled with data from OPEC (2013)

China. Traditionally relying on Saudi Arabia as its biggest source of imports, the United States has been successful in recent years in moderating this dependence. As the reader can see in Exhibit 2.21, it is now Canada that accounts for over one-quarter of US imports, with Saudi Arabia having dropped to second place and Venezuela to third. The development of the Canadian oil sands has been a boon to the United States as it has been for Canada, as imports from the politically safe and predictable North American neighbour have been used to leverage the US position in its quest for energy independence. However, despite this development, it is worth noting that just under half of total US imports still come from OPEC members. This is perhaps another figure that will be changing rapidly as the United States continues developing its own indigenous oil reserves.

China, on the other hand, had to quickly develop a portfolio of more traditional and newly developed suppliers to satisfy its rapidly increasing demand for crude oil, particularly in recent years. In addition to traditional suppliers in the Middle East, who have been all too keen to supply Asia Pacific's fastest growing economy with their crude oil, Chinese imports also come from West Africa, South America and the Pacific coast of Russia. The latter has also been particularly keen to promote its hydrocarbon exports, both crude oil and natural gas, to the three largest economies in Asia Pacific, Japan, South Korea and, most of all, Russia. Exhibit 2.22 provides more detailed information.

The Middle East continues to dominate world crude oil exports, generating some 46 per cent of them in 2012. The second and third most important exporting regions are the former Soviet republics and West Africa, respectively,

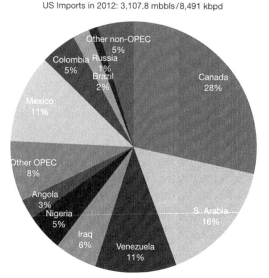

US Imports in 2012: 3,107.8 mbbls/8,491 kbpd

Exhibit 2.21 US crude oil imports by country of origin

Source: Author, compiled with data from EIA (2013b)

Chinese Imports in 2012: 1,987 mbbls/5,444 Kbpd

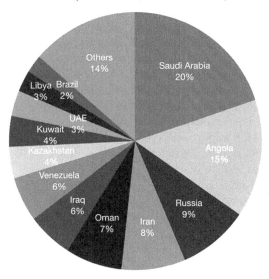

Exhibit 2.22 Chinese crude oil imports by country of origin
Source: Author, compiled with data from ITC (2013, code 2709)

as shown in Exhibit 2.23. Even more interesting is the role of OPEC as a crude oil exporter. As shown in Exhibit 2.24, the organisation is responsible for over 60 per cent of world exports, proportionately much higher than the over 40 per cent of crude oil production for which it is responsible. This shows the importance that OPEC still has in the international oil market, a role that is unlikely to change for the foreseeable future, especially in view of the rising demand for oil from emerging economies.

When it comes to individual exporters, Exhibit 2.25 shows the 12 top countries, led by Saudi Arabia and Russia, and followed effectively by all the remaining OPEC members, with the exception of Canada, Mexico and Norway. Given that OPEC generates approximately 25 mbpd of exports, in 2012 Saudi Arabia contributed almost 30 per cent of all OPEC exports, and nearly one-fifth of total world exports. Russia is, of course, another paramount exporter, generating about 15 per cent of world crude oil exports. The next five exporters in the list exported between 2 and 2.5 mbpd, which may not seem that big on an individual basis, but when one considers that the oil market becomes a lot more jittery when spare capacity contracts to less than 2 mbpd, it becomes evident that each and every one of these exporters is significant in its own right.

One final comment: since 2000, it has become increasingly apparent that the emerging economies of Asia Pacific generated the vast majority of growth in oil trade. At the beginning of 2010, the region has become the main focus of oil exports, particularly by OPEC members, and even more so by Middle

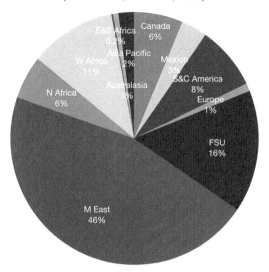

Exports in 2012: 1,927.3 Mt/38,599 Kbpd

Exhibit 2.23 Crude oil exports by major region
Source: Author, compiled with data from BP (2013a)

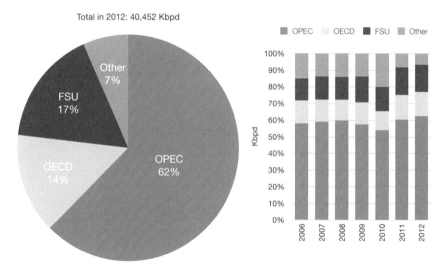

Total in 2012: 40,452 Kbpd

Exhibit 2.24 Crude oil exports by major country bloc
Source: Author, compiled with data from OPEC (2013)

Eastern members of the organisation. Exhibit 2.26 shows this in the context of all the crude oil flows out of OPEC members, whereas Exhibit 2.27 shows the relative importance of Asia Pacific, which generates a hefty 57 per cent of export flows, some 14.4 mbpd in 2012.

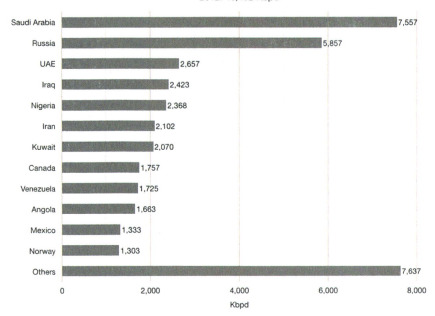

Exhibit 2.25 Top crude oil exporters
Source: Author, compiled with data from OPEC (2013)

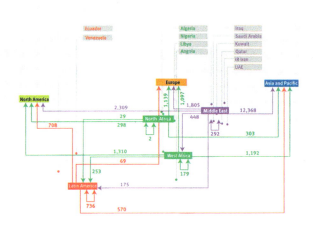

Exhibit 2.26 OPEC crude oil export flows
Source: OPEC (2013, p. 48)

Exports in 2012: 25,281 Kbpd

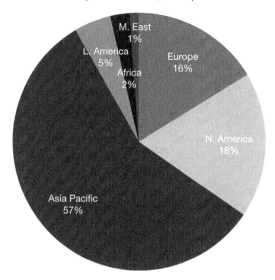

Exhibit 2.27 OPEC crude oil exports by destination
Source: Author, compiled with data from OPEC (2013)

A brief history of pricing in the oil industry

Probably the most interesting aspect of the oil industry is the procedure used to price the commodity. Oil's pricing mechanism has changed several times since the inception of the industry. It has followed closely the patterns of ownership and control of the commodity itself, and has gone through phases of perfect competition, to monopolistic and oligopolistic price determination, and finally to the modern competitive pricing mechanism that is in place today. In this section, we look at the development of oil price determination until the mid-1980s, through the history of the struggle for power in the oil industry. We focus on contemporary mechanisms and the use of benchmark pricing later in the chapter, when we discuss the most important physical crude oil markets. To put some context in the current discussion, Exhibit 2.28 shows the annual average price for crude oil, from 1861 to 2012.

Price volatility characterised the oil industry since its beginnings in the 1860s. New discoveries attracted many wildcat drillers who pumped the new crude as quickly as they could get away with, flooded the market and caused prices to collapse. As soon as deposits were depleted, prices soared once more, until the circle was repeated with discoveries. That situation changed when Standard Oil gradually took control of the industry at all stages of the supply chain: production, refining, transportation and retail sales. Until 1911, Standard Oil had an essential monopoly of oil in the United States.

The situation was not the same in the international oil market, however. American oil was competing with oil from Russia – extracted by the Nobel

Exhibit 2.28 Oil price history, 1861–2012

Source: Author, compiled with data from BP (2013a)

brothers – and from Indonesia – produced and carried by Royal Dutch Shell. After 1911, the situation became more complicated. The dissolution of Standard Oil left the United States with a number of smaller companies with different expertise and different degrees of vertical integration. Some of the 'baby' Standards were in fact quite big, such as Standard Oil of New Jersey. Most of the smaller 'baby' Standards, however, had to struggle to find new upstream suppliers – often abroad – or form downstream alliances with companies that had adequate retail sales networks.

In the meantime, the international market had two more contenders: Burmah, which exploited the oil reserves in Burma; and Anglo-Persian, which was owned by the British Government, Burmah and private shareholders, and operated in Persia. Shell had ventured in the American market, with the foundation of Aguila in Mexico in 1919, after the setback of its Russian venture by the Soviet Revolution. The picture was completed by Royal Dutch, with its Asiatic ventures and a few minor producers such as Romania. As all those companies were striving to secure supplies of crude and markets for their products, a price war, mainly between American and European companies, broke out that lasted almost until the end of the 1920s.

In August 1928, some of the most influential men in the oil business convened at Achnacarry in the Scottish Highlands: Henri Deterding of Royal Dutch Shell, Walter Teagle and Heinrich Riedemann of Standard Oil of New Jersey, Sir John Cadman of Anglo-Persian, William Melon of Gulf, and Col. Robert Stewart of Standard of Indiana. Although the meeting was to be on an informal and rather secretive basis, news of an oil company cartel soon leaked around the world. The agreement by the initial members of the cartel was to stop price wars and maintain current market shares intact. Although small at the beginning, the cartel had about 20 companies in the mid-1930s and controlled most of the international oil trade. The meeting remained known for posterity as the 'Achnacarry' or 'As is' or 'Pool association' agreement, and it was there that the *Gulf-plus* pricing formula was born.

This system was used by oil majors internationally until it was phased out soon after the Second World War. Prices were quoted on a CIF (cost, insurance, freight) basis, based on oil's FOB (free on board) price at the US Gulf, plus the hypothetical shipment cost from the US Gulf to the final destination. The system essentially applied a blanket price for all crudes, irrespective of their origin, effectively overpricing Middle East crude exported to Europe and Japan.

Underlying *Gulf-plus* prices were *US posted* prices. These were standard well head prices for crude oil from local producing fields, quoted from individual US refiners. These prices represented domestic prices for the US market only, and were often distorted by federal government controls. They were generally higher than the world market, reflecting the protectionism of US domestic oil markets. From 1974, however, US posted prices were generally lower than international prices, reflecting the attempt of the US government to dampen the effect of the huge increase in oil prices. After 1981, the Reagan administration phased out most controls on its domestic oil industry, so that US posted prices became directly competitive to export prices of non-US crudes.

After the Second World War, the *Gulf-plus* system was phased out due to clamours from the British and American Navies, initially, and the European Co-operation Administration, which supervised the implementation of the Marshall Plan. Under this pressure, oil companies started quoting FOB prices ex-Middle East (in 1950) and ex-Venezuela (in 1952). The new system was know as the *dual basing point system* and was more representative of the international price of oil, rather than the US domestic market.

Meanwhile, in the Middle East, the end of the First World War left the Allies with a difficult problem to resolve: the dissolution of the Ottoman Empire. British, French and Americans were all very keen on the potential of the deserts of Iraq, primarily, and the Arab Peninsula. This led to the 'Red Line Agreement', as discussed earlier in this chapter, which formed the IPC consortium from cooperation in the upstream sector between Anglo-Persian, Shell, CFP and a consortium of American companies. The important development in this period was the change of the host-company agreement for the Iranian concession, which changed from profit sharing to royalty crude. This arrangement formed the basis of several subsequent host-company agreements around the world.

This gradual shift in the role of national governments in pricing oil did not start in the Middle East, however. From the beginning of the twentieth century, both the American and the British had shown interest in Mexico's potential as an oil producer. The trouble was, though, that since 1917, Article 27 of the Mexican Constitution named the state as the sole owner of the country's subsoil rights. Successive governments tried vigorously to enforce that article, resulting in a long dispute that was finally ended with the bitter retreat of both American and British interests in the country, after the Mexican government took complete control and agreed to compensate the companies.

After the Mexico fiasco, the next obvious target for American oil companies was Venezuela, with its promising reserves under the bed of Lake Maracaibo. Although pressures for nationalisation were also strong in Venezuela, oil companies were essential for the development of the industry and were welcome, but the Venezuelan government clinched a 50/50 sharing agreement with the companies. The scheme meant that the government took 50 per cent of the net profits of oil companies' operations after deduction of royalties and other contractual payments to the state. The 'Venezuelan-style' sharing agreement soon paved the way to improved remuneration of host countries for the exploitation of their natural resources, and was later extended to the Middle East.

Before that, Middle East governments collected 50 per cent of oil companies' profits from operations, but that 50 per cent included royalties and other contractual obligations. Many countries felt that the 'Middle-East-style' 50/50 sharing was not adequate anymore. It was Iran that voiced its objection to, in fact, any sharing agreement at all, with the attempt of Prime Minister Dr Mossadegh to oust Anglo-Persian and nationalise the industry. Although that attempt was only short-lived, it set the tone for any subsequent sharing agreements between states and oil companies.

The Iranian nationalisation was only the beginning of what proved to be a long history of turmoil in the Middle East, which revolved around the oil industry. Later in the same decade, the Suez Canal was closed by the Egyptian government, leading to a massive increase in transport requirements for oil, which now had to be transited around the Cape of Good Hope, resulting in shortages and rationing of oil in Western Europe.

The 1950s and 1960s also witnessed a considerable decrease in the price of oil in the open market. On the supply side, production was increasing, particularly in the Middle East, exerting downward pressure on posted prices (which can be seen in Exhibit 2.28, especially when looking at prices in current day money). This, coupled with the expansion of several independently owned refineries, gave rise to an increased number of arm's-length deals (i.e. an open market in crude oil). By the end of the 1950s, almost all arm's-length deals were priced at a discount to official prices, a trend accentuated by the dumping of Soviet oil to the world market.

Depressed oil prices attracted the stern criticism of producing countries, resulting in the formation of OPEC in 1960. Soon enough, OPEC countries asked the oil companies for 'Venezuelan style' 50/50 sharing. The compromise reached in the ensuing negotiations became known as the 'OPEC royalty-expensing formula', and essentially allowed a 50/50 sharing of profits after royalties, in return for several concessions on the part of host countries.

The persistent discounting of prices during the 1950s and 1960s made oil considerably cheaper than coal and boosted its share of total energy consumption in the Western world. The oil embargo and the second Suez closure in 1967 failed to interrupt the growth of oil consumption and trade, as Western European countries had accumulated considerable stocks, and were also able to import crude from countries outside the embargo, which could import as much oil as they asked for from the Middle East. Shortages due to the longer haul around Cape of Good Hope were of no importance either, as a large part of Middle East crude was being carried by very large vessels (VLCCs), which could not transit Suez anyway.

Supply restrictions proved ineffective in raising oil prices, but it was excessive demand that spurred the first oil price shock. The first rumblings started with Colonel Qaddafi's demand for increased Libyan postings, on the basis that Libyan crude should command a premium for its quality and proximity to Western markets. This led to the Tripoli Agreement in 1971, which allowed increased Libyan postings with a wide Libya-Middle East differential, no discounting of posted prices, and a schedule for future increase of postings between 1971 and 1975.

In the meantime, the United States had dramatically increased its dependence on crude oil imports in the early 1970s, particularly so in 1973. A seller's market was very much in place, but it was the oil companies that skimmed it. With the outbreak of the Yom Kippur War, the Arab producers seized their chance to flex their muscle and demand higher prices. On 16 October 1973, OPEC imposed unilateral postings increases, and the following day it also decided on production cutbacks.

It was at this time that *official OPEC* posted prices (or *official OPEC postings*) came into existence. These were the prices quoted by OPEC countries. Their determination represented the consensus of member countries regarding their target prices, although they were at times violated by members. OPEC postings drove international crude oil markets from late 1973 to the first part of the 1980s. Prices were quoted for the Saudi Arabian 34° API light crude, FOB Ras Tanura, which was the *marker* or *benchmark* crude. Most other OPEC crudes were priced as discounts or premiums to Arabian light. Nowadays, many OPEC members still quote their own posted prices, which are usually calculated on the basis of one or more benchmark crudes, typically Brent, WTI or Dubai-Oman, depending on which market the oil is sold to.

Although the whole OPEC movement looked well orchestrated, it was in fact improvised along the way. There was no initial agreement over market shares among OPEC members, whose national interests frequently came into conflict. Some countries pushed for successive increases; others advocated restraint. The result was a stop-go pattern of oil price increases, which eventually stabilised above $10/bbl, in nominal terms, although in real terms the price of oil decreased through the 1970s. The Iranian Revolution and the outbreak of the Iran–Iraq War spurred fresh confusion in the oil market. Libya, on the one hand, followed a 'leapfrogging' pricing tactic, while Saudi Arabia tried to moderate the situation by adopting a price of $24/bbl, and advising restraint. It was only in June 1980 that OPEC managed to determine a price band of $32–37, which was acceptable by all members.

The new market situation prompted the increased participation of non-OPEC producers in the international oil market, both for security reasons but also because the new higher prices incentivised exploration and production of oil, which was far more expensive. The availability of several independent suppliers (i.e. not controlled by the state or any major oil company), coupled with the dismantling of the remaining price controls in the US market, gave way to a more transparent and liberal trading environment, at least in the US and Western Europe. One major piece in the new jigsaw was now North Sea oil. The production of Brent crude in the UK sector was in direct competition with Nigerian Bonny Light crude, both in terms of quality and in terms of markets. As most of Nigeria's revenues came from oil exports, the country's economy was particularly hurt from intense competition by Brent. As a result, Nigeria started undercutting OPEC's official posted prices, with the aim to recapture market share.

The lack of production and price discipline within OPEC resulted in spot oil prices spiralling downwards, and getting more and more out of touch with the organisation's official postings. OPEC's dismay was exacerbated by falling demand for energy worldwide and a considerable erosion of oil's share in primary energy consumption. OPEC remained a substantial, but residual, producer. Within OPEC, Saudi Arabia remained the *swing* producer. With tumbling oil prices, however, Saudi Arabia denounced its role in 1985 and started quoting prices to refiners on a *netback* basis. In general, netback prices were prices attached to crude oil, which have been calculated from prices of products, using the netback method. This means that the crude oil price is the residual of the product's price after subtracting the refiner's profit margin, the cost of refining and the cost of transport and insurance. This system means, of course, that the crude producers effectively accept the market risk, and at the same time guarantee the refiner's profit. Saudi Arabia was now ready to assume the price risk, with the aim to defend its market share. The immediate effect of this action was for market prices to tumble rapidly. Prices were now set in international commodity exchanges, notably the New York Mercantile Exchange (NYMEX), rather than OPEC ministerial meetings. In 1986, a barrel of crude oil was sold for under $12 and on certain days it dipped below $10. The path of oil prices since the mid-1980s has already been discussed earlier in the chapter. The key structural change was that now arm's-length spot transactions for physical oil cargoes and paper transactions for futures contracts contingent on the physical commodity were the ones determining oil prices. This competitive market pricing, which distils the market information on current demand, supply and expectations thereof, is still in place today, and we will look at it in the following section.

Physical crude markets

The discussion of oil's physical characteristics earlier in this chapter implies that there is a large variety of crude oils available in the open market, most of which are priced on a purely competitive basis. It is, therefore, important to know the physical characteristics, as well as the location of a particular crude, as these are key determinants of its final price. One such market that developed and matured in the 1980s is the market for Brent crude, which is extracted in the British sector of the North Sea. The presence of Brent crude prices in the pricing formulae of several crudes around the world justifies its placement at the top of the list of the crude oil covered in this section.

Brent and other North Sea

Brent is the name of a system of oilfields in the North Sea that includes the Brent, Cormorant, Hutton, Thistle, Murchison and Dunlin fields, whose output is used to create a standard blend. The output of the Brent system is comingled with that from the Ninian system, which includes the Ninian, Alwyn North and Agnus fields, and together they produce what is known as the Brent-Ninian Blend (BNB). Exhibit 2.29 shows the northern part of the North Sea, which includes the majority of the British oilfields and also depicts gas and condensate fields in the UK, as well as the Norwegian and Danish sectors.

Historically, it was in 1976 that the first consignments of Brent crude were loaded at Brent Spar, and in 1979 the terminal at Sullom Voe became operational. In the early 1990s, the production of Brent blend amounted to

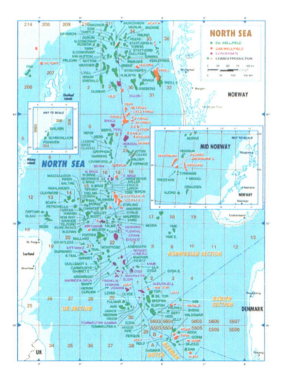

Exhibit 2.29 Map of oil and gas fields in the northern part of the North Sea

Source: Acorn Petroleum Services, www.acorn-ps.com/web/page/oilgas/nsfields/nnsmap.htm

about 850 Kbpd. In the early 2000s, this figure was down by more than half, and nowadays industry estimates put the production of the Brent and Ninian fields to ca. 220 Kbpd. The rapid decline of the physical base Brent blend created the potential threat of price manipulation, which would have undermined the position of Brent as a world pricing benchmark for oil. This was quickly addressed by the industry from the early 2000s, and the result was the addition of three more North Sea crude oils in the physical base: Forties and Oseberg (in 2002) and Ekofisk (in 2007); the first is in the UK sector, the latter two in the Norwegian sector of the North Sea. The four of them together form BFOE, the physical base of what the wide world still refers to as 'Brent crude', with their combined production amounting to ca. 1 mbpd.

Brent blend is denominated as a light, sweet crude, with a specific gravity of 38.5° API and a sulphur content of 0.41 per cent. Its constituent crudes, however, have a specific gravity in the range of 30–40° API, and a sulphur content of 0.2–1 per cent. Standard quality is, of course, important, since market participants expect at least some security in terms of the blend's properties.

Another important issue is the ownership of the fields, as control by a limited number of companies might create oligopolistic tendencies, and hence supply squeeze. In the case of the North Sea fields, including Brent, the UK government ensures that ownership interests are as widespread as possible. In 2010, for example, there were over 170 companies with ownership interests, but the ownership structure is never the same, as takeover activity is considerable. Some companies, however, are more important than others, in terms of ownership shares in – or entitlements to – Brent blend. The leading companies are Shell, ExxonMobil, BP, Chevron, Total and CNR, with Shell (who made the first discovery of this crude and named the field) being the key operator.

Brent is very much an international crude, with the majority of it being exported. Nowadays, most of the exports are directed to Europe, with Rotterdam in the Netherlands and Wilhelmshaven in Germany the main recipients. There are, however, other flows across the Atlantic to the United States and Canada, and even further away to South Korea. In the US market, Brent competes with other domestic light sweet crudes, such as WTI, or imported ones, such as Nigerian Bonny Light.

Brent is one of a number of crude oils produced in the North Sea. In the UK sector, blends from the Forties and Flotta sectors also compete in the export markets, and the former is already included in the BFOE physical base, as discussed earlier.

In the Norwegian sector, the most prominent fields are Ekofisk, Oseberg, Statfjord and Gullfaks. All of them enter the international market, as most of the Norwegian production is exported. The first two are already part of the BFOE physical base, whereas the other two are priced against Brent/BFOE. Norwegian crude production is primarily exported to European countries, with the United Kingdom being the major customer, followed by the Netherlands, Sweden and Germany. Some of the non-European importers of Norwegian production are the United States, South Korea and Canada.

WTI and other North America

While Brent crude is an extremely important benchmark for world oil prices, it is still in competition with what used to be the original pricing benchmark – WTI. It is worth remembering that the United States is the world's largest consumer of oil, accounting for nearly 20 per cent of world consumption, and also the world's largest importer. At the same time, the country is also the world's third largest producer, with an output of crude oil and NGLs at nearly 9 mbpd, which is set to rise with the advent of shale oil in the last few years. There are several crude oils, which are traded heavily, albeit only domestically, as crude oil exports are effectively banned since the mid-1970s. The country itself is divided into five *Petroleum Administration for Defence Districts* (PADDs): East Coast (PADD 1), Midwest (PADD 2), Gulf Coast (PADD 3), Rocky Mountain (PADD 4) and West Coast with Alaska and Hawaii (PADD 5) – Exhibit 2.30 shows the five districts and which states they include. Of these districts, the most important one is PADD 3, which produces nearly 60 per cent of total US crude oil. PADD 3 includes, of course, Texas, the biggest producing state, and the federal offshore fields in the US Gulf, which collectively form the second largest producing region. This district also holds half of the country's operable refining capacity, nearly 8.4 mbpd (of a total 16.3 mbpd) as of August 2013.

The most prominent crude in the United States, West Texas Intermediate is a blend of several crudes with specific gravities between 34 and 45° API and sulphur content below 0.5 per cent. The par grade is 40° API and has 0.4 per cent sulphur content, which is slightly lighter and as sweet as Brent. The

Exhibit 2.30 United States PADDs

Source: Author, with information from EIA (2013a)

physical base consists of crude deliveries at the end of the pipeline or suitable storage facilities at Cushing, Oklahoma. Although WTI is the par grade, there are several other crude oils that are actively traded. Sweet light crudes, similar to WTI, include: Louisiana Light Sweet (LLS), New Mexico Sweet, Oklahoma Sweet, South Texas Sweet and Low Sweet Mix (Scurry Snyder). The list does not stop there, however. The offshore fields of the US Gulf yield a number of different grades, including Mars, Thunder Horse, SGC (Southern Green Canyon), Poseidon and Eugene Island, all of them heavier and sourer than WTI. The list of PADD 3 grades would close with West Texas Sour and Heavy Louisiana Sweet, if it were not for the most recent and most exciting addition: Eagle Ford. This is a shale play that yields a number of different qualities, all of them very light (condensates) and sweet.

Another important crude is the one produced in Alaska. Alaskan North Slope (ANS) is a relatively sour and heavy crude, which is extracted from the fields in the North of Alaska at Prudhoe Bay and then moved via the Trans-Alaskan pipeline to Valdez. From there, it is shipped by tankers to the US West Coast and the US Gulf. The picture of crude oil production in the United States is completed with the Bakken shale play in the north of the country, in the states of North Dakota and Montana, as well as the Canadian provinces of Manitoba and Saskatchewan.

Over the border in Canada, crude oil production boomed throughout the 2000s. The existence of oil-bearing sands had been known for nearly three centuries and production attempts had been made since the late 1960s. The international oil prices, however, were not high enough to justify production at such a high cost. With oil prices on the ascent since 2000, however,

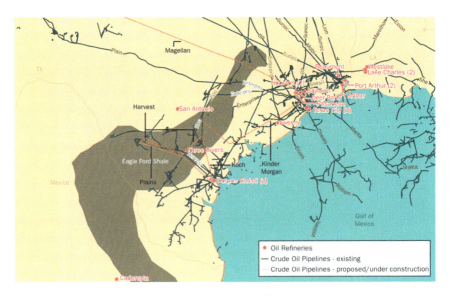

Exhibit 2.31 Eagle Ford shale play: formation, pipelines and refineries

Source: Platts (2013, p. 4)

production came on stream again in 2003 and has expanded since then. Today, Canada is the world's eighth largest crude oil producer and third largest reserve holder, behind Venezuela and Saudi Arabia, with over 170 billion barrels. Around half of its production comes from the Alberta oil sands, with the rest coming from the eastern Canadian provinces, such as Ontario, Newfoundland and Nova Scotia. From the eastern provinces come grades such as Terra Nova, Hibernia and White Rose, all medium to light sweet varieties. From Alberta come grades such as Lloyd Blend (a heavy and very sour grade), Mixed Sweet and Light Sour Blend, as well as Syncrude Sweet. The latter is produced after extracting bitumen from the oil sands and upgrading it to light crude by fluid coking, hydroprocessing, hydrotreating and reblending. The result is known as synthetic crude oil (SCO) or Syncrude, and is shipped via pipeline to Canadian and US refineries.

Dubai and other Middle East Gulf

The Middle East is the biggest exporter of crude in the world and plays, therefore, a key role in regulating the supply side of oil trade. The role of the Middle East was extensively discussed earlier in the chapter, so there is no need to repeat it in this section. As we know, Saudi Arabia is the world's largest producer and exporter, and produces a variety of crude grades, from the Arab Heavy to the Arab Extra Light. For many years, one of the most commonly quoted crudes for many years was Arab Light, and it still is one of the 12 constituent crude oils of the OPEC basket.

Since the 1980s, Dubai crude oil has been steadily rising as a new pricing benchmark, particularly for cargoes delivered East of Suez, mainly to Asia Pacific. This is a medium crude of 31° API and contains around 2 per cent sulphur. Its physical base has been steadily declining, so now it relies on two other regional crudes, Oman and Upper Zakum (Abu Dhabi), which are of similar quality and can be delivered in lieu of Dubai.

There are several other crude oils in this area, as it produces substantial amounts of both oil and gas, which are exported to the international market. These include: Basra Light (Iraq), Murban and Lower Zakum (Abu Dhabi), Qatar Land, Qatar Marine, Ras Gas condensate and Shaheen (Qatar), and South Pars condensate (Iran).

West Africa

A substantial amount of international oil trade is generated from the west coast of Africa, where the producing countries are Nigeria, Angola, Gabon, Congo, Cameroon and, more recently, Ghana. Their target markets are primarily transatlantic, notably the United States, but also Europe. In recent years, the other prime destination, particularly for Angolan crude oil, has been China. There are several types of crude coming out of the region, some better known than others. Historically, Bonny Light has been the most well known and is also one of the 12 OPEC basket crudes. Other grades include: Forcados,

Escravos, Brass River and Qua Iboe (Nigeria), Cabinda, Kuito, Nemba and Girassol (Angola), Kole and Lokele (Cameroon), N'Kosa and Djeno (Congo), Mandji and Rabi Light (Gabon), and Jubilee (Ghana). All of the above crudes use mainly Brent as a marker crude, but pricing on WTI is not uncommon, especially for cargoes destined for the US Gulf.

Black Sea/Mediterranean

In the Mediterranean, the main producers participating in the spot market have traditionally been Libya, Egypt, Syria and Algeria. Iran and Russia are also very active and important despite not having a Mediterranean coast; the former via the SUMED pipeline, which receives oil at Ain Sukhna in the Red Sea and transfers it to the Sidi Kerir terminal on the Mediterranean coast of Egypt, and the latter from the port of Novorossiysk in the Black Sea. Russia has now consolidated its position as the world's second largest exporter. The main Russian crude grade is Urals, a medium sour crude, which is transferred via a network of pipelines to the port of Novorossiysk in the Black Sea, from where it is shipped in tankers through Bosporus and on to its final destination. Urals crude is also exported via Russia's port in the Baltic Sea, Primorsk and Ust-Luga. In addition to Urals, Russia produces Siberian Light, a light and sweet grade, which it also exports via Primorsk and Novorossiysk.

The latter port is also the recipient of crude oil from Russian production platforms in the Caspian Sea, as well as large quantities of Tengiz, a light and sweet crude produced in the Kazakh section of the Caspian Sea. This is done via the CPC (Caspian Pipeline Consortium) pipeline, which delivers its CPC Blend to Yuzhnaya Ozereevka, near Novorossiysk. Kazakhstan also produces the Kumkol grade further to the east of the country, which it plans to export to China with the construction of the Kazakhstan-China pipeline from Atasu to Alashankou, which will connect to Kumkol and extend further westwards to eventually connect to Atyrau in the north of the Caspian Sea and the beginning of the CPC pipeline. Strategically, this is important for Kazakhstan as it will allow the country to market the production from its most recent project, Kashagan, both to the west and the east, depending on prices and contractual commitments.

The third crude oil producer in the Caspian Sea is Azerbaijan. Its Azeri Light, a medium to light sweet crude, is exported from the port of Baku, via two pipelines. The Baku-Supsa pipeline carries the oil to the Georgian port of Supsa on the Black Sea coast, from where it is loaded on tankers. The BTC (Baku-Tbilisi-Ceyhan) pipeline takes the oil from Baku, via Tbilisi in Georgia, and then down to the port of Ceyhan in the south-eastern corner of Turkey, from where it is also loaded to tankers for export. From Syria come two rather small streams of crude, Syrian Light and Souedie, a heavy and very sour crude. However, under the current (late 2013) political climate, not a lot of it finds its way to the international market.

Coming now to the main Mediterranean basin, there are several crude oils that are traded alongside Urals, CPC and Azeri Light. From Egypt comes the

Suez Blend, a medium sour grade, alongside Iranian Heavy and Iranian Light crude (provided the embargo on Iranian oil is terminated), which are lifted at Sidi Kerir. Iraqi Kirkuk Blend is exported from the Kurdistan region of the country's north, via the Kirkuk-Ceyhan pipeline, to the port of Ceyhan. Moving on towards the western part of the Mediterranean, Algeria and Libya are the other two main exporters. Algeria's Saharan Blend and Zarzataine are both light sweet crude oils. Libya's Es Sider, on the other hand, is slightly heavier, but still a very important oil for European markets, especially for Italy. Once again, the aftermath of the Arab Spring is affecting Libyan exports. At the time of writing, there were frequent disruptions to Libya's exports, to the point that less than 10 per cent of its 1.25 mbpd capacity was operative.

Latin America

This part of the world has been an important oil producer and exporter for a very long time now. The natural destination for exports from these regions is the United States. Indeed, in 2012, the US sourced 11 per cent of its imports from Mexico and the same amount from Venezuela, with smaller flows coming from Colombia and Brazil.

Venezuela is, of course, the world's largest reserve holder, and PDVSA, the state oil company, produces a number of different grades of crude oil, most of the heavy to medium and sour variety. Bachaquero is probably the best known of Venezuelan grades and Merey is the one included in the OPEC basket. Both of them are very heavy and sour, in the range of 12–16° API, and sulphur content of ca. 2.5 per cent. Other grades include Tia Juana Light and Mesa 30, both of which are medium and sour.

Mexico has been a long-standing exporter, particularly to the United States. The country was among the first to nationalise its hydrocarbons, and did so in 1938. After 75 years, Mexico finds itself with declining production and exports and with great difficulties to incentivise foreign oil companies to come and boost its exploration efforts. Its main crude grade is the heavy and sour Maya, most of which is exported to the United States. Isthmus and Olmeca are its lighter grades, which tend to be directed to Mexico's own refineries.

Brazil is Latin America's second largest producer, after Venezuela, with ca. 2.2 mbpd in 2012. Domestic consumption of ca. 2.8 mbpd, however, means that the country is a net importer. Over 90 per cent of its crude oil comes from offshore fields and is, unusually, heavy sweet. Typical grades are Marlim and Roncador. The country's position as a sizeable oil producer may be boosted further when development of its Libra oilfield goes ahead in the next few years. The possibility of Brazil becoming a sizeable exporter, particularly to the North American and European markets, is certainly on the cards.

Colombia is a relatively small producer, compared to its South American neighbours, but its production has increased steadily since 2008 due to increasing exploration and development. Its crude oil is mostly heavy and sour, with Cano Limon the lightest and relatively sweetest of the lot. The remaining countries in the region are relatively less significant oil producers, although several crude grades find their way to the international markets. Argentinian Escalante, Ecuadorian Oriente and Peruvian Loreto are such examples. Again, all of them are relatively heavy crudes (19–24° API) and mostly sour.

Asia Pacific

As a region, Asia Pacific is in huge deficit in terms of oil. According to BP (2013a), the region produced 8.3 mbpd in 2012 and consumed 29.8 mbpd in the same year. Inevitably, the region relies on substantial imports, particularly from the Middle East, West and North Africa, and Russia.

Half of the region's production comes from a number of onshore and offshore fields in China. There are several grades, some of which are: Daqing, Nanhai Light and Shengli. They have a range of qualities, from sour, to light and varying degrees of sulphur content. Indonesia is another established producer, although its declining production made the country a net importer and caused it to lose its place as an OPEC member. Still, there are several streams of Indonesian crude that are traded regionally. The longest-standing one is Minas, but other grades include Attaka (light), Duri (heavy) and Senipah (condensate), although this list is far from exhaustive.

Another key producer in the region is Malaysia, with its Tapis Light, sweet crude oil being extensively traded regionally and used as a key local benchmark in Singapore. Other Malaysian grades traded regionally are Miri Light and Labuan. The two relatively most recent participants in this regional market are Australia and Vietnam. Both countries have intensified their exploration and production efforts in the last decade or so. Vietnam's Bach Ho and Australia's Gippsland are the two most commonly traded crude grades, although other grades, such as Su Tu Den, Cossack and Enfield, are also traded in the region.

Finally, Russia is also a keen exporter to the region of the oil it produces in several fields in Eastern Siberia. The production from these fields is collected by the ESPO (East Siberia Pacific Oil) pipeline, which delivers the light and sweet ESPO Blend to the port of Kozmino, from where it is lifted by tankers for delivery to Chinese, South Korean and Japanese buyers.

Pricing methodology

Historically, crude oil has been sold on the basis of long-term contracts, sometimes as long as the life of a particular field. Life-of-field contracts rarely exist nowadays, if at all. Term contracts do exist, of course, but the way they are priced has also evolved during the course of oil's history. Whereas term contract quantities and prices were all fixed at the beginning of the contract, the increased irritation of host producing countries towards the prices paid to them by Western oil companies meant that the original term contracts had to be replaced with ones that allowed at least some degree of price renegotiation driven by market demand and supply dynamics.

As we saw in the history of oil earlier in this chapter, oil pricing has evolved from pricing essentially dictated by international oil companies, to those negotiated between the same companies and host nations asserting their right to extract a higher economic rent for their natural resources, to administrative pricing by OPEC members and finally to a brief period of netback pricing, whereby crude oil prices were simply pegged to prices for refined products as they were competitively determined in the open markets of developed economies. For a more detailed review of the evolution of oil pricing and a detailed discussion of the current pricing system, see Fattouh (2011). From 1986 onwards, we have witnessed the transition of the oil pricing mechanism to a market-led system, with spot physical transactions for a multitude of crude oil grades of different specifications and locations, on the one hand, and a number of layers of derivative paper products, including futures, options, swaps, some of which are traded in commodity exchanges and some as over-the-counter (OTC) products. In this section, we focus on the pricing of physical crude oils using a number of benchmark crudes and how these benchmarks operate. We defer the discussion on derivative products for later in the text.

The side effect of the third oil price shock of the mid-1980s and partly what led to that was the emergence of the spot – or cash – market and prices. These are prices quoted in one-off, arm's-length deals. Before the 1980s, spot prices were quoted primarily for refined products. If there were any occasional spot market transactions for crude oil, there was no publicly reported information about them, so that spot prices for crude oil were inferred from product prices.

Although the term 'spot' may allude to the immediacy with which a cargo of oil is delivered, this is not true and in fact impractical. First of all, the oil itself needs to be produced, perhaps blended and then placed in port/terminal storage tanks awaiting lifting. Even when spot transactions are done on an FOB (free-on-board) basis, which is the norm, there is a time lag between agreeing the purchase and lifting it. The next phase involves waterborne transportation, typically by large crude oil carriers, with voyages lasting from a few days (say from the North Sea to Northwest European ports), to a few weeks (say from the Middle East Gulf to Pacific Rim ports) or even over a month (say from the Middle East Gulf to US Gulf ports via Cape Good Hope). When the transaction takes place after lifting, which is quite common in the oil industry, further adjustments are made to the final price, which is now a CIF (cost, freight and insurance) basis, or any other contract terms that make the seller more involved in the delivery of the cargo to the buyer. In both cases, it is quite common to price the cargo around the time of its lifting from the export terminal (FOB basis), or its arrival at the final destination (CIF basis).

In addition to the prevailing contract terms, the price for a particular crude oil P_c is determined on the basis of a formula such as $P_c = P_B \pm \Delta$, where P_B is the benchmark price and Δ is the differential. So, at the minimum, a particular crude oil will trade at a premium or a discount to the benchmark price and the differential may depend on a number of factors, including quality, desirability of the particular crude, availability of other competitive crude grades and so on. This means that both the underlying benchmark price and the differential can and will fluctuate.

Following on from this, it is now common to use spot prices, or rather an agreed spot price average, to price term contracts, in some cases on a cargo-by-cargo basis. So although the contractual agreement to supply/purchase the crude oil is long-term, the price is set on a much more short-term basis and is market-driven.

The final link in this pricing system is the existence of a reliable source of market information on the various crude oils and, especially, the benchmarks. This is a function performed by the price reporting agencies, or PRAs. There are two main PRAs, when it comes to crude oil prices – Platts (owned by publishers McGraw-Hill) and Argus Media (thereafter Argus). There are a few more PRAs publishing price information for refined products and chemicals, but Platts and Argus are the de facto market leaders. What the PRAs deliver is a series of price assessments at the end of every day. They do this by contacting market participants (oil majors, upstream producers, oil traders, refiners and so on) to find out whether they have bought/sold specific cargoes and from/to whom. They then cross-check this information with the respective counterparties, in order to establish the accuracy of the information and whether it can be included in the calculation of the bid-ask price range for the particular crude oil for the day. The two PRAs follow slightly different methodologies. Platts uses a specific time window during each day, which it calls 'market-on-close' or MOC methodology. Argus, on the other hand, uses a weighted average of prices for cargoes bought/sold during the course of a particular day. Both agencies publish a daily report for crude oil prices around the world, including the key benchmarks. A sample of Platts report is shown in Exhibit 2.32.

Having established how important spot prices and benchmark prices are, it is time to turn to the three key crude oil benchmarks that are currently predominant in the pricing of crude oils around the world: Brent, WTI and Dubai.

Brent pricing

Brent production was boosted after the first two oil price shocks, when it became profitable to extract the rather high-cost oil under the very dangerous rough waters of the North Sea. This new light sweet crude was not only used in the domestic UK market, but it was sought after by many refiners in developed economies on both sides of the Atlantic. Its quality made it highly competitive against West African crude oils, primarily Bonny Light, and its production in a politically safe environment meant that supply disruptions were highly unlikely. The licensing system used by the UK government meant that Brent had widespread ownership, so that no individual producer could squeeze the market in order to artificially raise prices.

High quality, which leads to high marketability, and broad ownership are the two fundamental prerequisites for the establishment of a price benchmark in any market. With NYMEX light sweet crude (essentially WTI) fulfilling

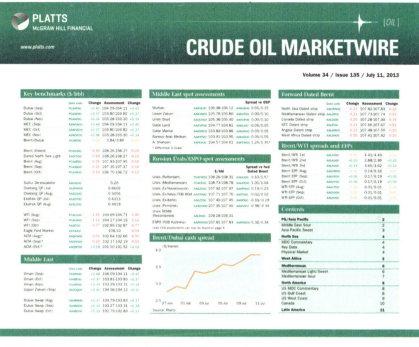

Exhibit 2.32 Sample of Platts Crude Oil Marketwire
Source: www.platts.com

this role in the US domestic market, Brent became the obvious choice for internationally traded crude oil. The market developed on two levels: 'wet' cargoes, which were due for delivery in the next 7–15 days; and 'paper' cargoes, or forward contracts, which were bought and sold between market participants, until they were eventually linked to specific cargoes with a particular delivery window. The two markets that developed were *Dated* (DTD) Brent and *15-day* (or *forward* or *paper*) Brent, respectively. Over time, the declining quantity of physical Brent necessitated the inclusion of additional North Sea crude oils to increase the physical base to what is now the BFOE, as discussed earlier in the chapter. In addition to this, the pricing window for Dated Brent has expanded from 7–15 days, to 10–21 days, and currently to 10–25 days, in order to allow more cargoes to enter the pricing window and ensure that the prices are truly competitive. As a result, the forward market for Brent is known as *25-day Brent* (or *25-day cash BFOE* or *25-day paper BFOE*), reflecting the arrangements in the pricing process of Dated Brent. So, let us now have a look at how this process works.

The orderly operation of Dated (DTD) Brent is important to ensure its price formation is not subject to unexpected disruptions, given that it is used to price so many other crude oils around the world. There is, therefore, a standard procedure for its delivery, which consists roughly of the following steps:

- Equity holders nominate their intention to deliver Dated Brent cargoes (which can be any of the BFOE constituent crude oils) to be produced in any month by the beginning of the previous month. Soon after that, the loading schedule is released. For example, loading dates for cargoes to be delivered during November 2013 were released on 7 October 2013.
- Cargoes are lifted in standard parcels of 600,000 bbls, with a tolerance of ±1 per cent (i.e. ±6,000 bbls). For standard Brent quality, this would equate to ca. 79,000–80,000 tonnes, the size of a typical Aframax tanker.
- Each cargo is given a number and a loading (or lay-can) window, during which the cargo has to be loaded on a designated vessel. Each window is typically three days long, with the first day of the first window starting on the first day of the month, and the last day of the last window ending on the last day of the month. So, for November 2013, the first window (assuming a three-day lay-can) would be 1–3 November, and the last 28–30 November.

These specific dated and numbered cargoes form the basis of the physical Brent/BFOE market, and these are the cargoes that are bought/sold between market participants in the spot market. As mentioned earlier, spot does not mean immediate delivery in the oil market. Typically, it implies a time lag between the transaction and the actual cargo delivery. In this market, the earliest delivery is normally 10 days after the spot transaction and the delivery window can extend to 25 days forward. For this reason, when the PRAs assess spot prices, they refer to them as Dated Brent/BFOE prices for loading 10–25 days ahead. For example, on 20 October, price assessments will be for cargoes due to be delivered between 30 October and 14 November. Price assessments on 21 October will be for cargoes to be loaded between 31 October and 15 November and so forth. Platts publishes these assessments under the name 'Dated Brent', whereas Argus uses the name 'North Sea Dated'. The underlying commodity is the same (one of the four BFOE constituents), the principle of the assessment is the same (the most competitive of the four grades on each day), but the methodology of the calculation is different (Platts uses MOC and Argus uses averaging).

Given the nature of the Dated Brent/BFOE market operations and the size of each parcel, the Dated Brent market is really for large companies, who either need the cargoes for their own refineries or sell them to international buyers. These companies are usually oil majors, independent oil traders, independent refiners, upstream producers and occasionally financial institutions who may have a presence in the physical North Sea oil market.

Having seen how the Dated Brent market works, we now turn to the *25-day cash BFOE*, essentially the forward market for BFOE. As far as forward markets are concerned, this is an unusual one, in that practically all the aspects of the contract are standardised, rather than customised. The cargo parcel is standard at 600,000 barrels (although partial cargoes of 100,000 barrels are also possible), the quality of the cargo is standard (current quality Brent-Ninian Blend, Forties, Oseberg or Ekofisk, the latter three with appropriate price adjustments for quality) and so is delivery (Sullom Voe or appropriate terminal for each grade). What remains unknown for both transacting parties is the precise loading window for the cargo and of course the price, which is negotiable.

Forward BFOE contracts can be bought/sold between parties for delivery as far in the future as the two parties wish, but for practical purposes it is the next three months forward that are more actively traded and for which the PRAs provide daily price assessments. Contracts for 25-day cash BFOE can be sold and bought at any point in time, all the way up to 25 days before the delivery date (the first day of the three-day loading window) of the Dated Brent cargo. After this deadline, the particular 25-day BFOE becomes 'wet' and can only be traded as Dated Brent. Based on this principle, the front (next forward) month becomes 'wet' when its first cargo becomes 'wet', which is on the fifth day of a 30-day month. For example, July 25-day BFOE will expire on 5 June, but prices for the rest of June will continue to be assessed until 30 June. On 1 July, August becomes the front month, September becomes the second month and October becomes the third month.

For the market participants, there are two ways to clear their positions – *nominations* or a *paper, cash* or *dry book-out*. Once the seller of a 25-day BFOE has the precise details of a cargo (number and lay-can), he can hand a nomination (i.e. a document notifying the details of the cargo) to the buyer. At this point, the buyer can: (a) hold on to the nomination and sell it on as a Dated Brent cargo; (b) hold on to the nomination and take delivery of the cargo, in which case he has to nominate a vessel to lift the cargo; or (c) pass the nomination to another party to whom he had sold a 25-day BFOE at a different point in time. If the buyer chooses (c), this is known as 'passing the parcel' and can continue up to 5:00 p.m. London time, 25 days before the first day of the lay-can for the specific cargo.

Most of the times, however, buying or selling 25-day BFOE is done purely for hedging or speculation purposes. As a result, a party may have bought a cargo at one point in time for delivery in a specific month and at another point in time he may have sold another cargo for delivery in the same month. In a typical futures market, say the Intercontinental Exchange where Brent futures contracts are traded, this would be equivalent to the party reversing his position, cashing his profit or loss, and exiting. In the 25-day BFOE, however, this is not done automatically. To cancel out their positions, the various transacting parties need to communicate with each other and agree to form a *book-out circle*, in which participants cancel their contracts with each other by making cash settlements for the difference between contract price and reference price. An example of a book-out is given in Exhibit 2.33.

In this example, A has sold one contract to B at $98/bbl, B has sold one contract to C at $97.80/bbl and C has sold one contract to A at $98.20/bbl. Each transaction has most probably taken place at different times and at different prices. If the circle (A-B, B-C, C-A) is identified, then the parties can agree to forego delivery of the physical cargo, and settle the transaction with accounting entries in their books. If all parties agree, then C buys back

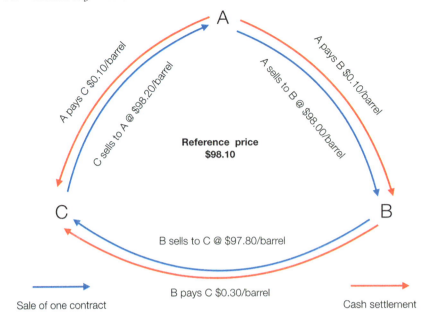

Exhibit 2.33 A book-out circle

Source: Author

from A, B from C, and A from B. The price of each contract is compared against the reference price at the day of the book-out and the appropriate cash transfers are made. In our example, A has agreed to sell to B at $98/bbl below the reference price of $98.10/bbl, which means that he has to pay the difference of $0.10/bbl to B to settle in cash. The payment will, of course, be for one cargo (i.e. 600,000 bbls or $60,000). In a similar fashion, B has agreed to sell to C at a price below the reference price, and he now has to make a payment of $0.30/bbl to C (i.e. $180,000). Trader C, on the other hand, has agreed to sell at a price above the reference price, so in order to settle in cash he must receive the difference of $0.10/bbl from A, or a payment of $60,000. Looking at the individual cash positions for each party, we see that:

- A pays $60,000 to B and $60,000 to C, a total loss of $120,000, or $0.20/bbl.
- B pays $180,000 to C and receives $60,000 from A, a total loss of $120,000, or $0.20/bbl.
- C receives $180,000 from B and $60,000 from A, a total profit of $240,000, or $0.40/bbl.
- The total profit for C equals the losses of A and B put together – a zero-sum game.

Book-outs are not always as easy as they sound. Circles might involve a lot more than three parties and can be very difficult to identify. Once identified, all parties must be willing to participate, and no party can be obliged to do so. Despite all these complications, however, it is estimated that about two-thirds of the 25-day BFOE market is cleared by book-outs every month.

A final note on the Brent/BFOE market concerns the possibility of using contracts for differences (CFDs). The need for this instrument stems from the fact that although the agreement to buy/sell a Dated Brent cargo is made now, the actual pricing of the transaction is done around the loading window of the cargo, which is a few weeks into the future. Between now and the loading window, the Dated Brent price will most probably change, leaving the trans-acting parties with risk to manage. This risk can perhaps be managed with the use of the second month forward contract, but there is still a basis risk (i.e. the risk that the price movement of the forward contract will not exactly match that of Dated Brent, as the two are not perfectly correlated). This is where the CFDs become useful. They are relatively short-term swaps, assessed by the PRAs for several weeks ahead (four by Argus and eight by Platts), and represent the market differential between Dated Brent and a forward month BFOE, typically the second forward month. The CFD swap is between the uncertain, or floating, price of a Dated Brent/25-day BFOE differential and a certain, or fixed, such differential, which is assessed by the PRAs based on market trades.

To give a more practical example, consider the following. On 11 July, a crude oil producer has sold a cargo of Forties for loading 24–26 July (13–15 days from the current date), with the price set as the Dated Brent averaged over five days around the loading time (i.e. the average over 22–26 July). The current Dated Brent price is $108.26, but he is afraid that the Dated Brent price may decrease (i.e. he may end up receiving a lower price). To hedge against this risk, he may wish to sell the second forward month (September) at the current price of $107.36 and also sell a CFD for week 2 (22–26 July) for $0.60.

When the time comes to sell his cargo, the five-day average Dated Brent price (22–26 July) has gone down to $107.95, which is what he actually gets for selling his cargo spot. In the meantime, the price of the September forward contract has gone to $107.02. By buying back this contract, he has made a profit of ($107.36 –$107.02 =) $0.34, which can be added to his spot price of $107.95. In addition, he buys back his CFD, which is now priced at $0.70, making him a loss of ($0.60 – $0.70 =) $0.10. His effective sale price then becomes:

$$\$107.95 + \$0.34 - \$0.10 = \$108.19.$$

In the end, he sold his cargo for only slightly less than what the Dated Brent price was a the time of the spot transaction and he managed this with the help of the profit from the second forward month hedge, although his CFD trade made him a loss.

WTI pricing

Like Brent, WTI is a very actively traded crude oil and it has a long history as a price benchmark, both for the US domestic and international markets.

Unlike Brent, WTI has a much simpler pricing structure and a much more straightforward link with the light sweet crude oil contract traded on NYMEX, which is now part of the CME Group. This futures contract was launched in March 1983 and rose to prominence during the third oil price crisis in 1986. With the world economy in recession and demand for oil, especially OPEC oil, suffering, OPEC members struggled to keep to their quotas, tried to undercut each other's prices in spot market sales in order to gain market share, and eventually prompted Saudi Arabia, the swing producer who kept decreasing its production to maintain the overall quota levels, to resort to netback pricing. With netback prices in force, it became paramount to have a market-determined price for refined products, from which refining margins and transportation costs could be deducted, in order to calculate the next price of the crude oil payable back to the producers. Since late 1978, there was already a heating oil futures contract traded on NYMEX. With the introduction of the light sweet crude contract, the netback link between products and crude was established. As the United States was very much the most dominant demand market for crude oil and refined products, the world looked to the futures market in New York to establish a world price for crude oil and WTI, the main physical crude oil deliverable against the futures contract, became the de facto world benchmark.

The physical base of WTI has already been described earlier in this chapter. Physical trading takes place at the pipeline hub in Cushing, Oklahoma, and the crude oil is delivered at the end of a pipeline or in suitable storage tanks in the area. The physical delivery of WTI and other acceptable substitutes is specified in the CME/NYMEX traded contract:

> Delivery shall be made free-on-board ('F.O.B.') at any pipeline or storage facility in Cushing, Oklahoma with pipeline access to Enterprise, Cushing storage or Enbridge, Cushing storage. Delivery shall be made in accordance with all applicable Federal executive orders and all applicable Federal, State and local laws and regulations.
>
> At buyer's option, delivery shall be made by any of the following methods: (1) by interfacility transfer ('pumpover') into a designated pipeline or storage facility with access to seller's incoming pipeline or storage facility; (2) by in-line (or in-system) transfer, or book-out of title to the buyer; or (3) if the seller agrees to such transfer and if the facility used by the seller allows for such transfer, without physical movement of product, by in-tank transfer of title to the buyer.[9]

The WTI contract is more flexible than Dated Brent, with contracts only 1,000 barrels large and deliveries typically in parcel of 50,000–100,000 barrels. The WTI futures market is also very forward-looking, with months open until nine years ahead. More specifically, consecutive months are listed for the

---

9 CME (2013).

current year and the next five years; in addition, the June and December contract months are listed beyond the sixth year. Finally, WTI contracts are also more flexible than Brent contracts, in that they allow a considerable number of alternative crudes to be delivered. Specific domestic crudes with 0.42 per cent sulphur by weight or less, not less than 37° API gravity nor more than 42° API gravity. The following domestic crude streams are deliverable (as of November 2013): West Texas Intermediate, Low Sweet Mix (Scurry Snyder), New Mexican Sweet, North Texas Sweet, Oklahoma Sweet, South Texas Sweet. Also, specific foreign crudes of not less than 34° API nor more than 42° API are deliverable. The following foreign streams are deliverable: Brent Blend, for which the seller shall receive a 30¢-per-barrel discount below the final settlement price; Norwegian Oseberg Blend is delivered at a 55¢-per-barrel discount; Nigerian Bonny Light, Qua Iboe, and Colombian Cusiana are delivered at 15¢-per-barrel premiums.

Despite all these attractive attributes, however, in recent years WTI seems to have lost its crown as the world's prime crude oil benchmark, while Brent has consolidated itself in this role. Increasingly, WTI is a US domestic benchmark, with prices used for other US crude oils, as well as cargoes imported into the North American market. The relationship between WTI and Brent is often observed in the co-movement between their two prices. Historically and all the way up to 2010, WTI prices have been above those for Brent. The explanation was quite straightforward: the differential was due to quality and location. Brent was a crude imported into the United States and to make it competitive with WTI, it needed an FOB price below that of WTI, to reflect the slightly lower quality and also the freight that had to be added to deliver Brent to US refineries. Exhibit 2.34 shows the spot price series for the two benchmarks since the beginning of 2000 until the end of October 2013, plotted as solid lines and measured on the left axis. Their price differential (WTI *minus* Brent) is plotted as an area and measured on the right axis. It is evident that until mid-2010, WTI traded above Brent, with the WTI premium fluctuating mostly around $0–5/bbl, although in some instances it did trade at a discount. From mid-2010 onwards, however, the WTI discount versus Brent has been consistent, and even exceeded $25/bbl between August and October 2011. More recently, in Q3 2013, the discount has shrunk and is currently (end October) ca. $10/bbl.

Why is this, then? Market analysts have identified several causes: the increased domestic oil production, which has created a glut; the irreversibility of domestic oil pipelines, which are geared towards receiving, rather than exporting, the various crude oils; and the short supply of storage facilities. The latter two causes seem to have been addressed in recent months, but the issue of increased domestic production remains outstanding and may possibly become more problematic with more shale oil coming on stream. Whatever the future development may be, it seems that, for now, WTI is primarily a North American benchmark, suitable for crude oils produced domestically or imported in the area. For cargoes trading all over the rest of the world, Brent seems to have established itself as the prime choice for benchmark pricing.

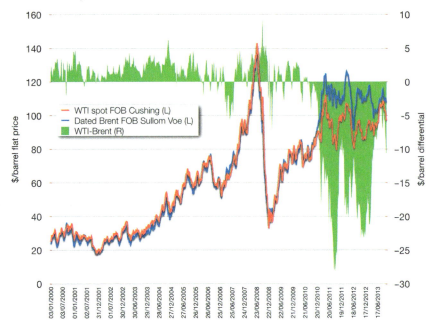

Exhibit 2.34 WTI and Brent weekly average prices, 2000–2013 (weekly averages)

Source: Author, compiled with data from Thomson Reuters Datastream (codes used: CRUDOIL and OILBRNP)

Dubai pricing

Dubai is the newest of the three benchmark crudes and gained prominence from 2000, when the ascent of emerging economies in Asia Pacific meant that much larger quantities of crude oil, especially from the Middle East and West Africa, found their way into the region. Dubai is a Middle Eastern crude oil, coming from the smallest (in terms of oil) emirate. Although it was produced in relatively small quantities, it was one of the very few Gulf crudes that could be traded in the spot market. The rapid decline in the production of Dubai crude has created a similar situation to that for Brent. Although Dubai is still the name of the benchmark, it is frequently Oman or Upper Zakum crude that is delivered instead, as Dubai crude production is estimated to be below 60 Kbpd. As Fattouh (2012, p. 3) notes, 'Dubai has turned into a brand, or index, representing a basket of mid-sour crudes'. These are crude oils travelling predominantly from the Middle East to Asia Pacific, a trade flow that has grown substantially in recent years, as emerging economies in the latter region are expanding their refining capacity, in anticipation of the growth in their demand for oil. As a result, many official selling prices (OSPs) for Middle East Gulf grades tend to be formula-priced using Dubai and/or Brent, for cargoes due to Asia Pacific and Europe, while also using WTI for any cargoes due to North America.

Earlier in the chapter, we saw that Dubai is a heavy and sour crude, and hence expected to trade at a lower price than Brent. Exhibit 2.35 shows that this is indeed the case, but it also shows the pricing paradox with regard to WTI, a light sweet crude, which is trading below Dubai as well.

Asia Pacific markets

This region has been a bit of an oddity in terms of pricing benchmarks. As noted earlier, there are several regional crude grades available, coming primarily from Indonesia and Malaysia, but also from Australia, China and Vietnam. The region, however, is largely dependent on imports, predominantly from the Middle East, but also from West Africa and even the North Sea. As a result, there are several crude grades traded in the region, some of which we discussed earlier. In addition to these grades, three regional indices have also been developed over the years: APPI, ICP and JCC.

The Asian Petroleum Price Index (APPI) is assessed twice weekly by a panel of traders, producers and refiners. It is based on a basket of crude oils traded in the Asia Pacific region, including imported and regionally produced ones. The Indonesian Crude Price index is assessed once a month by Pertamina, the Indonesian state oil company, and is effectively an Official Sale Price (OSP)

Exhibit 2.35 Dubai prices versus Brent and WTI prices, 2000–2013 (weekly averages)

Source: Author, compiled with data from Thomson Reuters Datastream (codes used: CRUDOIL, OILBRNP and DUBC)

Exhibit 2.36 JCC versus Brent and Dubai prices, 2000–2013 (weekly averages)

Source: Author, compiled with data from Thomson Reuters Datastream (codes used: OILBRNP, DUBC and CRUDJCC)

for the various crude oils it produces, led by Minas. The Japan Crude Cocktail is calculated by the Petroleum Association of Japan (PAJ) and is an average of the DDP prices[10] of the various crude oils landing in Japan. The JCC is extensively used as a marker of crude oil prices in the region, but also to price LNG (liquefied natural gas) cargoes traded in Asia Pacific. Historically, this was justified by the fact that oil and gas are competitive substitutes for a number of energy uses: natural gas versus fuel oil for electricity generation; natural gas versus LPG for domestic use; and natural gas versus naphtha for petrochemical manufacture.

All of these price indices, however, have a common fundamental characteristic – they are reactive. This means that they are calculated, with some time lag, after the prices of the individual crude oils have been set. The result is that they are not really benchmark prices; they are rather market activity indices, reflecting the level of prices based on recent transactions. Behind these prices, one can ultimately trace the effects of the three key benchmarks, especially Brent and Dubai.

10 DDP stands for Deposit Duty Paid. This is one of the 11 Incoterms used in international trade. It includes the cost of the commodity, insurance, freight, and any export and import taxes. It is effectively the CIF price plus customs taxes, which is how the crude oil prices landing in Japan enter the JCC calculation.

Conclusion

Oil continues being right at the heart of world energy, although its role and significance has changed over the years. The history of the oil industry is, of course, fascinating, but knowledge of it does not offer just pleasure; it also helps build an understanding of the economics of the industry. The previous chapter focused on the economics of energy production and consumption; this chapter concentrated on the particulars of crude oil supply, as well as oil pricing. After the oil price collapse of the mid-1980s, the world witnessed a notable switch to open market pricing. This led to the emergence of three key benchmarks: Brent, WTI and Dubai. Although not commanding an important part of world production or trade, their prices are instrumental in the trading of the many different types of crude oil around the world, and they also act as indispensable reference prices for the industry at large, including derivative paper contracts (futures, options, swaps and so on), royalty/taxation and production sharing contracts, and they even influence the prices of other energy commodities, such as natural gas, as we shall see later.

The next chapter will deal with the downstream part of the oil industry, as we focus on petroleum refining and trade in oil products.

References

Adelman, M.A. (2002) 'World oil production and prices 1947–2000', *Quarterly Review of Economics & Finance*, 42: 169–191.

Alhajji, A.F. and Huettner, D. (2000) 'OPEC and world crude oil markets from 1973 to 1994: cartel, oligopoly, or competitive?', *Energy Journal*, 21: 31–59.

Bentzen, J. (2007) 'Does OPEC influence crude oil prices? Testing for co-movements and causality between regional crude oil prices', *Applied Economics*, 39: 1375–1385.

BP (2013a) *Statistical Review of the World Energy 2013*, British Petroleum, accessed online at: www.bp.com/statisticalreview.

—— (2013b) *World Energy Outlook 2030*, British Petroleum, accessed online at www.bp.com/en/global/corporate/about-bp/statistical-review-of-world-energy-2013/energy-outlook-2030.html.

CME (2013) *Light Sweet Crude Oil (WTI) Futures*, Chicago Mercantile Exchange, accessed online at: www.cmegroup.com/trading/energy/crude-oil/light-sweet-crude_contract_specifications.html.

EIA (2013a) *PADD Definitions*, Energy Information Administration, accessed online at: www.eia.gov/oog/info/twip/padddef.html.

—— (2013b) *US Imports by Country of Origin*, Energy Information Administration, accessed online at: www.eia.gov/dnav/pet/pet_move_impcus_a2_nus_epc0_im0_mbblpd_a.htm.

Fattouh, B. (2011) *An Anatomy of the Crude Oil Pricing System*, Working Paper WPM40, Oxford: Oxford Institute of Energy Studies.

—— (2012) *The Dubai Benchmark and its Role in the International Oil Pricing System*, Oxford Institute of Energy Studies, accessed online at: www.oxfordenergy.org/wpcms/wp-content/uploads/2012/03/The-Dubai-Benchmark-and-its-Role-in-the-International-Pricing-System.pdf.

Gülen, S.G. (1996) 'Is OPEC a cartel? Evidence from cointegration and causality tests', *Energy Journal*, 17: 43–57.

Horan, S.M., Peterson, J.H. and Mahar, J. (2004) 'Implied volatility of oil futures options surrounding OPEC meetings', *Energy Journal*, 25: 103–125.

ITC (2013) *Trade Statistics*, International Trade Centre, accessed online at: www.trademap.org.

Kaufmann, R.K., Dees, S., Karadeloglou, P. and Sanchez, M. (2004) 'Does OPEC matter? An econometric analysis of oil prices', *Energy Journal*, 25: 67–90.

Kohl, W.L. (2002) 'OPEC behavior, 1998–2001', *Quarterly Review of Economics & Finance*, 42: 209–233.

Lin, S.X. and Tamvakis, M. (2010) 'OPEC announcements and their effects on crude oil prices', *Energy Policy*, 38: 1010–1016.

Loderer, C. (1985) 'A test of the OPEC cartel hypothesis: 1974–1983', *Journal of Finance*, 40: 991–1006.

Marcel, V. (2006) *Oil Titans: National Oil Companies in the Middle East*, London: Chatham House/Brookings.

Norwegian Ministry of Finance (2013) *Taxation of Petroleum Activities*, accessed online at: www.regjeringen.no/en/dep/fin/Selected-topics/taxes-and-duties/bedriftsbeskatning/Taxation-of-petroleum-activities.html?id=417318.

OPEC (2013) *Annual Statistical Bulletin*, Organisation of the Petroleum Exporting Countries, accessed online at: www.opec.org/opec_web/en/publications/202.htm.

Platts (2013) *Special Report: New Crudes, New Markets*, Platts, accessed online at: www.platts.com/IM.Platts.Content/InsightAnalysis/IndustrySolutionPapers/NewCrudesNewMarkets.pdf.

Raymond, M.S. and Leffler, W.L. (2005) *Oil and Gas Production in Nontechnical Language*, Tulsa, OK: PennWell Books.

Wirl, F. and Kujundzic, A. (2004) 'The impact of OPEC conference outcomes on world oil prices 1984–2001', *Energy Journal*, 25: 45–62.

Yergin, D. (1993) *The Prize: The Epic Quest for Oil, Money and Power*, New York: Simon & Schuster.

3 Refined oil products

So far, our discussion of the oil industry has focused primarily on the upstream: looking at what drives crude oil demand, supply and pricing. It is now time to turn our attention to the downstream. We begin with a brief description of the refining process, continue with the main categories of refined products and, finally, discuss production, consumption, pricing and trade patterns for major regions, including North America, Europe and Asia Pacific.

Petroleum products and the refining process

Although the majority of oil industry economics revolve around crude oil, it is the finished products that are used by end consumers. Crude oil is rarely usable in its natural state and has to be refined and broken down into products adequate for final consumption. What follows is a simplified expression of what, in real life, is a set of complex processes. The aim is to gain an appreciation of the complexity of refining, from the standpoint of economics, rather than chemical engineering. For a more detailed discussion, the keen reader is advised to refer to either Leffler (2008) or Gary et al. (2007), with the latter providing a much more involved discussion of all aspects of refining economics. To aid the discussion that follows, Exhibit 3.1 gives a simplified visual representation of the basic flows in a refinery. A more detailed diagram, which will help with the understanding of the more complex processes described later, is given in Exhibit 3.2.

The fundamental principle on which oil refining is based has not changed since the nineteenth century: crude oil is heated until it is vaporised and then the vapours are condensed separately, according to the boiling points of their constituent molecules; the procedure is called distillation. However, the complexity and sophistication of the refining process has evolved over time, in order that modern refineries can cope with the increasingly heavier and sourer crude oils to which they have access. Based on the sophistication of their equipment, refineries can be broadly classified into simple (also known as 'topping' or 'hydroskimming'), complex (or 'cracking') and very complex (or 'coking') refineries.

The outputs of the refining process are classified into three broad categories: light, middle and heavy distillates. Light distillates – also known as white or

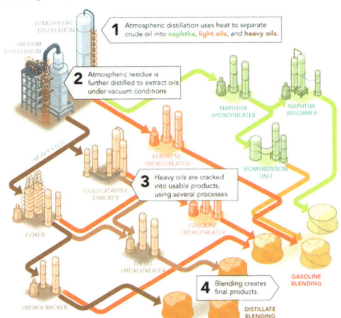

Exhibit 3.1 Simple refinery flow diagram

Source: http://supplychainn.blogspot.co.uk/2012/09/crude-oil-refining.html

top-end cuts – include ethane, propane, butane (collectively known as the LPGs), gasoline (also known as petrol), naphtha (which is used as feedstock for petrochemicals or treated further and eventually used in gasoline blending), kerosene (including jet kerosene) and other industrial spirits. Middle distillates (or middle cuts) include gas oil, diesel, marine diesel, and medium- and high-grade fuels. Finally, heavy distillates – also known as black or bottom-end cuts – include heavy fuels, paraffins, lubricating waxes and greases.

Fractioning, vacuum flashing and hydrotreating

In all types of refinery, crude oil is stored in large tanks and from there it is desalted and then pumped continuously through a series of steel tubes into a furnace. From there, it is pumped to the bottom of a tall cylindrical tower, usually 8–24 feet in diameter and 100–150 feet in height. This is called the 'fractioning' tower, or CDU (crude distillation unit). The CDU is divided into 'floors', with perforated trays, which allow vapours to pass from lower to higher floors. The hydrocarbon vapours with highest boiling points condense first, on the bottom floors, and those with the lowest boiling points condense last, higher up the tower. The shorter the hydrocarbon molecule, the easier it vaporises and the higher it rises. At the top of the CDU come LPGs (propane, butane and ethane), which typically vaporise at less than 90° F (32° C). These are followed by gasoline (petrol), which vaporises at 90–220° F (32–104° C),

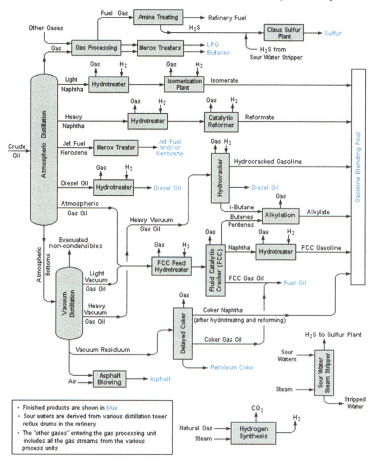

Exhibit 3.2 Refinery flow chart

Source: Wikimedia Commons, http://commons.wikimedia.org/wiki/File:RefineryFlow.png, licensed under the terms of the GNU FDL

and naphtha at 220–315° F (104–157° C). Lower down comes kerosene at 315–450° F (157–232° C) and gas oil at 450–800° F (232–427° C). Right at the bottom remains the atmospheric residue, which requires much higher temperatures (800° F or 426° C).

In a simple refinery, this very basic distillation process yields about 20 per cent light distillates (LPGs, gasoline, naphtha) from an average crude oil, and falls considerably short of the commercial need for petrol. At the same time, the process yields heavier products in quantities that exceed consumption requirements. In fact, each individual crude oil yields very different proportions of the various refined products. These proportions of the various products that can be recovered from a barrel of oil are collectively known as the 'barrel cut' or 'product slate'. They depend on the physical characteristics of the oil, including its specific gravity, its viscosity and the proportions of the various types of hydrocarbons it contains. Exhibit 3.3 illustrates how two different types of crude oil yield different volumes of refined products. For example, the heavier crude oil (blue line) yields a cumulative total of ca. 25 per cent of butanes, gasoline and naphtha, whereas the lighter crude (green line) yields ca. 45 per cent of the same light distillates. Conversely, the heavier crude yields 50 per cent residue (from 50 to 100 on the horizontal axis), whereas the lighter crude yields 30 per cent (from 70 to 100 on the horizontal axis). This illustration is, of course, a hypothetical example, but it demonstrates how different crude oils produce different product slates. Simple refineries are normally geared up to deal with a very limited range of such quality specifications.

The next stage is to remove the sulphur from the light distillates, including the butanes, gasoline, naphtha and kerosene (jet fuel or jet kero). A Merox treater is normally used to remove the sulphur from LPGs and kerosene, whereas a hydrotreater (using hydrogen) is used to desulphurise the naphtha. The desulphurised naphtha can then be used for further industrial applications, typically to produce chemicals or plastics. However, more often than not, part of the naphtha will go through further processing. Lighter naphtha molecules are passed through an isomerisation unit in order to convert linear carbon molecules to higher-octane branched molecules, which can then be used for gasoline blending. Heavier naphtha molecules, on the other hand, are processed in a catalytic reformer, using platinum and a silica-alumina agent, in order to convert them into a high-octane 'reformate', which is then also used for gasoline blending.

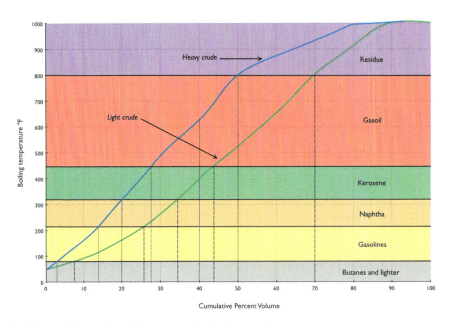

Exhibit 3.3 Illustration of fractional distillation yields

Source: Author

The atmospheric distillation unit, the cat(alytic) reformer and the various hydrotreaters comprise the basic equipment at the disposal of a simple refinery. For this reason, simple refineries typically seek lighter and sweeter crude oils, from which they can extract the highest possible yield of light products straight from the main CDU (i.e. 'straight-run' products). They can then clean up the sulphur and produce reformate from the naphtha, which they use in their gasoline blending. They also desulphurise their kerosene and diesel oil and market them as well. However, there is little they can do with their residual heavy fuel oil. Some of it they may sell for marine bunkers, but the rest they will probably sell at a lower price to another refinery, which has the necessary equipment to further process it.

In addition to the equipment and processes described above, a complex refinery can perform a number of additional, value-adding processes. To start with, the relatively large amount of atmospheric residue from the CDU passes through a further distillation cycle, this time under low pressure and relatively lower temperature, in a vacuum distillation unit (VDU), also known as a 'vacuum flasher'. Vacuum distillation yields additional quantities of vacuum gas oil (VGO), which is then desulphurised and cracked to produce additional amounts of gasoline for the blending pool.

Thermal cracking

Cracking is the process used, in several different forms, to break the long hydrocarbon chains into smaller ones (i.e. lighter products that can be sold off much more profitably, such as gasoline and diesel). A complex refinery employs at least one, frequently more, of a number of methods to crack hydrocarbons. These methods are broadly classified into *thermal* and *catalytic* cracking. As the names indicate, the former employs high temperatures, while the latter uses a catalyst.

Thermal cracking was developed early in the history of refining, as early as the end of the nineteenth century. It relies on the simple principle that by increasing the temperature, long-chained hydrocarbons are agitated and break down into shorter-chain molecules. The term thermal cracking is used to describe a number of processes in this category, including *steam cracking*, *visbreaking* and *coking*. In steam cracking, a feed of saturated hydrocarbons, typically naphtha, ethane, butane, gas oil or residues, is broken down using steam at high temperatures (ca. 1,500° F or 815° C). The high temperature encourages the feed to break down into a number of lighter hydrocarbons, some of which can then be used for the manufacturing of chemicals, or alternatively be sent to the gasoline blending pool. The precise yield of the various products of the steam cracking process depends on the feed used, the proportion of steam in the mix, the temperature and the amount of time (only a few seconds) that the feed is exposed to this temperature.

Visbreaking is a relatively simpler process, which has the aim to 'break' the 'viscosity' of the relatively high amounts of residue from either the vacuum or the straight-run distillation. It is a somewhat milder thermal cracking process.

The residual from the distillation tower is heated at about 900° F (482° C), cooled with gas oil and then fed to a fractioning tower, where it is separated into a mix of light and middle distillates. The new residue of that process can then be passed through a vacuum fractioning tower to yield additional amounts of heavy gas oil and tar.

While steam cracking and visbreaking units may be found in a complex refinery, a coking unit tends to be associated with very complex refineries. This process targets all the heavy residues, which would normally be burned to produce electricity or supply the energy needs of heavy industry. With less demand for such use nowadays and the predominance of heavier and sourer crude oils, which tend to yield higher quantities of residue, the installation of a coker is a valuable investment for any refinery that wants to extract more value out of the refining chain. 'Coking can be considered as a severe thermal cracking process in which one of the end products is primarily carbon' (Gary *et al.* 2007, p. 97). There are three main versions of this process: *delayed coking*, *fluid coking* and *flexicoking*.

Delayed coking evolved out of the industry's experience in heating residual oil at high temperatures in order to extract lighter products. Initially, heating at very high temperatures had the undesired side effect of accumulating coke in the furnace tubes, which resulted in substantial expense and inconvenience to clean the tubes frequently. Over time, it was observed that it was possible to raise the temperature of the residue without significant coke formation, by reducing the amount of time the residue is retained in the heater. The furnace outlet temperatures range between 900 and 930° F (482 and 500° C) and the furnace tubes have to be decoked every three to five months (Gary *et al.* 2007, p. 99).

In fluid coking, the heavy residue from the flasher (CDU) is fed into the coker and coke is separated from the hydrocarbons using cyclones. Coke is then sent to a gasifier and hot air is blown on it. This produces a fuel gas, which is made up of a mix of short-chain hydrocarbons (C_4 or lower) and can be burned to produce heat and electricity. The process leaves some residual coke, which is drawn from the bottom of the coker and recycled into the main reactor.

Flexicoking is a more sophisticated version of fluid coking, with the aim being to reduce the amount of net coke produced by the process. To achieve this, a second gasifier is added, which is fed with any residual coke and produces additional amounts of fuel gas, as described above.

Catalytic cracking

Catalytic cracking (or *cat cracking*) is the method most widely used nowadays for extracting additional value from a barrel of crude. The fundamental principle of the process is the same as for thermal cracking – expose the heavier products from the straight run to higher temperatures, so that the longer hydrocarbon chains break into shorter chains, yielding more valuable, lighter products. The key difference here is the addition of a catalyst, which facilitates or accelerates the chemical reaction, but which remains chemically unchanged. Gary *et al.* (2007, p. 121) explain the cat cracking process as follows:

> The hot oil feed is contacted with the catalyst in either the feed riser line or the reactor. As the cracking reaction progresses, the catalyst is progressively deactivated by the formation of coke on the surface of the catalyst. The catalyst and hydrocarbon vapours are separated mechanically, and oil remaining on the catalyst is removed by steam stripping before the catalyst enters the regenerator. The oil vapours are taken overhead to a fractionation tower for separation into streams having the desired boiling ranges.

There are various cat cracking processes that have evolved over time, but the predominant one is fluid catalytic cracking (or *FCC*). The feed for the FCC is typically composed of heavier products, such as heavy atmospheric or vacuum gas oil. The process is named after the fluid-like behaviour of the catalysts used, known as *zeolites*. These are micro-porous, aluminosilicate minerals, commonly made from alumina-based clay. Although there are several such zeolites that occur naturally as minerals, refineries increasingly use synthetically produced zeolites with precise molecular dimensions and mineral content. This facilitates the production of more gasoline, with higher octanes, and less heavy fuel oils and light gases. The light gases that are produced tend to be olefins, such as ethylene and propylene, which are then used as feedstock for the petrochemical industry.

Hydrocracking

In simple terms, hydrocracking is cat cracking in the presence of hydrogen (H_2). Although invented in the late 1920s in Germany, it was not until the 1950s and 1960s that the process was used on an industrial scale by refineries in the USA. As the name suggests, there are two processes working in tandem here: hydrogenation and catalytic cracking. The feed can be light or heavy gas oil (often the latter), coming as straight-run from the CDU, or as VGO from the vacuum flasher, or even as the output of a previous cycle of cat cracking. Under high pressure and moderate temperature, the feed first passes through the catalyst and the heavy hydrocarbons break into lighter, unsaturated hydrocarbons – this reaction absorbs heat (endothermic). Second, the excess hydrogen in the reactor saturates the molecules giving off heat (exothermic reaction). Thus, the heat generated by hydrogenation is used to keep the catalytic cracking going, with hydrogen acting as the temperature controller. The hydrocarbon mix from the reactor is cooled down, separated from the excess hydrogen that is then fed back to the reactor and fed to a fractionator, which splits it into jet fuel, diesel, kerosene and other useful products. Whatever gas oil is left at the bottom is channelled to a second reactor, which repeats the process, typically under higher pressure and temperature.

Catalytic reforming

One of the most sought after, and hence most valuable, refined products is gasoline. It was the birth of the automobile that saved the oil industry from extinction in its nascent stage. It was the automobile again after the end of the Second World War that generated the ever-increasing demand for high-quality gasoline. To respond to that demand, refineries had to find ways to produce copious quantities of high-octane gasoline from blending components that typically include low-octane, heavy naphthas. In the 1940s, the process of catalytic reforming was invented and the first industrial plant set up by Universal Oil Products (UOP) in 1949. Since then, a number of similar reforming processes have been invented and improved by other refiners.

The chemistry of catalytic reforming is quite complex for the layman, and hence beyond the scope of this text. However, it is worth grasping some of the key components of the process. The feed is typically straight-run naphtha, although hydrocracked naphtha may also be used. As Leffler (2008, p. 91) states, 'these naphtha streams typically have a high concentration of normal paraffins and naphthenes . . . the cat reformer causes many of these components to be reformed into isoparaffins and aromatics that have much higher octane numbers'. Why is this good? Because the higher the octane number (or rating), the more compression the gasoline can withstand and the lower the probability of *engine knocking*.

The reforming process requires a catalyst, as the name implies, which is typically platinum, but can also be rhenium or palladium. The by-product of cat reforming is hydrogen, an extremely useful element, which is invariably used for both the hydrotreating and hydrocracking processes.

Gasoline blending

Gasoline is probably the one petroleum product most people, or at least motorists, are familiar with. The widespread use of the motorcar and the increased demand for higher performance vehicles have made gasoline one of the most sought after refined products. Gasoline is the fuel of choice for the four-stroke internal combustion engine. Although there are several quality attributes to an individual gasoline blend, the two key ones are vapour pressure and octane number.

Put simply, vapour pressure (or Reid Vapour Pressure – RPV) is an indication of how easily a hydrocarbon vaporises (i.e. how volatile it is). This is a desirable feature, as it is the vapours mixed with the oxygen from the air that combust in the cylinder (with the aid of a spark plug) to generate the power that pushes the piston down and turns the crankshaft. The gasoline blend has to achieve an RPV that is high enough to ignite when the engine is cold, but not so high that the vapour expands so much that it does not leave space for air to be injected in the chamber and thus causes an engine stall. To achieve the desired RPV, refiners blend a number of hydrocarbons, including straight-run gasoline, straight-run naphtha, reformate (from the cat reformer), hydrocrackate (from the cat hydrocracker), alkylate (from the alkylation unit), cat-cracked gasoline, coker gasoline and butane (C_4H_{10}), both normal (nC_4) and isobutane (iC_4). The latter two have much higher RPV values than the rest of the blending components, and are particularly valuable for the refinery, especially during the summer months (in the northern hemisphere), when gasoline demand peaks.

Octane is probably the best known quality attribute of gasoline, and the average motorist is familiar with the fact that the higher the octane number (say 97), the less chance there is that the engine will *knock*. Knocking occurs when the gasoline-air vapour self-ignites at the wrong point in the four-stroke cycle, resulting in the piston pushing the crankshaft in the wrong direction, which ultimately reduces the efficiency of the engine and increases the wear of the mechanical parts. Blending is once again the process used to achieve the required octane number, mixing the hydrocarbon components mentioned in the previous paragraph.

Mixing these components, each with their own RPV and octane values, in order to optimise both the RPV and octane number of the blend is not a trivial undertaking. It is with the aid of linear programming that such a problem can be solved, especially in the current operating environment where gasoline quality specifications are strictly regulated by government bodies, requiring at least the same performance, but with lower emissions of CO_2 and other pollutants.

Distillate and residual fuels

Although one may presume that a refinery is predominantly geared up to produce hydrocarbons for gasoline blending, there are several other distillates produced for a variety of uses. Kerosene, jet fuel (or jet kero), heating oil, automotive diesel oil and heavy fuel oil are the most common ones. Jet fuel is effectively kerosene, but with a stricter specification, particularly when it comes to its freezing point, which needs to be low (ca. $-40°$ C), so that crystals do not form when flying at high altitudes. Kerosene was the basis of the expansion of Standard Oil at the outset of the oil industry, and it is still utilised for cooking, heating and lighting, especially in rural areas where electricity is not available or is intermittent.

Automotive diesel oil is an equally sought after distilled product as gasoline. It is the fuel used mostly in diesel passenger cars and heavy goods vehicles, but also for construction equipment, small generators, pumps, compressors and so forth. Although in the USA it takes second place to gasoline for passenger cars, in Europe its use is more widespread, on account of a more dominant preference for diesel cars. As a result, US refineries usually have a surplus of diesel, which they export to Europe and, conversely, European refineries export their surplus gasoline to the USA.

Heating oil bridges the gap between kerosene and residual fuel oil and comes in a number of different specifications, for a variety of uses. These include lighting, heating, combustion fuel for marine diesel engines, industrial fuel oil, oil-fired power plants and bunker fuel. Of these, the best-known grade is

No. 2 Heating Oil, typically used as domestic heating oil, which is traded as a futures contract on the New York Mercantile Exchange.

Residual fuel, as the name implies, is the leftover of the various refining processes, at the bottom of the CDU or the VDU. It is the least useful product, quite heavy and viscous, with a high concentration of sulphur and other heavy metals, and less valuable than the crude oil it was cut from. The two typical uses are either as boiler fuel or marine bunkers. For the latter use, residual fuel comes in two versions – heavy fuel oil (HFO) with a viscosity of 380 cSt, or intermediate fuel oil (IFO) with a viscosity of 180 cSt.

Other refinery processes

Several more processes may potentially take place in a refinery, depending on the complexity of its equipment. It is beyond the scope of this text to look at these processes in detail, but a short description, for completeness, is given below.

Alkylation – This is effectively the inverse of cracking, as alkylation puts together shorter chain hydrocarbons to create longer chain ones. The process was devised to deal with lighter molecules too unstable to dissolve in gasoline blends. With alkylation, the lighter molecules are combined into longer chain hydrocarbons, which can be added to the gasoline blend and increase the octane rating.

Isomerisation – In mainstream chemistry, it is the chemical process by which a compound is transformed into any of its isomeric forms (i.e. forms with the same chemical composition but with different structure or configuration, and hence generally with different physical and chemical properties). From the point of view of refining, the process is used to convert straight chain hydrocarbons (typically pentane and hexane, which are abundant in straight-run gasoline) into branched hydrocarbons (isopentane and isohexane), which have much higher octanes and are, therefore, more desirable in gasoline blending.

Asphalt – At the bottom of the distillation tower remain the most complex hydrocarbons, called asphaltenes. They consist of very long-chained molecules with a very high carbon-to-hydrogen ratio and frequently bonded with sulphur and heavy metals such as vanadium and nickel. The refinery processes these hydrocarbons to remove any unwanted elements and then produces asphalt in a number of different specifications, according to the intended final use. For its most common use, asphalt is mixed with aggregates to create tarmac for road surfaces.

Lubricants – Also known as *lube oils*, these products have a very wide range of applications. These include: automotive engines, marine engines, railroad engines, refrigeration units, bearings, gears, hydraulic equipment, metal working, electrical insulation, tire manufacturing and many more. Motor oil is the largest lube oil category, followed by engine oils and oils for other applications. Because of this wide range of applications, quality specifications among lube oils vary considerably. Lube oils typically consist of oil base stock (ca. 90 per cent) and chemical additives, depending on the end-use requirements. The oil base stocks are prepared from selected crude oil by distillation and special processing, which adds to the refinery's added value and complexity index.

Ethylene plant – Ethylene (or ethene – C_2H_4) and propylene (or propene – C_3H_6) are two of the simplest unsaturated hydrocarbons; both of them have a simple double bond. Both hydrocarbons, and particularly ethylene, form the basic building blocks of the chemical and petrochemical industry. Ethylene is used in the production of a variety of articles, including plastics (such as the thin polythene film used for carrier bags), textiles, toiletries, detergents, paints, antifreeze, lightweight car components and medical supplies. Propylene is also the building block for a variety of plastics and other consumer products, the most common of which is polypropylene. This is used for the production of packaging materials, caps, plastic bottles and so on. An ethylene (or olefin) plant produces these two compounds, as well as butylene and butadiene. Feedstocks used comprise LPGs such as ethane, propane and butane, but naphtha is also commonly used. A typical ethylene plant uses an ethane/propane mix, which is fed to the cracking furnaces where it is mixed with steam and heated at a very high temperature (over 800° C) for a very short period of time (under a second). The ethane/propane mix breaks down into ethylene and small amounts of other gases. When the maximum amount of ethylene is produced, the process is quickly cooled down (quenched) in order to stop it producing lighter compounds such as methane. The ethylene is then passed though a fractionator in order to separate it from any other hydrocarbons and yield a product of at least 99 per cent purity.

Refinery complexity

Earlier on, we introduced the concept of the simple and the complex refinery. A simple refinery only has basic equipment and relies on cutting a limited number of crude oils in order to produce mostly straight-run distilled products. As more refining processes are added to a refinery, its level of complexity increases. But how can one measure this complexity? The problem was tackled by Wilbur Nelson in the early 1960s when he wrote a number of articles for the *Oil & Gas Journal*, where he developed his idea of devising an index to measure the secondary conversion capacity of a refinery in comparison to its primary distillation capacity. It indicates the investment intensity, or cost index, of the refinery, as well as the value addition potential.

How is this definition translated in practical terms? First, the atmospheric distillation unit (CDU) of the refinery is assigned a complexity factor of 1. Second, the cost of all other units is expressed relative to the cost of atmospheric distillation. Consider the following example:

- A crude distillation unit of 100,000 BPSD[1] capacity costs $10 million, which implies that the unit cost per day is $100/BPSD.

---

1 BPSD stands for *barrels per stream day*. It is the maximum number of barrels of input that a distillation facility can process within a 24-hour period when running at full capacity under optimal crude and product slate conditions with no allowance for downtime (EIA 2013).

- A 20,000 BPSD catalytic reforming unit costs $10 million, implying that the unit cost per day is $500/BPSD.
- The complexity of the cat reformer, then, is $500 ÷ $100 = 5.

Exhibit 3.4 gives an example calculation of Nelson's complexity index for one of ExxonMobil's refineries in the US. The atmospheric distillation unit is the base against which all other units are compared. The capacity of the CDU and all other processes is given in column [1]. Column [2] expresses all the capacities as a percentage of the CDU's capacity. Column [3] lists the complexity factors for each process, with a factor of 1 for the CDU. Column [4] calculates the contribution of each process to the complexity index as the simple product of percentage of distillation capacity and the complexity factor ([2] × [3]). Finally, the sum of the figures in column [4] gives the overall complexity index for the refinery.

Refining capacity and throughput

The supply of oil products is very much dependent on the available refining capacity around the world. In fact, refining capacity sets the upper limit to the supply of distillates. As can be seen in Exhibit 3.5, world refining capacity amounted to just over 93 mbpd in 2012, with the USA leading the table with over 17 mbpd, or nearly 19 per cent. Other large refiners include China and Russia, although the EEA (EU plus Switzerland and Norway) could be in second place with ca. 14.5 mbpd, if considered as a single area.

Although useful, this is a rather static picture of refining capacity. Exhibit 3.6, on the other hand, shows the development of refining capacity in major

ExxonMobil's Baton Rouge Complexity Index (2005)

Process operation	Capacity (BPSD) [1]	Percent of dist. capacity [2]	Complexity factor [3]	Complexity Index [4] = [2] x [3]
Atmospheric distillation	501,000	100.0	1	1.00
Vacuum distillation	227,000	45.3	2	0.91
Coking	112,500	22.5	5.5	1.24
Catalytic cracking	229,000	45.7	6	2.74
Catalytic reforming	75,500	15.1	5	0.75
Catalytic hydrocracking	24,000	4.8	6	0.29
Catalytic hydrotreating	333,500	66.6	1.7	1.13
Alkylation	140,000	27.9	11	3.07
Polymerisation	9,500	1.9	9	0.17
Lubes	16,000	3.2	60	1.92
Oxygenates	7,000	1.4	10	0.14
Hydrogen (MCFD)	12,000	2.4	1	0.02
Cumulative complexity index				13.38

Exhibit 3.4 Example of Nelson's Index

Source: Gary *et al.* (2007, p. 32)

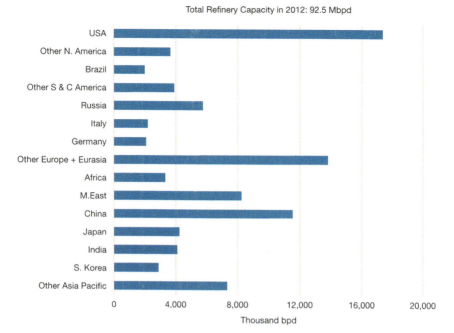

Exhibit 3.5 Refining capacity
Source: Author, compiled with data from BP (2013)

regions over the last 40 years. The picture is quite diverse. Europe and Eurasia, which include Russia and the former Soviet republics, appears to be in terminal decline. Capacity has been decreasing, with older refineries decommissioned and new refineries practically impossible to build, due to cost but also planning and environmental regulations. North America, on the other hand, has increased its capacity from the 1990s onwards, following a decline during the 1980s. In addition, what the graph obscures is the fact that not only has US capacity expanded, it has also increased in complexity. US refiners have invested in additional equipment, which allows the distillation of heavier and sourer crudes and the extraction of larger quantities of valuable light products. See, for example, in Exhibit 3.7 the average profitability of a coking (very complex) refinery in the US Gulf Coast, distilling heavy sour crude, compared to a cracking refinery in Northwest Europe, using light sweet crude, and a hydrocracking refinery in Singapore, using medium sour crude.

The most impressive growth in refining capacity is demonstrated by China, particularly between 2000 and 2012 when capacity doubled, and there are plans for further expansion until 2017. The other two rising refining centres are the Middle East and India. Both have expanded substantially, especially in the last couple of decades, albeit possibly for different reasons. The Middle East aspires to process a lot more of its own crude oil and export the higher value distilled products instead. India, on the other hand, faces a rising domestic demand for refined products as its economy develops and there is

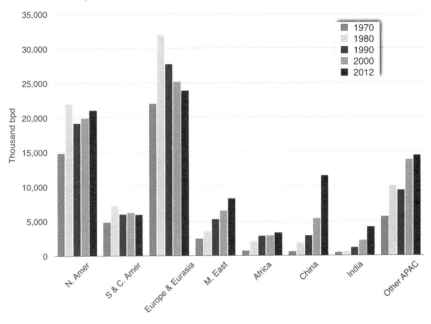

Exhibit 3.6 Development of refining capacity

Source: Author, compiled with data from BP (2013)

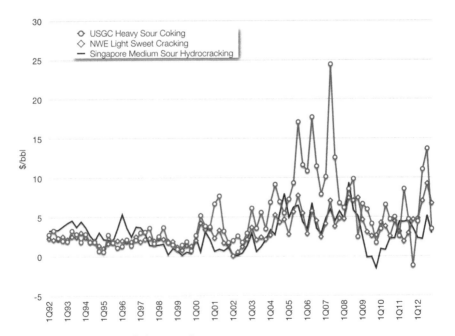

Exhibit 3.7 Indicative refining margins

Source: Author, compiled with data from BP (2013)

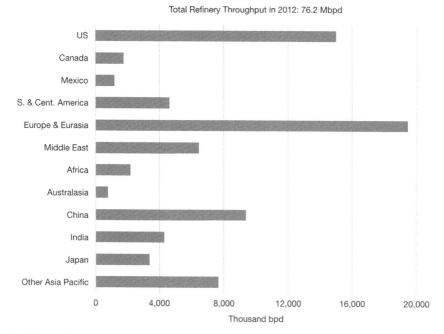

Total Refinery Throughput in 2012: 76.2 Mbpd

Exhibit 3.8 Refinery throughput
Source: Author, compiled with data from BP (2013)

more demand for road transport. One could argue, however, that India may also wish to be a refining centre, being located between a prime source of crude oil (Persian/Arabian Gulf) and the developed and emerging economies of Pacific Asia.

What is also key in terms of production is the refinery throughput: the quantity of oil being processed by refineries per annum. This also allows the calculation of refinery utilisation rates, a figure crucial for the profitability of a refiner. For example, the average utilisation for the US was just over 86 per cent in 2012, compared to 81 per cent for China and 78 per cent for the Middle East. These are, of course, averages and should be used cautiously, as they may disguise mixed information, such as refineries that are mothballed, or the diversity of capacity utilisation among refineries in the same country.

Finally, we can assess the global picture of distilled products output, as shown in Exhibit 3.9. It is no surprise that the USA leads the table, with China and Russia in second and third place, respectively. The reader may notice that the data do not concord with those in previous exhibits – this is due to the different sources used for these exhibits. Refinery throughputs and consumption of oil products give a broad framework for the study of patterns in international trade in oil products. As we will learn later, however, trade flows are much more complicated, and there is often exchange of similar products between countries that produce all distillates, but in varying proportions. This

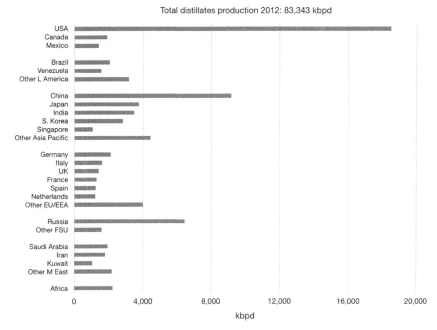

Exhibit 3.9 Distillate producers

Source: Author, compiled with data from OPEC (2013)

is, in fact, a classic case of intra-industry trade, as is that of the exchange trade in diesel and gasoline between the USA and Europe, mentioned earlier.

Consumption and trade patterns

Consumption patterns influence both the short- and the long-term balance of the market. Different regions have different tastes for oil products, depending on their economic activities, climatic conditions and other consumption habits. Although refinery yields can change to match demand, imbalances do arise, and trade flows are generated in order to cover them. The world as a whole has a great appetite for light and middle distillates. A typical example of the former category would be gasoline, and of the latter would be diesel. Exhibit 3.10 shows the total consumption of petroleum products in 2012, where it can be seen that light and middle distillates account for two-thirds of the total.

As Exhibit 3.11 demonstrates, the US is not only a major producer of refined products, but it also dominates consumption, with just over one-fifth of the world's total. The EEA countries collectively account for about one-sixth of global consumption, while Asia Pacific accounts for one-third of the same, with China now the leading country in the region, having overtaken Japan in 2002.

Having considered the overall picture, it is interesting to highlight the development of refined products consumption in some of the key geographical

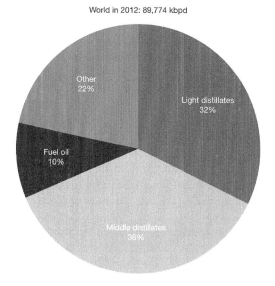

Exhibit 3.10 Products consumption by type of product
Source: Author, compiled with data from BP (2013)

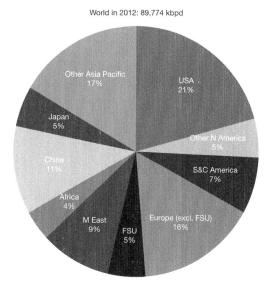

Exhibit 3.11 Production consumption by region
Source: Author, compiled with data from BP (2013)

areas. North America remains the largest consumer with just over 23 mbpd, although it is evident that consumption has readjusted since the 2008 financial crisis and it is slowly declining. This may be caused by the state of the economy, but may also be attributed to the fuel efficiency policies that are promoted by the US government in particular. One more notable feature of the time series in Exhibit 3.12 is the dominant role of light distillates (e.g. gasoline), which account for nearly half of North American consumption. This is in contrast to the ever-declining part of fuel oil, whose consumption has steadily declined over the last four decades.

Europe has exhibited similar consumption trends over the last five to six years (i.e. declining overall demand, after a slow but steady demand expansion from the mid-1980s onwards). Like the US, European product consumption increased rapidly from the mid-1960s, only for this growth to be interrupted by the two oil crises in 1973 and 1979. The one notable difference from the US is Europe's larger appetite for middle distillates, in comparison to light ones. This is evidenced by the preference of European motorists for diesel vehicles and has resulted in the steady decline of gasoline, as shown in Exhibit 3.13.

Japan went through a meteoric rise in its consumption of oil products from the 1960s to the late 1970s. Its consumption increased every single year until 1979, with the exception of 1974 and 1975, the two years after the first oil crisis. After the second oil crisis, products consumption experienced a downturn that lasted until about 1987, after which Japan and the rest of the world economy started coming out of economic recession. As Exhibit 3.14 shows, Japan's expansion in the early years was predominantly based on fuel oil, which was used in its heavy industry and for electricity generation. As the

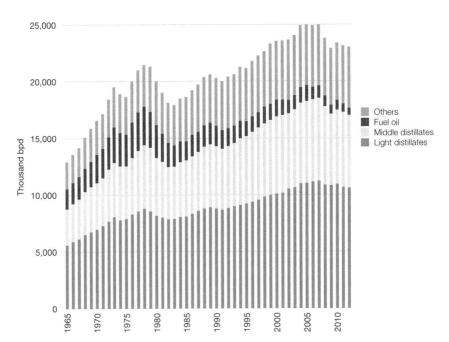

Exhibit 3.12 Development of refined products consumption in North America

Source: Author, compiled with data from BP (2013)

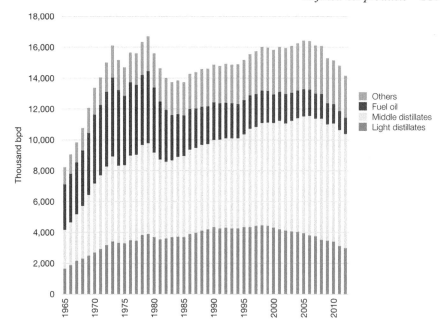

Exhibit 3.13 Development of refined products consumption in Europe (excluding FSU)

Source: Author, compiled with data from BP (2013)

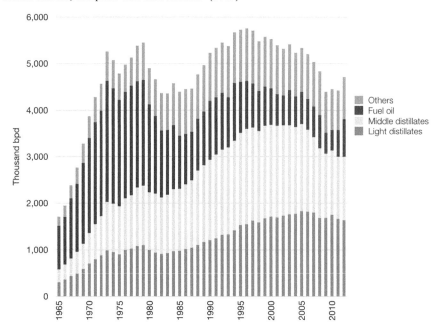

Exhibit 3.14 Development of refined products consumption in Japan

Source: Author, compiled with data from BP (2013)

Japanese economy sought ways to redress its vulnerability to oil prices after 1973, there was a relentless pursuit of energy efficiency and the switch from heavy manufacturing to consumer electronics and knowledge-based industries that were less energy intensive. This was reflected in the decline of fuel oil consumption and the increase of both light and middle distillates. From the 1990s onwards, as Japan entered a long period of economic stagnation, the rate of consumption growth slowed down, until the overall trend eventually became negative.

Starting from very modest consumption levels, Chinese economic growth has driven products consumption to an exponential increase, especially from the beginning of this millennium. As shown in Exhibit 3.15, China currently consumes ca. 10 mbpd of refined products, most of which are middle and light distillates. Middle distillates consumption has increased faster than other products, as they are widely used in domestic freight and passenger transportation, as well as for small-scale electricity generation from diesel generators where the electricity grid has not yet reached. Light distillate consumption is also increasing rapidly, as the middle classes are expanding and have a greater appetite for consumer goods such as passenger cars. China is now the world's largest car manufacturer and second largest in car ownership, despite the country having a very low ratio of cars per thousand inhabitants.[2] There is a

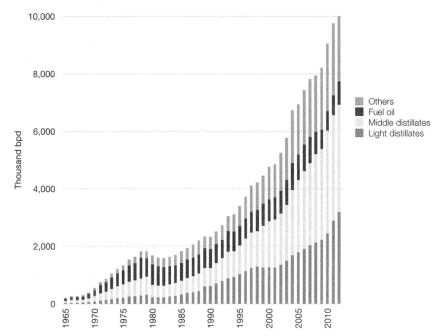

Exhibit 3.15 Development of refined products consumption in China

Source: Author, compiled with data from BP (2013)

2 In 2010, China had 58 vehicles per 1,000 inhabitants, compared to 797 in the US, 590 in Japan and 563 in the OECD on average.

great potential for this strong demand to continue as incomes rise and people acquire the taste for more consumer goods, such as cars.

In comparison to international trade in crude oil, refined products trade is much smaller, but still substantial. Exhibit 3.16 shows the development of trade in both crude oil and products since 1975. It shows how trade has grown continuously after the mid-1980s, with the exception of 2009, when oil trade felt the effect of the world financial crisis. In 2012, trade in refined products amounted to just over 800 million tonnes (or 16.7 mbpd), compared to 1,927 million tonnes (or 38.6 mbpd) of crude oil. However, over the last 10 years, the trend has been for products trade to grow faster than crude oil trade, so that the former is now nearly 30 per cent of the total trade.

Finally, Exhibit 3.17 displays exports and imports of refined products for the key geographical areas. It is interesting to note that every single region is both an importer and an exporter, although in all cases there is an imbalance between the two. The US, for example, is the world's largest exporter, but also imports vast amounts of products, coming second only to Europe (excluding FSU). On the other hand, the former Soviet republics are the leading net exporters, and so are the Middle East and India. China and Japan, on the other hand, are the two leading net importers, followed by Singapore and other Asia Pacific economies.

The graph does conceal the detail of these trade flows, which may be important. For example, it is well known that Russia tends to export large amounts of dirty products (e.g. heavy fuel oil), which it cannot process in its

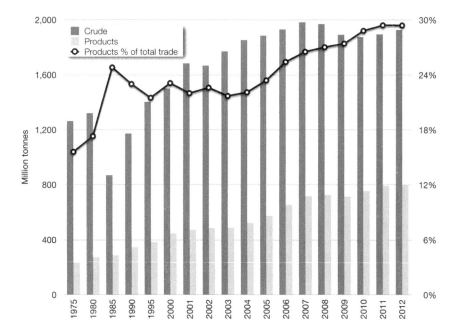

Exhibit 3.16 Crude versus refined products trade

Source: Author, compiled with data from BP (2013)

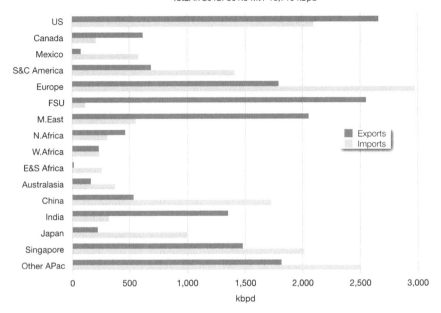

Exhibit 3.17 Refined product imports

Source: Author, compiled with data from BP (2013)

own refineries. This is owing to the fact that many of these refineries are mostly hydroskimming ones, without catalytic cracking or coking facilities, so that residual products often have to be sold off to other more complex refineries to be further processed. However, this trend is very likely to be reversed, as Russia launched an extensive programme of refinery upgrading in 2013 and 2014, with the aim to process more of its residual fuel into valuable ULSD (ultra low sulphur diesel) for export to EU markets.

Conclusion

Although crude oil is the most discussed energy commodity and the one almost constantly in the limelight, it is refined products that reach the end consumers and provide energy for a number of needs, including transportation, heating and petrochemicals. The transformation of the large variety of crude oils to the refined products we use every day takes place in large, capital-intensive refineries. Over the last few decades, refining technology has evolved and many countries have made substantial investments in new refining capacity, which can process a wide array of even the most difficult crude oils and yield large amounts of the most valuable refined products such as gasoline and light gas oil.

Over the last decade, we have witnessed the erosion of refining capacity in Europe, while China, India and the Middle East have substantially increased theirs. It is apparent that the centre of gravity for products consumption is steadily shifting towards the emerging economies of Asia, and international trade and shipping are already feeling the effects of this shift.

This chapter concludes the rather lengthy journey through the economics and markets for crude oil and products. We will now continue with what many still anticipate to be the hydrocarbon fuel that will bridge the transition of energy generation from oil to renewables: natural gas.

References

BP (2013) *Statistical Review of the World Energy 2013*, British Petroleum, accessed online at: www.bp.com/statisticalreview.

EIA (2013) *Glossary*, Energy Information Administration, accessed online at: www.eia.gov/tools/glossary/.

Gary, J.H., Handwerk, G.E. and Kaiser, M.J. (2007) *Petroleum Refining Technology and Economics*, 5th edn, Boca Raton, FL: CRC Press.

Leffler, W.L. (2008) *Petroleum Refining in Nontechnical Language*, Tulsa, OK: PennWell Books.

OPEC (2013) *Annual Statistical Bulletin*, Organisation of the Petroleum Exporting Countries, accessed online at: www.opec.org/opec_web/en/publications/202.htm.

4 Natural gas

Natural gas has occurred naturally for millennia, having manifested its presence through natural seepages from underground, which were often treated as much with curiosity as with fear and reverence. The technology to capture, clean up, store and transport natural gas only became available later in the history of the hydrocarbon industry, and hence natural gas only came to prominence in the second half of the twentieth century. This was helped by the laying, in the 1930s and 1940s, of several pipelines in the United States and, in the 1960s onwards, by the large pipeline infrastructure projects in Europe, such as *Brotherhood*, which connected the West Siberian fields of the then Soviet Union to Eastern Europe.

As a result, natural gas is considered the newest of hydrocarbons, and many people believe it to be the future of energy, at least in the medium term. In the last 30 or so years, natural gas has experienced an impressive growth in terms of reserve discovery, field development and production. On the demand side, gas consumption has rapidly expanded to contest coal's second place as a source of primary energy. This is particularly evident in electricity generation, whereby gas is increasingly becoming the fuel of choice, replacing coal, which is less efficient and more polluting, although coal remains the less expensive of the two fuels.

Physical characteristics and supply

Gas formation is similar to that of oil. Organic matter, which has been compressed and heated for millennia, is the source of all hydrocarbons, including natural gas, of course. At greater depths, both higher pressure and higher temperatures favour the production of gas over oil. This is why gas is normally associated with deep oil deposits and, as the depth increases, so does the probability of finding fields that contain almost pure methane. Most gas comes from 'conventional' fields, which allow the extraction of the commodity using existing cost-efficient technology. As Exhibit 4.1 shows, however, there are additional 'non-conventional' gas reserves, which are technically more difficult to exploit. Such reserves include: deep gas, tight gas, coalbed gas, shale

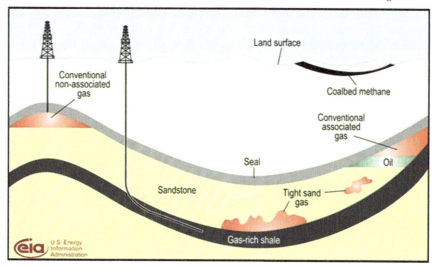

Exhibit 4.1 The variety of conventional and non-conventional gas reserve formations
Source: US Energy Informational Administration

gas and gas hydrates.[1] Of these, shale gas is the one that has captured the imagination of the industry, particularly so in the United States, where the take-off of shale gas exploration and extraction has changed the economics of hydrocarbons not only in the domestic economy, but also on a worldwide scale. The issue of shale gas will reappear in the following sections.

Although often a by-product of oil production, most of the world's natural gas production comes from dedicated gas fields. In its 'dry' form, natural gas consists primarily of methane (CH_4 often up to 90 per cent), small amounts

---

1   *Deep* natural gas exists in deposits very far underground, typically over 5 km or deeper, beyond 'conventional' drilling depths. *Tight* gas is stuck in a very tight formation underground, trapped in unusually impermeable, hard rock, or in a sandstone or limestone formation that is unusually impermeable and non-porous (tight sand). *Coalbed methane* (CBM) is associated with many coal seams, either within the seam itself or the surrounding rock. It is trapped underground, typically adsorbed on the coal surface, and is generally not released into the atmosphere until coal mining activities unleash it. In the past, it used to be a nuisance for coal mining, but now it can be extracted and injected into natural gas pipelines for resale, used as an industrial feedstock, or used for heating and electricity generation. *Shale* is a very fine-grained sedimentary rock, which is easily breakable into thin, parallel layers. It is a very soft rock, but can be as impermeable as concrete and does not disintegrate when it becomes wet. Hence, extracting gas from such a formation is much more expensive. Hydraulic fracturing, or *fracking*, has been used for several decades in North America, but it is only after 2005 that the technology became economical enough to use on a wide scale and has since been responsible for the shale gas boom experienced in North America. *Methane hydrates* are the most recent form of unconventional natural gas to be discovered and researched. They are molecule formations made up of a lattice of frozen water, which forms a 'cage' around molecules of methane. These hydrates look like melting snow (which can burn!) and were first discovered

of other hydrocarbons such as ethane, propane and butane, and even smaller amounts of carbon dioxide (CO_2), oxygen (O_2), nitrogen (N_2), hydrogen sulphide (H_2S) and rare gases (A, He, Ne, Xe). Gas exploration is similar to, and associated with, oil exploration. Once gas is produced at the well head, it goes through a purification process that removes NGLs ('wet' gases, which can be further processed and marketed separately), water vapours, carbon dioxide, sulphur compounds[2] and oil (if the gas is associated with an oil well). This is required for the 'dry' gas to be of suitable quality for pipeline transportation and further distribution. A sophisticated network of pipelines[3] is used to collect the gas from the well head, channel it through the processing plant for purification, store it if necessary and distribute it to its final destination; or channel it to a port facility for cryogenic liquefaction, load it on specialised LNG carriers, unload it at a regasification facility at the other end and deliver it again by pipeline to its final destination.

Natural gas can be measured in many different ways, which were covered earlier in Chapter 1. To quickly recap here, for trading purposes, volume is important, and hence the most common measurement units are cubic feet (*cbf* or *cf*) and cubic metres (*cbm* or *cm*); gas reserves are quoted in trillion cubic feet or trillion cubic metres (*tcf/tcm*). For consumption purposes, gas is normally measured in therms or BTUs to reflect the amount of energy consumed. For pricing, probably the most widely used unit is the BTU, in fact $/MMBTU, although pence/therm is the price quotation in the United Kingdom. To calculate its equivalence in other fuels, the amount required to produce a standard electricity unit (e.g. MWh) is used instead.

Reserves and production

Like oil, substantial amounts of gas reserves are held by those who do not consume them heavily. The picture is similar, but not identical, to that of oil.

---

in permafrost regions of the Arctic, but are also abundant in marine sediments. According to the US Geologic Survey, gas hydrate reserves (*gas in place* or *GIP*) have been estimated in the last 15 years in ranges between 100,000–300,000,000 TCF, although the technically recoverable reserves are only a subset of these figures and the pool of economically recoverable reserves is even smaller. In a recent study, Boswell and Collett (2011) put the estimate of ultimate global recoverable volumes to approximately 10^{16} cbf (10,000 tcf or 283 tcm). To put this in context, total proved 'conventional' gas reserves stood at 6,614 tcf (187 tcm) and there is an estimated additional 7,200 tcf (203 tcm) of technically (but not necessarily economically) recoverable shale reserves. However, the USGS warns, gas hydrates do have hazards and for the time being they are uneconomical. In the meantime, it continues investigating technical, economical and environmental aspects through its USGS Gas Hydrates Project, which runs at the Woods Hole Coastal and Marine Science Center (http://woodshole.er.usgs.gov).

2   These sulphur compounds (mercaptans) can be re-injected in micro-quantities later on, in order to give natural gas its distinctive 'rotten eggs' smell, which acts as a warning sign in case of leakage.

3   This network includes associated compressor, metering and control stations, all necessary for a seamless operation and all adding to the cost.

Reserves are concentrated in a few regions and are controlled by relatively few governments. In 2012, there were 187.3 tcm (6,641 tcf) of gas reserves in the world, and the development of gas reserves since 1980 is shown in Exhibit 4.2. Of these, 50.4 tcm (1,780.7 tcf, 26.9 per cent) were located in Russia and Turkmenistan, and 80.5 tcm (2,842.9 tcf, 43 per cent) in the Middle East. Within the latter region, two countries hold the majority of reserves: Iran and Qatar. In fact, combining the reserves of these two countries with those of Russia and Turkmenistan (i.e. the top four reserve holders), they amount to about 58.3 per cent of the world's total. It is no wonder, then, that when these four, together with several more medium-sized and smaller producers decided to found the Gas Exporting Countries Forum (GEFC) in 2001, they sent jitters to all major gas consumers, especially Europeans. Although GEFC still remains a 'forum', it will be interesting to observe whether it could ultimately turn into a 'gas-OPEC'.

Relatively smaller reserves are located throughout the world (see Exhibit 4.3), but the regions that use it most – North America, Western Europe and Asia Pacific – control less than 20 per cent of the world's reserves.

The key development in terms of reserves is of course the prospect of non-conventional gas, especially shale gas. What is now termed 'the shale gas revolution' in the US is the culmination of more than 20 years of efforts to make shale gas extraction both technologically and economically feasible. On the technological front, the breakthrough came with the introduction of hydraulic fracturing, or *fracking* as it is more commonly known. Although the

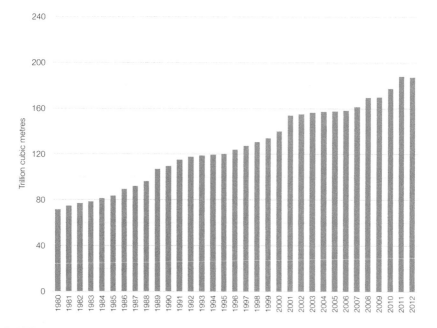

Exhibit 4.2 Development of gas reserves

Source: Author, compiled with data from BP (2013)

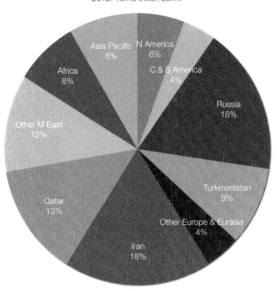

2012: 187.3 trillion cu.m.

Exhibit 4.3 Distribution of world gas reserves
Source: Author, compiled with data from BP (2013)

process itself is much older, it was with the persistence of pioneers such as George Mitchell, who started experimenting since the early 1980s, which eventually made fracking work nearly 20 years later. Aided by directional (e.g. horizontal) drilling to increase accuracy and effectiveness, fracking consists of pumping a high-pressure fracturing fluid in the borehole that has been drilled. The fracturing fluid is typically a slurry of mostly water, with about 10 per cent sand and several chemical additives. The water's viscosity can be controlled with additives (e.g. guar gum), so that high viscosity fluid is used to cause large dominant fractures, whereas lower viscosity ('slickwater') fluid is used to produce smaller, distributed micro-fractures. The sand in the mixture (e.g. silica sand, or other man-made ceramics) is known as the 'proppant'. Its role is to stay in the fractures and increase the porosity of the shale, so that the gas (and oil) trapped in it can escape more easily and then be directed towards a collecting line, which allows the hydrocarbons to rise to the surface. The chemicals in the fracking fluid have a number of uses. Some are there to increase viscosity, others to prevent corrosion and yet others to reduce friction.

The effect of shale gas has been quite dramatic in the energy profile of the US. According to EIA data, nearly one-third of gas produced in the US is shale gas. The immediate effect of this relative abundance was a collapse of domestic gas prices, from a high of ca. \$13/MMBtu in July 2008, to ca. \$4/MMBtu around the same time in 2013. The secondary, and for some more important, effect has been that of consumption substitution. Cheap gas has meant that it is now more price-competitive against coal for power generation, as well as against naphtha as feedstock to the chemical and petrochemical industries. More avenues are sought to absorb shale supply, including the use of LNG for powering trucks (and perhaps ships in the near future) and, ultimately, exports of gas in the form of LNG. At the time of writing, four such licences have been granted and construction is under development, with several applications being considered by the US Department of Energy.

Although at the time of writing shale gas has been an exclusively US success story, plans are afoot in several countries around the world to verify the estimated probable reserves and start production, where technologically and economically feasible. In a recent report, the EIA (2013b) estimates that the total technically recoverable shale gas reserves amount to almost 7,300 tcf (207 tcm). Exhibit 4.4 shows the geographic location of these reserves, based on the estimates of the EIA report, while Exhibit 4.5 lists the top 10 holders of technically recoverable reserves. As one can clearly see, the shale gas potential is enormous, in fact as much as the current conventional gas reserves. However, 'technically' recoverable reserves rarely equate to 'economically' recoverable ones, so it remains to be seen how many of these reserves it will be feasible to monetise.

When it comes to production figures, the world's two largest producers, by far, are the United States and Russia. Between them, they produced 1,273 bcm (billion cubic metres, or 44.95 tcf) of gas in 2012, or 38 per cent of the world output. They are followed by Iran, Qatar, Canada, Norway, China, Saudi Arabia, Algeria and Indonesia, while the remaining producers are shown in Exhibit 4.6. The presence of the US, with 20 per cent of world production, is, of course, justified, as it is also the world's largest consumption market. Moreover, the US is also ahead of the game in terms of competitiveness and

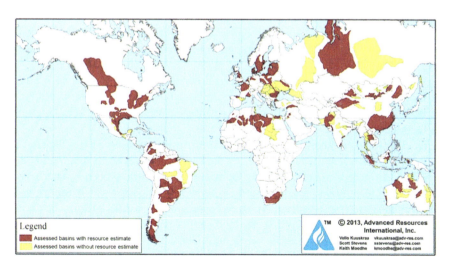

Exhibit 4.4 Map of basins with assessed shale oil and shale gas formations, as of May 2013

Source: EIA (2013b, p. 5)

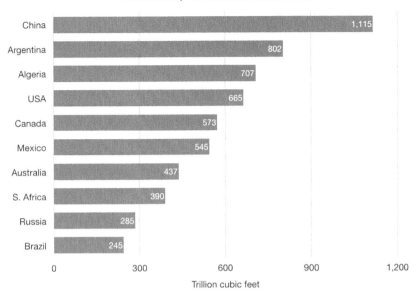

Exhibit 4.5 Top 10 countries with technically recoverable shale gas reserves
Source: EIA (2013b, p. 10)

deregulation, and has further increased its production with the shale gas revolution. The salient feature of production, however, is once again the dominance of Russia, which contributed nearly 18 per cent to the world's output in 2012, and is the dominant supplier of gas to the European Union. Of the remaining producers, Canada directs large quantities of its gas to the US market and Qatar has been impressively active in exporting its gas in the form of LNG, while all other important producers, perhaps with the exception of Iran, market their production internationally.

As is evident from the short description, the existence of a technically competent, cost-effective and low-risk transportation network is vital for the commodity to flow in either domestic or international markets. This is much easier said than done, however.

Pipelines are expensive and time-consuming to lay down. The decision to invest requires a host of factors to be taken into consideration: technical (e.g. pipeline diameter, route, sourcing of materials, safety aspects, sourcing of skilled staff); political (e.g. obtaining licences and approvals, adhering to national and international regulations, crossing or bypassing country borders); and economic (e.g. supply flow from reserves and their duration, existence of adequate demand at the receiving end) are but a few of the obstacles (or 'opportunities') created by a pipeline project. The decision to build a pipeline, or use seaborne transportation, is itself complex. Broadly speaking, pipelines are more suitable when the distance is below 5,000 km, although it depends on the diameter of the pipeline and the annual flow of natural gas in terms of

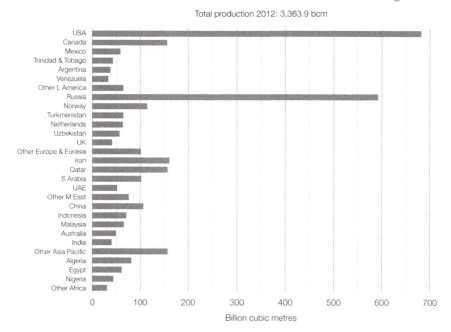

Exhibit 4.6 Major natural gas producers

Source: Author, compiled with data from BP (2013)

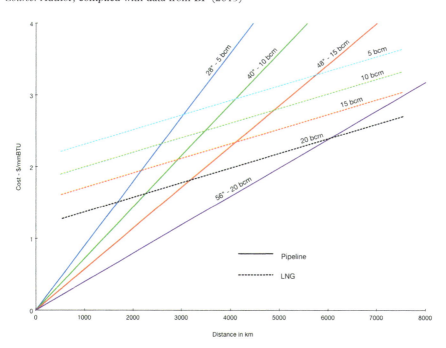

Exhibit 4.7 Pipeline versus LNG transportation cost

Source: Total

bcm per annum. LNG transportation, on the other hand, is more efficient in bringing 'stranded' gas reserves to distant markets.

Probably the most interesting aspect of the supply side of gas, as indeed of oil, are the geopolitics and the resultant effects on security of supplies. We have already seen how gas reserves are concentrated in Russia and the Middle East. To complicate matters even more, the supply corridors from producers to consumers are often ridden with problems. Pipelines are the most effective means to move gas from A to B, but they typically have to cross one or more countries, which can often be a headache for all parties involved. More on this, however, later in this chapter.

Demand determinants

Natural gas consumption has experienced remarkable growth; in the last nearly 50 years since 1965, its consumption has increased fivefold, from 650 bcm to over 3,300 bcm. The average growth rate during these 50 years was 3.5 per cent per annum, compared to the 2 per cent recorded by oil. A host of factors have contributed to this development. The rapid increase in reserves, noted above, certainly provided a springboard for this. The clean-burning properties of natural gas, in the face of increasingly urgent environmental concerns, was another factor. Practically all new power generation projects these days favour CCGT (combined cycle gas turbine) technology. Increased affluence (at least in developed and rapidly developing economies), combined with an environmental conscience, make gas an ideal choice for the modern consumer. This does not mean that gas's increased importance has gone unchallenged. During the 2000s, aided by China's impressive growth of energy demand, coal has again risen to prominence, as seen in Chapter 1. At the time of writing, coal remains the most price-competitive fuel for power generation, at least outside the US, but more on this in the next chapter.

Gas was first marketed in the USA in the late nineteenth century. It was not until the 1930s, however, when technological improvements made possible the laying of high-pressure pipelines over long distances, that it was extensively marketed throughout the country. This started the very long history of gas in the country, which makes it the world's largest consumer of the commodity; over 720 bcm of gas were consumed in the USA in 2012.

In Europe, gas was discovered in small quantities at Lacq (France) and the Po Valley (Italy) in the 1950s. The first substantial discovery came about in 1959 at Groningen in the Netherlands, while Britain made the first commercially exploitable discoveries in its sector of the North Sea in 1965. Since then, gas has had a predominant position in domestic consumption. As can be seen from Exhibit 4.9, in the European Union the UK still remains the largest consumer of gas, with 78 bcm consumed in 2012, although this figure was down from a high of nearly 100 bcm in 2008 and again in 2010. The UK is followed closely by Germany and then Italy and France. The EU, as a group, consumes a total of nearly 460 bcm, more than Russia, but still well behind US consumption. In Russia, gas overtook oil as the main source of primary

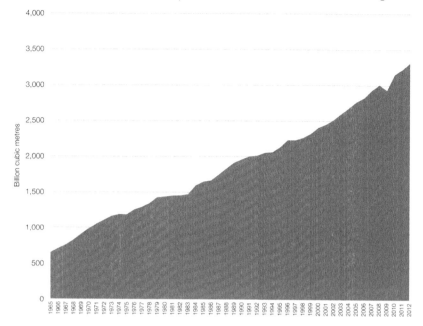

Exhibit 4.8 Gas consumption development

Source: Author, compiled with data from BP (2013)

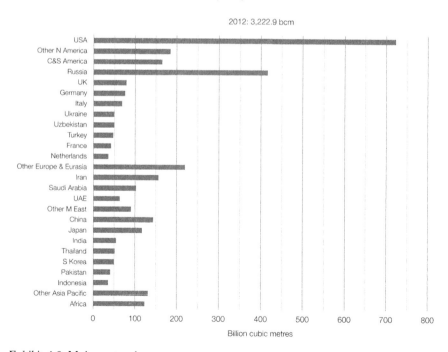

Exhibit 4.9 Major natural gas consumers

Source: Author, compiled with data from BP (2013)

energy consumption in the early 1980s. Since then, it has remained firmly at the top, and Russia is today the second largest gas consumer in the world, with 416 bcm in 2012.

In the Middle East, the most prominent consumer is Iran, with 156 bcm in 2012, practically absorbing all its indigenous production of 160 bcm. It is a surprise that one of the biggest reserve holders is not a prime exporter, but, on the one hand, Iranian consumption has doubled in the past 10 years, and, on the other, the country has been struggling for years to put the investment in place necessary to boost production and become an influential exporter. In Asia Pacific, China and Japan are the two largest consumers, with the former being the most rapidly increasing throughout the 2000s, and eventually overtaking the latter in 2009.

Having seen the leading consumers in absolute terms, it is also worth observing the degree of penetration natural gas has achieved in primary energy consumption. We have already seen in Chapter 1 that gas contributes ca. 24 per cent to world primary energy consumption, but Exhibit 4.10 breaks this down to show the relative shares of the main fuels in broad regions around the world. The picture presents us with some obvious contrasts, but there are a few hidden ones as well. In North America (which includes Mexico), and Europe and Eurasia, which includes Russia, gas accounts for at least 30 per cent of consumption. In South and Central America and Africa, this share is lower, 22 per cent and 27 per cent, respectively. In the Middle East, as expected, gas accounts for 48 per cent of primary energy consumption, the balance being covered by oil. Asia Pacific sources less than 5 per cent of its energy consumption from gas, with over 50 per cent coming from coal.

An illustrative contrast is that between Russia and Asia Pacific: in the former, gas has assumed an even more commanding position, accounting for 54 per cent of total consumption; in the latter, gas has a very modest share, with coal still having a stronghold, especially in China and India. Given that this is the key growth region currently and in the foreseeable future, it will be interesting to observe how gas consumption will develop, given that the region as a whole is in deficit (i.e. has to rely on gas imports, particularly from the Middle East). The region is already showing a voracious appetite for any type of energy, but as environmental concerns assume urgency, gas becomes a more palatable choice. The development of the Sakhalin II project (LNG) on Russia's Pacific coast, as well the various offshore gas projects in the north-west continental shelf of Australia, shows how well aware regional governments and IOCs are of the huge growth potential of Asia Pacific in gas consumption. And from a geopolitical viewpoint, Russia's expansion to the lucrative Asian markets shows how diversification of consumer markets has become a strategic priority for the country.

Another important aspect of gas consumption is its end use. Exhibit 4.11 shows how gas used in a sample of OECD countries, in various OECD country groupings and also in the OECD as a total. Overall, over one-third (37 per cent) of the gas used is for generating electricity and heat in combined cycle plants. This figure changes dramatically when one looks at OECD Asia and

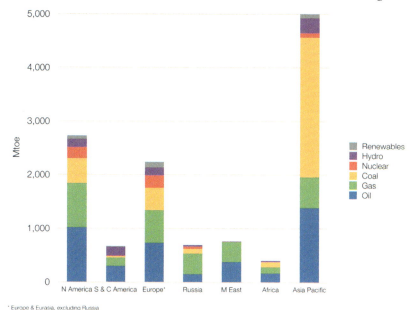

Exhibit 4.10 Regional gas shares in primary energy consumption
Source: Author, compiled with data from BP (2013)

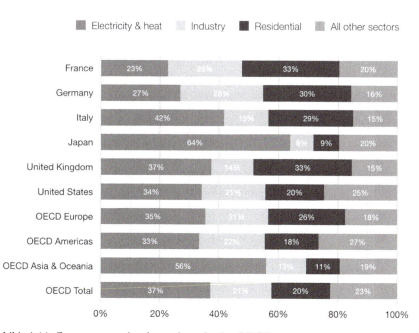

Exhibit 4.11 Gas consumption by end use in the OECD
Source: Author, compiled with data from IEA (2013), Natural Gas Information (Edition: 2013),
Mimas, University of Manchester, DOI: http://dx.doi.org/10.5257/iea/ng/2013

Oceania, however. This figure is dominated by Japan, which uses substantial amounts of imported LNG for power generation; in fact, Japan uses 64 per cent of the gas it consumes to generate electricity and heat. The other sectors accounting for the total gas consumption are industry (e.g. chemicals and petrochemicals, food processing, pulp paper and printing), residential consumption (for heating and cooking), and other sectors (including commercial buildings, agriculture, energy industry's own consumption, transportation and many more). Throughout the 2000s, gas absorption by power plants grew cumulatively by over 50 per cent, with more CCGT plants coming into operation. It will be interesting to observe how growth in other sectors, especially the rather negligible transportation, will change the map of how gas is utilised by final consumers.

Storage

Just like oil, gas also has storage requirements. There are various regulatory and economic reasons for doing so. Demand fluctuation has traditionally been one such reason. Increasingly, gas is being used for power generation; uninterrupted power supply requires a steady supply of gas and stored gas helps avoiding disruptions. Typically, two types of storage are required: baseload and peak load. Baseload storage is designed to address long-term demand patterns through the consumption year; for example, higher demand in winter months, which implies that gas is injected in the storage during the summer months and retrieved at slow and predictable rates during the winter. Larger depleted reservoirs tend to be used for this storage, which are slower in responding to sudden demand surges. Peak-load storage, on the other hand, is designed for exactly this purpose: sudden demand surges, which require quick delivery of relatively smaller amounts of gas. Salt caverns tend to be used for this type of storage, as well as storage in LNG form.

To give an idea of the fluctuations of storage requirements during the year, Exhibit 4.12 shows the level of base and working gas held in US storage facilities. 'Base gas' is required to be in the storage site in order to maintain overall pressure, whereas 'working gas' is injected and withdrawn, depending on what the consumption requirements are. For example, in the US, working gas levels are at their lowest in March, then they start building up during the spring and summer months, reaching their peak around October or November. Increased withdrawals of gas during the autumn and, especially, winter months bring down the overall storage levels to their lowest point, in March, whence the seasonal cycle starts again.

Trade

Natural gas is not as extensively traded as oil and coal; its physical characteristics make it more difficult to handle and its high flammability makes precision and care imperative. In the 1970s, gas entering world trade increased and new countries appeared on the scene, such as the Netherlands, Norway,

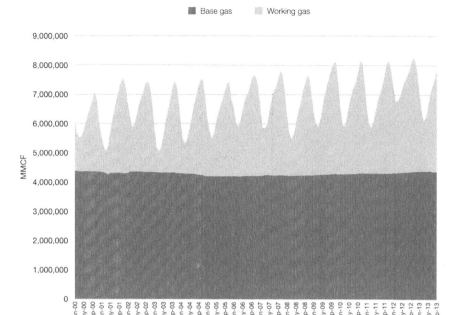

Exhibit 4.12 US monthly gas storage levels
Source: EIA (2013a)

the Soviet Union, Iran and Mexico. The 1980s saw the opening of the TransMed (or Enrico Mattei) submarine pipeline between Algeria and Italy via Tunisia, the beginning of trade between Malaysia and Japan, and the expansion of Soviet gas exports. With the collapse of the Soviet Union in the 1990s, Russian oil and gas exports expanded even more and increasingly larger quantities of pipeline gas found their way to the European Union and the former Soviet republics, through which pass the pipelines carrying the gas from the Yamalo-Nenets district in West Siberia to most countries on the eastern EU front. In the meantime, Japan became the dominant importer of liquefied natural gas, a position it still holds today. In the 2000s, there were two notable developments that affected international trade in gas: the rapid ascent of Qatar to become the world's second largest gas exporter (mostly as LNG); and the advent of US shale gas, which changed the industry dynamics not only in terms of production, but also in terms of the direction of trade flows.

In 2012, just over 30 per cent of the world production entered international trade; the remaining 70 per cent was consumed domestically. World trade amounted to a total of 1,033.4 bcm in that year, with about two-thirds of it being via pipeline and the one-third as LNG. Exhibit 4.13 shows an overview of the major gas trade flows and Exhibit 4.14 lists the key gas exporters in terms of pipeline and LNG flows, whereas Exhibit 4.15 shows the key importers.

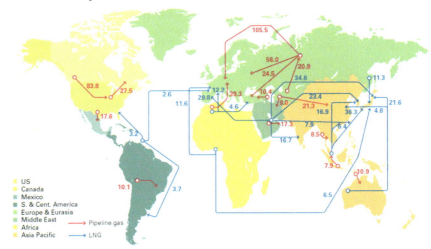

Exhibit 4.13 World gas trade flows
Source: BP (2013, p. 29)

Pipelines

Just over 700 bcm of natural gas was exported by pipeline in 2012, representing ca. 20 per cent of the total gas produced for that year. Pipeline exports are predominant between Canada and the United States (83.8 bcm southbound and 27.5 bcm northbound), and between Russia and the rest of Europe (130 bcm, of which more than half were exported to Germany [30 bcm], Turkey [24.5 bcm] and Italy [13.6 bcm] alone), in addition to another 56 bcm exported to Ukraine, Belarus and other former Soviet republics. Pipeline gas also flows in large quantities from Norway (106.6 bcm), the Netherlands (54.4 bcm) and Algeria (32.8 bcm) to Europe. The other growing force in pipeline exports is Turkmenistan. This former Soviet republic typically exported ca. 20 bcm a year, mostly to Russia and Iran. However, in 2007, the country signed a 30-year contract to supply gas to China, and the gas started flowing in 2010. This has now become Turkmenistan's biggest export flow. Of the 41.1 bcm exported in 2012, 21.3 bcm were destined to China, with the remaining to Russia and Iran, in almost equal quantities.

As mentioned earlier in this chapter, a pipeline is the most obvious technology choice for transporting natural gas. Methane is carried in its natural gaseous form, with only the need to have compression stations at regular intervals, in order to maintain adequate pressure that will keep the gas flowing. The capacity of the pipeline is dictated by its diameter, so that modern 'trunk' pipelines typically have diameters of 48 or 56 inches. Although technically less demanding than a liquefaction plant, pipelines are expensive to lay, especially where the terrain is challenging. More importantly, laying a pipeline assumes that supply of and demand for gas will last for several decades, so that investing in a fixed transportation medium is economically justifiable.

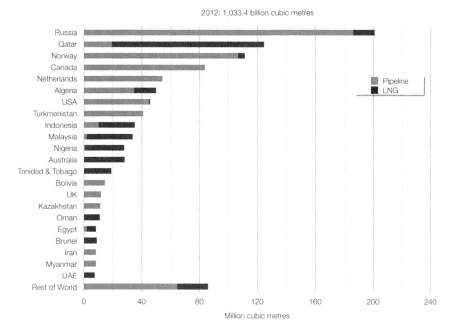

Exhibit 4.14 Top gas exporters

Source: Author, compiled with data from BP (2013)

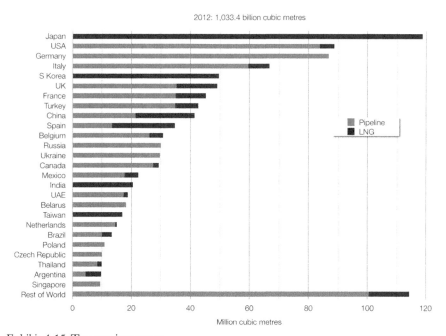

Exhibit 4.15 Top gas importers

Source: Author, compiled with data from BP (2013)

Even more crucial than the technical and economic aspects is the geopolitical significance of pipelines. A case in point is Russia, most of whose gas production is channelled to its most important EU customers via third countries. One of these pipelines is the Yamal-Europe, which carries the gas through Belarus and Poland, before reaching its main customer, Germany. Exhibit 4.16 shows the path of this pipeline, together with the compressor stations along the way.

The stand-off between Ukraine and Russia in late 2005, whose Soyuz/ Brotherhood gas pipeline crosses through the former, is well documented and exemplifies the type of political tensions created. At the time of writing in 2013, a way forward seems to have been found, which involved considerable negotiations between the two countries. As highlighted in BBC News (2013), in December 2013, Ukraine suspended a deal on closer EU ties and signed an aid agreement with Russia instead. The article carries on to state that 'Russia has agreed to buy $15bn (£9.2bn, 11bn euros) of government bonds and slash the price of gas'. However, developments in 2014 quickly overturned the status quo yet again. The pro-Russia Ukrainian government was ousted, a new pro-EU government was voted in and the treaty with the EU was quickly signed. At the same time, Russia annexed Crimea and there is currently continuing conflict in the eastern provinces of Ukraine, between government forces and separatist groups that wish to maintain their alignment with Russia. At the time of writing, there is no sign of a permanent resolution to the situation.

Another example, in the same vein, is Russia's decision to lay a new major pipeline to Western Europe on the seabed of the Baltic, rather than through the territories of old foes. This refers, of course, to the Nord Stream pipeline project (jointly owned by Russia's Gazprom and Germany's Wintershall and E.On Ruhrgas, the Netherlands' Gasunie and France's GDZ-SUEZ), which

Exhibit 4.16 Yamal-Europe gas pipeline

Source: Gazprom, www.gazprom.com/about/production/projects/pipelines/yamal-evropa/

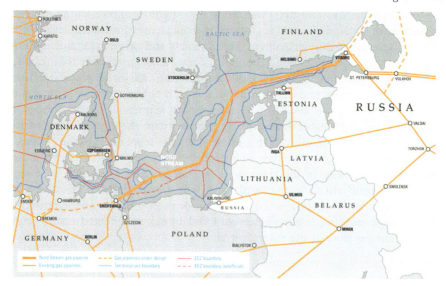

Exhibit 4.17 Nord Stream gas pipeline

Source: www.gazprom.com/about/production/projects/pipelines/nord-stream/

started operating in 2011. The project directly links Vyborg in Russia to Greifswald in Germany using twin pipelines, 1,224 km long, 45 inches (115 cm) wide, with a total capacity of 55 bcm per annum. Exhibit 4.17 shows Nord Stream, alongside other gas pipelines in the region.

At the time of writing, pipeline geopolitics are still at the forefront of European energy policy. On the one hand, the Nord Stream pipeline aims to secure uninterrupted supply of Russian gas to Europe, by linking Russia directly to Germany and bypassing Ukraine. On the other hand, the EU is also trying to secure alternative sources of gas supply, in order to counter-balance the dominance of Russian gas exports. To this effect, the EU has explored alternative sources of gas from the Caspian region, particularly from Azerbaijan, which is the most viable alternative at the moment.[4] One such alternative, the Nabucco pipeline, is all but defunct due to lack of funding. Instead, the Trans-Adriatic Pipeline (TAP), in combination with the Trans-Anatolian Pipeline (TANAP), was selected as the preferred route for Azeri gas exports from the Shah Deniz field in the Caspian Sea. In the meantime, Russia gave up in 2014 its South Stream pipeline project, which would carry its gas via the Black Sea to Bulgaria and from there to Serbia, Hungary, Slovenia and, eventually, the north of Italy.

Not all pipelines are ridden with geopolitical issues. In the US, the early expansion of the gas pipeline network has allowed the freer movement of

4 Other alternatives could be Turkmenistan and Iran. Turkmenistan is currently focusing on its exports to China and any direct exports to the EU would require the completion of the Trans-Caspian pipeline first. Iran is a much more remote possibility. First and foremost, it requires the resolution of the political problems between Iran and the West and, second, it requires substantial investment in exploring and producing Iranian gas reserves in the Caspian.

the fuel around the country. Welded steel pipelines allowed long-distance transmission and gave birth to interstate commerce. From the mid-1980s started the gradual deregulation of gas contracts and prices, which eventually led to the current system, which consists of several gas marketers that transact directly with the final large-scale consumers (e.g. gas-fired power stations, industrial consumers and distributors of gas to retail consumers). For this to become possible, the building of a complex interstate pipeline network was necessary. An idea of this network, together with the key gas flows within the US, is given in Exhibit 4.18. As can be seen from the graphic, there is convergence of several pipelines to create one very big flow from the south-east to the north-east of the country. This reflects the concentration of large cities and conurbations in the north-east, where both gas and electricity are consumed in large quantities. Equally, the location of some of the country's biggest gas-producing states, Texas and Oklahoma, is reflected in the origin of the main gas flow in the same graphic.

LNG

Liquefied natural gas entered international trade in a very modest way in the 1960s. The first experimental voyages with LNG carriers were carried out in the 1950s, but the first commercial trip was in 1964, between Algeria and the UK. A year later, LNG cargoes began flowing from Algeria to France, while in 1969 trade between Alaska and Japan was initiated.

An interesting characteristic of the LNG market is the fact that the transport element was traditionally only the last in a long chain of planning decisions

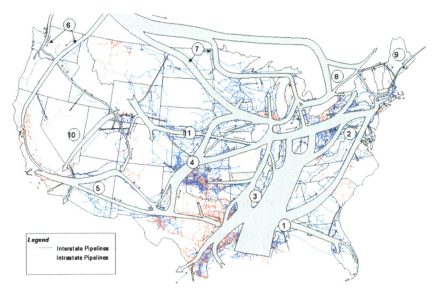

Exhibit 4.18 US gas pipelines

Source: EIA, as stated in the graphic

that have to be made for any individual project. Still today, LNG ships are probably among the most sophisticated and technology-intensive in the world, with prices in the region of $200 million for a ship with a typical capacity of 160,000 cbm, built in the Far East.

LNG projects are extremely capital-intensive, usually requiring billions of dollars of funds, of which a substantial part has to be provided by equity holders. Projects are usually set up as joint ventures between developed and developing countries, and involve long lead times, usually between 7 and 10 years. Some of the factors that need to be in place for a project to be successful include: a big enough reserve of gas, which is unlikely to be consumed domestically for the next 20 years at least; one or more buyers willing to enter long-term purchase contracts; a host government willing to be flexible on fiscal issues; expertise in technical and safety areas; and willingness of all parties to view the projects on a long-term, cooperative basis.

These factors will undoubtedly continue being important in the future. However, through the 2000s, we have witnessed a gradual, but persistent, increase in the amount of LNG cargoes that move on a short-term basis, as can be seen from Exhibit 4.19.

This was not a great surprise, though. With a lot more buyer interest and more governments willing to export their production, LNG projects took off since the beginning of the new millennium. According to GIIGNL (2012), there were 89 liquefaction trains in 18[5] exporting countries in 2012, with a total capacity of 282 mtpa (million tonnes per annum). As seen in Exhibit 4.20, Qatar currently holds the largest LNG production capacity, with 14 liquefaction trains operating at Ras Laffan, by the two production companies, Qatargas and Rasgas. Over the last decade, Qatar invested heavily in these facilities, in order to monetise its large gas reserves and, as we have seen earlier,

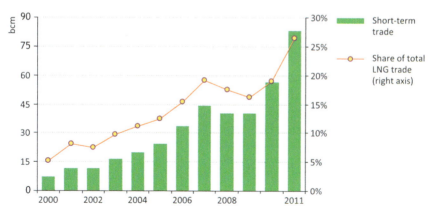

Exhibit 4.19 Share of short-term contracts in the LNG market

Source: GIIGNL and IEA, as stated in the graphic

5 Libya is one of these 18 countries, although its LNG terminal remained mostly closed during 2012.

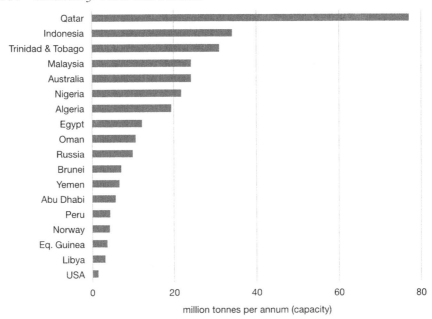

Exhibit 4.20 Liquefaction terminals around the world

Source: Author, compiled with data from GIIGNL (2012, pp. 20–2)

it is now the world's largest LNG exporter, as well as the second largest overall gas exporter.

On the consumer side, there were 93 LNG regasification facilities, including 11 floating ones, with half of this capacity located in Asia. Figures for regasification facilities are not immediately comparable with those for liquefaction ones. A regasification facility typically comprises one or more docks where LNG vessels can moor in order to offload their cargo, a set of pipelines that carry the gas in its liquid form to cryogenic storage tanks, a number of vaporisers that turn the liquid methane into its gaseous form, and finally another set of pipelines that connect the facility to the main gas pipeline grid. What is, therefore, measured is the storage capacity and the nominal 'send-out' capacity (i.e. the amount of methane in gaseous form that can be put on to the gas grid, assuming that the regasification plant has a continuous supply of LNG to vaporise). This nominal capacity is measured in the more familiar bcm units. On this base, we can see in Exhibit 4.21 that Japan is by far the largest holder of regasification capacity. The other large capacity holder in the region is South Korea, whereas in Europe it is Spain and the UK holding the top two places. The US, albeit the world's second largest capacity holder, is a bit of an anomaly. In 2012, only about 2 per cent of this capacity was utilised. Quite a few of these regasification terminals were built or expanded in the early part of the 2000s, in anticipation of a surge in US gas imports. But then, the shale gas revolution hit the US market and many of these plants have remained seriously underutilised. However, with the possibility of a sizeable expansion

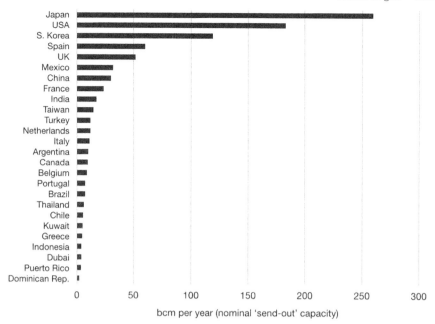

Exhibit 4.21 Regasification plants around the world

Source: Author, compiled with data from GIIGNL (2012, pp. 28–31)

of US exports of shale gas, several plans are afoot for converting some of these plants into liquefaction terminals. Only time will show how successful these ventures will be.

Once an LNG project, including the transport element, is in place, the buyer and seller face the risk of operating a successful and profitable venture. Notwithstanding any technical or operational issues, the key risk is profitability. The buyer requires a long-term, steady stream of income; the seller requires a competitively priced, highly marketable, easily transferable commodity. Long-term contracts (LTCs) have, therefore, been the obvious choice for LNG partners. This is not a novelty; iron ore and other mineral commodities have been traded for decades on the back of LTCs. In this contractual arrangement, the seller normally takes the price risk and the buyer assumes the volume risk. LTCs normally have take-or-pay (TOP) clauses, whereby a buyer is obliged to pay for a certain amount of cargo, even if he does not lift it. Often, there are destination clauses: the cargo can only be destined to certain markets; it cannot be sold further on, to more lucrative markets. However, as we mentioned earlier, this traditional long-term buyer-seller relationship has been challenged, with more shipments made on a short-term basis and more flexibility added to LTCs to reflect the new market dynamics.

LNG trade accounts for only about 10 per cent of world natural gas production and is rather small compared to trade flows of other energy commodities; but because of the complexity of its transport logistics, LNG flows have been meticulously documented on a voyage-by-voyage basis, since the very beginning in the 1960s. The carriage of the liquid itself is only one of several steps of a carefully planned procedure, which includes carriage of gas from the point of production to the port liquefaction facility; loading; regasification at the port of destination; and transport to the point of consumption. LNG contracts have been extensively documented and are being regularly quoted in special publications by organisations such as Cedigaz and the International Group of Liquefied Natural Gas Importers. Details of contracts are given in GIIGNL (2012), and a small excerpt for Qatar contracts is given in Exhibit 4.22. As one can clearly see, the vast majority of contracts are for durations in excess of 20 years, and in some cases they extend over 30 years, an indication of how important long-term commitment from both buyers and sellers is essential.

Natural gas trade, be it by pipeline or LNG, will continue to rise in importance in the next two decades and even beyond. The human race is looking for ways to respond to rising energy demand, as discussed in Chapter 1, while at the same time dealing with less abundant (or some would say 'scarce') supply and the need to put the rate of greenhouse gas (GHG) emissions, especially CO_2, under some form of control. More and more nations are adding gas to their energy portfolio, and in order to achieve this they will have to resort to trade. Pipelines, despite their shortcomings, will continue

Seller	Buyer	Nominal quantity mtpa	Duration	Contract type
Qatargas I	Chubu Electric	4	1997/2021	FOB
	Tohoku Electric, Tokyo Gas, Osaka Gas, The Kansai Electric, The Tokyo Electric Power Co.	2	1998/2021	DES
	Gas Natural Aprov.	0.66	2001/2012	FOB
	Gas Natural Aprov.	0.66	2002/2012	DES
	Gas Natural sdg	0.75	2005/2024	DES
	Gas Natural sdg	0.75	2006/2025	FOB
	The Tokyo Power Electric Co	1	2012/2021	DES
Qatargas II T1	ExxonMobil	7.8	2009/2034	DES
Qatargas II T2	CNOOC	2	2009/2034	DES
	Total	1.85	2009/2034	DES
	Total	1.5	2009/2034	DES
	Total	1.15	2009/2034	DES
	Total	0.7	2009/2034	DES
	ExxonMobil	0.6	2009/2033	DES
Qatargas III	ConocoPhillips	7.8	2010/2035	DES
Qatargas IV	Shell	3.8	2011/2041	DES
	Petrochina	3	2011/2036	DES
	Marubeni	1	2011/2031	DES
Rasgas I	KOGAS	4.92	1999/2024	FOB
	ENI	0.73	2004/2024	DES
Rasgas II T1	Petronet LNG	5	2004/2028	FOB
Rasgas II T2	Edison	4.6	2009/2034	DES
	Endesa	0.74	2005/2025	DES
Rasgas II T3	EDF Trading	3.4	2007/2012	DES
	CPC	3.08	2008/2032	FOB
	ENI	2.05	2007/2027	DES

Exhibit 4.22 LNG contracts for Qatar in 2012

Source: Author, compiled with data from GIIGNL (2012, pp. 34–5)

being very important. For LNG, the issue will always be that of the huge capital outlay required to build the liquefaction and regasification terminals, as well as the ships themselves, in the face of a market that seems to require more flexibility while still operating on the basis of LTCs. This is why new technology solutions are being tried out, such as floating facilities, both for liquefaction (FNLG unit, such as the Prelude, which is currently being built by Shell) and regasification (FSRU – floating storage and regasification unit).

Pricing

Crude oil, an inherently heterogeneous commodity, has managed to settle on a system of benchmark pricing, as discussed in Chapter 2. This creates a global market, allowing, of course, for transportation costs and regional demand and supply, and supply imbalances.

Natural gas, an inherently homogeneous commodity, is characterised by a number of different pricing regimes, as well as considerable differences in levels among regions and countries. To get a glimpse of these variations, let us look at Exhibit 4.23. One can instantly see that there are considerable discrepancies between three of the key benchmark indices: US (Henry Hub), UK (Heren NBP index) and Japan (cif LNG). In 2012, the US price averaged $2.76/MMBtu, with the UK equivalent average price at $9.46 and the Japanese at $18.82. The Japanese price does include the cost of, rather expensive,

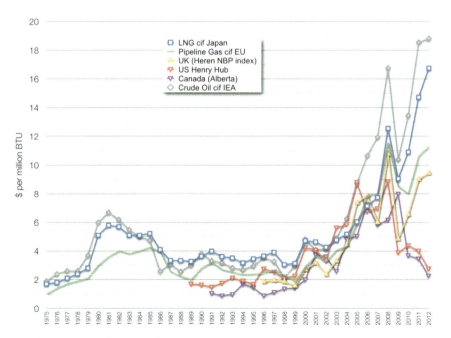

Exhibit 4.23 Indicative gas prices around the world

Source: Author, compiled with data from BP (2013)

transportation, but even taking this into account the difference is quite substantial.

Why all this variety, then? Historically, the most challenging issue for the economics of the industry has been the relation of gas and oil prices. Traditionally, gas prices were determined on the basis of its calorific equivalence to oil. This is what is known as *oil indexing*, or *oil price escalation*. The rationale behind this system is not difficult to understand. Until the last 10 or so years, gas has been used for the production of peak electricity (i.e. electricity that is produced to respond to short-term, sharp peaks in demand), and gas has the advantage of being able to produce this at very short notice. A major competitor to gas in such an operation is fuel oil. Although nowadays this may not be true in North America and the EU, it is still true in Japan. In addition, gas also competes with naphtha as a feedstock to the chemical and petrochemical industry, which is another strong reason to index gas prices on oil. As a result, LNG cargoes destined for Japan are routinely indexed on the JCC.

At the other end of the spectrum of pricing regimes, we have gas pricing in an open, competitive market, with a close correlation between the spot price of gas and the next available futures contract (*front month*). This is commonly known as *gas-on-gas* pricing, and it is the prevalent pricing method in the US. We have already seen how gas flows within the US; to facilitate this movement, the gas pipeline network has a number of *hubs*, big interchange points, where gas travels through, can change direction, can be bought or sold, and also stored if necessary. It is at these nodal points that pricing takes place, and this is also the reason why *gas-on-gas* pricing is also known as hub pricing. The largest and most liquid of them is Henry Hub in Louisiana, and the Henry Hub price is the benchmark price for gas in the US.

Somewhere in between these two regimes is where the EU finds itself. As of the end of 2013, and despite the EU Commission's continued efforts to create a single competitive market in gas, there is a number of different pricing regimes, depending on which end of the EU one is. Move towards the west border, for example the UK and the Netherlands, and pricing leans more towards gas-on-gas pricing. Move towards the east border, for example Germany, and pricing is still dominated by oil indexing, with a measure of gas-on-gas pricing as well. When it comes to Russian imports, oil indexation is still prevalent, as can be seen in Exhibit 4.24. For a further discussion on the progress of gas pricing in continental Europe, Stern and Rogers (2011) is a good starting point.

The issue of pricing will remain one of the hottest issues in the gas market for the foreseeable future, especially as trade expands, more pipelines are being laid, more LNG cargoes move more flexibly worldwide, buyers increasingly ask for more gas-market-related (gas-on-gas) prices, while sellers continue to resist giving up oil indexing formulas. Over the last few years, the International Gas Union has been producing market surveys on how wholesale gas prices are formed. In their most recent survey (IGU 2013), the majority of gas consumed around the world is priced on a gas-to-gas basis, however this is

Exhibit 4.24 Prices of Russian gas imported in Germany

Source: Author, compiled with data from www.indexmundi.com and IMF

biased by what happens in North America (which also includes Mexico), where gas-on-gas pricing is used almost exclusively. Exhibit 4.25 shows the proportion of world gas consumption that is priced under the variety of existing regimes. In addition to gas-on-gas (GOG) and oil indexing (OPE), there are several state-regulated regimes (RCS, RSP and RBC) whereby the price is set on the basis of recovering costs, or on a social/political basis, or even below cost in order to subsidise domestic consumption. The list of regimes is completed with bilateral monopoly (BIM, whereby two states fix the prices after negotiations, often for a long time), netback (NET, whereby the price of gas is a function of the price of the final good the buyer produces, e.g. the price of ammonia for a chemical plant using gas as feedstock), no price (NP, where the gas is flared or given for free), and not known (NK, where no data are available).

Exhibit 4.26 juxtaposes the pricing of traded gas via pipeline and LNG and, as one can see, oil indexing is still predominant.

Finally, Exhibit 4.27 compares pricing regimes in some of the key consuming regions, which confirms our earlier discussion. North America used gas-on-gas pricing almost exclusively. Europe, on the other hand, relied almost equally on both oil indexing and gas-on-gas pricing, and it will be interesting to see whether the trend towards the latter continues. Finally, in China, the Indian subcontinent and the rest of Asia Pacific, oil indexing remains strong, followed by regulated (non-market) prices, particularly in China, India, Bangladesh, Malaysia, Indonesia and Vietnam.

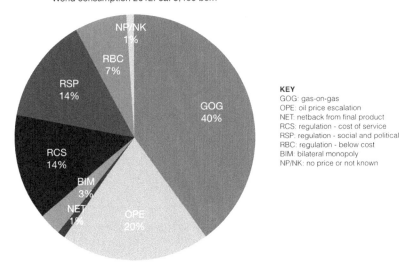

Exhibit 4.25 Gas pricing regimes – worldwide consumption
Source: IGU (2013, p. 15)

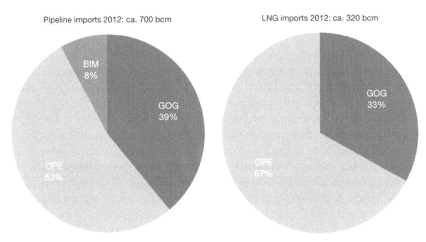

Exhibit 4.26 Gas pricing regimes – traded gas
Source: IGU (2013, p. 14)

Conclusion

To encapsulate a market as complex, diverse and exciting as gas in a few pages is impossible. Natural gas is, for many, the imminent future of energy, in the face of rapidly declining oil reserves and environmental concerns about the use of coal. The industry has progressed by leaps and bounds in the last 30 or so years. It started with the extensive deregulation of the US market.

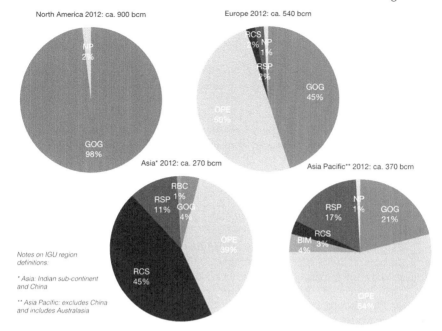

Exhibit 4.27 Gas pricing regimes – regional consumption

Source: IGU (2013, pp. 16–17)

This allowed for a lot of integrated services to 'unbundle' into their constituents (i.e. gas production, transmission, storage, marketing, distribution and ancillary services, and competitive pricing) to become more prominent. In Europe, progress has been slower, but it is picking up pace. In Asia, gas has started playing a bigger role in the large emerging economies of China and India, but there is still plenty of room for development. Gas consumption is also increasing markedly in the Middle East, alongside oil consumption.

Deregulation, however, is only one force for change. Demand increase, especially for power generation; competition between coal, gas and renewables for electricity generation; the rise of Russia as *the* dominant gas exporter to Europe; pipeline geopolitics; growth in the volume and diversity of LNG trade flows; the potential for additional conventional gas production from Africa; the shale gas revolution in the US and the knock-on effect on world markets; and the rise of the environmental conscience have all acted as harbingers of change. The list can go on and on, as will our interest in this endlessly fascinating energy source.

References

BBC News (2013) 'Russia deal saved Ukraine from bankruptcy – PM Azarov', *BBC Online*, 18 December 2013, accessed online at: www.bbc.co.uk/news/world-europe-25427706.

Boswell, R. and Collett, T.S. (2011) Current perspectives on gas hydrate resources. *Energy and Environmental Science*, 4: 1206–15.

BP (2013) *Statistical Review of the World Energy 2013*, British Petroleum, accessed online at: www.bp.com/statisticalreview.

EIA (2013a) *US Underground Natural Storage Data*, Energy Information Administration, accessed online at: www.eia.gov/dnav/ng/ng_stor_sum_a_EPG0_sat_mmcf_m.htm.

—— (2013b) *Technically Recoverable Shale Oil and Shale Gas Resources: An Assessment of 137 Shale Formations in 41 Countries Outside the United States*, Energy Information Administration, accessed online at: www.eia.gov/analysis/studies/worldshalegas/pdf/fullreport.pdf.

GIIGNL (2012) *The LNG Industry in 2012*, The International Group of Liquefied Natural Gas Importers, accessed online at: www.giignl.org/sites/default/files/publication/giignl_the_lng_industry_2012.pdf.

IEA (2013) *Natural Gas Information (Edition: 2013)*, accessed on line at: http://dx.doi.org/10.5257/iea/ng/2013.

IGU (2013) *Wholesale Gas Price Survey – 2013 Edition: A Global Review of Price Formation Mechanisms 2005–2012*, International Gas Union, accessed online at: www.igu.org/gas-knowhow/publications/igu-publications/.

Stern, J. and Rogers, H. (2011) *The Transition to Hub-Based Gas Pricing in Continental Europe*, The Oxford Institute of Energy Studies, accessed online at: www.oxfordenergy.org/wpcms/wp-content/uploads/2011/03/NG49.pdf.

5   Coal

Coal was the first ever hydrocarbon in human history to be used on an industrial scale. Coal, and especially peat, has been used for centuries for rudimentary household cooking and heating, in the form of open-hearth fires. As the power of steam was discovered and harnessed to mechanise every type of production activity from agriculture, to mining, to metallurgy, to manufacturing, to lighting and transportation, coal was the fuel that powered the Industrial Revolution from the early eighteenth to the early twentieth century, until it eventually took second place to oil.

Physical characteristics

Coal is a solid mineral, composed primarily of carbon; other components of coal are volatile hydrocarbons, sulphur and nitrogen, and the minerals that remain as ash when the coal is burned.

Most of the coal in the earth's crust was formed during the Carboniferous period – between 280 and 345 million years ago. At that time, much of the world was covered with luxuriant vegetation growing in swamps. Many of these plants were types of ferns, some as large as trees. This vegetation died and became submerged underwater, where it gradually decomposed. As decomposition took place, the vegetable matter lost oxygen and hydrogen atoms, leaving a deposit with a high percentage of carbon. As time passed, layers of sand and mud settled from the water over some of the Carboniferous deposits. The pressure of these overlying layers, as well as movements of the earth's crust and sometimes volcanic heat, acted to compress and harden the deposits, thus producing coal.

Coal is classified in several subtypes, primarily according to its carbon content. Peat, the first stage in the formation of coal, has a low fixed carbon content and a high moisture content, but it does not have the same uses as commercial coal.

Commercial coal is usually classified in two broad categories – brown and hard. The first category includes lignite – the lowest rank of coal – and sub-bituminous coal. Both of these types are invariably used for power generation and, because of their low quality, they are consumed in domestic markets. Lignite is usually brownish-black in colour and often shows a distinct fibrous or woody structure. Lignite is inferior in calorific value to ordinary coal because of its high water content and low (25–35 per cent) carbon content; the high content of volatile matter causes the lignite to disintegrate rapidly upon exposure to air. Sub-bituminous coal is a bit better in terms of carbon content (ca. 35–45 per cent), but still not high enough to make it up to export quality standard. As a result, practically all lignite and lower-quality coal is consumed domestically, typically for power generation, but also for cement manufacturing and other industrial uses, especially because higher-quality coal is more expensive or perhaps not easily available.

The term 'hard coal' comprises all the remaining high-quality types of coal, from bituminous coal to graphite. Bituminous coal has more carbon than lignite and a correspondingly higher heating value. It is primarily used for generating power, although coals closer to anthracite are suitable for further processing into coke for steel production.

Anthracite is a hard coal with the highest fixed-carbon content and the lowest amount of volatile material of all types of coal. It typically contains over 86 per cent carbon, ca. 9–10 per cent ash and ca. 4–5 per cent volatile matter. Anthracite is glossy black, with a crystal structure; although harder to ignite than other coals, anthracite releases a great deal of energy when burned and gives off little smoke and soot. Anthracite is ideal for reduction into coke, which is then used to fire iron ore in order to produce molten iron.

Coke is a vital input in the steelmaking process. Coke is the name given to the hard, porous residue left after the destructive distillation of coal; it is

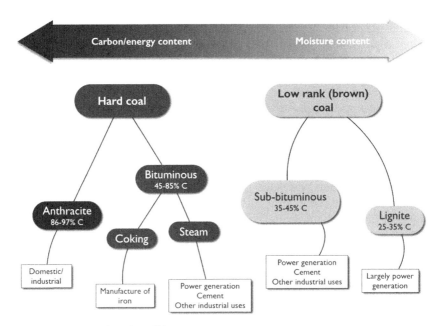

Exhibit 5.1 Range of coal qualities

Source: Author

blackish-grey, has a metallic lustre and is composed largely of carbon – usually about 92 per cent. It has excellent burning properties, with a gross calorific value of 12,000–13,500 Btu/lb, which makes it appropriate for use as a reducing agent in the smelting of pig iron. Coke was first produced as a by-product in the manufacture of illuminating gas. The growth of the steel industry, however, produced a rising demand for metallurgical coke, making it inevitable that coke should be manufactured as a chief product rather than as a by-product.

The earliest method of coking coal was simply to pile it in large heaps out of doors, leaving a number of horizontal and vertical flues through the piles. These flues were filled with wood, which was lighted, and which, in turn, ignited the coal. When most of the volatile elements in the coal were driven off, the flames would die down; the fire would then be partly smothered with coal dust, and the heap sprinkled with water.

A later development was the coking of coal in the beehive oven, so named because of its shape. As in open-air coking, no attempt was made to recover the valuable gas and tar that were by-products of the process. Beehive ovens have now been almost entirely supplanted by the modern by-product coke ovens. These ovens, usually arranged in batteries of about 60, are narrow vertical chambers with silica-brick walls, heated by burning gas between adjoining ovens. Each oven is charged through an opening in the top with anywhere from 10 to 22 tons of coal, which is heated to temperatures as high as 1,482° C for about 17 hours. During this period, the gases from the oven are collected through another opening in the top. At the end of the coking period, the red-hot coke is forced by a ram, out of the oven, directly into a car that carries it to the quenching hood, where it is sprinkled with water. The emptying process takes only about three minutes, so that the oven is ready for recharging with little loss of heat.

Although we are mainly concerned with coal for power generation and steelmaking, it is worth taking note of another form of coal – graphite – and a coal by-product – coal tar – both of which have a variety of industrial uses.

Graphite is one of the three allotropic forms of carbon; the other forms are diamond and amorphous carbon. It occurs in nature as a mineral invariably containing impurities. It is widely distributed over the world; important deposits are found in Siberia, England, Madagascar, Mexico, Sri Lanka, Canada, and numerous localities in the United States. Graphite is made artificially by baking a mixture of petroleum coke and coal tar pitch at 950° C for 11–13 weeks, then transferring the baked product to electric graphitising furnaces and heating it to about 2,800° C for four or five weeks.

Although graphite is chemically the same as diamond, it differs greatly from that mineral in most of its physical properties. Graphite is black, opaque, metallic in lustre, and has a specific gravity of 2.09 to 2.2. Graphite is extremely soft, it smudges anything with which it comes into contact, and it feels greasy or slippery to the touch. It is the only non-metal that is a good conductor of electricity; unlike other conductors of electricity, it is a poor conductor of heat.

The cores of 'lead' pencils contain no lead, but are made of graphite mixed with clay. Graphite is used as electrodes in electrochemical industries where corrosive gases are given off, and for electric arc furnaces that reach extremely high temperatures. It is used as a lubricant either by itself or mixed with grease, oil, or water. It is also used in crucibles that must withstand extremely high temperatures, and in certain paints.

Coal tar is a viscous black liquid produced in the destructive distillation of coal to make coke and gas. Coal tar is a complex mixture of organic compounds, mostly hydrocarbons. Its composition varies with the coal, the temperature at which it is formed, and the equipment used. Coke is usually produced at about 1,000° C, and coal tar formed in that temperature range consists mostly of aromatic hydrocarbons, plus phenols and some compounds containing nitrogen, sulphur, and oxygen. The variation in composition means that most of the compounds in coal tar are formed during the coking process and are not present, as such, in the original coal. Some 300 distinct compounds have been identified in coal tar, of which about 50 are separated and used commercially. Separation is achieved through distillation, which produces benzene, toluene, naphthalene, xylene, anthracene, phenanthrene and other valuable products. The processing may be varied to give different proportions. Left, after distillation, are residues of pitch used in making roads, in roofing mixtures, and in electrodes for the production of aluminium.

Coal tar was once regarded as a useless nuisance. Since then, however, it has led to a whole new field of chemistry, and its compounds are indispensable to a vast number of products, including dyes, drugs, explosives, food flavourings, perfumes, artificial sweeteners, paints, preservatives, stains, insecticides and resins. Coal tar is also the chief source of creosols, a group of chemicals used in antiseptics, creosote oil, paint removers and plastics.

As we noted earlier, coal normally contains a number of other compounds, mainly sulphur and metallic elements, which form the ash. When burnt, coal generates a number of undesirable by-products, which have largely contributed to the image of coal as a 'dirty' source of energy. Carbon reacts with oxygen to produce carbon monoxide (CO) and dioxide (CO_2). Increased emissions of these two gases have contributed to the greenhouse effect on the earth's atmosphere, with detrimental long-term consequences for global climate. When burnt, the sulphur contained in coal reacts with oxygen to form sulphur dioxide (SO_2), a gas that has several useful industrial applications. If the gas is released in the atmosphere, however, it mixes with water (H_2O) in a lethal combination – sulphuric acid (H_2SO_4) – that returns to earth as acid rain. Finally, coal burning also produces a number of nitrogen oxides (NOX), which also have detrimental effects on the earth's atmosphere.

As the coal industry is trying to improve the image of the commodity, several attempts have been made to improve its combustion, with the aim to reduce emission of impurities, such as sulphur and nitrogen oxides, and increase the efficiency of energy production. Clean coal technologies (CCTs) may be increasingly commercially attractive in the twenty-first century, provided there are adequate incentives (say a substantially high price for carbon emissions) to make their use more widespread. In general, these technologies are cleaner, more efficient, and less costly than conventional coal-using processes. A wide variety of CCTs exist, but all of them alter the basic structure of coal before, during or after combustion. CCTs include: improved methods of cleaning coal; fluidised bed combustion; integrated gasification combined cycle; furnace sorbent injection; and advanced flue-gas desulphurisation.

Supply characteristics

The supply determinants of coal have essentially been discussed in Chapter 2, together with other hydrocarbons. One definite advantage of coal over all other fossil fuels is its sheer abundance. World coal reserves were estimated at over 860 billion tonnes at the end of 2012, with an R/P ratio of 120 years. With R/P ratios of 60 years for natural gas, and 45 years for oil, coal seems likely to continue playing a very important role on the world energy mix in the long term. Another very interesting statistic is that while just between 10 and 15 per cent of oil and natural gas reserves are located in OECD countries, over 40 per cent of coal reserves are located in the OECD area, which makes coal a 'politically safe' source of energy.

With such obvious advantages, then, why is coal not the most popular source of energy in most countries around the world? The answer lies very much in the economics of coal mining and the challenge to coal by the 'new' fuels – oil and natural gas.

As in any project for the extraction of mineral resources, there are three main stages in coal recovery: exploration, development and production. Exploration may last a few years, until proper geological surveys point with high probability to the existence of reserves. Several exploratory shafts may have to be constructed in order to assess the quality and extent of the deposits. Costs at this stage can be substantial and are sunk. The development stage involves the construction of an open pit (if the developer is lucky enough to find coal near the ground surface) or the digging of an underground mine. Again, costs at this stage are sunk, and further costs might have to be incurred at later stages of a project in order to improve and/or extend capacity.

At the production stage, most of the costs are operating costs, which tend to increase as reserves are being depleted and more effort is required to extract them. This is particularly true when underground mining is the method of production. Another important difference of coal mining from oil and gas extraction is that coal has to be moved at every stage, whereas oil and gas flow naturally; coal requires a lot more effort to break and extract, while oil simply requires a steady pressure that will keep it flowing out of the well, naturally.

Another important characteristic of the coal industry, which is also evident throughout the mineral sector, is the large extent of heterogeneity in production costs. Depending on the geomorphology of the field and local climatic conditions, costs can vary considerably from one region to the next. Indonesia, South Africa and Colombia, for example, are low- to medium-cost producers, while countries such as Germany and the UK produce coal at such high costs that it is much cheaper to import the commodity from distant, low-cost exporters. Apart from regional differences, one should also expect different production costs between surface and underground coal mines, as well as differences arising due to inland transportation costs. Russia, for example, has free-at-mine costs comparable to those of cheap producers, such as Indonesia and Colombia. However, the cost of inland transportation, in order to bring the coal to an export terminal, is as much as the mining production cost. Exhibit 5.2 shows the range of FOB supply costs for internationally traded steam coal, together with the average price levels in 2011. The width of each bar gives an indication of the amount of coal available for the export market from each supply country.

Although capital, land and fuel are the most important contributors to extraction costs, one should not underestimate the role of labour in coal production. Taking into account the fact that coal is largely produced in OECD countries, labour costs become quite sizeable, and labour relations are central to the uninterrupted running of a coal mine; one has only to recall the huge disruption caused, in the UK economy, by the long strike of coal miners at the beginning of the 1980s.

Reserves and production

Coal is found in nearly every region of the world, but deposits of present commercial importance are confined to Europe, Asia, Australia and North America (see Exhibit 5.3 for the key reserve holders as of 2012). Great Britain, which led the world in coal production until the twentieth century, has deposits in southern Scotland, England and Wales. In Western Europe, coalfields are found throughout the Alsace region of France, in Belgium, and in the Saar and Ruhr valleys in Germany. The French and Belgian production is rather small, with the latter disappearing altogether after 1993. Germany is still the

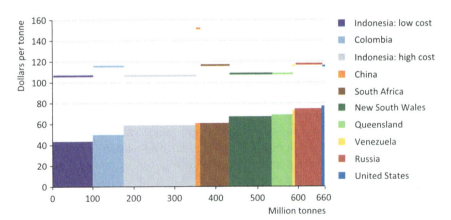

Exhibit 5.2 Average FOB supply cash costs and prices for internationally traded steam coal, 2011

Source: IEA (2012b, p. 177) and others, as stated in the graphic

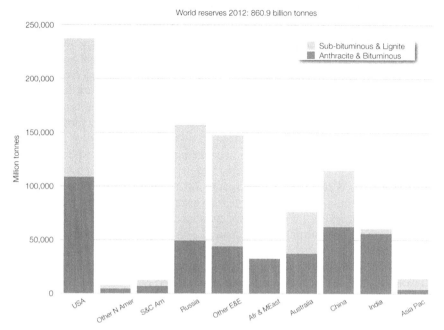

Exhibit 5.3 World coal reserves

Source: Author, compiled with data from BP (2013)

most important Western European producer, but its production has been falling steadily for the last 10 years. Most of Germany's deposits contain brown and sub-bituminous coal, which are of lower calorific value, and hence decrease total German production in oil-equivalent terms.

Eastern European deposits include those of Poland, the Czech Republic, Romania, Bulgaria and Hungary. The most extensive and valuable coalfield in the former Soviet Union is that of the Donets Basin between the Dnepr and Don Rivers; large deposits have also recently been exploited in the Kuznetsk Coal Basin in Western Siberia. The Russian Federation holds the world's second largest reserves of coal, with some 157 billion tonnes in 2012, which was behind US deposits of 237 billion tonnes. Apart from Russia, Ukraine and Kazakhstan are the other two former Soviet republics to hold substantial reserves. As in Western Europe, coal production in Eastern Europe experienced a declining trend through the 1990s. This trend, however, started a reversal in the late 1990s, with coal production showing an increase as we have moved into the twenty-first century. Unlike Germany, the former Soviet republics – especially Ukraine and Kazakhstan – produce primarily hard coal.

The coal reserves of the United States are divided into six major regions. Only three of these regions, however, are mined extensively. The most productive region is the Appalachian field, which includes parts of Pennsylvania, West Virginia, Kentucky, Tennessee, Ohio and Alabama. In the Midwest, one large field covers most of Illinois and sections of Indiana and Kentucky. A thick field extends from Iowa through Missouri, Kansas and Oklahoma. These three regions produce the majority of the coal mined in the United States. There are large deposits of lignite and sub-bituminous coal in North Dakota, South Dakota and Montana. Sub-bituminous and bituminous coal deposits are scattered throughout Wyoming, Utah, Colorado, Arizona and New Mexico. The Pacific Coast and Alaska have small reserves of bituminous coal. Almost all the anthracite in the United States is in a small area around Scranton and Wilkes-Barre, in Pennsylvania. The best bituminous coal, for coking purposes, comes from the Middle Atlantic states.

Canada does not have the massive coal reserves of the United States, but it produces very good quality anthracite, large quantities of which it exports to Japan, as well as Western Europe. Most of Australia's coal reserves are located in Western Australia, close to the large iron ore reserves. Australia is the world's fourth largest reserves holder, albeit at some distance from the top three. However, it is a substantial producer, and a top exporter of coal, particularly to the Pacific Rim.

The coalfields of north-western China, among the largest in the world, were little developed until the twentieth century. Today, however, China is the world's largest coal producer, although its reserves are only about half those located in the United States; the Chinese economy is a very intensive user of the commodity and has, indeed, driven the phenomenal growth coal consumption experienced during the 2000s.

Finally, the most important producer in Africa and the Middle East is South Africa, with reserves of over 30 billion tonnes. The country is essentially the only significant producer of coal in the African continent, with a production of 260 million tonnes in 2012, all of which was hard coal.

Turning our attention to production now, Exhibit 5.4 shows the development of coal production for the last 30 years. Note the big expansion recorded by Asia Pacific from 2000 onwards, accounted for mostly by China, but also by other economies in the region, such as Indonesia and Australia, who expanded their production in order to satisfy Chinese demand for imports of the commodity. Production in the rest of the world remained rather static otherwise. Exhibit 5.5 shows essentially the same information, this time split by type of coal produced, from anthracite (highest rank) to lignite (lowest rank).

Finally, Exhibit 5.6 lists the largest coal producers, starting with China, which is head and shoulders above everyone else, having produced ca. 45 per cent of the world's total coal output in 2012.

Demand characteristics

All types of coal have some value; as an old saying in the coal industry goes: 'anything pale brown will burn'. This, of course, does not necessarily mean that it will burn efficiently. Although peat is frequently used as a fuel in rural communities and, more recently, peat and lignite have been made into briquettes for burning in furnaces, it is brown and hard coals that are consumed extensively; and, of these two, only hard coal is traded internationally.

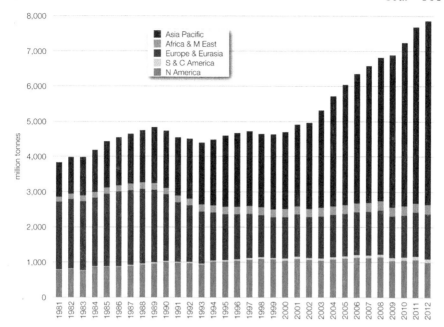

Exhibit 5.4 Coal production by major region

Source: Author, compiled with data from BP (2013)

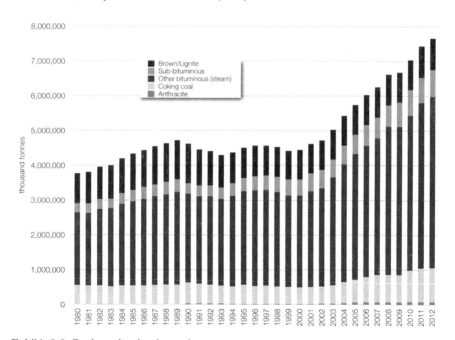

Exhibit 5.5 Coal production by major type

Source: Author, compiled with data from IEA (2013), Coal Information (Edition: 2013), Mimas, University of Manchester, DOI: http://dx.doi.org/10.5257/iea/coal/2013

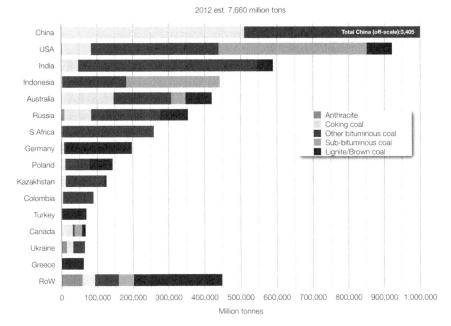

Exhibit 5.6 Major coal producers – countries and types of coal

Source: Author, compiled with data from BP (2013)

If one were to point at a single factor that has tremendously affected the fortunes of the coal industry, this would be its cross-substitutability with oil and natural gas. In Chapter 1, we saw that energy is needed for residential, industrial, transport and 'other' consumption. Although oil fits very well into all types of consumption, this is no longer the case for coal. Coal has been substituted by oil and natural gas in domestic consumption; in transport, coal burns inefficiently and is quite bulky to carry around; in industry, however, it is still used extensively.

Coal has two main uses – power generation, and as a fuel in the production of other industrial materials. Exhibit 5.7 shows the major categories of coal consumption and one can see how power generation dominates. Coal is used extensively in power plants with coal-fired electricity generators, as well as in other industrial processes that use coal-fired generators. In industry, coal is used in the production of steel and cement. For the latter, coal is mixed with limestone and other materials, and fired to produce clinker – the raw material that is pulverised to become cement. In steelmaking, the procedure is not that simple; coal has to be carbonised (i.e. purified) in special furnaces, in order to produce coke, a coal of a quality very close to that of graphite. Coke is then mixed with iron ore and a flux, and fired in a blast furnace, to yield pig iron, as we will describe in a later chapter.

Only anthracite and high-quality bituminous coal can be used for coking; coal with such attributes is known as coking coal. All other coal is used for

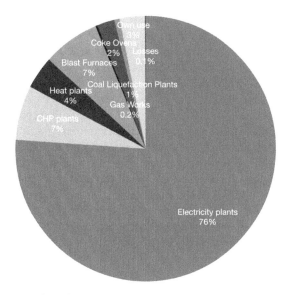

Exhibit 5.7 Consumption of coal by end use

Source: Author, compiled with data from IEA (2012a)

power generation, and is known as steam coal. These two new groupings of coal should not be confused with brown and hard coal. By definition, all lignite and sub-bituminous coal is steam coal, and so is the lower-quality bituminous coal; anything of higher quality is suitable for coking.

Steam coal is a very important input in power generation, accounting for about 80–90 per cent of the variable cost of producing coal-fired electricity. Demand for steam coal depends on the price of the commodity itself, the price of other substitutes – such as oil and natural gas – and the ease with which a power plant can switch between different fuels. After the first oil price shock, although coal became affordable, it was rather difficult for coal to capture a large market share, because most power generators were geared to use oil as fuel. During the 1970s, it became evident that oil was getting too expensive and too unsafe to be relied upon; the result was increased popularity for coal, which was readily available from politically safe areas. With electricity companies and other industries changing their generators to accommodate coal, it was little surprise to see a massive boost in coal consumption and trade after the second oil price shock.

While steam coal is by far the most important cost contributor in electricity generation, this is not the case with coking – or metallurgical – coal, which is estimated to account for about 30–40 per cent of the finished cost of steel. There is no substitute for coal in blast furnace steel production; instead, the whole steelmaking process has to be replaced with an electric arc furnace. The increased popularity of EAFs has curtailed the share of blast furnaces in crude steel production and has, therefore, undermined the demand for coking coal as well. While this is true, however, new smelting reduction techniques for making steel utilise coal once again, and thus increase the demand of coal.

Power generation, steelmaking and cement production are not the only uses of coal, however. Coal was also used, from the early nineteenth century to the Second World War era, for the production of fuel gas, just as coal liquefaction techniques were used to produce liquid oil products. In the 1980s, several industrialised nations showed interest in developing CTL (coal-to-liquids), but the popularity of the environmentally friendlier natural gas and the availability of cheaper oil after the mid-1980s hampered the rapid development of such technologies. With the resurgence of oil prices since the mid-2000s, interest in such technologies remains active, albeit still marginal. Finally, coal has a number of additional minor uses. For example, it is used as a raw material for the manufacturing of carbon electrodes; also, in pulverised form, it is directly injected in blast furnaces for steel production.

Turning our attention to coal consumption, one can see from Exhibit 5.8 that coal consumption experienced a resurgence since the beginning of the new millennium. Between 2000 and 2012, coal consumption increased by ca. 60 per cent, in contrast to the mostly uneventful 1990s. Note that the data are given in tonnes of oil equivalent, rather than metric tons, but the message given is the same. This growth was driven entirely by Asia Pacific, in particular China and India, two countries who used coal extensively to power their economic growth.

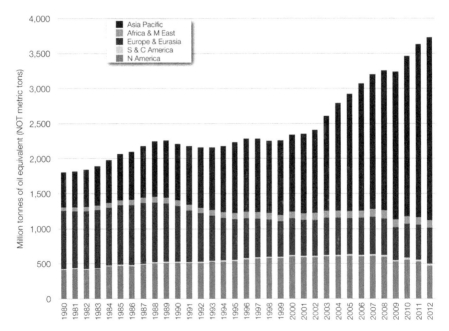

Exhibit 5.8 Development of coal consumption by region

Source: Author, compiled with data from BP (2013)

Exhibit 5.9 gives the list of the key coal consumers around the world. It is evident that China dwarfs every other nation, while India was the third largest consumer, after the US, in 2012. China alone consumed almost exactly 50 per cent of the world's coal in the same year. This was not surprising, given the country's massive expansion of its steel industry, as well as the large amounts of energy, especially electricity, required to power its rapidly expanding manufacturing activity.

Even more poignant, however, are the projections about the future of coal consumption. Both the EIA and the IEA broadly agree on the big role coal will have to play, in order to satisfy the growing energy consumption requirements over the next 20 to 30 years. Exhibit 5.10 shows the projections made by the EIA all the way to 2040. As one can see, overall coal consumption is expected to increase from a total of ca. 150 quads (quadrillion Btu) to ca. 220 quads by 2040. Throughout this time, OECD consumption is expected to remain stable at ca. 40–45 quads, with all the remaining demand being generated by non-OECD economies, particularly the emerging ones in Asia Pacific.

Based on such projections, it is difficult to see how the world can reduce its dependence on coal, even though it is the most polluting of the hydrocarbons. Indeed, coal provides a stable, secure and cost-efficient source of electricity generation. Providing cheap and reliable electricity is very much a priority for most emerging economies, whose populations still consume less energy per

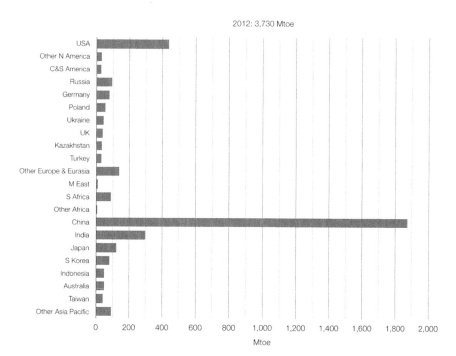

Exhibit 5.9 Major coal consumers

Source: Author, compiled with data from BP (2013)

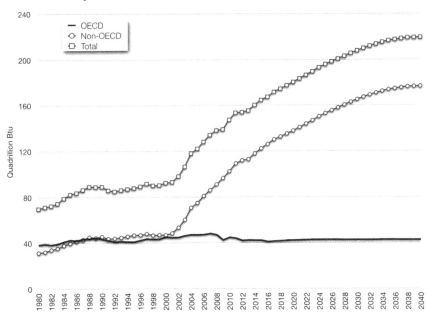

Exhibit 5.10 Projections for future world consumption of coal to 2040

Source: Author, compiled with data from EIA (2013)

capita, and large parts of these populations do not even have continuous access to electricity. Developed economies may, of course, continue trying to reduce their coal consumption as a way of reducing their carbon emissions. In some cases, this may be achieved by more stringent environmental regulations, as in some EU countries. In other cases, this may be a by-product of market forces, as in the US, where cheap shale gas is substituting coal in power generation. The fact remains, however, that the world as a whole still has a great appetite for coal, and the commodity will continue resisting those predicting or calling for its demise, for years to come.

Trade

Not all coal produced is marketed internationally. Brown coal has a high humidity content, which makes it susceptible to spontaneous combustion, and therefore difficult to transport. Moreover, its low carbon content makes brown coal uneconomical to export. Hard coal, however, is quite actively traded, and a total of about 1.25 billion metric tons of coal were traded in 2012. Hard coal traded is made up of steam coal and coking coal. Steam coal trade is the larger of the two, but coking coal is actually the most actively traded. In 2012, about 30 per cent of coking coal was traded, compared to about 15 per cent for steam coal. Exhibit 5.11 shows the development of coal trade since 1980. From 2000 onwards, coal trade started increasing rapidly, and in the space of just over 10 years it doubled in size. From the same exhibit, one can also see

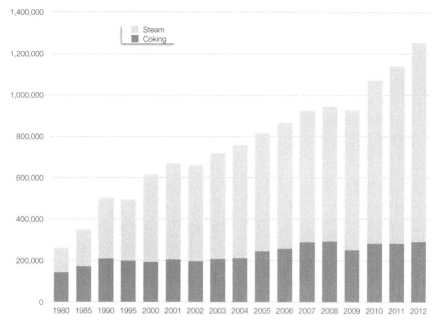

Exhibit 5.11 International hard coal trade

Source: Author, compiled with data from IEA (2013), Coal Information (Edition: 2013), Mimas, University of Manchester, DOI: http://dx.doi.org/10.5257/iea/coal/2013

the relative proportion of the two coal types. Steam coal accounted for just over 75 per cent of total trade, with coking coal making up the balance.

The list of top exporters of coal differs somewhat from that of top producers. Some of the most important producers of coal use it domestically; the case of China is an extreme example, whereby the country is also the world's largest importer. At the other extreme, Indonesia and Australia channel over 85 and 70 per cent, respectively, of their production to the export market, while the United States presents a mixed picture, with substantial quantities of coal (ca. 90 per cent) disappearing through domestic demand. Exhibit 5.12 shows the world's top coal exporters. For many years, it was Australia that topped the list, but since 2011 Indonesia overtook its rival, having exported some 380 million tonnes in 2012, 30 per cent of which went to China and a further 25 per cent to India. Despite losing its top place, however, Australia still accounts for about one-eighth of total steam coal trade and, more importantly, nearly half of the coking coal trade. This latter trade is dominated by only a handful of countries. Australia is one of them; the other two are the US (ca. 20 per cent of coking coal trade in 2012) and Canada (a further 10 per cent), with Mongolia and Russia contributing another 6 per cent each to the trade.

Being responsible for 45 per cent of the world's coal production, one would expect that China would have enough to satisfy its domestic demand. Yet, the country is the world's largest importer, with nearly 290 million tonnes imported

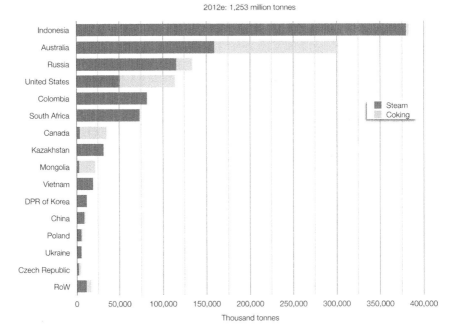

Exhibit 5.12 Major hard coal exporters

Source: Author, compiled with data from IEA (2013), Coal Information (Edition: 2013), Mimas, University of Manchester, DOI: http://dx.doi.org/10.5257/iea/coal/2013

in 2012, most of them from Indonesia (ca. 40 per cent) and Australia (ca. 20 per cent). With the exception of China, which has risen to prominence relatively recently, the list of the remaining key importers has remained practically unchanged. Japan is now the world's second largest importer, strengthening its position after the Fukushima nuclear incident, which meant that the country had to accelerate its coal (and gas) imports in order to make up for the lost power generation capacity after the shutdown of its nuclear reactors. South Korea and Taiwan are also sizeable importers, using coal both for power generation and steelmaking, while several EU countries make up most of the rest of the list.

Coking coal imports are directed primarily to Asia nowadays, with only smaller amounts directed to European countries. In contrast to the past, China has overtaken Japan as the largest single importer of coking coal, sourcing most of its needs from Australia. Japan has dropped to second place, and third place is India, which has expanded its steel production in recent years. Of the Europeans, Germany is still the biggest coking coal importer, while Turkey is a close second, also having expanded its steel producing output over the last decade.

We talked about the countries involved in producing and trading coal; how about the companies? It is no surprise that four out of the 10 largest coal-mining companies in 2010 were in China, with another two in that list from

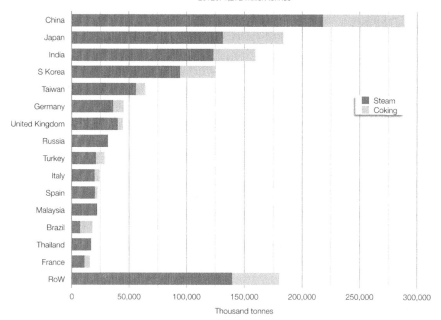

2012e: 1,272 million tonnes

Exhibit 5.13 Major hard coal importers

Source: Author, compiled with data from IEA (2013), Coal Information (Edition: 2013), Mimas, University of Manchester, DOI: http://dx.doi.org/10.5257/iea/coal/2013

the US and one from Australia. Yet, the world's largest coal miner is Coal India. The remaining companies are shown in Exhibit 5.14, and include international mining companies (such as BHP Billiton, Xstrata, Rio Tinto and Anglo American), as well as large national mining companies (such as Sasol in South Africa, Kompania Węglowa in Poland and RWE in Germany). What the list does not provide are the various coal trading companies, which may not always be producers themselves, but they are the ones who procure coal supplies from mines around the world and market them internationally to large industrial users, such as power stations and steel mills. Glencore is one such company, which owned a third of Xstrata, a company listed as a coal miner, until it eventually it took over the company to form GlencoreXstrata in 2012. Vitol is another such trader, better known for its large share of crude oil trade. There are numerous other commodity trading companies that trade coal and have been doing so with increasing success, as the market for coal took off in the 2000s.

Pricing

In the 'good old days', when coal was a less exciting commodity, pricing was a rather mundane business, with prices set on an annual basis, typically based on a 'cost plus' methodology. This methodology relied on a mutual agreement

Company	Corporate base	Production (Mt) 2010	Company	Corporate base	Production (Mt) 2010
Coal India	India	431	Alpha Natural Resources	USA	77
Shenhua Group	China	352	Rio Tinto	UK-Australia	73
Peabody Energy	USA	198	Consol Energy	USA	66
Datong Coal Mining Group	China	150	PT Bumi Resources	Indonesia	59
Arch Coal	USA	146	Kuzbassrazrezugol	Russia	50
China National Coal Group	China	138	Banpu	Thailand	43
BHP Billiton	Australia	104	Sasol	S. Africa	43
Shanxi Coking Coal Group	China	101	PT Andaro Indonesia	Indonesia	42
RWE Power	Germany	99	Kompania Węglowa	Poland	40
Anglo American	UK	97	Massey Energy	USA	34
SUEK	Russia	89	Drummond	USA	32
Cloud Peak Energy	USA	85	Patriot Coal	USA	28
Xstrata	UK-Switz	80	Total		2,775

Exhibit 5.14 Top 25 coal mining companies
Source: IEA (2011, p. 419)

between buyer and seller on the cost elements of the commodity (fixed and variable production costs, inland transportation, international shipping), before negotiating on a profit margin for the producer that reflected the demand and supply conditions in the international markets for steel and energy.

This was particularly true of coking coal, a commodity supplied by only a handful of countries and companies, whose prices were closely associated with iron ore, the other key input in steel production. For thermal coal, the market was somewhat more competitive, as steam coal is more abundant and there are many more buyers and sellers, so that trading occurred on the spot market, as well as longer horizons.

In the 2000s, China's impact on the coal market was decisive. Coal prices started an unprecedented ascent, which culminated to all-time high prices in the summer of 2008, just before the world financial crisis. Exhibit 5.15 shows the development of coal prices, as measured by three different price benchmarks, from the beginning of 2008. The data range captures the last surge in prices, before they started their rapid descent from July 2008 to March 2009. This rapid price rise brought about structural changes in the pricing of the commodity.

Coking coal followed the rising price trends not only of coal in general, but also of iron ore, whose price also experienced a phenomenal increase through the 2000s. As a result, when iron ore pricing changed from annually negotiated prices between steel mills and mines to quarterly prices based on a spot market index, coking coal process followed suit, using exactly the same methodology.

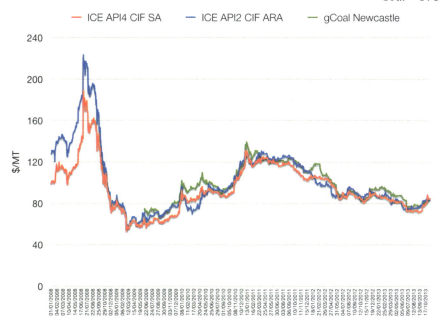

Exhibit 5.15 Indicative coal prices

Source: Author, compiled with data from Thomson Reuters Datastream

Trade in steam coal doubled, as we saw earlier. As a result, there were a lot more transactions and quoted market prices, so much so that price-reporting agencies, such as Argus Media and Platts, became interested in reporting them.

So if we take the example of a power plant procuring coal in the international market, what are the key considerations when negotiating prices? Coal quality is, of course, at the centre of the pricing mechanism and it is determined by a number of parameters, such as its calorific value (measured in kcal/kg); per cent content of volatile matter, moisture, ash, and sulphur; hargrove; and initial deformation point. Coal quality is important, because low-quality coal results in: energy losses; excessive waste material that has to be disposed of; increased corrosion, and hence increased maintenance costs; and increased expenses for desulphurisation.

As far as the supplier is concerned, a power plant needs a counterpart with adequate infrastructure, in an area of relative political stability, with a healthy financial position, a long-term attitude to doing business, and commitment to quality development, and cost control. Moreover, the supplier should preferably have prior export experience, which will help overcome any difficulties that may arise.

The contract is, of course, the most important part of the agreement, and should be fair and equitable, which will keep both partners happy throughout its duration. After all, the contract provides security of supplies for the buyer, while income security is the main benefit for the coal producer, together with

Phys DES ARA (physical cargoes, delivered ex-ship, Amsterdam - Rotterdam - Antwerp range)

For Shipments originating from:	RB (Richards Bay)	AUS (Australia)	COL (Colombia)	POL (Poland)	RUS (Russia)	US
Calorific Value (kcal/kg NCV*)	6,000	6,000	6,000	6,000	6,000	6,000
Total Moisture (as received basis)	12% (max)	15% (max)	14% (max)	14% (max)	14% (max)	12% (max)
Volatile Matter (as received basis)	22% (min)	24% - 35%	31% - 37%	25% - 32%	26% - 35%	27% - 35%
Ash (as received basis)	15% (max)	15% (max)	11% (max)	15% (max)	15% (max)	14% (max)
Sulphur (as received basis)	1% (max)	0.75% (max)	0.85% (max)	1% (max)	0.75% (max)	1% (max)
HGI**	45 - 70	45 - 70	45 - 70	45 - 70	45 - 70	45 – 70
Nominal Topsize	50 mm	50 mm	50 mm	50 mm	50 mm	50 mm
IDT*** (degrees celsius)	1,250 (min)	1,250 (min)	1,200 (min)	1,150 (min)	1,250 (min)	1,430(min)
Calcium Oxide in ash (dry basis)	12% (max)	7% (max)				
Chlorine (as received)						0.15% (max)

* NCV: Net calorific value
** HGI: Hardgrove grindability index (the higher, the easier to pulverise)
*** IDT: Initial deformation temperature

Exhibit 5.16 Typical qualities of internationally traded steam coal

Source: Global Coal, www.globalcoal.com/scota/scotaSpecs.cfm

This table is to be used in conjunction with globalCOAL's Standard Coal Trading Agreement (SCoTA) – download a copy at www.globalcoal.com © Global Coal Ltd – reproduced with permission

the ability to use the contract as a loan collateral. Although contracts usually include long lists of clauses for every eventuality, it is always preferable to keep them simple, since arbitration is expensive and time-consuming. Finally, contracts also make proper arrangement for the transportation of coal from source to destination. More than 90 per cent of the world trade in coal is carried by sea – over 1 billion tonnes in 2012. Coal is in fact – with iron ore – the largest seaborne dry bulk commodity, providing employment for all sizes of dry bulk carriers, but particularly for Capesize and Panamax vessels. Interestingly, freight rates for both ship sizes also experienced unprecedented increases through the 2000s, adding to the cost of transportation included in the delivered price of coal and thus further adding to the coal prices witnessed during that period.

Conclusion

In this chapter, we discussed the supply and demand economics of coal. One distinction that should be made when studying coal is that between steam and metallurgical, or coking, coal. Demand for the former is driven by demand for other energy commodities, while the latter depends on the fortunes of the steel industry.

Coal is considered a 'safe' commodity, because it is largely located in OECD countries; it also suffers from the negative image of the 'dirty' fuel, which is always lagging behind oil – and at some point was almost overtaken by natural gas.

The new millennium saw a surge in the demand for coal, both for power generation and steelmaking. Coal production, trade and prices rose to levels never seen before. As for the future of coal, forecast energy demand can only be satisfied on the assumption of abundant supplies of cheap coal. Although coal is the dirtiest of the three main hydrocarbons, its price competitiveness makes it an indispensable part of the energy mix of many countries, especially the rapidly emerging economies of Asia Pacific. Unless there is a drastic and rapid change in the urgency with which governments and citizens respond to climate change, coal's future as an energy source is secure for many more years to come.

References

BP (2013) *Statistical Review of the World Energy 2013*, British Petroleum, accessed online at: www.bp.com/statisticalreview.

EIA (2013) *International Energy Outlook 2013*, Energy Information Administration, accessed online at: www.eia.gov/forecasts/ieo/pdf/0484(2013).pdf.

IEA (2011) *World Energy Outlook 2011*, International Energy Agency, accessed online at: www.worldenergyoutlook.org/publications/weo-2011/.

—— (2012a) *Key World Energy Statistics 2012*, International Energy Agency, accessed online at: www.iea.org/publications/freepublications/publication/kwes.pdf.

—— (2012b) *World Energy Outlook 2012*, International Energy Agency, accessed online at: www.worldenergyoutlook.org/publications/weo-2012/.

—— (2013) *Coal Information (Edition: 2013)*, accessed on line at: http://dx.doi.org/10.5257/iea/coal/2013.

6 Electricity

Electricity is not a commodity in the traditional sense of the word. Although ubiquitous in our everyday lives, and uninterrupted access to it is a measure of prosperity and economic development, electricity cannot be stored, in commercially large enough quantities, and is traded cross-border only among a relatively small number of countries.

Yet, in the last two to three decades, the deregulation of electricity markets in several economies in the Americas and Europe has led to substantial changes in the way this good is supplied, consumed and traded.

This chapter aims to complete the discussion on energy commodities and also provide the reader with a primer on the key industry characteristics on a global basis, as well as in selected key markets.

Physical characteristics

Electricity is a form of energy caused by the presence of electrical charges in matter. In an atomic nucleus, each proton carries a unit of positive electric charge and each electron circling the nucleus carries a unit of negative electric charge. Electric current is the movement of electrons through an electric conductor driven by differential concentrations of electrons that repel each other. This movement can create heat (e.g. to fire up a kettle or light a conventional lamp), or movement through electromagnetic action (e.g. to move a motor). Electricity moves in closed loops or *circuits*. When we flip a switch, we close the circuit and allow the current to flow through, in order to produce a useful function.

For the total novice, it is worth listing a few key properties of electricity. An electric current is the rate at which electric charges flow through a circuit and is measured in *amperes*. Potential difference is commonly known as *voltage*, whereby one *volt* is the difference in electric potential across a wire when an electric current of one ampere dissipates one watt of power. Electrical power is the amount of work available from an electric current. It is defined as the product of voltage and current and measured in *watts*, whereby one watt is the work produced by a current of one ampere with a potential difference of one watt.

In commercial terms, the latter of the three properties above is the most important. The capacity of a power station or an electricity line is measured in watts (or rather kW, MW or GW). Taking this one step further, multiplying watts by time, we can calculate the amount of electricity produced and consumed over time. For example, the use of one kW constantly over one hour results in the consumption of one kWh of electricity. Another example is that of a power station that has a generation capacity of 10 MW; if it produces at its *nameplate* maximum capacity every single day of the year, it can theoretically produce 8.76 GWh in a year.[1]

There are many different ways of producing electricity, but the resulting electrical currents are of two main types: direct (DC) or alternating (AC). A battery, or a photovoltaic cell, produces a steady voltage and a steady direct current. In contrast, a spinning electromagnet generates alternating electricity, whereby the voltage reverses its direction from positive to negative several times per second. In the early stages of the electricity industry, during the late nineteenth and early twentieth centuries, both DC and AC suppliers were competing, as each type had both advantages and disadvantages.[2] In the end, AC supply prevailed, primarily because of the efficiency of being able to step up the voltage for long-distance transmission and then step it down again to a voltage appropriate for industrial and residential users of electricity. It is worth noting, however, that DC remains the favourable option for the electrical interconnection between countries, as it does not have the problems of synchronising the frequency and phase of modern AC three-phase electricity. As a result, countries or regions wishing to exchange electricity convert their supply from AC to DC, transfer it through a high voltage direct current (HVDC) cable and then convert it back again to AC at the other end.

The physical attributes covered above are the bare essentials for understanding the economic fundamentals of electricity and the challenges posed by both demand and supply factors. Let us start with demand.

Demand characteristics

Non-storability is the key characteristic of electricity, which sets it apart from all other commodities. Theoretically, the fuel used to generate electricity can be thought of as proxy storage. So a tank of natural gas or oil, a load of coal, a lake full of water or rods of uranium can all be thought of as stores of potential electricity. Yet, all of these fuels need to be transformed into electricity first and this can be done in varied amounts of time depending on the fuel itself. Electricity itself cannot be stored as such, except perhaps in batteries, which can be rather expensive and quite cumbersome.[3]

---

1 This is calculated as 10 MW × 365 days × 24 hours = 8,760 MWh or 8.76 GWh.
2 For a more detailed and illustrative discussion of the history and key characteristics of electricity, see Everett *et al.* (2012, Chapter 9).
3 In recent years, a substantial amount of research is being directed towards electricity storage technology. Any developments on this front would be exceptionally welcome, as it would help address the interruptibility of many renewable sources and the time mismatch between the supply and demand of the electricity produced by them.

In modern societies where access to electricity is *universal*,[4] we do not have to think twice before flipping a switch to consume electricity at any time of the day or night. We expect the electricity grid to be able to provide adequate amounts of electricity to satisfy demand from industrial, commercial and residential consumers. As electricity is not normally rationed, all users are free to consume whenever they like. This typically results in large amounts of *coincident load* (i.e. the amount of electricity required simultaneously by many users at certain points in time). Hence, electricity demand displays repeated patterns during the course of a day (*diurnal*), which may differ between a weekday and the weekend. Over the course of a year, demand displays seasonal patterns, and over the period of several years it may also show long-term trends.

To demonstrate how this works from the point of view of the load on an electricity system, consider Exhibit 6.1, which shows the diurnal patterns of UK electricity demand during three days in the winter of 2013, plotted over the course of 24 hours, in 48 half-hourly intervals. Note how demand is at its lowest from midnight to approximately 5:00 a.m. – this is known as *baseload* demand and, from the exhibit, it can be seen that it was at around 25 GW.[5] As people wake up and start preparing to go to work and as industry and businesses start their daily production cycle, demand starts rising quite steeply until it levels off to ca. 45 GW between 9:30 a.m. and 2:30 p.m. From about 3:00 p.m., many households begin their late afternoon routine, which typically involves switching on high-consumption appliances (e.g. a cooker or an oven for the preparation of supper). In this case, there is also more need for lighting, as dusk starts falling during this time of the year. With these patterns repeating in more and more households, there is usually a peak in demand between 4.30 p.m. and 7:30 p.m, when demand reaches its highest point at ca. 50 GW – this is known as *peakload* demand. Thereafter, demand falls steeply, as the various high-consumption household activities come to an end and people eventually go to sleep, by which time demand starts falling towards the baseload point. The pattern is repeated during the weekend, although it is worth noting that the 'morning rush' in demand takes place 1–2 hours later than during the week and the level-off plateau is also lower, as there is less requirement for electricity by commercial and industrial consumers.

If we collate the daily data over a period of time, we start getting a fuller picture of how demand varies during the year and from one year to the next (i.e. we can observe seasonal patterns and annual trends). Exhibit 6.2 demonstrates how the UK daily electricity load fluctuated over the whole of 2013 and Q1 2014. Note how the range of loads fluctuates during the year, with the higher levels occurring in January and the lower ones in July.

---

4   This typically means that the entire population has uninterruptible access to electricity 24 hours a day, 365 days a year.

5   This is, of course, winter baseload demand. In the summer, baseload demand in the UK tends to be lower, at around 20 GW. In contrast, in the US, baseload demand, and electricity consumption in general, is at its highest during the summer months (especially in July) due to the need for more air conditioning of commercial buildings and households.

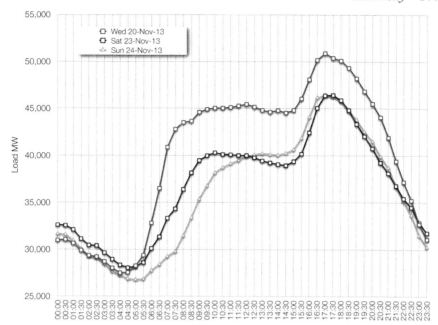

Exhibit 6.1 Diurnal electricity load curve – UK

Source: Author, based on data from National Grid (2014)

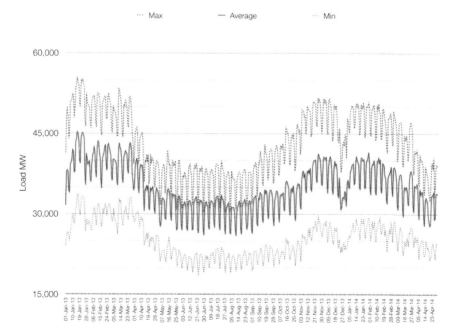

Exhibit 6.2 Annual electricity load, 2013–Q1 2014 – UK

Source: Author, based on data from National Grid (2014)

Similar observations can be made in Exhibit 6.3, where the data series is extended to the beginning of 2010. We can also observe a longer-term trend of lower electricity demand across time, with demand peaks being progressively lower year after year, which is partly on account of the economic downturn.

The next step in our analysis is to construct a cumulative distribution function (CDF) of demand loads over a period of time in order to gain a better understanding of how much electricity is required for how much of the time. This is what is depicted in Exhibit 6.4, and is known as the *load duration curve*. The curve summarises the ca. 75,900 half-hourly observations of demand loads during the chosen period by clustering the loads into categories (1,000 MW each) and then counting the percentage of times that demand loads fall into each category. How is this graph useful in understanding electricity demand? By simply connecting points on the curve with the two axes, we can ascertain how much electricity we need for how much of the time. For example, the red arrows indicate that, 50 per cent of the time, the load is ca. 37,000 MW. Conversely, the green arrows show that a load of over 45,000 MW is required for ca. 15 per cent of the time. From the same exhibit, we can also observe that the minimum load required at all times is ca. 18,000 MW.

The load duration curve is a useful tool for planning purposes. It gives information about long-term demand requirements and can help an electricity network designer decide what types of generation to build in the system. For

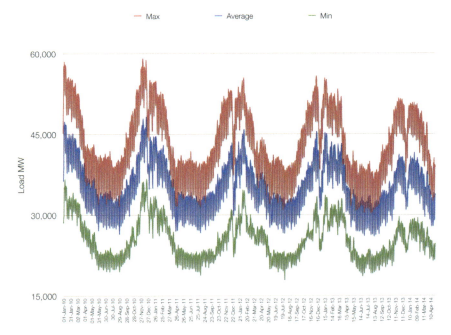

Exhibit 6.3 Annual electricity load, 2010–Q1 2014 – UK

Source: Author, based on data from National Grid (2014)

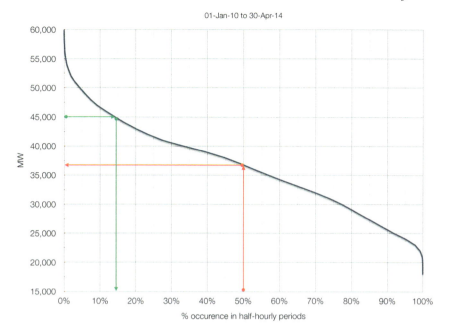

Exhibit 6.4 Demand load curve, 2010–Q1 2014 – UK

Source: Author, based on data from National Grid (2014)

example, nuclear or coal generation may be used to cover demand up to a certain threshold, before using additional generation from other fossil fuels or renewables.

Supply characteristics

In 2012, the world produced just over 22,500 TWh of electricity, as can be seen in Exhibit 6.5. The top two countries, China and the US, generated ca. 40 per cent of global electricity, and if we add to them Japan, Russia and India, the share goes to 55 per cent. A substantial amount of electricity (ca. 13 per cent) was also produced in the EU and European Economic Area (EEA). In contrast, the entire continent of Africa generated less than Germany, which is the biggest producer among European countries.

Where does it all come from, then? Electricity can be generated using a multitude of different sources, the largest of which is currently fossil fuels. As demonstrated in Exhibit 6.6, two-thirds of global electricity is generated using coal, gas and oil. They are followed by hydroelectricity, nuclear power and finally all other renewables. Let us briefly review the range of available generation sources:

• *Coal* is the most widespread generation fuel. Anything from lignite to high-quality bituminous (steam) coal can be used. Because of its lower calorific

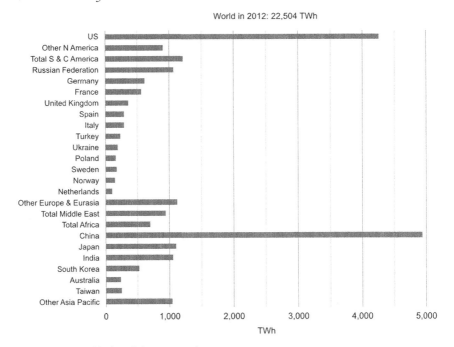

Exhibit 6.5 World electricity generation

Source: Author, compiled with data from BP (2013)

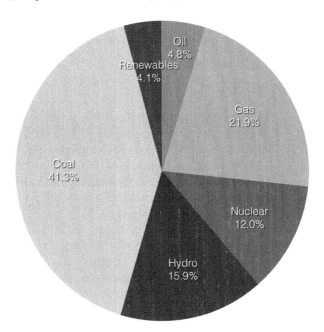

Exhibit 6.6 World electricity generation by fuel

Source: Author, based on data from BP (2013) and IEA (2013)

value, lignite tends to be used domestically in several countries (e.g. Germany and Greece in Europe, China and Indonesia in Asia Pacific). As we have seen in Chapter 5, steam coal is used extensively around the world, and is in fact one of the largest commodities traded exactly for this reason: to be burnt in order to produce steam, which in turn generates electricity.

- *Natural gas* is the cleanest of the fossil fuels used for generation.[6] In recent years, its use has expanded in North America, Western Europe and Asia Pacific, as numerous combined cycle gas turbine (CCGT) power stations have been built to take advantage of the increased efficiency of using gas and the positive externalities of reducing CO_2 emissions.
- *Oil* typically refers to a number of middle or heavy oil products, which can be burnt to produce electricity. In some cases, this can be heavy gas oil (i.e. lower-quality diesel, with a higher sulphur content), but typically it is heavy fuel oil, one of the least desirable and most plentiful products of the distillation process. Oil-fired capacity was reduced substantially after the first two oil crises, and a lot more electricity has been generated by coal instead. It is, however, still present in most countries around the world.
- *Nuclear* refers to the use of the fission of heavy atoms, typically of uranium, to generate heat, which is then used to produce steam and eventually electricity. Nuclear capacity has declined since the Fukushima accident in March 2011,[7] and this is reflected in the reduced share of nuclear generation in Exhibit 6.6. Leading nuclear electricity producers include the USA, France, Russia, South Korea, China and Canada.
- *Hydro* refers to hydroelectricity, which is the largest renewable source of generation. Leading hydroelectricity producers include China, Brazil, Canada, the USA, Russia and Norway.
- *Renewables* refers to the long list of generation sources that are classed either as inexhaustible or can be replenished regularly, with the exception of hydroelectricity, which is listed separately. These include: wind[8] (offshore and onshore), solar[9] (photovoltaic and concentrated thermal), geothermal, biomass, tidal, wave, post-use waste and several more.

---

6 On average, gas emits 0.42 tonnes of CO_2, whereas coal emits 0.85 tonnes, for each megawatt-hour of electricity produced.

7 In the aftermath of the Fukushima accident, practically all of Japan's nuclear capacity was shut down for immediate inspection and only a small part of it has come back into operation. In the meantime, Germany has decided to phase out nuclear generation and replace it with a lot more renewables and conventional fossil fuels (coal and gas) instead, which has also contributed to the reduction of global nuclear generation.

8 The largest producers of wind electricity are the EU (led by Germany, Spain and the UK), the USA and China. Together, they account for 90 per cent of global wind generation.

9 The largest producer of solar electricity is the EU (led by Germany, Italy and Spain), which accounted for two-thirds of global generation. Other important producers include the USA, Japan and China.

The extent to which the different sources of generation are used to provide shares of the total electricity produced in a country or region is referred to as the *fuel mix*. The choice of fuel mix is a mixture of strategic decisions (e.g. the use of nuclear and renewable generation) and market-based criteria (e.g. the use of fossil fuels, depending on domestic availability and import prices). Exhibit 6.7 uses the US as an example of fuel mix and how electricity has been generated there since 2000. In the same exhibit, note how generation has stagnated since 2005, with a dip in 2009, and also how natural gas has increased its share at the expense of coal, as a result of the advent of US shale gas. The UK case is shown in Exhibit 6.8, where we can observe how electricity demand has declined from 2008 onwards and how coal has made a late surge as generation fuel of preference, due to its lower cost, in comparison to natural gas, in Europe.

It is evident from the previous discussion that electricity networks have several choices as to the range of fuels they may use, as well as how frequently they may use each fuel in the course of a typical day. The latter is due to the fact that different sources of generation have different technical and operational characteristics.

For example, a nuclear plant requires a large initial capital expenditure, but the subsequent operating cost of producing a megawatt-hour of electricity is relatively small. In addition, a nuclear plant normally operates throughout the day, as it is not flexible to shut it down and restart it very quickly. The same

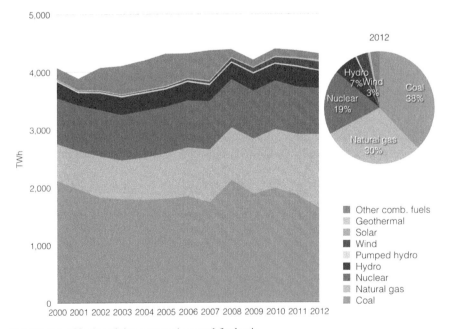

Exhibit 6.7 US electricity generation and fuel mix

Source: Author, compiled with data from IEA (2013), Electricity Information (Edition: 2013), Mimas, University of Manchester, DOI: http://dx.doi.org/10.5257/iea/coal/2013

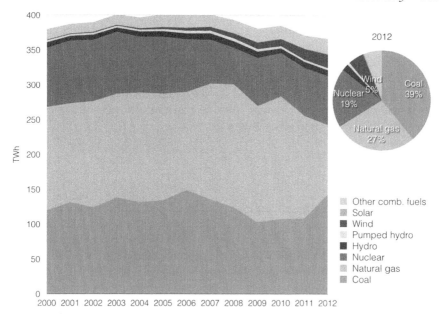

Exhibit 6.8 UK electricity generation and fuel mix

Source: Author, compiled with data from IEA (2013), Electricity Information (Edition: 2013), Mimas, University of Manchester, DOI: http://dx.doi.org/10.5257/iea/coal/2013

can be said for a coal-fired plant and, as a result, both coal and nuclear generation are used to cover baseload electricity demand throughout the year. Gas and oil-fired plants, on the other hand, are relatively more straightforward to build and incredibly flexible in producing electricity at very short notice (in just a few minutes), but they also have higher operating costs, due to the price of the fuel they use. As a result, they tend to be used to cover high-demand periods or, in the industry parlance, *peak shaving*.

This relationship may change if the economic fundamentals change. An example of this is mentioned above, whereby low-priced, abundant shale gas has displaced coal in baseload generation in the US. In contrast, the relatively cheaper coal exports from the US to Europe have incentivised the use of the relatively dirtier fuel in the continent, at the expense of gas whose oil-indexed price makes it more expensive.

Finally, renewable electricity is treated as a 'must-have' generation (i.e. any amount that can be produced is sent to the electricity network) and it is only limited by the operational efficiency of the renewable source (e.g. whether 'the wind blows' or 'the sun shines').[10]

10 Occasionally, the network operator may ask renewable generators to stop producing, if there is an oversupply of electricity, which may result in system overload and physical damage to the network infrastructure.

From the discussion above, it is evident that not all sources of generation produce electricity all the time, and different sources are used at different points during the day to satisfy varying levels of demand. This variability in the utilisation of a particular plant is known as *capacity factor*.

The concept is quite simple: the capacity factor is the amount of electricity that a plant produces over a period (say a year), divided by the maximum theoretical or operational capacity that the plant has during the same period. The simple formula used to calculate it is:

$$CF = \frac{MWh \ produced \ in \ period \ t}{Max \ capacity \ MW \times hours \ in \ period \ t}.$$

Consider the following example: a coal plant has a nameplate capacity of 30 MW and during the course of a year it has produced 185 GWh of electricity. Its annual maximum nameplate capacity is 30 MW × 365 days × 24 hours = 262,800 MWh = 262.8 GWh. Hence, the capacity factor is simply 185 ÷ 262.8 = 70.4 per cent. If we know that the plant had to shut down for 10 24-hour periods for maintenance, then its annual maximum operating capacity would be 30 MW × 355 × 24 = 255.6 GWh, in which case its operating capacity factor is 185 ÷ 255.6 = 72.4 per cent.

It is quite straightforward to comprehend, why nuclear and coal plants tend to have larger capacity factors, whereas open cycle gas turbine (OCGT) and oil-fired power stations have very small capacity factors as they are mostly used for peak shaving. Exhibit 6.9 demonstrates this for electricity plants in the US and the UK.

The supply chain of electricity

So far, we have only talked about generation of electricity. However, there are several more links in the supply chain that connect the power stations with the final consumers. The electric current produced by most generators is AC,[11] but the voltage needs to be stepped up in order to transmit it efficiently over long distances. The network of high-voltage cables and pylons is known as the *grid*. Electricity is transmitted through the grid at around 400 kV,[12] but before it can be distributed to industrial, commercial and residential consumers, its voltage has to be stepped down. This is done through a series of substations, until eventually the voltage comes down to the familiar 220–240 V or 100–120 V, which is used by households and offices all over the world. In addition to these essential links, some electricity networks also have interconnections

11 Although solar PV is DC, which has to be transformed to AC before being transmitted to the electricity network.
12 kV or kilovolt is the abbreviation for 1,000 volts. Transmission voltages do vary from one network to another, so 400 kV is only an indicative number.

US Annual Capacity Factors by Fuel (percent)

	Coal	Petroleum	Natural Gas CC	Natural Gas Other	Nuclear	Hydro Conventional	Wind	Solar PV	Solar Thermal	Geothermal
2008	73.4	15.6	40.1	12.4	91.1	37.2	31.7	22.5	19.5	74.7
2009	65.1	14.5	39.8	11.2	90.3	39.6	28.1	20.6	23.6	73.3
2010	67.9	13.5	43.8	11.4	91.1	37.6	29.8	20.3	24.5	71.9
2011	63.7	12.0	43.6	12.4	89.1	45.9	32.1	19.1	23.9	71.8
2012	56.7	12.8	51.1	12.8	86.1	39.6	31.8	20.3	23.8	68.2
2013	59.7	11.7	46.5	10.7	90.1	38.1	32.3	19.4	17.8	66.0

UK Annual Capacity Factors by Fuel (percent)

Percent	2007	2008	2009	2010	2011	2012
CCGT	64.7	71.0	64.2	61.6	47.8	30.4
Nuclear	59.6	49.4	65.6	59.3	66.4	70.8
Pumped storage hydro	16.1	16.9	15.3	13.1	12.0	12.3
Conventional thermal	44.6	39.3	33.2	34.5	34.7	48.6
of which coal	46.7	45.0	38.5	40.2	40.8	57.1
System load factor	66.1	67.7	64.5	64.6	66.6	66.3

Exhibit 6.9 US and UK annual capacity factors

Source: Author, compiled with data from DECC (2013a) and EIA (2014)

within the geographic borders of a country, or across the border linking two or more countries. Cross-border interconnectors are usually large HVDC cables, in order to bypass the technical issues of the difference in voltage and frequency that may exist among neighbouring countries.

It is still quite common in many countries for the entire network to be owned, operated and managed by one state-owned power company, which also meters the electricity at the consumption point and invoices the customers. Since the 1990s, however, electricity markets in several economies have been deregulated and privatised. This development was initiated in the 1980s in South America and subsequently spread to the US, as well as the UK and many more European countries.

This progressive deregulation usually began with the introduction of independent power producers (IPPs, often generators of renewables) who were allowed to enter long-term power purchase agreements (PPAs) with the state utility. The next development was the break-up of the state utility into autonomous units, in preparation for their eventual privatisation. This process came to be known as *unbundling* and was popularised in the UK in the 1990s.

The result of this unbundling was the separation of the supply chain into individual stages and the introduction of competition at each and every stage. Hence:

- *Generation* consists of several generating companies, each with one or more power plants (e.g. coal, gas, nuclear, oil, wind, solar, hydro and so on), which compete with each other to supply various tranches (e.g. baseload or peak load) of electricity.
- *Transmission* consists of one or more *independent system operators* (ISOs),[13] whose role is to maintain and modernise the high-voltage *grid* and provide third-party access to both generators and suppliers. See Exhibit 6.10 for an example.
- *Distribution* refers to the companies that own and operate the substations and the cables (colloquially known as the *wires*), which bring the low voltage electricity to wholesale and retail consumers.
- *Marketing of supply* refers to the companies (or suppliers) who buy large quantities of wholesale electricity from generators and then sell it on to commercial and residential customers.
- *Trading* can take place among generators, suppliers and large industrial consumers, and this takes place on a daily basis, but also for delivery at various future dates.
- *Metering and technical services* form the final part of the supply chain and encompass the companies that install, maintain and monitor electricity meters at the point of consumption. They report their readings back to the suppliers, who can then invoice the customers and receive their income.

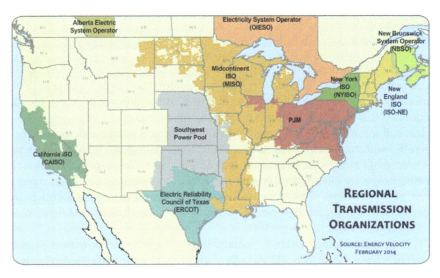

Exhibit 6.10 Regional Transmission Organisations (RTOs) and Independent System Operators (ISOs) in North America

Source: Federal Energy Regulatory Commission, www.ferc.gov/industries/electric/indus-act/rto. asp

13 Also known as transmission system operators (TSOs).

Balancing demand and supply

So far, we have observed how demand fluctuates during the course of a day, week, month of year, and also how supply can come from a variety of different sources, which may (or may not) be owned and operated by the same financial entity. Given the non-storability of electricity and the fact that it has to be produced the very second it is demanded, how are supply and demand balanced?

On a daily basis, all participants in the electricity supply chain have a forecast of the diurnal demand pattern for the *day ahead* (i.e. the one-day-forward market). This forecast may be based on past historical data and may also be informed by anticipated events that may create demand peaks (e.g. an anticipated sharp drop in temperatures, which is likely to generate additional demand for electrical heating). The forecast usually splits the day into time periods or intervals, with different levels of expected demand for each period. These periods may last for a few hours, a single hour, half an hour or even shorter. In most European countries, for example, the interval is hourly, whereas in the UK it is half-hourly.

Every day, each generator (e.g. a nuclear plant, a coal power station or a large wind farm) is prepared to offer a certain amount of electricity for each hourly or half-hourly interval for the next 24 hours (day-ahead market). Likewise, wholesale buyers (e.g. a regional supplier, or a large industrial consumer) put bids for quantities of electricity they will require. Buyers and sellers of electricity can transact on a bilateral basis and notify the ISO, which is ultimately responsible for maintaining system integrity.

Given the multitude of generation sources, how is the decision made whose electricity to use first? This issue is resolved using a very basic premise: the lowest-cost generation source dispatches first until its maximum is reached, before the next, more costly, source is called upon, until the demand at any given moment is satisfied. As a result, there is an ordering of generation sources according to their cost, starting from the cheapest and ending with the most expensive.

This is known as *merit order dispatch*, and Exhibit 6.11 demonstrates an example of this. What is shown here is a snapshot of the demand-supply balance of a network at a particular point in time (e.g. during a particular hourly interval during the day). During this interval, demand is determined by the collective activities of consumers and it is inflexible, hence the demand curve is vertical. The supply curve is a staggered line, created by ordering the generators from the least to the most expensive. Right at the bottom of the merit order is generator A, which is designated as a 'must-run'. This may be a renewable generator (e.g. a wind farm), which is guaranteed to sell its entire production. Generators B–E are the next ones to be called upon. Each of them produces varying amounts of electricity, depending on their capacity, and these are represented by the width of the bar. The height of the bar indicates their cost or the price at which they are prepared to offer their electricity for. As can be deduced from the exhibit, the last and most expensive generator that

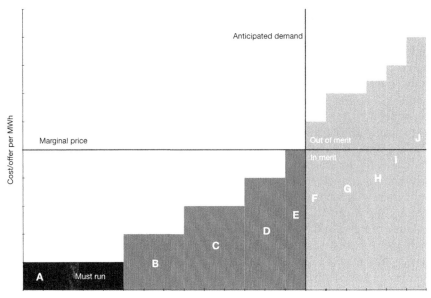

Exhibit 6.11 Merit order dispatch
Source: Author, based on Harris (2006, p. 167)

needs to be called upon in order to match demand (in this case, E) is also the one that sets the marginal price for the particular time interval. As we move through the day, demand changes and so the vertical demand curve will shift to the right if demand increases, or to the left if it decreases. In the former case, additional, more expensive, generators will be brought in, whereas in the latter case, some generators will be asked to rump down production or switch off altogether.

Occasionally, a supply disruption or a system constraint may require the ISO to take off one generator and replace it with a higher-cost one. In Exhibit 6.12, we can see what happens when generator D has to come off the grid and is replaced by G, pushing the marginal price up as well.

As the reader may have noticed from the discussion above, the ISO has a crucial role in ensuring that demand and supply balance every second of the day and the electricity system remains stable at all times. In a deregulated, competitive electricity market, where multiple supply and demand units engage in bilateral transactions, the ISO has continuous oversight of real-time demand requests and full access to generators from whom it can request additional generation when necessary. In the UK, for example, the counter-parties can engage in bilateral transactions up to one hour before the beginning of each half-hourly interval. This point in time is known as *gate closure*, after which the *balancing mechanism* kicks in, which is overseen by the ISO. Units large enough to be part of the balancing mechanism submit series of bids (if they are consumers) or offers (if they are generators) that the ISO

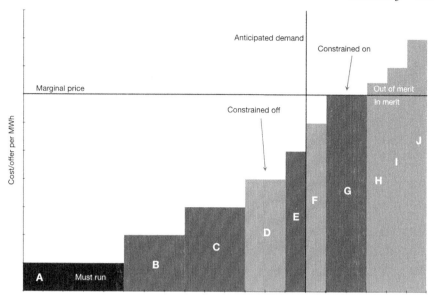

Exhibit 6.12 Merit order dispatch with constraint

Source: Author, based on Harris (2006, p. 168)

can call against. So if there is an unexpected demand surge, or a supply failure, the ISO can request plants with *hot spinning reserve*[14] to ramp up production in order to maintain system stability.

Comparing costs across different types of generation

As it has become evident from the merit order discussion, there is considerable variability in the cost of producing a megawatt-hour of electricity, depending on the technology, capital costs, fuel costs and so on. In order to be able to make comparison across the various technologies, a methodology has been devised to calculate a *levelised cost of electricity* (LCOE), which takes into account the very diverse factors that determine the cost of electricity using, for example, coal or natural gas or wind, so that a fair comparison can be made among them. The factors that enter LCOE calculations are given in Exhibit 6.13. Here, we can see that the levelised cost is affected by the fixed cost of building and operating the generating plant (cost of capacity), as well as the variable cost of producing the electricity.

14 This refers to the ability of a plant to produce electricity at very short notice, within a few minutes. A gas or oil-fired power station, or a hydroelectric plant, are good examples of generators that have short response times. A coal-fired plant, on the other hand, has very little flexibility to do so at short notice.

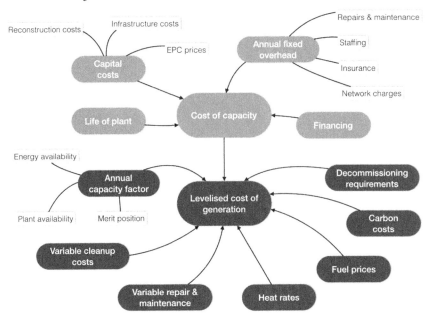

Exhibit 6.13 Factors entering LCOE calculations

Source: Author, based on MacDonald (2010, p. 3)

All of these costs are added up on an annual basis, from the construction phase of the plant, all the way to the end of its life. The costs are discounted by an appropriate discount factor and added up to produce a total present value of the cost of generation. This is divided by the total amount of electricity that the plant is expected to produce over its lifetime, in order to produce the present value of the cost of producing a megawatt-hour of electricity. Two examples of such calculations for various types of generating technologies are given here. In Exhibit 6.14, we can observe that there is variability on the LCOE in the US, with figures ranging from ca. $65/MWh for advanced supercritical coal, to over $250/MWh for solar thermal generation. In Exhibit 6.15, the relevant UK figures are displayed. Observe the large share of fuel cost in gas generation (both combined cycle and open cycle). Also noteworthy is the relatively large share of capital costs in the LCOE for wind and solar generation and the (expected) absence of any fuel costs.

Conclusion

In this chapter, we examined the economic fundamentals of electricity. Although not a traditional energy commodity, electricity has become the focus of public attention since the 1980s, as the industry has been deregulated and at least partly privatised in several countries around the world. Electricity is traded competitively between generators and wholesale consumers within countries and increasingly across national borders. Two of the three main fossil

Plant	Capacity factor %	Levelized capital cost	Fixed O&M	Variable O&M (incl. fuel)	Transmission investment	Total system levelized cost
Conventional coal	85	65.7	4.1	29.2	1.2	100.2
Advanced coal	85	84.4	6.8	30.7	1.2	123.1
Advanced coal with CCS	85	88.4	8.8	37.2	1.2	135.6
Natural gas fired						
Conventional CC	87	15.8	1.7	48.4	1.2	67.1
Advanced CC	87	17.4	2.0	45.0	1.2	65.6
Advanced CC with CCS	87	34.0	4.1	54.1	1.2	93.4
Conventional combustion turbine	30	44.2	2.7	80.0	3.4	130.3
Advanced combustion turbine	30	30.4	2.6	68.2	3.4	104.6
Advanced nuclear	90	83.4	11.6	12.3	1.1	108.4
Geothermal	92	76.2	12.0	0.0	1.4	89.6
Biomass	83	53.2	14.3	42.3	1.2	111.0
Wind	34	70.3	13.1	0.0	3.2	86.6
Wind - offshore	37	193.4	22.4	0.0	5.7	221.5
Solar PV	25	130.4	9.9	0.0	4.0	144.3
Solar thermal	20	214.2	41.4	0.0	5.9	261.5
Hydro	52	78.1	4.1	6.1	2.0	90.3

Exhibit 6.14 US levelised costs of electricity generation

Source: Author, compiled with data from EIA (2013)

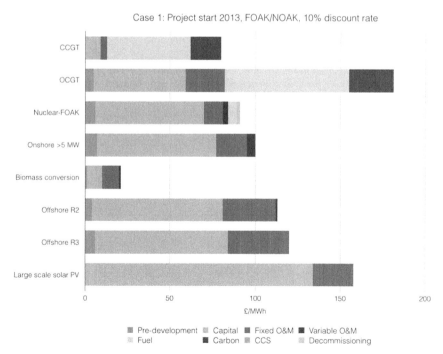

Exhibit 6.15 UK levelised costs of electricity generation

Source: Author, compiled with data from DECC (2013b)

fuels, coal and natural gas, are predominantly used for electricity generation, hence a discussion of this 'secondary' form of energy was necessary.

Nevertheless, a detailed discussion of the large array of renewable and alternative forms of generation is beyond the scope of this textbook. The reader is referred instead to the excellent work by Boyle (2004), Kaltschmitt *et al.* (2007) and Everett *et al.* (2012), who provide extensive discussion of the technical and economic aspects of renewable sources of energy.

It is time now to complete our analysis of energy commodities with a look at energy derivative markets in the next chapter.

References

Boyle, G. (ed.) (2004) *Renewable Energy: Power for a Sustainable Future*, 2nd edn, Oxford: Oxford University Press.

BP (2013) *Statistical Review of the World Energy 2013*, British Petroleum, accessed online at: www.bp.com/statisticalreview.

DECC (2013a) *Digest of UK Energy Statistics (DUKES) July 2013*, Department of Energy and Climate Change, accessed online at: www.gov.uk/government/publications/electricity-chapter-5-digest-of-united-kingdom-energy-statistics-dukes.

—— (2013b) *Electricity Generation Costs 2013*, Department of Energy and Climate Change, accessed online at: www.gov.uk/government/publications/decc-electricity-generation-costs-2013.

EIA (2013) *Annual Energy Outlook 2013*, Energy Information Administration, accessed online at: www.eia.gov/forecasts/aeo/pdf/0383(2013).pdf.

—— (2014) *Electric Power Monthly – April 2014*, Energy Information Administration, accessed online at: www.eia.gov/electricity/monthly/epm_table_grapher.cfm?t=epmt_6_07_b.

Everett, B., Boyle, G., Peake, S. and Ramage, J. (eds) (2012) *Energy Systems and Sustainability: Power for a Sustainable Future*, 2nd edn, Oxford: Oxford University Press.

Harris, C. (2006) *Electricity Markets: Pricing, Structures and Economics*, Chichester: Wiley.

IEA (2013a) *Electricity Information (Edition: 2013)*, accessed on line at: http://dx.doi.org/10.5257/iea/elec/2013.

IEA (2013b) *Key World Energy Statistics 2013*, International Energy Agency, accessed online at: www.iea.org/publications/freepublications/publication/KeyWorld2013.pdf.

Kaltschmitt, M., Streicher, W. and Wiese, A. (2007) *Renewable Energy: Technology, Economics and Environment*, Berlin: Springer.

MacDonald, M. (2010) *UK Electricity Generation Costs: Update 2010*, Department of Energy and Climate Change, accessed online at: www.gov.uk/government/publications/uk-electricity-generation-costs-mott-macdonald-update-2010.

National Grid (2014) *Historical Demand Data for Electricity*, accessed online at: www2.nationalgrid.com/UK/Industry-information/Electricity-transmission-operational-data/Data-Explorer/.

7 Energy derivative markets

In the preceding chapters, we examined the economic fundamentals of the key energy resources, and analysed how demand and supply drivers interact to reach equilibrium in terms of the quantity consumed and the price paid for each commodity. We also considered the various pricing regimes for different commodities and alluded to the fact that energy prices may change rapidly and often exhibit considerable volatility.

In this chapter, we observe the key characteristics of energy price series and set the scene with regard to the risk implied by price movements. We then tackle the financial derivative instruments that can be used to hedge this risk and use a number of examples to demonstrate simple hedging strategies.

Overview of energy prices

As most commodities, energy prices tend to be highly volatile, especially in comparison to other asset classes such as equities and bonds. There are both demand and supply factors that contribute to this volatility. On the demand side, it can be seasonal changes in consumption, long-term changes and trends in consumer tastes, or even substitution between different sources of energy. On the supply side, production is usually stable through the year, but disruptions to this stability do happen, whether due to technical reasons, accidents, political events or other random factors. In addition, there are long-term trends in supply, reflecting the overall abundance or scarcity of a particular energy commodity.

In order to acquire a view of how energy prices have moved in recent years, we use daily data from 1 January 2007 to 31 March 2014. The selected period focuses deliberately on the last few years and also includes the effects of the 2008 financial crisis on the prices of energy commodities. Exhibit 7.1 shows spot prices for four types of crude oil, three of which are key benchmark indicators (WTI, Brent and Dubai). It can be seen that all four series display similar movements, particularly the big price drop from Q3 2008 to Q1 2009, in the aftermath of the financial crisis after the collapse of Lehman Brothers. It is also worth noting that not all prices followed exactly the same path. WTI did not rise as strongly from Q3 2010 to Q1 2011, as a result of the oversupply of the domestic US market with domestically produced light sweet crude. More on this when we discuss spreads late on in this chapter.

Exhibit 7.1 Crude oil prices

Source: Author, based on data from Thomson Reuters Datastream

Exhibit 7.2 displays the price series of four typical refined products: gasoline, naphtha, gas oil (i.e. diesel) and fuel oil. Note that each series is measured in its own specific units, but the price movement shows a similar pattern to that of crude oil prices, marked by a sharp decline in Q4 2008 and a rebound lasting through most of 2009 and 2010.

Moving over to gas and coal prices, Exhibit 7.3 shows the development of the two key indices for coal (API2 for coal imported on a CIF basis in Northwest Europe and API4 for coal exported on an FOB basis from South Africa), as well as NBP gas prices in the UK and Henry Hub gas in the US. It is interesting to note here that although coal prices fell sharply in late 2008, they rebounded to ca. $120/mt by 2011, until their steady decline from the end of that year until the end of Q1 2014. Also notable is the divergence of the UK and US gas prices, in accordance to what was discussed with regard to gas pricing in Chapter 4.

Finally, Exhibit 7.4 displays prices for baseload electricity from four quite different markets: the Phelix index in Germany in the top-left quadrant; PJM prices in the US in the top-right quadrant; Nordpool average daily prices in Scandinavia in the bottom-left quadrant; and UK prices in the bottom-right quadrant. As one can see, the common characteristic among the four price series is their intense fluctuation, or 'spikiness', which reflects the volatility normally associated with electricity prices.

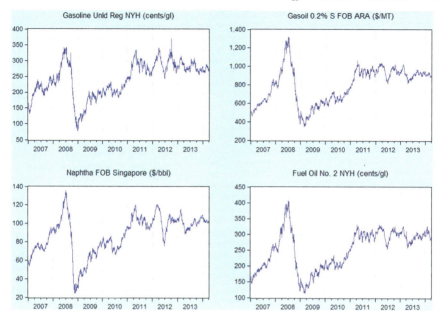

Exhibit 7.2 Refined product prices

Source: Author, based on data from Thomson Reuters Datastream

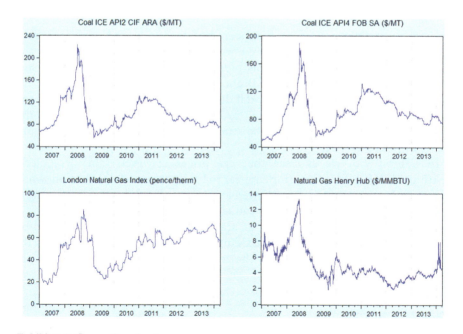

Exhibit 7.3 Gas and coal prices

Source: Author, based on data from Thomson Reuters Datastream

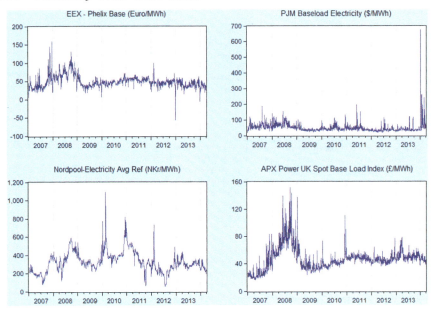

Exhibit 7.4 Electricity prices

Source: Author, based on data from Thomson Reuters Datastream

Price series characteristics

As with most financial price series, commodity prices tend to depart from the normal assumption that they are normally distributed. A quick look at the following few exhibits confirms this premise. Exhibit 7.5 displays the histogram and descriptive statistics for Brent (top) and WTI (bottom) crude oils. Brent prices seem to follow a bimodal distribution, with low kurtosis and the Jarque-Bera statistic, and associated probability leads us to safely reject the null hypothesis that this is a normal distribution. We reach a similar conclusion for WTI prices as well.

In Exhibit 7.6, we can see that gas prices are even more irregularly distributed. UK NBP prices (top) appear to have a trimodal distribution, while Henry Hub prices appear to be skewed and have excess kurtosis. For both sets of data, the normality assumption can also be safely rejected.

Finally, even more excess kurtosis and non-normality is demonstrated by the two electricity price series in Exhibit 7.7, where descriptive statistics for UK baseload prices are shown at the top and US PJM baseload prices are shown at the bottom.

Returns and volatility

We conclude this brief overview of energy price series with a look at two more aspects: returns and volatility. The return on any asset, be it a stock, bond

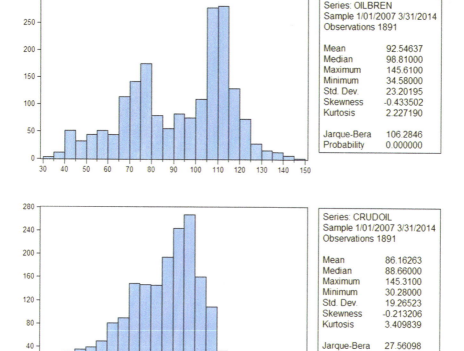

Exhibit 7.5 Histogram and descriptive statistics for Brent and WTI crude oil prices

Source: Author, based on data from Thomson Reuters Datastream

or commodity, is defined as the percentage difference of the price of the asset between two points in time. This is expressed more formally by the equation

$$R_t = \frac{S_t - S_{t-1}}{S_{t-1}} \, ,$$

where R_t is the return in period t, and S_t and S_{t-1} are the prices in periods t and $t-1$, respectively.

For example, say that the price for Brent crude at the close of the market on 1 March is \$102.00/bbl and at the close of 2 March it is \$103.55. The daily return is then calculated as $(103.55 - 102.00) \div 102.00$, or alternatively, $(103.55 \div 102.00) - 1$, and this is equal to 0.0152 or 1.52 per cent.

An alternative method to calculate returns, which is commonly used in finance, is to use the natural logarithm of the ratio of prices between two points in time. This means that

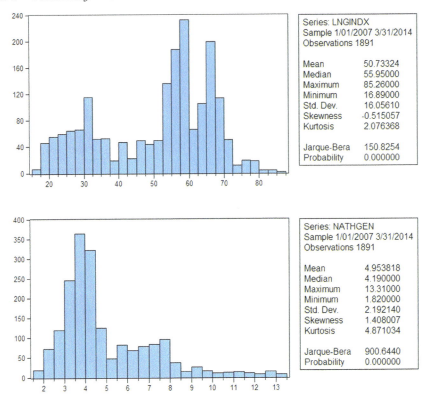

Exhibit 7.6 Histogram and descriptive statistics for NBP and Henry Hub gas prices

Source: Author, based on data from Thomson Reuters Datastream

$$R_t = \ln \frac{S_t}{S_{t-1}}.$$

In the previous example, the return would be calculated as $\ln(103.55 \div 102.00)$, which is equal to 0.01508 or 1.51 per cent. The result is close to the result in the previous paragraph, but somewhat lower, as this method implies that returns are continuously (rather than discretely) compounded. This method has the additional advantage that returns are additive. For example, to calculate the returns on an asset in a particular week of trading days, it suffices to calculate the natural logarithm of the ratio of the last day over the first day. The result will be the same if we calculate each daily return and then add them up.

Having defined returns and how we calculate them, we now proceed to observe the returns on a selection of energy commodities and how these returns are distributed. Exhibit 7.8 displays the returns for Brent and WTI crude prices (top and bottom left), where we can observe how they fluctuate around a mean that is very close to zero. We can also observe that the majority of returns fluctuate in the 5 per cent range around the mean, with the period between

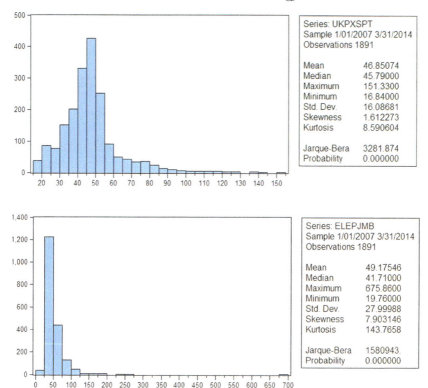

Exhibit 7.7 Histogram and descriptive statistics for UK and US baseload electricity prices

Source: Author, based on data from Thomson Reuters Datastream

Q4 2008 and Q1 2009 characterised by much sharper fluctuations around the mean. The frequency distribution of returns for both series is shown on the right of the same exhibit. They show the same leptokurtic distribution, which is common among financial price series, as well as commodities in general. Similar observations can be made for all other energy commodities included in Exhibits 7.9–7.12

The second aspect examined here is the volatility of commodity returns. Having defined returns in the previous paragraphs, volatility is simply the standard deviations of these returns from their mean. More formally, this is expressed as

$$\sigma_T = \sqrt{\frac{1}{T-1}\sum_{i=1}^{T}\left(R_i - \bar{R}\right)^2},$$

where T is the time period over which we calculate the volatility. A final adjustment needs to be made, with regard to the frequency (or periodicity) of the data we use to calculate the volatility. We should not be comparing

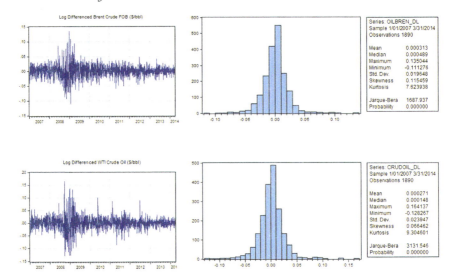

Exhibit 7.8 Returns and their distribution for Brent and WTI
Source: Author, based on data from Thomson Reuters Datastream

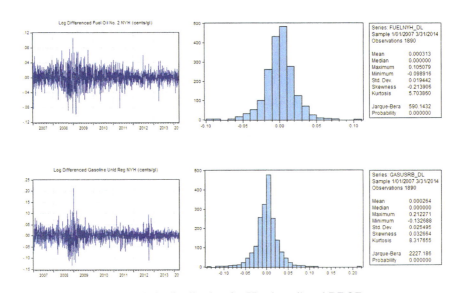

Exhibit 7.9 Returns and their distribution for Heating oil and RBOB
Source: Author, based on data from Thomson Reuters Datastream

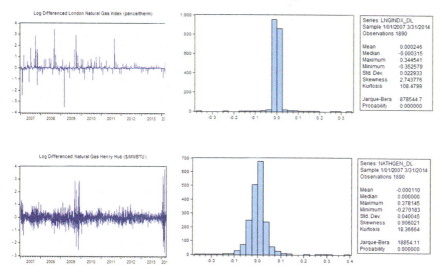

Exhibit 7.10 Returns and their distribution for UK and Henry Hub gas

Source: Author, based on data from Thomson Reuters Datastream

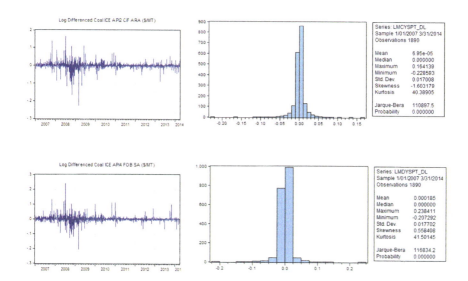

Exhibit 7.11 Returns and their distribution for API2 and API4 coal

Source: Author, based on data from Thomson Reuters Datastream

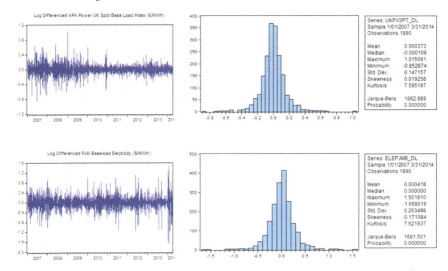

Exhibit 7.12 Returns and their distribution for UK and PJM electricity

Source: Author, based on data from Thomson Reuters Datastream

volatilities between daily and monthly data, for example. To make the various calculated volatilities comparable, we need to annualise them by multiplying our σ by the square root of the number of periods in a year. More formally,

$$\sigma = \sigma_T \sqrt{P},$$

where P is 12 for monthly, 52 for weekly and 250–252 for daily return observations in a year. For example, if σ_T for daily returns over a period is 0.02, then volatility

$$\sigma = \sigma_T \sqrt{250}$$

is equal to 0.3162 or 31.62 per cent. On the other hand, if σ_T of weekly returns over a period is 0.02, then volatility

$$\sigma = \sigma_T \sqrt{52}$$

is equal to 0.1442 or 14.42 per cent.

Using the definition given above and a rolling window of 60 days, we calculate the volatility for various energy commodities in the exhibits that follow. In Exhibit 7.13, we can observe the volatilities of Brent and WTI crude oil returns, as well as those of heating oil and RBOB gasoline. Note how all volatilities jumped to between 30 and 45 per cent during Q4 2008 and Q1 2009, soon after the financial crisis that also caused the dramatic drop of oil prices in the same period. Towards the end of the period covered (Q1 2014), volatilities have decreased to ca. 5–10 per cent for all four commodities.

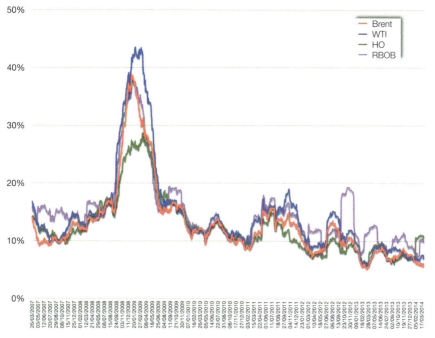

Exhibit 7.13 60-day rolling volatility for crude oil and refined products

Source: Author, based on data from Thomson Reuters Datastream

Using the same type of calculation, in Exhibit 7.14 we can observe the much higher volatilities recorded for natural gas, especially for Henry Hub in the US, compared to the relatively low ones for coal over the same period.

Finally, in Exhibit 7.15, we can see the comparative volatilities for UK and US electricity, both base and peak. Worthy of noting here are: the relatively lower volatilities for UK electricity; the fact that peak electricity returns are more volatile than base electricity for both countries; and the seasonality of volatility in the US, where the peak is reached in the summer months, due to the peak demand for air conditioning requirements.

Modelling the price processes for energy and other commodities has attracted considerable attention in academic literature. Various models have been put forward, many of them emanating from theorists studying mainstream financial markets. Hence, the very first step is normally to investigate the randomness of commodity prices and attempt to model it using a Brownian motion with a drift. In particular, the Geometric Brownian Motion (GBM) has been used to model returns in financial assets, be it stocks or commodities. The model postulates that the return on the asset (e.g. stock price) is given by the equation

$$\frac{dS_t}{S_t} \mu \cdot dt + \sigma \cdot dW_t \, ,$$

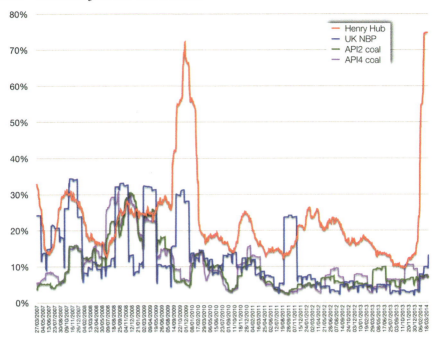

Exhibit 7.14 60-day rolling volatility for natural gas and coal

Source: Author, based on data from Thomson Reuters Datastream

whereby μ is the drift of the process and $dW(t)$ is a Wiener process that introduces the element of randomness in returns from one period to the next.

As the GBM contains a drift term, it implies that the price of the underlying asset grows with time, which is a reasonable assumption for stocks. In commodity markets, this assumption often breaks down, as commodities tend to display a tendency to revert to a long-term equilibrium price. To address this problem, an alternative equation has been proposed instead, which is

$$\frac{dS(t)}{S(t)} = k(\theta - \ln S_t)dt + \sigma dW(t) \; ,$$

where θ is the long-term mean to which returns revert to and k is the speed of the mean reversion. Even a mean-reverting GBM process tends to produce price return trajectories that are relatively continuous. How can we represent then the often-violent upward and downward movements in stock, commodity and other asset prices? Merton (1976) introduced the jump diffusion model, where a jump component is added to the diffusion term, so that the equation now becomes

$$\frac{dS(t)}{S(t)} = \mu dt + \sigma dW(t) + U_t \, dN_t,$$

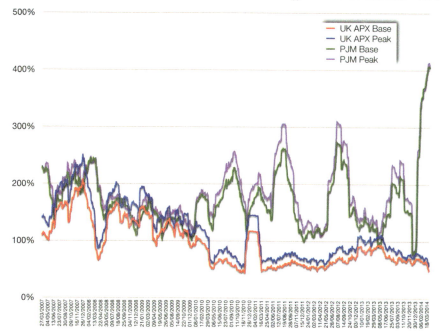

Exhibit 7.15 60-day rolling volatility for electricity

Source: Author, based on data from Thomson Reuters Datastream

where N_t denotes a Poisson distribution with intensity λ accounting for the arrival of jumps, and U_t is a real valued random variable as jumps may be positive or negative. Various other propositions have been made that extend the accuracy of the various models used to capture the diffusion process of commodity price returns. For example, Gibson and Schwartz (1990) propose a state variable model to capture the diffusion process of oil prices, whereby the two states are those of contango and backwardation and account for the change in the convenience yield. For a more expansive discussion of this and several other methods of modelling commodity prices, the reader is referred to authors such as Eydeland and Wolyniec (2003), Geman (2005), Burger *et al.* (2007), Pilipovic (2007), Geman (2008), Edwards (2010) and Pirrong (2012).

Participants in energy derivative markets

There are several types of participants in the energy derivative markets. They may be producers and consumers of the various types of fuels and energy, as well as transformers (e.g. refiners or power stations) and traders. They are typically companies, but they may also be private individuals who simply want to bet on the direction that energy prices may move.

With regard to the reasons that the various participants get involved in these markets, we can differentiate among three types: hedgers, speculators and arbitrageurs. Hedgers typically have an exposure to the physical commodity and need to offload their price risk by opening equivalent and opposite exposure in an appropriate derivative. For example, an upstream oil E&P company has a natural long position in the physical oil market and is afraid that the oil price may decline in the future and it will lose revenue. It may wish to hedge its risk by assuming a short (sell) position in a derivative instrument, such as a futures contract. In contrast, an airline company that regularly buys jet kerosene to fuel its fleet has a natural short position in the physical market for this particular refined product. It may wish to hedge its risk by assuming a long (buy) position in an appropriate derivative instrument. For example, it may buy call options that give it the right to buy jet kerosene at a certain price, the *strike* price, which can be exercised if the market price is higher than the strike price.

Speculators do not have an underlying position on the physical commodity. Instead, they assume long and short positions on derivative instruments because they have a particular view of where the market price may go. They effectively bet on the price movement, based on their own analysis of all the fundamental and technical factors that may affect price movement. Although speculators have often been blamed for causing excessive price volatility with their buy/sell actions, they are an essential part of each and every derivative market. Their participation enhances market liquidity, and they are the ones who are prepared to take on the risk that hedgers wish to offload.

Prices for a commodity between markets and across time may occasionally be out of balance. Arbitrageurs are those who seek such imbalances and act quickly to take advantage of such mispricing opportunities in order to make riskless profits. They are essential for keeping price relationships in balance and also provide additional liquidity, which is vital for the hedgers who want to be able to open and close derivatives positions quickly and effectively.

The relationship between spot and futures prices

Before we move on to the futures and other instruments, it is worth looking at the temporal element of commodity prices, and in particular the relationship between spot and futures prices. Many authors have looked at this relationship, and among the first to do so was Keynes. He posited that futures prices are generally downwards-based estimates of future spot prices. As a result, spot prices should 'normally' exceed forward prices by the amount that a producer is ready to sacrifice in order to hedge himself – a sort of 'insurance premium'. This theory is also known as the theory of normal backwardation.

In his seminal paper, Working (1949) offered an alternative explanation of the spot-future price relationship. Known as the *theory of storage*, Working's explanation links spot and future prices with the cost of capital, the storage cost and the convenience yield. The latter variable is more difficult to observe directly, but can be indirectly calculated using market data for spot and future prices, storage costs and borrowing costs.

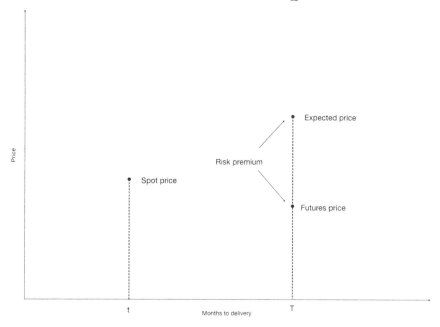

Exhibit 7.16 Spot and futures prices in the theory of normal backwardation
Source: Author

Working observed that the difference between spot and future prices, known as the *basis*, is inversely related to the level of stocks of a particular commodity. The higher the stocks, the higher the expectation that future price will be higher than the spot price, and vice versa.

Putting this in the context of an energy commodity such as oil, consider the following. If stocks of crude oil are low,[1] market participants, such as refineries that need the physical commodity in order to process it into refined products, will be prepared to pay a premium in order to acquire the commodity now. Their *convenience yield* for holding the physical commodity is high. Conversely, if stocks are abundant and users of the physical commodity can easily acquire it in the spot market, there is less upward pressure on the spot price, which tends to be lower than the future price.

To express the spot-future price relationship more formally, we can use the equation

$$F_t^T = S_t(1 + r_{T-t} + c_{T-t} - y_{T-t}) \, ,$$

which states that the current price (time t) of the futures contract for a commodity which is due to be delivered at time T in the future is F_t^T and equals

1 Stock indicators could be the level of OPEC's spare production capacity, stocks held by oil companies, IEA country reserves and so forth.

the spot price at time *t*, plus the cost of storage and insurance *c* for the period *T − t*, plus the cost of capital *r* used to acquire the commodity and hold it over the same period, minus the convenience yield *y*. To express the same relationship using continuous compounding, we can simply restate the previous equation as

$$F_t^T = S_t \cdot \exp{(r + c - y)(T - t)} .$$

Returning to Working's observation, the higher the stocks, the lower the convenience yield (approaching zero) and the more the price of the futures contract exceeds the spot price by the full *cost of carry* (storage, insurance and cost of capital). This relationship is graphically expressed in Exhibit 7.17.

From the previous discussion, we can deduce that there are two states with regard to the relationship between spot and future prices (i.e. the basis). If we define the basis as $F_t - S_t$ when the future price is higher than the spot, the basis is positive and the market is said to be in *contago*. Conversely, when the future price is lower than the spot, the basis is negative and the market is said to be in *backwardation*.

Depending on supply and demand conditions and market expectations, a market can switch between contango and backwardation, even on a daily basis. However, as the futures contract approaches its expiry date, the closer it comes to becoming the physical commodity (at least theoretically) and the more its

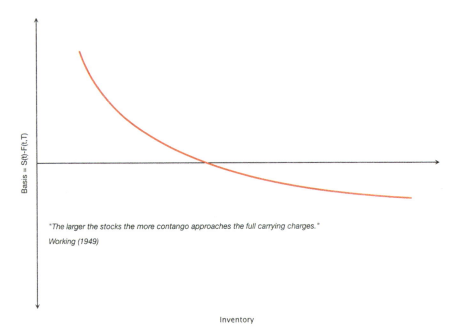

Exhibit 7.17 Relationship between inventory and basis
Source: Author

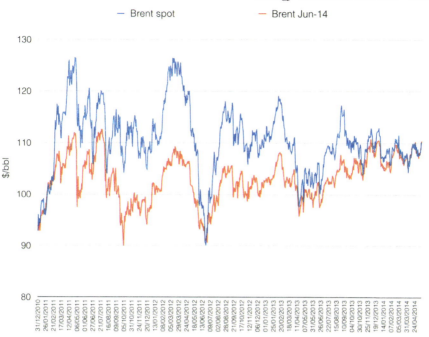

Exhibit 7.18 Price convergence of Brent spot and June-14 futures contract
Source: Author, based on data from Thomson Reuters Datastream

price will converge to the spot price. This premise is known as *price convergence*, and we can observe it in Exhibit 7.18 for the Brent spot and June-14 contract, when we eventually have convergence on the contracts expiry on 15 May 2014.

Going a step further from the discussion above, we can also look at the relationship among the prices of a number of sequential contracts for a particular commodity, for deliveries at various points in the future. When doing so, we are building the forward curve of the particular commodity. The forward curve may be useful for a number of reasons. First of all, it shows how the market prices the commodity for various future delivery dates, and hence tells us where the future spot prices will be according to rational expectations. The forward curve allows us to extract the convenience yield between two different maturities. Finally, it provides forward prices for the pricing of forward contracts, options, swaps and, in general, for the many risk management calculations. Exhibit 7.19 shows the forward curves for WTI and Brent prices on a particular date in June 2014.

Derivative contracts

There is a wide array of derivative products that are contingent on energy, and indeed several other commodities. Forwards, futures, swaps and options are some of the most commonly used ones, and we will examine them all in brief.

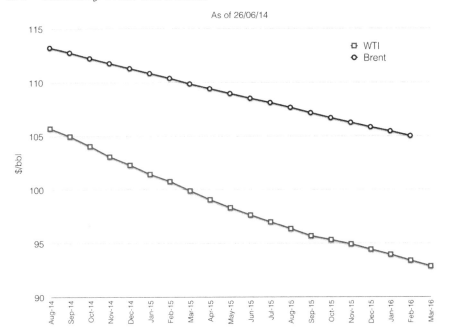

Exhibit 7.19 Forward curves for WTI and Brent

Source: Author, based on data from Thomson Reuters Eikon

Forward contracts

A forward contract is the simplest and most straightforward means for two parties to agree the physical sale and purchase of a commodity. The quantity, quality, delivery specifications and price are all negotiable between the buyer and the seller, hence a forward contract is fully customisable and very flexible. However, once written, a forward contract cannot be reversed, unless the two parties mutually agree to do so and are prepared to incur any contingent penalties. In addition, the contract cannot be sold on to a different party as there is not a secondary market for these instruments. Finally, one of the key risks of a forward contract is that either party may default on their obligations, in which case the entire transaction simply collapses.

Futures contracts

In contrast to the bilateral transaction model of the forward market, a futures market brings all transactions under the umbrella of the exchange. When a party buys (goes *long*) or sells (goes *short*) a contract for the commodity, the counterparty is the exchange clearing house, which guarantees that the transaction will be honoured. To achieve this, market participants are required to make an initial deposit (the *initial margin*) with the exchange, proportional to the value of the position they open and then maintain their deposit at a minimum level required by the exchange (the *maintenance margin*), until they decide to terminate their position. For the exchange and the market participants at large, this system calculates the profits and losses of each position on a daily basis (*marking to market*) and any participants with an account balance below the required maintenance margin is required to pay up additional amounts of money (*margin calls*) in order to continue trading.

This is best illustrated by an example. Let us assume that Max Profit, a seasoned oil trader, decides to open a long position on the NYMEX light sweet crude contract for September 2014, because he feels that the price of oil will be rising. On 10 June, he puts an order to buy five Sep-14 contracts (each for 1,000 barrels of WTI) and his broker fills the order at a price of $103.25/bbl. In order to open the position, Max has to deposit an initial margin of $3,000 per contract (i.e. a total of $15,000 for his overall position). He also has a maintenance margin of $2,750 per contract (i.e. his overall balance should not fall below $13,750, otherwise he will be asked for a margin call high enough to restore his balance to the initial margin).

Over the next few days, he maintains his position, but as the market moves, so does the balance of his account that his broker keeps on his behalf with the exchange. Exhibit 7.20 shows how the settlement price of the Sep-14 contract fluctuates on a daily basis and the result on Max's margin account, until he decides to close his position and exit.

Date	Day	Price ($/bbl)	Daily P&L ($)	Margin account ($)	Variation margin ($)
09/06/14	1	102.60		15,000.00	
10/06/14	2	102.49	-550.00	14,450.00	0.00
11/06/14	3	102.69	1,000.00	15,450.00	0.00
12/06/14	4	104.82	10,650.00	26,100.00	0.00
13/06/14	5	105.07	1,250.00	27,350.00	0.00
16/06/14	6	105.33	1,300.00	28,650.00	0.00
17/06/14	7	105.02	-1,550.00	27,100.00	0.00
18/06/14	8	104.84	-900.00	26,200.00	0.00
19/06/14	9	105.30	2,300.00	28,500.00	0.00
20/06/14	10	105.97	3,350.00	31,850.00	0.00
23/06/14	11	105.42	-2,750.00	29,100.00	0.00
24/06/14	12	105.32	-500.00	28,600.00	0.00
25/06/14	13	105.72	2,000.00	30,600.00	0.00
26/06/14	14	105.11	-3,050.00	27,550.00	0.00
27/06/14	15	105.04	-350.00	27,200.00	0.00
			Net P/L	**12,200.00**	

Exhibit 7.20 Marking to market for NYMEX light sweet crude oil contract
Source: Author

If Max decides to close his position, he is most likely to do this by *offsetting*. This means that he simply has to sell the same number of an identical futures contract (for the same commodity and the same delivery month), incurring the normal brokerage fees and taking any profit or loss he may have made on his position.

Offsetting is one of four methods that may be available for closing a futures position. The other three are: exchange of futures for physical, cash settlement and physical delivery.

An *exchange of futures for physical* (EFP) involves two parties, one with a long and one with a short futures position. The two parties can identify each other with the mediation of the commodity exchange and agree to swap their futures position, and at the same time enter a transaction on the physical commodity. They may do so before the expiry of the specific contract, but they have to carry out the transaction under the supervision of the exchange authorities. It is also required that their futures positions match the size of the physical transaction on the commodity.

To illustrate this, consider the following. We are in May and two traders, OilCo and RefCo, have previously opened a short and a long futures position, respectively, using the ICE July Brent futures. OilCo has sold 600 contracts and RefCo has bought 600 contracts. At some point during May, before the expiry of the July contract, the two parties decide they wish to engage in an EFP transaction. They approach the exchange authorities and request their mediation to find an appropriate match. The exchange puts the two traders in contact and gives them the go-ahead to engage in the transaction. RefCo and OilCo agree to exchange their futures positions, so that both parties clear their respective paper transactions. At the same time, they agree that OilCo will sell to RefCo a physical Brent crude oil cargo. The transaction happens privately between the two parties, but the price and transaction particulars have to be reported back to the exchange authorities, who verify that this is a *bona fide* commercial transaction. Note also that the two paper positions that have been exchanged (600 contracts) equate the quantity of the physical Brent cargo (600,000 bbls). A similar example can be constructed using the CME/NYMEX light sweet crude futures contract. The number of contracts that need to be swapped here may be smaller, though, as WTI physical deliveries at Cushing are usually for smaller volumes.

If there is no offsetting or EFP transaction before the expiry of a futures contract, market participants, whether long or short, can simply settle their positions in cash. *Cash settlement* is available for most futures contracts, and in some cases it is the only alternative to offsetting (i.e. no type of physical delivery is allowed). It simply requires traders to make payments to settle their gains or losses at the expiration of the contract.

If no other method is used, and the exchange regulations allow it, an open position can be settled by making a *physical delivery* of the commodity underlying the contracts. In this situation, it is typically the short position holder that notifies the exchange of the need to arrange a physical delivery. The exchange tries to find suitable long position holders and put them in touch with the short position holder, who normally determines exactly which commodity (of the ones allowed by the futures contract specification) and where it is delivered. The price can be negotiated between the two parties, but it is normally a differential from the official exchange price and has to be reported back to the exchange, as in the case of the EFP.

In our earlier example, Max Profit opened a long position at a certain market price. If the price moves higher than the price he bought at, then he will be making a profit, which he may decide to realise by reversing his position and closing out the contract. If he maintains his position and the price falls below his initial purchase price, then he will make an overall loss. For a graphical demonstration of the profits or losses from a long futures position, see Exhibit 7.21. On the horizontal axis is the price of the commodity, which rises as we move from left to right. On the vertical axis is the profit the trader makes in relation to the price at which he opened the long position. The pay-offs are represented by a positively sloping line (from the bottom left to the top right).

Conversely, Exhibit 7.22 demonstrates the pay-offs of a short futures position. As the price falls (towards the left of the horizontal axis), the short position becomes profitable. The trader can simply reverse it by buying back at a lower price and booking the profit. If the price increases, on the other hand, the position is loss-making. He can either reverse it and take the losses, or maintain it and make any necessary margin payments to keep his account in credit.

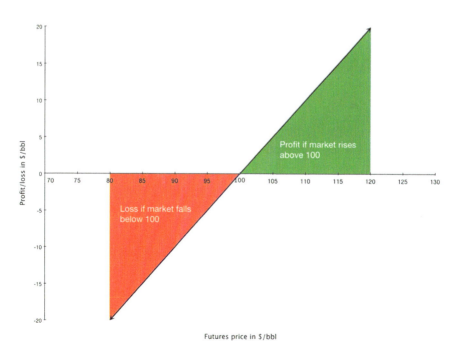

Exhibit 7.21 Pay-offs from a long futures position

Source: Author

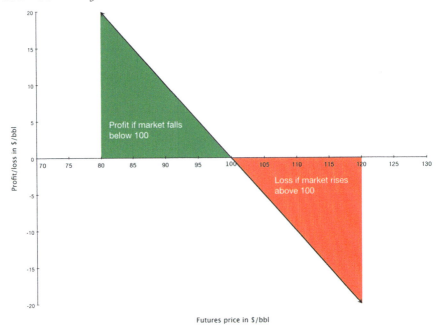

Exhibit 7.22 Pay-offs from a short futures position
Source: Author

There are several commodity exchanges listing futures contracts for an array of energy commodities, including crude oil, refined products, natural gas, coal and electricity. The two key exchanges, where most trading activity takes place, are the Intercontinental Exchange (ICE) and the New York Mercantile Exchange (now part of CME Group – CME/NYMEX). Other exchanges include TOCOM in Japan and MCX in India, although the list is not exhaustive.

ICE lists one of the two most popular and liquid crude oil contracts: Brent crude. The contract, in its current form, was launched in June 1988 by the predecessor of ICE, the International Petroleum Exchange. It is for 1,000 barrels of current quality Brent blend, deliverable at Sullom Voe, although the physical base is supported by the additional three types of North Sea crude oil that form BFOE, as discussed earlier. The contract size is comparable to that of the equally successful light sweet crude contract on the New York Mercantile Exchange (NYMEX). The physical base for this contract is the WTI crude, but several more US domestic crude oils, as well as a few imported qualities, can also be delivered against it. Exhibit 7.23 lists a selected number of futures contracts trading on CME/NYMEX and ICE.

Contract name	Exchange	Price quotation Tick	Contract size	Contracts traded	Contract expiry
Light sweet crude oil (WTI)	CME	US$ and cents/bbl $0.01/bbl	1,000 barrels	Consecutive monthly contracts for current and next 5 years. June and December contracts for an additional three years	Third business day before the 25th calendar day of the month preceding the delivery month
Brent crude oil	ICE	US$ and cents/bbl $0.01/bbl	1,000 barrels	Consecutive monthly contracts for the next six years	The 15th calendar day before the first calendar day of the delivery month or, if this is not a business day, the first business day prior to that
NYH ULSD (diesel)	CME	US$ and cents/gl $0.0001/gl	42,000 gallons	Consecutive monthly contracts for current year, plus three years, plus one month	Last business day of the month preceding the delivery month
RBOB gasoline	CME	US$ and cents/gl $0.0001/gl	42,000 gallons	Monthly contracts for 36 consecutive months	Last business day of the month preceding the delivery month
Diesel 10 ppm (UK) NWE cargoes	ICE	US$ and cents/mt $0.001/mt	1,000 metric tons	Monthly contracts for 60 consecutive months	Last trading day of the contract month
UK NBP gas	ICE	pence Sterling/th 0.01 p/th	1,000 therms per day per delivery period	Up 42 daily contracts, balance-of-week (5 business days), weekend, balance-of-month	Business day prior to the start of the delivery period
Henry Hub gas	CME	US$ and cents/ mmBtu $0.001/mmBtu	10,000 mmBtu	118 consecutive months	Three business days prior to the first day of the delivery month
API2 coal (CRF ARA)	CME	US$ and cents/mt $0.05/mt	1,000 metric tons	Monthly for 5 consecutive months	The last Friday of the contract month
API4 coal (FOB Richards Bay)	CME	US$ and cents/mt $0.05/mt	1,000 metric tons	Monthly for 5 consecutive months	The last Friday of the contract month
UK APX baseload electricity	ICE	£ and pence/MWh 1 p/MWh	1MWh per hour per day per delivery period	54-59 consecutive months, 6-7 consecutive quarters, 7-8 consecutive seasons	Two business days prior to the first calendar day of the delivery month, quarter or season
PJM Western Hub Off-peak electricity	CME	US$ and cents/ MWh $0.05/MWh	5 MWh	72 consecutive months	Last business day of the contract month (only financial settlement)

Exhibit 7.23 List of energy futures contracts
Source: Author

Spread contracts

It is not always relevant to trade in simple (or *plain vanilla*) long and short positions. Frequently, one can construct a hedge for a more complex position, or indeed find a profitable opportunity, by using simultaneous positions in two ore more closely associated contracts. Hence, the exposure is not on the full (or *flat*) price of the commodity, but on the price differential (or *spread*) instead. In energy, as indeed in other commodities, there are opportunities to construct three key type of spreads: *calendar, cross-commodity* and *raw material-product*.

A calendar spread involves a long position in a futures contract for delivery in one month and a short position in another contract for delivery in a different month. The spread is then known by the name of the two months. For example, a Jan-Feb Brent spread is a one-month calendar spread and involves the two futures contracts for Brent for January and February. When the trader goes long the closest month and short the furthest month, he buys the spread. Conversely, selling a Jan-Feb spread would involve selling January and buying February contracts. With spreads, the trader takes a position on the price differential between the two months (i.e. the level of contango or backwardation, rather than the flat price movement of the underlying commodity).

A cross-commodity spread involves the sale a purchase of two contracts for different but related commodities, usually for the same delivery month.

A typical cross-commodity spread in energy is that for two different crudes, also known as an *inter-crude* spread. The most popular version is the WTI-Brent spread, whereby a trader may buy a WTI contract for a certain delivery month and at the same time sell a Brent contract for the same month. For example, going long, the May WTI-Brent spread implies the purchase of May WTI contracts and the sale of the same number of May Brent contracts. In this example, the trader anticipates that the price differential between the two crude oils will narrow (i.e. WTI will become relatively more expensive and Brent relatively cheaper). Changes in the spread could be explained by factors such as quality differentials, delivery terms, transport costs and supply/demand imbalances in the respective markets of the different crude oils.

Similar spreads can be constructed between other energy commodities. For example, the HH-NBP spread reflects the differential in gas prices between the US (Henry Hub) and the UK (NBP). The list can continue with more pairs of appropriate futures contracts listed in the various commodity exchanges, and may also extend to spread trades between several more types of energy contracts in the OTC (over-the-counter) market.

In the context of energy commodities, there are two raw material-product spreads: the *crack* and the *spark* spread. We will look at both of them in turn.

The crack spread is relevant to the petroleum industry, as it is constructed to replicate the refining process and reflects the underlying refining spread. For refiners, this is an important tool for hedging their gross refining margins. With this principle in mind, a number of different crack spreads can be constructed to replicate different refining scenarios. For example, if a refiner processes a barrel of crude oil to produce half a barrel of gasoline and half a barrel of heating oil, he can replicate this by buying the paper equivalent of two barrels of crude oil and selling one barrel of gasoline and one barrel of heating oil. This splitting of a barrel of crude into equal parts of gasoline and heating oil (very) loosely approximates the product slate of a northern hemisphere refinery during the winter, when roughly equal amounts of middle and light distillates are needed in order to satisfy demand both for heating and transportation. Hence, this approximation is commonly known as the *2:1:1*, or *winter crack*. To replicate this using futures contracts on CME/NYMEX, the refiner would have to buy two light sweet crude contracts (each for 1,000 bbls) and sell one contract of RBOB gasoline (42,000 gls or 1,000) and one contract of heating oil (also for 42,000 gls or 1,000 bbls). During the summer months in the northern hemisphere, consumers require relatively higher volumes of gasoline and less heating oil, as the driving season starts (especially in the US) and the weather is warmer. As a result, refineries normally shut down sequentially for maintenance and are reconfigured to produce larger quantities of lighter distillates. In this case, the product slate can is better approximated by a 2:1 proportion between gasoline and heating oil. This implies that the refiner would buy three barrels of crude and cut it into two barrels of gasoline and one barrel of heating oil. This is commonly known as the *3:2:1*, or *summer crack*. More sophisticated spreads can be constructed to replicate more complicated refining compositions, such as the 5:3:2 crack and so on. Exhibit 7.24 demonstrates the volatility of the 3:2:1 crack spread using WTI crude, RBOB gasoline and heating oil prices. The exhibit also shows the same crack spread using West Texas Sour (WTS), a heavy and sour crude oil, which is typical of the crude oil quality used in many complex US refineries, as it leaves a higher profit margin.

The *spark* spread is similar to the crack spread, but it is relevant to the power generation industry and comes in a number of different versions, depending on the fuel used to generate the electricity and whether the cost of carbon emissions is taken into account or not.

The simple spark (or *raw spark*) spread reflects the price differential between the price of one MWh of electricity and the cost of producing this using natural gas. To calculate this, we need to take into account not only the cost of gas, but also its heat rate (i.e. how much of the heat energy contained in a unit of gas is converted to electrical energy). On average, the heat rate for a CCGT power plant is approximately 50 per cent, although this will vary from plant to plant and may be higher for more modern plants. To illustrate how the spark spread is calculated, consider Exhibit 7.25, which gives the example of a CCGT plant in the UK, with prices for electricity and gas given in £/MWh and pence/therm, respectively. Columns [1] and [2] show the calculations for the raw spark and the clean spark, respectively.

In a similar way, the *dark spark* is the differential between the price of one MWh of electricity and the cost of producing it using coal. Once again, we

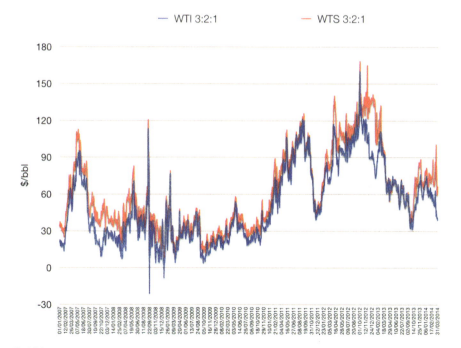

Exhibit 7.24 WTI/WTS:RBOB:HO crack spreads

Source: Author, based on data from Thomson Reuters Datastream

Spread type	Raw spark [1]	Clean spark [2]	Dark spark [3]	Clean dark [4]
Electricity price		£40/MWh		
Energy conversion	1MWh = 3.412 mmBtu & 1mmBtu = 10 therms ⇒ 1MWh = 34.12 therms		Coal calorific value = 6,000 kcal/kg 1 mt coal = 6,000,000 kcal 1MWh = 860,000 kcal ⇒ 1 mt = 6.98MWh	
Cost of fuel	Gas price = 35 p/therm Gas heat rate = 50% £0.35x34.12÷0.5 = £23.88/MWh		Coal price = $75/mt @ £/$1.70 Coal heat rate = 35% $75÷1.70÷6.98÷0.35 = £18.06/MWh	
Cost of emissions		€6/tCO₂ @ £/€1.25 €6÷1.25 = £4.80/tCO₂ £4.80x0.42 = £2.02/MWh		€6/tCO₂ @ £/€1.25 €6÷1.25 = £4.80/tCO₂ £4.80x0.85 = £4.08/MWh
Spread	£40 - £23.88 = **£15.12/MWh**	£40 - £23.88 - £2.02 = **£14.10/MWh**	£40 - £18.06 = **£21.94/MWh**	£40 - £18.06 - £4.08 = **£17.86/MWh**

Exhibit 7.25 Examples of spark spread calculations

Source: Author

need to take into account the heat rate, which is lower than that of gas, as coal tends to be less efficient, with only about 35 per cent of the generated heat energy being converted to electrical energy, on average. This again depends on the individual plant, with more modern plants[2] achieving higher heat rates. To illustrate the calculation of the dark spread, consider columns [3] and [4] of Exhibit 7.25, for an example of a coal-fired power station in the UK, which imports its coal from abroad and with prices given in £/MWh for electricity and $/mt for coal.

Finally, Exhibit 7.26 shows the movement of the raw and dark spark in the UK over the last seven years. Note how much the raw spark has declined in relation to the dark spread, as coal has become relatively less expensive than gas. A similar story is given by Exhibit 7.27, which shows the same sparks in the US market.

Swap contracts

As discussed earlier on, a forward contract can be used to hedge price risk exposure for a particular time in the future for any commodity, as long as the

---

2 For example, with fluidised bed combustion (FBC), supercritical and ultra-supercritical boilers, and integrated gasification combined cycle (IGCC) technologies.

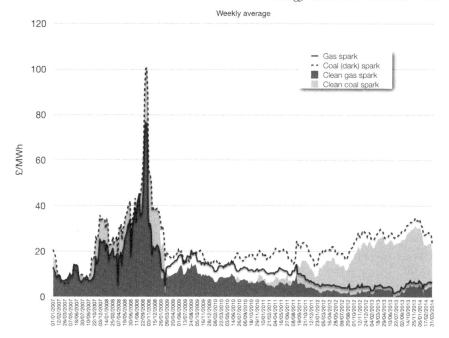

Exhibit 7.26 UK spark spreads

Source: Author, based on data from Thomson Reuters Datastream

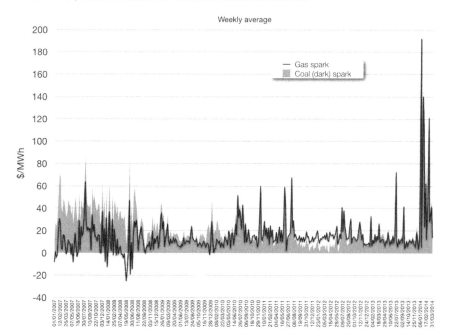

Exhibit 7.27 US spark spreads

Source: Author, based on data from Thomson Reuters Datastream

two transacting parties agree the commodity quality and quantity. This gives both parties flexibility on the contract specifics, but leaves both parties exposed to each other's default risk. Alternatively, a hedger can use the futures market to cover his price risk exposure in the physical market. In this case, the counterparty risk is undertaken by the commodity exchange, but the hedger may be limited in terms of the futures contracts that are available and may not match the precise quality and delivery specification of his physical cargo.

To resolve these shortcomings, financial intermediaries developed the *swap*, a derivative instrument that is essentially an exchange of a fixed for a floating price. Swaps are routinely used by traders to hedge exposures in the physical market for numerous energy commodities. As long as there is a published, commonly accepted price benchmark for a commodity of a specific quality and delivery, a swap can be constructed. The swap transfers the price risk from the commodity seller (producer) or buyer (consumer) to a financial inter-mediary – the swap provider – who warehouses the risk. In exchange, the swap provider can benefit from movements of the market in his favour. Once the provider has entered the swap agreement, he has to cover the risk exposure. Ultimately, the ideal way to cover this risk may be to arrange a counter-balancing swap with another financial institution, for an equal and opposite position.

An example here will help clarify the concept and the mechanics of a swap. Assume that there are three parties: 'RefCo' is an oil refinery; 'OilCo' is a crude oil producer; and 'FinCo' is the swap provider (e.g. a bank). RefCo is short the physical and will need to buy crude oil in the open market; it is, therefore,

Exhibit 7.28 Oil swap example

Source: Author

exposed to the risk of rising oil prices. OilCo is long the physical and will need to sell its production in the open market; the risk here is a downward price swing. RefCo can enter a swap agreement with FinCo, for a specified amount of crude oil at a specified price and over a specified period of time, typically for several months. For simplicity, let us assume that the swap is for 1 million barrels of Urals crude at a price of $105.50/bbl. In a similar but opposite way, OilCo enters a swap agreement with FinCo, also for 1 million barrels of Urals crude at $105.40/bbl. Both parties require the swap for a period of six months.

Let us now assume that at the end of the first month, the average market price for Urals[3] has been $105.30/bbl. The swap provider will make a payment to OilCo – because the average market price has been below the swap price – equal to $0.10/bbl (a total of $100,000). In an analogous way, the provider will receive a payment of $0.20/bbl from RefCo (a total of $200,000), because the average market price has been below the swap price. The net position of the swap provider is a profit of $100,000.

Once again, real life is rarely as straightforward as the preceding example. To start with, the quantities agreed in swaps are unlikely to be equal, and the price movements are not always favourable for the swap provider. Any mismatched risk has, therefore, to be appropriately covered. If the provider, for example, has a net long position, then taking an adequate long position on the futures market might cover his exposure.

One can think of many different swap examples, using the appropriate energy commodities and hedging parties. For example, an airline would enter a consumer swap for jet fuel, whereas a refiner would enter a producer swap for the same refined product. A gas-fired power station would enter a consumer swap for natural gas, whereas an upstream gas company would enter a producer swap and so on. Exhibit 7.29 shows the setup of a typical swap agreement, using the example of an airline company that wishes to hedge its jet fuel costs. The lower part of the exhibit shows the payoffs over the length of the swap contract, while Exhibit 7.30 conveys the same information in a diagram.

The swaps described above are also known as *plain vanilla* swaps. There are more sophisticated versions of these transactions, which allow more flexibility on the terms of the swap for either of the two parties. For example, in a *differential* swap, the counterparties exchange the difference between two floating prices (e.g. WTI-Brent) for a fixed price differential. A *double-up* swap gives the swap provider the option to double the notional volume of the swap, before the pricing period starts. On the other hand, an *extendable* swap gives the swap provider the right to extend the swap, at the end of the period, for an additional predetermined period. A final example is that of a *swaption*, whereby the buyer has the option to decide, up to an expiry date, whether to initiate the swap or not. There may be more types available depending on the risks the counterparties are trying to hedge and their creativity.

---

3 The average price is calculated as the simple arithmetic mean of the daily prices over the calendar month as reported by a recognised agency such as Platts.

Contract	Jet Fuel, FOB Singapore
Payer of fixed	Airline
Payer of floating	Bank
Period of swap	12 months, starting May 2011
Notional amount	10,000 mt per month
Settlement	Monthly
Price source	Platts APAG in $/mt
Floating reference price	Spot price FOB Singapore published daily
Reference price calculation	Arithmetic average of the floating reference price per month

Date	Swap price	Average market price (Platts)	Price diff	Payment to airline
May-11	127.50	128.87	1.37	13,700
Jun-11	127.50	127.51	0.01	100
Jul-11	127.50	129.36	1.86	18,600
Aug-11	127.50	124.69	-2.81	-28,100
Sep-11	127.50	123.91	-3.59	-35,900
Oct-11	127.50	123.50	-4.00	-40,000
Nov-11	127.50	128.07	0.57	5,700
Dec-11	127.50	123.06	-4.44	-44,400
Jan-12	127.50	126.93	-0.57	-5,700
Feb-12	127.50	132.39	4.89	48,900
Mar-12	127.50	136.31	8.81	88,100
Apr-12	127.50	133.43	5.93	59,300
			Total Net	**80,300**

Exhibit 7.29 Jet fuel swap for an airline – set-up and monthly pay-offs
Source: Author

Option contracts

Forward, futures and swap contracts share one common element: they are all designed to counterbalance the profit or losses made in the physical market. This is welcome when the hedger makes a loss in the physical, as his profit in the paper market will compensate for all or most of his loss. Conversely, however, any profits made in the physical market will also be wiped out by losses in the paper market. Ultimately, this is the nature of hedging, unwelcome though it may be on some occasions.

One way of hedging against unfavourable market movements, while still being able to take advantage of the upside potential of favourable market swings, is to use options contracts. Traded options contracts were introduced by both NYMEX and IPE (the predecessor of ICE), soon after the launch of the benchmark futures contracts for WTI and Brent crude oil. Currently, there are numerous options contracts written on most futures contracts, which are traded in the major commodity exchanges. In addition, there are countless more OTC contracts that are designed to deal with specific aspects of risk,

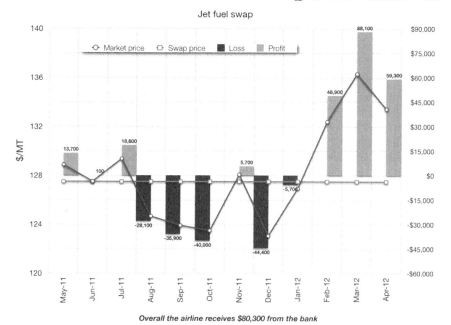

Exhibit 7.30 Jet fuel swap for an airline – monthly pay-offs graph
Source: Author

both in terms of the price and in terms of the volume of the commodity in question.

Basic definitions and contract types

Let us start, though, with a brief definition of the key types of options contracts and how they work. An option gives the right, but not the obligation, to the buyer to buy or sell a commodity (the underlying asset) at a specified price (the *strike* price), up to a certain point in the future (the *expiry* date). For the privilege, the buyer of the option has to pay an upfront fee (the *premium*) to the seller (or writer) of the option.

Options may grant the right to buy (*call* option) or sell (*put* option). For some options, this right can only be exercised at expiry (*European-style* option), while for others it can be exercised on any day up to expiry (*American-style* option).

Now that the basic characteristics of plain-vanilla options have been stated, it is time to discuss how each type of option works. Panel A of Exhibit 7.31 demonstrates the pay-offs for the buyer (long) call option written on crude oil, with a strike price of $100/bbl, with an expiry at the end of November 2014 and for which a premium of $5/bbl has been paid. The horizontal axis shows the price of the underlying asset, while the vertical axis shows the profit or loss made for each price. If the price remains below $100, there is no benefit from exercising the option and the buyer simply loses his premium. As the price rises to $100 and above, the option becomes valuable and can be exercised. Once the price rises enough to equate the strike price plus the premium, the overall position yields a profit. For example, if exercised when the underlying price is $110, the buyer will buy his crude oil at the strike price of $100 and, as he has already paid a premium of $5, he will have a net purchase price of $105. He can then sell his oil at the market price of $100 and realise a profit of $5/bbl.

The opposite pay-off takes place for the buyer (long) of a put option (panel B), who gets a profit out of exercising the option when the market price falls below the strike price of $100. When the market price falls to, say, $85, he will exercise his option to sell his oil at the strike price of $100. Having paid a $5 premium already, he will receive a net price of $95, which will leave him $10/bbl better off than the current market price.

Panels C and D of Exhibit 7.31 show the pay-offs from the point of view of the option seller (short). In the case of a short call, as long as the underlying price remains below the strike price, the option will remain unexercised and he will simply receive his premium of $5/bbl. If the price rises above the strike price, he will have to pay to the buyer of the call the difference between the market price and the strike price. The seller of a put has a pay-off schedule that is the mirror image of a short call and the reader can work this out easily from panel D.

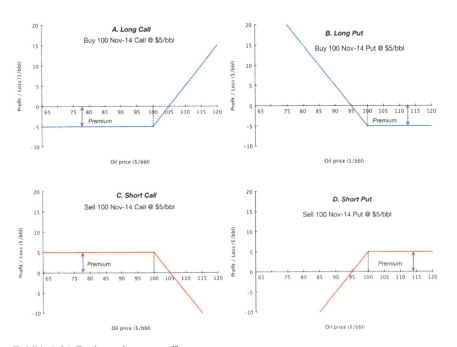

Exhibit 7.31 Basic option pay-offs

Source: Author

Although options can be used on their own simply to speculate, they are normally part of a hedging portfolio for market participants with a physical exposure in the underlying commodity. For example, a refinery that is short on crude oil on the physical side may want to protect itself from paying an excessively high price for its oil input, but is happy to take advantage of the higher profitability when oil prices (i.e. its input costs) fall. To do this, the refinery may wish to buy a call option, which, in combination with its physical position, will help it form a *cap* on the price it pays for its crude oil. This combination is also called a *covered call*, and its pay-offs are shown in Exhibit 7.32. The refiner's short physical position (-S) is depicted by the downward-sloping red line, while the pay-off of the long call option is shown by the now familiar green line, which implies that the strike price is $90 at a premium of $5. If the market price of crude oil rises above the strike price, the option can be exercised. When the market price rises above $95 (the strike price plus the premium), any additional losses in the physical market (in the form of higher crude oil purchase costs) will be cancelled out by the payment that the refiner will receive, which will equal the differential between the market price and the strike price. The combined pay-offs are depicted by the blue line, which sets a cap to the loss of profitability as the market price rises above $90. This means that the effective purchase price for the crude oil cannot exceed (is capped at) $95/bbl.

To help us understand how a cap works, consider the example given in Exhibit 7.33. Here, a refinery has a commitment to supply refined oil products

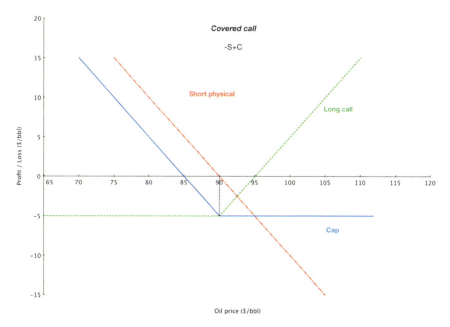

Exhibit 7.32 Covered call (cap)

Source: Author

On 01-Mar-14 a refinery enters into a deal to supply gasoline, diesel oil and several other refined products to be delivered by end of May-14. To fulfill the order it will require to purchase 30,000 bbls of crude oil at the end of Apr-14

It decides to hedge the crude oil cost by buying a call option

Oil price at 01-Mar-14 = $105/bbl

Oil required at the end of Apr, so expiry is 30-Apr-14

Amount required is 30,000 bbls

Buy Apr 14 Call with strike price $110/bbl @ premium $5/bbl

Cap hedge for April 2014

Physical market	Options market
Oil price on 01-Mar-14: $105/bbl	Buy Apr-14 call, strike price $110/bbl @ $5/bbl
Current cost of oil: $3,150,000 (=30,000 x 105)	Call cost: $150,000 (=5 x 30,000)

First scenario - Falling oil prices

Oil price on 30-Apr-14: $95/bbl	Strike price ($110) > Settlement price ($95)
Actual cost of oil: $2,850,000	Option NOT exercised

Total crude oil cost (incl. option premium) = 2,850,000 + 150,000 = $3,000,000
or $100/bbl

Second scenario – Rising oil prices

	Strike price ($110) < Settlement price ($120)
Oil price on 30-Apr-14: $120/bbl	Option IS exercised
Actual cost of oil: $3,600,000	Payoff from options
	(120-110) x 30,000 - 150,000 = $150,000

Total crude oil cost (incl. option payoff) = 3,600,000 - 150,000 = $3,450,000
or $115/bbl

Exhibit 7.33 Cap hedge example
Source: Author

and will need to buy a certain quantity of crude oil at the end of a specified period. The refinery decides to hedge the risk of rising oil prices by buying a call option at the specified price and premium. The exhibit provides the specific information on prices and data and then sets out two scenarios: one of falling and one of rising oil prices. Note how, in the second scenario, the effective purchase price for the refinery (the cap) is set at $115/bbl (i.e. the strike price plus the premium).

Just like a purchaser of the commodity is afraid that the market price will rise, a producer wants to hedge against prices going down, which will result in a loss of income from selling the commodity. In this case, the producer is interested in fixing a minimum price (a *floor*) at which he can sell his production if prices fall, while still being able to take advantage of favourable price upswings. In this case, the producer may wish to enter a *protective put*, as described in Exhibit 7.34. Here, an oil producer has a long physical exposure to crude oil, which is depicted by the upward-sloping red line. The more the market price falls, the more he stands to lose. He can, therefore, buy (long) a put option that will establish a floor for the price he gets for his oil. This is depicted by the now familiar green line, which implies that the put option has a strike price of $90 and a premium of $5. If the market price of crude oil falls below the strike price, the option can be exercised. When the market price

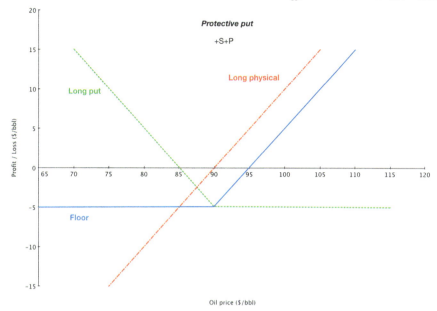

Exhibit 7.34 Protective put (floor)

Source: Author

falls below $85 (the strike price minus the premium), any additional losses in the physical market (in the form of lower income from selling crude oil) will be cancelled out by the payment that the oil producer will receive, which will equal the differential between the market price and the strike price. The combined pay-offs are depicted by the blue line, which sets a floor to the loss of income as the market price falls below $90. This means that the effective sale price for the crude oil cannot fall below (has a floor of) $85/bbl.

To help us understand how a floor works, consider the example given in Exhibit 7.35. Here, an oil producer is worried about the market price he will manage to get for his crude oil in the last quarter of the year. The producer decides to hedge the risk of falling oil prices by buying a strip of put options at the specified prices and premiums. The exhibit provides the specific information on prices and data and then sets out two scenarios: one of rising and one of falling oil prices. Note how, in the second scenario, the effective sale price for the oil producer (the floor) is set at $108/bbl (i.e. the strike price minus the premium). The example only gives the results for the Oct-14 part of the strip, but the reader should be able to work out the remaining two months with little additional effort.

Useful though a protective put may be, it does create a substantial outflow of cash in the form of the upfront premium payment. In the previous example, the premium cost just for one month amounts to $6 million, whereas for the whole Q4 strip, it is $20.4 million. It is not surprising, therefore, that option buyers are keen on constructing hedges that are less expensive.

In 01-Jun-14 an oil producer is worried about the uncertainty of the oil market and would like to hedge its revenue from selling crude for the last quarter (Oct-Dec) of 2014. He decides to buy a strip of three put options as described below

Oil price at 01-Jun-14 = $100/bbl

Production 100,000 bbls/day => 3,000,000 bbls/month

Buy a strip of puts for Q4-14

Oct-14 put, strike $85/bbl @ premium $2/bbl; Nov-14 put, strike $85/bbl @ premium $2.3/bbl;

Dec-14 put, strike $85/bbl @ premium $2.5/bbl

Floor hedge for Q4 2014 - October payoffs	
Physical market	**Options market**
Oil price on 01-Jun-14: $100/bbl Current revenue per day: $10,000,000 (=100,000 x 100)	Buy Oct-14 put, strike price $110/bbl @ $2/bbl Put cost: $200,000 (= 2 x 100,000) or $6,000,000 for the month
First scenario - Rising oil prices	
Oil price on 30-Oct-14: $115/bbl Actual revenue per day: $11,500,000 Per month: $345,000,000	Strike price ($110) < Settlement price ($115) Option NOT exercised

Total crude oil revenue (incl. option premium) = 345,000,000 - 6,000,000 = $339,000,000
or $113/bbl

Second scenario – Falling oil prices	
Oil price on 30-Oct-14: $80/bbl Actual revenue per day: $8,000,000 Per month: $240,000,000	Strike price ($110) > Settlement price ($80) Option IS exercised Payoff from options (110 - 80) x 100,000 x 30 - 6,000,000 = $84,000,000

Total crude oil revenue (incl. option payoff) = 240,000,000 + 84,000,000 = $324,000,000
or $108/bbl

Repeat for Nov-14 and Dec-14, using the appropriate option premium

Exhibit 7.35 Floor hedge example

Source: Author

A *collar* is a good example of such a hedge, and works as follows. Imagine that the oil producer in the previous example still wants to create a floor on the price that he receives for his oil, but he is willing to forego some of the profit opportunity he may have if the oil price rises. To do this in practice, he can sell (write) a call option, for which he will receive a premium, but which may require him to make payments to the buyer of the call if the oil price rises. Exhibit 7.36 shows this combination of a long put (green line) and a short call (blue line), with the oil producer's natural long physical position (red line) on the commodity. As implied by the diagram, while the market price stands at $90, the oil producer has bought an out-of-the-money put at a strike price of $80 and sold an out-of-the-money call at a strike price of $100. As long as the market price fluctuates between these two prices, the oil producer will simply get the market price, and the premium of $5 he pays for the put will be covered by the $5 premium he receives for the call (zero cost). If the price drops below $80, his put option will become valuable and worth exercising. Let us say that the price drops to $70. This means that he will receive $70 from the market for his oil, as well as $10 from the option writer, a total of $80, which is $10 below the original market price of $90. Conversely, if the price rises above $100, he will be making higher profits on the physical side, but he will have to make payments to the buyer of the call option. For example, if the price

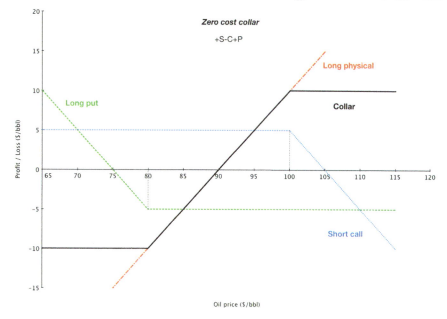

Exhibit 7.36 Zero-cost collar

Source: Author

climbs to $110, he will be receiving $110, but he will have to pay $10 to the call buyer, leaving him a net income of $100. In short, using a zero-cost collar, the oil producer has created a collar between $80 and $100, and hence protects himself from excess losses, but also foregoes excess profits.

In addition to plain-vanilla options and combinations thereof, several more complicated (or *exotic*) options have developed over time, in response to the needs of market participants and the peculiarities of certain commodities. One such type is an *average price* or *Asian* option. This is a European option with a settlement price calculated as an arithmetic average of underlying prices (e.g. spot or futures) over a period of time, typically one calendar month. More formally, the value of an Asian option is given as

$$V_{AP} = \max(A_T^t - K, 0) \, ,$$

where

$$A_T^t = \frac{\sum_{i=t}^{T} S_t}{T - \tau}.$$

This type of option is popular in all commodity groups and in general for commodities or assets where the physical trade is done over a monthly or longer period, or where the underlying price is not easily identifiable or can be easily influenced.

Often, the main risk is not found in the flat price of a commodity, but on the price differential between related commodity prices (i.e. the price spread). Spreads were discussed earlier, and one can simply envisage the purchase of options on the various types of spreads we encountered, such as calendar, inter-crude and crack spreads.

The vast majority of options are written with regard to the price of the underlying asset. Frequently, however, the risk does not emanate solely from the price. There is also risk associated with the volume of the commodity that is to be delivered. For commodities such as natural gas or electricity, it is quite common to use such *volumetric* options, where the option is written on the contract volume, rather than the price.

Three such volumetric options are *swings*, *nominations* and *recalls*. A swing option gives the customer the right to vary the amount of the commodity delivered, within a certain range. Given that there are N dates during which the commodity is delivered (say $N = 30$ in a month), the right to change the volume delivered can be exercised K times, where $K N$. To put this in a more practical context, consider a CCGT power station that purchases the same quantity of natural gas, say 10,000 mmBtu/day, throughout the month of January. The utility knows that weather extremes may change the demand for electricity generation, and hence the need to purchase varying amounts of gas. It expects that on 10 days during the month, its actual need for gas might be different, say 5,000 or 15,000 mmBtu instead of the usual 10,000. The utility can buy its gas forward at a predetermined price (say a differential to one of the gas price benchmarks) together with 10 swing rights to alter the nominated amount to either 5,000 or 15,000 mmBtu. It can buy these rights by paying an upfront premium, or simply embed the premium in the price that it pays for its gas.

A nomination is similar to a swing option, with the main difference that the level of the volume delivered is adjusted upwards or downwards for the remainder of the contracts, until the next nomination right is exercised. Finally, a recall is essentially a swing bought by the supplier of the commodity. It is an option to interrupt delivery under stressful circumstances and typically involves substantially fewer rights than a swing.

A final type of options that are quite interesting are *quantos*. A quanto is a composite option, combining price risk hedging of the underlying commodity price in the currency in which the commodity is traded, as well as risk hedging of the exchange rate between the commodity currency and the user's base currency. For example, consider a Japanese utility that buys LNG from the international market, in order to distribute it to its domestic customers. The LNG is bought at international prices, which are volatile and are denominated in US dollars. On the other hand, the utility is obliged to sell its gas to its customers in Japanese yen and is only allowed to vary its sale prices at regular intervals (say quarterly or semi-annually). The risk faced by the utility is not only the commodity price risk from gas, but also the $/¥ currency risk. A quanto option allows the utility to hedge both risks at the same time with one instrument.

Basics of option pricing

As can be seen from the above discussion, options offer ample opportunities to hedge a variety of risks, both in terms of the price and the volume of the underlying commodity. Calculating the value and price of an option has been a challenging task, tackled by numerous authors, until the breakthrough by Black and Scholes (1973), who discussed pricing of European stock options. Their formula for pricing a European call option on a stock, $C_t^{K,T} = S_t N(d_1) - Ke^{-r(T-t)}N(d_2)$, is an elegant closed-form solution, whereby $C_t^{K,T}$ is the price at time t of a call option with strike price K and maturity T, $e^{-r(T-t)}$ is the discount factor until maturity and $N(x)$ is the cumulative normal distribution function. Once the price of a call is known, the put price can be calculated from the put-call parity: $P_t^{K,T} = S_t = C_t^{K,T} + Ke^{-r(T-t)}$, where $P_t^{K,T}$ is the price at time t of a put option and the other terms are as described earlier. This solution does come with a number of assumptions, however. These include continuous trading of the underlying stock, lack of tax and transaction costs, lack of dividend payments, knowledge and non-variability of the short-term interest rate, as well as the assumption that the price of the underlying stock is driven by a GBM process.

Merton (1973) extended the B-S pricing model by allowing interest rates to be stochastic, the option to be American-style and the stock to pay dividends. This latter property is quite relevant to commodities, as the convenience yield for a commodity works in a similar way as a dividend payment for the value of the stock. Hence, the formula for a European call option written on a spot commodity price can now be written as $C_t^{K,T} = S_t e^{-y(T-t)}N(d_1) - Ke^{-r(T-t)}N(d_2)$, where y is the convenience yield. In a further breakthrough, Merton (1976) tackled the assumption of the price dynamics being described by a continuous-time diffusion process. He introduced the jump-diffusion process (mentioned earlier in this chapter), which allows the coexistence of both a continuous price motion and a jump stochastic process.

Black (1976) discussed the pricing of options written on futures contracts, which is particularly relevant to commodities, as many of the options written are of this type. The price for a call option with a strike price K and expiry time T, written on a futures contract F with expiry T_1, is given by the formula $C_t^{K,T} = F_t^T e^{-r(T-t)}N(d_1) - Ke^{-r(T-t)}N(d_2)$. Finally, Cox et al. (1979) extended the option pricing literature by introducing their binomial option pricing methodology, which allows itself to generalisation and can be used to price more complex options.

A final note in this analysis is the brief mention of the sensitivity of an option value with respect to changes in the market parameters. These are commonly known as the *Greeks*. Starting with *delta* (Δ), this is the partial derivative of the call price C with respect to the price S of the underlying asset and it is positive (negative for a put option). *Gamma* (Γ) is the rate of change (i.e. the derivative) of Δ. *Theta* (θ) is the partial derivative of the option price with respect to time, and is negative for both a put and a call option, representing the loss of the value of the option due to time decay. *Vega* is the rate of change of the option price with respect to the volatility σ, and is positive for puts and calls – the higher the volatility, the higher the chance that the option will be exercised. Finally, *rho* (ρ) is the partial derivative of the option price with respect to the risk-free interest rate *r*.

The purpose of the preceding discussion was to only briefly expose the reader to some of the most important literature in the area of options and their pricing. For a more expansive discussion of option pricing methodologies for commodities, the reader is referred to Burger *et al.* (2007, Chapter 2), Eydeland and Wolyniec (2003, Chapter 8), Edwards (2010, Chapters 3.4–3.6) and Geman (2005, Chapters 4–6).

Conclusion

This chapter completes the review of energy markets undertaken in the previous six chapters. The focus was placed on the characteristics of the various energy commodity prices and the instruments available for hedging the price risk posed by the market. Although there is considerable overlap with respect to the range of derivative instruments available to the various commodity groups, we have geared the analysis primarily towards energy derivative contracts. It is now time to turn our attention to the next major group of commodities – metals.

References

Black, F. (1976) 'The pricing of commodity contracts', *Journal of Financial Economics*, 3: 167–179.

Black, F. and Scholes, M. (1973) 'The pricing of options and corporate liabilities', *Journal of Political Economy*, 81: 637–654.

Burger, M., Graeber, B. and Schindlmayr, G. (2007) *Managing Energy Risk: An Integrated View on Power and Other Energy Markets*, Chichester: Wiley.

Cox, J.C., Ross, S.A. and Rubinstein, M. (1979) 'Option pricing: a simplified approach', *Journal of Financial Economics*, 7: 229–263.

Edwards, D.W. (2010) *Energy Trading and Investing: Trading, Risk Management and Structuring Deals in the Energy Markets*, McGraw-Hill.

Eydeland, A. and Wolyniec, K. (2003) *Energy and Power Risk Management: New Developments in Modeling, Pricing and Hedging*, Hoboken, NJ: Wiley.

Geman, H. (2005) *Commodities and Commodity Derivatives: Modeling and Pricing for Agriculturals, Metals, and Energy*, Chichester: Wiley.

—— (2008) *Risk Management in Commodity Markets: From Shipping to Agricuturals and Energy*, Chichester: Wiley.

Gibson, R. and Schwartz, E. (1990) 'Stochastic convenience yield and the pricing of oil contingent claims', *The Journal of Finance*, 45: 959–976.

Merton, R.C. (1973) 'The theory of rational option pricing', *Bell Journal of Economics and Management Science*, 4: 141–183.

—— (1976) 'Option pricing when underlying stock returns are discontinuous', *Journal of Financial Economics*, 3: 125–144.

Pilipovic, D. (2007) *Energy Risk: Valuing and Managing Energy Derivatives*, 2nd edn, McGraw-Hill.

Pirrong, C. (2012) *Commodity Price Dynamics: A Structural Approach*, Cambridge: Cambridge University Press.

Working, H. (1949) 'The theory of price of storage', *American Economic Review*, 39: 1254–1262.

8 Fundamental mineral economics

After covering energy, probably the most important group of commodities, at least in terms of trade volume, we move on to the second major group – metals.

Metals have always had a central role in human history, proved by the fact that two of the prehistoric ages of mankind are named after metals – the Bronze Age and the Iron Age. Moving from the hard and brittle stone, the development of the ability to extract metal from ore and then shape it into tools and weapons was crucial for the survival of many warring nations. Tribes with copper weapons were overpowered by those with bronze ones, and the latter were in turn besieged by invaders with iron weapons.

The advent of iron casting technology was also crucial for the advancement of agriculture, replacing the softer and less resistant bronze plough. Despite these advances, however, metal casting technology remained quite basic until the fifteenth century, and production techniques, as we know them today, did not evolve until the nineteenth century, when new advances meant that the production of large quantities of relatively cheap metal became feasible.

In this chapter, we will be first looking at the basic characteristics of the organisation of metal markets. This will include a taxonomy of the most important metals, the determinants of demand and supply for metals and their ores, and some of the procedures of metal price formation. We will then proceed, in the next chapter, to look at the most important of metal commodities – iron and steel. In the following two chapters, we will discuss two also very important base metals – copper and aluminium.

Taxonomy

In chemistry, metals are defined as a group of elements that: are normally solid at ordinary temperatures; are non-transparent except in very thin films; are good electrical and thermal conductors; and have a crystalline structure when in the solid state. Elements that are normally classified as metals are: aluminium, barium, beryllium, bismuth, cadmium, calcium, cerium, chromium, cobalt, copper, gold, iridium, iron, lead, lithium, magnesium, manganese, mercury, molybdenum, nickel, osmium, palladium, platinum, potassium, radium, rhodium, silver, sodium, tantalum, thallium, thorium, tin, titanium, tungsten, uranium, vanadium and zinc.

There is also another category of elements that fall between metals and non-metals as they have chemical properties from both. This category comprises boron, silicon, germanium, arsenic, antimony, tellurium, polonium and astatine. The reader will have already recognised silicon as the single most important element in this category, since it is the material used for the manufacture of microchips, as well as solar photovoltaic cells, among other applications.

Metals are distinguished by their uses and rarity, and, for commercial purposes, they are usually classified into five main categories: precious metals; iron; base metals; light metals; and alloying metals. Precious metals include gold, silver and platinum. They form a special category because they are rare to find and difficult to extract. They have several industrial uses,[1] but are also distinguished for their use as storage of wealth. Gold, in particular, has been used as money since time immemorial and still constitutes an anti-inflationary instrument in many investment portfolios.

Iron is in a category of its own, since it is the most widely produced and traded metal, present in most household and industrial uses. The raw material for its production, iron ore, has also been extensively traded, particularly since the 1950s.

Base metals include copper, lead, tin and mercury, and are called such because of their great significance to many civilisations throughout history. Copper, lead and tin were the first metals ever to be used and they still have a wide range of applications. Tin is used as an anti-corrosive coating for steel (tinplate), in wire form for soldering, and in several other alloying applications;[2] lead is used extensively in batteries, but also in ammunition and pipes; copper and its uses are going to be discussed more extensively in a later chapter.

Light metals are named so because of their lightweight properties that make them invaluable in applications where weight reduction without loss of strength is crucial.[3] Such metals include aluminium, titanium and magnesium, and they are used on their own or in alloys.

Alloying metals are named so because they are almost always used with other major metals to form alloys for special uses. Manganese, nickel, chromium, molybdenum and vanadium fall into this category, but other metals are also used. One of the most commonly used alloys is stainless steel, a mixture of steel, with added quantities of nickel and chromium.

The rest of the metals are usually classified together, and are usually given the collective title 'minor metals'. Because most of these minor metals are rare and are normally used for the construction of high specification alloys, which are exposed to extreme conditions, they are also commonly referred to as 'advanced materials'.

In recent years, a group of more 'exotic', less abundant, metals has captured the attention of news headlines. They are known as 'rare earths', and they refer

---

1 Platinum, for example, is used for its electrical conductivity properties; gold is used in dentistry for its durability and non-toxicity.
2 Tin is added to copper to make bronze.
3 The aerospace industry, for example, is a heavy user of aluminium and other light metals.

to the group of elements on the periodic table called lanthanides. They include metals with not-so-frequently-used names such as neodymium, europium, dysprosium and, of course, lanthanum, after which the group is named – the elements in the group are shown in Exhibit 8.1. Many of these metals have excellent magnetic properties in relatively small quantities, and are hence used as permanent magnets in many applications. Modern electronics (e.g. smartphones), electric-powered vehicles, wind turbine generators and several other modern technologies rely on these materials. It is, therefore, not surprising that the availability of rare earths is a highly contentious issues, especially when presently more than 95 per cent of the world's supply comes from one country – China.

Within the broad definition of metals, some of their common characteristics include: hardness, the resistance to surface deformation or abrasion; tensile strength, the resistance to breakage; elasticity, the ability to return to their original shape after deformation; malleability, the ability to be shaped by hammering; fatigue resistance, the ability to resist repeated stresses; and ductility, the ability to undergo deformation without breaking. Despite these broad similarities, however, large variations do exist between metals: most of them are greyish in colour, but copper is red, gold is yellow and bismuth is pinkish; their melting points range from −39° C for mercury to 3,410° C for tungsten; iridium is the densest of the metals (specific gravity 22.4) and lithium is the least dense (specific gravity 0.53); bismuth has the lowest electrical conductivity and silver the highest.[4]

As we will see, several of these properties are crucial for the choice of the appropriate metal for each use. Hence, steel is preferred for its hardness, but also for its elasticity, in building. Copper has excellent ductility and high conductivity, which makes it suitable for electricity transfers.[5] Also, several metallurgical techniques have been developed over the years with the aim to improve (or eliminate) some of the physical properties that are desirable (undesirable).

Supply determinants

Like other minerals, metals are classified as exhaustible – or non-renewable – natural resources. They have, therefore, the same characteristics as those described for energy commodities. The central concept behind the supply of mineral commodities is the determination of a feasible rate of extraction, which will neither deplete the resource too quickly nor leave it unexploited for too long. Let us start at the beginning, however.

---

4 Conductivity observed at normal temperatures; under extreme temperatures, conductivity properties change.
5 Copper, however, is relatively heavy, as opposed to, for example, optic fibres.

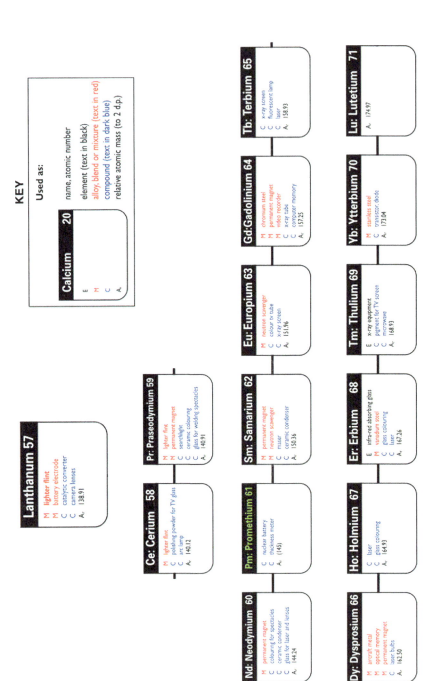

KEY

Used as:

name, atomic number

element (text in black)
alloy, blend or mixture (text in red)
compound (text in dark blue)
relative atomic mass (to 2 d.p.)

Calcium	20
E	
M	
C	
A_r	

Lanthanum 57
M lighter flint
M battery electrode
C catalytic converter
C camera lenses
A_r 138.91

Ce: Cerium 58
C lighter flint
C polishing powder for TV glass
C arc lamp
A_r 140.12

Pr: Praseodymium 59
M lighter flint
M permanent magnet
C searchlight
C ceramic colouring
C glass for welding spectacles
A_r 140.91

Nd: Neodymium 60
M permanent magnet
C colouring for spectacles
C ceramic condenser
C glass for laser and lenses
A_r 144.24

Pm: Promethium 61
C nuclear battery
C thickness meter
A_r (145)

Sm: Samarium 62
M permanent magnet
M neutron scavenger
C maser
C ceramic condenser
A_r 150.36

Eu: Europium 63
M neutron scavenger
C colour tv tube
C x-ray screen
A_r 151.96

Gd: Gadolinium 64
M chromium steel
M permanent magnet
C video recorder
C x-ray tube
C computer memory
A_r 157.25

Tb: Terbium 65
C x-ray screen
C fluorescent lamp
C laser
A_r 158.93

Dy: Dysprosium 66
M aircraft metal
M optical memory
M permanent magnet
C laser bulbs
A_r 162.50

Ho: Holmium 67
C laser
C glass colouring
A_r 164.93

Er: Erbium 68
E infra-red absorbing glass
M vanadium steel
C glass colouring
C laser
A_r 167.26

Tm: Thulium 69
E x-ray equipment
C pigment for TV screen
A_r 168.93

Yb: Ytterbium 70
M stainless steel
C transistor diode
A_r 173.04

Lu: Lutetium 71
A_r 174.97

Exhibit 8.1 'Rare earth' elements

Source: Adapted from a poster by ABPI, www.abpi.org.uk/our-work/library/posters/Pages/table-of-elements.aspx

Exhibit 8.2 Escondida copper mine in Chile
Source: BHP Billiton

Extraction

The first stage of mineral supply is the extraction of the metal-bearing ore. This depends on a number of factors, ranging from geological conditions to the market price of the commodity.

Geological conditions

The geological formation of the mineral-bearing area determines the extent and quality of reserves. Large proved reserves are necessary for any mineral project to even begin, as the whole process takes a long time and is extremely capital-intensive. In fact, long lead times – normally more than four years – are characteristic of mineral projects, and the process of turning a mere suspicion of possible reserves into a fully fledged ore-producing unit consists of several consecutive phases:[6]

- exploration for economic concentration of the mineral;
- evaluation of mineralisation during exploration;
- discovery;

6 Trocki (1990).

- evaluation and feasibility study of discovery;
- construction of the mine, which can be an open or an underground pit;
- mining of the ore;
- ore processing and refining; and
- distribution of the ore to the final markets.

At the exploration stage, the aim is to collect as much information as possible at the lowest possible cost. The techniques usually employed include aerial surveys and geochemical sampling, and these will provide a first indication of mineral concentration in an area. Once geological anomalies indicate possible mineralisation, more precise – and costlier – methods are used to determine the extent and quality of reserves.

These methods include more frequent sampling and a more detailed geologic mapping. The precision of the mapping will be verified by drilling the prospect – a technique identical to wildcat drilling in oil exploration. When adequate samples have been tested and indicate, with a satisfactory degree of certainty, that the project has the required size and quality characteristics, it is registered as a discovery.

The next stage is to carry feasibility studies regarding the development of the project. This will include plans about the development of underground or open-pit mines, and the design of a proper transport network to transfer the ore from pit to consumption point. Another issue that is increasingly taken into account is the effect of the mining project on the flora and fauna of the area, so that landscaping is now an integral part of many new ventures.

Once all the studies are in place, and finance has been arranged, the project enters the developmental stage. This includes the purchase of capital equipment and the hiring of labour in order to construct the mine and put in place all the accompanying infrastructure. This stage might take 1–2 years to complete, assuming that there are no major natural obstacles to overcome.

The procedure does not end, however, with the extraction of the mineral. The raw material is usually processed before leaving the country of origin,[7] and then has to be transported from the processing plant to the export terminal. From there, distribution is usually the responsibility of the metal fabricator, but this can vary from case to case.

The above description is applicable for a project starting from scratch – a so-called greenfield project. Not all mining ventures are greenfield, however. In fact, they are classified into several categories:

- ancient mines, which have been mined for several centuries;
- previously mined deposits, which were abandoned in the past, but are now redeveloped, perhaps with the introduction of new technology;
- expansions, which are attached to already existing mines;

---

7 Crushing is usually the minimum, while further processing might also take place, such as pelletising in the case of iron ore.

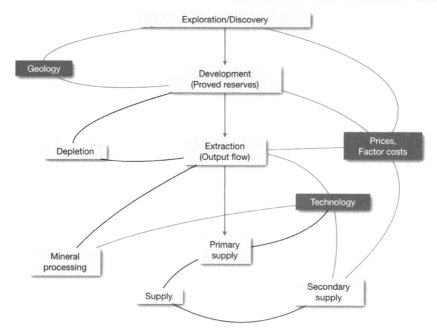

Exhibit 8.3 The mineral supply process
Source: Author

- previously known mineralisations, which have been known in the past but have never been drilled or defined;
- previously known deposits, which have been drilled and defined, but were not previously mined because they were considered of inferior quality;
- greenfield discoveries, which are projects starting from scratch, as was discussed before; and
- related discoveries, which are usually brought to light soon after major greenfield discoveries.[8]

Technology

Technology does, of course, play a great role in determining the rate of extraction and the degree to which probable reserves turn into proven reserves. In fact, technology might even make the difference in reaching the decision to develop a project. One particular area where technology plays a crucial role is transport. A typical example of this is found in the history of iron ore: exports of the raw commodity jumped in the 1950s and 1960s with the introduction of larger vessels that made economical the transportation of that relatively cheap commodity, over long distances.

8 Trocki (1990).

Improvements in mining technology are also important, especially when underground excavation is used. Technological advances, for example, changed the face of coal mining, from a labour-intensive to a capital-intensive production process. Technology is also the parameter that might make some – previously uneconomical – reserves worth exploiting.

Metals can also be manufactured from recycled material. In fact, scrap may be an important source of secondary supply for some metals (e.g. aluminium), and may originate from the manufacturing process of crude metal or metal manufactures (manufacturing scrap), or from obsolete final products (recycling scrap), such as aluminium from cans, and steel plate from car bodies and ships. Advances in technology affect the extent to which metal supply originates from primary or secondary sources. In the aluminium industry, for example, it is actually quite cost-effective to recycle, while, in the steel industry, technological advances in the electric arc furnace allow steel to be produced entirely from scrap material.

Technological advances may also alter the way production is organised in metal manufacturing, which affects in turn the way mineral supply responds to new manufacturing procedures. We will see in more detail how the advent of 'mini-mills' has affected the way the steel industry has restructured its supply contracts with mineral producers.[9]

Economic conditions

Geological and technological conditions alone do not determine the decision to develop a mineral resource. Several economic parameters come into play, and these include capital and labour intensity, the cost of inputs, and the price of the extracted ore itself. The cost of capital and labour – the fixed and variable production inputs – together with the specific geological conditions, determine the final combination of these inputs and the shape of the production curve. Assuming that the producing firm has the objective of maximising its profits, production will expand until marginal cost equals marginal revenue from the sale of the commodity.

The main drawback of the analysis used before is that it is, by definition, static. When dynamic price determination is of importance, a number of additional considerations enter the model, such as the nature of long- and short-term supply of production inputs, and the way these inputs are phased into production. As was discussed before, mineral production is a large-scale process that requires several years to set up, in order to run it at the minimum possible cost. As a result, any decision to alter production fundamentals cannot be implemented immediately; a number of time lags intervene between the decision to change production and the actual change itself. Labys (1980) lists three different types of lags:

---

9 Note, however, that technological progress was not the only reason for change; economic conditions played an even more important role.

(1) an implementation lag [1–2 years], which is the time lag between a change in price and the reaction by decision makers; (2) a technological or developmental lag [1–4 years], which is the time required to place new mining capacity into full production; and (3) an exploration lag [≥4 years], which is the time between the decision to explore for new deposits and the utilisation of the deposits in production.

The existence of so many lags implies that the response of supply, to changes in prices, is rather slow. As a result, supply conditions remain fairly stable for long periods and simply absorb – rather than react to – demand changes. Hence, capital-intensive low-variable-cost mines prefer to continue operating under unfavourable prices, as long as operating costs are covered. Such a behaviour, for example, has been observed in the copper market, whereby copper producers prefer to hold inventories when prices are low, and ration supplies when prices are high, in order to sustain short-term price stability.

Despite any attempts for price stability, however, long-term price trends cannot be ignored. Supply will eventually have to adjust to any structural changes of demand. The problem, however, is that with total lead times of well over 6–8 years, the effect of new projects coming into production could be devastating to a market much different from what it was when the project began. One such example of a new mining project that was heavily criticised for its bad timing was the Carajás project, a massive iron ore development in the north of Brazil. Production from that project was added to international iron ore supply at a time when prices were under immense pressure and, in fact, several steel mills had to cancel liftings of the ore that were specified in their contractual obligations with the mines.

Finally, supply decisions are very much affected by the economic objectives set by the mining company. Profit maximisation is a central assumption in the classical supply model, but other objectives – such as employment, foreign exchange earnings and so on –may assume greater importance.

Resource ownership and concentration in supply

Until now, we have looked at considerations facing the individual producer of the metallic ore. It is often, however, that production and investment decisions are dictated by the structure of the industry, its participants, and the degree of concentration of supply. Mineral projects require substantial capital investments, which impose an entry barrier for new participants. The firms that are already in the market are few and large, and their commitment is imposed by the level of exit costs.[10] Similar considerations arise in the case of metal manufacturers, who also tend to be large in size and vertically integrated.[11]

10 Costs incurred when a firm decides to liquidate its investment and abandon the sector.
11 With vertical integration, we mean the concentration of all stages of metal casting and shaping in the same plant, in order to take advantage of more efficient production and economies of scale.

With this kind of operational constraint, it is not surprising that, in most mineral and metal markets, power is concentrated in the hands of a few countries or companies. In many cases, governments – especially in developing countries – are largely involved in the development of mining projects, because they view them as an integral part of their economic development plans. In doing so, they tend to assume a majority stake in such projects, in order to retain control of the foreign exchange earning capacity of the mining operation.

Of course, ownership concentration in the hands of a few companies only gives rise to oligopolistic – or, in some extreme cases, in the past, even monopolistic – behaviour. The copper industry in the United States, for example, has been scrutinised for price-setting oligopolistic behaviour, and their aluminium industry was monopolised by Alcoa at the beginning of the century, before the company was broken down – much like what happened to Standard Oil. Oligopolistic behaviour does not always imply collusion among suppliers; firms might be following the pricing decisions of one of the bigger firms (although not necessarily the biggest), which becomes the market leader. One such example is the case of US Steel, the largest North American steel manufacturer, which has often assumed a price-setting role in the US market, with the remaining steel manufacturers following suit.[12]

One should note, however, that the mere existence of just a few producing firms does not necessarily imply oligopolistic behaviour. Sometimes demand structure has a considerable bearing on suppliers' behaviour. In the market for iron ore, for instance, procurement of imports is often undertaken by private or government agencies representing a country's steel manufacturers; this effectively creates a monopsony in the particular country and, if imitated by other importing countries, an oligopsony on a global basis. The situation then becomes much less clear, but it certainly puts a lot more pressure on suppliers to behave competitively.

Metallurgy

Metallic ores themselves are of no use to the final consumers. Metals have to be extracted from the ore and then refined and processed, in order to give them the required characteristics for use in myriads of industrial processes.

An entire field of science – metallurgy – is concerned with the extraction, refining and preparation of metals for their final use, and the study of methods to enhance their properties. In the following two chapters, we will look at some of the most important aspects of metallurgy that are important to the metals in question from an economic and trading point of view.

Generally speaking, metallurgical processes are classified into two types of operations: concentration, involving the separation of the metal or metallic compound from the useless rock material, or gangue, which is attached to it;

---

12   This behaviour is also called *signalling*. See, for example, Martin (1994, p. 157), where the case of US Steel is described.

and refining, which involves processing until the metal reaches a pure or nearly pure state. Both operations may use chemical, electrical or mechanical means to achieve their ends.

One of the simplest methods of mechanical separation takes advantage of the difference in specific gravity between metals, or metal compounds, and the rock materials. When crushed ore is suspended in water or an air blast, the heavier metal or metallic mineral particles fall to the bottom of the processing chamber, and the lighter gangue is blown or washed away. One of the most popular methods of mechanical separation is flotation. In this process, fine ore, water and a small proportion of oil – called a flotation reagent – are mixed; metal particles, with the aid of the oil, float at the top of the solution, and can thus be removed and further processed.

The most well-known chemical separation method is smelting, which is usually the second stage after mechanical concentration. Smelting is used for the extraction of iron, aluminium, lead, nickel and other metals, from their ores.

Electrostatic separation employs an electric field to separate minerals of different electrical properties by exploiting the attraction between unlike charges and the repulsion between like charges.

Several other processes are also used at later refining stages, such as pyrometallurgy, distillation and electrolysis. Electrolysis, for example, is the method used to refine copper to a 99.9 per cent degree of purity; it is also used for nickel, zinc, silver and gold. We will look at some of these processes in more detail, when we discuss iron, aluminium and copper.

Demand determinants

Although agricultural commodities are more closely related to human subsistence, metals had a central role in rendering agriculture more productive, and it is metals – together with fossil fuels – that have shaped the world we live in today. We drive cars made of steel; we work in office blocks that have steel and aluminium to reinforce their construction; we move electricity in cables that are made of copper; we fly in aeroplanes made mostly of aluminium; we use computers driven by silicone-based microchips; the list is endless. To try to identify every single end use of metals is a bewildering task. Some major industrial sectors are, however, identified in order to study consumption patterns for various metals – construction, car manufacturing, shipbuilding, machinery and aerospace are representative examples of such broad classifications.

While end users are quite clearly on the demand side, and ore producers are also clearly on the supply side, metal fabricators provide the vital link between the two and stand with one leg on each side of the demand/supply equation. For the student of international trade in metals and their ores, the two-tier structure of the market makes necessary the separate study of the market for the metal and that of its ore, while keeping in mind that the two form a continuous production process that must remain uninterrupted in order to work efficiently.

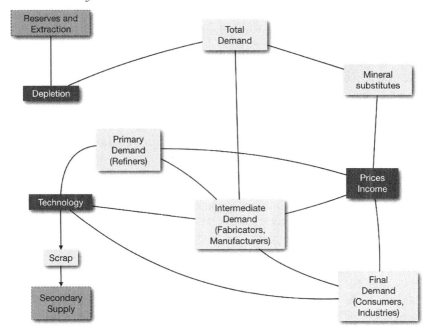

Exhibit 8.4 The mineral demand process
Source: Author

Demand for a metal – and, consequently, for its ore – ultimately depends on the industrial sectors that use the metal. In order to estimate demand, one has to study demand trends and patterns on a sector-by-sector basis, and then compile an aggregate forecast.

A second consideration is the fact that metals are used to manufacture durable goods. This implies that consumers will reinvest in a similar product, only after a few years have passed; think, for example, how often you invest in a new car or a new washing machine. In a similar manner, a growing economy builds up its capital stock[13] for a number of years until it reaches a plateau, after which construction is undertaken primarily for the upkeep and renewal of existing stock.

Metals, of course, are not used only for durable goods. Packaging material is an example of an end product making use of metals; if the consumption of the packaged goods increases, demand for the metal also increases. Such was the case for soft drink cans, for instance; aluminium replaced tin in cans and any change in the demand for canned soft drinks affects demand for aluminium. New products may also come on the market, which introduce a

13 Capital stock may include all conceivable durable goods, which almost invariably contain metals in one form or another. Examples would be: steel beams for construction of infrastructure and transport equipment; copper for telecommunications cabling; and aluminium for construction and engineering.

new use of an old metal; such is the case of aluminium – yet again – whose consumption was boosted by the advent of compact discs.

As for any other good, demand for metals depends on their market price, and the flexibility of demand is expressed by their price and income elasticities. Both elasticities depend very much on the elasticity of the demand for the final good, in whose production the metal is used. Copper, for instance, has been estimated to have a unitary income elasticity[14] and a very low price elasticity.

A major factor in determining demand for metals is their cross-substitutability. In many applications, metals can substitute each other and, in some cases, substitution may be permanent.[15] Substitution may also take place between metals and other materials. In the packaging industry, once again, metal may be substituted by glass, wood or plastic, depending on the product. Although most of the examples are from metals, rather than mineral ores, any changes in the demand for metals is usually directly transmitted to the demand for their ores, as ores are almost exclusively used for the production of a specific metal.

A final important consideration is the concentration of control on the demand for mineral commodities and metals. As was pointed out in the previous section, metal fabricators stand between mineral producers and final consumers, and thus act both as consumers (of raw materials) and suppliers (of final products).

In their first capacity, metal fabricators may negotiate with the ore producers on an individual or on a collective basis; the first method implies competition, the second indicates an attempt to concentrate control on demand. An example of collective bargaining can be found in the iron and steel industry, where Japanese steel mills negotiate collectively their iron ore contracts with their main suppliers in Australia, and the same is true for German mills and Brazilian ore producers.

As suppliers, metal fabricators sell their products to a number of industrial sectors that make use of the metal for the construction of yet more complex products that will eventually reach the final consumer. Some of the largest of these users are bound to have some degree of demand power. Car manufacturers, for example, are heavy users of steel, and their procurement decisions have a considerable impact on the demand for this product.

Price formation

The most interesting feature of the markets for metallic ores is the procedure for price determination. A variety of different types of prices are quoted for each ore and metal, depending on the type of market and the type of the transaction.

Pricing may differ between ores and the finished metals, although there is typically a link (on a netback basis) between the two. Ores are usually required

14 Lord (1993, p. 192).
15 Like aluminium has substituted tin in canned drinks.

on a continuous basis, in order to keep the mill or smelter running on a continuous basis, as shutting down such an operation can be quite expensive. Stocks are typically held both by the mine and the smelter, but there is hardly any public information on available stocks, unless one is prepared to incur considerable costs to acquire market intelligence.

To maintain the continuous running of such an operation, a mix of contracts is typically used, including long-term contracts (LTCs, typically ca. for 10 years or even longer), medium-term ones (3–5 years perhaps) and short-term ones (typically for one year, or even for individual shipments on the spot market). In many cases, the ore itself contains very large amounts of waste material, which makes it uneconomical to ship as is. As a result, the ore is processed to remove as much waste material as possible in order to create a concentrate, which is what is eventually shipped. A good example of this is copper, which is typically found in concentrations of 0.5–5 per cent in copper-bearing ores. As a result, copper ores are processed to produce copper concentrates, which typically contain at least 25 per cent copper, or more.

At the other end of the spectrum, we have the finished metal, often both as a pure metal and in the form of alloys, as well as shaped products. For example, steel is traded in several shapes (slabs, billets, coils and so on), as well as several specifications in terms of its content of alloying metals and other elements. In addition, steel is also traded in the form of alloys, the most popular of which is stainless steel. On the other hand, copper is almost entirely traded in its pure form, typically as cathodes or bars, before it is further processed and mixed with other alloying metals by fabricators.

Given the variety of the ways that metals and their minerals are produced, processed and traded, it is not surprising that a number of different pricing practices have evolved. For example, for some ores and concentrates, prices may be fixed throughout the duration of the contract or may be renegotiated at regular intervals. Although such prices may be publicised, the full details of the contracts, such as quantities, delivery details, freight and so on, frequently remain confidential, so that no two prices are directly comparable.

Export prices for ores are usually quoted on an FOB basis, in which case the importer needs to make adequate allowances for freight and insurance costs. In some cases, however, prices are also quoted on a CIF basis.

Prices should also be distinguished according to the ownership relation between the buyer and the seller. In the 1950s and 1960s, most metal manufacturers had made direct investments in mining capacity, in order to guarantee supply of raw materials. Pricing between parent and subsidiary (i.e. transfer pricing) rarely reflected real market conditions. As many fabricators moved out of, or reduced their stake in, mining operations, deals were increasingly done on an arm's-length basis, thus ensuring a greater degree of pricing transparency. Deals, of course, are not made on a long-term basis solely. Spot markets do exist, but in most cases they are used to top up supply, especially in periods of increased demand.

As LTCs became the dominant way of trading in ores, it became quite common to sign the contract for a long period to secure the quantity of the ore, but renegotiate the price on an annual basis in order to review the market demand and supply conditions and reflect them in the price. In more recent times, particularly from the mid-2000s onwards, annual price negotiations for some metals (notably iron ore) have given way to more market-driven pricing. As a result, it is now more common to observe LTC prices being reset in shorter intervals (e.g. quarterly) and determined on the basis of spot prices.

Similar to ore producers, metal fabricators invariably keep stocks, in anticipation of demand fluctuations. Stocks are used not just for satisfying spot market needs, but also to fulfil contractual obligations in the future. This gives rise to a substantial market of contracts for forward delivery and, for some metals that are easy to standardise,[16] a futures market has emerged. The three most valuable functions of a futures market are: to provide risk hedging; to facilitate price discovery; and to be a last resource for the supply of the metal. It is the second function that has prevailed as the most competitive method to set prices, even for cash transactions. Futures prices, particularly those set at the London Metal Exchange (LME), have permeated pricing not only for the finished metals, but also in many cases for the ore or its concentrates. So, instead of negotiating a direct price for an ore or concentrate, market participants use LME prices (where possible) to determine the price of the

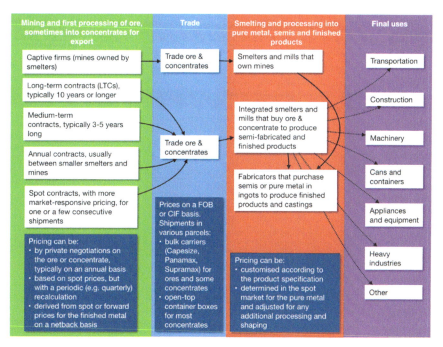

Exhibit 8.5 Price formation for minerals and metals

Source: Author

16 Such metals are aluminium, copper, tin, zinc and lead.

metal contained in the ore or concentrate (on a percentage basis) and then adjust it for any treatment and refining charges that need to be incurred in order to smelt the metal out of the concentrate. These treatment charges and refining charges are often known in their shorthand form as TCRC.

Unfortunately, not all metals have homogeneous qualitative characteristics, so that prices may need to be set for a wide range of custom-made products. The most notable case is that of iron and steel. Iron ore comes in many different qualities, which are determined by the degree of iron content. Because of this large variability in quality, prices have to be quoted for each individual ore. The same is true for steel products, which come in a large array of completely different specifications, and therefore have to be priced separately. Although steel futures contracts are now traded on the LME and other commodity exchanges, prices are quoted for only certain qualities of steel, typically billets or rolled coil.

We will return to pricing of, and price risk hedging for, metals and minerals in subsequent chapters, but for now a generalised overview is given in Exhibit 8.5.

References

Labys, W.C. (1980) *Market Structure, Bargaining Power and Resource Price Formation*, Lexington, MA: Lexington Books.

Lord, M.J. (1993) *Imperfect Competition and International Commodity Trade: Theory, Dynamics and Policy Modelling*, Oxford: Oxford University Press.

Martin, S. (1994) *Industrial Economics, Economic Analysis and Public Policy*, New York: Macmillan.

Trocki, L.K. (1990) 'The role of exploration in iron and copper supply', *Resources and Energy*, 12: 321–338.

9   Iron ore and steel

Iron is the most widespread of all metals. It is used almost invariably in the form of steel, which is present in almost every aspect of our everyday life. The buildings we live and work in; the cars we drive; the electrical appliances we use; the drills to extract oil; the machines we construct to manufacture new goods – all are made of, or contain, steel because of its strength and flexibility. As Fish (1995) puts it, 'Steel is a material essential for the modern world. The industrial revolution would not have been possible without the development of iron and steel'.

Iron, however, is not a new metal; its use has been widespread for several thousand years.[1] It was the development of technology that could produce it cheaply and in large quantities that made it indispensable for the Industrial Revolution.

Physical characteristics

Iron – or *ferrum* as it is known in Latin – is a magnetic, malleable, greyish-white metallic element. In the periodic table of elements, its symbol is Fe; it has a specific gravity of 7.86; it melts at 1,535° C; it boils at 2,750° C; and it loses its magnetic properties at about 790° C. The metal exists in three different forms: ordinary, or α-iron (alpha-iron); γ-iron (gamma-iron); and δ-iron (delta-iron). The internal arrangement of the atoms in the crystal structure of the molecule changes in the transition from one form to another. Iron is an allotropic element (i.e. each of its forms has different physical properties). Allotropy and the difference in the amount of carbon taken up by each of the forms play an important role in the formation, hardening and tempering[2] of the steel.

Chemically, iron is an active metal. It combines with fluorine, chlorine, bromine, iodine, sulphur, phosphorus, carbon and silicon. It burns in oxygen to form ferrosoferic oxide (Fe_3O_4). When exposed to moist air, iron becomes

---

1 The earliest specimen known today, a group of oxidised iron beads in Egypt, dates from about 4000 BC.
2 Tempering is the process of bringing steel to proper hardness and elasticity by heating after quenching.

corroded, forming a reddish-brown, flaky, hydrated ferric oxide, commonly known as rust.

Iron is one of the most abundant elements, estimated to make up ca. 5 per cent of the earth's crust. It is very rare for metallic iron to appear in free form; instead, it is most frequently found in chemical compounds (i.e. ores). In general, grades of iron ore around the world range from 30 to over 70 per cent Fe. The principal ferrous ores are:

*   hematite (Fe_3O_4), which is the most common and, in its pure form, contains 70 per cent iron;
*   magnetite (Fe_2O_3), which, when pure, contains about 72 per cent iron;
*   limonite ($HFeO_2$);
*   ilmonite ($FeTiO_3$);
*   siderite ($FeCO_3$), containing about 48 per cent iron;
*   pyrite (FeS_2), containing 47 per cent iron; and
*   taconite, containing 15–35 per cent iron.

The first four oxides are the most widely used iron ores. Pyrite – an iron sulphide – is the least common because of the difficulty in extracting the metal from the compound. Taconite is the ore with the most impurities, and has to be beneficiated and agglomerated before it can be used; some North American ores are taconites, and this is where pelletisation has been heavily used. Beneficiation and agglomeration will be discussed in the following section.

Sometimes, iron ore deposits also contain valuable minerals of copper, titanium, phosphorus, vanadium, cobalt and, occasionally, even gold and silver. In the past, gold has been recovered from iron ore operations in Minas Gerais in Brazil; copper, cobalt, minor accounts of nickel, and unspecified amounts of gold and silver occur in the ore at Hierro, Peru.[3] Therefore, it is common for the ores to be processed before they leave their origin in order to recover any of the above metals.

Supply determinants

Iron is a metal that can be found in almost every country around the world. The problem is that it may be found in quantities that are too small, or formations that are too impure, to exploit. In North America, taconite formations are found in the Mesabi range in the Lake Superior region. Most North American iron formations contain 30 per cent or more total iron, 60–80 per cent of which is economically recoverable.

Better quality iron formations are found in South America, especially Brazil. Brazilian itabirites are usually richer in iron content; the term was applied originally in Itabira, Brazil, to a high-grade massive specular hematite ore (66 per cent Fe), and is now used to describe formations in which ore is present in thin layers of hematite, magnetite, or martite. Iron ore may also be present

3 Bolis and Bekkala (1987, p. 9).

in riverbed deposits, such as the Robe River deposit in Australia; or in manganiferous or titaniferous compounds, such as the ores found in Canada, India and New Zealand.

Before we look at individual countries, however, we need to discuss in more detail the production characteristics and initial processing of iron ore.

Iron ore processing

As we have seen, iron is abundant and can be found in a variety of compounds. However, not all ores can be used directly for the ironmaking process. Plain, unconcentrated iron ore as it leaves the mine is classified as crude ore. If this ore can be used with minimal crushing and screening, it is considered as direct-shipping ore. This is also frequently known as lump ore, and refers to any relatively unbeneficiated product, with granules generally sized between 6 and 30 mm.

Usually, however, most ores need to be beneficiated (i.e. processed until a considerable part of the gangue[4] has been removed and their iron content improves). Hematite and magnetite are concentrated by means of magnetic separators. Other ores, however, are concentrated by screening or flotation. In all cases, the products of the beneficiation process are called concentrates.

After beneficiation, the ore has the proper iron content, but may not be suitable yet for use in the blast furnace, because the size of the ore particles is too small.[5] At this stage, iron ore is usually known as fines, a term that refers mainly to the size of the ore granules, and is very important because it affects the usability of the ore in the blast furnace.

Most iron ores with a particle diameter of less than ¼-inch must be agglomerated. *Agglomeration* is a process in which small particles are combined to produce larger, permanent masses. There are two principal types of agglomerates – sinter and pellets.

Sinter is produced by firing a mixture of fine ore, lime or limestone, and coke on a moving horizontal grate. The result is a rather brittle product, suitable for blast furnace feed, but sensitive to handling and transportation; this is the reason why almost all sintering facilities are located next to steel mills.

Pellets are the product of a process whereby very fine iron ore (pellet feed) is rolled into 'green'[6] pellets, using bentonite[7] as a binder, and then fired at 1,250–1,350° C in a furnace to produce the final indurated product. Pellets are normally between 9 and 16 mm, with less than 5 per cent below 5 mm; have excellent burning characteristics, and hence are ideal for blast furnace feed; and are also resistant to handling and transportation, which is why pelletising plants are usually located near mines.

---

4 Non-metallic part of the ore.
5 If the ore is too fine, it cannot be fed in the blast furnace, because it 'chokes' it and results in lower recovery rates of pure iron at a higher cost.
6 I.e. unfired.
7 A type of clay.

Exhibit 9.1 Iron ore pellets
Source: LKAB

Pelletising normally yields products of at least 60 per cent Fe content, with the average being 65 per cent Fe. The process was originally used in the United States and Canada as a means of recovering more iron from the low-grade taconite ores that were available domestically. North America still possesses the largest pelletising capacity in the world, with over 80 million tons for the USA and Canada combined. In free-market economies, Brazil and Sweden have considerable facilities, while Russia (combined with Ukraine and Kazakhstan) has over 65 million tonnes of capacity in place. Finally, China has very rapidly grown its pelletising capacity, as its steel industry has expanded, rising to first place in the world.

Reserves and production

Although iron ore deposits can be found in most countries, their distribution is not even. As can be seen in Exhibit 9.3, four countries dominate the list of top reserve holders and control ca. two-thirds of world reserves: Australia, Brazil, Russia and China.

The face of the iron ore industry has changed dramatically since the beginning of the twentieth century. Until the 1950s, most of the iron ore used in Europe was produced domestically – mainly in France, Sweden, Spain and Germany. As domestic reserves were depleted and post-war reconstruction multiplied the need for steel, iron ore had to be imported from abroad, often over long distances. Today, only Sweden has any reserves worth mentioning. In North America, the United States and Canada have traditionally been

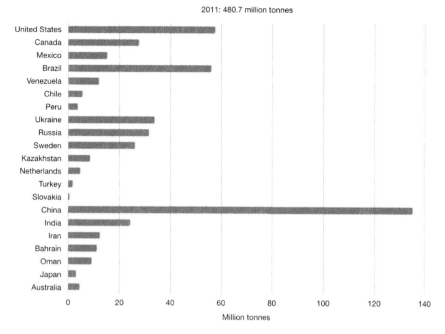

Exhibit 9.2 World pelletising capacity
Source: USGS (2013, Table 15)

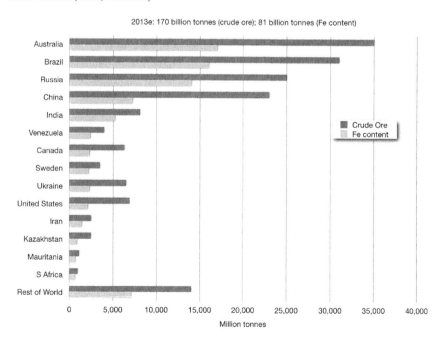

Exhibit 9.3 Iron ore reserves
Source: USGS (2014)

important producers of iron ore, but their entire output is consumed domestically, or channelled in intra-regional trade. South America rose to prominence after the 1950s, especially Brazil, which competes directly with Australia in the export markets.

China remains the world's largest producer, but none of its production finds its way into the international market. On the contrary, because of the astounding domestic absorption, the country is in fact the world's largest importer. Australia is the world's second largest producer and emerges as Asia's prime supplier of iron ore. African production is predominantly channelled to China and Europe, with most of the deposits located in Western Africa and South Africa.

Exhibit 9.4 summarises the key iron ore producers and how their output has developed in the five years from 2008 to 2012. It will serve as a useful *aide memoire* as we turn our attention to the individual geographic regions.

Western Europe

Today, Sweden is the only important Western European producer, with Austria and Germany the only other countries in the region registering any production at all. Sweden's deposits are estimated in the range of 3.5 billion tonnes (with an iron content of 2.2 billion tonnes) and are produced mainly in the northern part of the country. Some of these deposits are located above the Arctic Circle, and contain some of the world's most important high-grade

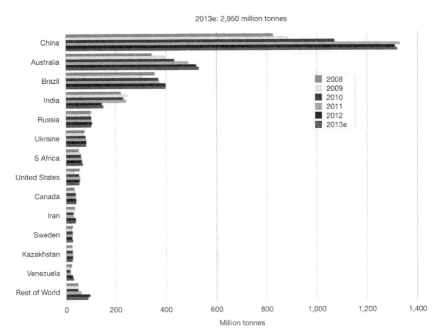

Exhibit 9.4 Iron ore production

Source: USGS (2014)

iron ore; the ore bodies of the Kiruna district – Kirunavaara, Luossavaara, Malmberget and Svappavaara – account for over 90 per cent of Swedish exports. The rest of Swedish production originates in the Grangesberg area in central Sweden, with the principal mines about 150 km west of Stockholm.

The country's iron ore production and exports are dominated by Luossavaara-Kirunavaara AB (LKAB), a state-owned mining company, which was established in 1890. The company ships a number of ore grades with %Fe-content ranging from 61.8 per cent for KDFs (Kiruna D Fines – high phosphoric), to 70.6 per cent for MAFs (Malmberget A Fines – low phosphoric). One important characteristic of Swedish mines is the fact that they are underground, as opposed to the open-pit mines in countries such as Brazil and Australia, which are less costly to operate, and thus more competitive in pricing their products.

North America

Most of the available iron ore reserves in North America are located in the United States. Crude ore reserves are estimated in the region of 6.9 billion tonnes for USA and 6.3 billion tonnes for Canada, with Fe content of 2.1 and 2.3 billion tonnes, respectively. Most resources are primarily low-grade, taconite-type ores, of the Lake Superior district, that have to be processed in order to be suitable for commercial purposes.

Apart from the Lake Superior region, other iron ore resources of the United States are widely distributed in several geographical regions, including Alaska and Hawaii. Several of the old mines are now out of action, however, and the main iron-ore-producing region is around Lake Superior, which includes the Mesabi, Cuyna, Vermillion and Fillmore ranges in Minnesota, the Black River Falls and Baraboo districts in Wisconsin, the Gogebic Range in Wisconsin and Michigan, and the Marquette and Menominee districts in Michigan.

There are several mining companies producing iron ore in the United States and Canada. In the United States, Cliffs Natural Resources (formerly Cleveland Cliffs) is the most dominant. They produce a number of iron ore products, with sinter and pellets being the most common. In Canada, production is dominated by the Iron Ore Company of Canada (IOC).[8] The other two producers are ArcelorMittal Mines Canada (formerly Quebec Cartier Mining – QCM)[9] and Wabush Mines – owned by Cliffs Natural Resources.[10]

---

8 IOC is owned by Rio Tinto, Mitsubishi Corporation and the Labrador Iron Ore Royalty Income Fund.

9 QCM was sold in 1989 by US Steel to the USA's Dofasco (50 per cent), Japan's Mitsui (25 per cent) and Brazil's Caemi (25 per cent). In 2005, Dofasco acquired all of Caemi's shares. In February 2006, Arcelor acquired 88 per cent of Dofasco's shares. And in June 2006, Arcelor announced its merger with Mittal Steel, to form ArcelorMittal, the world's largest steel producer. Eventually, QMC was renamed to ArcelorMittal Mines Canada.

10 In early 2014, Cliffs announced that Wabush mines were not competitive any longer and that the operation would shut down.

Production in the United States and Canada should be examined as one, since all of the iron ore output is used in the regional steel industry, especially in steel mills in the United States.

South America

Brazil rose to prominence by becoming Japan and Western Europe's most important supplier. In the 2000s, China attracted most of the Brazilian exports, as we will see later. Brazilian resources are estimated in the region of 29 billion tonnes (with an estimated 16 billion tonnes of iron content), and are located primarily in two states – Minas Gerais (in the southern, more developed part of the country) and Para (in the northern, more remote and less developed Amazon region). In the south, the deposits are found mainly in the 'Quadrilatero Ferrifero',[11] while in the north they are found near the municipality of Maraba in the Carajás range. The mines in the Quadrilatero Ferrifero have provided most of Brazil's production and exports, while production from the Carajás project started only in the mid-1980s. However, the Carajás resources are of magnificent abundance and quality; some 18 Bmt are estimated to be in place; their grade is in the region of 66 per cent Fe; and the project is designed to yield some 35 Mmt per annum, at full capacity.

Brazilian iron ore production is dominated by a massive state-owned company, with considerable interests in other metal and non-metal commodities: Vale, which started life as Companhía Vale do Rio Doce (CVRD). Vale produces about 80 per cent of the country's iron ore, with grades ranging from 61 to 67 per cent Fe. Samarco, a joint venture between BHP Billiton and Vale, is the only other sizeable iron producer in the country. Several other smaller companies were primarily joint ventures between Vale and steel companies from Germany, Japan, Italy and Spain. Most of these companies have been absorbed into Vale and exist as long-term partners in pelletising plants.

Other Latin American producers include Venezuela, Chile and Peru. Of these, Venezuela is the most important, with reserves estimated at 4 billion tonnes of crude ore, and production about 15–20 million tonnes per year. The entire production is handled by the state-owned CVG Ferrominera Orinoco, which operates four principal mines at Cerro Bolívar, El Pao, San Isidro and Los Barrancos. With the exception of El Pao, all the mines are in the 'Bolívar Iron Quadrilateral', which is located in the valley of River Orinoco and its tributary Caroni.

Oceania

After China, the most important producer of iron ore in the Pacific Rim is Australia. Production was at an all-time high of 525 million tons in 2012, most of which is exported, with iron ore reserves estimated at about 29 billion tons

11 Iron Ore Quadrilateral.

of crude ore. Most of the Australian output is exported to other Pacific Rim countries, particularly China, Japan, South Korea and Taiwan. About half of Australia's iron ore comes in the form of lumps, while the remaining is usually pelletised at destination, although a small pelletising capacity of 4 mtpa is in place. As Bolis and Bekkala (1987) note:

> Australia is one of the lowest cost producers of iron ore in the world, making its operations very competitive on the world market. This is attributable to several factors – large, high-grade deposits; high production; highly automated nature of the industry in both mining and shipping; and short distances from [Chinese and] Japanese markets.

Most Australian deposits are located in Pilbara, Western Australia, with a few mines in the state of South Australia and the island of Tasmania. A handful of mining companies control the iron ore industry in Australia, and are also involved in the mining of most other metallic ores. The largest of these companies is BHP Billiton, which operates its own mines and also participates in joint ventures with other producers.

Hamersley Iron used to be the other major iron ore producer, and almost as influential as BHP in Australia's economy and politics. The company is wholly owned by Rio Tinto, which started life after the merger of two British companies with interests in Australian mining. Nowadays, the name Hamersley Iron survives only in older annual reports, and the mines are managed by Pilbara Iron, a wholly owned subsidiary of Rio Tinto. The company's mines are also located in the Pilbara region, and include Yandicoogina, Hope Downs, Mt Tom Price, West Angelas, Greater Paraburdoo, Mt Brockman and Marandoo. Savage River Mines is one of the few projects not located in Western Australia. It is majority-owned by Grance Resources, with a minority stake by the UK's Stemcor, and the mine is located in Tasmania.

Asia

Asian output is dominated by two main producers – China and India. The latter was traditionally a considerable iron ore exporter, especially to the Pacific market. In the 2000s, exports have declined, as India's own requirements for domestic steel production have increased and the government imposed an export tax on the commodity.

India has been producing about 200–245 million tons of crude ore per annum, which come from a number of private and state-owned companies. The National Mineral Development Corporation (NMDC) has mines in Bailadila (470 km from the port of Visakhapatnam), and in Donimalai (in the Bellary-Hospet region, 500 km from Madras). NMDC's entire production is handled by the state-owned Minerals & Metals Trading Corporation of India (MMTC), and it is sold to the Asia Pacific market, mainly China and Japan.

Apart form MMTC, there are a number of private companies that produce – and trade in – iron ore. There are two other important production zones in

India – Kudremukh and Goa. The first is operated by KIOCL, while in the second there are several mines (in Sanquelim, Sonsbi, Orasso Dongor, Rivona, Guelliem and Codli), which are run by Sesa Sterlite, a subsidiary of the privately owned Vedanta Resources. Other prominent iron ore producers/ traders include Dempo, Salgaocar, Chowgule and several smaller companies.

China produced some 1.3 billion tonnes of crude ore in 2012, and is also the world's largest importer of further quantities, which come from Australia, Brazil, South Africa, India and Peru. Traditionally, the country's imports were handled by the state-owned China National Metallurgical Import & Export Corporation (CNMIEC), but its role diminished, with the major steel plants of the country, instead becoming more active in procuring their own needs in iron ore. The major Chinese steel producers – Hebei, Baoshan Iron & Steel (Baosteel) and Wuhan Iron & Steel (WISCO) – are already large importers and often seek to secure long-term imports by participating in mining investments around the world.

Africa

The most significant iron ore producers on this continent are located in the west and south of Africa. Traditionally, Liberia was the most important iron ore producer in Western Africa, but civil unrest hit production after 1988. As a result, Mauritania has now emerged as the second most important African producer, after South Africa.

Liberian production was mined at the Nimba mountains and exported through the port of Buchanan. The concession was given in 1953 to the Liberian-American-Swedish Company (LAMCO). Operations were ceased in 1989, and the concession was surrendered because of the civil war. Since 2003, when the former president Charles Taylor lost power and the new transitional government came to power, attempts were made to attract new investors to the Nimba project. In August 2005, Mittal Steel (ArcelorMittal) won the concession for 25 years.

In Mauritania, production is in the region of 10 million tonnes per annum, and is controlled by SNIM SEM (Société Nationale Industrielle et Minière), a joint venture between the state, Kuwait Real Estate Investment Consortium, Arab Mining, Iraq Fund for External Development, BRPM-Morocco, and the Islamic Development Bank. The company exports its production through the port of Nouadhibou.

The Republic of South Africa is the top iron ore producer in Africa, with about 60 million tonnes produced in 2012. Most of the production comes from the Sishen mine, which is located in the heart of the country, north of the Orange River. Production was handled by Iscor, the originally state-owned (but later privatised) company, which also operated the electric railway that transports the iron ore from the mine, over a distance of 860 km, to Africa's deepest port – Saldhana Bay. From 2002, Mittal Steel started acquiring minority interests in Iscor, until 2004 when the company came under the complete control of the group and became Mittal Steel South Africa. Saldhana

Bay is also used for exports from the Khumani and Beeshoek mines, which is located some 930 km inland and operated by the Associated Manganese Mines of South Africa (Assmang).

A few other African countries also produce iron ore, but in quantities that are rather insignificant for the international market, although their production is important for their domestic needs. These countries are Algeria, Tunisia, Zimbabwe, Nigeria, Morocco and Egypt, and deposits are also present in Gabon, Ghana, Cameroon and Côte d'Ivoire.

Eastern Europe

The combined production of all of its constituent democracies places the former Soviet Union at the top of the world league of iron ore producers. Although production has been falling since the late 1980s, FSU production is in the region of 200 Mmt per year, which nowadays accounts for less than 7 per cent of world production. Soviet ores are mostly low-grade, with %Fe contents ranging from 20 to 50 per cent. All ores undergo beneficiation and have to be agglomerated to sinter or pellets. This is the reason why the FSU has considerable pelletising capacity – some 74 million tonnes – which accounts for ca. 15 per cent of global capacity.

Of the former Soviet states, Russia, Ukraine and Kazakhstan are the most important producers, with Azerbaijan making a small contribution as well. In Russia, there are several mines, most of which have annual run-of-mine capacities in excess of 10 Mmt. These are: Bogolovsky Mine in the Sverdlosk region in Urals; Lebedinsky Mining & Dressing Plant in Belgorod; Michailovsky Mine in the Kursk region; Sibruda – Siberian Scientific & Industrial Mining Amalgamation in the Kemerovo region; Stoilensky Mine in Belgorod; and Uralruda Mining Production Amalgamation in the Sverdlovsk region in Urals. Many of these mines have rather low-grade ores – often as low as 20 per cent Fe – which decreases the quantities of high-grade ore that can be produced after beneficiation and agglomeration. Evraz is today one of the leading iron ore, steel and coal producers not only in Russia, but also in Ukraine, North America, South Africa, and several EU countries. Another well-known producer is Severstal, with mines in the Karelia Republic and the Murmansk Region. Like Evraz, Severstal is also mainly known as a major steel producer.

In a similar manner, most Ukrainian mines have run-of-mine capacities in excess of 10 million tonnes per annum. Most mines are located in the Dnepropetrovsk region: Inguletsky Ore Mine & Concentrator; Krivbassruda Ore Mining Amalgamation; Krivorozhsky Central Mine; Krivorozhsky Yuzhny Ore Mine; Novokrivorozhsky Mine; Poltavsky Mine; and Severny Mine.

Kazakhstan has five mines, three of which have annual capacities of over 10 Mmt. These are: Kotomukshky; the Lisakovsky; and Sokolovsko-Sarbaisky. Finally, Azerbaijan has the much smaller Severo-Zapadny mine, which produces just about 2 million tonnes per year. As in the case of Russia,

Ukrainian, Kazakh and Azeri ores have an average 30 per cent Fe content, which needs considerable beneficiation and agglomeration.

Steel manufacturing

Iron ore is almost exclusively used in the production of steel. There are, however, a few chemical compounds of iron that have a variety of other minority uses. Ferrous sulphate ($FeSO_4$), called 'green vitriol', is used as a mordant in dyeing, as a tonic medicine and in the manufacture of ink and pigments. Ferric oxide, an amorphous red powder, is used as a pigment, known as either iron red or Venetian red; as a polishing abrasive, known as rouge; and as the magnetisable medium on magnetic tapes and disks. Ferric ferrocyanide ($Fe_4[Fe(CN)_6]_3$) is a dark-blue amorphous solid, called Prussian blue; it is used as a pigment in paint and in laundry bluing to correct the yellowish tint left by the ferrous salts of water. Finally, potassium ferricyanide ($K_3Fe(CN)_6$), called red prussiate or potash, is used in processing blueprint paper.

Despite all these 'exotic' uses of iron, however, steel production remains the main force that drives the iron ore industry. Steel, in its simplest forms, is the most basic good needed for the industrialisation process of any economy. In fact, crude steel production is often a signal of a buoyant manufacturing sector. The steel sector, of course, is not defined just by crude steel. Advanced steel products and steel alloys are goods of high added value, in which many industrial countries specialise, leaving the bulk of the production of 'plain', unalloyed steels to developing countries, with low labour costs.

Demand for steel products is derived from a variety of industries, and it is therefore segmented. The biggest consumers of steel products are: transportation; construction; machinery; cans and containers; appliances and equipment; mineral exploration industries; and any other sector that is not covered above.

The analysis of demand determinants for crude steel and steel products falls within the framework of the analysis of demand for metals, as was discussed in Chapter 8; there is therefore no need for further discussion. We are, however, going to focus our attention on the production process of iron and steel products, in order to gain an understanding of the areas where steel is most commonly used.

Ironmaking

The first step in processing the beneficiated – and possibly agglomerated – ore is its reduction to iron. There are two main processes for doing so: blast furnace reduction and direct reduction. Blast furnace reduction is the most widespread method, so we are going to discuss it first.

Blast furnace

The blast furnace is a 'tower', specially built to withstand high temperatures, into which sinter or pellets, coke and limestone are fed from the top. Coke is nothing more than coal that has been 'carbonised' in ovens, in order to improve its burning properties.

As these products fall in the tower, they encounter the rising hot reducing gases and eventually settle on previous loads fed from the top. To keep the process going, hot air[12] is blasted through special nozzles – tuyères – so that the temperature of the coke remains at about 2,000° C. The iron in the iron ore, sinter or pellets is melted out to form a pool of molten metal – known as pig iron – in the bottom – or hearth – of the furnace. As iron accumulates in the hearth, it is removed periodically from the furnace – an operation called tapping. The limestone combines with impurities and molten gangue from the ore, forming a liquid slag that, being lighter than the metal, floats on top of it, and is also removed periodically. The charging system at the top of the furnace also acts as a valve mechanism to prevent the escape of gas, which is taken off through large-bore pipes to a gas cleaning plant. Exhibit 9.5 shows production development in key countries over the last five years. It is no surprise that China stands head and shoulders above the rest, with its pig iron production growing without interruption even after the 2008 financial crisis.

Blast furnaces rely on two important economic factors: first, that the process is continuous; and, second, that substantial quantities of pig iron are produced, in order to take advantage of scale economies. A modern blast

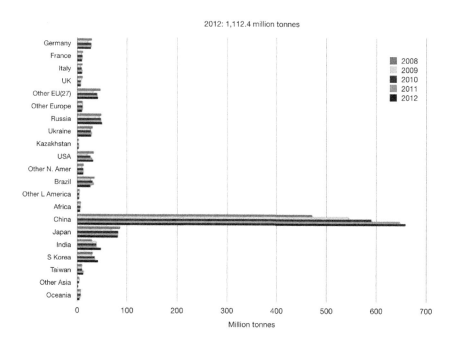

Exhibit 9.5 Pig iron production

Source: Author, compiled with data from World Steel Association (2013)

12 Frequently, hot air is enriched with oxygen.

furnace produces about 1 mtpa, while an integrated steel facility should have a turnover of about 3 mtpa, in order to operate efficiently.

Direct reduced iron

An alternative reduction process was developed by Midrex and HYL, whereby iron ore is mixed with coke or natural gas, and heated to about 900° C, in order to increase its iron content, normally to over 80 per cent. The result of the process is not pig iron, but a product known as sponge iron, which can be fed directly to an electric arc furnace (EAF) to produce steel. Sponge iron – or direct reduced iron (DRI) – is more desirable than scrap in EAF steel-making, because it has a lower level of metallic residuals and other impurities than recycled scrap.

The main drawback of this method is its high requirement for fuel. As a result, DRI plants are primarily located in energy-rich countries, such as Venezuela, Mexico, Iran, Saudi Arabia, India and Indonesia.

There are a few more ironmaking methods, which are of small significance right now, but might have a bigger effect in the future. Most of these techniques are still in the developmental stage – although for a few, commercial production has already started – and are: Eldred, Inred, Plasmamelt, DIOS, HIsmelt, Krupp-COIN, Combismelt, and Corex. The common characteristic of all the above is that they employ direct smelting or smelting reduction technology. This process, which was originally developed by Nippon Kosan and Kawasaki,

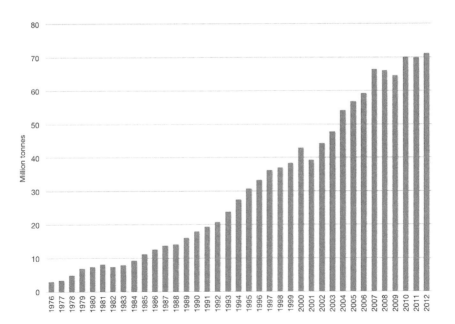

Exhibit 9.6 DRI production development

Source: Author, compiled with data from World Steel Association (2013)

allows the smelting and reduction of iron ore in a single process, and has four main objectives:

1   the direct input of iron ore, without need for sintering or agglomeration;
2   the substitution of coal for coke;
3   lower capital and operating costs; and
4   production on a smaller, and ecologically more sound, basis.

The Saldhana plant of Mittal Steel South Africa uses the Corex/Midrex method into a continuous chain, producing some 1.2 million tonnes of hot roll steel coil (HRC) per annum. The gist of the Corex process is that it uses coal instead of (more expensive) coke, and the whole process has a useful by-product – gas – which can be used as fuel to produce hot-briquetted iron.

Steelmaking

The manufacture of steel is quite a separate procedure from that of iron, although both procedures coexist in large, integrated steel mills. There are two methods of making steel, which are the most important – the basic oxygen furnace/converter (BOF/BOC), and the electric arc furnace (EAF). Before these two, steel was produced with the open-hearth method, but this process is now obsolete, although antiquated open hearth furnaces still exist in the FSU. Exhibit 9.7 shows the shares of the different steelmaking methods.

Before focusing on the two main steelmaking methods, it is worth having an overall look at the key steel producing regions, as shown in Exhibit 9.8. With Asia being the *de facto* manufacturing centre of the world, it is little

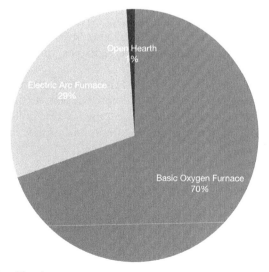

Exhibit 9.7 Steelmaking by process

Source: Author, compiled with data from World Steel Association (2013)

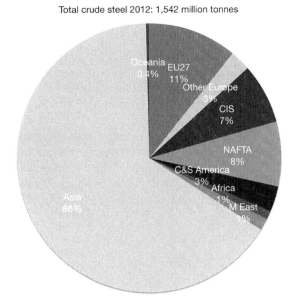

Total crude steel 2012: 1,542 million tonnes

Exhibit 9.8 Crude steel production by region

Source: Author, compiled with data from World Steel Association (2013)

surprise that it produces ca. two-thirds of the global steel output. The EU, North America and the FSU represent the old generation of steel producers and collectively generate ca. another quarter of world production.

A more detailed list of the top crude steel producers is shown in Exhibit 9.9. China is, of course, the great outlier, forging ca. 45 per cent of world steel. Japan, India and South Korea are the top Asian producers, with Germany, Turkey, Italy and France in Europe; Brazil and Mexico in Latin America; and other traditional producers, such as the US, Russia and Ukraine, completing the list.

Finally, Exhibit 9.10 lists the top 25 steel-producing companies. The reader may notice that although Arcelor Mittal and Nippon & Sumitomo[13] top the list, there are also 10 Chinese producers on the list that collectively produced ca. 300 million tonnes, representing less than half of the total production of the country in 2012.

Basic oxygen furnace

In the BOF method, scrap (25 per cent) and molten iron (75 per cent) are charged into a vessel – the converter. A water-cooled oxygen lance is lowered into the furnace and high-purity oxygen is blown on the metal at very high

---

13 The full name of the company is Nippon Steel & Sumitomo Metal. The two companies merged in 2012.

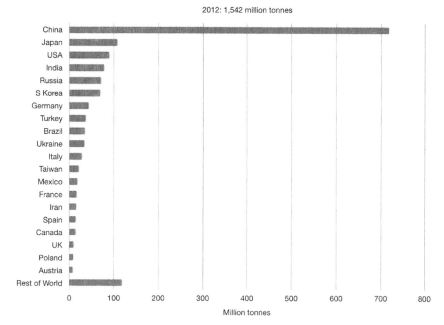

Exhibit 9.9 Top crude steel producers

Source: Author, compiled with data from World Steel Association (2013)

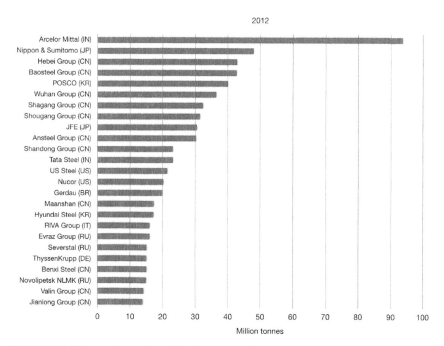

Exhibit 9.10 Top crude steel-producing companies

Source: Author, compiled with data from World Steel Association (2013)

pressure. The oxygen combines with carbon and other unwanted elements, thus eliminating the impurities from the molten charge.

These oxidation reactions produce heat, and the temperature of the metal is controlled by the quantity of the scrap added. The carbon leaves the converter as a gas (carbon monoxide) that can, after cleaning, be collected for reuse as a fuel. During the 'blow', lime is added as a flux to help carry off the other oxidised impurities as a floating layer of slag. Modern converters will take a charge of up to 350 tons at a time and convert it into steel with a charge-to-tap time of 40 minutes or less.

Electric arc furnace

Cold scrap, or sometimes DRI, is the only input of the EAF process. As its name implies, the process uses a powerful AC or DC electric current to melt the scrap or DRI. The furnace consists of a circular 'bath' with a movable roof, through which three graphite electrodes can be raised or lowered. At the start of the process, the electrodes are withdrawn and the roof swung clear. The steel scrap is then charged into the furnace from a large steel basket lowered from an overhead travelling crane. When charging is complete, the roof is swung back into position and the electrodes lowered into the furnace.

When the current passes through the charge, an arc is created, and the heat generated melts the scrap. Lime is added as flux and oxygen is also blown into

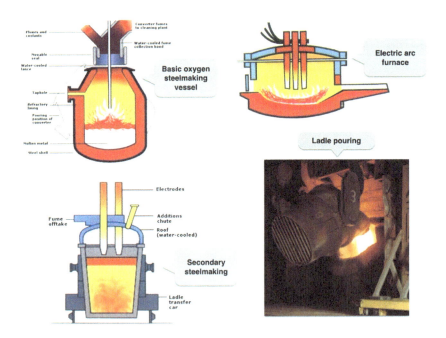

Exhibit 9.11 Steelmaking

Source: www.worldsteel.org

the melt, so that impurities form a liquid slag and are removed at the end of each charge. Modern electric furnaces can make up to 150 tonnes of steel in a single melt, in less than an hour and a half.

Other methods

With the exception of open-hearth steelmaking, which is now obsolete, the only other alternative method is the high frequency induction furnace. The process uses electricity to melt a charge of cold scrap, but it does it using a coil, rather than cathodes. Furnaces of this type are usually less than 5 tonnes capacity.

A number of secondary metallurgy methods are used to rid the steel from some harmful elements, which result from the oxygen process. More specifically, secondary metallurgy methods are used to: improve homogenisation of temperature and composition; remove deleterious gases, such as nitrogen, oxygen and hydrogen, in the steel; allow careful trimming of composition to exact ranges of analyses; remove phosphorus and sulphur; and refine the quantity of other metallic elements in the steel.

Steel processing

When the molten steel forms at the bottom of the oxygen converter, or the electric furnace or after secondary processing, it is poured – or tapped – into a ladle; at this stage, the steel has an average carbon content of less than 1 per cent and any alloying elements that need to be added are charged to the hot metal at this stage. The next step is moulding, which aims to form the steel in usable final products.

Moulding

Before steel can be rolled or formed into products for sale – such as plates, sheets, strips, beams, bars, tubes or sections – it has to solidify and be formed into standard basic shapes called *billets*, *blooms* or *slabs*.[14] To achieve this, the molten metal has to be cast in ingot moulds where it is left to solidify; this process is called teeming. Almost always, the metal needs to be reheated and reworked into more intricate shapes.

The most popular moulding technique used today is continuous casting. In this process, instead of going through the ingot stage before being reheated and rolled, the molten metal is teemed directly into a casting machine to produce billets, blooms and slabs. Continuous casting, therefore, eliminates the need for primary and intermediate rolling mills, as well as the need for large numbers of ingot moulds.

---

14 Typical cross-section dimensions for these products would be: slabs (rectangular) – 1,500 mm to 2,000 mm wide and 50 mm to 250 mm thick; blooms (square) – 150 mm each side; billets (square or round) – 150 mm each side or in diameter.

The process works as follows:

- a ladle of steel is brought to the continuous casting plant by overhead crane;
- after pre-treatment, which may involve stirring by the injection of an inert gas (argon), the open mouth of the ladle is covered by an insulating lid, to reduce heat loss;
- the whole unit is lifted by crane on to a rotating turret – this makes sequence casting possible (i.e. a number of ladles of the same grade steel can be cast without stopping the machine);
- the ladle nozzle is opened, allowing the steel to flow out of the ladle, through a gas-tight tube, into the tundish, a reservoir supplying the water-cooled copper mould of the casting machine, at a controlled rate; and
- with only its outer shell solidified, the steel is then drawn downwards from the bottom of the mould through a curved arrangement of support rolls and water sprays until it emerges horizontally as solid steel from the discharge end of the machine, where it is cut by automatic gas cutting equipment to the lengths required.

Hot rolling

Almost all semi-finished steel products undergo further processing at temperatures of 800–1,250° C, in order to produce steel in finished form and in shapes and sizes that are requested by the customer.

Hot rolling is essentially any procedure that involves the reduction of the cross-section of the semi-finished product, by using rolls to exert pressure on the hot metal. The inputs in these procedures are slabs, blooms and billets, and some of the most common products of the process include:

- heavy plates and strips (from slabs);
- rods and bars from billets;
- structural sections, which come in a variety of standard shapes (H, I, U and L sections) and are normally used in construction;
- seamless tubes; and
- custom-made complex steel structures, produced by forging or extrusion.[15]

Cold working

Hot-rolled products are frequently processed further, after they have cooled down. This is done mainly to improve the finished quality of the product's surface or to improve its strength. Cold processing usually involves rolling of the steel, or drawing in order to produce wire, and tube and bar products.

---

15 Forging uses opposing forces to deform the steel into the desired shape; in extrusion, the steel is forced through a die cut to the required shape and dimensions of the finished product.

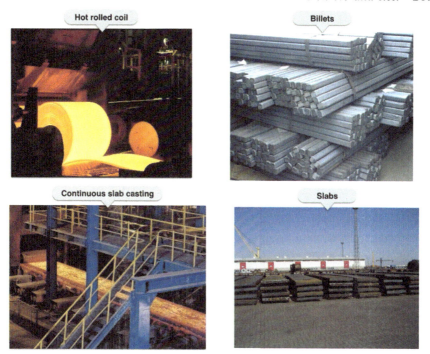

Exhibit 9.12 Casting, rolling, billets and slabs
Source: www.worldsteel.org

The process yields a number of finished goods, such as: cold-rolled wide coil; cold-rolled narrow strip; cold-rolled plate; cold drawn bar; cold-finished bar; cold-drawn tube; and blackplate.

Coating

To improve its anti-corrosive properties, steel is often covered with a variety of metallic and non-metallic coatings. The two most popular types of coated steel are tinplate and galvanised steel, which use tin and zinc, respectively. Galvanised steel, for example, has recently become popular with automobile manufacturers, who have introduced galvanised bodies as a feature in their new models. Apart from tin and zinc, a number of other metals are used for coating steel, such as nickel, aluminium and chrome, which may be used on their own or in alloys specially developed for steel coating.

Non-metallic coatings include paints, plastic lamination (using hard plastic strip) and plastic film. The coating may be necessary for the final good that uses the steel, or just to protect the steel (usually steel plate and coils) while in storage.

Pricing and trade

From the discussion above, three main points emerge, which have a bearing on the way international markets for iron ore are organised:

1   iron ore is almost exclusively used for the production of steel;
2   steel mills are the only customers of iron ore mines and, although scrap can be used to a certain extent, iron ore is by far the most important raw material for steelmaking; and
3   there are only very few dominant iron ore producing countries, which have large capacities and low costs, and dominate the supply side.

Because of these peculiarities, the procurement of iron ore supplies is handled directly by iron ore producers and steel mills. There is less scope for the existence of trading companies, although such companies do exist and frequently act as agents between smaller mines and steel mills.

As we have seen, steelmaking is a continuous procedure. A blast furnace needs a minimum throughput in order to operate at all, and production cannot be halted, except for necessary repairs to the refractory lining; it is paramount that iron ore feed be continuous and guaranteed. It is not surprising, therefore, that steel producers have always tried to achieve some stability and security in the procurement of their iron ore requirements.

In the 1950s and 1960s, many steel mills, particularly in the United States, tackled the problem of supply security through the acquisition of equity stakes in both domestic and foreign iron ore mines. The Japanese, on the other hand, followed a strategy of arranging long-term contracts (LTCs) – usually of 10–20 years, but some of them even evergreen – that would guarantee their supply requirements. Such contracts were also desirable for the mines because they provided them with a substantial collateral, on the back of which debt could be incurred to finance further expansion.

Today, even though direct equity stakes are still in existence, most steel mills secure their supplies through LTCs. Iron ore contracts come in a variety of formats, depending upon the time and duration of the agreement. However, while in the 1970s LTCs of 10 years or more were commonplace, in the 1990s it became difficult to find any contracts with terms more than five years. The 2000s saw a dramatic change in iron ore trading, with the advent of a number of smaller or larger Chinese steel mills who wanted access to higher volumes and quality of iron ore and started tapping the international market. Although LTCs were used, quite a lot of the trade was done on the basis of spot and short-term (less than a year) basis.

Originally, most LTCs were quoted on FOB terms, with the exception of contracts between Australian mines and European mills, which were negotiated on a CFR basis. Nowadays, the key price indices report prices for iron ore delivered on a CFR basis in Chinese ports. Some of the most important features of LTCs include: quantity, term and delivery schedule; loading and discharge terms; quality and quantity monitoring; pricing and payment method; provisions in the case of *force majeure* and/or disputes; and any additional requirements, such as taxes, duties, export licences and so on.

Pricing

Since the first LTCs were initiated in the 1970s, price determination for iron ores was a most intriguing and perplexing procedure, taking place once a year. Since 2009, this has changed, with prices now more reflective of spot market conditions. The price quotation itself is fairly straightforward, at least in comparison to other metals, although rather different to other commodities.

There is no truly 'international' reference price for iron ore, in the way that the price of a barrel of Brent crude is. Ore qualities differ widely, and it is common that ores from different mines have their own quotations. It is also common that prices are quoted for different types of ore; usually, lumps, fines, pellets and sinter.

Prices are quoted in two different ways. The first one is to simply quote the price per dry metric ton (dmt)[16] of ore, while at the same time specifying the type of ore shipped (e.g. lump ore, fines, pellets and so on), as well as the amount of iron contained in the ore as a percentage, known as the *%Fe* content.

The alternative method is to quote prices on the basis of dry metric ton units (dmtu).[17] This simply means that the price is quoted in cents per dmtu (i.e. per 1 per cent Fe in a dmt). Exhibit 9.13 contains a sample of quoted prices for various types of iron ores for the pricing periods Apr-04 to Mar-05 and Apr-05 to Mar-06, the point in time that saw a major shift in the price levels. If we take Hamersley fines as an example, and assuming that they have 62 per cent Fe content, their price in March 2006 would be [61.72¢ × 62 =] $38.27/dmt.

Prior to 2009, prices in the iron ore market were renegotiated and settled once a year. There were two distinct markets: Japan and Europe. The Japanese steel mills started negotiations, around November each year, with each of the Australian ore producers and with Vale (then CVRD) of Brazil. In the European market, negotiations started at about the same time, and were usually conducted between CVRD and two agencies representing interests of German steel mills – Rohstoffhandel and Erzkontor. Price negotiations usually carried through to the beginning of the following year, developing into a 'war of words', with suppliers and consumers trying to demoralise each other.

Although the annual price negotiations were somewhat cumbersome, both mines and steel mills had settled quite happily in this regime, which resolved the pricing issue in a market that was essentially a bilateral oligopoly.[18] The

16 A dry metric ton (or dmt) has the same mass as a normal metric ton, but the material has been dried to remove excess moisture and limit to a maximum amount, which is agreed between the two transacting parties. It is the most common unit of measurement for metallic minerals and concentrates.

17 A dry metric ton unit (or dmtu) is simply an extension of the dmt concept. A dmtu is simply 1 per cent metal content per dry metric ton.

18 See Tamvakis (1999) for a more detailed economic analysis of the iron ore market up until the end of the 1990s.

Country and Producer	Type of Ore	Apr 2004 - Mar 2005	Apr 2005 - Mar 2006
Australia			
Hamersley	Lump ore	45.93	78.77
Hamersley	Fines	35.99	61.72
Robe River	Fines	28.69	49.20
BHP Billiton (Yandi)	Fines	33.83	58.02
Brazil			
Vale Carajás	Fines	32.76	56.18
Vale Itabira	Fines	32.27	55.34
MBR	Lump ore	34.78	59.65
Chile			
MDP (Huasco)	Pellets	59.10	110.32
MDP (El Romeral)	Fines	29.51	50.61
India			
MMTC (Bailadila)	Lump ore	45.25	77.6
Peru			
Shougang Hierro Peru	Pellet feed	25.08	43.01

Exhibit 9.13 Iron ore prices to the Japanese market

Source: Tex Report (2008), prices in US cents/dmtu

status quo started creaking from the mid-2000s, particularly from 2005 onwards. The steep growth of the China was largely fuelled by the expansion of heavy industry and manufacturing. At the centre of this growth was the expansion of the steel industry, which provided the much-needed products for new construction, engineering and infrastructure projects. Domestic iron ore production was not sufficient, so many Chinese steel mills turned to the international market. Only a handful of Chinese steel mills, however, had the bargaining power to negotiate LTCs with mines, or even invest in mines to secure supplies. Numerous small Chinese steel mills had to resort to the spot and short-term market to secure iron ore shipments, and to do this they frequently had to pay well above prices for LTCs.

This practice gave rise to a parallel spot market whereby prices continuously and increasingly exceeded annually negotiated prices and increased the temptation for many mining companies to sell spot rather than commit their production to LTC contracts. What was a temporary market anomaly eventually became the new market reality.[19] Mining companies, led by BHP Billiton, pushed for a switch to a market-led pricing system. Eventually, from late 2009, LTC contracts started being priced on a quarterly basis, with prices calculated as averages of the prevailing spot prices in the three previous months.

The reader can observe this development in Exhibit 9.14, which shows monthly prices for iron ore fines imported in the port of Tianjin in northern China. Prices remained stable from 1978 to 2004, with changes implemented every 12 months and only modest fluctuations between $20 and $30/dmt. Between 2005 and 2009, there was a big price hike, although changes are still implemented only once a year. From the beginning of 2010, prices fluctuated

19 Crowson (2008, pp. 243–244) discusses the strong growth of the spot iron ore market and also mentions the push by some mines to alter the pricing regime.

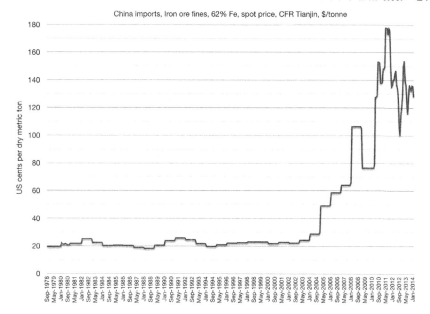

Exhibit 9.14 Iron ore price development

Source: Author, compiled with data from Thomson Reuters Datastream

freely and changes are observed every month, effectively reflecting spot market transactions.

Since the paradigm shift in pricing, market reporting agencies have taken a more active role in reporting iron ore prices. Three key price indices have emerged: MBIO,[20] IODEX[21] and TSI.[22] With the spot market at the heart of the current pricing system, these benchmarks are necessary for market participants, whether in physical cargo deals or for settling financial derivatives used for hedging purposes.

Steel pricing

Pricing of steel products can be quite complicated, because of the large diversity of products, in terms of quality and shape. In Europe and the United States, things are simplified by the publication of official lists of prices by individual mills, which are usually valid for a year. Prices are quoted primarily for the most basic steel products, which have low-grade and shape specifications. Any additional finishing, shaping, cutting to size or coating is charged as an extra to the *basis* price. Steel mills and consumers normally limit their price negotiations to the determination of the basis price and of any quantity discounts that

20 Metal Bulletin Iron Ore Index.
21 Produced by Platts.
22 The Steel Index is produced by SBB (Steel Business Briefing), which is now part of Platts.

may be offered for bulk purchases. In Europe, surcharges are usually accepted by buyers, who concentrate on negotiating basis prices. In the United States, even surcharges are the object of negotiations.

Pricing of steel exports is usually further simplified – in order to facilitate transport and paperwork – and prices are usually quoted on an average, per ton basis. Quotations are also available on an FOB, CFR or CIF basis.

In Japan, prices are less transparent and also less volatile. If there is a need for drastic changes, the burden is usually shared between mills and consumers.

While steel pricing is quite straightforward in Europe, Japan and the United States, other nations (in particular Eastern European mills) do not normally work with price lists. There, all quotations are on a client-to-client basis *as per request*. Export pricing is also on the same basis.

The most important development in recent years is the introduction of the steel billet futures contract on the London Metal Exchange. The discussion of this contract is deferred for a later chapter, but the impact on the market was substantial as it created a pricing benchmark for basic steel and gave rise to other contracts for steel products to be listed as well.

Trade

About 40 per cent of the world production in iron ore is traded internationally, and Exhibit 9.15 shows details of the key exporters. In 2012, world exports stood at between 1.1 and 1.2 billion tonnes, over 70 per cent of which were

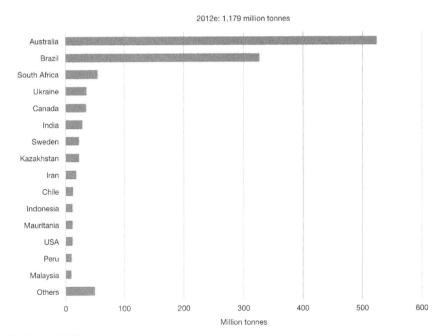

Exhibit 9.15 Top iron ore exporters

Source: International Trade Centre and World Steel Association (2013)

shared by just two countries – Australia and Brazil. Other important – although much smaller – exporters were South Africa, Ukraine, Canada, India and Sweden. Australian exports are almost exclusively destined for Asia Pacific, primarily China, Japan, South Korea and other countries in the region, with only a small flow to the EU market. Brazilian exports also have a bias towards Asia Pacific, owing to Chinese and Japanese demand, although there are still sizeable quantities channelled to EU countries.

Canadian exports are primarily directed to the United States; however, Canadian companies are also very active selling their ore to Europe. Indian exports, although much reduced in recent years, compete directly with those of Australia in Asian markets, while South Africa targets both European and Asian markets. Finally, Sweden exports practically all of its production to other European countries.

As demonstrated by Exhibit 9.16, iron ore imports are even more biased towards Asia Pacific – primarily China, but also Japan and South Korea. In 2012, China imported two-thirds of total iron ore traded internationally, while the rest of Asia imported another 20 per cent of it. Trailing behind are EU countries who collectively imported the majority of the remaining imports, ca. 13 per cent. Exhibit 9.17 shows the details of bilateral iron ore trade flows between they key trading regions.

The vast majority of iron ore trade, over 90 per cent, is carried by sea. The remaining tonnage is accounted for by trade between the United States and Canada, and between the former Soviet republics and other Eastern European

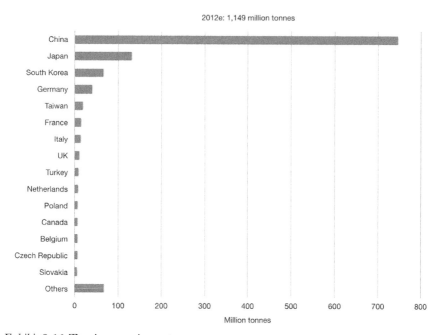

Exhibit 9.16 Top iron ore importers

Source: International Trade Centre and World Steel Association (2013)

Exporters → ↓ Importers	EU(27)	Other Europe	CIS	NAFTA	C&S America	Africa & M East	Asia	Oceania	Total Imports	of which extra-regional
EU(27)	21.4	2.8	31.0	10.4	57.0	12.2	0.2	10.7	145.7	124.3
Other Europe	1.2	0.0	1.7	0.5	3.9	0.4	0.0	0.0	7.7	7.7
CIS	0.0	0.0	3.1	0.0	0.0	0.0	0.0	0.0	3.1	0.0
NAFTA	0.2	0.0	0.0	10.7	1.3	0.1	0.0	0.0	12.3	1.6
C&S America	0.0	0.0	0.0	1.9	10.1	0.0	0.0	0.0	12.0	1.9
Africa & M East	5.6	0.0	0.1	1.0	23.8	0.1	0.0	0.0	30.6	30.5
China	2.3	1.6	35.7	24.2	189.2	65.2	60.3	366.8	745.3	685.0
Japan	0.0	0.0	1.2	1.4	39.3	5.6	2.7	80.9	131.1	128.4
Other Asia	14.1	1.6	0.5	0.9	28.6	7.4	0.5	63.6	117.2	116.7
Oceania	0.0	0.0	0.0	0.0	0.1	0.0	0.8	0.2	1.1	1.0
Total Exports	44.8	6.0	73.3	51.0	353.3	91.0	64.5	522.2	1,206.1	1,097.1
of which extra-regional	23.4	6.0	70.3	40.2	343.3	90.9	1.1	522.0	1,097.2	
Net Exports (EX-IM)	-100.9	-1.8	70.3	38.6	341.4	60.4	-52.5	521.0		

Exhibit 9.17 Iron ore trade matrix

Source: World Steel Association (2013)

countries. The major characteristic of iron ore transportation is the need to take advantage of scale economies, in order to justify the movement of such a bulky and relatively low-value cargo over long distances. Thus, the vast majority of iron ore is carried in vessels of over 100,000 dwt, typically Capesize bulk carriers, between 150,000 and 200,000 dwt. The largest ore carriers are twice that size, with the Valemax class of vessels just touching 400,000 dwt. Exhibit 9.18 demonstrates the development of iron ore trade since 1975. Throughout the 1980s and 1990s, trade fluctuated between 300 and 400 mtpa. From early in the new millennium, especially from 2005 onwards, trade expansion picked up pace, and within the space of just over 10 years tonnage has almost tripled – another manifestation of the sea change brought about in this commodity by the Chinese economic expansion.

Steel trade

World trade in steel products was about 415 million tonnes in 2012, a figure that – when compared with the ca. 1,540 million tonnes of crude steel production – indicates that ca. 25 per cent of world steel production enters international trade. This, however, might be an underestimate of the extent of steel trade, because not all of crude steel is turned into products; a part of it ends up as industrial scrap, and is usually recycled into the steelmaking process.

Steel is a textbook example of intra-industry trade (i.e. a commodity exchanged between geographic regions with similar production factor endowments). As a result, all regions are both exporters and importers of a variety of steel products, whether semi-manufactured or finished. Another interesting aspect of steel trade, which cannot be seen from the data given here, is the

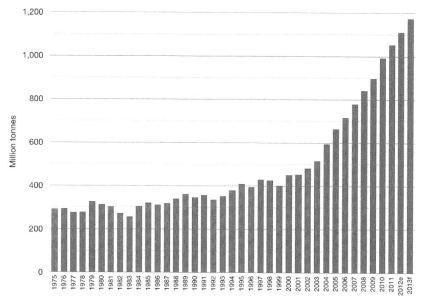

Note: 2012e = estimate; 2013f = forecast

Exhibit 9.18 Seaborne iron ore trade

Source: ISL Bremen Shipping Statistics & Logistics, based on data from Fearnleys (1975–1984); Clarksons Shipping Review & Outlook, Spring 2013, p. 101 (1985 to date)

value of steel products leaving different countries. Quite often, developed steel producers are associated with high-quality, high-value specialised steels and alloys, while developing producers have a comparative advantage in the production of lower-value, basic steel products, such as plates, bars and rods. Exhibit 9.19 shows a breakdown of the various types of steel products traded internationally.

Exhibit 9.20 shows the top 20 importers and exporters, while Exhibit 9.21 narrows down to the top 15 net exporters and importers and Exhibit 9.22 presents the full steel trade matrix. China is the top exporter, whether on a gross or net basis, while the United States holds the same position on the importers' list.

Other top net exporters include Japan, Ukraine and Russia. On the net importer side, Thailand, Indonesia, Saudi Arabia and Vietnam trail behind the Unites States. All are rapidly developing economies, and steel is the basis for the expanding construction, transportation and other infrastructure sectors.

In contrast to iron ore, steel products have mixed transport requirements: the more basic, semi-finished products are usually carried as bulk cargo; specialised finished products, on the other hand, are typically carried as unitised cargo, either in multipurpose or container vessels. Exhibit 9.23 shows examples of steel products stacked up and awaiting transportation. The two bottom pictures show steel coils and tube section loaded in the hold of a bulk carrier and being secured in place for transportation.

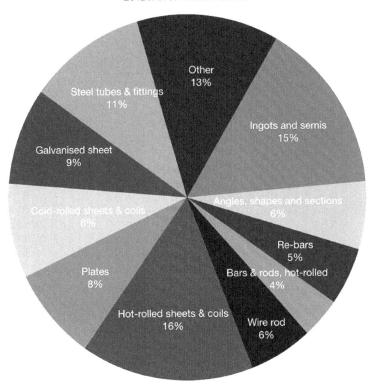

Exhibit 9.19 Steel trade by type of product
Source: World Steel Association (2013)

As mentioned earlier, there is also a smaller, but still quite substantial, trade in steel scrap. The extent of this trade is shown in Exhibit 9.24. One can observe that the EU and North America are the top net exporters, while China and Asia in general are net importers.

Conclusion

Iron ore and steel are the most basic commodities in all developed and developing nations. Steel consumption is synonymous with industrial growth and strength, and hence many developing nations seek to establish steel mills as the basis for heavy industry. Iron ore is almost exclusively used in the steelmaking process, and is therefore closely tied to the fortunes of the steel industry. Although iron ore can be found in most countries around the world, there are very few countries that produce it efficiently and export it in large quantities.

The stability and security required by the operational characteristics of steel plants have made the use of long-term iron contracts, for the procurement of

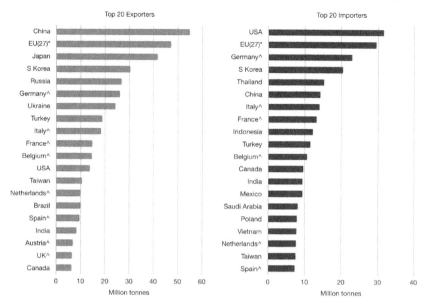

Exhibit 9.20 Top steel exporters and importers

Source: World Steel Association (2013)

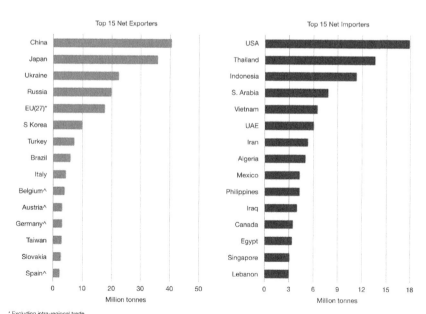

Exhibit 9.21 Top net steel exporters and importers

Source: World Steel Association (2013)

Exporters → ↓ Importers	EU(27)	Other Europe	CIS	NAFTA	Other America	Africa & M East	China	Japan	Other Asia	Oceania	Total Imports	of which extra-regional
EU(27)	101.8	4.5	17.0	0.6	1.0	0.6	3.9	0.4	3.6	0.0	133.3	31.6
Other Europe	10.3	0.7	5.4	0.1	0.1	0.1	0.5	0.6	0.5	0.0	18.3	17.6
CIS	1.9	0.8	9.5	0.0	0.0	0.0	2.1	0.2	0.6	0.0	15.1	5.6
NAFTA	7.1	1.7	2.0	19.4	4.6	0.3	3.1	3.5	8.3	0.3	50.2	30.8
Other America	2.0	1.3	0.8	2.6	3.5	0.1	5.0	1.1	1.6	0.1	18.2	14.7
Africa	8.2	3.6	3.2	0.2	0.1	1.4	3.2	0.7	1.5	0.0	22.1	20.7
M East	2.9	8.6	9.0	0.3	0.2	0.3	4.6	2.0	5.7	0.1	33.6	33.3
China	1.1	0.1	0.3	0.1	0.0	0.0	•	5.8	6.1	0.0	13.6	13.6
Japan	0.1	0.0	0.0	0.0	0.0	0.0	0.9	-	4.7	0.0	5.7	5.7
Other Asia	5.9	0.6	7.9	0.9	2.0	0.6	30.6	26.8	24.0	0.3	99.5	75.6
Oceania	0.4	0.1	0.0	0.1	0.1	0.0	1.0	0.4	2.6	0.3	4.9	4.6
Total Exports	141.5	21.9	55.1	24.4	11.5	3.5	54.8	41.5	59.2	1.1	414.5	
of which extra-regional	39.8	21.2	45.7	4.9	8.1	1.8	54.8	41.5	35.2	0.8		253.7
Net Exports (EX-IM)	8.2	3.6	40.0	-25.9	-6.6	-52.2	41.2	35.8	-40.3	-3.8		

Exhibit 9.22 Steel trade matrix

Source: World Steel Association (2013)

Exhibit 9.23 Steel products in transit

Source: www.wordsteel.org

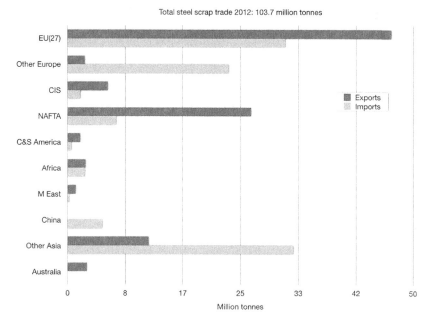

Exhibit 9.24 Steel scrap trade
Source: World Steel Association (2013)

iron ore, indispensable. However, the emergence of China as a major steel manufacturer has shifted the focus of the whole industry entirely to Asia Pacific. This has not only changed the structure of production, consumption and trade; it has also brought about changes in the pricing structure of iron ore, with the introduction of quarterly repricing based on spot market prices.

References

Bolis, J.L. and Bekkala, J.A. (1987) *Iron Ore Availability – Market Economy Countries*, US Bureau of Mines.

Crowson, P. (2008) *Mining Unearthed*, London: Aspermont.

Fish, P.M. (1995) *The International Steel Trade*, Cambridge: Woodhead.

Tamvakis, M. (1999) *An Economic Model of the Iron Ore Trade*, PhD thesis, London: City University.

Tex Report (2008) *Iron Ore Manual*, Tokyo: Tex Report.

USGS (2013) *2011 Minerals Yearbook: Iron & Steel*, United States Geological Survey, accessed online at: http://minerals.usgs.gov/minerals/pubs/commodity/iron_&_steel/myb1-2011-feste.pdf.

—— (2014) *Iron Ore Mineral Commodity Summary*, Unites States Geological Survey, accessed online at: http://minerals.usgs.gov/minerals/pubs/commodity/iron_&_steel/mcs-2014-feste.pdf.

World Steel Association (2013) *World Steel in Figures*, accessed online at: www.worldsteel.org/publications/bookshop?bookID=704c467d-8c30-4980-8720-04a743f91965.

10 Aluminium

Aluminium is the most abundant metal in the earth's crust and the third most abundant of all elements, coming after oxygen and silicon. It is, however, a relatively new metal, isolated only in the first quarter of the nineteenth century by a Danish chemist. Since then, aluminium has come a very long way, and is currently the second most widespread metal after iron, having penetrated several industrial sectors, and having displaced traditional metals, such as copper, tin, and iron itself.

Physical characteristics

Aluminium – denoted Al – is a lightweight, tin-white metal, which has a specific gravity of 2.7, melts at 658° C and boils at 2,467° C. Aluminium is an extremely reactive metal; in contact with air, it rapidly becomes covered with a tough, transparent layer of aluminium oxide, which gives the metal excellent anti-corrosive properties. The metal also reduces many other metallic compounds to their base metals. For example, when thermite – a mixture of powdered iron oxide and aluminium – is heated, the aluminium rapidly removes the oxygen from the iron; the heat of the reaction is sufficient to melt the iron. This phenomenon is used in the thermite process for welding iron.

Most of all, aluminium is sought for its desirable lightweight properties; it has an excellent strength-to-weight ratio, making a given volume of aluminium more than three times lighter than the same volume of steel.

Because of its reactiveness, aluminium is never found on its own naturally. It forms compounds with a number of other elements, including oxides, hydroxides, silicates and sulphates. It is, however, chemically difficult – and therefore expensive – to extract aluminium from most of these compounds. The commercial source of aluminium is bauxite, an impure hydrated aluminium oxide (Al_2O_3 = aluminium trioxide), which has been used extensively since antiquity, in its primary form – clay. Even today, some of the best refractory bricks are made from bauxite clay.

Despite knowledge of bauxite, aluminium metallurgy did not commence until the third quarter of the nineteenth century, and may still have a long way to go. In 1886, Charles Martin Hall in the United States and Paul L.T. Héroult in France, while working independently, discovered the same procedure for separating aluminium from one of its oxides – alumina. They observed that alumina would dissolve in fused cryolite (Na_3AlFe_6) and could then be decomposed electrolytically to a crude molten metal. The process was later enhanced by K.J. Bayer's research in the refining of alumina and gave birth to today's methods of producing aluminium, although modern techniques make much more efficient use of production inputs.

Supply determinants

Bauxite is the raw material used in the production of aluminium; the name denotes any ore that has in its composition more than one-third aluminium oxides. The usual marketable quality of bauxite – the basis grade – contains 40–55 per cent alumina (Al_2O_3), of which about half can be retrieved as pure aluminium; this implies that it takes about 4–5 metric tons of bauxite to produce 1 metric ton of aluminium.

The production process is divided into three distinctive phases: mining, refining and smelting. As for any mineral resource, bauxite has to occur in large enough quantities in order to be worthwhile mining. Production of bauxite usually takes place in open-pit mines, with capacities in excess of 1 million tonnes, although underground mines are also in operation. Almost all extraction is by giant earth-moving equipment, which digs up bauxite after removing overburden, which may vary from less than a metre to a dozen metres deep.

Most bauxite reserves are located in developing countries, with the notable exception of Australia, which holds about one-quarter of total world reserves of bauxite. Other regions that are rich in bauxite reserves are: Western Africa, especially Guinea; Central and South America, especially Brazil and Jamaica; the former Soviet Union, especially Russia and Kazakhstan; India; China; and Greece in Southern Europe. Exhibit 10.1 shows the key regions where

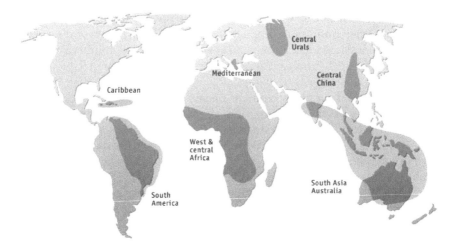

Exhibit 10.1 Location of main bauxite reserves

Source: www.aluminiumleader.com/

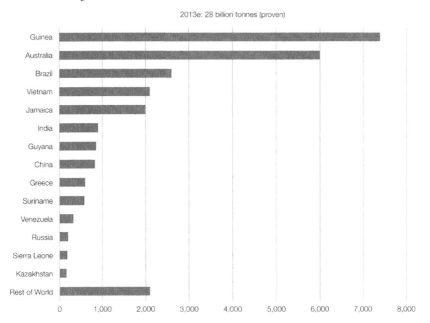

Exhibit 10.2 World bauxite reserves by country
Source: USGS (2014b)

bauxite reserves are available, while Exhibit 10.2 lists the key reserve-holding countries.

Production of bauxite has demonstrated an increasing trend over the last 20 or so years. In 2013, an estimated 258 million tonnes of bauxite were produced around the world, 30 per cent of which originated in Australia. In the Americas, production is dominated by Brazil and Jamaica, followed by Suriname and Venezuela; while African production is almost monopolised by Guinea. Other important producers include China (the world's second largest), Indonesia, India, Russia and Kazakhstan. In Southern Europe, Greece, Bosnia and Serbia are rather minor producers. Exhibit 10.3 lists the top bauxite producers.

The next stage of supply is refining. Bauxite contains many impurities and cannot be used directly for aluminium production. The raw material must undergo a process of beneficiation, after which it turns into a reddish-brown powdery substance – alumina. Alumina refining typically happens close to where primary aluminium is produced, although there are exceptions to this, as one can observe in Exhibit 10.4. China, for example, is the world's largest consumer of aluminium, so it is little surprise that it is also the top alumina producer. Australia and Brazil, on the other hand, export a lot of their production of bauxite and alumina, but also have sizeable domestic production. Conversely, Guinea does not even feature in the list of alumina producers, as all of its bauxite production is simply exported and is refined at facilities owned by the aluminium smelters.

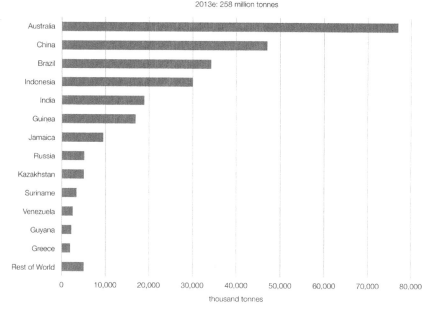

Exhibit 10.3 Top bauxite producers
Source: USGS (2014b)

World alumina production is in the region of 90[1] million tonnes per annum, and it takes place primarily in China, Australia, Central and South America, North America, Western Europe, and the former Soviet Union. The vast majority of alumina production, more than 90 per cent, is of 'metallurgical grade' (i.e. used for aluminium). There is a small amount, less than 10 per cent, which is of 'chemical grade' (i.e. used for all other purposes).

The most important stage in aluminium production is the third one – smelting. Despite significant improvements, aluminium is still produced with the Bayer/Hall-Héroult method. This method has been refined to yield a final commercial product of at least 99.5 per cent purity, although further refinement to 99.99 per cent purity is also achievable.

There are three main inputs in the smelting process: alumina; cryolite, which is now usually synthetic; and electricity. Smelters are large, continuous electrolytic plants, comprising cells – known as pots – arranged in rows – known as potlines. Like the blast furnace in steel production, the aluminium smelters have to produce a minimum rate every year in order to be operational. A modern smelter has a capacity of not less than 100,000 mtpa, while it can produce perhaps as much as 500,000 mtpa. Electricity in massive amounts arrives at the plant, where it is converted to 1,000 V DC at 200,000–250,000 amps. A modern smelter would typically require some 13 MWh per ton of aluminium produced. Production takes place in huge cells, where carbon cells

1 About one-third of bauxite production.

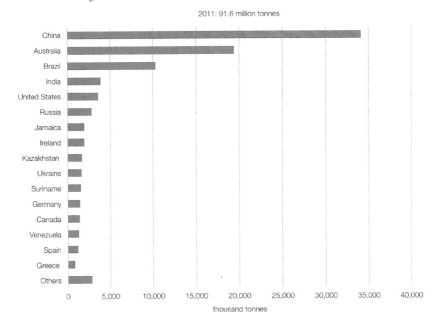

Exhibit 10.4 Top alumina producers
Source: USGS (2013a, Table 12)

– made of pre-baked petcoke – are used as anodes, while the carbon lining of the cells serves as the cathode. The electrolyte is formed by a mixture of alumina and cryolite, and is kept molten by the heat generated by the passage of the electric current. Molten aluminium is formed at the bottom of the cell, as a result of electrolysis, and it is siphoned every 24–48 hours in order to be cast into standard shapes.

As the reader may have guessed, electricity is absolutely central to the smelting process. First of all, it has to be readily available and continuous, as any disruption will cause the electrolyte to solidify, a situation that would take several months of heavy labour to rectify. Second, the cost of electricity is the most important production parameter. Alumina accounts for just about 15 per cent of the cost of final aluminium products, with the remaining going to electricity, capital and labour costs. It is not surprising, therefore, that aluminium production costs and final prices are very sensitive to the cost of energy.

After production of pure aluminium, products can be manufactured with the usual methods of drawing, extracting, forging and rolling. Aluminium products can be formed in many intricate shapes, without any need for further processing.

Primary aluminium production showed an increasing trend through the second half of the 1980s, and stabilised to a total of just over 20 million tonnes worldwide. From 1995 onwards, production surged forward to reach 25 million tonnes by 2000. Since then, aluminium smelting capacity and production have been dominated by the massive expansion of China. In the

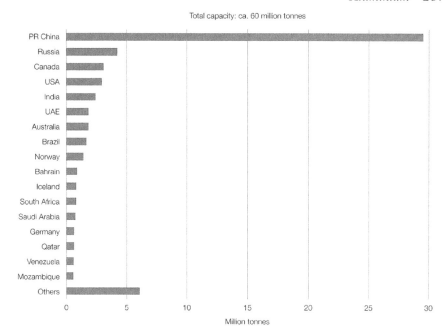

Exhibit 10.5 Primary aluminium smelting capacity

Source: Author, based on data from Pawlek (2012)

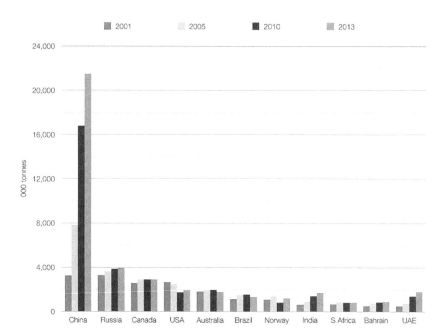

Exhibit 10.6 Primary aluminium production trends in top producers

Source: US Geological Survey, Aluminum Mineral Commodity Summaries 2002–2014

space of just over 10 years, Chinese primary aluminium production increased almost sevenfold. No other country was able to match this, and in fact very few countries recorded an increase, as can be seen in Exhibit 10.6.

Exhibit 10.7 shows the state of affairs in 2013, and one can clearly observe that China produced ca. half of the world's total aluminium. Of the rest, Russia and Canada are the next two most important producers, with the US lagging behind and Australia having been overtaken by the UAE.

Another source of aluminium is the recycling of aluminium scrap. In fact, aluminium recycling is a very efficient process, provided that it is used for large enough quantities. This is the reason why secondary aluminium production is usually undertaken by large smelters, rather than small ones.

Because of the large production costs, the firms involved in the production of aluminium found it necessary to undertake extensive vertical integration from the very beginning. The case of Alcoa – the Aluminium Company of America – is still a textbook case for the study of monopoly in a domestic market. Like Standard Oil, Alcoa's monopoly was brought to an end by legal action, but the need for large-scale, integrated operations has been deeply embedded in the industry's behaviour.

At the time of writing, there are four major companies, each with a production capacity over 3.5 mtpa;[2] seven medium-sized producers, each with

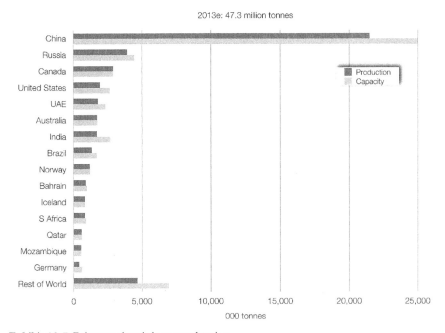

Exhibit 10.7 Primary aluminium production

Source: Author, compiled with data from USGS (2014a)

2 Alcoa, Rio Tinto Alcan, UC Rusal and Chinalco. Canada's Alcan merged with Switzerland's Alusuisse in 2000 and acquired France's Pechiney in 2003, before being taken over by Rio

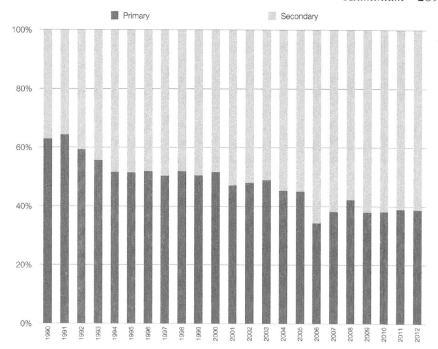

Exhibit 10.8 Primary and secondary aluminium production trend in the US

Source: Author, compiled with data from USGS (2013b, Table 1)

capacities between 0.5 and 1.5 mtpa;[3] a few Japanese *sogo sosha*, which tend to focus on high-end aluminium products (for chemical and computer applications);[4] commodity traders with interests on the mineral side;[5] a few new smelters that are being set up in the Middle East;[6] and a final layer of smaller smelters and fabricators that operate mainly in domestic markets.

Tarring and Pinney (1989) note three factors that have affected the trend of vertical integration in the aluminium industry:

1   the growth of the independent extrusion business, which allowed smaller specialist manufacturers of aluminium products to thrive and decreased the need for extensive vertical integration;

Tinto in 2007. United Company (UC) Rusal was formed in Russia from the merge of several smaller smelters, as well as SUAL and the alumina assets of Glencore. Chinalco has become the world's largest aluminium producer after the consolidation of several smaller state-owned smelters into one larger entity.

3 Hydro (Norway), BHP Billiton (Australia), Dubal (UAE), Alba (Bahrain), Century Aluminium (USA), CVG (Venezuela) and Hindalco (India).

4 Sumitomo, Mitsui, Mitsubishi, Nippon Light Metal.

5 GlencoreXstrata is one such example.

6 Qatalum (Qatar), EMAL (UAE), Sohar (Oman). In 2013, Dubal and Emal agreed to merge into Emirates Global Alumnium (EGA), a company that is expected to be the fifth largest smelter in the world.

2   the increasing competitiveness of aluminium in the cable industry, which made the manufacturing of aluminium an increasingly independent operation and led to the creation of smaller aluminium-cable fabricators; and

3   the growth of secondary aluminium manufacturing, which brought business back to the large integrated aluminium smelters.

Despite tendencies for a more competitive structure of aluminium supply, the fact remains that the majors still have a considerable weight in the international market for aluminium and continue to be very actively involved in all stages of production, from mining bauxite to manufacturing aluminium alloys.

Demand determinants

As for steel, demand for aluminium depends very much on disposable income. Aluminium is the major input in industries that are normally associated with countries at an advanced stage of development – such as the aerospace and automotive industries. Aluminium, however, has several other more 'modest' uses, in which it replaces base metals, such as steel, tin and copper; its cross-price elasticity is therefore very important.

The lightweight properties of aluminium make it indispensable for the construction of aircrafts, railroad cars, automobiles, and for other applications where reduction of weight is the most important requirement. Aluminium is also increasingly used in construction as roofing, cladding and siding on factories, agricultural and residential buildings, and in windows, doors and screens.

Another major use of aluminium is in electricity transfers. Strictly speaking, aluminium is about 35 per cent less effective in transferring electricity, but it is also 60 per cent lighter. Compared to copper wires, aluminium wires are thicker, but still manage to be much lighter. This weight advantage makes aluminium more efficient to use when electricity is transferred through bare (overhead) wires, over long distances, because it reduces the number of pylons that would have to be built to support the much heavier copper wires. Aluminium cables are now used to transmit electricity at 700,000 volts or more; normally, aluminium is stranded on a core of galvanised steel or high-strength aluminium alloy to ensure that cables can be strung in long lengths between towers.

Aluminium has also proved quite popular in the packaging industry, and is used extensively as canning and wrapping material.[7] In fact, it has been so successful that it managed to displace tin as the primary raw material for cans.

Aluminium alloys are also very versatile, offering hardness, corrosion resistance and the advantage of reduced weight in advanced applications. They are used in the defence industry, especially as armour plate for tanks, personnel

7   Think, for example, of the versatility of aluminium foil in everyday household uses.

carriers, and other military vehicles. Alloys are also used in the aircraft and automotive industries, for parts that need to operate under extreme conditions of temperature and pressure.

Aluminium is not the lightest of all metals – lithium, beryllium and magnesium are even lighter; and magnesium in particular may pose a threat to aluminium's widespread use. For the time being, however, magnesium's prices remain high, often because its fabricators refuse to be more flexible. Moreover, magnesium is extremely reactive and burns more violently in air, which has inhibited many applications due to fear of fires and explosions.

In a nutshell, if light weight and strength are vital, aluminium is the answer. In low-value applications, it competes with steel, which is cheaper but heavier; in high-value applications, it competes with other advanced materials, which are lighter but more expensive.

Trade and pricing

An estimated 40–50 per cent of the world's bauxite production is traded internationally, with four countries dominating the export market. The world's largest exporters are Indonesia, Guinea, Australia, Brazil and Jamaica. In recent years, Indonesia made a considerable impact on the export market, driven by the fast-rising import demand from China. China, once again, tops the list of major importers, accounting for over half of world imports. Following at some distance is the United States, which used to be the world's largest importer a decade earlier. More details on key exporters and importers are given in Exhibits 10.9 and 10.10.

Bauxite and alumina constitute the biggest of the minor bulk commodities carried by sea, providing considerable employment for the world's Panamax-sized fleet. Seaborne trade in bauxite and alumina has followed closely the development of the industry through the 1980s. After 1985, when the world economy entered its recovery period, trade increased considerably, from 40 to 50 million tonnes. In recent years, with the demand generated by China, the bauxite and alumina trade has grown even more.

In aluminium, the picture is quite different. Industrial nations are the main exporters of primary (unwrought) aluminium, led by Russia, Canada, the UAE, Australia, Norway and Iceland, as shown in Exhibit 10.11. As far as importers are concerned, the list is topped by the US, Japan, Germany and South Korea, as shown in Exhibit 10.12.

The picture changes again when one looks at international trade not only of primary aluminium, but of its finished products as well. Exhibits 10.13 and 10.14 record the top exporters and importers, respectively, in terms of value of trade, for 2012.

As we discussed earlier, the industry is characterised by vertical integration, with many smelters having equity stakes in bauxite mining projects. Where this is not possible, smelting companies secure long-term supply contracts with bauxite producers, and then locate alumina refining facilities and aluminium smelters in their own countries.

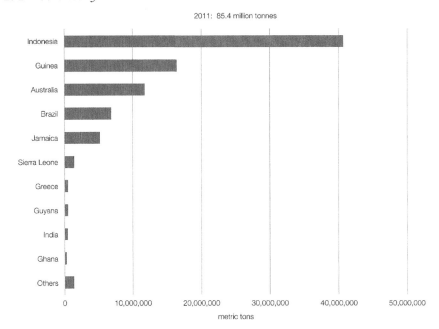

Exhibit 10.9 Top aluminium ore and concentrates exporters

Source: Author, compiled with data from www.trademap.org, SITC code 2606

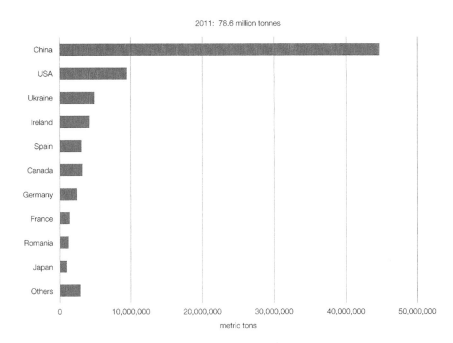

Exhibit 10.10 Top aluminium ore and concentrates importers

Source: Author, compiled with data from www.trademap.org, SITC code 2606

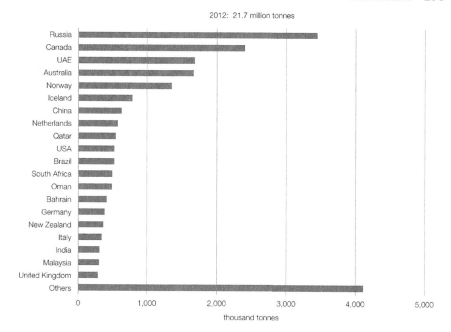

Exhibit 10.11 Top primary (unwrought) aluminium exporters

Source: Author, compiled with data from www.trademap.org, SITC code 7601

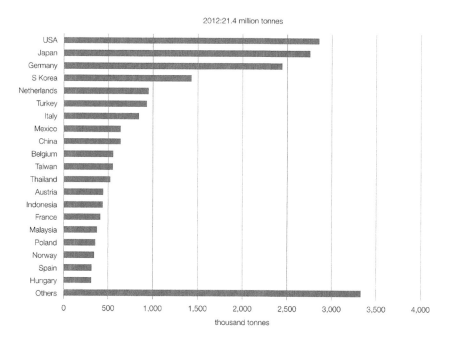

Exhibit 10.12 Top primary (unwrought) aluminium importers

Source: Author, compiled with data from www.trademap.org, SITC code 7601

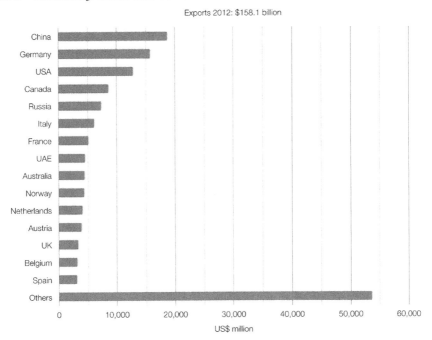

Exhibit 10.13 Top primary (unwrought and products) aluminium exporters, by value

Source: Author, compiled with data from www.trademap.org, SITC code 76

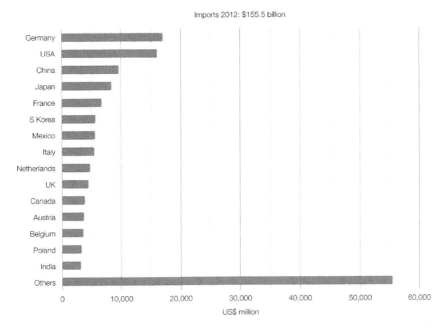

Exhibit 10.14 Top primary (unwrought and products) aluminium importers, by value

Source: Author, compiled with data from www.trademap.org, SITC code 76

This strategy found a substantial obstacle, particularly in the mid-1970s, when many producing countries – spurred by the success of OPEC in the oil industry – decided to tighten control on their own production and exports, and add value to their final product by expanding their alumina refining operations. This aspiration, however, was hindered by an important shortfall – the lack of adequate capital to invest in mining operations and alumina refining capacity.

On the other hand, smelters had the necessary funds, but could not really maintain control of mining operations, since the technological 'know-how' was rather basic and had already been passed on to the host countries. As a result, most smelters decided to channel money into expansion programmes for bauxite, and invest in alumina refining capacity, thus maintaining a secure source of raw material supply.

This interdependence between a few smelters (buyers) and a few producing countries (sellers) has created a situation similar to that in the iron ore market. Most business is done on the basis of long-term contracts, with a lack of either a spot market, or of any fairly representative international price quotations.

The situation is quite different for aluminium, however. Commercial aluminium comes to the market in two degrees of purity – 99.5 per cent and 99.7 per cent. It also comes in a number of standardised shapes: standard ingots – usually of 50 lb/piece; sows; T-bars, which are large pieces for mechanical handling – up to 1 ton each or more; rolling slabs; and billets.[8] The high standardisation of the product, and the existence of a large number of small fabricators and many buyers, creates a competitive environment, and scope for the participation of traders and dealers.

As a result, aluminium is traded very competitively around the world, both on a spot and a forward basis. It is also actively traded in organised futures markets, on the London Metal Exchange (LME), the Shanghai Futures Exchange (SHFE) and the MCX in India.[9] Aluminium and aluminium alloy contracts are used for hedging purposes, but their trading also performs the very important role of price discovery. In a later chapter, we will see how futures contracts in metals can be used for risk management and how they relate to the spot market.

Conclusion

Aluminium is one of the most abundant elements and the most widespread metal on the earth's crust. It is a relatively new metal, but has a wide range of uses, and has replaced a number of other base metals, such as steel, copper and tin, because of its lightweight and anti-corrosive properties. Currently, it is the second most widely used metal, after iron (including steel).

8 Tarring and Pinney (1996, p. 90).
9 Aluminium was also traded on the COMEX division of NYMEX, but the contract was eventually suspended by the current exchange owner, CME Group.

Aluminium smelting is an extremely energy-intensive operation, which needs to take advantage of economies of scale and must be kept in continuous operation. Because of these supply characteristics, aluminium production is dominated by a handful of large, integrated smelting companies, which also have interests in the mining and refining side of the business.

This situation is similar to that of steel, with the difference that the final product here – aluminium – is fairly standardised and is, as a result, traded actively both on spot and futures markets.

References

Pawlek, R. (2012) *Primary Aluminium Smelters of the World*, Light Metal Age, accessed online at: www.lightmetalage.com/producers_primary.php.

Tarring, T.J. and Pinney, G. (1996) *Trading in Metals*, 3rd edn, London: Metal Bulletin.

USGS (2013a) *2011 Minerals Yearbook: Bauxite & Alumina*, United States Geological Survey, accessed online at: http://minerals.usgs.gov/minerals/pubs/commodity/bauxite/myb1-2011-bauxi.pdf.

—— (2013b) *2012 Minerals Yearbook: Aluminum*, United States Geological Survey, accessed on line at: http://minerals.usgs.gov/minerals/pubs/commodity/aluminum/myb1-2012-alumi.pdf.

—— (2014a) *Aluminum Mineral Commodity Summary*, Unites States Geological Survey, accessed online at: http://minerals.usgs.gov/minerals/pubs/commodity/aluminum/mcs-2014-alumi.pdf.

—— (2014b) *Bauxite & Alumina Mineral Commodity Summary*, Unites States Geological Survey, accessed online at: http://minerals.usgs.gov/minerals/pubs/commodity/bauxite/mcs-2014-bauxi.pdf.

11 Copper

Copper is one of the oldest metals known to mankind, and definitely the first one to be used extensively. The use of copper signalled the beginning of the progression from the Stone Age to the emergence of the first identifiable civilisations. This transitive period was named Chalcolithic Age, because of the use of both stone (λίθος) and copper (χαλκός). The first alloy ever to be manufactured also involved copper, when it was discovered that adding a small quantity of tin immensely improved copper's durability. The next long period in human history – the Bronze Age – was named after this alloy, and trading activities often emerged because of the need to find new sources of copper and tin.

Copper objects have been found among the remains of many ancient civilisations, including those of Egypt, Asia Minor, China, South-Eastern Europe, Cyprus (from which the word copper is derived) and Crete. It was also known to ancient American civilisations, and European explorers found evidence of extensive use of the metal for utilitarian and ornamental purposes.

Copper was valued for its attractive red lustre, its malleability, and its resistance to corrosion, and was used extensively for the construction of tools and weapons. With the advent of iron, the use of copper was restricted to more domestic and ornamental uses, but during the Middle Ages and in the early modern era, the use of copper in the manufacture of brass cannons and other military supplies greatly increased the consumption of the metal.

At the beginning of the Industrial Revolution, almost all of the world's refined copper was produced in Britain, but as the revolution proceeded, other countries soon overtook Britain, and one of them – Chile – came to be the most important producer and exporter after the 1850s, holding this position until today.

Physical characteristics

Copper – denoted Cu – is a brownish-red metallic element, which melts at 1,083° C, boils at 2,567° C, and has a specific gravity of 8.9. Because of its many desirable properties, such as its conductivity of electricity and heat, its resistance to corrosion, its malleability and ductility, and its beauty, copper has long been used in a wide variety of applications.

Overall, copper is about the 25th most abundant element in crustal rocks. It is usually found admixed with other metals, such as gold, silver, bismuth and lead, and exists in small specks in rock, but individual masses weighing as much as 420 metric tons have been found. Copper occurs in a variety of ores, but unlike aluminium and iron, which are found in relatively large concentrations, it is contained only in small quantities – at best, 5–6 per cent, sometimes as low as 0.5 per cent.

Copper occurs in three types of minerals – sulphides, carbonates and silicates. The principal copper compounds are chalcopyrite and bornite, mixed sulphides of copper and iron. Other important ore minerals are chalcocite and covellite, sulphides of copper, which are found in Arizona and Nevada in the United States, and in Cornwall in England. Enargite, a sulpharsenate of copper, is found in various parts of the United States. Azurite, a basic carbonate of copper, is found in France and Australia; and malachite, also a basic carbonate of copper, in the Ural Mountains. Tetrahedrite, a sulphantimonide of copper and various other metals, and chrysocolla, a copper silicate, are both widely distributed. Cuprite, an oxide, is found in Cuba; and atacamite, a basic chloride, in Peru.

Supply determinants

Copper deposits are usually classified into three main categories: porphyry, strata-bound, and massive sulphide. Porphyry are the most common deposits, primarily found in Chile, Peru, south-west United States, northern Mexico, western Canada, Papua New Guinea and the Philippines. The grade and size of these deposits vary considerably: typical deposits in Chile and Peru contain 1–2 per cent Cu; in the United States and Mexico, ores typically have 0.4–0.8 per cent Cu; the Philippines and Canada have ores with a 0.3–0.5 per cent Cu content. Exhibit 11.1 shows the key reserve holders, among which Chile is the largest with over one-quarter of the world's total reserves.

Strata-bound deposits are typically silicates and carbonates, but also sulphides. They are not as important and widespread as porphyry deposits, but they usually have the largest copper content. They are encountered mostly in Zaire and Zambia; Zambian deposits are sulphides with 2–4 per cent Cu content; Zairian deposits are carbonates and silicates, with 4–6 per cent Cu content. Finally, massive concentrations of sulphide minerals also contain copper, and occur mainly in eastern Canada, Australia, South Africa and the Philippines; they usually contain 1–5 per cent copper.

The metallurgy of copper varies with the composition of the ore. The most important ores – the sulphides – must first be crushed and concentrated by flotation. The outcome of the flotation is a product containing 22–32 per cent copper by weight. On the other hand, carbonates, silicates and oxides usually undergo a process known as leaching.[1]

---

1 In leaching, the copper ore is treated with a chemical solution. The copper is then extracted from the copper-bearing solution either by precipitation on scrap iron, or by recovering it directly as copper metal in electrolytic cells.

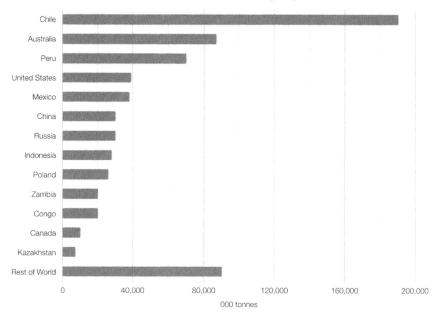

Exhibit 11.1 Copper reserves

Source: Author, based on data from USGS (2014)

After crushing, the concentrates are roasted – or smelted – in furnaces, which yield crude metallic – or blister – copper, approximately 98 per cent pure. There are two main types of furnaces used for roasting: reverbatory furnaces, which are rather old-fashioned, and inefficient in burning the sulphur in the concentrates, and the flash furnace, which uses oxygen to remove iron and sulphur in the form of slag.

Flash smelting is a more efficient method, especially because it yields a desirable by-product, sulphur dioxide, which can be recovered in a sulphuric acid plant. Some of the variants of this method include the Noranda, Mitsubishi and Outokumpu processes.

An alternative to smelting (pyrometallurgy) is the use of hydrometallurgy, whereby copper concentrates are leached in an acid solution, and separated with the method described in note 1. There are several hydrometallurgy processes, the most well known being: Cymet (by Cyprus Corp.); CLEAR (by Duval); and Arbiter (by Anaconda).

Whether pyrometallurgy or hydrometallurgy is used, the result is crude copper, which is further purified by electrolysis, yielding bars – or copper cathodes – exceeding 99.9 per cent purity. Finally, copper can also be manufactured from recycled copper scrap.

Pure copper is soft but can be hardened somewhat by being worked; the product is then known as wrought copper. Alloys of copper, which are far harder and stronger than the pure metal, have higher resistance and so cannot be used for electrical purposes. They do, however, have corrosion resistance

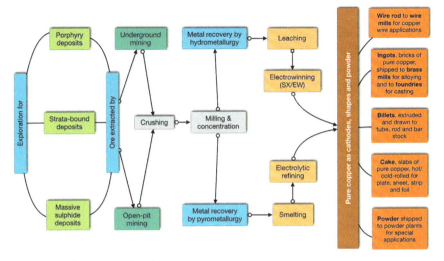

Exhibit 11.2 Copper production processes
Source: Author

almost as good as that of pure copper, and are very easily worked in machine shops. The two most important alloys are brass, a zinc alloy, and bronze, a tin alloy. Both tin and zinc are sometimes added to the same alloy, and no sharp dividing line can be drawn between brass and bronze. Both are used in enormous quantities. Copper is also alloyed with gold, silver and nickel, and is an important constituent of such alloys as Monel metal, gunmetal and German silver.

Production

One of the main prerequisites for a successful mining project is that the metal occurs in large enough concentrations, and large enough quantities. In the case of copper, this becomes even more important, because copper is found in rather small concentrations in its ores. Copper manufacturers normally extend their interests in mining as well, with the biggest of them having interests on a worldwide basis.

As of 2013, Chile remains the world's largest producer of copper ore, with almost one-third of world production, as can be seen in Exhibit 11.3. China has increased its presence in mine production, following its rapid industrialisation from 2004 onwards; it is currently the second largest producer of copper ore, with over 1.5 million metric tons of copper content. Other important producers include Peru, the USA, Australia and Russia.

Only a few years ago, Chile was also the world's leading copper smelter. From 2005 onwards, however, China rose head and shoulders above Chile and other important copper smelters, such as Japan and Russia. This leading group is followed by India, Germany, South Korea, the USA, Poland and Zambia (see Exhibit 11.4).

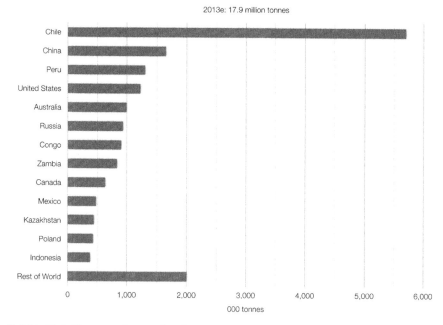

Exhibit 11.3 Copper mine production

Source: Author, based on data from USGS (2014)

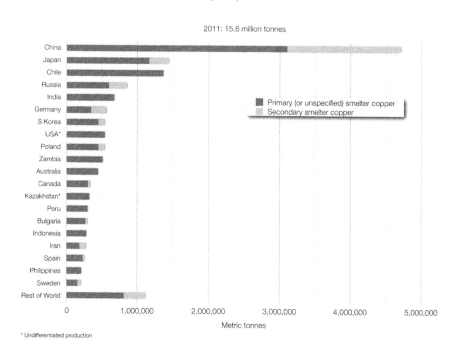

Exhibit 11.4 Copper smelter production

Source: Author, based on data from USGS (2014)

This change in leadership follows through to refined copper production, with China at the top, followed at some distance by Chile, Japan, the USA and Russia (see Exhibit 11.5). Other important refined copper producers include Germany, India, South Korea, Poland and Zambia.

For the same reasons as for the aluminium industry, there are strong tendencies for concentration in the copper industry as well. With the emergence of China and India as new dynamic economies based on manufacturing and IT (both requiring copper resources), it became evident that the formerly neglected copper sector became a prime target for investment once again. As a result, the first few years of the new millennium saw substantial takeover activity.

The world's biggest producer of copper is Codelco, the state-owned Chilean company. It was followed by the US's Phelps Dodge, which was taken over by Freeport-McMoRan (also known as FCX) in 2007. FCX now claims to be the world's largest 'publicly listed' copper producer. In addition to Phelps Dodge, it owns PT Freeport of Indonesia, whose principal asset is the Grasberg mine, the world's largest copper and gold mine; and Atlantic Copper, its European subsidiary, which operates in Spain.

BHP Billiton emerges again as a key player in the copper market; it claims third place as a copper producer, with operations in Chile (through its subsidiary Escondida), Peru (Antamina) and Australia (Olympic Dam). Another major player in the US is Kennecott, now a wholly owned subsidiary of Rio Tinto. Rio Tinto also owns part of Escondida in Chile and has copper

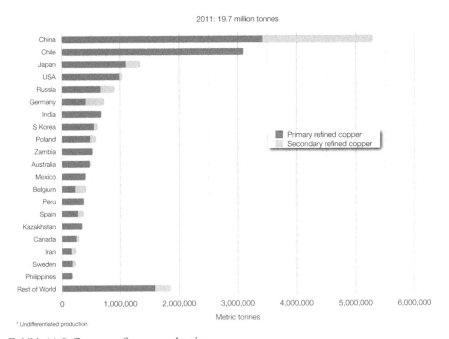

Exhibit 11.5 Copper refinery production

Source: Author, based on data from USGS (2014)

operations in Australia and South Africa. Finally, it owns 40 per cent of the Grasberg mine in Indonesia. Xstrata (now GlencoreXstrata) is another global mining corporation with substantial copper interests. It claims to be the world's fourth largest copper producer, with operations in the USA (where it acquired Falconbridge in 2006), Peru, Chile, Argentina, Papua New Guinea and the Philippines.

Other important producers include Southern Copper Corporation (with operations in Peru and Mexico), Anglo American (with operations in Chile, having bought Disputada from ExxonMobil, and South Africa) and KGHM Polska Miedź (which produces copper in Poland). Finally, several other companies have smaller interests in copper mining and smelting. Brazil's Vale explores for copper in the Carajás region, not far away from its own iron ore operations, as well as in Peru through its association with Antofagosta. India's Vedanta has a controlling share in Zambia's KCM (Konkola Copper Mines) and also has copper operations in India.

Demand determinants

Copper is a versatile metal, used in a wide range of applications. Pipes for plumbing, telecoms cable, power generation and transmission and a variety of automotive components are just a few examples of such applications. Exhibit 11.6 shows the shares of some of copper's main end uses in the United States.

One of its principal uses is for electrical products, because of copper's extremely high conductivity, which is second only to that of silver. Because

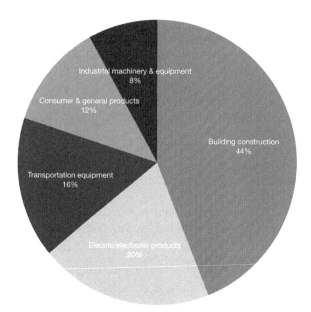

Exhibit 11.6 Copper end uses in the United States

Source: Author, based on data from USGS (2013)

copper is very ductile, it can be drawn into wires of any diameter from about 0.025 mm upwards. The tensile strength of drawn copper wire is about 4,200 kg/cm; it can be used in outdoor power lines and cables, as well as in house wiring, lamp cords, and electrical machinery such as generators, motors, controllers, signalling devices, electromagnets, and communications equipment.

Copper has been used for coins throughout recorded history and has also been fashioned into cooking utensils, vats, and ornamental objects. Copper was at one time used extensively for sheathing the bottom of wooden ships to prevent fouling. Copper can easily be electroplated alone, or as a base for other metals. Large amounts are used for this purpose, particularly in making electrotypes – reproductions of type for printing.

Certain copper solutions have the power of dissolving cellulose, and large quantities of copper are, for this reason, used in the manufacture of rayon. Copper is also used in many pigments and in such insecticides as Paris green and such fungicides as Bordeaux mixture, although it is being largely replaced by synthetic organic chemicals for these purposes.

As for any other metal, demand for copper is affected by the income disposable to consumers; copper is normally used in goods that have high income elasticities – such as cables, cars, machinery and so on – and is therefore more responsive to income changes when the absolute level of income is low (i.e. when the economy is edging out of the 'pre-industrial' and into the 'take-off' stage. On the other hand, mature economies with high disposable incomes grow accustomed to goods, which are considered luxuries in less-well-off countries, so that demand for these products – and their components – becomes less income-elastic.

The use of copper in an economy is also affected by the degree of substitution between this metal and other metals (e.g. aluminium). In recent years, copper has been challenged by competitive materials on three main fronts – electricity transfers, telecommunications and building construction. In electricity transfers, copper is challenged by aluminium, which displays a low weight-to-conductivity ratio, and is therefore preferable, especially for long-distance transfers of high-voltage current, using overhead cables. In telecommunications, copper is increasingly challenged by optic fibres, which have an edge when transferring signals from the source of emission to distribution centres; copper wires, however, are still very much used for connecting individual consumers to distribution points. Finally, in building construction, copper is being challenged by plastics and other materials, which are now extensively replacing copper in plumbing and weatherproofing.

Trade and pricing

Copper is shipped from the refinery in five different shapes: cathodes, wirebars, continuous cast rod, billets and cakes. Billets are normally used to produce seamless copper tubes, while cakes are large slabs of copper, used by fabricators to make plates, sheets, strips and bars.

It is the largest of anode copper producers that offer all of these products on the market, while a host of smaller, independent copper fabricators produce a wide range of finished copper, bronze and brass products, including tubes, plates, extrusions in many shapes and types, and, of course, cable.

Copper was among the world's top 10 traded commodities in 2012, with a turnover of just over $170 billion for trade in copper ores, concentrates, and semi-fabricated and finished products (see Exhibit 11.7). Compared to steel and aluminium ores and products, however, copper generates only small *volumes* of trade. Crude copper ores are almost never traded, because they contain uneconomically small concentrations of copper.

Instead, copper concentrates are exported to large copper refiners, such as China and Japan (see Exhibit 11.8). Copper is often smelted at the place of production and exported in the form of either unrefined copper (anode/blister copper, ca. 98 per cent purity), refined copper (99.9 per cent purity) or alloyed products (see Exhibits 11.9 and 11.10).

As would be expected, Chile dominates international exports of copper in all forms. Other important exporters include: Peru, Australia, Zambia and Kazakhstan. In terms of importers, China features in all types of imports, accompanied by countries such as Japan, South Korea, Germany and the USA.

Pricing

From the analysis so far, it has become evident that the market for copper is very competitive, on an international basis. Copper pricing is quite similar

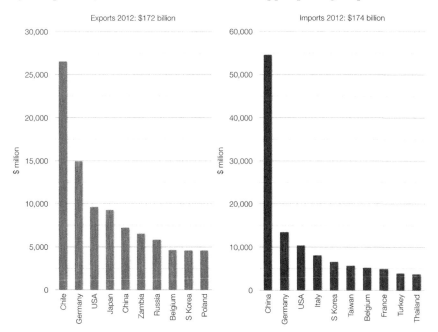

Exhibit 11.7 Top exporters and importers in copper and all products, by value

Source: Author, compiled with data from www.trademap.org, SITC 74

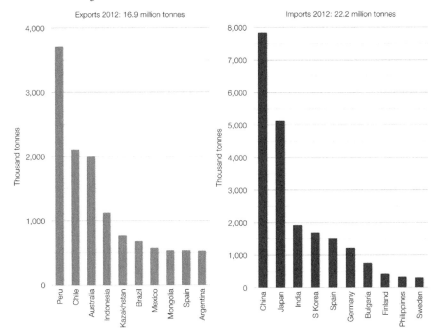

Exhibit 11.8 Top exporters and importers in copper concentrates
Source: Author, compiled with data from www.trademap.org, SITC 2603

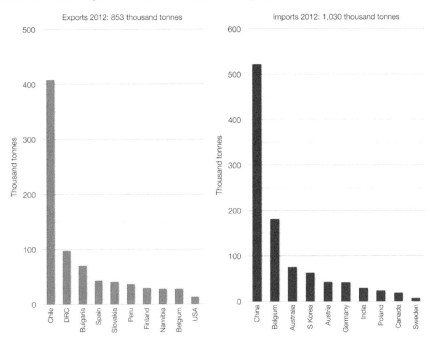

Exhibit 11.9 Top exporters and importers in unrefined copper anodes
Source: Author, compiled with data from www.trademap.org, SITC 7402

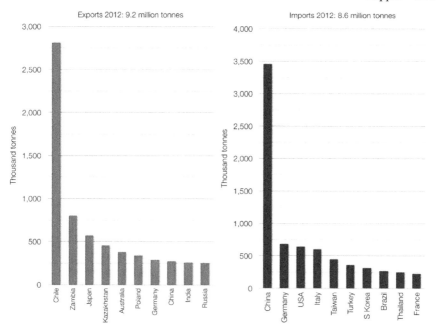

Exports 2012: 9.2 million tonnes   Imports 2012: 8.6 million tonnes

Exhibit 11.10 Top exporters and importers in refined and alloyed (unwrought) copper
Source: Author, compiled with data from www.trademap.org, SITC 7403

to aluminium, with benchmark prices for the finished metal set in the two most liquid metal exchanges – the London Metal Exchange (LME) and the COMEX division in the New York Mercantile Exchange (part of the CME Group). A variety of derivative instruments on copper are actively traded on both markets, and we shall discuss these in a later chapter.

The LME is considered as the price setter for the international copper market, and is also used as a benchmark for refined copper prices in domestic markets, as well as for differential pricing of copper concentrates. On the latter topic, it is worth expanding a bit more, as pricing copper concentrates reflects the common pricing practices for most non-ferrous base metals.[2]

As a concentrate contains only a certain proportion of the pure metal, which needs to be processed in order to extract the said metal, there are a number of adjustments that need to be made in order to calculate the price paid for a particular concentrate. These adjustments are commonly known by the acronym *TCRC*, and they are listed below together with some of the most common contract terms for concentrates:

- *Treatment charge (T/C)* – a deduction made by the processor for smelting the material, including receiving, handling, sampling and assaying.

---

2 For further discussion, the reader is directed to Tarring and Pinney (1996, Chapter 14) and Crowson (2008, Chapter 10).

- *Refining charge (R/C)* – a deduction made by processor for refining the smelted material into a marketable product.
- *Penalties* – deductions made from the value of the material representing the costs of treating and eliminating certain specified elements that are deleterious to the quality of the finished products.
- *Payable contents* – elements contained in the material that the processor is prepared to buy or attribute value to (e.g. precious metals).
- *Unit deductions* – agreed percentages that are deducted from the payable contents and represent the proportion of the materials that are unavoidably lost – or deemed to be lost – in the smelting or refining process.
- *Price participation* – a percentage of the benchmark price that the processor/smelter receives as part of his payment.
- *Price* – the market value of the refined product derived from the material being purchased (e.g. the price of copper on LME or COMEX).
- *Quotation period* – the period of time over which the buyer and the seller have agreed to fix the price of the material, and, in some cases, fix the conversion of any currency unit used to express the final invoice value.
- *Payment terms* – include the date(s) on which the buyer agrees to make the final settlement.

A practical example of pricing a metric ton of copper concentrate is given in Exhibit 11.11. In this example, we assume a concentrate with 31 per cent copper, 35 per cent iron, 32 per cent sulphur, 0.5 per cent bismuth, 0.5 per

Copper concentrate 31% Cu, 35% Fe, 32% S, 47ppm Au, 48ppm Ag 0.5% Bi, 0.5% As, 0.5% H_2O, other elements 0.5%	Prices and charges for one metric ton of concenrate
Price of LME copper (say 1M average) $7,000/tonne Unit deduction for Cu - 1% $7,000 x (31−1) =	$2100.00
Treatment charge: $100/tonne	−$100.00
Refining charge: $150/tonne	−$150.00
Penalties: $10 per each 0.1% of Bi and As over 0.1% 4 x $10 + 4 x $10 =	−$80.00
Payable contents: 47ppm Au minus 1ppm unit deduction Au: $1,250/tr.oz. 46 gr ÷ 31.1 gr/tr.oz. x $1,300	$1848.87
Payable contents: 48ppm Ag minus 1ppm unit deduction Ag: $20/tr.oz. 47 gr ÷ 31.1 gr/tr.oz. x $20	$30.23
Price participation: 5% on LME price $7,000 x 5% =	−$350.00
Total Price per metric ton of concentrate	**$3299.10**
Total TCRC	*−$680.00*

Exhibit 11.11 Pricing a copper concentrate

Source: Author

cent arsenic, 0.5 per cent water, 0.5 per cent other elements, and also 47 ppm gold (i.e. 47 grams per metric ton) and 48 ppm silver. Further assumptions on the various elements of TCRC are given in the exhibit, and the price per metric ton of concentrate is calculated at the end.

Conclusion

In this chapter, we examined the structure of the world's oldest metal, copper, which still plays a vital role in our modern society. Unlike steel, but like aluminium, copper is a fairly standardised metal, and both copper and aluminium are priced somewhat differently to steel. Both metals have been traded in organised exchanges for over a century, together with a few other base metals, such as lead, zinc, tin and nickel.

Trade in copper is mainly in refined products, rather than crude ore, and, compared to iron and aluminium, it is rather small. The international market for copper is very competitive, with prices being determined primarily on the LME, and also on COMEX/NYMEX for the US market. Due to the nature of its end uses, copper (like aluminium) is consumed primarily in developed and newly industrialising economies, such as China, Japan, India, North America and the EU.

References

Crowson, P. (2008) *Mining Unearthed*, London: Aspermont.

Tarring, T.J. and Pinney, G. (1996) *Trading in Metals*, 3rd edn, London: Metal Bulletin.

USGS (2013) *2011 Minerals Yearbook: Copper*, United States Geological Survey, accessed on line at: http://minerals.usgs.gov/minerals/pubs/commodity/copper/myb1-2011-coppe.pdf.

—— (2014) *Copper Mineral Commodity Summary*, United States Geological Survey, accessed online at: http://minerals.usgs.gov/minerals/pubs/commodity/copper/mcs-2014-coppe.pdf.

12 Metal derivative markets

In the preceding chapters, we examined the economic fundamentals of the key mineral and metal resources, and analysed how demand and supply drivers interact to reach equilibrium in terms of the quantity consumed and the price paid for each commodity. We also considered the various pricing regimes for different commodities and noted how most minerals are priced as a differential to the finished metal, which itself is priced on commodity exchanges, of which the most influential is the LME.

In this chapter, we observe the key characteristics of metal price series and set the scene with regard to the risk implied by price movements. We then tackle the financial derivative instruments that can be used to hedge this risk and use a number of examples to demonstrate simple hedging strategies.

Overview of metal prices

As most commodities, metal prices tend to be considerably volatile in comparison to other asset classes, such as equities and bonds, although probably less volatile than some energy commodities. There are both demand and supply factors that contribute to this volatility. On the demand side, it is mostly changes in industrial production, as manufacturing, construction and engineering are the key consumers of base metals. These changes are in turn instigated by changes in disposable consumer income, credit availability, as well as long-term changes and trends in consumer tastes and substitution between different metals. On the supply side, production is usually stable through the year, but disruptions to this stability do happen, whether due to technical reasons, natural disasters, political events or other random factors. In addition, there are long-term trends in supply, reflecting the overall abundance or scarcity of a particular metal commodity.

In order to acquire a view of how metal prices have moved in recent years, we use daily data from 1 January 2007 to 31 March 2014. The selected period focuses deliberately on the last few years and also includes the effects of the 2008 financial crisis on the prices of metal commodities. Exhibit 12.1 shows spot prices for four series, the first one a key mineral and the other three base metals, all of them benchmark indicators with futures contracts traded on the LME. It can be seen that not all four series display identical movements,

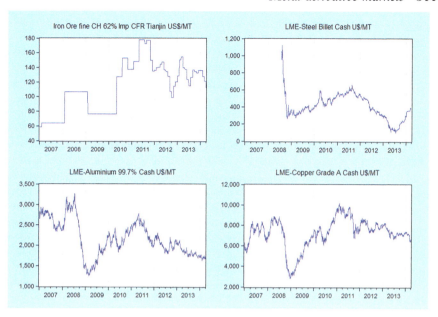

Exhibit 12.1 Iron ore, steel, copper and aluminium prices
Source: Author, based on data from Thomson Reuters Datastream

although the three metals do share the big price drop from Q3 2008 to Q1 2009, in the aftermath of the financial crisis after the collapse of Lehman Brothers. It is also worth noting that not all prices followed exactly the same path. Copper experienced a considerable increase in its price, managing to recover to levels around $10,000/mt in early 2011, although it has since declined, mostly owing to the slowdown of economic growth in emerging economies, such as China. Aluminium prices also rose considerably post-2008, but they have been in long-term decline since early 2011, due to the slowdown of economic growth and the chronic oversupply of physical metal in the market. Steel prices never quite recovered since 2008, and have in fact shown the steepest decline, reaching their lowest point in mid-2013, once again influenced by economic developments in emerging markets, in particular China, which dominates world steel production and consumption. Finally, iron ore seems to be the odd one out in this group. The price follows a stepwise pattern, with step changes becoming progressively more frequent from late 2010 onwards. This reflects the change in the pricing regime for this commodity, which came about in early 2010, as discussed in Chapter 9.

Exhibit 12.2 displays the price series of the remaining four key base metals: lead, nickel, tin and zinc. All series demonstrate the same steep decline in the second half of 2008, although nickel and zinc seem to have started their descent from the second half of 2007, possibly a precursor to the decline in steel prices that was going to follow. Lead, nickel and zinc shared the same 'sideways' price

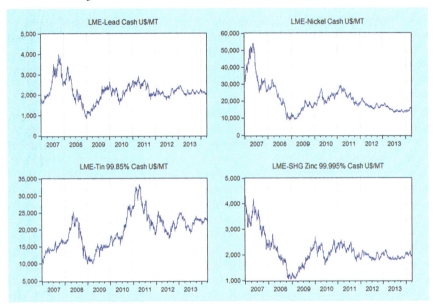

Exhibit 12.2 Lead, nickel, tin and zinc prices

Source: Author, based on data from Thomson Reuters Datastream

movement since 2011, while tin experienced further fluctuations until it also settled on a long-term price of around $20,000/mt.

Price series characteristics

As with most financial price series, commodity prices tend to depart from the normal assumption that they are normally distributed. A quick look at the following few exhibits confirms this premise. Exhibit 12.3 displays the histogram and descriptive statistics for copper (top) and aluminium (bottom) spot prices. Copper prices seem to be negatively skewed, with higher than normal kurtosis, and the Jarque-Bera statistic and associated probability leads us to safely reject the null hypothesis that this is a normal distribution. We reach a similar conclusion for aluminium prices as well.

In Exhibit 12.4, we can see that steel billet prices (top) are even more irregular, showing a bimodal distribution. The distribution of nickel prices (bottom) is skewed and leptokurtic. For both sets of data, the normality assumption can also be safely rejected.

Finally, even the price distributions for zinc (top) and lead (bottom) also demonstrate excess kurtosis and non-normality, as can be seen in Exhibit 12.5.

Returns and volatility

We conclude this brief overview of energy price series with a look at two more aspects: returns and volatility. The return on any asset, be it a stock, bond or

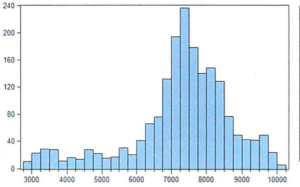

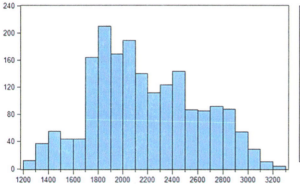

Exhibit 12.3 Histogram and descriptive statistics for copper and aluminium spot prices

Source: Author, based on data from Thomson Reuters Datastream

commodity, is defined as the percentage difference of the price of the asset between two points in time. This is expressed more formally by the equation

$$R_t = \frac{S_t - S_{t-1}}{S_{t-1}},$$

where R_t is the return in period t and S_t and S_{t-1} are the prices in periods t and $t-1$, respectively.

For example, say that the price for copper at the close of the market on 01-Mar is \$7,013.00/mt and at the close of 02-Mar it is \$7,087.50. The daily return is then calculated as $(7,087.5 - 7,013) \div 7,013$, or alternatively $(7,087.5 \div 7,013) - 1$, and this is equal to 0.01062, or 1.062 per cent.

An alternative method to calculate returns, which is commonly used in finance, is to use the natural logarithm of the ratio of prices between two points in time. This means that

$$R_t = \ln \frac{S_t}{S_{t-1}}.$$

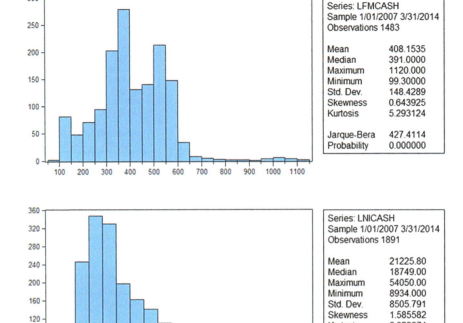

Exhibit 12.4 Histogram and descriptive statistics for steel billet and nickel prices
Source: Author, based on data from Thomson Reuters Datastream

In the previous example, the return would be calculated as ln(7,087.5 ÷ 7,013), which is equal to 0.01057 or 1.057 per cent. The result is close to the result in the previous paragraph, but somewhat lower, as this method implies that returns are continuously (rather than discretely) compounded. This method has the additional advantage that returns are additive. For example, to calculate the returns on an asset in a particular week of trading days, it suffices to calculate the natural logarithm of the ratio of the last day over the first day. The result will be the same if we calculate each daily return and then add them up.

Having defined returns and how we calculate them, we now proceed to observe the returns on a selection of metal commodities and how these returns are distributed. Exhibit 12.6 displays the returns for copper and aluminium prices (top and bottom left), where we can observe how they fluctuate around a mean that is very close to zero. We can also observe that the majority of returns fluctuate in the 4 per cent range around the mean, with the period between Q4 2008 and Q1 2009 characterised by much sharper fluctuations around the mean. The frequency distribution of returns for both series are

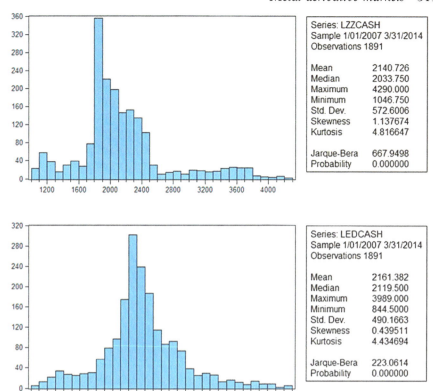

Exhibit 12.5 Histogram and descriptive statistics for zinc and lead prices

Source: Author, based on data from Thomson Reuters Datastream

shown on the right of the same exhibit. They show the same leptokurtic distribution that is common among financial price series, as well as commodities in general. Similar observations can be made for all other metal commodities included in Exhibits 12.7 and 12.8.

The second aspect examined here is the volatility of commodity returns. Having defined returns in the previous paragraphs, volatility is simply the standard deviations of these returns from their mean. More formally, this is expressed as

$$\sigma_T = \sqrt{\frac{1}{T-1}\sum_{i=1}^{T}\left(R_i - \bar{R}\right)^2},$$

where T is the time period over which we calculate the volatility. A final adjustment needs to be made, with regard to the frequency (or periodicity) of the data we use to calculate the volatility. We should not be comparing volatilities between daily and monthly data, for example. To make the various

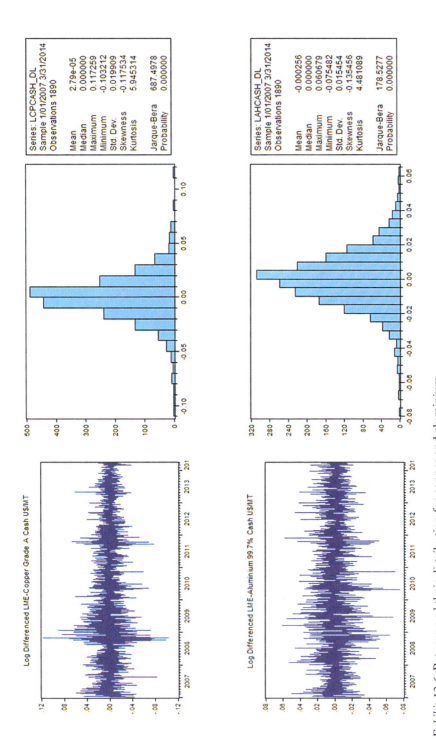

Exhibit 12.6 Returns and their distribution for copper and aluminium

Source: Author, based on data from Thomson Reuters Datastream

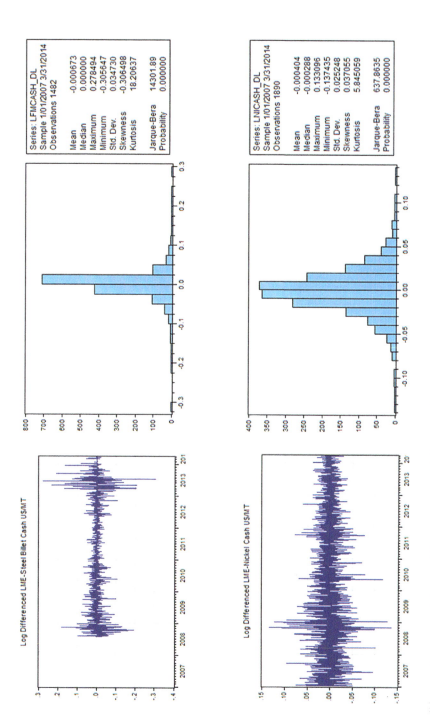

Exhibit 12.7 Returns and their distribution for steel billet and nickel

Source: Author, based on data from Thomson Reuters Datastream

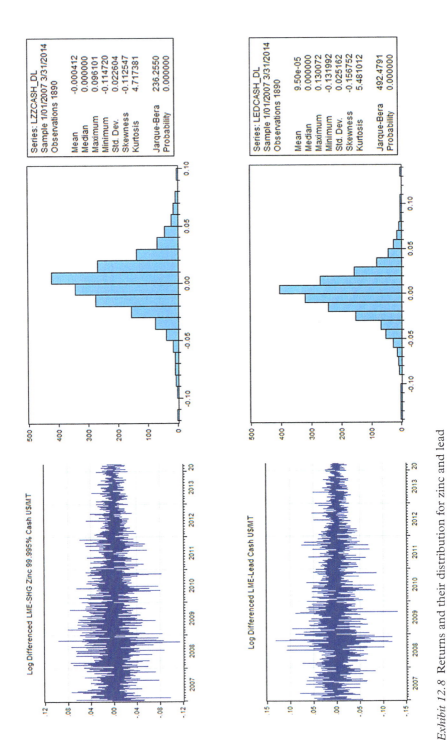

Exhibit 12.8 Returns and their distribution for zinc and lead

Source: Author, based on data from Thomson Reuters Datastream

calculated volatilities comparable, we need to annualise them by multiplying our σ by the square root of the number of periods in a year. More formally,

$$\sigma = \sigma_T \sqrt{P},$$

where P is 12 for monthly, 52 for weekly and 250–252 for daily return observations in a year. For example, if σ_T for daily returns over a period is 0.02, then volatility

$$\sigma = \sigma_T \sqrt{250}$$

is equal to 0.3162, or 31.62 per cent. On the other hand, if σ_T of weekly returns over a period is 0.02, then volatility

$$\sigma = \sigma_T \sqrt{52}$$

is equal to 0.1442, or 14.42 per cent.

Using the definition given above and a rolling window of 60 days, we calculate the volatility for various metal commodities in the exhibits that follow. In Exhibit 12.9, we can observe the volatilities of copper, aluminium and steel billet returns. Note how all volatilities jumped during Q4 2008 and Q1 2009, soon after the financial crisis, which also caused the dramatic drop of all metal

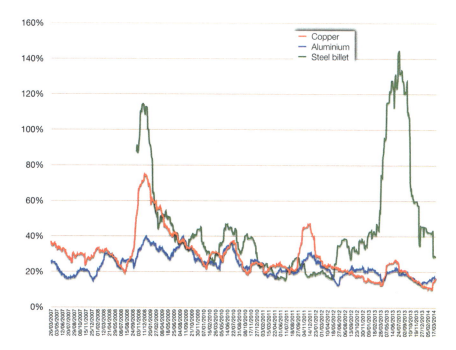

Exhibit 12.9 60-day rolling volatility for copper, aluminium and steel billet

Source: Author, based on data from Thomson Reuters Datastream

prices in the same period. Towards the end of the period covered (Q1 2014), volatilities have decreased to ca. 20 per cent for copper and aluminium, although steel returns remain more volatile and had a spike in volatility in the summer of 2013, as unfavourable news on Chinese steel production hit the markets and steel prices started tumbling down.

Using the same type of calculation, in Exhibit 12.10, we can observe similar volatilities recorded for the four minor base metals. All four had a spike in volatility around the financial crisis and, once again, all four have volatilities around 20 per cent, similar to these for the major base metals in the previous exhibit.

Modelling the price processes for metals and other commodities has attracted considerable attention in academic literature. Various models have been put forward, many of them emanating from theorists studying mainstream financial markets. Hence, the very first step is normally to investigate the randomness of commodity prices and attempt to model it using a Brownian motion with a drift. In particular, the Geometric Brownian Motion (GBM) has been used to model returns in financial assets, be it stocks or commodities. The model postulates that the return on the asset (e.g. stock price) is given by the equation

$$\frac{dS_t}{S_t} \mu \cdot dt + \sigma \cdot dW_t ,$$

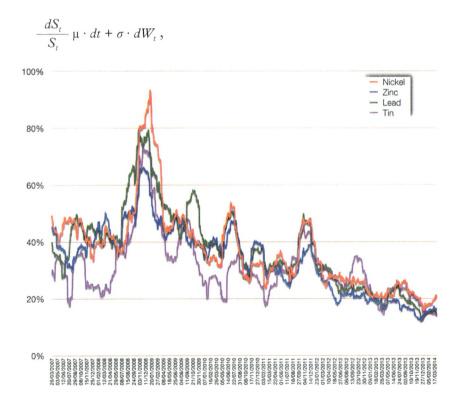

Exhibit 12.10 60-day rolling volatility for nickel, zinc, lead and tin

Source: Author, based on data from Thomson Reuters Datastream

where μ is the drift of the process and dWt is a Wiener process that introduces the element of randomness in returns from one period to the next.

As the GBM contains a drift term, it implies that the price of the underlying asset grows with time, which is a reasonable assumption for stocks. In commodity markets, this assumption often breaks down, as commodities tend to display a tendency to revert to a long-term equilibrium price. To address this problem, an alternative equation has been proposed instead, which is

$$\frac{dS(t)}{S(t)} = k(\theta - \ln S_t)dt + \sigma dW(t) ,$$

where θ is the long-term mean to which returns revert to and k is the speed of the mean reversion. Even a mean-reverting GBM process tends to produce price return trajectories that are relatively continuous. How can we represent then the often-violent upward and downward movements in stock, commodity and other asset prices? Merton (1976) introduced the jump diffusion model, where a jump component is added to the diffusion term, so that the equation now becomes

$$\frac{dS(t)}{S(t)} = \mu dt + \sigma dW(t) + U_t dN_t ,$$

where N_t denotes a Poisson distribution with intensity λ accounting for the arrival of jumps, and U_t is a real valued random variable as jumps may be positive or negative. Various other propositions have been made that extend the accuracy of the various models used to capture the diffusion process of commodity price returns. For example, Gibson and Schwartz (1990) propose a state variable model to capture the diffusion process of oil prices, whereby the two states are those of contango and backwardation and account for the change in the convenience yield. For a more expansive discussion of this and several other methods of modelling commodity prices, the reader is referred to authors such as Eydeland and Wolyniec (2003), Geman (2005), Burger *et al.* (2007), Pilipovic (2007), Geman (2008), Edwards (2010), and Pirrong (2012).

Participants in metal derivative markets

There are several types of participants in the metal derivative markets. They may be producers and consumers of the various metals, as well as transformers (e.g. copper wire mills or aluminium frame fabricators) and traders. They are typically companies, but they may also be private individuals who simply want to bet on the direction that metal prices may move.

With regard to the reasons that the various participants get involved in these markets, we can differentiate among three types: hedgers, speculators and arbitrageurs. Hedgers typically have an exposure to the physical commodity and need to offload their price risk by opening equivalent and opposite exposure in an appropriate derivative. For example, a mining company has a natural long position in the physical metal market and is afraid that the metal price may decline in the future and it will lose revenue. It may wish to hedge its risk by assuming a short (sell) position in a derivative instrument, such as a futures contract. In contrast, an automotive company that regularly buys metals for car bodies and engine components has a natural short position in the physical market for these particular metals. It may wish to hedge its risk by assuming a long (buy) position in an appropriate derivative instrument. For example, it may buy call options that give it the right to buy aluminium at a certain price, the *strike* price, which can be exercised if the market price is higher than the strike price.

Speculators do not have an underlying position on the physical commodity. Instead, they assume long and short positions on derivative instruments because they have a particular view of where the market price may go. They effectively bet on the price movement, based on their own analysis of all the fundamental and technical factors that may affect price movement. Although speculators have often been blamed for causing excessive price volatility with their buy/sell actions, they are an essential part of each and every derivative market. Their participation enhances market liquidity and they are the ones who are prepared to take on the risk that hedgers wish to offload.

Prices for a commodity between markets and across time may occasionally be out of balance. Arbitrageurs are those who seek such imbalances and act quickly to take advantage of such mispricing opportunities in order to make riskless profits. They are essential for keeping price relationships in balance and also provide additional liquidity, which is vital for the hedgers who want to be able to open and close derivatives positions quickly and effectively.

The relationship between spot and futures prices

Before we move on to the futures and other instruments, it is worth looking at the temporal element of commodity prices and in particular the relationship between spot and futures prices. Many authors have looked at this relationship, and among the first to do so was Keynes. He posited that futures prices are generally downwards based estimates of future spot prices. As a result, spot prices should 'normally' exceed forward prices by the amount that a producer is ready to sacrifice in order to hedge himself – a sort of 'insurance premium'. This theory is also known as the theory of normal backwardation.

In his seminal paper, Working (1949) offered an alternative explanation of the spot-future price relationship. Known as the *theory of storage*, Working's explanation links spot and future prices with the cost of capital, the storage cost and the convenience yield. The latter variable is more difficult to observe directly, but can be indirectly calculated using market data for spot and future prices, storage costs and borrowing costs.

Working observed that the difference between spot and future prices, known as the *basis*, is inversely related to the level of stocks of a particular commodity. The higher the stocks, the higher the expectation that the future price will be higher than the spot price, and vice versa.

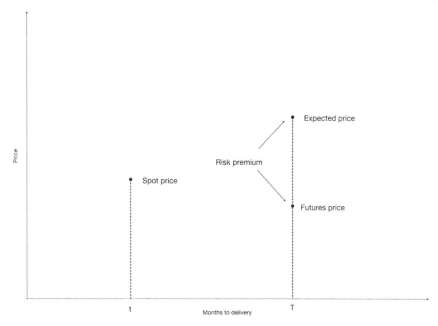

Exhibit 12.11 Spot and futures prices in the theory of normal backwardation

Source: Author

Putting this in the context of a metal commodity such as copper, consider the following. If stocks of copper are low,[1] market participants, such as fabricators that need the physical commodity in order to process it into finished products, will be prepared to pay a premium in order to acquire the commodity now. Their *convenience yield* for holding the physical commodity is high. Conversely, if stocks are abundant and users of the physical commodity can easily acquire it in the spot market, there is less upward pressure on the spot price, which tends to be lower than the future price.

To express the spot-future price relationship more formally, we can use the equation $F_t^T = S_t(1 + r_{T-t} + c_{T-t} - y_{T-t})$, which states that the current price (time t) of the futures contract for a commodity that is due to be delivered at time T in the future is F_t^T, and equals the spot price at time t, plus the cost of storage and insurance c for the period $T - t$, plus the cost of capital r used to acquire the commodity and hold it over the same period, minus the convenience yield y. To express the same relationship using continuous compounding, we can simply restate the previous equation as $F_t^T = S_t \cdot \exp\ [(r + c - y)(T - t)]$.

Returning to Working's observation, the higher the stocks, the lower the convenience yield (approaching zero), and the more the price of the futures contract exceeds the spot price by the full *cost of carry* (storage, insurance and cost of capital). This relationship is graphically expressed in Exhibit 12.12.

---

1 Stock indicators could be the level of OPEC's spare production capacity, stocks held by oil companies, IEA country reserves and so forth.

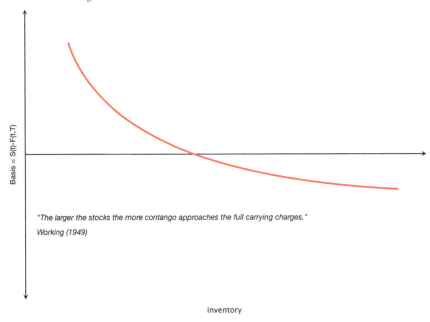

Exhibit 12.12 Relationship between inventory and basis
Source: Author

From the previous discussion, we can deduce that there are two states with regard to the relationship between spot and future prices (i.e. the basis). If we define the basis as $Ft - St$ when the future price is higher than the spot, the basis is positive and the market is said to be in *contago*. Conversely, when the future price is lower than the spot, the basis is negative and the market is said to be in *backwardation*.

Depending on supply and demand conditions and market expectations, a market can switch between contango and backwardation, even on a daily basis. However, as the futures contract approaches its expiry date, the closer it comes to becoming the physical commodity (at least theoretically), and the more its price will converge to the spot price. This premise is known as *price convergence*, and we can observe it almost working in Exhibit 12.13 for the spot copper cathode price and the CME/COMEX June-14 copper contract, although at the contract expiry on 26 June 2014 we do not have full convergence, which may be due to quality and delivery differences between the spot copper and the one stipulated in the futures contract specifications.

Going a step further from the discussion above, we can also look at the relationship among the prices of a number of sequential contracts for a particular commodity, for deliveries at various points in the future. When doing so, we are building the forward curve of the particular commodity. The forward curve may be useful for a number of reasons. First of all, it shows how the market prices the commodity for various future delivery dates, and hence tells us where the future spot prices will be according to rational expectations. The

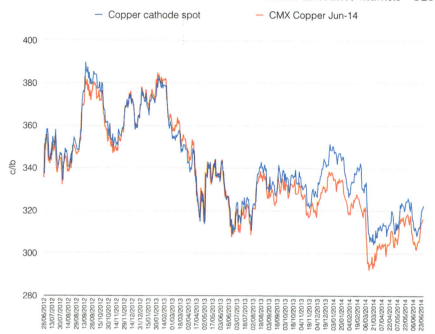

Exhibit 12.13 Price convergence of copper spot and June-14 futures contract
Source: Author, based on data from Thomson Reuters Datastream

Exhibit 12.14 Forward curve for COMEX copper
Source: Author, based on data from Thomson Reuters Eikon

forward curve allows us to extract the convenience yield between two different maturities. Finally, it provides forward prices for the pricing of forward contracts, options, swaps and in general for the any risk management calculations. Exhibit 12.14 shows the forward curve for copper prices on a particular date in June 2014.

Derivative contracts

There is a wide array of derivative products that are contingent on metals, and indeed several other commodities. Forwards, futures, swaps and options are some of the most commonly used ones and we will examine them all in brief.

Forward contracts

A forward contract is the simplest and most straightforward means for two parties to agree the physical sale and purchase of a commodity. The quantity, quality, delivery specifications and price are all negotiable between the buyer and the seller, hence a forward contract is fully customisable and very flexible. However, once written, a forward contract cannot be reversed, unless the two parties mutually agree to do so and are prepared to incur any contingent penalties. In addition, the contract cannot be sold on to a different party as there is no secondary market for these instruments. Finally, one of the key risks of a forward contract is that either party may default on their obligations, in which case the entire transaction simply collapses.

Futures contracts

In contrast to the bilateral transacting model of the forward market, a futures market brings all transactions under the umbrella of the exchange. When a party buys (goes *long*) or sells (goes *short*) a contract for the commodity, the counterparty is the exchange clearing house, which guarantees that the transaction will be honoured. To achieve this, market participants are required to make an initial deposit (the *initial margin*) with the exchange, proportional to the value of the position they open, and then maintain their deposit at a minimum level required by the exchange (the *maintenance margin*), until they decide to terminate their position. For the exchange and the market participants at large, this system calculates the profits and losses of each position on a daily basis (*marking to market*) and any participants with an account balance below the required maintenance margin is required to pay up additional amounts of money (*margin calls*) in order to continue trading.

This is best illustrated by an example. Let us assume that Max Profit, a seasoned copper trader, decides to open a long position on the COMEX copper contract for September 2014, because he feels that the price of copper will be rising. On 10 July, he puts an order to buy five Sep-14 contracts (each for 25,000 lb of copper) and his broker fills the order at a price of $3.5/lb. In order to open the position, Max has to deposit an initial margin of $3,000 per contract (i.e. a total of $15,000 for his overall position). He also has a maintenance margin of $2,750 per contract (i.e. his overall balance should not fall below $13,750, otherwise he will be asked for a margin call high enough to restore his balance to the initial margin).

Over the next few days, he maintains his position, but as the market moves, so does the balance of his account that his broker keeps on his behalf with the exchange. Exhibit 12.15 shows how the settlement price of the Sep-14 contract fluctuates on a daily basis and the result on Max's margin account, until he decides to close his position and exit.

If Max decides to close his position, he is most likely to do this by *offsetting*. This means that he simply has to sell the same number of an identical futures contract (for the same commodity and the same delivery month), incurring the normal brokerage fees and taking any profit or loss he may have made on his position.

Offsetting is one of four methods that may be available for closing a futures position. The other three are: exchange of futures for physical, cash settlement and physical delivery.

An *exchange of futures for physical* (EFP) involves two parties, one with a long and one with a short futures position. The two parties can identify each other with the mediation of the commodity exchange and agree to swap their futures position and at the same time enter a transaction on the physical commodity. They may do so before the expiry of the specific contract, but they have to carry out the transaction under the supervision of the exchange authorities.

Date	Day	Price ($/lb)	Daily P&L ($)	Margin account ($)	Variation margin ($)
09/06/14	1	3.04		15,000.00	
10/06/14	2	3.05	1,125.00	16,125.00	0.00
11/06/14	3	3.04	-1,500.00	14,625.00	0.00
12/06/14	4	3.02	-2,500.00	12,125.00	2,875.00
13/06/14	5	3.03	1,500.00	16,500.00	0.00
16/06/14	6	3.04	2,062.50	18,562.50	0.00
17/06/14	7	3.06	1,750.00	20,312.50	0.00
18/06/14	8	3.06	375.00	20,687.50	0.00
19/06/14	9	3.08	1,812.50	22,500.00	0.00
20/06/14	10	3.11	4,687.50	27,187.50	0.00
23/06/14	11	3.14	3,625.00	30,812.50	0.00
24/06/14	12	3.15	375.00	31,187.50	0.00
25/06/14	13	3.17	2,625.00	33,812.50	0.00
26/06/14	14	3.17	750.00	34,562.50	0.00
27/06/14	15	3.17	-500.00	34,062.50	0.00
			Net P/L	**16,187.50**	

Exhibit 12.15 Marking to market for COMEX copper contract
Source: Author

It is also required that their futures positions match the size of the physical transaction on the commodity.

If there is no offsetting or EFP transaction before the expiry of a futures contract, market participants, whether long or short, can simply settle their positions in cash. *Cash settlement* is available for most futures contracts and in some cases it is the only alternative to offsetting (i.e. no type of physical delivery is allowed). It simply requires traders to make payments to settle their gains or losses at the expiration of the contract.

If no other method is used, and the exchange regulations allow it, an open position can be settled by making a *physical delivery* of the commodity underlying the contracts. In this situation, it is typically the short position holder that notifies the exchange of the need to arrange a physical delivery. The exchange tries to find suitable long position holders and put them in touch with the short position holder, who normally determines exactly which commodity (of the ones allowed by the futures contract specification) and where it is delivered. The price can be negotiated between the two parties, but it is normally a differential from the official exchange price and has to be reported back to the exchange, as in the case of the EFP.

In our earlier example, Max Profit opened a long position at a certain market price. If the price moves higher than the price he bought at, then he will be making a profit, which he may decide to realise by reversing his position and closing out the contract. If he maintains his position and the price falls below his initial purchase price, then he will make an overall loss. For a graphical demonstration of the profits or losses from a long futures position, see Exhibit 12.16. On the horizontal axis is the price of the commodity, which rises as we move from left to right. On the vertical axis is the profit the trader makes in relation to the price at which he opened the long position. The pay-offs are represented by a positively sloping line (from the bottom left to the top right).

Conversely, Exhibit 12.17 demonstrates the pay-offs of a short futures position. As the price falls (towards the left of the horizontal axis), the short position becomes profitable. The trader can simply reverse it by buying back at a lower price and booking the profit. If the price increases, on the other hand, the position is loss-making. He can either reverse it and take the losses, or maintain it and make any necessary margin payments to keep his account in credit.

Unlike energy commodities, there are not that many contracts for base metals listed around the world. In the US, base (and precious) metals were listed on the COMEX division of NYMEX. In recent years, as CME has merged with NYMEX/COMEX, the only surviving base metals contract is that of copper. Contracts for base metals, such as steel products, copper, aluminium, nickel, zinc and lead, are increasingly available in Asian markets. Exchanges such as MCX in India and SHFE in China have launched several base metals contracts in recent years, as world metals consumption has shifted into these markets in a major way. However, the industry benchmark remains the London Metal Exchange, whose derivative contracts are the most widely used by market participants around the world, while LME prices form the basis for pricing physical trades and derivatives settlements.

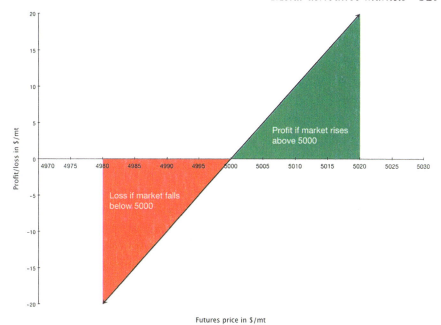

Exhibit 12.16 Pay-offs from a long futures position

Source: Author

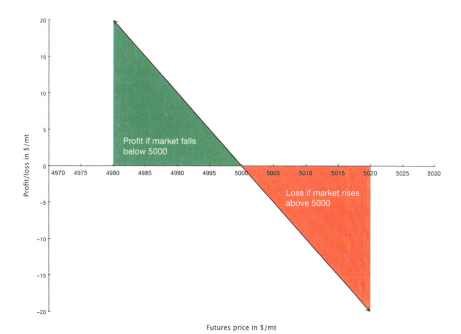

Exhibit 12.17 Pay-offs from a short futures position

Source: Author

Trading and hedging metals on the LME

The London Metal Exchange was set up in the mid-nineteenth century for the procurement of metals that were badly needed to sustain Britain's industrial growth. One thing that became evident from the start was the risk associated with metals trade, as most metal commodities had to be imported from a variety of distant origins. The problem was addressed with the introduction of a forward contract, which was designed to reflect the average period it took to take delivery of metals imported from abroad – three months.

This rather unique (if not slightly odd) instrument, the three-month contract, survives to date and is the key indicator of market activity and prices. The key difference between LME contracts and futures contracts on other exchanges is the 'continuous settlement' feature of the former. All LME three-month contracts are delivered exactly three months after having been opened – so a contract entered on, say, 15 June will be delivered on 15 September, and so forth.[2] Copper is the most liquid contract traded on the LME, but the exchange also offers contracts in aluminium, aluminium alloy, NASAAC (North American Special Aluminium Alloy Contract), tin, lead, nickel, zinc, steel billet, cobalt and molybdenum.[3]

In addition to the futures contracts being delivered daily out to three months, contracts can be delivered from three months to six months on a weekly basis (every Wednesday), and from seven months out to 63 months on a monthly basis (every third Wednesday of the month). Of these, the 15-month and 27-month contracts are often used as benchmarks for the medium- and long-term outlook of the metal's price. Finally, there is a cash market for immediate delivery, with cash settlement within two days of delivery.

Prices are quoted in $/mt terms, although all contracts may also be cleared in dollars, euros or yen. Prices are normally quoted for the three-month contract of each metal, with all other prices being determined as differential from the three-month contract.

To give an example of how this works, take a look at the top of Exhibit 12.18, panels A1 and A2. The bid-ask quotations for copper and aluminium are on the first line: aluminium is trading at $2,605/mt bid, and $2,606/mt ask; copper is at $7,498/mt bid, and $7,499/mt ask. For all other contracts, including the cash market, a bid-ask range of differential is given instead, with a letter indicating whether the market is in contango (C) or backwardation (B).

Suppose that the date is 15 March, and we want to calculate the bid-ask range for the cash contract for copper: first, write down the bid-ask quotations for the three-month contract; then read the cash/three-month differential from the table; because the market is in backwardation, cash prices are going to be above three-month prices, so you need to add the differentials to the three-

---

2 If the delivery falls on a weekend or holiday, it is transferred to the first available business day.

3 LME also offers 'LMEminis' for copper, aluminium and zinc. These are small size (5-tonne) contracts, delivered on a monthly basis out to 12 months and are traded electronically. Finally, it also offers a contract on LMEX, an index consisting of six of its most popular contracts.

A1. Aluminium				A2. Copper			
3 months	**$2605-6**	3M/Aug	10-12 C	**3 months**	**$7498-9**	3M/Aug	10-13 B
Cash/3M	29-30 C	3M/Sep	14-17 C	Cash/3M	37-38 B	3M/Sep	15-20 B
Apr/3M	20-21 C	3M/Oct	22-26 C	Apr/3M	29-30 B	3M/Oct	25-35 B
May/3M	15-16 C	3M/Nov	29-34 C	May/3M	15-16 B	3M/Nov	40-50 B
3M/Jun	2-3 C	3M/Dec	35-40 C	3M/Jun	4-5 B	3M/Dec	50-60 B
3M/Jul	6-8 C	3M/Jan	40-45 C	3M/Jul	7-8 B	3M/Jan	70-80 B

B1. Copper	Bid	Ask	B3. Aluminium	Bid	Ask
3M price	$7498	$7499	3M price	$2605	$2606
Cash/3M (B)	+ 37	+ 38	Cash/3M (C)	-30	-29
Cash Price	$7535	$7537	Cash Price	$2575	$2577
B2. Copper	**Bid**	**Ask**	**B4. Aluminium**	**Bid**	**Ask**
3M price	$7498	$7499	3M price	$2605	$2606
3M/Sep (B)	-20	-15	3M/Sep (C)	+ 14	+ 17
Sep price	$7478	$7484	Sep price	$2619	$2623

Exhibit 12.18 LME forward price quotations
Source: Author

month prices; the result is a bid-ask range of $7,535–7,537/tonne. The calculation is shown in panel B1, in the lower part of Exhibit 12.18.

Suppose now that you want to calculate the bid-ask range for the September copper contract (panel B2): write again the bid-ask range for the three-month contract; then read the three-month/Sep differentials from the table; because the market is still in backwardation, the contract closer to us (three-month) will be more expensive than the contract further away (July), so we need to subtract the differentials from the three-month quotations in order to obtain the July prices; doing so will give us a bid-ask range of $7,483–7,479/mt; this result, however, is irrational, since bid must always be lower than ask; this means that we need to make one more adjustment (i.e. cross-subtract the differentials from the three-month prices); this yields a bid-ask range of $7,478–7,484/mt, which is the required result. To calculate the cash and September contracts for aluminium, we use the same, but symmetrically oppo-site, methodology because the market there is in contango. The calculations are shown in panels B3 and B4 in the same exhibit.

Unlike other commodity exchanges, where each commodity is traded in its own pit, all metals are traded in the ring of the LME, in successive, five-minute market calls. Ring trading starts at 11:40 a.m. (London local time) with steel, and finishes with aluminium alloy at 4:15 p.m. (LLT). At 12:30 p.m. each day, prices are officially published for all metals; they are quoted in the financial press as AM official prices. The most interesting aspect of the LME, however, is that trading is not restricted to the ring; in fact, the market is very active around the ring – on the kerb – and electronically on computer screens, around the world, 24 hours a day. Kerb trading, contrary to what its name implies, is not a fringe activity, and prices for kerb trading are quoted next to AM official prices.

As in other futures markets, LME contracts[4] are standardised in terms of quantity and quality, so that market negotiations can focus on pricing alone. The LME, however, is a market that places considerable emphasis on the physical market, with proportionately more contracts being delivered at expiration. All contracts have a 2 per cent delivery tolerance; for the copper and aluminium contracts, which are specified at 25 tonnes, this means that the delivered quantity is allowed to vary between 24.5 and 25.5 tonnes. Although this may sound small, in a buoyant market it could make a considerable difference in the returns to the contracting parties. Apart from weight tolerances, the two parties must also be aware of additional issues, such as: freight costs; warehousing expenses; and the ability of warehouses to handle large quantities at short notice. All contracts are deliverable in LME designated warehouses to the bearer of LME warrants (i.e. documents of title to a quantity of metal of specific qualitative characteristics).

Although the LME is very much the market place for the physical trading of metals, its primary role is still to provide price discovery and risk hedging to its participants. As in all futures markets, participants in the LME can be distinguished as hedgers, speculators and arbitrageurs. For metals, an arbitrageur would look at the LME and COMEX for any mispricing opportunities. In doing this, he would take into account several items – such as freight charges, warehousing, insurance, duties and the cost of capital – and then see if the price differential is wider than what is justifiable.

In Exhibit 12.19, an example is given of a trader who faces a price of £4,790/mt of copper on the LME; if the price of copper is anything above $3.62/lb on COMEX, then it is worthwhile buying the metal in London, transferring it in the US, while selling the equivalent quantity of copper futures contracts on COMEX.[5]

Arbitrage is, of course, a very important activity, which keeps markets in balance and quickly eliminates pricing inefficiencies. The LME, however, is primarily used for hedging long and short positions in the physical market.

Take the example of an aluminium fabricator, who will have an exposure to price movements over the next three months. He will try to hedge the price risk by getting an equal – but opposite – exposure on the LME. The example and its pay-offs are shown in Exhibit 12.20.

---

4 LME contracts are known as *forward* contracts or *warrants*, but they are standardised, just like typical futures contracts.
5 One, of course, should take into account the difference of contract specifications between LME and CME/COMEX.

Assumptions
Home country is UK, home currency £, shipping from Felixstowe
Cargo is 25 metric tons of refined copper cathodes, or 1 LME contract
Destination country is US, shipping to Baltimore
CME copper futures 1-month ahead @ $3.48/lb

LME copper is £4,790/t (@ £/$1.6)	*$7,664.00*
Liner freight: $1,800 for 40' container	$72.00
Transfer to port customs, surcharges and other expenses £600/box @ £/$1.6	$38.40
Insurance @ 1% of value	$76.64
CIF Baltimore	*$7,851.04*
Duty on CIF @1%	$78.51
Customs clearance and transfer to warehouse $800/box	$32.00
Value at destination	$7,961.55
Cost of capital @ Prime (3.25%)+1.75% for 15 days	$16.36
Total Value	**$7,977.91**
CME copper equivalent price in $/lb (1 metric ton = 2,204.6lbs)	$3.62

Exhibit 12.19 Calculating an arbitrage opportunity
Source: Author

On 12 March, a fabricator tenders successfully for a contract to supply aluminium frames for a factory project, with delivery on 12 June.

Physical	LME Price	Futures
12-Mar: buys 1000 tonnes spot @ $2575/t	3M = $2605 Cash/3M = 30 (C)	Sells 40 3M warrants @ $2605/t
12-Jun: sells 1000 tonnes spot @ $2540/t	3M = $2570 Cash/3M = 30 (C)	Buys back 3M sale @ $2540/t spot
Loss of $35/t or total $35000	**Net profit of $30/t or total of $30,000**	Profit of $65/t or total of $65000

Exhibit 12.20 Short hedge in contango market
Source: Author

In a similar fashion, a party with a short position in the physical market will acquire a long futures position, in order to mitigate the effects of an unfavourable price movement. Of course, the net result of hedging need not be – and is not – always a net profit; it might very well be a loss. In either case, however, it will be better than a large loss on an unhedged position (see Exhibit 12.21).

Although the three-month contract is a very flexible instrument because it has a continuous settlement date, market participants frequently need to adjust their positions because of temporal mismatching. Exhibit 12.22 shows the case of a miner with initial short physical and long futures positions that needs to hedge his position for an additional 10 days, because delivery cannot be made on time. In this case, the miner – who is a short hedger – can extend his selling hedge by borrowing from the market. This he does by simultaneously

On 5 July, a copper wire manufacturer tenders successfully for a contract to supply telecom cable, with delivery in 3-months' time.

Physical	LME Price	Futures
5-Jul: orders 500 tonnes of copper for delivery in 3M, basis price ruling	3M = $7500 Cash/3M = 40 (B)	Buys 20 3M warrants @ $7500/t
5-Oct: receives 500 tonnes, basis @ $7690/t	3M = $7650 Cash/3M = 40 (B)	3M purchase @ $7500 matures; sells as spot @ $7690/t
Implied loss of $150/mt (7690-7540) or total of $75000	**Net profit of $40/t or total of $20,000**	Profit of $190/t or total of $90000

Exhibit 12.21 Long hedge in backwardation market

Source: Author

A miner expecting to ship copper concentrates fails to do so on time. He has to extend his hedge by 10 days. Market is in contango.

Physical	LME Price	Futures
Concentrates fail to arrive on due date	Cash = $7400/t 10 days over cash = $7410	Original 3M sale matures; buys back equal tonnage of cash; simultaneously sells same tonnage again for 10 days over cash
Concentrates delivered	Cash = $7350/t	Sells 10 days cash position and buys back spot @ $7350/t
Market fell by $50/t	**Net profit of $10/t**	Profit of $60/t

To extend a sell (short) hedge, you borrow, and such operation is favoured by contango

Exhibit 12.22 Miner extends selling hedge by borrowing

Source: Author

reversing his initial short futures position and re-initiating the same position for a few days only. This saves him from worrying about any unfavourable price movement during these few days.

The examples given above are commonly known as 'passive' hedging strategies; they all involve minimal use of the futures market, in order to hedge very specific exposures in the physical market. Life, however, is not always that straightforward. Indeed, the norm is for exposures in the physical market to develop as production progresses, so that hedging also needs to be an ongoing activity, with positions managed on a daily basis.

Consider, for example, the case of a smelter who receives a regular supply of concentrates, which he processes and needs to cover his long physical position. Assuming – for simplicity – that the estimated monthly throughput is 1,100 tonnes, and that there are 22 trading days per month, 50 tonnes of metal will be produced every day. This implies that each day, the physical exposure will need to be covered by the sale of an additional two contracts (2 × 25 tons each) on the LME.

Spread contracts

It is not always relevant to trade in simple (or *plain vanilla*) long and short positions. Frequently, one can construct a hedge for a more complex position, or indeed find a profitable opportunity, by using simultaneous positions in two or more closely associated contracts. Hence, the exposure is not on the full (or *flat*) price of the commodity, but on the price differential (or *spread*) instead. In metals, as indeed in other commodities, there are opportunities to construct three key types of spreads: *calendar*, *cross-commodity* and *raw material-product*.

A calendar spread involves a long position in a futures contract for delivery in one month and a short position in another contract for delivery in a different month. The spread is then known by the name of the two months. For example, a Jan-Feb copper spread is a one-month calendar spread and involves the two futures contracts for copper for January and February. When the trader goes long the closest month and short the furthest month, he buys the spread. Conversely, selling a Jan-Feb spread would involve selling January and buying February contracts. With spreads, the trader takes a position on the price differential between the two months (i.e. the level of contango or backwardation, rather than the flat price movement of the underlying commodity).

A cross-commodity spread involves the sale and purchase of two contracts for different but related commodities, usually for the same delivery month. A typical cross-commodity spread is that for two different metals. One could simply buy one metal, say copper, and sell the other, say aluminium. Changes in the spread could be explained by the various economic factors determining the use of each metal, as well as any substitution between the two metals, which would make one relatively more expensive than the other. Having said that, however, spread trades are not as common in metals as they are in energy commodities.

Swap contracts

As discussed earlier, a forward contract can be used to hedge price risk exposure for a particular time in the future for any commodity, as long as the two transacting parties agree the commodity quality and quantity. This gives both parties flexibility on the contract specifics, but leaves both parties exposed to each other's default risk. Alternatively, a hedger can use the futures market to cover his price risk exposure in the physical market. In this case, the counterparty risk is undertaken by the commodity exchange, but the hedger may be limited in terms of the futures contracts that are available and that may not match the precise quality and delivery specification of his physical cargo.

To resolve these shortcomings, financial intermediaries developed the *swap*, a derivative instrument that is essentially an exchange of a fixed for a floating price. Swaps are routinely used by traders to hedge exposures in the physical market for numerous energy commodities. As long as there is a published, commonly accepted price benchmark for a commodity of a specific quality

Exhibit 12.23 Iron ore swap example

Source: Author

and delivery, a swap can be constructed. The swap transfers the price risk from the commodity seller (producer) or buyer (consumer) to a financial intermediary – the swap provider – who warehouses the risk. In exchange, the swap provider can benefit from movements of the market in his favour. Once the provider has entered the swap agreement, it has to cover the risk exposure. Ultimately, the ideal way to cover this risk may be to arrange a counterbalancing swap with another financial institution, for an equal and opposite position.

An example here will help clarify the concept and the mechanics of a swap. Assume that there are three parties: 'SteelCo' is a steel mill; 'MineCo' is an iron ore producer; and 'FinCo' is the swap provider (e.g. a bank). SteelCo is short the physical and will need to buy iron ore in the open market; it is therefore exposed to the risk of rising prices. MineCo is long the physical and will need to sell its production in the open market; the risk here is a downward price swing. SteelCo can enter a swap agreement with FinCo, for a specified amount of iron ore at a specified price and over a specified period of time, typically for several months. For simplicity, let us assume that the swap is for 500,000 mt of iron ore at a price of $141.50/bbl. In a similar, but opposite, way, MineCo enters a swap agreement with FinCo, also for 500,000 mt of iron ore at $140.50/bbl. Both parties require the swap for a period of six months.

Let us now assume that at the end of the first month, the average market price for iron ore[6] has been $138.70/mt. The swap provider will make a

---

6   The average price is calculated as the simple arithmetic mean of the daily prices over the calendar month as reported by a recognised agency such as Platts or Metal Bulletin.

payment to MineCo – because the average market price has been below the swap price – equal to $1.80/mt (a total of $900,000). In an analogous way, the provider will receive a payment of $2.80/mt from SteelCo (a total of $1,400,000), because the average market price has been below the swap price. The net position of the swap provider is a profit of $500,000.

Once again, real life is rarely as straightforward as the preceding example. To start with, the quantities agreed in swaps are unlikely to be equal, and the price movements are not always favourable for the swap provider. Any mismatched risk has, therefore, to be appropriately covered. If the provider, for example, has a net long position, then taking an adequate long position on the futures market might cover his exposure.

The swaps described above are also known as *plain vanilla* swaps. There are more sophisticated versions of these transactions, which allow more flexibility on the terms of the swap for either of the two parties. For example, in a *differential* swap, the counterparties exchange the difference between two floating prices (e.g. copper-aluminium) for a fixed price differential. A *double-up* swap gives the swap provider the option to double the notional volume of the swap, before the pricing period starts. On the other hand, an *extendable* swap gives the swap provider the right to extend the swap, at the end of the period, for an additional predetermined period. A final example is that of a *swaption*, whereby the buyer has the option to decide, up to an expiry date, whether to initiate the swap or not. There may be more types available depending on the risks the counterparties are trying to hedge and their creativity.

Option contracts

Forward, futures and swap contracts share one common element: they are all designed to counterbalance the profit or losses made in the physical market. This is welcome when the hedger makes a loss in the physical, as his profit in the paper market will compensate for all or most of his loss. Conversely, however, any profits made in the physical market will also be wiped out by losses in the paper market. Ultimately, this is the nature of hedging, unwelcome though it may be on some occasions.

One way of hedging against unfavourable market movements, while still being able to take advantage of the upside potential of favourable market swings, is to use options contracts. Traded options contracts are available both on the LME and the CME. In addition, there are countless more OTC contracts that are designed to deal with specific aspects of risk, both in terms of the price and in terms of the volume of the commodity in question.

Basic definitions and contract types

Let us start though with a brief definition of the key types of options contracts and how they work. An option gives the right, but not the obligation, to the buyer to buy or sell a commodity (the underlying asset) at a specified price (the *strike* price), up to a certain point in the future (the *expiry* date). For the privilege, the buyer of the option has to pay an upfront fee (the *premium*) to the seller (or writer) of the option.

Options may grant the right to buy (*call* option) or sell (*put* option). For some options, this right can only be exercised at expiry (*European-style* option), while for others it can be exercised on any day up to expiry (*American-style* option).

Now that the basic characteristics of plain-vanilla options have been stated, it is time to discuss how each type of option works. Panel A of Exhibit 12.24 demonstrates the pay-offs for the buyer (long) call option written on copper, with a strike price of $5,000/mt, with an expiry at the end of November 2014 and for which a premium of $20/mt has been paid. The horizontal axis shows the price of the underlying asset, while the vertical axis shows the profit or loss made for each price. If the price remains below $5,000, there is no benefit from exercising the option, and the buyer simply loses his premium. As the price rises to $5,000 and above, the option becomes valuable and can be exercised. Once the price rises enough to equate the strike price plus the premium, the overall position yields a profit. For example, if exercised when the underlying price is $5,030, the buyer will buy his copper at the strike price of $5,000 and, as he has already paid a premium of $20, he will have a net purchase price of $5,020. He can then sell his copper at the market price of $5,030 and realise a profit of $10/mt.

The opposite pay-off takes place for the buyer (long) of a put option (panel B), who gets a profit out of exercising the option when the market price falls below the strike price of $5,000. When the market price falls to, say, $4,970, he will exercise his option to sell his copper at the strike price of $5,000. Having paid a $20 premium already, he will receive a net price of $4,980, which will leave him $10/mt better off than the current market price.

Panels C and D of Exhibit 12.24 show the pay-offs from the point of view of the option seller (short). In the case of a short call, as long as the underlying price remains below the strike price, the option will remain unexercised and he will simply receive his premium of $20/mt. If the price rises above the strike price, he will have to pay to the buyer of the call the difference between the market price and the strike price. The seller of a put has a pay-off schedule that is the mirror image of a short call, and the reader can work this out easily from panel D.

Although options can be used on their own simply to speculate, they are normally part of a hedging portfolio for market participants with a physical exposure in the underlying commodity. For example, a copper fabricator that is short on copper on the physical side may want to protect itself from paying an excessively high price for its copper purchases, but is happy to take advantage of the higher profitability when copper prices (i.e. its input costs) fall. To do this, the fabricator may wish to buy a call option that, in combination with its physical position, will help it form a *cap* on the price it pays for its copper. This combination is also called a *covered call*, and its pay-offs are shown in Exhibit 12.25. The fabricator's short physical position (-S) is depicted

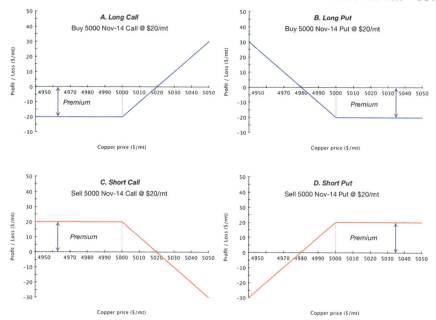

Exhibit 12.24 Basic option pay-offs

Source: Author

by the downward-sloping red line, while the pay-off of the long call option is shown by the now familiar green line, which implies that the strike price is $5,000 at a premium of $20. If the market price of copper rises above the strike price, the option can be exercised. When the market price rises above $5,020 (the strike price plus the premium), any additional losses in the physical market (in the form of higher copper purchase costs) will be cancelled out by the payment that the refiner will receive, which will equal the differential between the market price and the strike price. The combined pay-offs are depicted by the blue line, which sets a cap to the loss of profitability as the market price rise above $5,000. This means that the effective purchase price for the copper cannot exceed (is capped at) $5,020/mt.

To help us understand how a cap works, consider the example given in Exhibit 12.26. Here, a fabricator has a commitment to supply engine components and will need to buy a certain quantity of copper at the end of a specified period. The fabricator decides to hedge the risk of rising copper prices by buying a call option at the specified price and premium. The exhibit provides the specific information on prices and data and then sets out two scenarios: one of falling and one of rising copper prices. Note how, in the second scenario, the effective purchase price for the fabricator (the cap) is set at $5,050/mt (i.e. the strike price plus the premium).

Just like a purchaser of the commodity is afraid that the market price will rise, a producer wants to hedge against prices going down, which will result

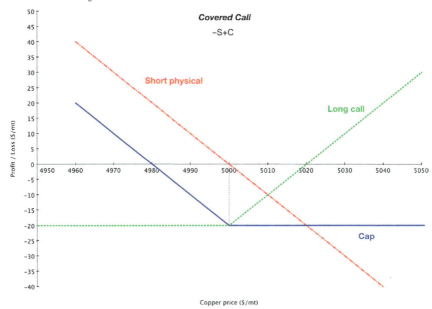

Exhibit 12.25 Covered call (cap)

Source: Author

On 01-Mar-14 a copper fabricator enters into a deal to supply engine components to be delivered by end of May-14. To fulfill the order it will require to purchase 500 metric tons of copper at the end of Apr-14

It decides to hedge the copper cost by buying a call option

Copper price at 01-Mar-14 = $4,970/mt

Copper required at the end of Apr, so expiry is 30-Apr-14

Amount required is 500 mt

Buy Apr 14 Call with strike price $5,000/mt @ premium $50/mt

Cap hedge for April 2014	
Physical market	**Options market**
Copper price on 01-Mar-14: $4,970/mt Current cost of copper: $2,485,000 (=4,970 x 500)	Buy Apr-14 call, strike price $5,000/mt @ $50/mt Call cost: $25,000 (=50 x 500)
First scenario - Falling copper prices	
Copper price on 30-Apr-14: $4,800/mt Actual cost of copper: $2,400,000	Strike price ($5,000) > Settlement price ($4,800) Option NOT exercised
Total copper cost (incl. option premium) = 2,400,000 + 25,000 = $2,425,000 or $4,850/mt	
Second scenario – Rising copper prices	
Copper price on 30-Apr-14: $5,500 Actual cost of copper: $2,750,000	Strike price ($5,000) < Settlement price ($5,500) Option IS exercised Payoff from options (5,500-5,000) x 500 - 25,000 = $225,000
Total copper cost (incl. option payoff) = 2,750,000 - 225,000 = $2,525,000 or $5,050/mt	

Exhibit 12.26 Cap hedge example

Source: Author

in a loss of income from selling the commodity. In this case, the producer is interested in fixing a minimum price (a *floor*) at which he can sell his production if prices fall, while still being able to take advantage of favourable price upswings. In this case, the producer may wish to enter a *protective put*, as described in Exhibit 12.27. Here, a copper miner has a long physical exposure to copper, which is depicted by the upward-sloping red line. The more the market price falls, the more he stands to lose. He can therefore buy (long) a put option that will establish a floor for the price he gets for his copper. This is depicted by the now familiar green line, which implies that the put option has a strike price of $5,000 and a premium of $20. If the market price of copper falls below the strike price, the option can be exercised. When the market price falls below $4,980 (the strike price minus the premium), any additional losses in the physical market (in the form of lower income from selling copper) will be cancelled out by the payment that the miner will receive, which will equal the differential between the market price and the strike price. The combined pay-offs are depicted by the blue line, which sets a floor to the loss of income as the market price falls below $5,000. This means that the effective sale price for the copper cannot fall below (has a floor of) $4,980/mt.

To help us understand how a floor works, consider the example given in Exhibit 12.28. Here, a copper miner is worried about the market price he will manage to get for his copper in the last quarter of the year. The miner decides to hedge the risk of falling copper prices by buying a strip of put options

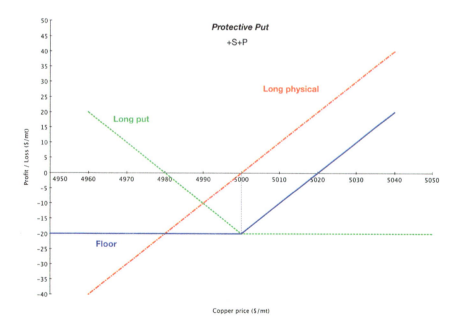

Exhibit 12.27 Protective put (floor)

Source: Author

at the specified prices and premiums. The exhibit provides the specific information on prices and data and then sets out two scenaria: one of rising and one of falling copper prices. Note how, in the second scenario, the effective sale price for the miner (the floor) is set at $4,860/mt (i.e. the strike price minus the premium). The example only gives the results for the Oct-14 part of the strip, but the reader should be able to work out the remaining two months with little additional effort.

Useful though a protective put may be, it does create a substantial outflow of cash in the form of the upfront premium payment. In the previous example, the premium cost just for one month amounts to $1.2 million, whereas for the whole Q4 strip it is $4.05 million. It is not surprising, therefore, that option buyers are keen on constructing hedges that are less expensive.

A *collar* is a good example of such a hedge, and works as follows. Imagine that the copper miner in the previous example still wants to create a floor on the price that he receives for his copper, but he is willing to forego some of the profit opportunity he may have if the oil price rises. To do this in practice, he can sell (write) a call option, for which he will receive a premium, but which may require him to make payments to the buyer of the call if the copper price rises. Exhibit 12.29 shows this combination of a long put (green line) and a short call (blue line), with the copper miner's natural long physical position (red line) on the commodity. As implied by the diagram, while the market

In 01-Jun-14 a copper miner is worried about the uncertainty of the copper market and would like to hedge its revenue from selling copper for the last quarter (Oct-Dec) of 2014. He decides to buy a strip of three put options as described below

Copper price at 01-Jun-14 = $5,000/mt

Production 1,000 mt/day => 30,000 mt/month

Buy a strip of puts for Q4-14

Oct-14 put, strike $4,900/mt @ premium $40/mt; Nov-14 put, strike $4,900/mt @ premium $45/mt;

Dec-14 put, strike $4,900/mt @ premium $50/mt

Floor hedge for Q4 2014 - October payoffs	
Physical market	**Options market**
Copper price on 01-Jun-14: $5,000/mt Current revenue per day: $5,000,000 (=5,000 x 1,000)	Buy Oct-14 put, strike price $4,900 @ $40/mt Put cost: $40,000 (= 40 x 1,000) or $1,200,000 for the month
First scenario - Rising copper prices	
Copper price on 30-Oct-14: $5,200/mt Actual revenue per day: $5,200,000 Per month: $156,000,000	Strike price ($4,900) < Settlement price ($5,200) Option NOT exercised

Total copper revenue (incl. option premium) = 156,000,000 - 1,200,000 = $154,800,000
or $5,160/mt

Second scenario – Falling copper prices	
Copper price on 30-Oct-14: $4,600/mt Actual revenue per day: $4,600,000 Per month: $138,000,000	Strike price ($4,900) > Settlement price ($4,600) Option IS exercised Payoff from options (4,900 - 4,600) x 1,000 x 30 - 1,200,000 = $7,800,000

Total copper revenue (incl. option payoff) = 138,000,000 + 7,800,000 = $145,800,000
or $4,860/mt

Repeat for Nov-14 and Dec-14, using the appropriate option premium

Exhibit 12.28 Floor hedge example

Source: Author

price stands at $5,000, the miner has bought an out-of-the-money put at a strike price of $4,980 and sold an out-of-the-money call at a strike price of $5,020. As long as the market price fluctuates between these two prices, the copper miner will simply get the market price, and the premium of $10/mt he pays for the put will be covered by the $10/mt premium he receives for the call (zero cost). If the price drops below $4,980, his put option will become valuable and worth exercising. Let us say that the price drops to $4,960. This means that he will receive $4,960 from the market for his copper, as well as $20 from the option writer, a total of $4,980, which is $20 below the original market price of $5,000. Conversely, if the price rises above $5,020, he will be making higher profits on the physical side, but he will have to make payments to the buyer of the call option. For example, if the price climbs to $5,040, he will be receiving $5,040, but he will have to pay $20 to the call buyer, leaving him a net income of $5,020. In short, using a zero-cost collar, the copper miner has created a collar between $4,980 and $5,020, and hence protects himself from excess losses, but also foregoes excess profits.

In addition to plain-vanilla options and combinations thereof, several more complicated (or *exotic*) options have developed over time, in response to the needs of market participants and the peculiarities of certain commodities. One such type is an *average price* or *Asian* option. This is a European option with a settlement price calculated as an arithmetic average of underlying prices (e.g. spot or futures) over a period of time, typically one calendar month. More formally, the value of an Asian option is given as $V_{AP} = \max(A^t_T - K, 0)$, where

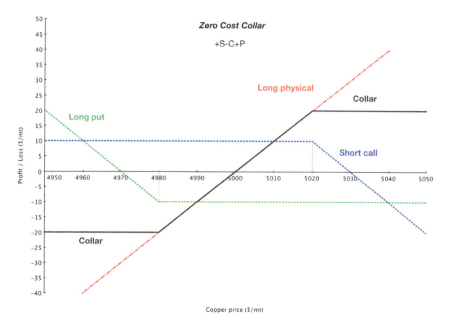

Exhibit 12.29 Zero-cost collar

Source: Author

$$A_T^t = \frac{\sum_{i=t}^{T} S_t}{T - \tau}.$$

This type of option is popular in all commodity groups and in general for commodities or assets where the physical trade is done over a monthly or longer period, or where the underlying price is not easily identifiable or can be easily influenced. As it happens, Asian options are particularly popular for base metals, and the LME offers this type of option, which it calls traded average price options (TAPOs), alongside its standard European-style options. All previous examples also work with the use of TAPOs, as long as we substitute the settlement price with the arithmetic average of the settlement prices of the previous month. This average is known as the monthly average settlement price (or MASP) at the LME.

Often the main risk is not found in the flat price of a commodity, but on the price differential between related commodity prices (i.e. the price spread). Spreads were discussed earlier, and one can simply envisage the purchase of options on the various types of spreads we encountered, such as calendar, cross-metal and ore-metal spreads.

The vast majority of options are written with regard to the price of the underlying asset. Frequently, however, the risk does not emanate solely from the price. There is also risk associated with the volume of the commodity that is to be delivered. As we saw in Chapter 7, for commodities such as natural gas or electricity, it is quite common to use such *volumetric* option, where the option is written on the contract volume, rather than the price. They can also be written on metals, although it is more common in metal markets for the buyer and the seller to agree a long-term contract of supply that guarantees the delivered quantity, while pricing is allowed to fluctuate in tandem with the spot market.

A final type of option that is quite interesting is *quantos*. A quanto is a composite option, combining price risk hedging of the underlying commodity price in the currency in which the commodity is traded, as well as risk hedging of the exchange rate between the commodity currency and the user's base currency. For example, consider a Chinese copper wire fabricator who buys copper from the international market, in order to manufacture telecom cable. The copper is bought at international prices, which are volatile and are denominated in US dollars. On the other hand, the fabricator is obliged to sell its copper wire to its customers in Chinese renminbi and is only allowed to vary its sale prices at regular intervals (say once or twice a year). The risk faced by the fabricator is not only the commodity price risk from copper, but also the $/RMB currency risk. A quanto option allows the fabricator to hedge both risks at the same time with one instrument.

Basics of option pricing

As can be seen from the above discussion, options offer ample opportunities to hedge a variety of risks, both in terms of the price and the volume of the underlying commodity. Calculating the value and price of an option has been a challenging task, tackled by numerous authors, until the breakthrough by Black and Scholes (1973), who discussed pricing of European stock options. Their formula for pricing a European call option on a stock, $C_t^{K,T} = S_t N(d_1) - Ke^{-r(T-t)}N(d_2)$, is an elegant closed-form solution, whereby $C_t^{K,T}$ is the price at time t of a call option with strike price K and maturity T, $e^{-r(T-t)}$ is the discount factor until maturity and $N(x)$ is the cumulative normal distribution function. Once the price of a call is known, the put price can be calculated from the put-call parity: $P_t^{K,T} = S_t = C_t^{K,T} + Ke^{-r(T-t)}$, where $P_t^{K,T}$ is the price at time t of a put option and the other terms are as described earlier. This solution does come with a number of assumptions, however. These include continuous trading of the underlying stock, lack of tax and transaction costs, lack of dividend payments, knowledge and non-variability of the short-term interest rate, as well as the assumption that the price of the underlying stock is driven by a GBM process.

Merton (1973) extended the B-S pricing model by allowing interest rates to be stochastic, the option to be American-style and the stock to pay dividends. This latter property is quite relevant to commodities, as the convenience yield for a commodity works in a similar way as a dividend payment for the value of the stock. Hence, the formula for a European call option written on a spot commodity price can now be written as $C_t^{K,T} = S_t e^{-y(T-t)}N(d_1) - Ke^{-r(T-t)}N(d_2)$, where y is the convenience yield. In a further breakthrough, Merton (1976) tackled the assumption of the price dynamics being described by a continuous-time diffusion process. He introduced the jump-diffusion process (mentioned earlier in this chapter), which allows the coexistence of both a continuous price motion and a jump stochastic process.

Black (1976) discussed the pricing of options written on futures contracts, which is particularly relevant to commodities, as many of the options written are of this type. The price for a call option with a strike price K and expiry time T, written on a futures contract F with expiry T_1 is given by the formula $C_t^{K,T} = F_t^T e^{-r(T-t)}N(d_1) - Ke^{-r(T-t)}N(d_2)$. Finally, Cox *et al.* (1979) extended the option pricing literature by introducing their binomial option pricing methodology, which allows itself to generalisation and can be used to price more complex options.

A final note in this analysis is the brief mention of the sensitivity of an option value with respect to changes in the market parameters. These are commonly known as the *Greeks*. Starting with *delta* (Δ), this is the partial derivative of the call price C with respect to the price S of the underlying asset and it is positive (negative for a put option). *Gamma* (Γ) is the rate of change (i.e. the derivative) of Δ. *Theta* (θ) is the partial derivative of the option price with respect to time and is negative for both a put and a call option, representing the loss of the value of the option due to time decay. *Vega* is the rate of change of the option price with respect to the volatility σ and is positive for puts and calls – the higher the volatility, the higher the chance that the option will be exercised. Finally, *rho* (ρ) is the partial derivative of the option price with respect to the risk-free interest rate r.

The purpose of the preceding discussion was to only briefly expose the reader to some of the most important literature in the area of options and their pricing. For a more expansive discussion of option pricing methodologies for commodities the reader is referred to Eydeland and Wolyniec (2003, Chapter 8), Geman (2005, Chapters 4–6), Burger *et al.* (2007, Chapter 2) and Edwards (2010, Chapters 3.4–3.6).

Conclusion

This chapter completes the review of metal markets undertaken in the previous four chapters. The focus was placed on the characteristics of the various metal commodity prices and the instruments available for hedging the price risk posed by the market. Although there is considerable overlap with respect to the range of derivative instruments available to the various commodity groups, we have geared the analysis primarily towards metal derivative contracts. It is now time to turn our attention to the next major group of commodities – agriculture.

References

Black, F. (1976) 'The pricing of commodity contracts', *Journal of Financial Economics*, 3: 167–179.

Black, F. and Scholes, M. (1973) 'The pricing of options and corporate liabilities', *Journal of Political Economy*, 81: 637–654.

Burger, M., Graeber, B. and Schindlmayr, G. (2007) *Managing Energy Risk: An Integrated View on Power and Other Energy Markets*, Chichester: Wiley.

Cox, J.C., Ross, S.A. and Rubinstein, M. (1979) 'Option pricing: a simplified approach', *Journal of Financial Economics*, 7: 229–263.

Edwards, D.W. (2010) *Energy Trading and Investing: Trading, Risk Management and Structuring Deals in the Energy Markets*, McGraw-Hill.

Eydeland, A. and Wolyniec, K. (2003) *Energy and Power Risk Management: New Developments in Modeling, Pricing and Hedging*, Hoboken, NJ: Wiley.

Geman, H. (2005) *Commodities and Commodity Derivatives: Modeling and Pricing for Agriculturals, Metals, and Energy*, Chichester: John Wiley.

—— (2008) *Risk Management in Commodity Markets: From Shipping to Agricuturals and Energy*, Chichester: Wiley.

Gibson, R. and Schwartz, E. (1990) 'Stochastic convenience yield and the pricing of oil contingent claims', *The Journal of Finance*, 45: 959–976.

Merton, R.C. (1973) 'The theory of rational option pricing', *Bell Journal of Economics and Management Science*, 4: 141–183.

—— (1976) 'Option pricing when underlying stock returns are discontinuous', *Journal of Financial Economics*, 3: 125–144.

Pilipovic, D. (2007) *Energy Risk: Valuing and Managing Energy Derivatives*, 2nd edn, McGraw-Hill.

Pirrong, C. (2012) *Commodity Price Dynamics: A Structural Approach*, Cambridge: Cambridge University Press.

Working, H. (1940) 'The theory of price of storage', *American Economic Review*, 39: 1254–1262.

13 Fundamental agricultural economics

The most fundamental human need is that to feed. Regular food production is what distinguished organised societies from nomadic tribes, and the beginning of civilisation coincided with the cultivation of land and domestication of animals in the Fertile Crescent, between the rivers Tigris and Euphrates.

Food commodities were also among the first to be traded among nations, be it cereals, oils or exotic spices. This and the following few chapters deal with the structure of some of the most important agricultural commodities internationally. We start with a discussion of the economics ruling the demand for, and supply of, food and the organisation of the sector. The next chapter deals more extensively with cereals, while the one after that focuses on the three most important of the 'soft' agricultural commodities, namely coffee, sugar and cocoa.

Sector organisation

Agriculture is a term collectively describing a set of distinctive but interdependent sectors, which are in the business of producing, processing and distributing a large array of commodities destined for human consumption and other industrial uses. Textbooks usually distinguish between three large subsectors: the farm sector, agri-business and the public sector.

Of the three, the first focuses on producing crops and rearing livestock. The second is further divided into the input subsector and the processing and marketing subsector. The input subsector deals with goods necessary for agricultural production, such as machinery, fertilisers and chemicals. Processing and marketing serves as a link between primary producers and final consumers, and very much shapes the way the latter perceive the function and role of the former.

The last of the aforementioned three subsectors is the public sector, which provides a regulatory framework, imposes taxes and grants subsidies to agricultural producers, all of which are extremely important functions for the uninterrupted operation of the agricultural sector, but also responsible for severe market distortions. The importance of government policies in agriculture cannot be exaggerated. Agriculture is the base of any society at the beginning of its economic development. The rural population in less developed societies is a large part of the total population, and has therefore the undivided attention of government officials. Even in developed economies, where the focus has long shifted to services, the agricultural lobby is strong and vociferous enough to attract the government's attention.

Apart from the lobbying power of the rural population, food availability and safety is high on the agenda of every nation, together with energy supplies and economic growth. As a result, food policy issues are of tantamount importance. Moreover, a host of other intrinsic characteristics of the industry call for government intervention: weather vagaries, international trade, environmental issues and technological advance are such examples.

Taxonomy

Agricultural commodities are normally split into crops,[1] animal produce, production inputs and processed foods. This classification should not be treated in a strict sense, as many commodities often fall into more than one category, and commodities in one class act as inputs in another class.

Food crops

Food crops are broadly classified in grains, legumes or pulses, fruits and vegetables, and other crops. Grains are the most prominent and most extensively traded of all other food commodities. These include wheat, coarse grains, rice and other minor grains.

Rice is usually examined separately, not only because of its different physical characteristics, but also due to the fact that it constitutes the staple food of most of the population in Asia, especially in Pacific Asia, and production is largely affected by massive governmental intervention. For this reason, we will look at it briefly at the end of the following chapter.

Minor grains and oilseeds include commodities such as sunflower seeds, rapeseed, tapioca and other commodities of minor importance, especially in terms of their importance for trade. Most of these commodities are used in composite animal feedstuffs, and hence end up indirectly in human consumption. Substantial quantities of these commodities are also pressed and their oils are consumed directly, or as margarines. In more recent years, these oils are also being used as feedstock for the production of biodiesel.

Coarse grains include maize, or 'corn' in the USA, barley, sorghum, oats, rye and millet. All of them are primarily used as inputs in the livestock industry, although some of them are used directly for human consumption, while a relatively small quantity is used in the production of alcoholic beverages. Corn is also extensively used for the production of ethanol, especially in the USA.

---

1 Crops include agricultural commodities for industrial use, such as forest products and natural rubber. These, however, will be treated separately; for the time being, we shall concentrate on food crops.

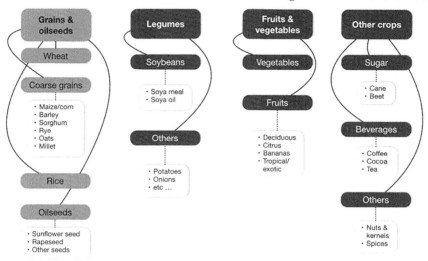

Exhibit 13.1 Food crops
Source: Author

Together with wheat, coarse grains will be discussed in detail in the following chapter.

Of the legumes, the most important are soya beans and their derivatives: soya meal and soya oil. Because of their cross-substitutability with coarse grains, soya beans are often studied together with them, and are also widely traded internationally.

The main difference between the fruits and vegetables and all the other classes of food crops is the length of time they can be kept in storage. Grains are storable for about a year, without loss of quality; coffee beans are often kept in storage for two or three years; fruits and vegetables, however, are classified as perishable commodities, and require quick and careful handling from harvest to final consumption. Because of their physical characteristics, therefore, they entered international trade only relatively recently, when adequate methods of refrigeration became available for long-haul transportation. Even so, however, many fruits and vegetables entering international trade may be considered as luxuries and are prone to large fluctuations due to changes in consumers' income.

The commodities grouped under 'other crops' are in fact quite significant in their own right. Three of these – sugar, coffee and cocoa – are important, if not in terms of tonnage, at least in terms of value, in international trade, and we will look at them in more detail in a later chapter.

Animal produce

Like fruits and vegetables, animal products are normally perishable commodities, which have to be kept under controlled conditions and consumed within a short period of time. Meat is traded primarily in frozen condition, although some countries prefer to import the animals themselves and then slaughter them domestically.

Fish is a rather unique case, as the commodity is caught, processed, packaged and refrigerated at sea, on the same or separate vessels. Fishing rights are also a hotly debated issue, because it steps up the competition among different nations, and raises the question of protecting the aquatic environment from excessive exploitation. In fact, the administration and monitoring of fisheries has often created friction between developed countries, such as Japan, the United States, Canada, Norway and Spain, among others.

Dairy products include eggs, milk (mainly powdered) and milk products. Like fruits and vegetables, dairy products are sensitive cargo and have to be maintained chilled at a constant temperature while in transit.

Agricultural inputs

A subsector that has received relatively little attention is that of agricultural inputs. Farm machinery falls in this category, together with fertilisers – both organic and inorganic – pesticides, seeds, and any other goods necessary for agricultural production. Fertilisers, seeds and pesticides are usually covered as part of the chemical industry; in fact, all of the world's major chemical manufacturers are heavily involved in the research, development, production and distribution of such agricultural inputs. In addition, firms involved in the trading of crops also deal in the sale of seed varieties, although they are not normally involved in their development.

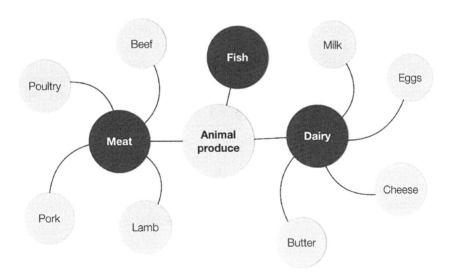

Exhibit 13.2 Animal produce

Source: Author

Supply of food

In economic terminology, crops are classified as renewable natural resources. The term 'renewable' is not a guarantee, however, of interminable supply. As with any production process, crops also display a convex yield curve, which means that output initially grows quickly – in comparison with the increase in the use of inputs – then reaches a plateau, and eventually tapers off as the soil becomes gradually devoid of those elements that are vital for the growth of the plants. Exhibit 13.3 shows the curves for total, average and marginal physical product. Note how marginal product may sometimes – but not necessarily always – become negative as more and more output is forced out of the land.

In the long term, all three curves respond dynamically to changes in technology. An improved seed variety, better protection with pesticides and the application of a fertiliser may all move the physical product curves upwards, representing the higher yields now achieved.

The production function

Crop production is a function of two sets of inputs: fixed and variable. Fixed inputs include: the amount of available arable land; the degree of mechanisation of agriculture; the quantity and quality of seeds, which can be considered as fixed in the short term; and the availability of irrigation. Variable inputs –

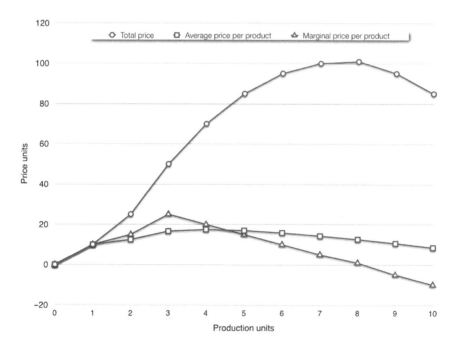

Exhibit 13.3 Total, average and marginal product

Source: Author

even in the short term – include: fertilisers; the amount of husbandry applied; the use of pesticides; and the use of labour.

Arable land is only the fourth largest type of land available around the world. Forests constitute 31 per cent of total land area, pastures are 26 per cent, while another 31 per cent of all available land is dedicated to other uses, mostly in urban areas for residential and industrial purposes (see Exhibit 13.4). Arable land is a mere 11 per cent of total land, and about 60 per cent of it shared among four regions: Africa, North America, South Asia and Eastern Europe (see Exhibit 13.5).

Land availability is not enough, however, to achieve production targets. Yields can be boosted with the use of fertilisers, and the deployment of mechanical means for preparing the soil, sowing and harvesting the crops. The application of fertilisers varies widely from one country to another and depends very much on the physical characteristics of the soil, and the capital available for their purchase. The use of agricultural machinery, in its turn, also depends on capital availability, but also on less obvious parameters, such as the average farm size, which determine the viability of such large investments.

Two more important agricultural inputs are labour and irrigation. The latter is not such an accurate indicator of agricultural efficiency, but it is a good proxy of the amount of capital and effort going into the sector. Labour, on the other hand, is – together with mechanisation – a reasonably good indicator of the modernisation of agriculture in any single country. The wide diversity of labour usage is shown in Exhibits 13.6 and 13.7, where a selection of countries is

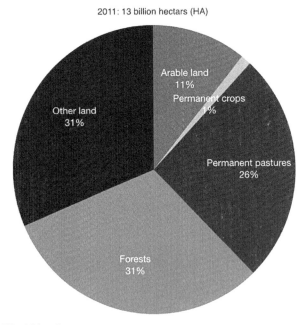

2011: 13 billion hectars (HA)

Arable land 11%
Permanent crops 1%
Other land 31%
Permanent pastures 26%
Forests 31%

Exhibit 13.4 World land use

Source: Author, based on data from FAO (2014)

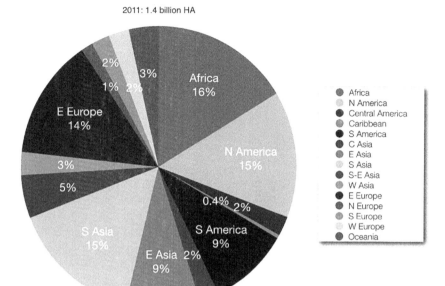

Exhibit 13.5 Shares of arable land
Source: Author, based on data from FAO (2014)

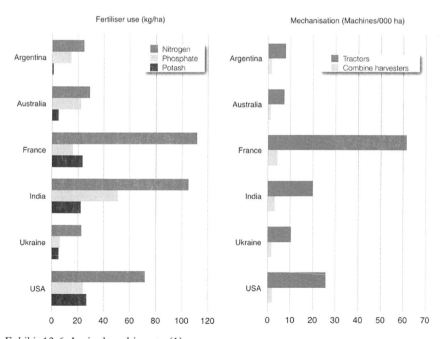

Exhibit 13.6 Agricultural inputs (1)
Source: Author, based on data from FAO (2014)

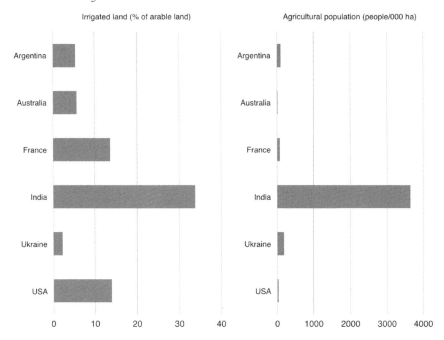

Exhibit 13.7 Agricultural inputs (2)
Source: Author, based on data from FAO (2014)

used to show the differences in the utilisation of fertilisers, machinery, land irrigation and labour.

Ultimately, all the factors discussed here are combined into one curve that represents the reaction of agricultural production to different market prices. This is the well-known supply curve, which is upward sloping. Determinants that may shift the supply curve are resource prices, technology, taxes and subsidies, prices of other similar goods, and expectations.

What is also interesting to note is how 'steep' or 'flat' the supply curve is. The term describing this characteristic is elasticity, which is very much dependent on time. In the short term, it is quite difficult to change decisions about crop production; once the seeds are sown or the new plants are put in the ground, production is fairly inflexible, if one disregards weather. Hence, the supply curve is very steep, perhaps vertical. In the long term, all parameters and decisions are variable, making the supply curve a lot more elastic. The medium term offers the chance to vary some production factors, but restrictions are still imposed by fixed production factors and costs.

One has to bear in mind, however, that the 'short', 'medium' and 'long' terms are periods that cannot be set consistently; they are usually imposed by the commodity itself. For annual crops, one year is the short term while the long term is the period after which all factors of production are variable. Grains are such crops, since they are sown and then harvested within the year. The situation is not that clear-cut for crops harvested from plants, such as coffee and cocoa. The life cycle of the coffee plant, for instance, can last for several years, with old and new plants contributing to production. This makes, of course, production decisions a lot less responsive to immediate changes in demand, and producers may have to live with their decisions for a long time.

In the next two chapters, we are going to discuss in more detail the supply characteristics of several agricultural commodities, which will help clarify and exemplify the supply framework given here.

Demand for food

The characteristics of the demand for food are not any different to that for any good, as described in standard economics textbooks.[2] Individuals consume goods because they derive some sort of utility from them. With each additional unit of the good, an additional amount of utility is derived. However, as the number of total units consumed increases, each additional unit gives less additional – or marginal – utility. This is depicted graphically in Exhibit 13.8; the utility from the consumption of the first unit is 50 'utils',[3] while for any additional units marginal utility remains positive but declines. In the extreme,

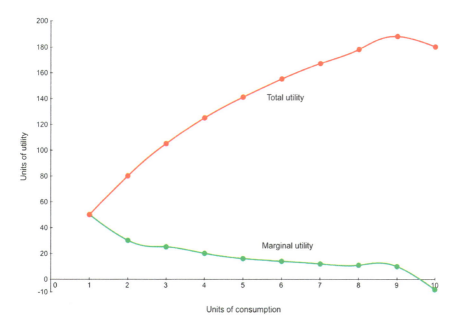

Exhibit 13.8 Total and marginal utility

Source: Author

2 See, for example, Seitz *et al.* (2001) and Lipsey and Chrystal (2007). For a discussion of consumer utility theory in the context of agriculture, see Cramer *et al.* (2001, Chapter 3).
3 The 'util' is an imaginary unit of measurement for utility, which belongs to the league of other economists' inventions, such as the widget and the numéraire.

marginal utility may even become negative,[4] causing a decrease in the level of total utility as well.

Unfortunately, the choices made by consumers are not only limited by their tastes, but also by their disposable income. In a simplified world of just two goods, consumers would be limited to those combinations of the two goods that are at or below their budget. This line is depicted in Exhibit 13.9, and shows how many units of one good must be given up in order to consume one unit of the other good; this is also known as the rate of substitution between the two goods. The budget line does not remain fixed over time; changes in technology, budget and prices may shift it or tilt it.

Exhibit 13.9 also shows the effects of an increase in consumer budget; the line shifts outwards, representing the fact that more units of both goods can be purchased. The change of the price of a good would also affect the slope of the budget line. Assuming that the price of good B increases, the consumer can now buy less units with his income. As a result, the budget line tilts clockwise around its intersection point with the axis of good A (see Exhibit 13.10).

Another concept used in demand analysis is that of indifference curves. This is a concave curve defined as the locus of combinations of goods A and B for which the consumer is indifferent. Combined with the budget constraint, the final consumption of the two goods should lie on the consumer's indifference

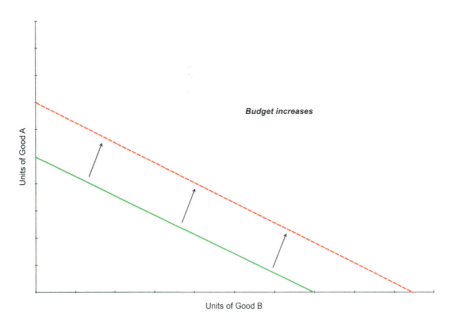

Exhibit 13.9 Budget change and the budget line

Source: Author

---

4 Imagine that the good in question is bars of chocolate, or gills of whiskey!

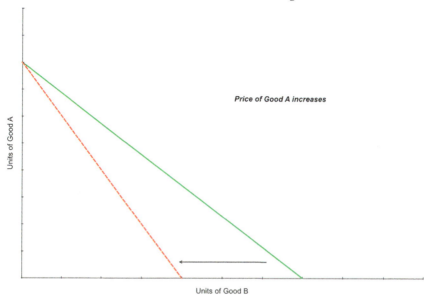

Exhibit 13.10 Price changes and the budget line
Source: Author

curve and not above the budget line. At the optimum, this is the point where the indifference curve is tangent on the budget line.

Exhibit 13.11 demonstrates a situation similar to that depicted in Exhibit 13.10. This time, good A becomes cheaper and the budget line tilts clockwise around its fixed intersection point with the horizontal axis. The improvement in the consumer's position is demonstrated by the shift of his indifference curve upwards to its tangent point with the new budget line.

If we repeat the previous process enough times, while keeping all other factors constant, we can plot prices against quantities and derive the demand curve for the good in question. Normally, the demand curve is concave and downward sloping, indicating the fact that, as the price of a commodity increases, consumers are only willing to buy ever-decreasing quantities of the commodity.

An interesting feature of demand is its responsiveness to price changes. The economic term is elasticity, and it can take the form of own-price, cross-price or income elasticity, depending on whether we measure demand responsiveness to the commodity's own price changes, changes in the price of its substitutes, or changes to disposable income.

Of these three types of elasticity, income elasticity seems to attract most interest. According to this criterion, food commodities – like all goods – can be classified into necessities and luxuries. The former have income elasticity between 0 and 1, while the latter have income elasticity of more than 1. Finally,

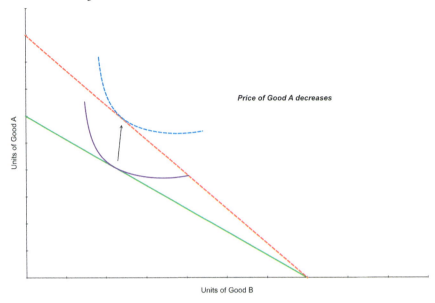

Exhibit 13.11 Consumption equilibrium

Source: Author

some food commodities may even have an elasticity of less than 0, in which case they are classified as inferior goods.[5]

Demand determinants

The main determinants of the demand for food commodities can be summarised into four items: population, tastes, income and prices.

Population

As one would expect, population directly affects the demand for food commodities around the world. The world's total population was estimated in 2010 to be just above 6.9 billion and to reach ca. 7.3 billion by 2015, with most of it located in Pacific and South Asia. The two most populous countries in the world are China and India, with about 1.34 and 1.2 billion, respectively. What is perhaps more interesting is that population growth in India is higher than China, and the former is projected to catch up with the latter around 2030 and to be ahead of it by 2050.

---

5 An example could be rice, whose consumption increases at a slower rate than income, but after a certain level of income its consumption declines, giving way to increases in the consumption of other grains, such as wheat. This example is particularly apt for Asian economies, where rice is the most widely used staple good. As average incomes have risen and tastes are changing in the region, rice consumption has given way to wheat and coarse grains. The increase in the consumption of coarse, in particular, is even more pronounced, as they are used for the production of meat, and are hence consumed indirectly.

1950			2010			2050		
Rank	Country	Population	Rank	Country	Population	Rank	Country	Population
1.	China	667.1	1.	China	1,337.7	1.	India	1,620.0
2.	India	449.6	2.	India	1,205.6	2.	China	1,385.0
3.	United States	180.7	3.	United States	309.3	3.	Nigeria	440.4
4.	USSR	119.9	4.	Indonesia	240.7	4.	United States	400.9
5.	Japan	92.5	5.	Brazil	195.2	5.	Indonesia	321.4
6.	Indonesia	88.7	6.	Pakistan	173.1	6.	Pakistan	271.1
7.	Germany	72.8	7.	Nigeria	159.7	7.	Brazil	231.1
8.	Brazil	72.8	8.	Bangladesh	151.1	8.	Bangladesh	201.9
9.	United Kingdom	52.4	9.	Russia	142.4	9.	Ethiopia	187.6
10.	Italy	50.2	10.	Japan	127.5	10.	Philippines	157.1
11.	Bangladesh	49.5	11.	Mexico	117.9	11.	Mexico	156.1
12.	France	46.6	12.	Philippines	93.4	12.	Congo DR	155.3
13.	Pakistan	45.5	13.	Ethiopia	87.1	13.	Egypt	121.8
14.	Nigeria	45.2	14.	Vietnam	86.9	14.	Russia	120.9
15.	Ukraine	42.7	15.	Germany	81.8	15.	Japan	108.3
16.	Mexico	38.7	16.	Egypt	78.1	16.	Vietnam	103.7
17.	Vietnam	34.7	17.	Iran	74.5	17.	Uganda	104.1
18.	Spain	30.5	18.	Turkey	72.1	18.	Iran	100.6
19.	Poland	29.6	19.	Thailand	66.4	19.	Turkey	94.6
20.	Egypt	28.0	20.	France	65.0	20.	Sudan	77.1

Exhibit 13.12 The 20 most populous countries in 1960 and 2010, and projections for 2050

Source: Author, based on data from UN World Population Division (2012)

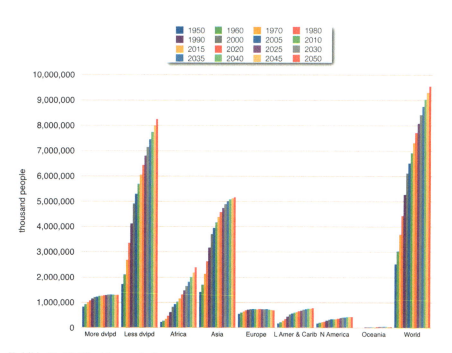

Exhibit 13.13 World population

Source: Author, based on data from UN World Population Division (2012)

Income and tastes

As was discussed earlier, income is a major determinant of food demand. A good approximation – but not an accurate indicator – of disposable income in different countries is their GDP per capita. One would expect higher demand for necessities, as well as luxuries, in countries with higher per capita income.

Income alone cannot determine consuming habits, however. Tastes play a very important role, both for the total consumption of food commodities and for the composition of this consumption. A common measure of the average level of food consumption is the dietary energy supply, or, put simply, the number of calories consumed per capita daily.

The composition of dietary energy supply is as important as its aggregate level, because it contains information on the tastes of the consumers. A larger proportion of animal sources of energy shows a preference of meat, which entails use of coarse grains in larger quantities, which might have to be imported. Although such measures of consumer tastes may be crude, they are very useful in long-term macroeconomic forecasts in food industries.

Prices

The final determinant of food demand is the actual price of the good in question. Earlier in this section, we mentioned the importance of own-price, cross-price and income elasticities. Although the latter seems to attract more attention, cross-price elasticity is also interesting for the student of food commodities. Agricultural goods are not immune to changes in the circumstances of similar or complimentary commodities; a large surge in the demand for chocolate will not only boost demand for cocoa, but also that for sugar; a switch to coffee will most probably affect the demand for tea; and so forth.

Another important element of the final price of the commodity is the transport cost. Low-value agricultural commodities rely on cheap freight rates for their competitiveness in foreign markets. On the other hand, rare and exotic foods target high-income households, and hence can afford to pay premium freight rates for fast and reliable delivery.

International trade in food commodities

Agricultural goods are quite actively traded around the world. Grains alone are the third largest dry bulk commodity transported by sea and provide considerable employment for the dry bulk carrier fleet. Fruits and vegetables have special handling requirements and provide employment to a large fleet of specialised reefer vessels; high-value fruit and vegetable varieties are also carried in special refrigerated boxes generating a considerable amount of container traffic. The rest of the agricultural commodities are generally traded as 'general cargo' (i.e. in small consignments together with other cargo, or in containerised form when it is affordable).

In terms of value, agricultural trade is only just over one-tenth of the value of all goods traded internationally. With the exception of rare or exotic crops,

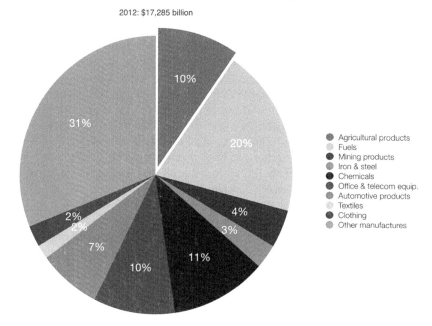

2012: $17,285 billion

- Agricultural products
- Fuels
- Mining products
- Iron & steel
- Chemicals
- Office & telecom equip.
- Automotive products
- Textiles
- Clothing
- Other manufactures

Exhibit 13.14 World merchandise trade by major products (% shares)
Source: Author, based on data from WTO (2014)

most commodities are of low to medium value, which implies that transport cost is a substantial part of the final price that the consumer has to pay. Further discussion of international trade in agricultural commodities is postponed until later, when we will focus our attention on individual commodities and analyse them in more detail.

Pricing of food commodities

Pricing methods are almost as numerous and diverse as the number of agricultural commodities. As a general rule, agricultural commodities are handled by governments who intervene to a lesser or greater extent, with the aim to support agrarian income.

Traditionally, the agricultural sector has a considerable bearing on governmental policies in many countries, even if it does not actually contribute that much to the gross domestic product. The sector's considerable lobbying power, together with the desire to promote and ensure security of food supplies, has led governments to regulate quite heavily and thus distort open market pricing mechanisms.

One can find examples of price distortions in almost every country, either directly or indirectly. In the European Union, for example, agricultural support is quite extensive and is formally given through the Common Agricultural

Policy.[6] In the United States, the system allows more participation from the private sector, and assistance is more pronounced for goods destined for export markets. In other countries, the governments are anxious to reduce income variability for their agrarian population and thus guarantee a minimum purchase price.

Despite all this regulation and intervention, however, there is plenty of scope for more competitive determination for the prices of most commodities. Exchanges trading in future claims to agricultural commodities exist in several countries, although the US and London Exchanges have a considerable advantage because of their liquidity. Such futures markets – although pricing just a portion of the total quantities produced and traded – are extremely important, as they provide an adequate mechanism for price discovery and risk hedging. Physical markets work very closely with futures markets, with cash prices often being determined as differentials of futures prices.

In the following chapters, we are going to discuss the pricing mechanisms for grains and soft commodities, both in spot and futures markets.

Conclusion

The aim of this chapter was to provide a general analytical background for the study of any agricultural commodity. In doing so, we looked at determinants that affect the demand and supply of agricultural commodities, which are produced for food uses. This discussion will prove useful – and clearer – when we concentrate on some of the most important agricultural commodities, but this chapter will also prove useful for the study of agricultural commodities with non-food uses (such as forest products and rubber), which we will encounter later in this textbook.

References

Cramer, G.L., Jensen, C.W. and Southgate, D.D. (2001) *Agricultural Economics and Agribusiness*, 8th edn, New York: John Wiley.

FAO (2014) *Faostat Database*, UN Food and Agriculture Organisation, accessed online at: http://faostat3.fao.org.

Lipsey, R. and Chrystal, A. (2007) *Economics*, 7th edn, Oxford: Oxford University Press.

Seitz, W., Nelson, G.C. and Halcrow, H.G. (2001) *Economics of Resources, Agriculture and Food* (McGraw-Hill Series in Agricultural Economics), 2nd edn, McGraw-Hill.

UN World Population Division (2012) *World Population Prospects: The 2012 Revision*, Department of Economics and Social Affairs, United Nations Secretariat, accessed online at: http://esa.un.org/unpp.

WTO (2014) *International Trade Statistics*, World Trade Organisation, accessed online at: http://stat.wto.org.

6 Since 2005, EU CAP's financing has been streamlined to two funds. The European Agricultural Guarantee Fund (EAGF) finances direct payments to farmers and measures to respond to market disturbances, such as private or public storage and export refunds. The European Agricultural Fund for Rural Development (EAFRD) finances the rural development programmes of the member states.

14 Grains

After setting the framework for the study of food commodities, we are going to turn our attention to the most important group of agricultural commodities: grains.

Grains include cereals, oilseeds, soya beans[1] and rice. We will first discuss the physical characteristics of cereals and the production procedure, with the aim to understand how these attributes have a bearing on the economics of the different commodities. We will then look at supply and demand parameters, and the trade patterns of grains around the world.

Trading of grains in the physical markets is the next focus, and we will also look at how these markets are organised in the world's largest market: the United States.

The futures markets in grains are the oldest in the world and still have an active and very important role today. We will look at their structure and how they function in conjunction with the physical markets, but this discussion is reserved for the last chapter in this textbook.

Physical characteristics

Grains are the fruits of relatively simple plants in the grass family. The importance of grains in the dietary requirements of all countries in the world cannot be overstated. Non-animal sources of food account for more than 60 per cent of dietary energy requirements around the globe, with grains accounting for most of this share. However, even when grains are not consumed directly by humans, they are used as animal feedstuff, and hence enter the food chain indirectly too.

Grains are grown for their nutritional value and they are an important source of both carbohydrates and proteins. Carbohydrates provide energy in the diet, both for humans and animals. But while animals can make do with a range of alternative sources of carbohydrates, humans are limited to their tastes. The fact, however, remains that – at least for animal feedstuff – competition from non-grain fodder, such as root crops, citrus pulp and fishmeal, does exist.

---

1 Strictly speaking, soya beans are legumes, but it is their direct competition with all types of grains that makes their inclusion here relevant.

Grains are also an important source of proteins. These are complex foods, made up of carbon, oxygen, hydrogen, nitrogen and sometimes sulphur, and are particularly important for nutrition at times of rapid growth. However, while some animals can synthesise proteins in their stomachs, humans need to receive proteins ready-made. In developed countries, proteins enter our diet mainly from animal products, while in developing countries they come mainly from grains.

Taxonomy

Grains – excluding rice – are classified in three major groups: wheat, coarse grains and other oilseeds. Soya beans are also incorporated in the analysis of grains because they are often used as a substitute for the latter. Coarse grains include corn, barley, oats, rye and sorghum. Of these, corn is the most important, and it will be covered in more detail together with wheat. Oilseeds include millet, sunflower seed, rapeseeds and other minor crops, which are used both for animal feedstuff and for oil and fats destined for direct human consumption.

Production specifics

There are several aspects of the process of growing grains and some of them are discussed under the individual grains later in the chapter. Some of the common production characteristics for all grains, however, are: soil preparation; variety selection and planting; feeding of the plant; protection from pests; and harvesting. The reader might wonder why so much detail is required for someone with no botanical interest in the subject. The coverage provided, however, is the minimum required for the understanding of the economics and pricing of the commodities.

Soil preparation

An important element for the growth of grains is the soil's characteristics and its adequate preparation. Soil has three main attributes: texture, which ranges from sand to clay; tilth, which is the way its particles are arranged; and its acidity or alkalinity. Wheat and barley, for example, require rich, grainy and not too acidic soils to flourish. On the other hand, oats can grow on soils that are too acidic for wheat or barley, and rye can even survive on poor, light, acidic soils where other grains would fail. Before planting, soil has to be adequately prepared. This usually involves inverting, bursting and mixing the topsoil, and encouraging water absorption while also maintaining adequate drainage.

Variety selection

Grains are usually distinguished by variety and class. A variety is described by the race and name of the cereal. Examples for wheat include 'Avalon', 'Apollo' and 'Galahad'. Class, on the other hand, represents the quality of the grains, which has been officially certified for trading purposes. An example would be 'Canadian Western Red Spring No.1'. These classes are extremely important for the standardisation of grains, which is a vital prerequisite for grains that are traded on commodity exchanges, such as wheat, barley and corn.

In recent decades, especially since the 1990s, variety production and selection has become a much more involved process, with changes taking place at the molecular level. We are, of course, referring to genetically modified (GM) crops, whereby the plants used have had their DNA changed using genetic modification techniques. The drivers behind the development of GM crops are several: improved shelf life, stress resistance,[2] herbicide resistance[3] and pathogen resistance[4] are key.

Feeding

To synthesise their food, grains use oxygen and carbon from air, oxygen and hydrogen from water, and a range of other elements from the soil, such as nitrogen, phosphorus, potassium, magnesium, calcium and sulphur. One important attribute of the soil, which regulates the availability of such elements, is its acidity or alkalinity. Steps to rectify acidity may be required, together with proper manuring and fertilisation.

Pests and diseases

Good weather and soil conditions also promote the growth of weeds, which restrict the growth of the crop plants themselves. Control is achieved with adequate soil preparation, straw burning before sowing, weeding before and after sowing, or through the use of chemical herbicides. Pests pose another threat to satisfactory crop yields. Protection from pests is usually achieved through treatment of crop residues, rotational cropping, good drainage and ploughing, and the use of pesticides.

Finally, diseases are not infrequent and may seriously affect the quality and/or yields of crops. Crop rotation has been the traditional way of preventing the development of diseases, but more recent techniques include the breeding of seed varieties resistant to disease and adequate selection and mixture of different varieties.

Harvesting

Harvesting is an important part of the production process, and its degree of mechanisation is the most visible criterion marking efficiency differences

---

2 Resistance to extreme conditions, such as drought, frost and increased water salinity.
3 One of the most common genetic modification aims to develop 'Roundup Ready', or glyphosate-resistant crops. The name comes from the widely used Monsanto herbicide, and it was the same company that developed the first GM variants resistant to its own product.
4 For example, corn, rice, potato and many other crops have been engineered to be resistant to a number of viral pathogens.

between various countries. In developed countries, specialised agricultural machinery is used to cut standing crops, but also to separate grains from straws, convey grains to a tank and then to a trailer, and discharge straws to the rear, or even chop them and tie them into bales. In developing countries, on the other hand, harvesting is very much dependent on the availability of ample and cheap labour, because machinery is too expensive to acquire, especially when the average farm size is too small to justify such an investment. In some cases, the production characteristics of a crop (e.g. rice grown in Asia) means that the crop can only be harvested manually.

Supply of grains

From the analysis so far, the main supply determinants for grains have become evident. Over the last 50 years, the production of grains has exhibited considerable volatility. When one looks more carefully, however, wheat and rice production have shown relative stability, which leaves much of the volatility to be accounted for by coarse grains.

Another characteristic of the sector is that while most of the increases in production before the Second World War came from increases in the areas cultivated, after the end of the war most gains came from increases in production yields. It has been estimated that in the period 1960–1983, 74 per cent of production growth came from increases in yields.[5]

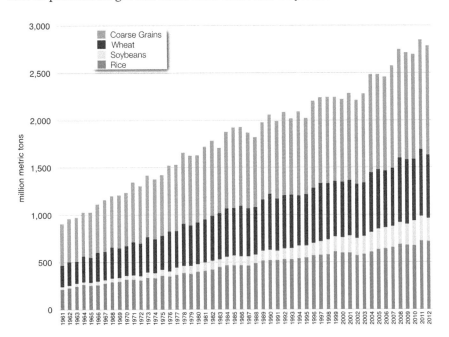

Exhibit 14.1 Historic development of primary grain crops (1961–2012)

Source: Author, based on data from FAO (2014)

5 Hazell (1985).

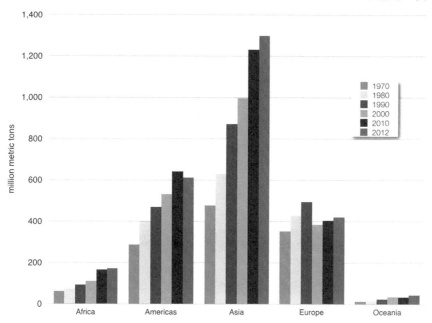

Exhibit 14.2 World production of primary cereals (excluding soya beans) by region
Source: Author, based on data from FAO (2014)

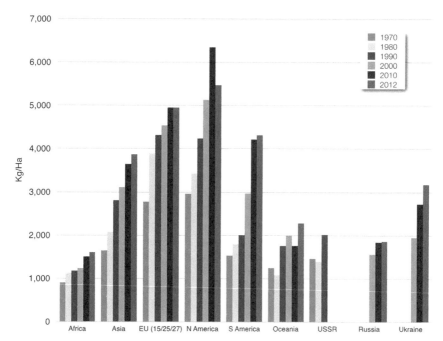

Exhibit 14.3 Development of regional cereal yields
Source: Author, based on data from FAO (2014)

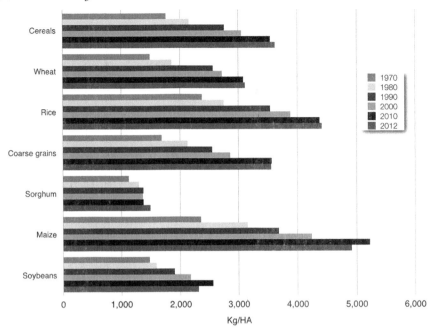

Exhibit 14.4 Development of cereal yields by product

Source: Author, based on data from FAO (2014)

On a regional basis, yields increased rapidly in the 1950s and the 1960s in developed countries, with little additional gains in subsequent decades. On the other hand, developing countries registered significant gains in productivity only after the 1970s, but even the highest yields in these countries are well below those in Western Europe and North America.

Exhibit 14.3 shows the development of average cereal yields by region, from 1970 to 2012, while Exhibit 14.4 highlights the yield development of individual cereals over the same period.

Wheat

Wheat is the most tolerant grain. It can be planted from as south as Australia and South America to a latitude of 60° N. It can be planted at sea level, but also as high as 3 km above it. Wheat grows in areas with rainfall between 25 and 180 cm per annum, and flourishes during long days with an average temperature of about 30° C. It is susceptible to frost, and winterkill sets in at temperatures of –15° C to –20° C, if the ground is not covered with snow. Even if the temperature is as high as 10° C, winterkill is still a risk if the ground is frozen and strong winds prevail.

Wheat has a growing period of anything from four months for spring wheat to eight months for winter wheat, and it goes through a number of distinct phases. These phases are recorded, usually on the basis of two similar scales:

Zadoks and Feekes (see Exhibit 14.5). The former is a two-digit scale, which tends to be more accurate, as each of the 10 digits it contains is further elaborated with a second digit, used to describe further intermediate stages in the growing process.

For winter wheat, the seed takes a few months to germinate, while for spring wheats the germination period is much shorter. In the spring, the head, which contains the kernels, develops at the tip of the stem while the stem is still very short [seedling growth and tillering]. The stem grows rapidly [stem elongation], pushing the head up (booting) and out of the top leaf sheath [ear emergence]. After the head emerges, [flowering] takes place and kernel development begins [milk development]. After the kernels have fully developed and filled [dough development], the leaves and stem lose their green colour [ripening], and the grain dries down quickly. When the grain dries down sufficiently (to 15 percent moisture or less), the fields are ready to harvest.

Climatic conditions affect all nodes on Zadoks' scale, but it is mainly nodes 71 and 89 that determine the amount of protein that the plant will have. Depending on their protein content, wheat varieties are broadly classified in

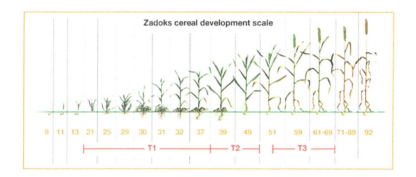

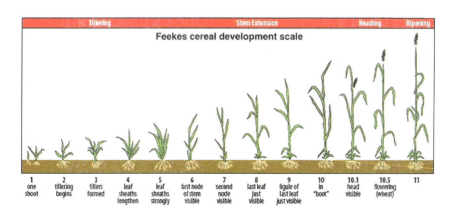

Exhibit 14.5 Zadoks and Feekes' scales of cereal growth

Source: Bayer Crop Science (2014)

hard and soft wheats, with several refinements in between. An example of protein ranges for US wheat classes is given in Exhibit 14.6.

Wheat is planted twice a year, and the two varieties are known as winter and spring wheat. Winter wheat is planted in autumn, during September or October. It grows to a height of about 10–15 cm, and can be grazed by cattle. During winter, the plant becomes dormant, and should ideally be covered by snow to prevent winterkill. As soon as spring arrives, the plant resumes growth and is normally ready to harvest in July. Spring wheat, on the other hand, is planted as early as possible in the spring, matures over the summer and is ready for harvest in September. Because the harvesting season begins with winter wheat in July, the beginning of the crop year for accounting and statistical purposes is also set then.

Wheat is produced in most countries, but a handful of these account for the majority of production and exports. The EU, South and East Asia and North America are the largest wheat-producing regions (see Exhibit 14.7). On an individual basis, China tops the lists of largest producers, followed by India, the USA, France and Russia (see Exhibit 14.8). Before its break-up, the FSU was a formidable wheat producer, leading the world's largest producing nations. Today, Ukraine is the second most important former Soviet republic, with production placing it in 12th position in the world. Both spring and winter wheat are grown in Russia and Ukraine. Yields have improved, but the weather extremities have created considerable instability in production from one year to the next. About 70 per cent of the total production is spring wheat, which is planted north of the Caspian Sea and east of the River Volga. Winter wheat is also planted in the vicinity of the Black Sea, Moldavia, Volga and northern Caucasus.

Problems with extreme weather conditions are also faced in Canada, where the main type planted is spring wheat. This is sown in April/May and harvested in July/August, mainly in the regions of Manitoba, Alberta and Saskatchewan.

In the United States, both winter and spring wheat is grown. The latter is about one-third of all US production, grown in a relatively narrow area in the states of North and South Dakota, Montana, Wyoming and Minnesota. Exhibit 14.9 highlights the acreage planted with winter wheat in 2013.

The most common type of wheat in Western Europe is red winter wheat, which is planted between September and November. It is harvested between June and August. The interesting story behind the stable growth of wheat

Wheat class	Protein range %
Hard Red Spring	12–18
Durum	10–16
Hard Red Winter	9–14
Soft red Winter	8–12
White	8–11

Exhibit 14.6 Protein ranges for US wheat classes

Source: Atkin (1995)

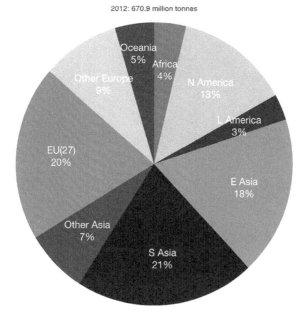

Exhibit 14.7 Regional production shares of wheat

Source: Author, based on data from FAO (2014)

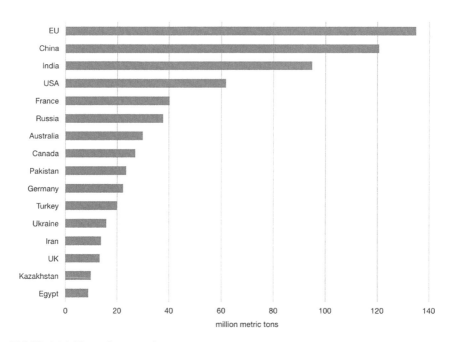

Exhibit 14.8 Top wheat producers

Source: Author, based on data from FAO (2014)

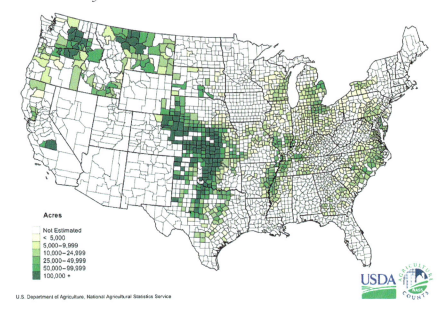

Acres

Not Estimated
< 5,000
5,000–9,999
10,000–24,999
25,000–49,999
50,000–99,999
100,000 +

USDA

U.S. Department of Agriculture, National Agricultural Statistics Service

Exhibit 14.9 Winter wheat in the United States
Source: USDA, National Agricultural Statistics Service

production in Western Europe is directly linked with the agricultural policies devised from 1967 onwards by the then European Economic Community. We will discuss this topic later in this chapter.

In China, wheat is grown throughout the country, but yields are better in the east and south regions, where climatic and soil conditions are better. Wheat is mainly sown in autumn and harvested in summer.

In Australia and Argentina, the two most important producers of the south hemisphere, both hard and soft wheat are sown in April/May (winter in the southern hemisphere) and harvested between November and January. Crops in Australia have manifested a great variability, mainly on account of drought seasons. In Exhibit 14.10, there are several examples of how Australian wheat production swings between extremes, as was the case in 1982, 1991, 1994, 2002 and 2006, when production was around 10 million tonnes. In contrast, during the bumper years of 1983, 1996, 1999, 2003, 2005, 2011 and 2012, production was well over 20 million tonnes.

Coarse grains

This broad category includes corn, sorghum, oats, rye and a few other minor grains. By far the most important of them is corn, which accounts for three-quarters of global production (see Exhibit 14.11).

Corn is planted in latitudes between 58° N and 40° S, and from sea level to 4 km above it. Rainfall should be at least 20 cm, but can be as high as

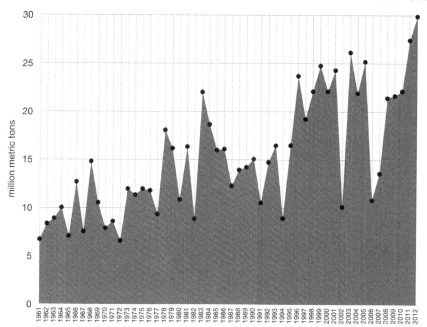

Exhibit 14.10 History of Australian wheat production

Source: Author, based on data from FAO (2014)

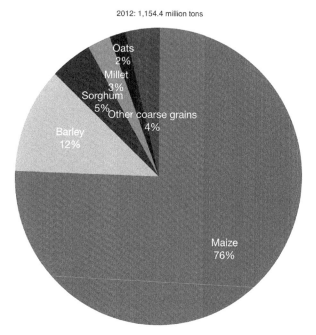

Exhibit 14.11 Coarse grains production by type

Source: Author, based on data from FAO (2014)

500 cm, per annum, with moisture levels adequately high during July and August (in the northern hemisphere). It is always planted in spring and has a growth period between 110 and 140 days. Corn flourishes in warm – but not hot – and sunny weather conditions, with temperatures between 20 and 30° C. Sunlight is in fact an important requirement, and one of the reasons why it is not widely grown in Northern Europe.

Weather conditions are also important for corn's protein content, and, together with soil characteristics, affect the amount of gliadin and determine the final use of the crop. A special type of corn with a genetic deficiency to convert sugars to starch is known to us as sweetcorn, while another variety with a very hard endosperm is the familiar popcorn. These varieties, however, hardly account for more than 1.5 per cent of total corn production. In the United States – the world's largest producer and exporter of corn – about 99 per cent of all corn production is dent corn, which is named from the indentation in the top part of the corn kernel caused by shrinkage of the starch.

Whether looking at coarse grains in total (Exhibit 14.12), or corn in particular (Exhibit 14.13), it is evident that North and Latin America and East Asia are the key producing regions.

Nearly one-third of global corn production is generated in the United States (see Exhibit 14.14). Of this, about 80 per cent is produced in the 'Corn Belt' (see Exhibit 14.15), where it is planted in May – but sometimes as early as March – and harvested in October. Corn is classified as yellow, white and mixed. Yellow dominates the markets for livestock feed and for wet milling into sweeteners, starches and other products for human consumption and

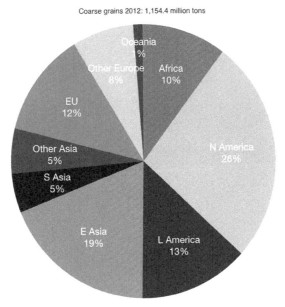

Coarse grains 2012: 1,154.4 million tons

Exhibit 14.12 Regional production shares of coarse grains

Source: Author, based on data from FAO (2014)

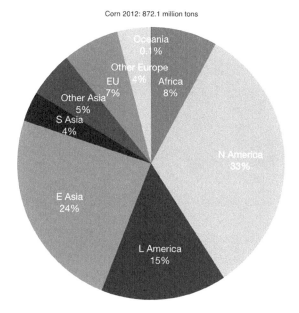

Corn 2012: 872.1 million tons

Exhibit 14.13 Regional production shares of corn

Source: Author, based on data from FAO (2014)

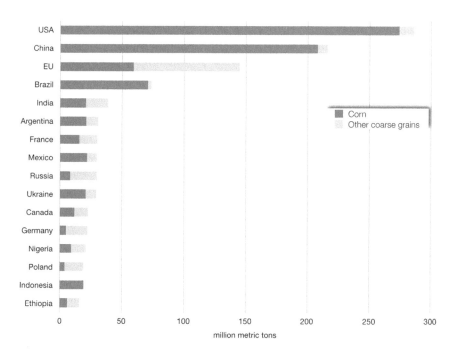

Exhibit 14.14 Top producers of corn and other coarse grains

Source: Author, based on data from FAO (2014)

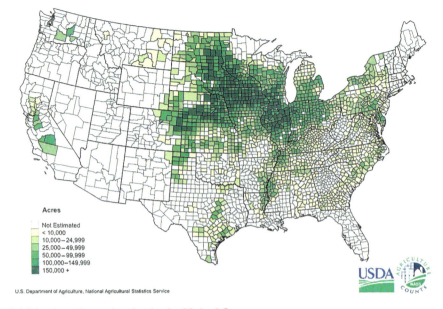

Acres

Not Estimated
< 10,000
10,000 – 24,999
25,000 – 49,999
50,000 – 99,999
100,000 – 149,999
150,000 +

U.S. Department of Agriculture, National Agricultural Statistics Service

Exhibit 14.15 Corn planting in the United States
Source: USDA, National Agricultural Statistics Service

industrial uses. White corn is more suitable for dry corn milling for the production of flour, hominy, grits and also industrial uses. Finally, mixed corn is mostly used for animal feedstuff.

The aforementioned concentration in production in the Corn Belt also means that if adverse weather hits that region, the international market in corn will almost certainly also be affected. Atkin[6] gives an illustrative example of the effect of a shortfall in US corn production:

> Consider the drought of 1988, which hit the mid-western states of the US very hard. As a result, US coarse grain production fell from 217 to 150 million tonnes whereas in the rest of the world, production increased only marginally from 588 to 590 million tonnes. Therefore, world production fell from 805 to 740 million tonnes, a fall of 8 per cent in global production simply because of adverse weather conditions in one region of the United States.

In more recent years, we have observed more such swings in US production in 2002, 2006 and the most recent drought in 2012 (see Exhibit 14.16).

A distant second to corn is barley, while sorghum and the remaining coarse grains are produced in relatively small quantities. Coarse grains are a bit more complicated to analyse, as a substantial part of their production never actually leaves the farm; it is used for animal feedstuff. Key producers of other coarse

6   Atkin (1989, p. 44).

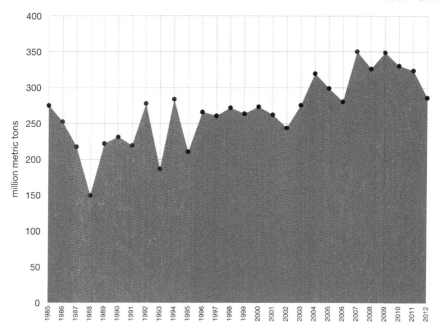

Exhibit 14.16 Historical US production of coarse grains

Source: Author, based on data from FAO (2014)

grains are the EU and Russia, with barley accounting for most of their production (see Exhibit 14.14).

Soya beans

Soya beans are botanically classified as a legume, but they are commercially classified as oilseeds, and their importance in the grains market is such that they are normally examined alongside other grains. Like in the case of corn, soya beans are extensively grown in the US, which produces one-third of global output per annum. The world's second largest producer is Brazil, with approximately one-quarter of world output. Other important producers include Argentina and China (see Exhibit 14.17).

In the United States, soya beans are planted in the same time of the year as corn, and the Corn Belt is their main production area, particularly the central and southern sections (see Exhibit 14.18). Of the more than 150 different varieties available, the yellow soya bean is the dominant class in commercial markets. Soya beans are traded in their original form, but most of them are usually processed into soya bean oil and meal.

Rice

Rice is a member of the grass family and its botanical name is *oryza*. Rice has been cultivated since the third millennium BC, originally in China, and from

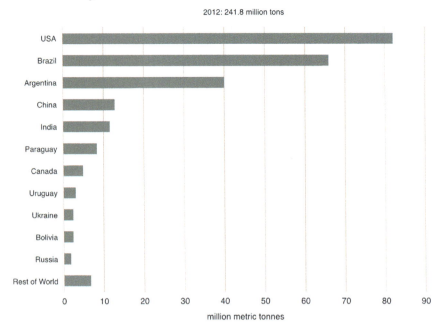

Exhibit 14.17 Top soya bean producing countries

Source: Author, based on data from FAO (2014)

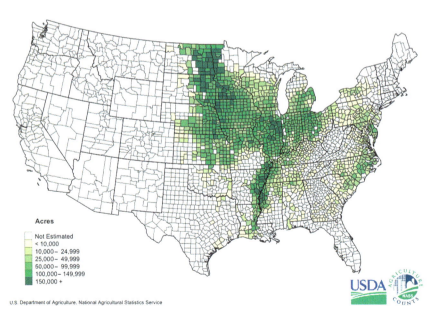

Exhibit 14.18 Soya bean planting in the US

Source: USDA, National Agricultural Statistics Service

there to India and the rest of South and East Asia. Although over 100 countries worldwide produce rice, Asia accounts for approximately 90 per cent of the world's production and consumption. Rice is an extremely important crop; it is a basic diet for over 50 per cent of the world's population.

Two species, *oryza sativa* and *oryza glaberrima*, have emerged as the most popular cultivated rice. Of these two, *oryza sativa* is primarily cultivated and is divided into two categories, *Indica* and *Japonica*, both of which include glutinous and non-glutinous varieties. A third category, *Javanica*, refers to the bulu and gundil varieties of Indonesia.

Indica rices are characterised by tall weak stems, long droopy leaves and their sensitivity to low temperature and photoperiod (day length). They produce longer slender grains that usually remain separate when cooked. This variety developed in the monsoon climates of South and Southeast Asia where the soils were relatively infertile, fields were unevenly flooded, and radiation from the sun was low due to cloud cover during the rainy season. Moreover, the temperatures were high at the time of planting, day length declined as the season progressed and the weed competition was intense. Indica grains are divided into long grain (greater than 6 mm) and medium grain (5–6 mm).

Japonica is a temperate-type plant, tolerant to lower temperatures, with short leaves and stems. It is sensitive to photoperiod, and therefore fares poorly in the short-day tropics. The variety developed in the moderate climate of China where the temperatures were lower at the time of seeding, rainfall more evenly distributed and the solar radiation was higher as a result of less cloud cover

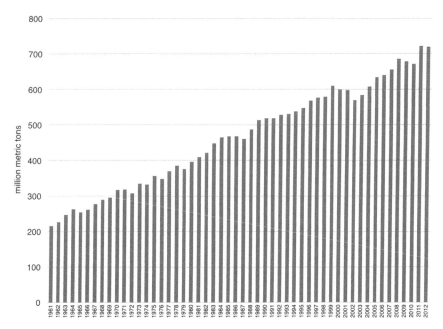

Exhibit 14.19 Development of paddy rice production

Source: Author, based on data from FAO (2014)

and longer days in summer. Moreover, the weed control was better, water depth more uniform and soil more fertile.

Japonicas produce shorter (4–5 mm in length), rounder and more translucent grains with low amylose content that makes the grain cohesive or sticky when cooked. They are also different in terms of taste and smell. Japonica is widely grown in China, Japan and Korea. The Javanica race is characterised by tall plants with thick stems and broad leaves with long panicles and large bold grains.

With the exception of Antarctica, rice is grown in every continent. It thrives in a wide range of altitudes, from sea level to about 3 km above sea level, and in varying climates, from tropical to temperate. Moreover, rice is grown on different soil types and on a range of ecological environments. Currently, rice is grown in approximately 100 countries. Rice production requires both copious amounts of water and extensive sunshine and high temperatures.

Rice can be cultivated either as a dry-land crop or, as is more common, in water. The varieties of seed differ according to the method of growth. When grown as a dry-land crop, it is sown and harvested as any other cereal crop. Water cultivation is a slightly more complicated method, and demands preparation of land contours and control of irrigation. Both methods have their advantages and disadvantages, although the yield is usually higher when rice is cultivated in water.

The different ecologies and environments in which rice is grown are classified thus: irrigated, rain-fed or lowland, upland and deep-water. In irrigated ecology, rice is grown in standing water impounded by bunds or levees (small mud walls). Rainfall supplements irrigation water. In rain-fed lowland ecology, the rice fields are generally submerged or flooded and the water depth can be up to 100 cm for a considerable period during the cropping season. The rice fields are usually waterlogged and the principal source of water is rainfall. In upland ecology, rice is grown with natural rainfall, no effort is made to impound the water and there is no natural flooding of the fields. Finally, the deep-water or floating rice is grown in low-lying areas that are flooded to depths of up to several metres. Rice is usually seeded prior to the arrival of the floods and little else is done until the harvest period. In certain areas, rice may have to be transplanted once or twice in order to save the plant from drowning if the floodwater rises too rapidly.

The average life cycle of the rice plant is between 110 and 115 days, although the duration from sowing to harvest can vary from 100 to 210 days. In temperate climates, the average duration is 130–150 days. The development of the rice plant, which can be divided into three phases, namely vegetative, reproductive and ripening, is affected by temperature and day length.

The quality of the rice at the time of the harvest is an important factor in the milling yield. Milling yield is the percentage of the crop that results in marketable whole grain rice. The moisture content of rice at the time of harvest ranges between 15 and 25 per cent, much too high for quality storage. If rice is allowed to dry out more prior to the harvest, excessive kernel damage may occur during the harvest operation.

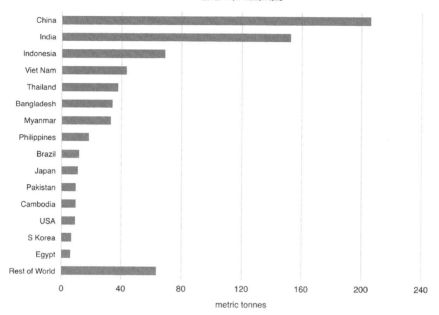

2012: 719.7 million tons

Exhibit 14.20 Top paddy rice producers
Source: Author, based on data from FAO (2014)

The harvested rice must therefore be dried and the moisture content brought down between 12 and 14 per cent in order to prevent spoilage. Although combine harvesters are the most efficient way of harvesting dry-land rice, hand harvesting is extensively carried out in Asia, where irrigated rice is predominant, with a sickle or a small sharp knife. Like other cereals, the rice harvest contains both straw and grains and the grains must be separated from the straw. This process is called threshing. Threshing can be performed by treading with the foot, beating sheaves against a ladder inside a tub, or by using machine-powered threshers. The husk and bran must also be cleaned off. This process, called winnowing, is performed by tossing rice in the air from a bamboo tray or sieve. The grain falls on the floor and the chaff is carried away by the wind.

Rice that has been properly dried can be stored for long periods without appreciably losing quality. The construction of bins is extremely important in order to exclude moisture, insects and rodents. High volume fans are often installed to provide temperature equalisation between the outside and the inside of the bin This helps prevent moisture condensation on the grain and possible deterioration as a result of rapid changes in the weather.

Rice usually remains in storage until it is needed to fill milled rice orders. The milling process begins by removing the outer inedible protective layer called hull or husk from the rough (paddy) rice. Rice with the hulls removed is called brown rice. The thin, brown, outer layer of the rice kernel after the hull has been removed is called rice bran. The familiar white rice is obtained by removing the bran using a process called polishing. Parboiled rice is rice that has been partially cooked before it is milled (i.e. the rough rice has gone through a steam pressure process before it is milled). Unlike some of the other traditional crops grown in developed countries where one crop per year is usual, rice can often produce two crops a year.

Agricultural policies

Extensive legislation regarding agriculture is common in most countries around the world. Atkin (1995) traces this tendency back to antiquity, when kings built large warehouses to store surplus production in years of prosperity, in order to use it in years of poor crops.

The obvious reason that drives governments to intervention is their desire to secure vital supplies of food. The same goal, one might say, could be achieved by securing adequate imports from more efficient producers abroad. Agriculture, however, has traditionally been a sector looked at with sympathy, especially in developed countries with a high degree of urbanisation. It may also be the case that rural populations exert considerable lobbying power to central government; power that is sometimes disproportionate to the number of people represented.

The fact remains, however, that government intervention creates distortions in prices, income distribution between producers and consumers and between countries themselves. Almost all countries have their own agricultural policies, interventionist to a greater or lesser extent. Among these policies, we can distinguish four main cases: European Union; United States; smaller export-oriented producers, such as Argentina and Australia; and Asian countries, both developing and developed. We will take a brief look at all of them.

European Union

The blueprints for the European Common Agricultural Policy (CAP) were being discussed soon after the signing of the Treaty of Rome in 1956. One of the aims of the treaty is to ensure the security of food supplies to country members, and wheat is of course central to this aspiration. It was not until 1967, however, that CAP came into force, with the aim to boost domestic production through a series of preferential measures: it raises prices to domestic producers, which are passed on to consumers who end up paying for the policy; restricts imports; and forces consumers, once more, to pay for the budgetary cost of the policy as well. The price control system introduced by CAP was also notorious for its complexity, with a long list of terms, indicating different degrees of intervention.

CAP and its effects have been a textbook case for the teaching of the costs and benefits of tariffs and customs unions to students of economics, while numerous studies have been made in order to assess the cost of so much intervention. The discrepancies between results from different studies are considerable, but all of them indicate that CAP results in an overall loss on the community's GDP.

What is more, CAP eroded the position of non-EU producers. First, imports of grains from efficient producers were substituted by more expensive domestic production; second, expensive grain surpluses were dumped in the international markets, eroding market shares of other producers.

As was expected, CAP became a hotly debated issue between the EU and other grain producers, particularly the United States. The latter threatened countervailing measures many a time and repeatedly pressed for the issue of protectionism in agriculture to become central in WTO negotiations.

With mounting pressure from both outside and inside, the EU Commission started revising CAP from the 1990s onwards. In the post-war, pre-1990 years, CAP was focused on boosting the production of certain agricultural commodities in order to achieve self-sufficiency. In the post-1990 years, the focus has shifted to boosting farming income, improving product quality and maintaining environmental sustainability. As a result, a new single payment scheme was introduced in 2003, which pays subsidies to each farm, on the basis of farmland maintained in an arable condition that adheres to stipulated environmental standards. This replaces the previous scheme, which relied on payments per unit of commodity produced. Further reforms have been implemented and, since 2005, EU CAP's financing has been streamlined to two funds. The European Agricultural Guarantee Fund (EAGF) finances direct payments to farmers and measures to respond to market disturbances, such as private or public storage and export refunds. The European Agricultural Fund for Rural Development (EAFRD) finances the rural development programmes of the member states.

It is still too early to judge the effects of the new CAP: on EU farmers (including those from the new member countries of EU-27), other developed agricultural producers (such as the United States and Canada), on developing economies that still largely rely on agriculture, on EU consumers, and on the EU budget. The fact remains, however, that a subsidy system does exist, albeit with an altered agenda.

United States

The agricultural sector in the USA is not that large as a percentage of GDP; it remains, however, substantial because of its sheer size and the impact it has on international markets for grains, particularly coarse grains. Atkin (1995) correctly observes that:

> The importance of the US to the world grain market is evident in two ways in particular that are relevant to a discussion of policy. The country is the largest exporter of grain, and large exporters typically find themselves with special responsibilities, as the examples of Saudi Arabia in the oil market and Brazil in the coffee market attest. Leading exporters often find it is in their interest to act as swing suppliers or important

stockholders, trying to ensure that prices do not fall too low. Secondly, world market prices for grain are established in the US, precisely because it is the key marginal supplier.

Current federal agricultural policy has remained fairly stable since the 1930s, when it was formulated as a reaction to the problems of economic depression. It has a three-prong approach: provide price support, make target price deficiency payments, and run efficiently production-control programmes.

The USDA has a different – if not unique – way of supporting prices. Instead of direct subsidies, there is a scheme of farm loans, funded by the Commodity Credit Corporation (CCC). Farmers place grain under loan for less than one year, with the loan rate set as a dollar amount per unit of the commodity. If the local cash price rises enough to pay back the loan and cover the interest cost, the loan is likely repaid and the farmer redeems the grain for sale in the cash market. If it is not redeemed, the CCC takes title to the grain and waives the interest on the loan. Thus, the loan rate is effectively the minimum acceptable price guaranteed by the government.

In the case of target price deficiency payments, a target price above the loan rate is established for each commodity. If the market price fails to reach the target, the difference between the target and the five-month average market price (or between the target price and the loan rate, whichever is less) is paid directly from the Treasury to the farmer. Linked to such payments is the stipulation that the farmer take out of production a designated number of acres of cropland.

This is one way of controlling production; the other way is through a 'payment-in-kind' (PIK) programme, which was passed in 1983 by Congress. To participate in the PIK programme, farmers were required to comply with the acreage-diversion programme and to set aside an additional percentage of acreage specified by the government. In return for not growing a particular crop, the government paid farmers in kind with government-owned stocks of grain or released the farmers' stocks, which were held under loan, back to them.

As far as export markets are concerned, the government has initiated several export-type programmes with the aim to 'help US farmers increase their competitiveness abroad'.[7] Among these are Public Law 480, and the Export Enhancing Programme.

Public Law 480 – or PL480 for short – was part of the Agricultural Trade Development and Assistance Act passed in 1954, just after the Korean War, and – although initiated as a short-term programme to help move growing surpluses of grain to foreign markets – has turned into a successful long-term programme in boosting US grain exports. PL480 provides for several types of possible government-to-government transactions, such as barter, food aid shipments, and financing by long- or short-term US government loans.

---

7 All these measures are no less interventionist than tariffs, quotas and subsidies. However, export-enhancing intervention is normally received better than import-restricting measures.

A more recent feature of US agricultural policy is its export enhancing programme (EEP), which was passed as part of the 1985 Farm Bill. Under the EEP, the private sector is responsible for organising and implementing the entire trading transaction; when the details of the transactions are finalised, the prospective exporter can submit a bid to the USDA requesting a subsidy. The USDA makes a decision about the validity of the bid after reviewing other similar bids for exports to the same country to attest their competitiveness. The subsidy – or 'bonus' – is paid to the US exporter and covers the cost difference between the price of grain paid in the United States versus a significantly lower price the exporter must sell grain for in other countries to be cost-competitive.

Argentina and Australia

Argentina and Australia have quite distinct approaches to agriculture, but they are similar in that they are both smaller but quite efficient producers, with a substantial part of their production destined for the export market.

In the market for grains, Argentina is frequently known as a cheap source of supply. Although this may not be always true, it is certain that Argentina is one of the most competitive producers in the world market. In fact, opposite to most countries, Argentina effectively penalises its agricultural sector by levying export taxes, restricting exports and underpricing the products in the domestic market for the benefit of urban populations.[8]

In Australia, the agriculture sector has lost the position it held in the 1950s as the country's top export income earner. Manufacturing and minerals have since become much more important elements of the country's exports, but export business is still key for the agricultural sector.

Australia suffers from notorious volatility in agricultural production and income. The federal government's policy has been, therefore, to reduce this volatility through intervention.[9] For this purpose, the Australian Wheat Board (AWB) was set up with the aim to coordinate production and exports. The board was authorised to make 'advance payments' to farmers for their production and do its best to market their products in the export markets. This means that AWB is also heavily involved in the handling, storage and transportation of grains from farm gate to export terminals. An interesting aspect of AWB is the change it has gone through in the last 20 years. Although it began as a government body, in 1999 it was privatised, with the ownership taken over by Australian farmers. In 2010, AWB was acquired by Agrium,[10] and in 2011 ownership passed on to Cargill.[11]

---

8 See, for example, *The Economist* (2014) for a more recent review of this continuing practice of intervention.
9 Not least because the agrarian population has substantial lobbying power and is largely represented by one of three major political parties.
10 Agrium is a US producer of fertilisers and other agricultural nutrients.
11 Cargill is one of the world's top commodity trading firms, with a very strong presence in the agricultural sector.

Asia

There is a wide range of policies across different countries in Asia, in particular East, Southeast and South Asia. The main theme of all policies, however, is the aim to achieve self-sufficiency in rice. To achieve this, most countries employ a series of import-restricting measures, notably tariffs and quotas, and several incentive schemes to boost local production of grains.

Southeast and South Asian countries feature as some of the heaviest importers of grains in the world. Particularly, China and Japan are among the largest importers of both wheat and coarse grains. In China, the government initiated a number of reforms in 1978, which had far-reaching effects in agriculture; yields in rice production improved with the use of high yield varieties and extensive irrigation, and so did yields in other grains such as wheat. Since the meteoric rise of the country's economy and the associated increase in average income, consumers have developed a taste for more wheat and meat in their diet, which is generating additional demand for imports of wheat (for direct human consumption), as well as coarse grains and soya beans (for animal feedstuff for meat production).

Japan is a mature economy, and the Japanese have acquired a taste for wheat and meat products, but still resist fiercely the calls from the US to mediate their overly protective policies. These policies were initially formulated in the 1950s, in the aftermath of the Second World War, and were understandably protective as the country was trying to reconstruct its economy. Progressively, policies became less restrictive, but the oil crisis in 1973 shook the Japanese administration, which felt threatened because of its dependence on other countries for both its food and its industrial raw materials, and resumed its protective policies forthwith. The remaining countries of the Pacific Asia region have similar policies promoting self-sufficiency.

And finally . . .

At the time of writing the first edition of this book, agriculture was one of no less than 40 items on the agenda of the Doha[12] Round of WTO negotiations. The agricultural mandate included topics such as 'improving market access, eliminating export subsidies, reducing distorting domestic support, sorting out a range of developing country issues, and dealing with non-trade concerns such as food security and rural development' (WTO 2014). At the time of writing the second edition of this book, the Doha Round is still ongoing and so are the negotiations on the agricultural agenda.

Demand for grains

As discussed earlier, grains are used both for direct consumption by humans and indirectly as livestock feeds. A proportion of production is also reserved

---

12 This is the ninth round of negotiations since the Second World War, and it started in Doha, Qatar, in 2001.

for industrial uses, some of which we will examine. The share of grains used for food, as opposed to that used for feeds, depends very much on consumer tastes and differ from country to country. As a rule of thumb, one would expect nations with lower income per capita to rely more on grains for direct human consumption, which are relatively cheaper; on the other hand, nations with more disposable income per capita can afford to switch to more expensive foods, such as meat and dairy products, implying a more extensive use of grains for livestock feeds.

When it comes to the types of grains used for direct (food) or indirect (feed) consumption, wheat is most commonly used for the former, whereas coarse grains are predominantly used for the latter. Exhibit 14.21 shows the world utilisation of wheat and coarse grains according to use, according to estimates for 2012–2013. It is worth noting that a substantial part of coarse grains (ca. 10 per cent) is used for the production of bioethanol. This reflects the widespread use of this type of biofuel in the United States as an additive to gasoline.

Wheat

The prime use of wheat is for the production of bread and other bakery products. Flour mills are the main purchasers of wheat, in order to produce a large variety of flours for general and speciality uses.

Wheat has been ground into flour since early human history. The millstone is probably the most well known tool to turn wheat into flour, and it is still in

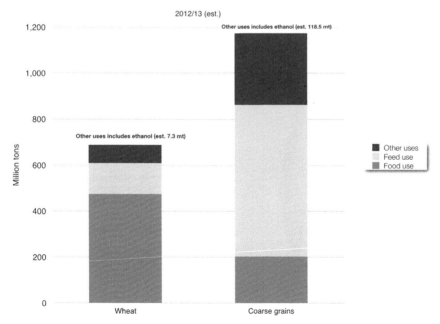

Exhibit 14.21 Food and feed uses of grains

Source: Author, based on data from FAO (2013)

use in less developed parts of the world. The first improvement in milling technology was made when the millstones were set further apart in order to gradually reduce the wheat grain to its constituents: the endosperm and the bran.

The endosperm is the floury inner part that contains the starch and the gluten; the bran is the outer covering that provides the fibre; finally, a third element, the germ, is the embryo inside the endosperm that contains the oil. The gluten contained in wheat is made of two proteins, gliadin and glutenin. Gluten is what gives wheat-flour dough its rubbery texture and makes it appropriate for bread production. At the same time, this property makes high-protein wheat unsuitable for animal feedstuff.

The varieties of wheat, discussed above, are extremely important because they determine the type and uses of the final product, wheat flour. Hard wheat – such as hard red winter wheat grown in Kansas, or hard red spring from North Dakota – is used to produce high-grade flour, which is in turn used in bread making.

Soft wheat flours, on the other hand, are low in protein and gluten, and lack the raising property necessary for bread making; they are used instead for bakery goods with a tender, flaky or crispy texture, such as cakes, cookies, crackers or pastry. White wheat flour is the most typical example.

All-purpose flour is another type, which is made from a blend of hard and soft wheats, and is not normally standardised. This is usually unsuitable for

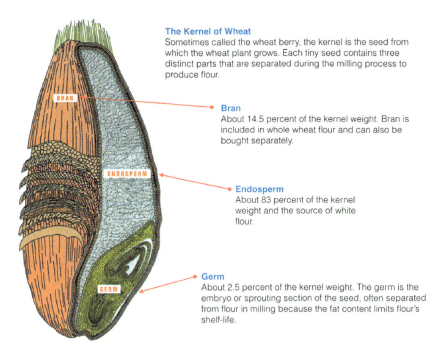

The Kernel of Wheat
Sometimes called the wheat berry, the kernel is the seed from which the wheat plant grows. Each tiny seed contains three distinct parts that are separated during the milling process to produce flour.

Bran
About 14.5 percent of the kernel weight. Bran is included in whole wheat flour and can also be bought separately.

Endosperm
About 83 percent of the kernel weight and the source of white flour.

Germ
About 2.5 percent of the kernel weight. The germ is the embryo or sprouting section of the seed, often separated from flour in milling because the fat content limits flour's shelf-life.

Exhibit 14.22 Cross-section of wheat kernel

Source: Author, adapted from Wheat Foods Council, www.wheatfoods.org

large bakeries, which require strictly controlled quality standards, but is quite acceptable for home baking.

The final category is durum wheat, the hardest of all wheats. This is milled differently than other wheats, resulting in a coarse, golden amber product, known as semolina. This is then mixed with water into a dough that is used to produce pasta in different shapes. Mixed with a proportion of egg solids or yolk, the same dough is used to produce egg pasta and noodles.

Wheat is a staple part of the diet in all developed countries, and a desirable commodity to which many developing countries switch as their income increases. One would expect that income elasticities for wheat would be low – even negative in some cases – in high-income countries. Those in middle-income countries should be somewhat higher, as consumers slowly turn from wheat to meat and dairy products. Finally, low-income countries could even display higher-than-unity elasticities, as wheat may be treated as a luxury when lower value staple foods – such as rice – are used (see Exhibit 14.23).

In terms of consuming countries, China is the world's largest consumer of wheat, closely followed by India. The United States, Russia and Pakistan complete the list of the top five wheat consumers in the world. The European Union is also a heavy user of wheat; in fact, as a bloc, the world's second largest consumer after China (see Exhibit 14.24).

Coarse grains

Coarse grains are primarily used for animal feed, although certain countries rely on them for direct human consumption. Parts of Africa, for example, use millet extensively, while corn is consumed heavily in Latin America. Because coarse grains are used heavily as an input in the production of meat and dairy goods, they are likely to be more affected by consumer income than by increases in population. This follows on from the fact that demand for meat products is more income-elastic, and so consequently will be the demand for their production inputs. In reality, such generalisations are not always discernible from hard facts, and this is because non-feed uses of coarse grains complicate the study of demand patterns.

	Wheat	Coarse grains
USA	–0.20	0.04
European Community	–0.37	0.04
Canada	–0.24	0.04
USSR	–0.42	0.10
India	1.06	2.13
Pakistan	0.62	1.50
China	0.75	1.69

Exhibit 14.23 Income elasticities of demand for grains

Source: Atkin (1995)

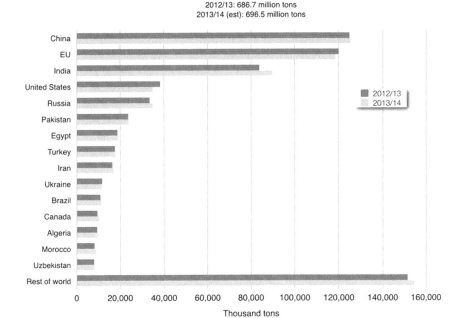

Exhibit 14.24 Top wheat consumers

Source: Author, based on data from USDA (2014b)

Corn

Corn is the dominant coarse grain; the majority of it is used for animal feed. This is not, however, its sole use. In fact, corn produces a bewildering array of products, with uses as diverse as corn oil, adhesives and sweeteners.

In the milling process, only corn kernels are normally used, since corn refiners do not utilise any other part of the plant. The kernel consists of the germ, the hull, the gluten and the starch. The germ contains most of the oil and is eventually pressed to extract corn oil. The hull contains mainly fibre and is frequently known as bran. Gluten (yellow) and starch (white) are usually intermixed throughout the endosperm.

There are two main milling processes for corn: the wet and the dry. In wet milling, the corn – after a first cleaning stage – is steeped or soaked in a solution of warm water and sulphur dioxide to retard undesirable fermentation and to aid in the extraction of soluble materials from the corn.

The solution goes through several stages, whereby the constituents of corn kernels are separated to produce oil, gluten feed, gluten meal and starch. These are then used in a multitude of applications, both edible and industrial.

Dry corn milling is similar to wheat milling, but the main difference is that while in wheat milling we are interested in extracting as much flour as possible, in corn milling we are more interested in the intermediate products, such as

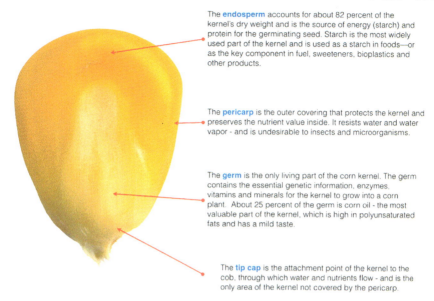

The **endosperm** accounts for about 82 percent of the kernel's dry weight and is the source of energy (starch) and protein for the germinating seed. Starch is the most widely used part of the kernel and is used as a starch in foods—or as the key component in fuel, sweeteners, bioplastics and other products.

The **pericarp** is the outer covering that protects the kernel and preserves the nutrient value inside. It resists water and water vapor - and is undesirable to insects and microorganisms.

The **germ** is the only living part of the corn kernel. The germ contains the essential genetic information, enzymes, vitamins and minerals for the kernel to grow into a corn plant. About 25 percent of the germ is corn oil - the most valuable part of the kernel, which is high in polyunsaturated fats and has a mild taste.

The **tip cap** is the attachment point of the kernel to the cob, through which water and nutrients flow - and is the only area of the kernel not covered by the pericarp.

Exhibit 14.25 Composition of corn kernel

Source: Author, image © Somchai Somsanitangkul/Dreamstime.com, text adapted from the National Corn Growers Association, www.ncga.com

crude oil, germ cake, brewers' grits and hominy feed. Flaking grits are sold to cornflake manufacturers, while the final and finest product of dry milling is corn flour.

The world's biggest consumers of corn are the US and China, followed at some distance by the EU (see Exhibit 14.26). In the US, corn consumption took off in the 2000s, as the use of corn ethanol expanded rapidly, in response to the introduction the Renewable Fuel Standard (RFS) in 2005, which stipulated the use of corn ethanol as an additive to gasoline blendstock to a proportion of 10 per cent (E10 gasoline). More recently, the US Environmental Protection Agency (EPA) introduced an update to this standard, RFS2, which proposed the introduction of E15 (15 per cent ethanol) gasoline. In China, corn consumption has been rising since the mid-2000s, in response to China's increasing disposable income and the changing consumption patterns of parts of the population, who have developed a taste for more meat products.

Oats

Oats are used mainly for cattle feed, but are also popular for human consumption, especially in regions with wet and cool conditions that favour their production. The most well known use of oats for human consumption is hot oatmeal porridge, but it is also used in multigrain breakfast cereals and in many baked goods.

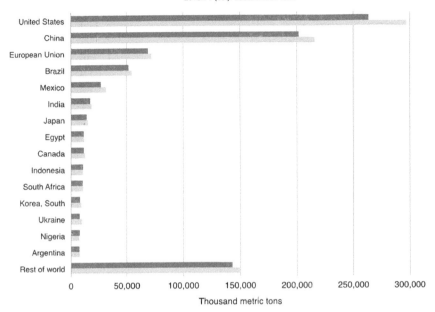

Exhibit 14.26 Top corn consumers

Source: Author, based on data from USDA (2014b)

Barley

Like oats, barley is primarily used for animal feedstuff. The most well known secondary use is in the brewing and distilling industries. The brewing industry uses barley malt, a product obtained by germinating moistened barley under controlled conditions. Malt is then mixed with water and heated under controlled conditions (mashing). After mashing, the liquid portion (wort) is separated from unconverted malt, and yeast is added to initiate fermentation that turns the mixture into beer. Finally, hops are added to the wort for flavour.

The distilling process is somewhat different, in that the starch is converted into sugar with fermentation. Distillation requires only the highest quality barley, but corn, oats and rye are often added. When corn is more than half of the starch, the whiskey produced is classified as bourbon.

Barley accounts for most of the consumption of coarse grains other than corn, as can be seen in Exhibit 14.27. The EU is the largest consumer of these grains, just over 80 million tons in 2012–2013, with barley accounting for 60 per cent of this figure.

Soya beans

Soya beans are among the oldest cultivated crops in the world. They became popular in the United States after the 1920s, and the country now has a

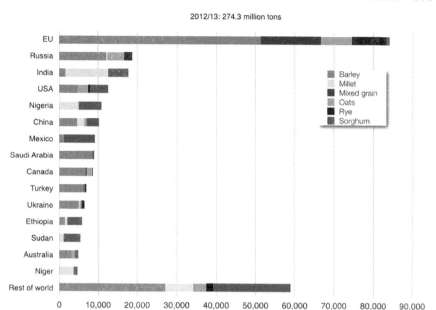

2012/13: 274.3 million tons

Exhibit 14.27 Consumption of other coarse grains

Source: Author, based on data from USDA (2014b)

position in the soya bean market as dominant as that in the corn market. In more recent years, this dominance was eroded by the ascent of Brazil, who are currently the world's second largest soya bean producer.

Soya beans are used in their original form, and are also processed into two main subordinate products: soya oil and soya meal. Soya meal is a prime feedstuff for cattle, pigs and poultry. Soya flour, a product similar to meal, is used in the food, cosmetics, pharmaceutical and chemical industries. Soya oil is a rich source of lecithin and is used in foods and medical goods, but also has a variety of technical uses in other areas. In fact, soya bean products are found practically everywhere. Edible uses of soya oil include coffee creamers, cooking oils, margarine, mayonnaise, salad dressings, chocolate coatings and pharmaceuticals. Technical uses include: anti-foam agent in alcohol and yeast; anti-spattering agent in margarine; dispersing agent in paint, ink, insecticides and rubber; epoxies; fungicides; plasticisers, vinyl plastics; waterproof cement; putty; antistatic agents; anti-corrosion agents; and many more. In addition, soya oil can be one of the feedstock oils used for the production of biofuels.

China, the US and Brazil lead the league table of soya product consumers, as can be seen in Exhibit 14.28. China in particular has rapidly increased consumption, for the same reasons discussed earlier in corn consumption. In the US, soya meal competes directly with corn meal as feedstuff for pigs and poultry, and soya oil is used in a myriad of applications, as indicated above.

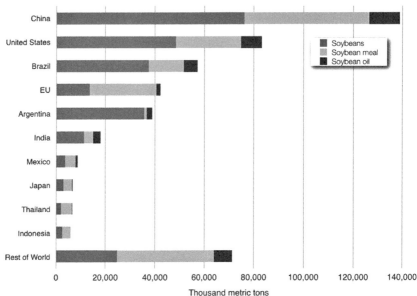

Exhibit 14.28 Top soya bean consumers

Source: Author, based on data from USDA (2014b)

Rice

Rice is divided into short-, medium- and long-grain varieties. Long-grain rice has a long slender kernel that is four times longer than it is wide. When cooked, the grains are separate, light and fluffy. Medium-grain rice is two to three times longer than it is wide. The cooked grains tend to be moist, tender and slightly clingy. The short-grain rice kernel is almost round and the grains cling together when cooked.

Rice is mostly used for human consumption. It is the staple food for almost two-thirds of the world's population. Very little rice is used as animal feed. Rice is a complex carbohydrate, and rice protein is one of the highest quality proteins, containing all of the eight essential amino acids. Rice has no fat, no cholesterol and no sodium. Rice has to be cooked before the human body can absorb the starch, which is the major component of milled rice. Rice bran is a good source of thiamine, niacin, phosphorus, iron, potassium, magnesium, vitamin B-6 and fibre, and is used as an ingredient in cereals and mixes and vitamin concentrates. It is also used to feed livestock. Rice bran can also be refined to produce a fine, clear oil that is low in fatty acids and is good for cooking and for protecting machinery from rust.

Rice flour is used to thicken sweets and sauces. Being non-allergenic, it can replace wheat flour in diets of people who are allergic to gluten and wheat flour products. Rice flours are used to make pasta, chips, cakes and other snacks, as well as breakfast cereals. Rice husks are used as fuel in rural areas and as insulation. They are also used for making lightweight bricks and as packing material. Broken rice is used to make liquors such as sake and arrak. Rice is also used to make beer.

The main factors that affect the growth in demand for staple grains are: (1) per capita income; (2) the growth rate of population; and (3) the change in prices relative to substitute crops. Rice is considered a luxury at low income levels, when meeting the energy needs is a major concern. As incomes increase, people tend to substitute low-cost sources of energy, such as coarse grains, cassava and sweet potato for rice. However, at high levels of income, rice becomes an inferior good. As incomes rise further, people consume diversified diets and prefer higher cost and quality foods, such as vegetables, fish, bread and meat, which contain more protein and vitamins. Moreover, the changes in food habits and the practice of eating outside that have come about as a result of urbanisation, which itself is a consequence of economic growth, lead to further reduction in the per capita rice consumption. Japan, South Korea and Taiwan are economies that have already passed these phases and have experienced a decline in the per capita rice consumption.

China is going through this phase currently, while nations such as India, Indonesia, Bangladesh, the Philippines and Vietnam have not yet reached the income threshold at which consumers start substituting rice for higher quality and more varied foods. These countries dominate the growth in rice consumption and account for approximately 40 per cent of the total rice

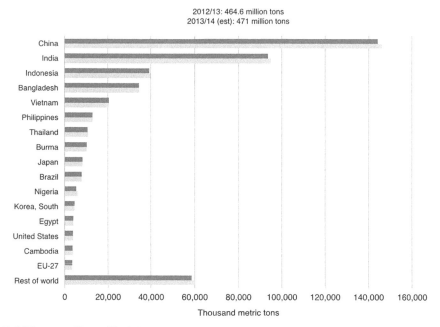

Exhibit 14.29 Top milled rice consumers

Source: Author, based on data from USDA (2014b)

consumption. The per capita rice consumption in these countries is expected to grow further with increased incomes and alleviation of poverty.

International trade in grains

Grains are one of the five major bulk commodities traded internationally today, but the history of trade in grains goes back to the beginning of civilisation, when grains were among the first commodities to be traded between local communities. With the advent and expansion of agriculture in the Fertile Crescent in Mesopotamia, the first surpluses of grains were exchanged for 'industrial' goods, such as pottery. Apart from such limited exchanges between communities, there did not seem to be any sizeable movement of grains, except perhaps for cases of famine due to severe crop failures.

Ancient Greeks in Athens built their external policies around the need of securing regular shipments of grains from the Black Sea. They saw the development of a strong naval base as the key to controlling and protecting the grain route from the Crimea, through the Hellespont across the Aegean to Piraeus. Even more pressing a problem was the import of grains in ancient Rome. The task of providing grains to Roman citizens was one of the greatest responsibilities of the central administration. Imports of grains were sourced from several regions around the Mediterranean, with Egypt as the principal supplier.

During the eras of Italian, German and Dutch domination of world trade in the early modern period, grains were never a much-favoured cargo, due to their low value compared to their volume. Instead, high value/low volume goods (such as spices and silk) were sought after, which would be sold at premium prices to the moneyed classes. Grain trade became important again after the repeal of Britain's Corn Laws in 1846. The surge in British imports made the transport of large – for the time – shipments of grains justifiable. Initially, imports originated from Odessa, across the Mediterranean, and from the Baltic ports across the North Sea. Later on, changed political and economic conditions both in Britain and the United States favoured imports from California and the Great Plains, across the Atlantic, to Liverpool.

In the modern era, the political economy of international grain trade circles around three notorious sources of turmoil: the dispute between the US and the EU over the latter's Common Agricultural Policy; an equally long-standing dispute between the US and Japan; and the 'special' relation between the US and Russia after the 1970s.

Probably the most complicated source of conflict was the dispute between the US and the EU, nearly cost the successful completion of the Uruguay Round of GATT negotiations.[13] Since the initiation of CAP in 1967, the US has been squeezed out of a very important market, and, in addition, they had to compete with substantial amounts of expensive surplus grains dumped in the international market by EU countries.

---

13 GATT (the General Agreement on Tariffs and Trade) was the precursor of WTO. The Uruguay Round was the eighth round of negotiations and lasted 1986–1994.

The dispute between the US and Japan over rice is still at the negotiating table, with the former asking the latter to lift some of the very considerable import restrictions as a goodwill gesture towards an American administration that is increasingly tempted to take countervailing measures.

The relation between Russia and the US was initiated in the 1970s, when the then Soviet administration decided to stop passing the shortfalls in grains production – especially wheat – directly to the consumers. Starting with the 'Great Grain Robbery' in the early 1970s, the FSU has been in the past a regular importer of US grains, going through several peaks and troughs, due to bad Soviet crops, lack of hard currency for imports, and a failed attempt by the Americans to impose a food embargo on the Soviets because of the latter's invasion of Afghanistan in 1979.

Finally, a small portion of international trade flows of grain are in the framework of the World Food Programme and other food aid programmes, administered primarily by the International Grains Council.[14]

Wheat and coarse grains

On a regional basis, Africa (North and Sub-Saharan) emerges as the largest importer of wheat (see Exhibit 14.30), whereas East Asia is the largest importing region for coarse grains (see Exhibit 14.32), each commanding just

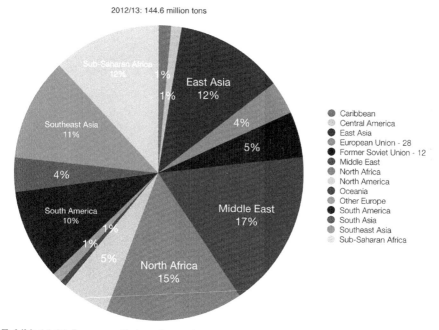

2012/13: 144.6 million tons

Legend:
- Caribbean
- Central America
- East Asia
- European Union - 28
- Former Soviet Union - 12
- Middle East
- North Africa
- North America
- Oceania
- Other Europe
- South America
- South Asia
- Southeast Asia
- Sub-Saharan Africa

Exhibit 14.30 Imports of wheat by region

Source: Author, based on data from USDA (2014b)

14 Formerly known as the International Wheat Council.

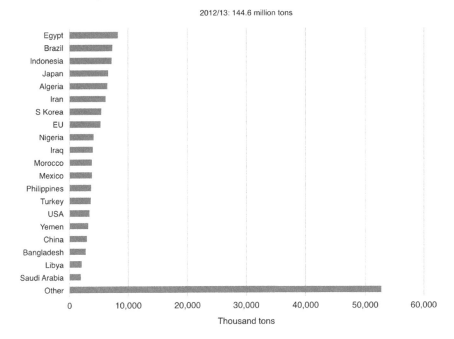

Exhibit 14.31 Top wheat importers

Source: Author, based on data from USDA (2014b)

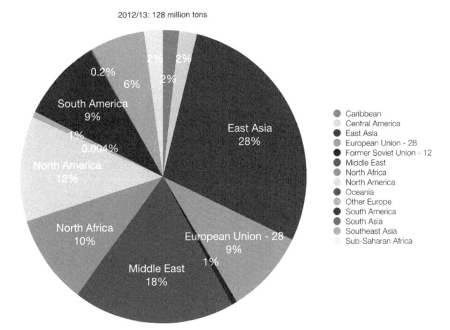

Exhibit 14.32 Imports of coarse grains by region

Source: Author, based on data from USDA (2014b)

under 30 per cent of the respective markets. The most important wheat importers are North Africa, the Middle East and the Far East (see Exhibit 14.31). In East Asia, Japan, South Korea and China are the most prominent importers (see Exhibit 14.33). All three countries have built their agricultural policies around the goal of self-sufficiency in rice. However, as the economies of these countries mature, their consumers have acquired a taste for wheat and meat products, necessitating imports of both wheat and coarse grains.

The rest of Southeast and South Asian countries base their diets on rice, with an increasing taste for wheat in emerging economies experiencing high growth rates in their economies. The Middle East, on the other hand, has traditionally been a deficit area, necessitating grain imports to satisfy most of their consumption requirements.

Africa is a net importer of grains, with several less developed countries receiving most of their grain as part of the World Food Programme. The only exception is South Africa, which is a minor exporter of grain, particularly to Western Europe. Some African countries feature in the list of top importers for both wheat and coarse grains. Notably, Egypt was the world's largest importer of wheat in 2012–2013, with Algeria and Nigeria also in the list of top 10 importers for the same commodity.

The former Soviet Union was a very important, and volatile, importer of grains, particularly wheat. Before the 1970s, the policy of the central government was to pass any shortfalls in production directly to the consumers, in the form of rationing or long queues for bread and meat products. After the 1970s,

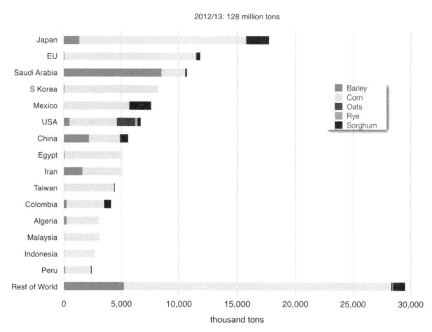

Exhibit 14.33 Top 10 coarse grains importers

Source: Author, based on data from USDA (2014b)

when fears of a potential civil unrest on account of the discontent with the food situation increased, the Soviet administration decided to top up the country's needs with imports. The obvious supplier was North America, and a 'special' relation was initiated between the US and the USSR, which was frequently forgotten by the general public, due to the more visible political antagonism between them. Even when the US administration decided to impose an embargo on grain exports to the USSR as a reaction to the latter's invasion of Afghanistan, the restriction was only on excess imports; the baseline agreement remained intact. After the collapse of the Soviet Union, the picture is much changed. Nowadays, Russia features in the list of top wheat exporters, with over 10 million tonnes leaving the country in 2012–2013. The other important wheat exporter is Ukraine, which has traditionally produced a substantial part of the FSU's grains. Currently, it is the world's fourth largest coarse grain exporter, with most of its exports accounted for by barley and corn.

The development of the EU's role in international grain trade can be seen through the development of the Common Agricultural Policy, discussed earlier. The main result is that the EU has not only become self-sufficient in grains, but has turned into the world's second biggest wheat exporter and a modest exporter of coarse grains, particularly barley. At the same time, some grain imports are also made, but these can be attributed to the fact that they have to satisfy certain tastes. For example, Italy imports most of its durum wheat for its pasta industry, because European wheat varieties are normally soft.

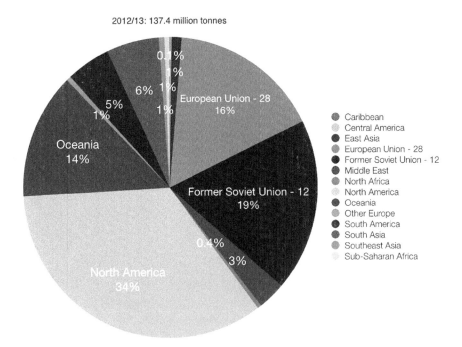

Exhibit 14.34 Exports of wheat by region

Source: Author, based on data from USDA (2014b)

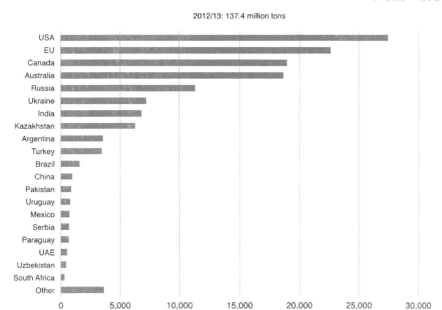

Exhibit 14.35 Top wheat exporters

Source: Author, based on data from USDA (2014b)

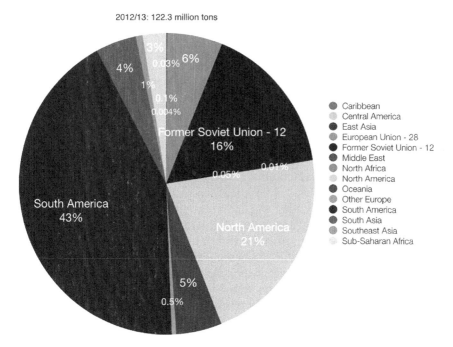

Exhibit 14.36 Exports of coarse grains by region

Source: Author, based on data from USDA (2014b)

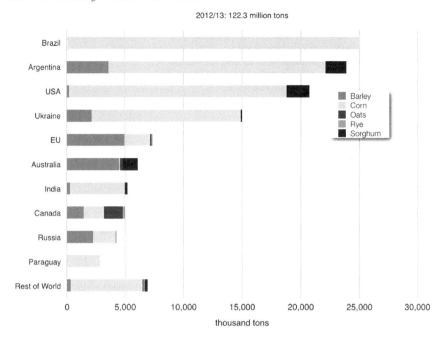

Exhibit 14.37 Top coarse grains exporters

Source: Author, based on data from USDA (2014b)

Continuing with exporters, North America dominates the scene, especially the United States in the market for wheat, where it is at the top of the list (see Exhibit 14.35), but also for coarse grains (see Exhibit 14.37). Canada, Australia, Russia and Ukraine as also important wheat exporters, whereas Brazil and Argentina top the list of major coarse grain exporters.

Rice

Although the world production of rice is slightly larger in comparison to the world production of wheat, a far smaller portion of rice enters world trade. This is mainly because China and India, the two largest producers of rice, in an average year need to keep almost all the rice they can produce to feed their own population. Moreover, it is difficult to point to a regular pattern of trade. For instance, it is not possible to say that most rice moves from developing to developed nations (or the reverse, as is the case for wheat). In fact, most trade takes place between developing countries, reflecting the vagaries of monsoon and natural and man-made disasters and their effects on rice production. As can be seen from Exhibit 14.38, about three-quarters of exports originate in South and Southeast Asia. Conversely, the major importing regions are Sub-Saharan Africa, the Middle East, and East and Southeast Asia (see Exhibit 14.40).

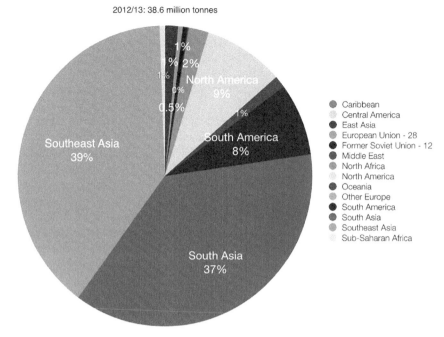

Exhibit 14.38 Milled rice exports by region

Source: Author, based on data from USDA (2014b)

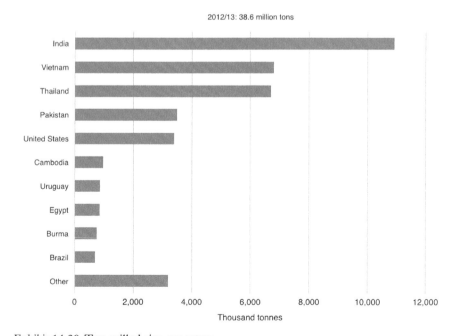

Exhibit 14.39 Top milled rice exporters

Source: Author, based on data from USDA (2014b)

World rice trade is affected by a variety of factors. Production, obviously, is one of the most important factors. Climate affects production, which in turn influences world trade. The amount of rainfall during the main growing season, for instance, is critical in determining the rice supply. Similarly, the use of fertilisers affects production. Other factors that influence world rice trade include prices of substitutes, income growth, currency values and foreign exchange reserves.

Long-grain (indica) and aromatic types, such as jasmine and basmati, account for almost 90 per cent of total trade, with the remaining being mainly medium-grain (japonica) rice. While India, Vietnam, Thailand, Pakistan and the USA are the major exporting countries (see Exhibit 14.39), China, Nigeria, Iran, Iraq, the Philippines and the EU are the major importers (see Exhibit 14.41).

A large proportion of the rice that is traded internationally is fully milled and bagged. A few countries, such as the USA, also export their paddy rice. Although 50 kg or 100 lb bags are a common size, the packing requirements in rice contracts can vary from a shipload full of bulk (loose) rice to 1 kg retail boxes.

Some other important factors that need to be considered when trading rice are the moisture content, chalkiness, proportion of brokens and the grain type (long, medium or short). Rice can be traded as paddy, cargo rice, white rice, broken rice, rice dust, rice meal or rice bran. Rice can be shipped either in

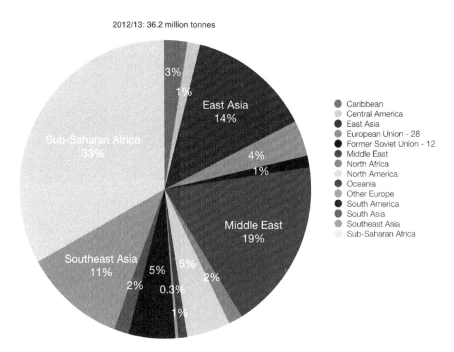

Exhibit 14.40 Milled rice imports by region

Source: Author, based on data from USDA (2014b)

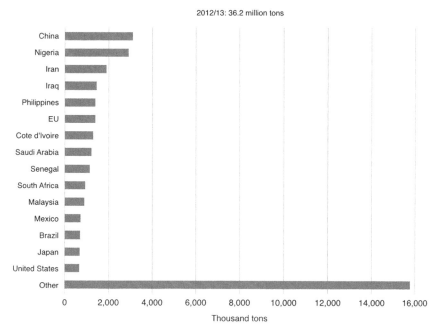

Exhibit 14.41 Top milled rice importers

Source: Author, based on data from USDA (2014b)

bags[15] or as bulk cargo. Because rice is susceptible to damage by strong odours, it should not be stowed together with scented and odiferous cargo. If damp or wetted in stowage, rice rots very quickly, generates heat and emits stench, all of which affects other rice in proximity. Bagged rice cargoes need to be ventilated in order to prevent condensation and should be dunnaged as normal bagged cargoes. When shipped in bulk, ship holds must be prepared as for grain cargo and loaded in compliance with grain rules. Rice bran is often infested, and should therefore be stowed away from goods likely to be contaminated by insect infestation.

Soya beans

As discussed earlier in this chapter, soya beans and its products (meal and oil) are important substitutes for most grains, particularly coarse ones. Soya beans are extensively traded internationally: ca. 40 per cent of the world's production is exported, just under 100 million tonnes in 2012–2013. In fact, soya, coarse grains and wheat provide a substantial part of employment for small- and medium- sized dry bulk carriers (Handysize, Supramax and Panamax class vessels).

---

15 This is most common and can be carried either by a break-bulk carrier or is, most commonly, containerised.

The three top soya bean producers also dominate world exports. Brazil, the United States and Argentina exported just over 85 million tonnes in 2012–2013 (i.e. 85 per cent of the world exports) (see Exhibits 14.42 and 14.43). In terms of imports, China is dominant, absorbing ca. two-thirds of world imports, with the EU following suit with 13 per cent of the total (see Exhibits 14.44 and 14.45).

Pricing

As with other commodities, price determination is a most interesting aspect of the marketing of grains. Price determination has repeatedly attracted the interest of extensive research. Some of the factors that affect prices and are a source of price differences among different grains are:

- qualitative differentiation;
- spatial differentiation;
- seasonality (temporal differentiation);
- cyclicality;
- trends; and
- irregular factors.

Irregular factors, such as weather conditions and wars, are often blamed for the large volatility of grain prices. True this as it may be in some cases, it is

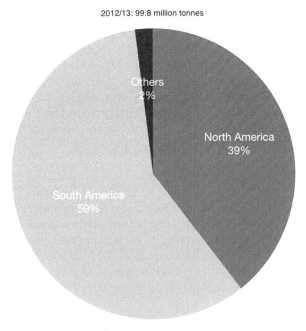

Exhibit 14.42 Soya bean exports by region

Source: Author, based on data from USDA (2014b)

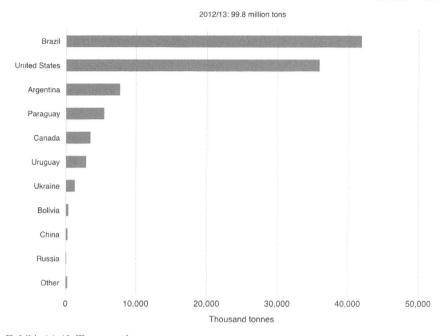

Exhibit 14.43 Top soya bean exporters

Source: Author, based on data from USDA (2014b)

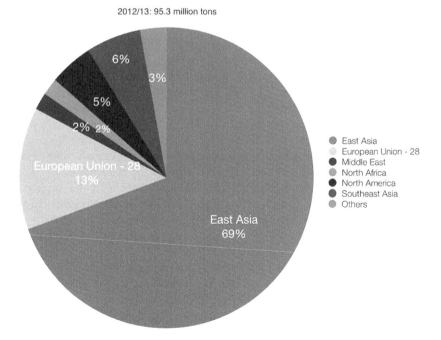

Exhibit 14.44 Soya bean imports by region

Source: Author, based on data from USDA (2014b)

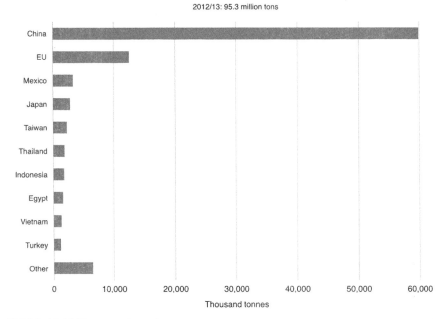

Exhibit 14.45 Top soya bean importers

Source: Author, based on data from USDA (2014b)

often the demand and supply characteristics of a particular commodity that create its price volatility.

Difference in quality between grains is a common source of price variations. Quality standards – known as grades – are normally strictly determined by government agencies in consultation with representatives of producers and marketing firms, and premia are paid for better qualities. A good example of the differences among various grades of wheat and corn is given in Exhibit 14.48.

Trends in agricultural prices are associated with general inflation and deflation in the economy and with factors specific to agricultural products, including changes in the tastes and preferences of consumers, increases in population and income, and technological changes in production.

Another source of price differentiation is the location of the supply and demand markets for the commodities. This is commonly known as spatial price differentiation, and the most important single variable used to build spatial equilibrium models is transfer costs. Seaborne transport is a source of such costs, for example.

Seasonal patterns are observed in all major grains. Take US winter wheat for instance; in an average year, prices are typically lowest during the harvest months of June and July when supplies are largest relative to demand. As the flow of newly harvested wheat into market channels tapers off and exports pick up, prices often move higher through the September–November period. Towards the end of the year, the approach of the southern hemisphere harvest tends to restrict foreign buying interest, and US prices generally reach a plateau by January or February. As soon as significant amounts of southern hemisphere wheat become available, foreign buying interest shifts away from US wheat. Prices then may trend lower through April or May, after which the US harvest gets under way and the cycle begins again.

In the case of corn, whose production and trade the US dominates, prices are normally lowest following harvest, usually between October and January. Prices often remain under pressure until April or May when planting gets underway, and then move steadily higher through the July–August pollination period. At that point, final crop size has been established, so prices usually turn lower until harvest, when the cycle begins again.

In a similar manner, soya bean prices are usually at their lowest between November and January when supplies are largest relative to demand. As the market absorbs these large supplies – if the harvest is good, of course – and both domestic use and exports pick up, prices often move higher through the May–June planting period. Once the crop is planted, prices usually begin trending lower, and, as long as growing conditions remain favourable, the downtrend often continues until sometime after harvest. At that point, the market typically bottoms out and the cycle begins again.

This sequence is generally regarded as the normal course of events. But unexpected weather developments, either favourable or unfavourable, can quickly alter this pattern and cause wide price swings. The direction of those price swings depends to a large degree on expectations: what actually happens compared to what the market expects will happen.

For example, if the market is expecting a drought, a period of rain and cooler temperatures could send prices lower as crop prospects improve. On the other hand, suppose a blast of bitter cold temperatures and high winds increase the possibility of an early killing frost. This might cause prices to rise as growing conditions become worse than expected.

Cyclicality is another characteristic of agricultural commodity prices. One of the models used to provide explanation of cyclical components in prices through time is the so-called 'cobweb model', which was first analysed by Ezekiel (1938). Put simply, the cobweb model views prices and quantities as being linked recursively in a causal chain (see Exhibit 14.46). A high price leads to large production; the large production results in low prices; low prices result in smaller production; this, combined with high demand, leads again to high prices and so forth. The model is based on three main assumptions:

1   A time lag exists between the decision to produce and the actual realisation of production.
2   Producers base production plans on current or recent past prices, hence realised production is a function of past prices.
3   Current prices are mainly a function of current supply, which, in turn, is mainly determined by current production.

The cobweb model, however, has not always given satisfactory results, mainly due to the assumption that current production is mechanistically determined

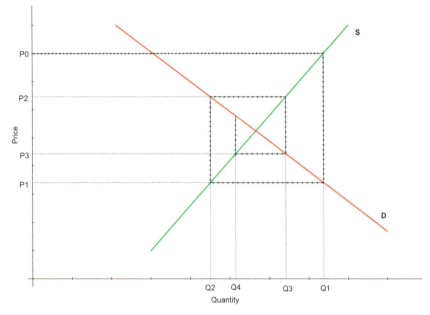

Exhibit 14.46 Convergent cobweb model
Source: Author

by last season's prices. This assumption has proved quite weak, since it is often disrupted by factors as diverse as weather conditions and government agricultural policies.

Marketing of grains in physical markets

Producers and consumers of grains eventually meet in the marketplace, where pricing takes place and transactions are completed. This marketplace need not be one specific location; it can be at the farmgate, at the elevator (silo), at the point of export, or even on the floor of an organised exchange. In fact, the Chicago Board of Trade (CBOT), the world's most renowned and liquid exchange in agricultural commodities, started its life in the second half of the nineteenth century as a meeting place for grain merchants and farmers who came into town with their harvested crops.

Marketing grains is a fairly simple operation – or at least it seems so in organised markets such as the US and the EU – since it only moves from the farmer to the processor and from there to the final consumer. It is notable, however, how the marketing system has failed in many developing countries, resulting in losses of valuable commodity, which ends up rotting in the open or in inadequate storage facilities.[16]

16 The former Soviet Union was a representative example of crop losses due to handling and transportation inadequacy, rather than weather conditions.

Grain marketing differs substantially from country to country in terms of the degree of involvement of the public and private sector. To get a better idea of the different types of the organisation of the whole operation, we will discuss the marketing chains in the United States (rather more extensively) and in Canada.

United States

As discussed earlier, the US is the world's most important grain producer and exporter, with a substantial share of the international wheat market, and a dominant position in the coarse grains market. The marketing chain consists of three phases: from farms to country elevators; from elevators to processing plants; and from elevators to the export markets.

Strict control of grain quality is essential not only for trade in the cash market, but also for the futures market. The quality of all grains entering the marketing chains are strictly scrutinised by the USDA, which establishes specific classes and subclasses of grains (see Exhibit 14.47), which are further categorised into grades, ranging from No. 1 to No. 5 (see Exhibit 14.48 for wheat and corn), under the Grain Standards Act.

The most important quality factors used for grain grading are:

*   test weight per bushel;
*   percentage of damaged kernels, including broken kernels;
*   foreign material, which may include broken kernels; and
*   other conditions, such as rot, sourness, mustiness, commercially objectionable foreign odour (COFO), and the presence of stones, insects or unknown substances.

Apart from the factors mentioned above, moisture is also of concern. It does not affect grain quality directly, but makes its long-term storage problematic.

Grain	Class	Subclass
Barley	Six-rowed barley	Six-rowed malting; Six-row blue malting; Six-rowed
	Two-rowed barley	Two-rowed malting; Two-rowed
Corn	White; Yellow; Mixed	
Soybeans	Yellow; Mixed	
Wheat	Hard red spring	Dark northern hard red spring; Northern hard red sring; Red spring
	Durum	Hard amber durum; Amber durum; Durum; Red durum
	Hard red winter; Soft red winter	
	White	Hard white; Soft white; White club; Western white
	Unclassed; Mixed	

Exhibit 14.47 Grain classification

Source: Author, based on USDA (2014a, Chapters 2, 4, 9, 10 and 13)

Wheat									
	Minimum limits of		Maximum limits of						
Grade	Test weight per bushel		Damaged kernels					Wheat of other classes	
	Hard red spring wheat or white club wheat (lbs)	All other classes and sub-classes (lbs)	Heat damaged kernels (%)	Total (%)	Foreign material (%)	Shrunken and broken kernels (%)	Defects (%)	Contrastin g classes (%)	Total (%)
US No. 1	58.0	60.0	0.2	2.0	0.5	3.0	3.0	1.0	3.0
US No. 2	57.0	58.0	0.2	4.0	1.0	5.0	5.0	2.0	5.0
US No. 3	55.0	56.0	0.5	7.0	2.0	8.0	8.0	3.0	10.0
US No. 4	53.0	54.0	1.0	10.0	3.0	12.0	12.0	10.0	10.0
US No. 5	50.0	51.0	3.0	15.0	5.0	20.0	20.0	10.0	10.0

Corn				
	Minimum limits of	Maximum limits of		
Grade	Test weight per bushel	Heat damaged kernels (%)	Damaged kernels total (%)	Broken corn and foreign material (%)
US No. 1	56.0	0.1	3.0	2.0
US No. 2	54.0	0.2	5.0	3.0
US No. 3	52.0	0.5	7.0	4.0
US No. 4	49.0	1.0	10.0	5.0
US No. 5	46.0	3.0	15.0	7.0

Exhibit 14.48 Wheat and corn grades and their specifications

Source: Author, based on USDA (2014a, Chapters 4 and 13)

This is the reason why grains need to be dried, and are usually dried before leaving the farm.

The first and most important stage is the transfer from farm to country elevator. The elevator – or silo, in Europe – is the point of receiving, grading, pricing, drying, storage and shipping of grains. Elevators are located in the countryside and at export terminals, and vary in size from 50,000 bushels to several million bushels. The closer we move to the export points, the bigger the elevators become. Elevators are owned by independent owners who operate them for a profit, by farmers themselves or their co-operatives, and by subsidiaries of grain merchants or grain processors.

As soon as a shipment of grain arrives, the elevator employees determine the quality of the consignment and grade it accordingly. The next stage is pricing; the elevator manager determines the price he will offer depending on any bid prices from processors, cash and futures prices at the Chicago Board of Trade (CBOT), prices offered by other competitors, previous sales or delivery commitments or contracts, freight charges to the best market, the elevator's costs and profit margin, and expectations for future prices.

The previous process is described as the *on-truck* or *to-arrive* method, and is essentially the spot market for the commodity. This implies that any further price risk, until the commodity reaches the final user, is undertaken by the grain merchant. Another way of doing business on the spot market is the *consignment* method, whereby the farmer consigns the grain to a merchant to a terminal market, but the merchant does not take ownership of the

Exhibit 14.49 Grain elevator

Source: Author, image © Zizagmart/Dreamstime.com

commodity; he merely tries to get the best possible price for the producer, effectively acting as a broker, while the price risk stays with the farmer.

While both methods are prevalent during harvest time when the crop is in hand, it is during periods of uncertainty about the crop level that both the farmer and the merchant want to establish some degree of certainty regarding prices. One common tool to achieve this is the *cash forward contract*, which allows the elevator operator and the farmer to lock in a price before actual delivery.

Exactly the opposite (i.e. pricing grain after actual delivery) is achieved with *delayed pricing* and *basis* contracts. Delayed pricing is a cash market alternative that allows the producer to deliver grain to the country elevator and price it at a later time. The time of pricing is negotiable between the farmer and the elevator manager. With a basis contract, the producer and the elevator operator lock in a basis that is over or under a specific futures contract. With the basis being fixed in advance, the cash price fluctuates with the futures price on CBOT.

Most of the methods discussed up to now make up the list of pricing options available to farmers in their transactions with elevator operators. Once the elevator operator, however, takes delivery of the commodity, he also assumes a considerable price risk. Unless the operator is fortunate enough to complete a *back-to-back* sale,[17] he will have to hedge his price risk exposure with futures and options contracts.

---

17 In a back-to-back sale, the elevator operator receives a bid by a processor, subtracts the elevator's cost and profit margin, and makes a bid to the producer.

Another important feature of grain marketing in the US is the availability of a highly developed inland transportation network, including road, rail and barge haulage. Highways and waterways are publicly funded and their networks are extensive and advanced, while barges are heavily used along the Mississippi and Missouri Rivers. More specifically, the interstate highway programme began in 1956, and since then it has increased the maximum weight limits on the interstate highway system, contributing to greater earnings per load for the trucking industry. In addition, the 1980 Motor Carrier Act deregulated pricing, boosting competitiveness in freight rates; similar changes were brought to the railroad sector with the introduction of the 1980 Staggers Act.

There is also substantial intermodal[18] and intra-modal[19] competition in transportation, which promotes competitive pricing of the services rendered. From the Eastern Cornbelt, grains are shipped, mainly by rail, to East Coast and Gulf Coast ports for export purposes. Western Cornbelt cargoes use both rail and barge to reach US Gulf ports for exports. Railroad, as well as barges along the Missouri, are used to carry crops from the Great Plains to Gulf ports. Finally, shipments from the Upper Great Plains are directed to Pacific Northwest ports for exports to the Far East.

Canada

Canada has set up a quasi-governmental organisation, the Canadian Wheat Board (CWB), which participates in every aspect of grain production, handling, transportation and export. The board has extensive control over every stage from production, to transportation and exports. It is charged with the responsibility to market as much grain as possible at the best possible price and, in doing so, it has the authority to use private companies as contractors.

To achieve this goal, the CWB posts an initial price for the grain it will accept before the beginning of the crop year, which is guaranteed to the farmers, and is effectively a floor to the market. At the end of the season, when all the delivered grain has been sold, the board makes an additional payment to farmers if the total realised returns from the crop are greater than those implied by the initial payment; if the returns are not high enough, the state pays up for the difference.

Finally, the board also has the authority to enter government-to-government transactions and arrange official credit for up to three years. Another responsibility for the CWB is the planning and handling of shipment schedules of grain consignments, in conjunction with the railroads and inland waterway carriers. The board also takes an active role in ensuring that all producers have equal access to markets, from silos to points of domestic consumption and to export terminals.

18 Between different modes of transport (e.g. railroad and barges).
19 Among different operators in the same transport mode (e.g. among railroad companies).

Purchase procedure

Irrespective of origin, we can find some common elements in the way wheat and coarse grains are traded internationally. The purchase of wheat in the international market primarily takes place in one of the three ways:

1 public tender;
2 private tender; and
3 spot market.

The public tender approach is commonly used by government agencies and their delegated semi-official representatives. The buyer issues a tender notice explicitly outlining the specifications and the terms and conditions of the intended purchase. The wheat class, grade, other quality aspects, volume, date of purchase, delivery period, terms of delivery, port of loading and discharge, and the method of payment are some of the details included in the tender. The exporters submit their bids (price offers) on a specified day. On the basis of the offers, the buyer chooses the most favourable supplier. Japan, Taiwan, the Philippines, Egypt, Tunisia and Algeria are among importers who use public tendering.

The private tender usually involves the buyer privately contacting wheat exporters and requesting them to make firm offers based on the buyer's specifications. Exporters send in their bids in writing. The buyer then selects the most appropriate/lowest bidder. There may, however, be further negotiations with this potential supplier, after which the tender is awarded. Private tendering is usually done when the buyers and suppliers are familiar with each other. This method of purchase is commonly used by privately owned mills in Eastern Europe. The wheat purchases in China, the former Soviet Union, most of Latin America and Southeast Asia are also undertaken using private tendering. Private tendering is by far the most commonly used form of import negotiation.

In the spot market, also called the open market, exporters offer wheat for sale based on its physical position and predetermined quality. The Rotterdam market, together with some of the other European ports, is a spot market where exporters offer wheat for immediate and future delivery depending upon its position in Rotterdam. The open market is frequently used by small mills and their brokers in Western Europe to procure their wheat requirements.

Irrespective of the method that the buyer uses to procure its wheat requirements, the following information is needed by the seller/exporter in order to make an offer:

1 Quality: the type of wheat required by the buyer depends on the planned end use. Class, grade, moisture content, protein content, dockage content, and so on are some of the quality factors that the buyer will need to specify.
2 Quantity: including the permitted tolerance.
3 Delivery: date and basis (FOB, CFR, CIF and so on), name of loading and discharge ports, any special discharge conditions, berthing charges, demurrage and rate of discharge, and so on.

4   Payment terms: letter of credit, cash against documents, and so on.
5   Vessel size, load rate guarantee.
6   Other special requirements.

While the import of wheat is primarily undertaken either by private flour mills and their agents or by official government food and supply agencies and their delegated semi-official representatives, the exporters range from:

1   large, vertically integrated, privately owned multinational companies with offices and/or representatives in importing countries;
2   smaller private companies who may not own or operate grain handling (e.g. silos) and transport facilities (e.g. vessels, barges) on their own (these companies do, however, maintain a network of agents in importing countries);
3   grower-owned co-operatives or co-operatively owned firms; and
4   statutory authorities.

Grain traders

Up to now, we have referred to farmers, processors, consumers, governments and quasi-governmental organisations, which are all directly involved in the grain trade. The last, but by no means least, important player in the international grain markets are the trading houses. Commonly known as 'grain houses', they do not restrict their activities to grain, but have diversified in other commodities, both agricultural and non-agricultural.

In the market, they are commonly known as the 'ABCD' group, which includes Archers Daniels Midland (ADM), Bunge, Cargill and Dreyfus (Louis Dreyfus Commodities). Glencore is also listed alongside the other four, but these days the company is mostly known for its trading activities in metals and oil products.

What has excited the imagination of many students of the grain markets, and attracted criticisms from many government officials, is the sheer size of these companies. It has been frequently argued that size is crucial for such companies because they rely on economies of scale and information to be able to take advantage of the relatively small margins of the grain trading business.

The origins of most of these companies can be traced to the second half of the nineteenth century, when grain trade regulation was in its infancy. Most of these companies were originally involved in the storage and/or transportation of agricultural commodities. Cargill started with a family-owned elevator in Conover, Iowa, and increased its strength in transportation, storage and finance to become the largest member of the grain establishment.[20] Louis Dreyfus Corporation, although privately owned and still under the control of

20   Continental was another large grain house, which was founded in 1813 in Arlon, Belgium, by Simon Fribourg. The company opened its first office in America in Chicago in 1921 and its dominance grew during the Second World War. It was eventually merged with Cargill in 2001.

the Louis-Dreyfus family, is also a co-operative under French law. It owns 49 per cent of the shares of UFC (Union Française des Céréales), better known as 'La Coopérative Lafayette'. UFC sells grain exclusively for itself and Dreyfus both within the European Community and to third markets. Bunge was originally a Dutch and then a Belgian company. Later, Ernesto Bunge and his brother-in-law, Jorge Born, extended their operations in Argentina to exploit the opportunities created in the growing Latin American market. Eventually, the company's headquarters moved to the United States.

In more recent years, a group of new contenders has emerged in the business of trading agricultural commodities. The so-called 'NOW' group consists of Noble Group, Olam and Wilmar. These are relatively younger companies, and all of them are now headquartered in Singapore but have operations around the world. All three have a strong base in agricultural commodities, particularly soft commodities and oilseeds. Increasingly, they are involved in the grain business, as they are located in the region that generates most of the world's import demand for this commodity group.

Alongside the previous companies, there are a number of very sizeable trading houses, mostly Japanese 'sogo soshas', who have a long-standing interest in the procurement of grains for the Japanese market. Such companies include Mitsui, Mitsubishi, Marubeni, ITOCHU, Nissho Iwai, Sumitomo and Zen-Noh (the latter being a large confederation of co-operatives). All of them were late entrants in the league. Mitsui, for example, took over the bankrupt Cook Industries in 1978, with a view to gaining a foothold in the US market and securing grain exports to Japan. Before the takeover, Cook Industries was the fourth largest trading firm in the world. Originally, it was a conservatively managed cotton-trading house that dated back to 1919. In 1963, the company moved away from cotton and into soya beans, and rose rapidly to become the newest member of the Big League. An exceptionally badly calculated bet on the soya bean market, however, brought the company to its knees. The new owner, Mitsui, has recently shown tendencies to become more international, despite its obvious commitment to the Japanese market.

The intermediary role played by grain houses involves the undertaking of a number of risks, one or more at a time. Imagine a flour mill in Japan that needs to import a consignment of wheat. For this purpose, the importer contacts a grain trader, who is prepared to offer the required quantity at a specific price and for a specified delivery date. Once the contract is signed, the trader has a number of risk exposures. The first is the risk implied by the volatility of the commodity price. If the wheat is purchased in the United States and the importer is prepared to pay in dollars, the trader does not have to worry about foreign exchange risk. If we assume, however, that the commodity is purchased in Australia in the local currency and sold to the Japanese importer in yen, and the grain trader has US dollars as his base currency, the currency risk is not negligible. In addition, assuming that the importer buys on a CIF basis, the grain trader will have to make arrangements for transport and bear the freight risk as well.

To deal with such diverse and closely related risks (but also opportunities for profits), the grain trader can only survive if these risks are diversified. Dealing with many countries, several currencies and different commodities is intended to diversify away country, currency, commodity price and credit risks. Survival in the marketplace has been the motto of all of these companies for over a century and a half, and this is the reason why most of them are closely controlled by family interests,[21] and refuse to go public or disclose the full extent and details of their business. This very persistence to avoid public scrutiny has often infuriated people and institutions[22] from the outside and has often led to criticism of cartelisation and distortion of the grain market. It would be reasonable to say, however, that:

> the damage done to global welfare by misguided agricultural and trade policies is far greater than any threat posed by grain traders, not least because the policy makers who enact these policies claim to act in the general interest. Innovative and competitive companies making money from trading certainly do not cause the kind of misallocation of resources that is generated by the EC's Common Agricultural Policy, a fact their critics would do well to recognise.[23]

Conclusion

This chapter has described and evaluated the mechanisms and organisation of the international markets for grains. By far the biggest and most heavily traded agricultural commodities, grains also have a long history of large price volatility and heavy interventionism. These features make theirs one of the most interesting markets to study. The inherent risk of the grain business is reflected in the fact that it was the first commodity to develop a market for futures in order to hedge part of this risk.

In the following chapter, we are going to deal with some of the smaller – but still important, in terms of value – agricultural commodities. Specifically, we will discuss the economics, trade patterns, pricing, physical and futures trading for coffee, sugar and cocoa.

References

Atkin, M. (1989) *Agricultural Commodity Markets: A Guide to Futures Trading*, 2nd edn, London: Routledge.

—— (1995) *The International Grain Trade*, 2nd edn, Cambridge: Woodhead Publishing.

Bayer Crop Science (2014) *Cereal Staging*, accessed online at: www.cerealcentral.ca/crop-management_cereal-staging.aspx?lang=en.

21 Cargill by the McMillans; Bunge by the Born and Hirsch families.
22 An investigation of grain trading houses was ordered by the US Congress in the 1970s, with little, if any, effectiveness.
23 Atkin (1995, p. 112).

Ezekiel, M. (1938) 'The cobweb theorem', *The Quarterly Journal of Economics*, 52: 255–280.

FAO (2013) *Food Outlook*, UN Food and Agriculture Organisation, November 2013, accessed online at: www.fao.org/docrep/019/i3473e/i3473e.pdf.

—— (2014) *FAOSTAT Database*, UN Food and Agriculture Organisation, accessed online at: http://faostat3.fao.org.

Hazell, P. (1985) 'Sources of increased instability in world cereal production', *Journal of Agricultural Economics*, 36: 145–160.

The Economist (2014) 'Argentina's wheat exports: against the grain', *The Economist Online*, 15 January 2014, accessed online at: www.economist.com/node/21594246.

USDA (2014a) *Grain Inspection Handbook – Book II Grain Grading Procedures*, USDA Grain Inspection, Packers & Stockyards Administration, accessed online at: www.gipsa.usda.gov/Publications/fgis/handbooks/gihbk2_insphb.html.

—— (2014b) *Production, Supply and Distribution Online*, USDA Foreign Agricultural Service, accessed online at: http://apps.fas.usda.gov/psdonline/.

WTO (2014) *Doha Round: What Are They Negotiating?*, World Trade Organisation, accessed online at: www.wto.org/english/tratop_e/dda_e/update_e.htm.

15 Soft commodities

Having discussed the main demand and supply determinants of agricultural products, and the markets for grains, we are now moving on to a set of minor agricultural commodities, which enter international trade quite frequently: coffee, sugar and cocoa. Apart from their obvious differences – in terms of production and consumption – from grains, these commodities are also special because they are almost exclusively produced in developing countries[1] and are central to the economies of those countries.

In a similar fashion to previous chapters, we first discuss the most important physical characteristics of the commodities in question, then we analyse the economics of their supply and demand, and, finally, we take a look at international trade and pricing in the physical markets. We defer the discussion of derivatives markets in these commodities to the final chapter of this textbook, where we look at all agricultural derivatives markets.

Coffee

Coffee is a relatively new crop, which originated in tropical Africa and was first picked from wild coffee trees. According to a 1,000-year-old legend, it was a goatskeeper – Kaldi – who first discovered the stimulating effects of caffeine when he observed that some of the goats were behaving very strangely if they ate the red berries of wild coffee bushes. Kaldi told his story to the abbot of a nearby monastery who decided to test the power of the berry for himself. He poured boiling water on to some berries to make a drink, which he found helped him to stay awake. He and other monks then drank this liquid each night and they no longer felt sleepy during their long hours of prayer.

It was in Yemen, in the fifteenth century, that coffee was first cultivated and also used as a beverage. From there, it spread to Southeast Asia in the seventeenth century, with the help of Dutch merchants. It was the French, however, who brought the coffee plant to Latin America, the Caribbean and the French territories in Africa.[2] In 1714, the French succeeded in bringing a

---

1 With the exception of sugar, although cane sugar is produced primarily in developing countries.
2 According to Wellman (1961), the spread of the coffee plant throughout the French Empire was a request of Louis XIV himself.

live cutting of a coffee tree to the island of Martinique in the West Indies, from where it spread to the rest of Latin America. Coffee reached Brazil in 1729, but Latin American countries became prominent producers in the nineteenth century, with Brazil being the world's dominant coffee producer since 1840.

Before then, world production originated mainly from South and Southeast Asia, especially Sri Lanka and Indonesia. However, 'much of the arabica coffee in Asia was decimated by leaf-rust epidemics during the last two decades of the 19th century'.[3]

As a result, most Asian countries introduced the more resistant robusta quality, or even switched altogether from coffee to tea cultivation.

Coffee is currently grown in most tropical countries throughout the world, but it is most widespread in Latin American and African countries. As we will see, this is due to the plant's physical characteristics and growth requirements, which necessitate warmth and relative humidity.

Physical characteristics

In botanical terms, coffee is the most important genus of the family Rubiaceae, which contains several hundreds of other genera. Officially known as coffea, the genus is further divided into four different species: Eucoffea, Argocoffea, Mascarocoffea and Paracoffea. Of these, only the first species is of commercial significance, and it is the plants of Eucoffea that yield the three main commercial varieties of green coffee beans: *robusta* (C. canephora), *arabica* (C. arabica) and *liberica* (C. liberica). Of these three varieties, only the first two are produced and traded extensively; the third one accounts for only about 1 per cent of total world production.

Exhibit 15.1 Coffee berries

Source: http://commons.wikimedia.org/wiki/File:Coffee_berries_1.jpg

---

3 de Graaff (1986, p. 24).

Each species is further subdivided in cultivars (i.e. varieties that are grown in different countries). Arabica, for example, can be found in several varieties, such as Colombian 'Medellín', Jamaican 'Blue Mountain', Costa Rican 'Tres Ríos', and many more. Canephora coffee also has a few cultivars, the most notable being 'Kouilou' and 'Robusta'; the latter is so significant that the entire species is named after it.[4]

The coffee plant is a shrub or small tree, 15–20 ft. high at maturity, bears shiny green, ovate leaves that last all year round, and has a life that can extend to 40 or more years. Production does not start until the plant is 3–5 years old, and full capacity is reached after the sixth year. From then on, production remains stable (provided weather conditions are not extreme) until the fifteenth to twentieth year of the plant. After that, production declines and the quality of beans may also deteriorate.

The coffee plant has a yearly cycle that starts with the appearance of white fragrant flowers. During the six or seven months after appearance of the flower, the fruit develops, changing from light green to red and, ultimately, when fully ripe and ready for picking, to deep crimson (see Exhibit 15.1). The mature fruit is called 'cherry' or 'berry', and grows in clusters on short stems. It usually contains two seeds, or beans, which are surrounded by several layers of skin and pulp.

The visible cover on the very top of the cherry is called outer skin and is the one that turns from green to red (or sometimes yellow) when the fruit ripens. Below this skin is a slippery sweet and mucilaginous pulp. Each of the two beans is covered by a loose yellowish skin – the parchment – underneath which is a thin tight membrane, called silverskin (see Exhibit 15.2).

Generally speaking, the soil in which coffee is grown must be rich, moist, and absorbent enough to accept water readily, but sufficiently loose to allow rapid drainage of excess water. The three marketable types of coffee have slightly different growth requirements, and hence appear in different parts of the world.

Arabica coffee is an upland species, growing between 650 and 2,800 m above sea level. As far as weather is concerned, an average annual temperature of 18–25° C is needed, with temperature extremes not below 13° C or above

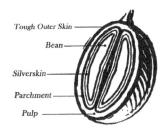

Exhibit 15.2 Cross-section of coffee berry

Source: www.coffee-machine.org/coffee-growing-and-harvesting/

---

4 As we will see later on, coffee varieties are further subdivided for commercial purposes.

30° C. Coffee trees are sensitive to frost; the crop will almost certainly be damaged, and if the plant itself is affected, future crops are also in peril. Because of this susceptibility to frost, altitude usually depends on latitude. Near the equator, arabica coffee can even be found as high as 2,500 m above sea level.

When grown further to the north or to the south, however, frost is more frequent at high altitudes, and the plant has to be cultivated closer to sea level.

Good conditions for arabica are found in Central America, Andean countries, some parts of Brazil and East Africa. Only a few areas are suitable in Asia, and these are mainly in India and Indonesia. Exhibit 15.3 highlights the main producing regions of the two coffee varieties.

Rainfall of 1,500–2,500 mm per annum is usually required, as the coffee plant is evergreen and needs moist soil all year round. In areas with low rainfall, irrigation is required, or alternative techniques to retain soil moisture are applied. Arabica coffee is also susceptible to certain diseases, such as leaf-rust, which necessitates the use of pesticides to fight them off and thus increases production costs.

Robusta coffee is a somewhat hardier species and is more resistant to pests and diseases. It is, however, more sensitive to climatic conditions. Robusta trees require an average yearly temperature of 24–26° C, and thrive in low altitudes of 300–800 m above sea level.

Required rainfall may vary between 1,000 and 2,500 mm per annum, with an optimum of 1,700 mm prevalent for about three-quarters of the year. Robusta trees also benefit from the existence of shade trees, which mitigate extremes of sunlight and humidity. Suitable zones for robusta are found over large tracts of West Africa, the lower regions of Central and South America, and in large areas of Southeast Asia.

Around the world, ca. 10 million hectares of land are used for coffee plants. Of these, over half are in Latin America, with over one-quarter located in just

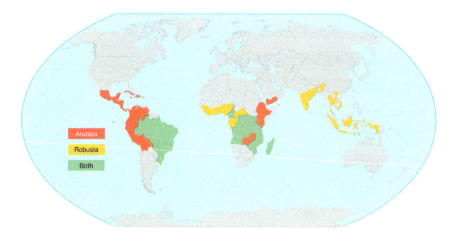

Exhibit 15.3 Coffee-growing regions

Source: Author, using Ortelius Mapping Software

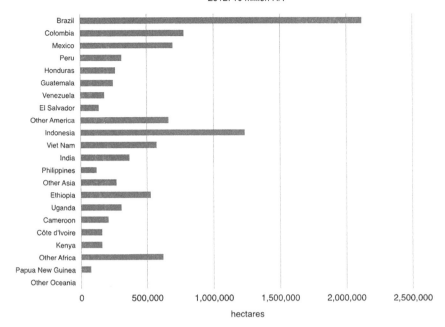

Exhibit 15.4 Area harvested for coffee

Source: Author, based on data from FAO (2014)

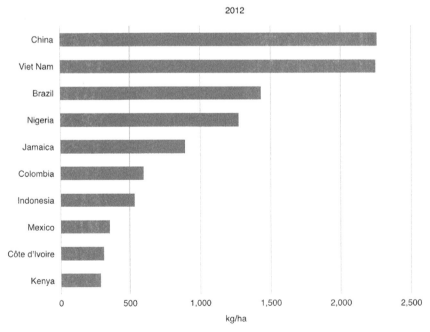

Exhibit 15.5 Indicative coffee production yields

Source: Author, based on data from FAO (2014)

two countries – Brazil and Colombia. Annual production figures imply that the average yield per hectare is between 700 and 900 kg. This figure is subject to wide variations that occur among countries, and even among farms in the same country.[5] Coffee yields range between under 100 to over 1,500 kg/ha. Exhibit 15.5 shows some indicative production yields for several countries around the world.

Supply of coffee

Historically, global coffee production has demonstrated an upward trend, especially after the major crop failure of Brazil in 1977. Yet this trend has been far from smooth. Fluctuations in production still occur on an annual basis, with some years producing bumper crops and others when production fails in some part of the world (notably Brazil) due to extreme weather conditions.[6] As mentioned above, in recent years, production has fluctuated between 115 and 150 million bags[7] per annum (equivalent to 7–9 million tonnes) (see Exhibit 15.6). Of this, ca. 60 per cent is accounted for by arabicas and the

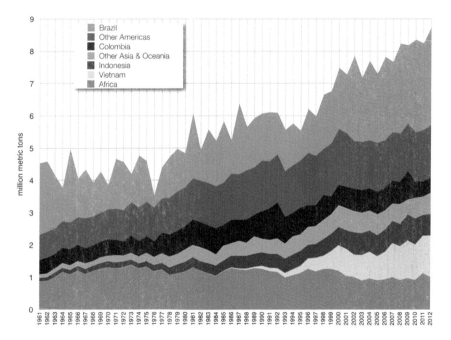

Exhibit 15.6 World coffee production development

Source: Author, based on data from FAO (2014)

5 Farm sizes vary from 'small' (2–5 ha.), to 'medium' (5–30 ha.) and 'large' (30 ha.).
6 Drought on the high Brazilian plains is a typical example of such weather extremes, which curtails coffee production. In addition, the cyclical El Niño phenomenon can also affect coffee production.
7 One bag of coffee is normally 60 kg.

rest by robustas, while liberica coffee has a negligible contribution to world production (see Exhibit 15.7).

New arabica plants take about five years to start yielding coffee berries, and reach full capacity at about their seventh year. Each tree produces an average of 0.5–1 kg of green coffee, and with spacing of about 10 m^2 for each plant, the average yield per hectare is about 750 kg. In contrast, robusta trees are spaced more widely, taking usually 15 m^2, or about 650–700 trees per hectare. Plants start yielding coffee cherries after about three years and reach their full production potential in their fifth year.

In either case, growing coffee has one very important difference from growing cereals or vegetables – planting decisions have a long-term effect on supply. Once producers decide to plant new coffee trees, they are faced with two crucial problems: production from the new trees will not reach the market before 3–5 years, when demand/supply conditions are likely to have changed; and once the new plants start producing, they will do so for the next 15 years at least.

Such production characteristics place substantial restrictions on the ability of supply to adapt to market conditions (i.e. supply price elasticity is low)[8] (see Exhibit 15.8). Another important characteristic of supply is its variability, due to the vagaries of the weather. As mentioned earlier, coffee plants are

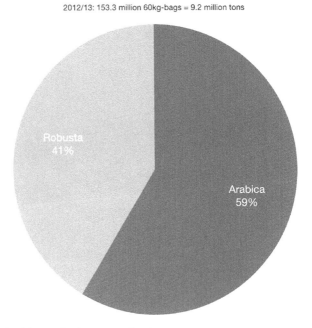

2012/13: 153.3 million 60kg-bags = 9.2 million tons

Robusta 41%

Arabica 59%

Exhibit 15.7 Arabica and robusta production

Source: Author, based on data from USDA (2014)

8 This is particularly true for the short term. Long-term supply elasticities are higher, as producers are able to adapt better to prices and other market conditions.

Country	2-year e^s	5-year e^s	10-year e^s
Brazil	0.03	0.10	0.36
Colombia	0.16	0.44	0.74
Costa Rica	0.11	0.15	0.41
Côte d'Ivoire	0.55	0.68	0.84
El Salvador	0.13	0.15	0.16
Guatemala	0.13	0.13	0.20
Indonesia	0.14	0.17	0.25
Mexico	0.02	0.06	0.13

Data coverage: 1968-1986

Exhibit 15.8 Supply elasticities for coffee
Source: Akiyama and Varangis (1990, p. 165)

susceptible to frost, and it is exactly this that has caused some of the severest supply disruptions in coffee history.

Although weather is a major determinant of coffee supply, it can also be called a 'wild card', implying that the estimation of its effects on annual production can only be ascertained close to harvest. Like any other agricultural commodity, coffee requires three major production inputs – land, labour and capital. Capital is required for the purchase of fertilisers, pesticides and new trees for planting, and also for the establishment and running of processing facilities on the farm. These costs are usually higher for arabica coffees, as they require more pesticides for protection and are usually processed with the 'wet' method, which is more costly. Robusta, on the other hand, requires less investment in processing facilities, and thus the largest part of the costs is allocated for labour.

Labour costs are incurred mainly during the crop season. Coffee cherries have to be picked by hand from the tree, although sometimes they may be shaken off the tree.[9] The picking season lasts for four months or slightly more, as coffee cherries ripen. Usually, labourers return to a tree every 10–14 days and pick the cherries that have gone from green to red. After collection, labour costs are also incurred for further processing by hand, especially for robusta coffee.

Further production costs include, of course, the transport cost from farms to export terminals, the freight from exporter to importer, administrative and set-up costs, and any export tax that may be levied on the commodity.

Coffee processing

As we mentioned coffee processing as a stage in the supply of coffee, it is now time to take a closer look at what it entails. When the cherries are collected, they need to be cleared of the hull in order to end up with just the green bean, which will be sold for roasting. There are two distinct phases: *initial processing* and *curing*.

9 This method is known as *strip picking*.

Initial processing is carried out using two alternative procedures – the 'wet' method and the 'dry' method. In the wet method, the first stage is to remove the pulp within the first 24–36 hours after harvesting. Subsequently, the beans – called *parchment* coffee at this stage – are thrown into fermenting tanks, where the mucilage is broken down naturally in 2–4 days. The beans are then washed, and dried either in the sun or mechanically. Through drying, the moisture content decreases dramatically from 53 per cent to 12 per cent.[10] It is mainly arabicas that are being processed with the wet method, and are thus called 'washed' arabicas.

The dry method is more suitable for areas with short supply of water and for robusta beans, which have a lower moisture content. In this method, the cherries are left on the tree to partially dry and are subsequently harvested. The cherries are then left to dry further in the sun for 3–4 weeks, or in drying machines for three days. As de Graaff (1986) notes:

> Dry processing after strip picking is common in those areas where the harvesting period is short, e.g. two to three months, as in Brazil and some parts of Central America and where wage rates are relatively high. A large labour force is required for such a short period and cannot always be employed economically in the long period between harvests. Since dry processing is generally cheaper, it is more appropriate for lower-quality coffee, and is therefore usually applied for robusta coffee.

After initial processing, coffee beans undergo further processing, which is known as curing. The first stage involves the stripping of the parchment shell and silverskin. The process is called *hulling* and is done mechanically. Polishing is also undertaken after hulling, in order to remove any silverskin remains.

Grading is the next phase, whereby the final product (called green coffee) is sorted by hand or machine to remove defective beans[11] and extraneous material,[12] and is then graded according to size. The objective of this stage is to create a final product as homogeneous and appealing to the customer as possible.

After initial processing and curing comes blending and roasting. Because of the closer relation of these two processes to consumers' tastes, and the fact that they usually take place in the importing countries, we will look at both of them in the section on coffee demand.

Policies

Brazil has been dominating the world coffee market since 1840. In fact, before the Second World War, exports from Brazil represented almost two-thirds of

10 de Graaff (1986, p. 46).
11 These may be pea-berries, elephant beans, triangular beans and *stinkers*, which can spoil the liquor of a good coffee.
12 Such as twigs, stones, husks, and sour and broken beans.

world coffee trade. The market had all the characteristics of an oligopoly with a dominant firm, whereby the dominant firm is the leader in setting quantities rather than prices. This was done through the *valoriscão* – or 'valorisation' – policy, whereby strict control of production and stocks was used to achieve acceptable prices. This often meant that in periods of glut, some of the coffee stocks had to be destroyed, rather than channelled into the market.

During the Second World War, Brazil traded almost exclusively with the United States. Because of the economic importance of coffee exports, a number of Latin American countries made arrangements before the war to allocate export quotas, so that each country would be assured a certain share of the United States coffee market. The first coffee quota agreement was arranged in 1940 and was administered by an Inter-American Coffee Board.

After the war, new producers entered the market with a view to capture a share for themselves. The most prominent competitor of Brazil was – and still is – Colombia, which markets its production aggressively and is there to benefit from any slip-up of Brazil. In more recent years, the most important competitor of both Brazil and Colombia is Vietnam, which entered coffee production in the mid-1980s and expanded rapidly from the mid-1990s onwards. This expansion can be seen in Exhibit 15.6, while Exhibit 15.9 lists the top 15 coffee producers. As the reader can see, the top four countries (Brazil, Vietnam, Indonesia and Colombia) produced two-thirds of global output (103 million bags) in 2012–2013.

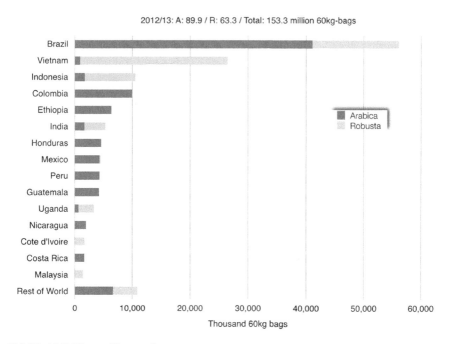

Exhibit 15.9 Top coffee producers

Source: Author, based on data from USDA (2014)

The idea of establishing coffee export quotas was occasionally put into practice by some countries during the 1950s, but it was adopted on a world-wide basis in 1962, when an International Coffee Agreement was negotiated by the United Nations. The aim was also to establish a buffer system that would help to stabilise world coffee prices through the purchase or release of stocks. During the five-year period when this agreement was in effect, 41 exporting countries and 25 importing countries acceded to its terms. The agreement was renegotiated in 1968, 1976 and 1983. The 1976 agreement was somewhat different, because it came after a severe frost in Brazil, which wiped out a large part of the production and affected crops in the following few years as well. It was, therefore, an agreement much more flexible than the previous two, allowing producing countries to increase their quotas to any extent that would not damage prices.

Participating nations failed to sign a new pact in 1989, however, and world coffee prices collapsed. For about a year – from mid-1989 to mid-1990 – prices remained at desperately low levels, with Brazilian arabicas hardly fetching 10 cents/lb in the world market. Prices eventually recovered in the second half of 1990 and remained fairly stable for about 3–4 years, although at levels below those achieved in the first half of the 1980s, when the market experienced another long period of relative stability.

Since 1990, coffee prices have demonstrated substantial volatility, as can be seen from Exhibit 15.10. In 1994, the severe frost caused the prices for Brazilian natural arabicas to jump from 97 cents/lb in April to 222 cents/lb in July of that year. There was another peak in 1997, which was followed by a long-term slump in coffee prices for most of the 2000s. It was only towards the end of that decade that coffee prices started picking up again, and in early 2011 coffee prices reached a 34-year high. This time, the price hike was not only due to the global shortage of good-quality Arabica beans, but also to the strength of demand in developed economies and rapid growth in new demand from emerging nations, such as China.[13]

Demand for coffee

Coffee contains a complex mixture of chemical components, some of which are not affected by roasting. Other compounds, particularly those related to the aroma, are produced by partial destruction of the green bean during roasting. Chemicals extracted by hot water are classified as non-volatile taste components and volatile aroma components. Important non-volatiles include caffeine, phenolic acids, amino acids, carbohydrates and minerals. Important volatiles are organic acids, aldehydes, ketones, esters, amines and mercaptans. The principal physiological effects of coffee are due to caffeine, an alkaloid that acts as a mild stimulant.

It is this stimulating effect that makes coffee a desirable beverage, but also a good that may not be necessary for everyday consumption. As such, coffee

13 At the time, consumers also blamed speculators for the price rally (Blas 2011).

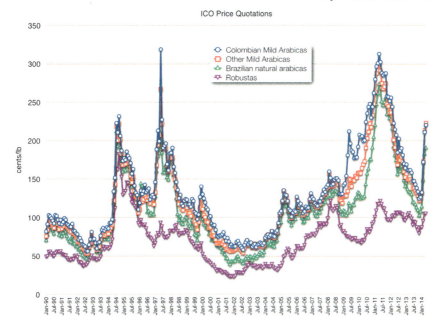

Exhibit 15.10 Coffee prices
Source: Author, based on data from ICO (2014a)

consumption is very much dependent on the level of income per capita and the extent of income elasticity. As can be seen from Exhibit 15.11, coffee is a luxury in some countries but a necessity in some others.

In the latter countries, coffee is part of everyday life and any attempt to expand consumption is usually targeted towards new users. In some cases, new occasions for drinking coffee might be promoted, or different ways of consuming coffee might be introduced in order to reduce seasonality in sales.

A slightly different pattern was followed in the United States since the late 1980s, whereby consumers changed their tastes towards 'speciality' coffees, which almost invariably imply the consumption of mild arabica varieties. These are produced in Colombia, Central America, Tanzania and Kenya, and expanding demand led producers in these countries to demand a proportionately larger share of the export market. It was this shift in consumer demand, many believe, that led to the failure of the 1989 ICA, whose quotas were regarded too inflexible by expanding countries.

The most important consumers of coffee are located in North America and the EU. Of these, the United States and Germany are the two leading consumers, with France, Italy, Spain, the UK and the Netherlands following suit. In the Far East, Japan is the biggest consumer, while Brazil is the largest consumer among coffee producers.

On a per capita basis, North European countries are consistently among the heaviest consumers, with Finland, Sweden, Norway and Denmark consuming

Country	Income	Own price
Austria	1.30	-0.54
Australia	1.72	-0.37
Belgium	0.36	-0.28
Canada	0.28	-0.13
Denmark	0.58	-0.43
United States	0.50	-0.46
France	0.68	-0.13
Germany	0.98	-0.17
Netherlands	0.89	-0.34
Ireland	2.89	-0.34
Italy	0.92	-0.18
Japan	2.03	-0.31
Norway	0.26	-0.14
Portugal	0.62	-0.28
Spain	1.07	-0.07
Switzerland	0.56	-0.24
Sweden	0.70	-0.29
United Kingdom	1.26	-0.51

Data coverage: 1968–1986

Exhibit 15.11 Demand elasticities for coffee

Source: Akiyama and Varangis (1990, p. 166)

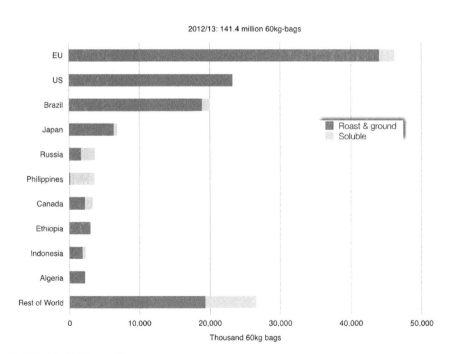

Exhibit 15.12 Top coffee consumers

Source: Author, based on data from USDA (2014)

between 8 and 12 kg/capita/year.[14] In contrast, Japan is at the bottom of the league of importing countries, with only one-quarter of the Scandinavian per capita consumption.

An important consideration in coffee consumption is competition from other beverages. Products such as tea, soft drinks, fruit juices, milk and drinking chocolate are such examples, although the term 'substitute' is not a good description, as more than one of them can be consumed by the same person at one time or another.

Blending and roasting

Two very important processing stages for coffee are blending and roasting, and they usually take place near the consumption markets, although roasting before export may also take place. There are several reasons why blending is important for coffee roasters:

- expensive varieties are mixed with lower quality beans, in order to control the cost of raw material input;
- beans of old and new crops can be mixed;
- beans with fermented taste can be spread among many consignments, instead of being wasted; and

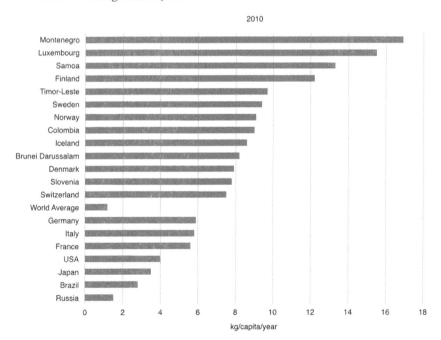

Exhibit 15.13 Per capita coffee consumption
Source: Author, based on data from FAO (2014)

14 This is ca. 22–33 grams per capita per day, or the equivalent of 3–5 espresso cups a day.

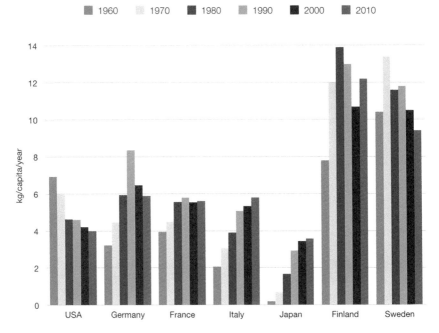

Exhibit 15.14 Development of per capita coffee consumption in selected countries
Source: Author, based on data from FAO (2014)

- when a reasonably stable quality is required, a blend with small quantities of many varieties is easier to reproduce year after year, even when there are major changes in the availability of certain beans.

Several varieties of green coffee are usually blended and roasted together to produce the tastes, aromas and flavours popular with consumers. The diversity of blends can be as large as the number of roasters, but some broad categories have been devised, in order to classify the strength of aromas and flavours. These are cinnamon, medium, medium high, city, full city, French, and Italian.

Roasting is undertaken in rotating, horizontal drums that provide a tumbling action to prevent uneven heating or scorching. Temperatures for roasting range from 193° C for a light roast, to 205° C for a medium roast, and to 218° C for a dark roast. The roasted beans are then cooled rapidly. Before the Second World War, it would normally take a full man-day to produce about 800 bags of coffee, with roasting lasting 15 minutes at almost 400° C. Nowadays, continuous roasters are used, which heat the beans for just five minutes at much lower temperatures and turn over 1,600 bags of coffee per man-day.

Roasted coffee may be packaged and shipped to retail stores, which custom grind it for the customers on purchase, or it may be ground in before shipment. Alternatively, coffee may be further processed into soluble granules. Instant coffee has a very large market around the world and actually makes more efficient use of coffee beans. A blend of arabicas and robustas is used, the first for flavour and aroma, the second for volume. In either case, the production process involves the extraction of liquor from ground roast coffee and the subsequent dehydration of the liquor. Dehydration is achieved by various methods, including the use of spray dryers or high-vacuum equipment. In freeze-dried coffee, the coffee extract is frozen and the water is removed by sublimation. The product is packed in vacuumed, sealed jars or in cans.

A final stage in coffee processing involves the removal of caffeine. Decaffeination can be achieved with chlorinated hydrocarbon solvents. The beans are roasted by ordinary procedures after removal of the solvents. Because the whole procedure removes so much of the beans' original aroma and flavour, cheaper robusta varieties are used for decaffeinated coffees.

Marketing and trade of coffee

The final product that enters the physical market is called green coffee and is classified into four major categories for trading purposes: Colombian milds; other milds; Brazilian and other arabicas;[15] and robustas. The first three groups are all arabicas, while the last group refers collectively to all the types of canephora coffee. The first two arabicas are also known as 'washed' arabicas, while Brazilian arabicas are usually unwashed; robustas are almost exclusively unwashed.

Brazilian arabicas consist principally of Santos, Paraná and Rio, named after the ports from which they are shipped. Milds are identified by the names of countries or districts in which they are grown, such as Medellín, Armenia and Manizales coffees from Colombia.[16]

There are several players participating in the market for coffee, both at the cash and the futures level. Before the commodity leaves its country of origin, it is handled by two different types of organisations: marketing boards and quasi-governmental coffee producers' associations.

Historically, marketing boards generally had a legal monopoly for purchasing the entire crop. They bought dried coffee cherries directly from local traders and producers, and undertook the responsibility to process, grade and store the commodity. Subsequently, they sold the coffee, through auctions, to registered exporters and local roasters. In more recent years, buying coffee crops at guaranteed minimum prices has proved financially cumbersome. As a result, coffee boards tend to avoid being central buyers and focus instead on other functions, such as: registration and licensing of coffee growers; formulate rules and regulations for the development of the sector; provide advisory services on coffee production and quality enhancement; and collect and analyse data relevant to the production, pricing and marketing of coffee. Some of the countries having such marketing boards include Tanzania, Kenya, Uganda and India. In francophone countries, the equivalent of the coffee board was the 'caisse de stabilisation'; examples of such countries are Cameroon and

15 This category is also known as 'Brazilian natural arabicas'.
16 These are frequently referred to as the 'Colombian MAMs'.

Côte d'Ivoire. Some 'caisse' converted to modern marketing boards, with their role being mostly regulatory and consultative.[17] Others retained part of their price-intervention powers, as well as undertaking the commercialisation of the commodity both domestically and in the export market.[18]

In a similar way, quasi-governmental coffee producers' associations used to assume a price-setting role, establishing minimum prices at which they will buy coffee from growers. In the 1990s, the role of these organisations was reviewed. Some were abolished altogether,[19] whereas others rescinded their price-setting role and focused on supporting farmers in different ways, such as improving coffee varieties and productivity, helping with export enhancement, collecting data and so forth.[20]

With the withdrawal of most coffee marketing boards and associations from setting prices, the importance of private traders has increased, as they provide the vital link between coffee growers and the international market. The extent to which traders participate in coffee marketing chains depends on the size and bargaining power (or lack thereof) of the coffee producers.

Exhibit 15.15 demonstrates the various stages of coffee marketing from production to final consumption. In some cases, large farms may sell their product directly to importers and roasters abroad, but, as a general rule,

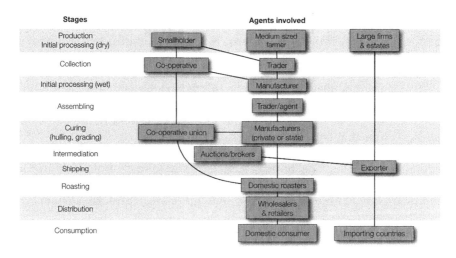

Exhibit 15.15 The marketing channels for coffee

Source: Author

17 Such is the case of Cameroon with its National Cocoa and Coffee Board (NCCB).
18 This is the case of Côte d'Ivoire and its Conseil du Café-Cacao. Part of its mission is to fix minimum purchase prices for coffee and cocoa from the producers and marketing the crop internationally, in addition to its other functions of market regulation, quality enhancement, and collection and analysis of statistical data.
19 An example is the Brazilian Coffee Institute, which was abolished in 1990, soon after the collapse of the ICA in 1989.
20 For example, the Colombian Coffee Growers' Federation (FedCafé).

producers are rather small to enter negotiations by themselves, and even co-operatives that buy the crop of small farmers do not always have the expertise to reach the big wholesale roasters themselves. It is here that the gap is filled by trading firms, which handle packaging and shipping of green beans from exporting countries to importing roasters.

Coffee is one of the most actively traded commodities, with ca. 80 per cent of production being channelled to the export market. As evidenced in Exhibit 15.16, exports have grown in tandem with production, but have also shown similar volatility. Brazil and Vietnam are by far the largest exporters of green coffee (see Exhibit 15.17). Brazil has been the world's largest exporter since the beginning of the industry. Vietnam, on the other hand, has had a truly astounding ascent from complete obscurity before 1990, to overtaking Colombia in 2000, and completely dominating robusta exports. In contrast, Africa has decreased in importance since 2000, largely due to underinvestment in planting new trees because of the relatively low coffee prices during most of the 2000s.

There are two more observations to make about coffee exports. Global exports are dominated by robustas and Brazilian and other unwashed arabicas, as can be seen in Exhibit 15.18, with ca. one-third accounted for by mild arabicas, such as the Colombian ones. Finally, Exhibit 15.19 displays the top exporters of processed coffee, which are led by Brazil once more.

The most important coffee consumers are also the most prominent importers of the commodity. The EU is the largest importing region, with

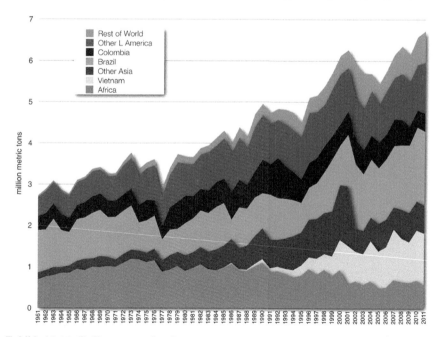

Exhibit 15.16 Coffee export development

Source: Author, based on data from FAO (2014)

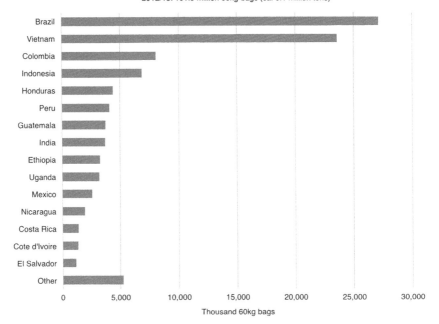

Exhibit 15.17 Top coffee bean exporters

Source: Author, based on data from USDA (2014)

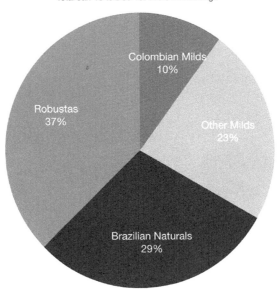

Exhibit 15.18 Coffee exports by type of bean

Source: Author, based on data from ICO (2014b)

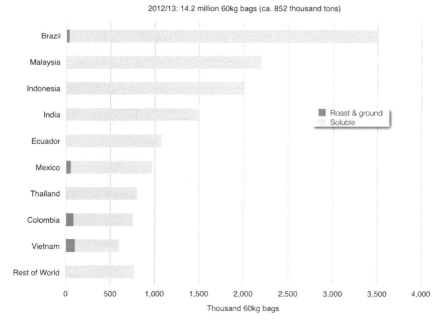

Exhibit 15.19 Top processed coffee exporters
Source: Author, based on data from USDA (2014)

Germany, France and Italy being among the largest importers of the group. The United States follows, but it is the largest individual country importer. The EU and the US absorb over two-thirds of global imports, while Japan is the largest importer from the rest of the world (see Exhibits 15.20 and 15.21). Finally, the top importers of processed coffee are shown in Exhibit 15.22, where the Philippines, Russia and Canada lead the list.

Coffee is available in the spot market, and prices are quoted on the basis of quality, origin, bean characteristics, place of purchase, and time of delivery. As mentioned above, coffees are divided into Colombian milds, other milds, Brazil and other (unwashed) arabicas, and robustas. Price quotations for all of the above varieties are provided by the ICO on a daily basis. These include prices for Colombian Mild arabicas, and an average price for Brazilian arabicas. As far as 'other milds' and robustas are concerned, quotations reflect changes in a basket of several cultivars from around the world. ICO prices for other milds are based on arabica crops of several countries, in Latin America, Africa and Asia. For robustas, the prices reflect crops from several African and Asian countries, with Vietnam being the most important one because of its large production.[21]

Some of the most important spot markets exist in large ports located in importing countries. In New York, for example, coffee is quoted on a spot basis, as well as on the Intercontinental Exchange (ICE). In Europe, the most

21 The development of these four price benchmarks can be seen in Exhibit 15.10.

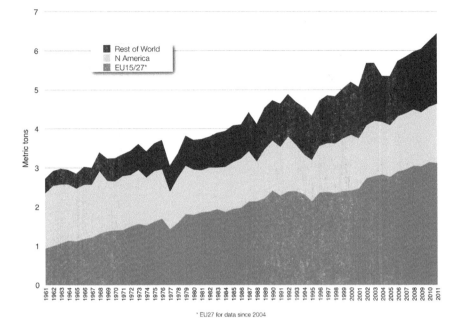

Exhibit 15.20 Coffee import development

Source: Author, based on data from FAO (2014)

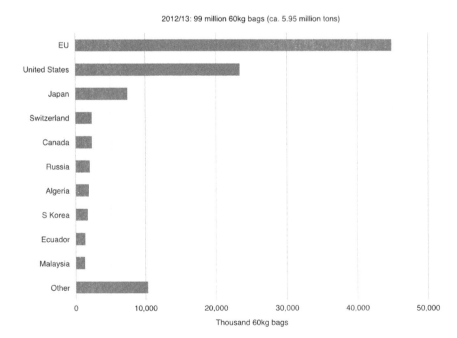

Exhibit 15.21 Top coffee bean importers

Source: Author, based on data from USDA (2014)

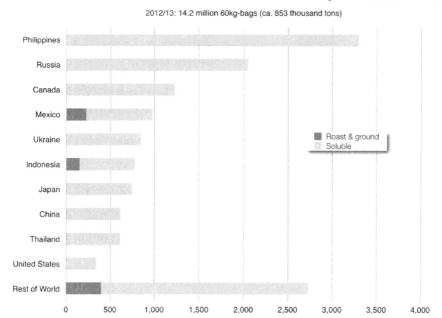

Exhibit 15.22 Top processed coffee importers

Source: Author, based on data from USDA (2014)

respected spot prices are quoted in Bremen and Hamburg and are reached after canvassing a number of brokers in both cities. In London, a coffee contract for robustas is quoted on NYSE-Euronext.[22]

In terms of spot market participants, seven large trading houses handle just over 50 per cent of the world trade in green coffee beans. These are: Rothfos, E D & F Man (who acquired Volcafé in 2004), CoffeeAmerica (who acquired Tardivat in 1997), ECOM Coffee (part of ECOM Agroindustrial, which also acquired Armajaro's physical operation in 2013) and NKG (Neumann Kaffee Gruppe).

In the retail market, the situation is quite different, however. The market is dominated by large roasting companies and, in some cases, by supermarket retailers who roast and grind their own-label coffee. Some of the most well-known participants in the roasted and instant coffee markets include: Kraft Jacobs Suchard, Nestlé, Sara Lee/Douwe Egberts, Lavazza, and Tchibo (who now also own Eduscho).

Conclusion

Coffee is one of the most important minor agricultural commodities, and indeed one of the most actively traded. Like several other minor agricultural

22 In late 2013, NYSE-Euronext was acquired by ICE, hence bringing all coffee futures contracts under the same organisation.

commodities, it is produced in developing countries that rely on exporting it to developed consumers. Due to its high value, coffee is important for the economies of the producing countries, especially the smaller ones.

Following the early domination of Brazil, the market is nowadays competitive, with the important functions of price discovery and price risk hedging being carried out by commodity exchanges in New York and London.

Control along the marketing chain changes as the commodity moves from the farm to the roaster and then to the final consumer. Governments, plantation owners, coffee traders, roasters and retailers; all play important roles in the marketing chain for coffee.

Cocoa

Although the history of cocoa is somewhat different to that of coffee, the economics of these two commodities are remarkably similar. Historical evidence suggests that beans of *xocoatl* had religious and pecuniary significance in the Aztec civilisation, and, according to myth, it was bequeathed to people by Quetzalcoatl – the Aztec god of air. It was this religious connotation perhaps that led Linæus to name the plant *theobroma cacao* (food of the gods) in the eighteenth century.

It was in the court of Montezuma that Cortes encountered the beans of the cocoa tree for the first time. He also saw how the beans were roasted and subsequently ground in order to make a drink. The pulverised beans were often mixed with spices and adulterated with maize to reduce cost. It was the discovery of this drink, rather than the beans themselves,[23] that made the product popular in the Spanish court. The recipe remained a closely kept secret and the drink remained very much a drink for the royalty. It was more than a century later, in the 1650s in England, that chocolate became available in the market, and then again it could only be afforded by the rich.

The new drink became popular in Europe in the mid-seventeenth century, when it was offered alongside coffee in the very popular coffee houses. Chocolate, however, remained a drink for the few, and for several decades it was mainly available from apothecaries and prescribed for medicinal purposes. A fading memory of that use today is the small proportion of cocoa for the production of theobromine, a mild heart stimulant that is contained in the bean.

The first signs of cocoa's future success were on the horizon when the first chocolate factory was opened in Bristol in 1728 by Joseph Fry. It was soon followed by shops that offered their own grindings of cocoa, such as Rowntree's, Terry's and Cadbury's.

The consumption of chocolate as a drink continued spreading in Europe and the Americas throughout the eighteenth century. The drink, however, had a somewhat fatty and gritty taste, and as a result research continued in finding ways to improve the palatability of the drink. Two advances in the preparation

23 Cocoa beans had been brought back to the Spanish Court by Columbus.

and use of chocolate became milestones in the history of cocoa. In 1828, C.J. van Houten discovered that by pressing the ground cocoa beans he could get rid of a significant amount of fat – the cocoa butter – leaving a powder that produced a much lighter and more palatable drink. He also discovered that by adding a small amount of alkali in the cocoa powder, he could enhance its flavour.[24]

The new process of extracting fat from cocoa grindings left manufacturers with an expensive residue – cocoa butter. It was Fry's who experimented by mixing cocoa powder, sugar and cocoa butter, to make the first commercially available eating chocolate in 1847. This new development created two quite separate processes, with the manufacturing of eating chocolate taking its own way and developing in subsequent years. It was this form of chocolate consumption that ended up as more popular and became more readily associated with the use of cocoa beans. Several further improvements were recorded after the commercialisation of eating chocolate: Fry's once again innovated by introducing the first filled chocolate bars with a non-chocolate centre in 1866; milk chocolate was developed in Switzerland in 1876 by Peter and Nestlé; in 1879, Lindt introduced a chocolate with a much smoother texture by repeatedly rolling the mixture with a grinding stone – called conching – until the particles of cocoa and sugar were finely ground and fully covered with the butter.

Physical characteristics

The cocoa tree belongs to the family of Sterculiaceae, whose genus theobroma has over 20 other species, one of which is cacao. There are two main types of trees (and beans) – the 'Criollo' and the 'Forastero'. Traditionally, it was the Criollo trees that were cultivated in Latin America and their beans that were exported to Europe and North America. With the introduction of Forastero trees around the beginning of the nineteenth century, production of Criollo cocoa diminished, and nowadays Criollo trees are very few.

The Forastero subspecies is further divided into two varieties – 'amelonado' and 'trinitario' cocoa. Amelonado is today the most widespread cocoa variety, due to its better colour and flavour characteristics.

The cocoa tree flourishes best in hot and wet conditions. Temperatures should be between 18 and 32° C, with rainfall ranging between 1,250 and 3,000 mm per annum. Rainfall all year round is preferable, but a relatively dry season of no more than three months can be withstood by the plants.

Like coffee, most of the cocoa-growing regions are in tropical and subtropical regions, within 8° north and south of the equator where climatic requirements are ideal. It is no surprise, therefore, that the entire world output of cocoa beans is produced in developing countries. Exceptions of the tree being grown in extreme latitudes do exist, notably in China, at about 20° N, and in São Paulo, at about 24° S.

---

24 In honour of van Houten, this process is called *dutching*.

Exhibit 15.23 Cocoa tree with pods

Source: NCA's Chocolate Council Association, http://thestoryofchocolate.com

The fruits of the tree are the cocoa beans, but, unlike coffee beans, they do not grow in the shape of cherries. Cocoa beans are enclosed in large pods, which grow straight out of the tree's trunk and branches.

The cocoa tree is susceptible to a variety of diseases, most of which usually cause the pod to rot, and hence waste a considerable proportion of production. Most of the diseases are of a fungous nature, and some of the most well known – and dangerous – ones include the black pod rot, and witch's broom. The second one affects branches initially, but it may extend to the pods and cause considerable losses.

The cocoa tree also requires some degree of husbandry, particularly pruning. Fertiliser application is usually necessary – especially in poor soils – during the initial growth of the new plant, and then after the first or second year of production, when some of the nutrients contained in the soil are likely to have diminished. Most of all, however, the cocoa tree requires shade, in order to avoid extremes of direct sunlight and to have some relative protection from the wind. Because of this requirement, cocoa trees are usually inter-cropped with other trees – such as coconuts and pawpaws – or, alternatively, are planted in thinned forests, when the cost of planting other trees is high.

The harvesting season starts in late September and the first beans are ready for export in October. This is the case, at least, in the most important producing countries, such as Côte d'Ivoire, Ghana and Brazil. It is customary, therefore, for the crop year to start in October and end the following September (see Exhibit 15.24).

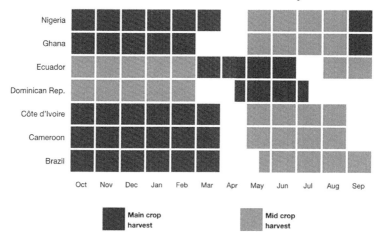

Exhibit 15.24 Cocoa harvesting seasons
Source: Author

Harvesting of cocoa is by hand and, like coffee, cannot be completed at once. Pickers have to go back to the tree every fortnight, in order to collect the ripe pods, which can be distinguished by their yellow-orange (Amelonado) or deep dark reddish-brown (Trinitario) colour.

The pods have to be opened by hand and the bean and placenta removed. The next part of the process, which is also the most intriguing, is to store the cocoa beans in heaps and let them ferment. Storage facilities vary from organised fermentaries, in larger farms, to makeshift heaps of beans stored between two layers of banana or plantain leaves. The beans are left there for not more than five days. During these five days, a series of chemical changes take place in the pulp and the beans, mainly with the help of bacterial oxidisation. The end result is that the cocoa beans acquire the colour and – later, after roasting – the distinctive chocolate flavour they are known for. The beans are then dried in the sun, cleaned in special machines, bagged and, finally, prepared for export. It is at this stage that they reach the importer, who is going to process them into the final products.

Supply of cocoa

The economics of cocoa supply are very similar to those of coffee. Cocoa is grown exclusively in developing countries and is an important source of income for thousands of smallholders, and of foreign exchange for the governments of the producing nations.

A handful of countries turn out almost the entire world production of cocoa beans. Before the beginning of the twentieth century, it was Latin America and the Caribbean that produced cocoa almost exclusively. From the 1900s to the 1920s, Africa produced as much as Latin America, and, since the 1930s,

African countries have been the world leaders in cocoa production. Despite this dramatic restructuring of cocoa supply, its history has been one of continuous growth, even for regions and countries whose market share diminished. Exhibit 15.25 displays the development of cocoa bean production across time in the main producing regions.

Another important player in the market is Asia, especially Southeast Asia. The region progressed from supplying just over 3 per cent of world cocoa output in 1980, to producing nearly 20 per cent in 2012. This rise to prominence is primarily driven by Indonesia, which is currently the world's second largest producer after Côte d'Ivoire (see Exhibit 15.26). It was achieved with intensive cultivation of the land and widespread use of fertilisers and pesticides, which resulted in high production yields that are now comparable to those of the more traditional producers, such as Côte d'Ivoire and Ghana (see Exhibit 15.27).

Although Indonesia stands out from the Southeast Asian producers, four of the top five producers are African countries. Côte d'Ivoire is the undisputed leader, producing one-third of total world output. In third place lies Ghana, which produces the best quality cocoa beans in the world – as Colombia does in the coffee market.

The remaining places in the league of the 10 largest producers are taken by Nigeria, Brazil, Cameroon, Ecuador, Mexico, the Dominican Republic and Peru. Latin American countries have fallen from world domination, although they still produce ca. 15 per cent of the world cocoa beans supply.

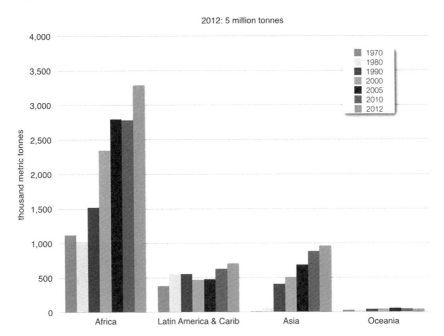

Exhibit 15.25 Cocoa production development in major regions

Source: Author, based on data from FAO (2014)

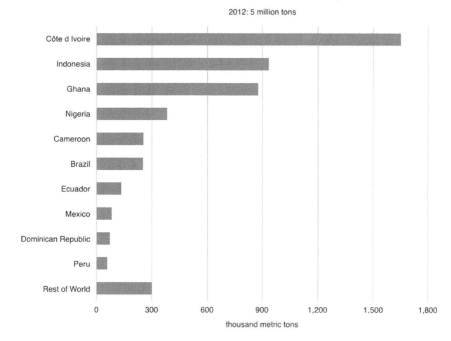

Exhibit 15.26 Top cocoa bean producers
Source: Author, based on data from FAO (2014)

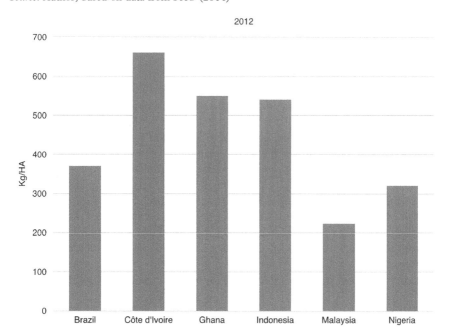

Exhibit 15.27 Representative cocoa production yields
Source: Author, based on data from FAO (2014)

In terms of the microeconomic structure of supply, labour costs play a significant role in the whole production procedure. Cocoa harvesting depends on the availability of cheap and reliable labour throughout the main crop season from October to April. Capital costs are incurred mainly for the production of seed material, the procurement of fertilisers and pesticides, and the construction of fermentaries. Any additional costs that may be incurred are due to taxation and administration charges.

The apportionment of costs and the role of government depends very much on the concentration of production in each country, and this may vary widely. As Dand (2010) notes, 'In the Côte d'Ivoire only 5 per cent of the cocoa grown comes from plantations larger than 40 hectares while in Malaysia the figure is 85 per cent, Indonesia 50 per cent and in Brazil it is above 55 per cent'.

In large farms, all stages of production are undertaken on site, leaving only the exports of the commodity to be administered by the state. In Africa, however, where most of the producers are smallholders, the government is involved in production at a much earlier stage. Producers are responsible for collecting the crop, but government may step in to provide proper fermentation facilities that can be used by many small producers. The state also undertakes the responsibility to market and export the commodity, and also provides advice to the farmers regarding production and the choice from several food and cash crops.

Much like coffee, cocoa is a substantial source of revenue for small producers and a considerable source of foreign exchange for the exporting country. Price variability is therefore undesirable, and attempts have been made to stabilise international market prices through international agreements on production quotas and buffer stocks.

The first International Cocoa Agreement (ICCA) was signed in 1972, and in 1973 the International Cocoa Organisation (ICCO) was set up to implement the agreement. Since then, another six agreements have been achieved, with the most recent one (seventh) signed in 2010 and having come into force at the end of 2012.

Like all typical international commodity agreements, attempts were initially made to mitigate price variability through price controls and buffer stocks. Earlier ICCAs involved a complex system of prices, which triggered different actions from the ICCO. The range of prices that was agreed was denominated in SDRs, rather than US dollars, and included a 'lower-intervention' price, a 'may-buy' price, a 'median' price, a 'may-sell' price and an 'upper-intervention' price. Unfortunately, depressed market conditions wiped out any hope of the ICCA for price stabilisation, as the agreement became too expensive for members to maintain.

During the last two decades, agreements have dispensed with trying to mitigate price variability with the use of buffer stocks. Recent ICCAs have a character and tone substantially different to their predecessors. The current agreement aims to strengthen cocoa economies through selecting and financing appropriate development projects; also, through collection of appropriate statistics and promotion of the consumption of cocoa and its products.

Demand for cocoa

Cocoa beans are roasted to bring out the chocolate flavour. This usually takes place in the country of final consumption, although a significant proportion of the beans – estimated at about one-third of global production – are roasted and ground in the country of origin (see Exhibit 15.28). After roasting, they are shelled in a crushing machine and ground into chocolate. During the grinding, the fat melts, producing a sticky liquid called chocolate liquor, which is used to make chocolate candy or is filtered to remove the fat and then cooled and ground to produce cocoa powder. Small percentages of various substances may be added, such as starch to prevent caking, or potassium bicarbonate to neutralise the natural acids and astringents and make the cocoa easy to dissolve in liquids. Cocoa has a high food value, containing as much as 20 per cent protein, 40 per cent carbohydrate and 40 per cent fat.

Like coffee, cocoa is a beverage used for the stimulating effects of the theobromine it contains. It is mainly used in the production of chocolate products, and may be viewed by consumers both as a necessity and as a luxury, depending on the country of reference. In countries with high consumption per capita, chocolate is largely viewed as a necessity, rather than a luxury. The heaviest consumers of chocolate are in the EU and the United States, averaging about 2 kg/capita/year, while in the rest of the world consumption stands at about 0.5 kg/capita.

True final consumption is rather difficult to estimate. The general level of consumption is usually monitored through cocoa grindings each year; this is

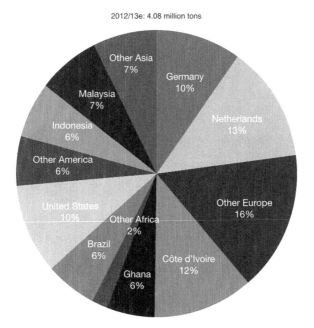

Exhibit 15.28 Cocoa bean grindings by country
Source: Author, based on data from ICCO (2014)

also a good indicator of processing activity in a country. Final consumption, however, is not necessarily represented by grindings alone. Imports of processed cocoa products, instead of the beans themselves, might be used, and stocks may also be utilised if needed.

Another characteristic of demand for cocoa products is that it is clearly split between demand for drinking chocolate and demand for eating chocolate. Cocoa powder is used for the manufacturing of drinking chocolate, while cocoa butter and chocolate liquor are used for the manufacturing of all other chocolate products – as is demonstrated in Exhibit 15.30. Finally, there is also a proportion of demand – for cocoa butter – that is generated by the cosmetics industry.

Marketing and trade in cocoa

Cocoa is very actively traded in the international markets, because it is consumed heavily in countries distant from the places of production. Marketing arrangements resemble those for coffee; there are government agencies as well as private companies participating at different stages of marketing. Marketing boards are the most common type of state organisation that get involved in cocoa exports. Their role is exactly the one described earlier for coffee.

In countries such as Brazil, Malaysia, Indonesia and Nigeria, there is a 'free market' system in place. The handling, distribution and pricing of the commodity is left to private traders, but the state is still actively involved in

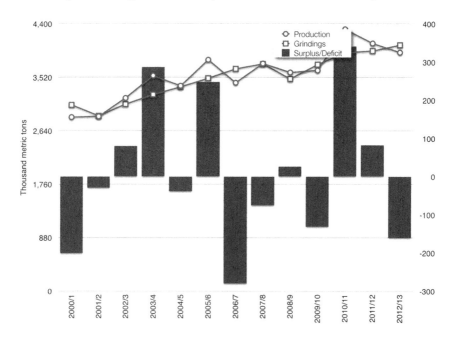

Exhibit 15.29 Cocoa bean production, grindings and implied surplus/deficit

Source: Author, based on data from ICCO (2014)

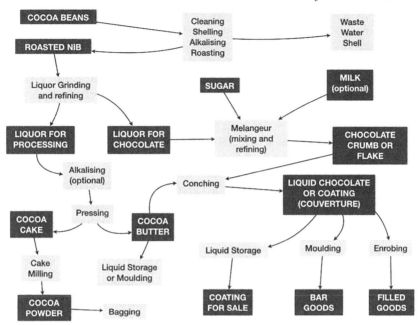

Exhibit 15.30 The cocoa processing chain
Source: Author

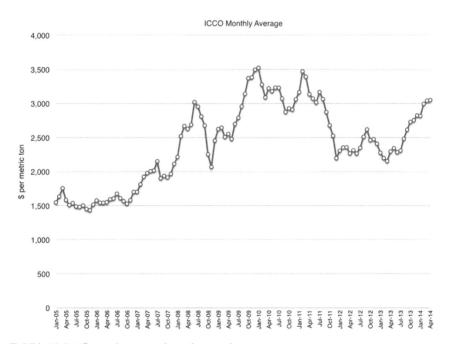

Exhibit 15.31 Cocoa beans and products prices
Source: Author, based on data from Thomson Reuters Datastream

the monitoring of bean quality, in order to ensure the country's reputation in the international market.

Chocolate manufacturers are not normally involved in cocoa production. They acquire their supplies in the open market, through brokers and dealers. The most active spot markets for cocoa beans are in New York and Amsterdam, and prices are usually quoted at a discount of Ghanian cocoa, which has the best and most reliable quality.

Market participants may also wish to use the futures markets, which operate in a similar manner to those for coffee. Cocoa contracts are quoted on ICE in New York, as well as on NYSE-Euronext in London.

Trade flows in cocoa products are quite straightforward – producing countries consume very little (with the exception of Brazil perhaps), and thus export their output to developed consumers. Côte d'Ivoire and Ghana lead the bean exporters, followed by Nigeria, Indonesia and Cameroon. Also in the list of top exporters are the Netherlands, Germany and France, by virtue of their re-exports of beans, as well as processed cocoa products: paste, butter and cocoa powder (see Exhibit 15.32).

Importers, on the other hand, are led by the Netherlands, followed by the United States, Germany and Malaysia. These are followed by mostly European and also Asian countries (see Exhibit 15.33).

The total trade in cocoa beans was ca. 3.2 million tonnes in 2012, representing ca. 64 per cent of the world production, which shows how actively

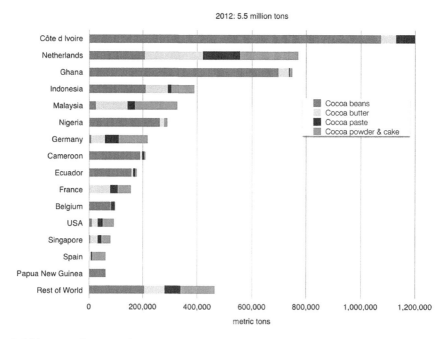

Exhibit 15.32 Exports of cocoa beans and products

Source: Author, based on data from FAO (2014)

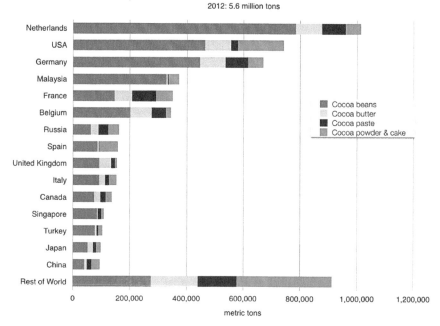

Exhibit 15.33 Imports of cocoa beans and products
Source: Author, based on data from FAO (2014)

the commodity is traded. Trade in cocoa products is equally active, with a total of 2.3 million tonnes entering international trade in 2012.

Conclusion

Cocoa is the smallest of the three commodities discussed in this chapter. It is, however, a very actively traded commodity, and one of significant importance for many trading houses. At the same time, cocoa is an important cash crop for several developing countries, and it is no wonder that they have been anxious to exercise some control over its price variability. Africa and Latin America dominate cocoa production and exports, but it is Asian newcomers – especially Indonesia – that are currently the most dynamic producers, much like African countries were, when they overtook Latin America in the 1920s.

Sugar

Sugar is believed to have been known to humans for some 2,000 years, and is thought to have originated in New Guinea, from where it spread to the rest of Southeast Asia, India and China. The plant was introduced to Latin America during the voyages of discovery at the end of the fifteenth century, when Columbus brought it with him to Hispaniola. From there, cultivation of sugar canes spread to the rest of the Caribbean islands, Central America and Brazil.

Sugar production was closely linked with the colonisation of the Americas, and during the English domination of international trade it became one of the region's main exports and was the main input in rum production. The sector, however, was also linked to the abominable slave trade, which furnished sugar cane plantations with much needed labour.

Physical characteristics

Sugar is a generic term applied loosely to any of a number of chemical compounds in the carbohydrate group that are: water-soluble, colourless, odourless, crystallisable, and relatively sweet in taste. Sugars are divided into several subgroups, normally distinguished by the number of carbon atoms contained in the molecule. Among the commercially important sugars are glucose, lactose and maltose; most important, however, is sucrose, also called saccharose or cane sugar.

Sucrose can be also obtained from other plants, including sugar maple and various palms. Sugar beet, however, is the most efficient and most widespread alternative to sugar cane for the production of sucrose. Thus, the sugar industry is quite clearly segmented into two sub-sectors, which revolve around these two sources of the commodity.

Exhibit 15.34 Cut sugar canes

Source: Wikimedia Commons, http://commons.wikimedia.org/wiki/File:Cut_sugarcane.jpg, licensed under the Creative Commons Attribution-Share Alike 2.0 Generic Licence

Sugar is a relatively homogeneous product, although it might be supplied in several stages of refinement, according to consumer tastes.[25] Cane sugar is produced best in the hot and humid conditions of the tropical and subtropical climates, and almost exclusively by developing nations. It is also cultivated, however, in parts of the United States and Australia. Sugar beet, on the other hand, is produced in temperate climates, with the United States, EU countries and Eastern Europe accounting for almost 80 per cent of world beet sugar output.

Sugar cane

Sugar cane is a perennial, monoculture crop, requiring about 1,500 mm of rain per annum and a moderately warm temperature of 20° C. The cane is planted in autumn or spring and takes about 12–16 months to mature. It

Exhibit 15.35 Types of sugar

Source: Author, with photo by Romain Behar, Wikimedia Commons, http://commons.wikimedia.org/wiki/File:Sucre_blanc_cassonade_complet_rapadura.jpg

25 This is not the case with beet sugar, however, because it is produced directly in refined form.

is capable of producing 8–10 good crops before yields begin to deteriorate. Cropping is once a year, although in many countries two crops a year are achievable.

Once harvested, sugar canes have to be processed fairly quickly because they are susceptible to rot and to a reduction in their sucrose content. The first stage is to strip the stems from the leaves. The stripped canes are carried to the mill, which is usually located close to the plantation. At the mill, the canes are cut into smaller pieces and then shredded. The shredded canes are fed into several milling rollers, which extract the dark juice containing the sugar. The remaining is known as bagasse and is normally used as a fuel for the mill.

The next stage is to extract the sugar from the juice. First, the juice is clarified by adding lime and boiling it under pressure.[26] The clear syrup passes through a number of evaporators, at the end of which most of the water has been removed. The concentrated syrup is boiled again to remove water until the massecuite – a mixture of raw sugar crystals and syrup – is formed. The mixture is placed in a centrifuge turning at a rate of 1,000 to 1,500 rpm; the centrifuge walls are perforated so that the molasses are forced out during centrifuging. The yellowish or brown sugar removed during the centrifuging process is called first sugar, or raw sugar. The raw sugar is sprayed with water to remove any molasses that may have clung to the crystals, and is then moved to the refinery. The molasses may be boiled again and re-evaporated in an attempt to crystallise out some of its rich sucrose content. The molasses are a valuable by-product of the sugar industry, being used in the manufacture of ethyl alcohol and rum, as table syrup and food flavouring, and as animal feedstuff.

At the refinery, the raw sugar goes through a number of further processing stages, similar to the ones described above. The first one – called affination – involves the separation of any remaining impure syrup from the sugar crystals by heating and centrifuging. Carbon dioxide and lime are subsequently added to remove any remaining insoluble impurities. In the third stage, the liquid is passed through a series of decolourising columns, until white sugar can be extracted from the liquor. The last stage involves the crystallisation and drying of the sugar and its subsequent grading and packaging.

Sugar beet

The beet is a long white root, which flourishes in cool weather, thus making it most appropriate for temperate regions in northern latitudes. The vast majority of sugar beets are grown in developed countries, mostly in the EU and North America. The beet is planted in the spring and grows for about five months, with the harvest usually starting in September. In warmer climates, it may even be planted in early fall and harvested during the spring, thus maintaining round-the-year production. The crop is collected mechanically, and the tops and any surplus dirt are removed.

---

26   Often, the juice is treated with gaseous sulphur dioxide to bleach it.

Exhibit 15.36 Sugar beets

Source: Author, with images from Wikimedia Commons, licensed under Creative Commons Attribution-Share Alike: http://en.wikipedia.org/wiki/File:Entladung_Bunker.JPG; http://en.wikipedia.org/wiki/File:Sugar_beet_cossettes.jpg; http://en.wikipedia.org/wiki/File:SugarBeet.jpg

Sugar from beets is produced in a similar way to sugar from canes, but the process is much shorter. Once in the refinery, the roots are cut into cossettes, immersed in hot water, and crushed to remove the juice. The pulp remaining after the extraction of the juice is a rich source of carbohydrates and is used as animal feedstuff, usually mixed with molasses.

After extraction, a mixture of lime, carbon dioxide and sulphur dioxide is added to the juice to remove any impurities. The purified juice passes through a series of evaporators until it reduces to a thick, clear liquor. The liquor is subsequently boiled and seeded with pulverised sugar to form crystals. Like with cane sugar, the material is graded, dried and, finally, packaged.

Supply of sugar

As mentioned earlier, the sugar industry is clearly divided into the sugar cane and the sugar beet sectors. Sugar canes are grown in developing countries, while sugar beets are almost exclusively cultivated in developed countries. As a result, the economic parameters and policies affecting supply are quite diverse.

World production of sugar canes is dominated by Brazil, which produces nearly 40 per cent of global sugar cane output; other important producers in the Americas are Mexico, Colombia, Argentina, Guatemala, Cuba and the United States, although with comparatively much lower shares. Asian production is also dominated by one major player, India, which contributes ca. 20 per cent of global supply. Other important producers are China, Thailand, Pakistan, the Philippines and Indonesia. Finally, Australia is also a substantial producer and exporter in the region (see Exhibit 15.37).

Sugar beets are predominantly grown in developed countries, and they are located therefore near the points of final consumption. EU countries and the United States feature as the most prominent producers of sugar beets, although FSU countries – such as Russia, Ukraine and Belarus – cultivate the crop extensively, because it is suited to the climatic idiosyncrasy of the region. In the rest of the world, important producers are the United States, Turkey, China and Egypt, as can be seen in Exhibit 15.38.

Total world production is roughly split 80/20 between cane and beet sugar, with the latter remaining fairly stable, while most of the variability appears to occur in cane sugar production. The production pattern for sugar beets is reasonably justified by the fact that their cultivation has been substantially subsidised by the EU and is also equally favoured in the United States. It remains upon cane sugar producers in developing countries, therefore, to absorb any supply/demand imbalances that occur in the market.

The distinct geographical and economic split between cane and beet sugar has given rise to two different sets of supply characteristics. The cane sector depends largely on the availability of cheap labour for harvesting and

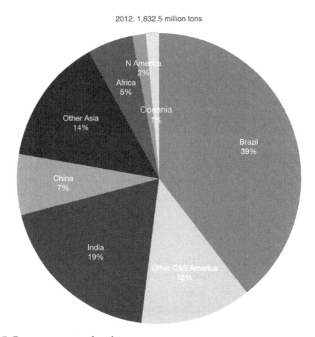

2012: 1,832.5 million tons

N America 2%
Africa 5%
Oceania 1%
Other Asia 14%
China 7%
India 19%
Other C&S America 13%
Brazil 39%

Exhibit 15.37 Sugar cane production

Source: Author, based on data from FAO (2014)

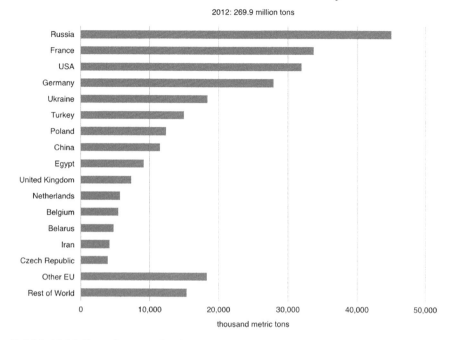

Exhibit 15.38 Sugar beet production

Source: Author, based on data from FAO (2014)

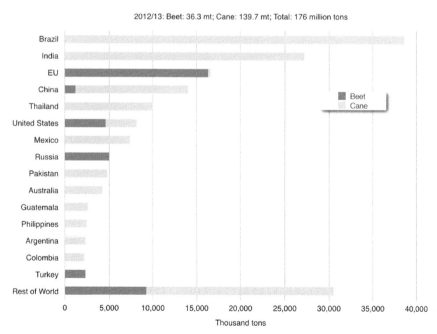

Exhibit 15.39 Centrifugal sugar (beet and cane) production

Source: Author, based on data from USDA (2014)

transporting the plants to the processing factories. Costs are predominantly variable, and the main problem is finding abundant labour just for seasonal employment. Another problem imposed by the nature of the plant is that it cannot be stored for long periods; once harvested, the 'kill-to-mill' time must be minimised, in order to avoid excessive wastage. In contrast to the first stage, the second stage of sugar processing is capital-intensive, and requires considerable investment in plant and equipment.

Quite frequently, owners of large farms set up their own milling operation, thus adding value to the product leaving their premises. This imposes, of course, often conflicting objectives – regular and widespread employment for the local population during harvesting, versus efficient capital-intensive operation of the milling installation with a minimum use of labour.

Practices differ largely from one country to another. Average farm sizes, for example, range from over 40 ha. in Brazil and Australia, but only 2 ha. in most Caribbean islands. Ownership of the farms is another issue; in most producing countries, farms belong to the private sector, but several governments take an active role in cane production – such as Jamaica and Trinidad, for instance.

For most agricultural commodities, prices in the international market display a large variability, which is most undesirable for producers whose income depends on their crops. Sugar is no exception, and has been the object of considerable government intervention, particularly in large consuming regions, such as the United States, the European Union and the former Soviet Union. Since the 1980s, the price of sugar in the open market has been fluctuating

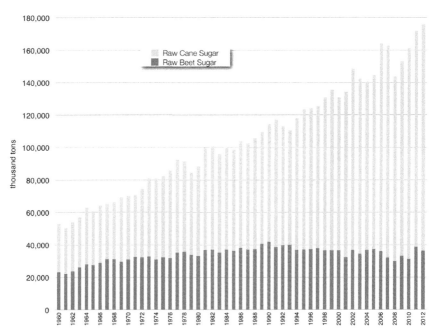

Exhibit 15.40 Sugar (beet and cane) production development

Source: Author, based on data from USDA (2014)

between 5 and 15 cents/lb ($110–330/tonne), with large drops recorded around the two major crises in 1990 and 1999. It was only from Q2 2007 that raw sugar prices started rising rapidly and hit a record of nearly 30 cents/lb in June 2011, before dropping again to 18 cents/lb in April 2014. Despite the relatively higher prices in the last five years, there is still considerable volatility, thus increasing uncertainty for producers' incomes. This situation has led producers in most countries to lobby their governments to operate compensatory schemes and remove some of the uncertainty of the international market.

The result was the creation of a complex net of subsidies, production controls, trade barriers and stockholding policies. In all cases, the policies had favourable effects on producers' welfare, but at the cost of consumers' welfare and the distorting effect of import diversion from other more efficient producers. Since the beginning of the 1970s, for example, prices paid to EU sugar beet growers consistently exceeded world prices, with the exception of the 1974 and 1980 price surges. In the United States, a similar situation exists, with the only difference that domestic prices were allowed to fluctuate with world prices during the two price shocks.

Despite this massive degree of intervention, occasionally there is scope for trade creation, even at low prices. The EU, for example, has signed successive Lomé Conventions with a number of African, Caribbean and Pacific Rim countries (ACP), covering a number of agricultural commodities – including a special 'sugar protocol' – for which trade barriers are lower. On a global scale, the Uruguay round of WTO (then GATT) also brought agricultural

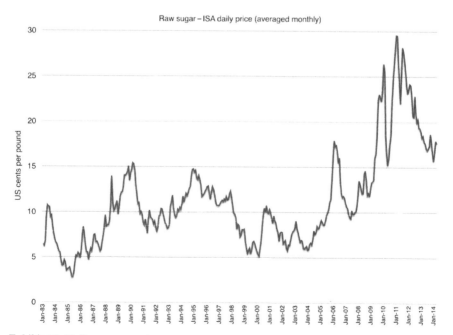

Exhibit 15.41 Raw sugar prices

Source: Author, based on data from Thomson Reuters Datastream

commodities into focus, with the aim to standardise and gradually bring down trade barriers, allowing efficient producers increased access to developed markets.

Attempts to control production and trade of sugar are not recent, however. Production controls date back to the time of the British Empire, when sugar was central to the distillation of rum, and thus of great importance to the economy. Producing countries (both of canes and beets) have repeatedly attempted to draft international agreements on production and trade since the beginning of the twentieth century. The first international sugar agreement (ISA) dates back to 1931, and grew out of the Chadbourne agreement between Cuba and the United States. Subsequent agreements were signed in 1937, 1953, 1958, 1968, 1977, 1984, 1987 and 1992. The 1977 agreement, however, did not include the EU, while the 1984 and 1987 ISAs were mostly of administrative agreements and statements of 'good intentions' for cooperation. The last agreement to be signed and the current one in existence is the 1992 agreement. This includes most of the world's producers of both cane and beet sugar, although the USA is not a member.

Since 1984, producing countries are less willing to enter new quota agreements and prefer to let market dynamics take care of prices. Moreover, there is a widespread view that no matter what agreement can be achieved, prices will succumb sooner or later to sugar's cyclical behaviour. This behaviour resembles very much the cobweb model that was described in an earlier chapter. Sugar producers are induced into planting more canes or beets by strong market prices. As they all rush to gain a bigger market share, prices are depressed, until production is reduced. Sometimes production is reduced so drastically that stocks are not enough to meet consumption requirements, so that large price hikes (such as the ones in 1974–1975 and 1980–1981) are not unlikely. In addition to the cyclicality described above, increased weather unpredictability also contributes to this volatility. Both Brazil and India, two of the world's largest market players, are often affected by extreme weather conditions, which play havoc with production, resulting in either shortages or surpluses from one crop year to the next. Brazil is affected by the El Niño weather phenomenon, which usually results in high temperatures and droughts, and significantly affects crop yields. In Q1 2014, the threat of this phenomenon was evident again (Agrimoney 2014). India's sugar production, on the other hand, relies primarily on natural rainfall, which is brought by the moist winds of the monsoons. When these winds are interrupted, production may not be enough to cover domestic demand, and, as a result, the Indian government is more likely to restrict or ban sugar exports, thus sending international prices sky-high.

Demand for sugar

Sugar is largely utilised for direct human consumption. It is used as a sweetening agent for foods and in the manufacture of sweets, cakes, puddings, preserves, soft and alcoholic beverages, and many other foods.

Although the most common uses of sugar are in home-produced and industrially produced foods, it is also used as the raw material from which

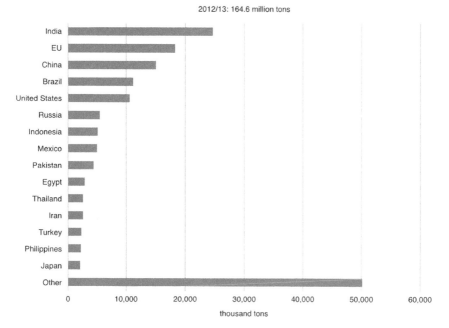

Exhibit 15.42 Top sugar consumers
Source: Author, based on data from USDA (2014)

fermentation produces ethyl alcohol, butyl alcohol, glycerine and citric acid. Sugar is an ingredient in some transparent soaps, and it can be converted to esters and ethers, some of which yield tough, insoluble and infusible resins. Of these products, ethyl alcohol has been the most popular, especially in Brazil. This is also known as ethanol, the biofuel that can be used as a gasoline additive, or entirely on its own in specially adapted car engines, and which was discussed in the energy section of this book.

Sugar consumption has the same basic economic characteristics of agricultural commodities, as described earlier. Total consumption is largely affected by the changes in total population, as well as by changes in tastes. Population growth after the end of the Second World War accounted largely for the increase in consumption. Consumption patterns, however, do differ among different groups of countries, and even among countries within the same economic grouping. High- and middle-income countries are large consumers of sugar, but have little scope for increasing their per capita consumption, which is believed to have reached a saturation point of about 45–50 kg per annum,[27] and have thus a low income elasticity of about 0.1 to 0.2.[28] On the

27 Estimates indicate that per capita sugar consumption per year is ca. 40 kg in the EU, 35 kg in Russia and most FSU countries, 60 kg in North America, 40 kg in South America, with Brazil at 42 kg. In contrast, in Japan per capita consumption is ca. 27 kg, in India 21 kg and in China 6 kg.
28 Abbot (1990, p. 25).

other hand, low-income countries have a low level of consumption per capita, with figures as low as 1–2 kg a year in the poorest of them. Income elasticities are estimated to be anything from 0.8 to 2.0, with the lower end of the range in countries with fast-rising income and changing dietary habits, which tend to regard sugar as less of a luxury and more of a necessity.

On a worldwide basis, a total of ca. 165 million metric tons of sugar were consumed in 2012–2013. Of these, 15 per cent is consumed in India, the world's largest consumer. The EU is the second largest consumption area, with Germany, France, the UK, Italy, Poland and Spain being the biggest consumers in this group. Following are China, Brazil and the United States. The remaining countries can be seen in Exhibit 15.42.

Although sugar is a most efficient sweetener, it has not been without contenders. The most widely adopted alternative source of sugar is high fructose corn syrup (HFCS), which is extracted from corn and is used as a sweetener in foods and beverages. In the United States, HFCS has substituted sugar to a great extent, especially in caloric soft drinks. Glucose and dextrose are other sources of caloric sweeteners, while increased demand for low calorie sweeteners has increased the market share of saccharin and aspartame.

Marketing and trade of sugar

Although production statistics usually group together cane and beet sugar under the common title 'raw centrifugal sugar', trade statistics distinguish between flows in raw and refined sugar. Between one-quarter and one-third of world sugar production is normally traded internationally. Latin America is the most active exporter of raw sugar, with Brazil being by far the top country in the region, generating half of the world's total exports. Thailand and Australia are the next two big exporters, both of them particularly important for the Asia Pacific Region, especially India and China. The EU used to be the largest exporter of refined (beet) sugar and a prominent exporter in general, but in recent years it has dropped down a few notches, as the contraction of the CAP has affected sugar surpluses (see Exhibit 15.43).[29]

Asia is the largest deficit region in sugar, and hence the largest importer. The EU and the United States are also net importers, mainly of raw sugar. Africa and the Middle East are two more deficit areas, and import mostly raw and some refined sugar. Beyond the top 15 importers, there are numerous more countries that import more modest quantities of sugar, so that the grouping 'Rest of the World' accounts for well over one-third of world imports (see Exhibit 15.44).

As in the case of coffee, sugar marketing is handled by different types of operators in the different stages through which the commodity goes before it reaches the final consumer. Although sugar plantations are usually owned by individuals, private companies or sometimes the state, it is government agencies

---

29 Another reason for the drop in EU exports may also been the more extensive use of beet sugar for the production of ethanol for use as an additive to motor gasoline.

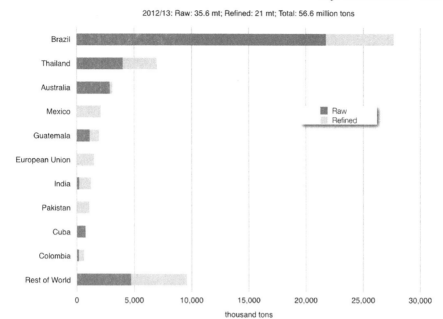

Exhibit 15.43 Top (raw and refined) sugar exporters
Source: Author, based on data from USDA (2014)

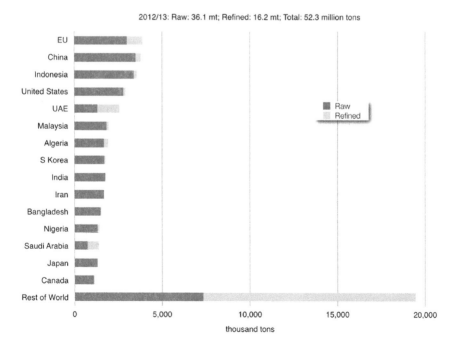

Exhibit 15.44 Top (raw and refined) sugar importers
Source: Author, based on data from USDA (2014)

that monopolise the handling and exporting of sugar in most developing and developed countries.

In many countries, state agencies handle the sale, purchase, distribution and exports of sugar. Sugar imports, on the other hand, are predominantly handled by private firms – trading houses or refiners. Frequently, private firms (especially refiners) undertake to refine and market the sugar on behalf of the exporting country.[30]

In some cases, however, government involvement is also evident in importing countries, especially when purchases are made by public tender, or when long-term supply contracts are negotiated with governments of exporting countries. Despite the existence of intergovernmental deals and the use of public tenders for sugar procurement, there is still scope for the participation of trading houses – either acting as brokers or operating on their own account – which perform the most important role of matching short-term demand and supply through the spot and forward/futures markets.

The most frequently quoted spot sugar prices are in New York (raw sugar) and London (refined sugar). The first reflects market dynamics both for the domestic sugar market and the import market for Central and South American sugar. London quotations mainly reflect the situation in the European market as refined sugar is most commonly associated with beet sugar. Finally, prices are also quoted extensively for Australian sugar, largely reflecting demand and supply conditions in the Pacific Rim. Sugar is also traded in the commodity futures markets, with a raw sugar contract traded in New York and a refined sugar contract traded in London.[31]

Conclusion

Like coffee and cocoa, sugar is an important cash crop for several developing countries. Unlike coffee and cocoa, however, sugar is also produced extensively in several developed countries, which are also the commodity's biggest consumers.

Price variability is a major concern for all producers. Developed countries have resorted to a barrage of protectionist measures, while developing countries have favoured restrictive production policies on an international scale in order to mitigate price variability. Neither approach has been particularly successful, however. International sugar agreements have become less and less relevant to the economics of supply and are essentially obsolete. Protectionist measures, on the other hand, are heavily criticised by more efficient developing exporters, and become increasingly difficult to justify to consumers, who have to pay the higher prices and bear the extra cost of administering support to producers.

30 This operation in known as *tolling*.
31 Currently (May 2014), the raw sugar contract is listed by ICE and the refined one by NYSE-Euronext-LIFFE. However, with the takeover of the latter exchange by the former, both contracts are traded and cleared under the same umbrella.

Trade is handled by a number of different types of operators: state agencies, trading companies and refiners. State agencies are usually responsible for channelling sugar in the international market; traders negotiate sales and purchases on behalf of their clients or for their own account; large refiners may also conduct transactions directly with producers, or may even undertake to refine and market sugar on behalf of producers.

References

Abbot, G.C. (1990) *Sugar*, London: Routledge.

Agrimoney (2014) 'Growing El Niño threat rattles sugar market nerves', *Agrimoney. com*, 25 March 2014, accessed onlune at: www.agrimoney.com/news/growing-el-nino-threat-rattles-sugar-market-nerves-6913.html.

Akiyama, T. and Varangis, P.N. (1990) 'The impact of the International Coffee Agreement on producing countries', *The World Bank Economic Review*, 4: 157–173.

Blas, J. (2011) 'Coffee still full of beans amid 34-year high', *FT Online*, 22 February 2011, accessed online at: www.ft.com/cms/s/0/26725f62-3ea9-11e0-834e-00144 feabdc0.html?siteedition=uk#axzz31DNEx9NE.

Dand, R. (2010) *The International Cocoa Trade*, 3rd edn, Cambridge: Woodhead.

de Graaff, J. (1986) *The Economics of Coffee*, The Netherlands: Pudoc.

FAO (2014) *FAOSTAT Database*, UN Food and Agriculture Organisation, accessed online at: http://faostat3.fao.org.

ICCO (2014) *Quarterly Bulletin of Cocoa Statistics, Vol. XL No. 2, Cocoa Year 2013/14*, accessed online at: www.icco.org/statistics/quarterly-bulletin-cocoa-statistics.html.

ICO (2014a) *ICO Indicator Prices: Annual and Monthly Averages*, International Coffee Organisation, accessed online at: www.ico.org/prices/p2.htm.

—— (2014b) *Trade Statistics*, International Coffee Organisation, accessed online at: www.ico.org/prices/m1.htm.

USDA (2014) *Production, Supply and Distribution Online*, USDA Foreign Agricultural Service, accessed online at: http://apps.fas.usda.gov/psdonline/.

Wellman, F.L. (1961) *Coffee: Botany, Cultivation and Utilization*, London: L. Hill.

16 Agricultural derivative markets

In the preceding chapters, we examined the economic fundamentals of the key agricultural commodities (thereafter abbreviated to *ags*) and analysed how demand and supply drivers interact to reach equilibrium in terms of the quantity consumed and the price paid for each commodity. We also considered the various pricing regimes for different commodities and alluded to the fact that agricultural commodity prices may change rapidly and often exhibit considerable volatility, especially due to weather effects that give rise to very variable crops from one year to the next.

In this chapter, we observe the key characteristics of ags price series and set the scene with regard to the risk implied by price movements. We then tackle the financial derivative instruments that can be used to hedge this risk and use a number of examples to demonstrate simple hedging strategies.

Overview of agricultural prices

As for most commodities, ags prices tend to be considerably volatile, especially in comparison to other asset classes such as equities and bonds. There are both demand and supply factors that contribute to this volatility, although supply is the most important in the short term. On the demand side, it can be seasonal changes in consumption, long-term changes and trends in consumer tastes, or even substitution between different types of ags as incomes increase and more expensive foods become more affordable and sought after.[1] On the supply side, production typically varies from year to year, due to weather effects, planting decisions, natural disasters and so on. These supply-side effects may differ from commodity to commodity, especially considering that some of them are annual and others perennial, but this annual variability in supply and stock availability through the year is evident for all ags. In addition, there are long-term trends in supply, reflecting the overall abundance or scarcity of land and other agricultural production inputs.

In order to acquire a view of how ags prices have moved in recent years, we use daily data from 1 January 2007 to 31 March 2014. The selected period focuses deliberately on the last few years and also includes the effects of the

---

1 The reader is referred to the discussion on income elasticity in Chapter 13.

2008 financial crisis on the prices of ags. Exhibit 16.1 shows spot prices for four representative commodities: wheat, corn, soya beans and soya bean meal. Technically, the first two are grains and the latter two come under the oilseed category, although all four compete to some extent with each other, as they are all consumed by humans either directly (processed in food preparations) or indirectly (as animal feed that is transformed into meat or in various other industrial uses).

None of the four series displays many similarities with any of the energy or metal commodities that we have seen in previous chapters. Although corn and soya beans show a steep decline from Q3 2008 to Q1 2009, the similarities end here. This is not surprising as ags tend to be staple commodities, with low-income elasticities, which means that demand does not display large cyclical fluctuations. On the other hand, note how all four price series peaked at the same time (Q3) in 2012, as a result of one of the worst droughts in the last 50 years hitting the US, affecting crops for that year.

Exhibit 16.2 displays the price series of the three key soft commodities: coffee (Colombian arabicas and robustas), cocoa and raw sugar. Note how each series follows essentially its own path, depending on the supply conditions that affect them, typically weather conditions (drought, El Niño cycles and so on).

Price series characteristics

As with most financial price series, commodity prices tend to depart from the normal assumption that they are normally distributed. A quick look at the

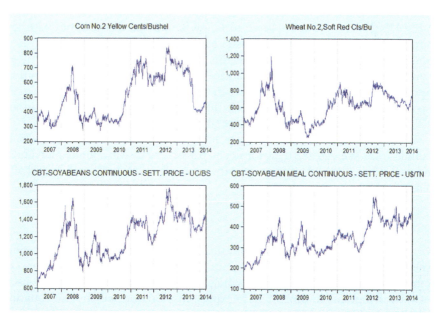

Exhibit 16.1 Corn, wheat, soya bean and soya bean meal prices

Source: Author, based on data from Thomson Reuters Datastream

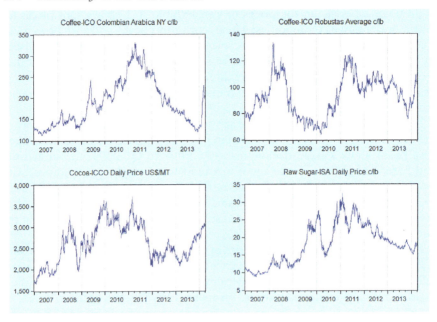

Exhibit 16.2 Agricultural commodity prices

Source: Author, based on data from Thomson Reuters Datastream

following few exhibits confirms this premise. Exhibit 16.3 displays the histogram and descriptive statistics for corn (top) and wheat (bottom) traded in the US. Both price series seem to follow a bimodal distribution, with low kurtosis, and the Jarque-Bera statistic and associated probability leads us to safely reject the null hypothesis that this is a normal distribution.

At the top of Exhibit 16.4, we can see that soya bean prices have a similar distribution and non-normality characteristics to those of corn and wheat. At the bottom of the exhibit, we can see the rather unusual looking distribution of Colombian coffee prices, which are also non-normally distributed.

Finally, the distributions of cocoa and raw sugar prices are displayed in Exhibit 16.5. We can see that, for cocoa prices, the distribution is platykurtic and non-normal, whereas, for sugar, it is trimodal, with low kurtosis and also non-normal.

Returns and volatility

We conclude this brief overview of ags price series with a look at two more aspects: returns and volatility. The return on any asset, be it a stock, bond or commodity, is defined as the percentage difference of the price of the asset between two points in time. This is expressed more formally by the equation

$$R_t = \frac{S_t - S_{t-1}}{S_{t-1}},$$

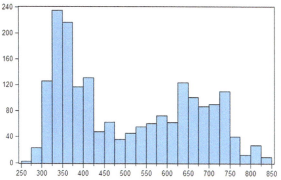

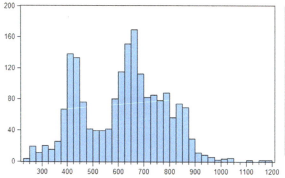

Exhibit 16.3 Histogram and descriptive statistics for corn and wheat prices

Source: Author, based on data from Thomson Reuters Datastream

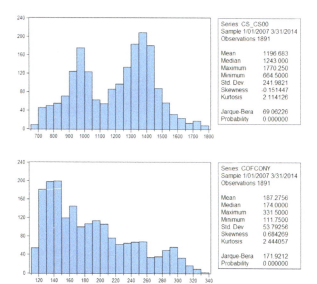

Exhibit 16.4 Histogram and descriptive statistics for soya beans and coffee prices

Source: Author, based on data from Thomson Reuters Datastream

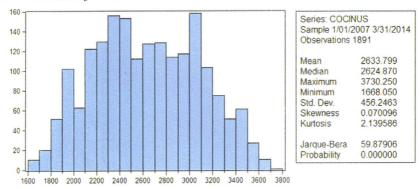

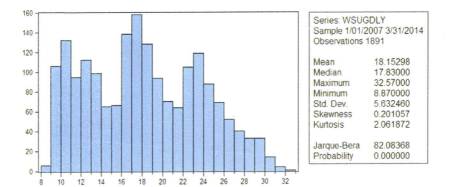

Exhibit 16.5 Histogram and descriptive statistics for cocoa and sugar prices

Source: Author, based on data from Thomson Reuters Datastream

where R_t is the return in period t, and S_t and S_{t-1} are the prices in periods t and $t-1$, respectively.

For example, say that the price for corn at the close of the market on 01-Mar is 632.25 ¢/bu and at the close of 02-Mar it is 642.50 ¢/bu. The daily return is then calculated as $(642.50 - 623.25) \div 632.25$, or alternatively $(642.50 \div 623.25) - 1$, and this is equal to 0.03089, or 3.09 per cent.

An alternative method to calculate returns, which is commonly used in finance, is to use the natural logarithm of the ratio of prices between two points in time. This means that

$$R_t = \ln \frac{S_t}{S_{t-1}}.$$

In the previous example, the return would be calculated as $\ln(642.50 \div 623.25)$, which is equal to 0.03042, or 3.04 per cent. The result is close to the result in the previous paragraph, but somewhat lower, as this method implies that returns are continuously (rather than discretely) compounded. This method has the additional advantage that returns are additive. For example, to calculate the returns on an asset in a particular week of trading days, it suffices to calculate the natural logarithm of the ratio of the last day over the first day. The result will be the same if we calculate each daily return and then add them up.

Having defined returns and how we calculate them, we now proceed to observe the returns on a selection of argicultural commodities and how these returns are distributed. Exhibit 16.6 displays the returns for corn and wheat (top and bottom left), where we can observe how they fluctuate around a mean that is very close to zero. We can also observe that the majority of returns fluctuate in the 5 per cent range around the mean, although in 2008 there were much sharper fluctuations around the mean. The frequency distribution of returns for both series are shown on the right of the same exhibit. They show the same leptokurtic distribution that is common among financial price series, as well as commodities in general. Similar observations can be made for all other agricultural commodities included in Exhibits 16.7 and 16.8.

The second aspect examined here is the volatility of commodity returns. Having defined returns in the previous paragraphs, volatility is simply the standard deviations of these returns from their mean. More formally, this is expressed as

$$\sigma_T = \sqrt{\frac{1}{T-1}\sum_{i=1}^{T}\left(R_i - \bar{R}\right)^2},$$

where T is the time period over which we calculate the volatility. A final adjustment needs to be made, with regard to the frequency (or periodicity) of the data we use to calculate the volatility. We should not be comparing volatilities between daily and monthly data, for example. To make the various calculated volatilities comparable, we need to annualise them by multiplying our σ by the square root of the number of periods in a year. More formally,

$$\sigma = \sigma_T\sqrt{P},$$

where P is 12 for monthly, 52 for weekly and 250–252 for daily return observations in a year. For example, if σ_T for daily returns over a period is 0.02, then volatility

$$\sigma = \sigma_T\sqrt{250}$$

is equal to 0.3162, or 31.62 per cent. On the other hand if σ_T of weekly returns over a period is 0.02, then volatility

$$\sigma = \sigma_T\sqrt{52}$$

is equal to 0.1442, or 14.42 per cent.

Using the definition given above and a rolling window of 60 days, we calculate the volatility for various ags in the exhibits that follow. In Exhibit 16.9, we can

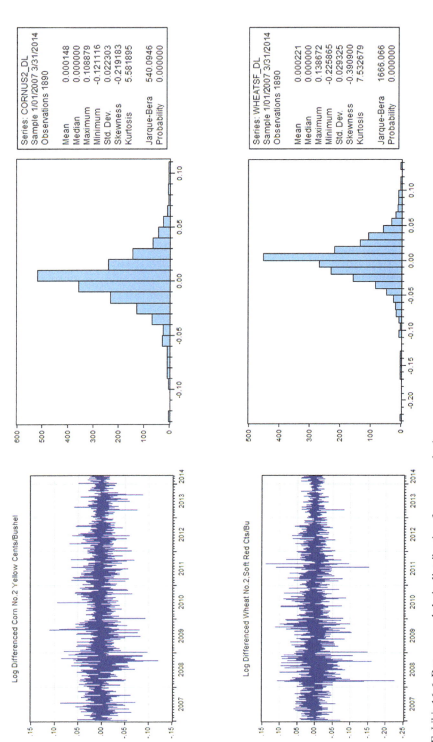

Exhibit 16.6 Returns and their distribution for corn and wheat

Source: Author, based on data from Thomson Reuters Datastream

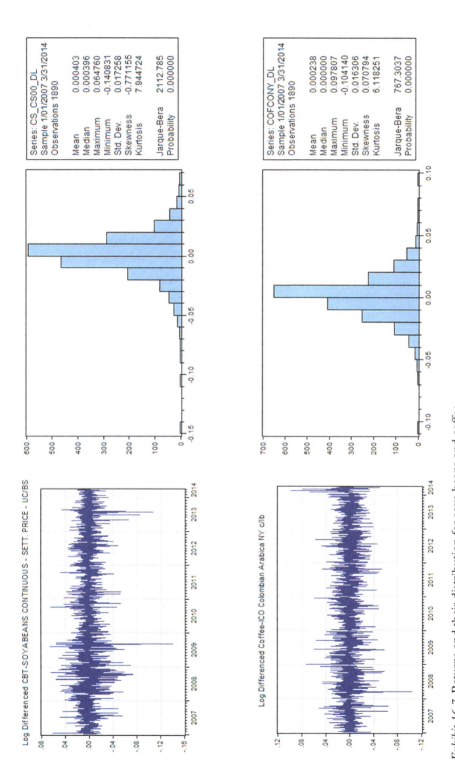

Exhibit 16.7 Returns and their distribution for soya beans and coffee

Source: Author, based on data from Thomson Reuters Datastream

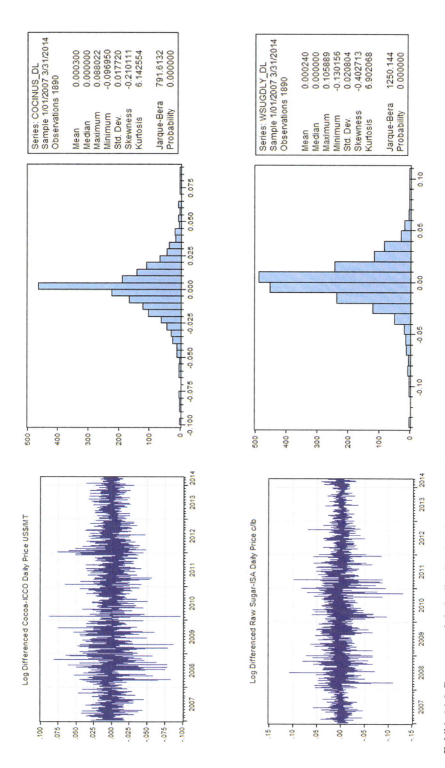

Exhibit 16.8 Returns and their distribution for cocoa and sugar

Source: Author, based on data from Thomson Reuters Datastream

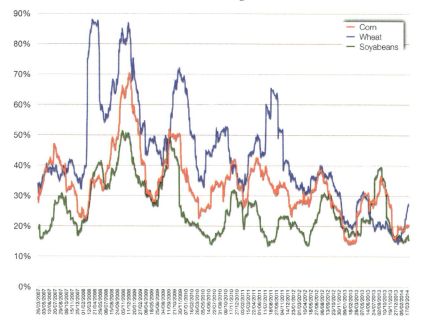

Exhibit 16.9 60-day rolling volatility for corn wheat and soya beans

Source: Author, based on data from Thomson Reuters Datastream

observe the volatilities of corn, wheat and soyabean returns. Note how all wheat volatility jumped to nearly 90 per cent soon before the 2008 harvest, which was affected by drought. Later on that year, return volatility for all three commodities jumped to between 50 and 85 per cent, as uncertainty increased about the possible impact of weather on the crops of these commodities in the southern hemisphere. In contrast to this, volatilities have settled to between 15 and 30 per cent for all three commodities in Q1 2014.

Using the same type of calculation, in Exhibit 16.10 we can observe the relatively lower range of volatilities recorded for coffee, cocoa and sugar returns.

Modelling the price processes for ags and other commodities has attracted considerable attention in academic literature. Various models have been put forward, many of them emanating from theorists studying mainstream financial markets. Hence, the very first step is normally to investigate the randomness of commodity prices and attempt to model it using a Brownian motion with a drift. In particular, the Geometric Brownian Motion (GBM) has been used to model returns in financial assets, be it stocks or commodities. The model postulates that the return on the asset (e.g. stock price) is given by the equation

$$\frac{dS_t}{S_t} = \mu \cdot dt + \sigma \cdot dW_t,$$

Exhibit 16.10 60-day rolling volatility for coffee, cocoa and sugar

Source: Author, based on data from Thomson Reuters Datastream

where μ is the drift of the process and $dW(t)$ is a Wiener process that introduces the element of randomness in returns from one period to the next.

As the GBM contains a drift term, it implies that the price of the underlying asset grows with time, which is a reasonable assumption for stocks. In commodity markets, this assumption often breaks down, as commodities tend to display a tendency to revert to a long-term equilibrium price. To address this problem, an alternative equation has been proposed instead, which is

$$\frac{dS(t)}{S(t)} = k(\theta - \ln S_t)dt + \sigma dW(t) ,$$

where θ is the long-term mean to which returns revert to and k is the speed of the mean reversion. Even a mean-reverting GBM process tends to produce price return trajectories that are relatively continuous. How can we represent, then, the often-violent upward and downward movements in stock, commodity and other asset prices? Merton (1976) introduced the jump diffusion model, where a jump component is added to the diffusion term, so that the equation now becomes

$$\frac{dS(t)}{S(t)} = \mu dt + \sigma dW(t) + U_t dN_t ,$$

where N_t denotes a Poisson distribution with intensity λ accounting for the arrival of jumps, and U_t is a real valued random variable as jumps may be positive or negative. Various other propositions have been made that extend the accuracy of the various models used to capture the diffusion process of commodity price returns. For example, Gibson and Schwartz (1990) propose a state variable model to capture the diffusion process of oil prices, whereby the two states are those of contango and backwardation and account for the change in the convenience yield. For a more expansive discussion of this and several other methods of modelling commodity prices, the reader is referred to authors such as Eydeland and Wolyniec (2003), Geman (2005), Burger *et al.* (2007), Pilipovic (2007), Geman (2008), Edwards (2010) and Pirrong (2012).

Participants in agricultural derivative markets

There are several types of participants in the agricultural derivative markets. They may be producers and consumers of the various types of agricultural commodities, as well as transformers (e.g. sugar refiners, flour mills or soya bean processors) and traders. They are typically companies, but they may also be private individuals who simply want to bet on the direction that ags prices may move.

With regard to the reasons that the various participants get involved in these markets, we can differentiate among three types: hedgers, speculators and arbitrageurs. Hedgers typically have an exposure to the physical commodity and need to offload their price risk by opening equivalent and opposite exposure in an appropriate derivative. For example, a farmer has a natural long position in the physical grain (e.g. corn) market and is afraid that the grain price may decline in the future and he will lose revenue. He may wish to hedge his risk by assuming a short (sell) position in a derivative instrument, such as a futures contract. In contrast, an ethanol plant that regularly buys corn to convert to ethanol has a natural short position in the physical market for corn. It may wish to hedge its risk by assuming a long (buy) position in an appropriate derivative instrument. For example, it may buy call options that give it the right to buy corn at a certain price, the *strike* price, which can be exercised if the market price is higher than the strike price.

Speculators do not have an underlying position on the physical commodity. Instead, they assume long and short positions on derivative instruments because they have a particular view of where the market price may go. They effectively bet on the price movement, based on their own analysis of all the fundamental and technical factors that may affect price movement. Although speculators have often been blamed for causing excessive price volatility with their buy/sell actions, they are an essential part of each and every derivative market. Their participation enhances market liquidity and they are the ones who are prepared to take on the risk that hedgers wish to offload.

Prices for a commodity between markets and across time may occasionally be out of balance. Arbitrageurs are those who seek such imbalances and act quickly to take advantage of such mispricing opportunities in order to make riskless profits. They are essential for keeping price relationships in balance and also provide additional liquidity, which is vital for the hedgers who want to be able to open and close derivatives positions quickly and effectively.

The relationship between spot and futures prices

Before we move on to the futures and other instruments, it is worth looking at the temporal element of commodity prices, and in particular the relationship between spot and futures prices. Many authors have looked at this relationship, and among the first to do so was Keynes. He posited that futures prices are generally downwards-based estimates of future spot prices. As a result, spot prices should 'normally' exceed forward prices by the amount that a producer is ready to sacrifice in order to hedge himself – a sort of 'insurance premium'. This theory is also known as the theory of normal backwardation.

In his seminal paper, Working (1949) offered an alternative explanation of the spot-future price relationship. Known as the *theory of storage*, Working's explanation links spot and future prices with the cost of capital, the storage cost and the convenience yield. The latter variable is more difficult to observe directly, but can be indirectly calculated using market data for spot and future prices, storage costs and borrowing costs.

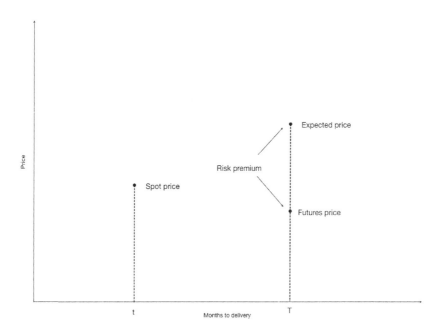

Exhibit 16.11 Spot and futures prices in the theory of normal backwardation
Source: Author

Working observed that the difference between spot and future prices, known as the *basis*, is inversely related to the level of stocks of a particular commodity. The higher the stocks, the higher the expectation that the future price will be higher than the spot price, and vice versa.

Putting this in the context of an agricultural commodity such as wheat, consider the following. If stocks of wheat are low, market participants, such as mills that need the physical commodity in order to process it into flour, will be prepared to pay a premium in order to acquire the commodity now. Their *convenience yield* for holding the physical commodity is high. Conversely, if stocks are abundant and users of the physical commodity can easily acquire it in the spot market, there is less upward pressure on the spot price, which tends to be lower than the future price.

To express the spot-future price relationship more formally, we can use the equation

$$F_t^T = S_t(1 + r_{T-t} + c_{T-t} - y_{T-t}) \,,$$

which states that the current price (time t) of the futures contract for a commodity, which is due to be delivered at time T in the future is F_t^T and equals the spot price at time t, plus the cost of storage and insurance c for the period $T - t$, plus the cost of capital r used to acquire the commodity and hold it over the same period, minus the convenience yield y. To express the same relationship using continuous compounding, we can simply restate the previous equation as

$$F_t^T = S_t \cdot e^{(r+c-y)(T-t)} \,.$$

Returning to Working's observation, the higher the stocks, the lower the convenience yield (approaching zero) and the more the price of the futures contract exceeds the spot price by the full *cost of carry* (storage, insurance and cost of capital). This relationship is graphically expressed in Exhibit 16.12.

From the previous discussion, we can deduce that there are two states with regard to the relationship between spot and future prices (i.e. the basis). If we define the basis as $F_t - S_t$ when the future price is higher than the spot, the basis is positive and the market is said to be in *contago*. Conversely, when the future price is lower than the spot, the basis is negative and the market is said to be in *backwardation*.

Depending on supply and demand conditions and market expectations, a market can switch between contango and backwardation, even on a daily basis. However, as the futures contract approaches its expiry date, the closer it comes to becoming the physical commodity (at least theoretically) and the more its price will converge to the spot price. This premise is known as *price convergence*, and we can observe it in Exhibit 16.13 for the corn spot and June-14 contract, when we eventually have convergence on the contracts expiry on 3 July 2014.

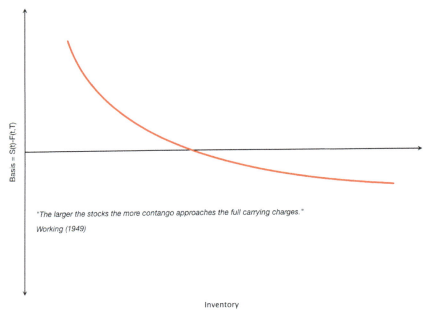

Exhibit 16.12 Relationship between inventory and basis

Source: Author

Exhibit 16.13 Price convergence of corn spot and July-14 futures contract

Source: Author, based on data from Thomson Reuters Datastream

Going a step further from the discussion above, we can also look at the relationship among the prices of a number of sequential contracts for a particular commodity, for deliveries at various points in the future. When doing so, we are building the forward curve of the particular commodity. The forward curve may be useful for a number of reasons. First, it shows how the market prices the commodity for various future delivery dates, and hence tells us where the future spot prices will be according to rational expectations. The forward curve allows us to extract the convenience yield between two different maturities. Finally, it provides forward prices for the pricing of forward contracts, options, swaps and, in general, for any risk management calculations. Exhibit 16.14 shows the forward curves for corn and wheat prices on a particular date in June 2014.

Derivative contracts

There is a wide array of derivative products that are contingent on energy, and indeed several other commodities. Forwards, futures, swaps and options are some of the most commonly used ones and we will examine them all in brief.

Forward contracts

A forward contract is the simplest and most straightforward means for two parties to agree the physical sale and purchase of a commodity. The quantity,

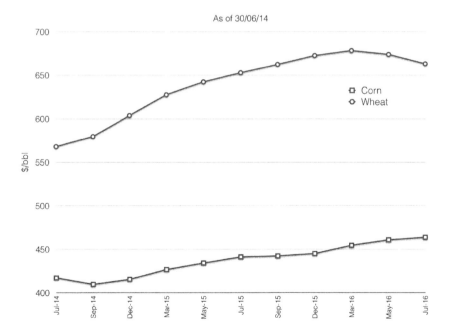

Exhibit 16.14 Forward curves for corn and wheat

Source: Author, based on data from Thomson Reuters Eikon

quality, delivery specifications and price are all negotiable between the buyer and the seller, hence a forward contract is fully customisable and very flexible. However, once written, a forward contract cannot be reversed, unless the two parties mutually agree to do so and are prepared to incur any contingent penalties. In addition, the contract cannot be sold on to a different party as there is no secondary market for these instruments. Finally, one of the key risks of a forward contract is that either party may default on their obligations, in which case the entire transaction simply collapses.

Futures contracts

In contrast to the bilateral transaction model of the forward market, a futures market brings all transactions under the umbrella of the exchange. When a party buys (goes *long*) or sells (goes *short*), a contract for the commodity, the counterparty is the exchange clearing house, which guarantees that the transaction will be honoured. To achieve this, market participants are required to make an initial deposit (the *initial margin*) with the exchange, proportional to the value of the position they open, and then maintain their deposit at a minimum level required by the exchange (the *maintenance margin*), until they decide to terminate their position. For the exchange and the market partici-pants at large, this system calculated the profits and losses of each position on a daily basis (*marking to market*), and any participants with an account balance below the required maintenance margin is required to pay up additional amounts of money (*margin calls*) in order to continue trading.

This is best illustrated by an example. Let us assume that Max Profit, a seasoned corn trader, decides to open a long position on the CME corn contract for September 2014, because he feels that the price of corn will be rising. On 9 June, he puts an order to buy five Sep-14 contracts (each for 5,000 bushels of corn) and his broker fills the order at a price of 447.50 ¢/bu. In order to open the position, Max has to deposit an initial margin of $3,000 per contract (i.e. a total of $15,000 for his overall position). He also has a maintenance margin of $2,750 per contract (i.e. his overall balance should not fall below $13,750, otherwise he will be asked for a margin call high enough to restore his balance to the initial margin).

Over the next few days, he maintains his position, but as the market moves, so does the balance of his account that his broker keeps on his behalf with the exchange. Exhibit 16.15 shows how the settlement price of the Sep-14 contract fluctuates on a daily basis and the result on Max's margin account, until he decides to close his position and exit.

If Max decides to close his position, he is most likely to do this by *offsetting*. This means that he simply has to sell the same number of an identical futures contract (for the same commodity and the same delivery month), incurring the normal brokerage fees and taking any profit or loss he may have made on his position.

Offsetting is one of four methods that may be available for closing a futures position. The other three are: exchange of futures for physical, cash settlement and physical delivery.

Date	Day	Price (c/bu)	Daily P&L ($)	Margin account ($)	Variation margin ($)
09/06/14	1	447.50		15,000.00	
10/06/14	2	441.25	-1,562.50	13,437.50	1,562.50
11/06/14	3	437.50	-937.50	14,062.50	0.00
12/06/14	4	440.00	625.00	14,687.50	0.00
13/06/14	5	443.00	750.00	15,437.50	0.00
16/06/14	6	436.75	-1,562.50	13,875.00	0.00
17/06/14	7	434.00	-687.50	13,187.50	1,812.50
18/06/14	8	435.50	375.00	15,375.00	0.00
19/06/14	9	444.25	2,187.50	17,562.50	0.00
20/06/14	10	448.25	1,000.00	18,562.50	0.00
23/06/14	11	439.00	-2,312.50	16,250.00	0.00
24/06/14	12	436.75	-562.50	15,687.50	0.00
25/06/14	13	435.75	-250.00	15,437.50	0.00
26/06/14	14	439.00	812.50	16,250.00	0.00
27/06/14	15	442.25	812.50	17,062.50	0.00
			Net P/L	-1,312.50	

Exhibit 16.15 Marking to market for CME corn contract
Source: Author

An *exchange of futures for physical* (EFP) involves two parties, one with a long and one with a short futures position. The two parties can identify each other with the mediation of the commodity exchange and agree to swap their futures position and at the same time enter a transaction on the physical commodity. They may do so before the expiry of the specific contract, but they have to carry out the transaction under the supervision of the exchange authorities. It is also required that their futures positions match the size of the physical transaction on the commodity.

To illustrate this, consider the following. We are in May and two traders, FarmCo and MillCo, have previously opened a short and a long futures position, respectively, using the CME July corn futures. FarmCo has sold 10 contracts and MillCo has bought 10 contracts. At some point during May, before the expiry of the July contract, the two parties decide they wish to engage in an EFP transaction. They approach the exchange authorities and request their mediation to find an appropriate match. The exchange puts the two traders in contact and gives them the go ahead to engage in the transaction. MillCo and FarmCo agree to exchange their futures positions, so that both parties clear their respective paper transactions. At the same time, they agree that FarmCo will sell to MillCo 50,000 bushels of corn. The transaction happens privately between the two parties, but the price and transaction particulars have to be reported back to the exchange authorities, who verify that this is a *bona fide* commercial transaction. Note also that the two paper positions that have been exchanged (10 contracts) equate to the quantity of the physical corn quantity (50,000 bushels).

If there is no offsetting or EFP transaction before the expiry of a futures contract, market participants, whether long or short, can simply settle their positions in cash. *Cash settlement* is available for most futures contracts, and in some cases it is the only alternative to offsetting (i.e. no type of physical delivery is allowed). It simply requires traders to make payments to settle their gains or losses at the expiration of the contract.

If no other method is used, and the exchange regulations allow it, an open position can be settled by making a *physical delivery* of the commodity underlying the contracts. In this situation, it is typically the short position holder that notifies the exchange of the need to arrange a physical delivery. The exchange tries to find suitable long position holders and put them in touch with the short position holder, who normally determines exactly which commodity (of the ones allowed by the futures contract specification) and where it is delivered. The price can be negotiated between the two parties, but it is normally a differential from the official exchange price and has to be reported back to the exchange, as in the case of the EFP.

In our earlier example, Max Profit opened a long position at a certain market price. If the price moves higher than the price he bought at, then he will be making a profit, which he may decide to realise by reversing his position and closing out the contract. If he maintains his position and the price falls below his initial purchase price, then he will make an overall loss. For a graphical demonstration of the profits or losses from a long futures position, see Exhibit 16.16. On the horizontal axis is the price of the commodity, which rises as we move from left to right. On the vertical axis is the profit the trader makes in relation to the price at which he opened the long position. The pay-offs are represented by a positively sloping line (from the bottom left to the top right).

Conversely, Exhibit 16.17 demonstrates the pay-offs of a short futures position. As the price falls (towards the left of the horizontal axis), the short position becomes profitable. The trader can simply reverse it by buying back at a lower price and booking the profit. If the price increases, on the other hand, the position is loss-making. He can either reverse it and take the losses, or maintain it and make any necessary margin payments to keep his account in credit.

There are several commodity exchanges listing futures contracts for an array of agricultural commodities, including grains, oilseeds and soft commodities. The two key exchanges, where most trading activity takes place, are the Intercontinental Exchange (ICE) and CME Group (which incorporates the Chicago Board of Trade). Other exchanges include TOCOM in Japan and MCX in India, although the list is not exhaustive. A small selection of some of the most popular contracts is given in Exhibit 16.18.

CME lists the three most popular and liquid grain contracts: corn, soya beans and wheat. It also lists several contracts for other grains (such as oats and rough rice), livestock (for cattle and hogs), dairy and forest products. ICE, on the other hand, lists the most popular contracts for soft commodities, including its flagship coffee 'C' contract for arabicas, sugar No. 11 for raw sugar and cocoa. In addition, the exchange lists contracts for canola (rapeseed), robusta coffee, cotton and frozen concentrated orange juice (FCOJ).

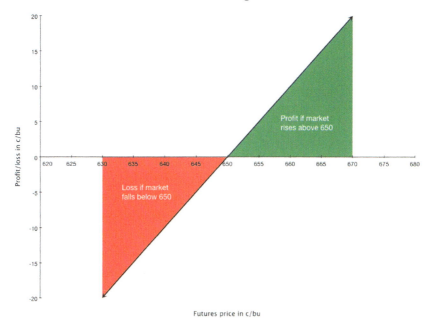

Exhibit 16.16 Pay-offs from a long futures position

Source: Author

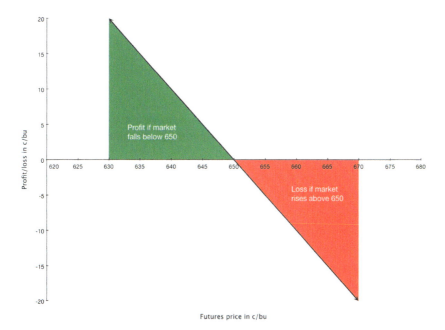

Exhibit 16.17 Pay-offs from a short futures position

Source: Author

Contract name	Exchange	Price quotation Tick	Contract size	Contracts traded	Contract expiry
Corn	CME	cents/bu 1/4 cent/bu	5,000 bushels	March, May, July, September, December	The business day prior to the 15th calendar day of the contract month
Soya beans	CME	cents/bu 1/4 cent/bu	5,000 bushels	March, May, July, September, December	The business day prior to the 15th calendar day of the contract month
Soft red winter wheat	CME	cents/bu 1/4 cent/bu	5,000 bushels	March, May, July, September, December	The business day prior to the 15th calendar day of the contract month
Soya bean meal	CME	$ and cents/st 10 cents/st	100 short tons	January, March, May, July, August, September, October, December	The business day prior to the 15th calendar day of the contract month
Soya bean oil	CME	cents/lb 1/100th cent/lb	60,000 lbs	January, March, May, July, August, September, October, December	The business day prior to the 15th calendar day of the contract month
Rough rice	CME	cents/CWT 1/2 cent/cwt	2,000 hundredweights (cwt)	January, March, May, July, September, November	The business day prior to the 15th calendar day of the contract month
Coffee 'C' Arabica	ICE	cents and 1/100 c/lb 5/100 c/lb	37,500 lbs	March, May, July, September, December	Eight business days prior to the last business day of the delivery month
Coffee Robusta	ICE	$ per metric ton $1/ton	10 metric tons	January, March, May, July, September, November	Last business day of the delivery month
Cocoa	ICE	$ per metric ton $1/ton	10 metric tons	March, May, July, September, December	Eleven business days prior to the last business day of the delivery month
Sugar No. 11	ICE	cents and 1/100 c/lb 1/100 c/lb	112,000 lbs	March, May, July, October	Last business day of the month preceding the delivery month
FCOJ-A Frozen concentrate orange juice	ICE	cents and 1/100 c/lb 5/100 c/lb	15,000 lbs orange juice solids	January, March, May, July, September, November	14th business day prior to the last business day of the month

Exhibit 16.18 List of agriculture futures contracts
Source: Author

Spread contracts

It is not always relevant to trade in simple (or *plain vanilla*) long and short positions. Frequently, one can construct a hedge for a more complex position, or indeed find a profitable opportunity, by using simultaneous positions in two ore more closely associated contracts. Hence, the exposure is not on the full (or *flat*) price of the commodity, but on the price differential (or *spread*) instead. In ags, as indeed in other commodities, there are opportunities to construct three key type of spreads: *calendar*, *inter-commodity* (or cross-commodity) and *raw material-product*.

A calendar spread involves a long position in a futures contract for delivery in one month and a short position in another contract for delivery in a different month. The spread is then known by the name of the two months. For example, a May-July corn spread is a one-contract calendar spread and involves the two adjacent futures contracts for CME corn for May and July. When the trader goes long the closest month and short the furthest month, he buys the spread. Conversely, selling a May-July spread would involve selling May and buying July contracts. With spreads, the trader takes a position on the price differential between the two months (i.e. the level of contango or backwardation, rather than the flat price movement of the underlying commodity).

A cross-commodity spread involves the sale and purchase of two contracts for different but related commodities, usually for the same delivery month. A typical cross-commodity spread in ags is that for two different grains. The most popular version is the corn-wheat spread, whereby a trader may buy a corn contract for a certain delivery month and at the same time sell a wheat contract for the same month. For example, going long the September corn-wheat spread implies the purchase of September corn contracts and the sale of the same number of September wheat contracts. In this example, the trader anticipates that the price differential between the two grains will narrow (i.e. corn will become relatively more expensive and wheat relatively cheaper). Changes in the spread could be explained by factors such as quality differentials, delivery terms, transport costs, and supply/demand imbalances in the respective markets of the different grains.

In the context of agricultural commodities, there are two raw material-product spreads: the *soya bean crush* and the *corn crush* spread. We will look at both of them in turn.

The soya bean crush refers to the gross processing margin (GPM) of a soya bean processor who buys soya beans and processes (*crushes*) them to produce soya meal and soya oil. This typically means that a bushel of soya beans weighing an average of 60 lb is crushed to produce 48 lb of soya meal and 11 lb of soya oil, leaving 1 lb of hulls and waste. The processor is exposed, therefore, to the price risk of all three commodities and his GPM has considerable volatility, as can be seen from Exhibit 16.19.

He may wish to hedge this risk by using the corresponding CME futures contracts. As it happens, the three contracts are traded in entirely different

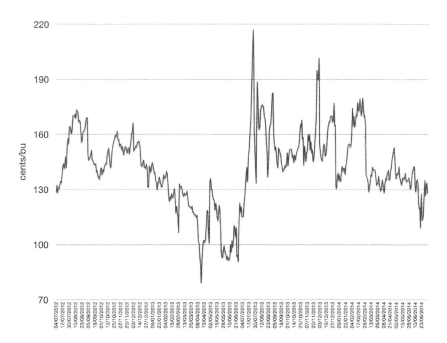

Exhibit 16.19 Soya bean crush spread

Source: Author, based on data from Thomson Reuters Datastream

units: soya beans in bushels (5,000 bu per contract), soya meal in short tons (100 st per contract) and soya oil in pounds (60,000 lbs per contract). To illustrate the use of a soya bean crush hedge, consider the example in Exhibit 16.20. Note the implied GPM at the beginning of the hedging period (137.5 ¢/bu) and how it has declined at the end of the period (118.2 ¢/bu). His profit from the futures market helps him increase his effective GPM and leaves him better off.

In a similar way, the corn crush spread refers to the GPM of an ethanol producer who buys corn, processes it and sells ethanol and distiller's dried grains (DDGs, which are used as animal feedstuff). This typically means that a bushel of corn yields an average of 2.8 gallons of ethanol and 17 lb of DDGs. The processor is exposed, therefore, to the price risk of all three commodities and his GPM has considerable volatility, as can be seen from Exhibit 16.21.

He may wish to hedge this risk by using the corresponding CME futures contracts. As it happens, the three contracts are traded, again, in entirely different units: corn in bushels (5,000 bu/contract), ethanol in gallons (29,000 gls/contract) and DDG in short tons (100 st/contract). To illustrate the use of a corn crush hedge, consider the example in Exhibit 16.22.

Note the implied GPM at the beginning of the hedging period (11.9 ¢/bu) and how it has almost been wiped out at the end of the period (2.7 ¢/bu). His profit from the futures market helps him increase his effective GPM to 13.2 ¢/bu and leaves him in a much better position.

On 01-Mar-14 a soya bean processor enters into a deal to supply soya meal and soya oil to customers in early May-14. To fulfill the order he will require to purchase 50,000 bushels of soya beans at the end of Apr-14

He decides to hedge his GPM by purchasing soybean contracts and selling soya meal and soya oil contracts

His physical exposure is for 50,000 bu of soya beans ⇒ buy 10 x 5,000 bu May bean contracts

He will produce 50,000 x 48 lbs = 2,400,000 lbs meal = 1,200 short tons ⇒ sell 12 x 100 st May meal contracts

He will produce 50,000 x 11 lbs = 550,000 lbs oil ⇒ sell 9 x 60,000 lbs May oil contracts (to closer whole contract)

Soya bean crush hedge for April 2014		
	Physical market	**Futures market**
01-Mar-14	Soya beans: 1506 c/bu Soya meal: $490/st Soya oil: 42.50 c/lb *Implied GPM: $68,750 or 137.5 c/bu*	Buy 10 May bean @ 1530.75 c/bu Sell 12 May meal @ $503.90/st Sell 9 May oil @ 42.38 c/lb
30-Apr-14	Buys cash soya beans @ 1395 c/bu Sells cash soya meal @ $438/st Sells cash soya oil @ 42 c/lb	Sell 10 May bean @ 1409.25 c/bu Buy 12 May meal @ $450.50/st Buy 9 May oil @ 41.88 c/lb
	Beans cost: 1395 c/bu x 50,000 = - $697,500 Meal revenue: $438/st x 1,200 = + $525,600 Oil revenue: 42 c/lb x 550,000 = + $231,000	Bean: -121.5c/bu x 10 x 5,000 = - $60,750 Meal: +$53.4/st x 12 x 100 = + $64,080 Oil: +0.50 c/lb x 9 x 60,000 = + $2,700
	Cash GPM = $59,100 or 118.2 c/bu	Futures profit = + $6,030

Net GPM = 59,100 + 6,030 = $65,130 or 130.26 c/bu

Exhibit 16.20 Example of soya bean crush hedge

Source: Author

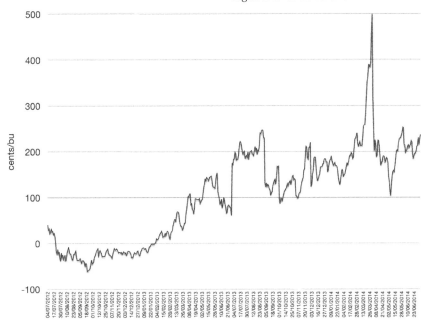

Exhibit 16.21 Corn crush spread

Source: Author, based on data from Thomson Reuters Datastream

On 01-Mar-14 an ethanol producer enters into a deal to supply ethanol to customers in early May-14. To fulfill the order he will require to purchase 50,000 bushels of corn at the end of Apr-14

He decides to hedge his GPM by purchasing corn contracts and selling ethanol and DDG contracts

His physical exposure is for 50,000 bu of corn ⇒ buy 10 x 5,000 bu May bean contracts

He will produce 50,000 x 2.8 gls = 140,000 gls ethanol ⇒ sell 5 x 29,000 gls May ethanol contracts (to closer whole contract)

He will produce 50,000 x 17 lbs = 850,000 lbs DDG = 425 short tons ⇒ sell 4 x 100 st May DDG contracts (to closer whole contract)

Corn crush hedge for April 2014		
	Physical market	**Futures market**
01-Mar-14	Corn: 715 c/bu Ethanol: $2.28/gl DDG: 114/st *Implied GPM: $5,950 or 11.9 c/bu*	Buy 10 May corn @ 727 c/bu Sell 5 May ethanol @ $2.30/gl Sell 4 May DDG @ $115/st
30-Apr-14	Buys cash corn @ 750 c/bu Sells cash ethanol @ $2.33/gl Sells cash DDG @ $118/st	Sell 10 May corn @ 756 c/bu Buy 5 May ethanol @ $2.35/gl Buy 4 May DDG @ $120/st
	Corn costs: 750 c/bu x 50,000 = - $375,000 Ethanol revenue: $2.33/st x 140,000 = + $326,200 DDG revenue: $118/st x 425 = + $50,150	Corn: + 29c/bu x 10 x 5,000 = + $14,500 Ethanol: - $0.05/gl x 5 x 29,000 = - $7,250 DDG: - $5/st x 4 x 100 = - $2,000
	Cash GPM = $1,350 or 2.7 c/bu	Futures profit = + $5,250
	Net GPM = 1,350 + 5,250 = $6,600 or 13.2 c/bu	

Exhibit 16.22 Example of corn crush hedge

Source: Author, based on data from Thomson Reuters Datastream

Swap contracts

As discussed earlier, a forward contract can be used to hedge price risk exposure for a particular time in the future for any commodity, as long as the two transacting parties agree the commodity quality and quantity. This gives both parties flexibility on the contract specifics, but leaves both parties exposed to each other's default risk. Alternatively, a hedger can use the futures market to cover his price risk exposure in the physical market. In this case, the counterparty risk is undertaken by the commodity exchange, but the hedger may be limited in terms of the futures contracts that are available, and which may not match the precise quality and delivery specification of his physical commodity.

To resolve these shortcomings, financial intermediaries developed the *swap*, a derivative instrument that is essentially an exchange of a fixed for a floating price. Swaps can be used by traders to hedge exposures in the physical market for numerous agricultural commodities. As long as there is a published, commonly accepted price benchmark for a commodity of a specific quality and delivery, a swap can be constructed. The swap transfers the price risk from the commodity seller (producer) or buyer (consumer) to a financial intermediary – the swap provider – who warehouses the risk. In exchange, the swap provider can benefit from movements of the market in his favour. Once the provider has entered the swap agreement, he has to cover the risk exposure. Ultimately, the ideal way to cover this risk may be to arrange a counterbalancing swap with another financial institution, for an equal and opposite position. As swaps are less frequent in the context of agricultural commodities, the reader is referred to Chapters 7 and 12, where there is a more detailed discussion on energy and metal swaps.

Option contracts

Forward, futures and swap contracts share one common element: they are all designed to counterbalance the profit or losses made in the physical market. This is welcome when the hedger makes a loss in the physical, as his profit in the paper market will compensate for all or most of his loss. Conversely, however, any profits made in the physical market will also be wiped out by losses in the paper market. Ultimately, this is the nature of hedging, unwelcome though it may be on some occasions.

One way of hedging against unfavourable market movements, while still being able to take advantage of the upside potential of favourable market swings, is to use options contracts. Traded options (on futures) contracts are traded on both CME and ICE. In addition, there are countless more OTC contracts that are designed to deal with specific aspects of risk, both in terms of the price and in terms of the volume of the commodity in question.

Basic definitions and contract types

Let us start, though, with a brief definition of the key types of options contracts and how they work. An option gives the right, but not the obligation, to the buyer to buy or sell a commodity (the underlying asset) at a specified price (the *strike* price), up to a certain point in the future (the *expiry* date). For the privilege, the buyer of the option has to pay an upfront fee (the *premium*) to the seller (or writer) of the option.

Options may grant the right to buy (*call* option) or sell (*put* option). For some options, this right can only be exercised at expiry (*European-style* option), while for others it can be exercised on any day up to expiry (*American-style* option).

Now that the basic characteristics of plain-vanilla options have been stated, it is time to discuss how each type of option works. Panel A of Exhibit 16.23 demonstrates the pay-offs for the buyer (long) call option written on corn, with a strike price of 650 ¢/bu, with an expiry at the end of November 2014, and for which a premium of 20 ¢/bu has been paid. The horizontal axis shows the price of the underlying asset, while the vertical axis shows the profit or loss made for each price. If the price remains below 650, there is no benefit from exercising the option and the buyer simply loses his premium. As the price rises to 650 and above, the option becomes valuable and can be exercised. Once the price rises enough to equate the strike price plus the premium, the overall position yields a profit. For example, if exercised when the underlying price is 690 ¢/bu, the buyer will buy his corn at the strike price of 650 ¢/bu and, as he has already paid a premium of 20 ¢/bu, he will have a net purchase price of 670 ¢/bu. He can then sell his corn at the market price of 690 ¢/bu and realise a profit of 20 ¢/bu.

The opposite pay-off takes place for the buyer (long) of a put option (panel B), who gets a profit out of exercising the option when the market price falls below the strike price of 650 ¢/bu. When the market price falls to, say, 620 ¢/bu, he will exercise his option to sell his corn at the strike price of 650 ¢/bu. Having paid a 20 ¢/bu premium already, he will receive a net price of 630 ¢/bu, which will leave him 10 ¢/bu better off than the current market price.

Panels C and D of Exhibit 16.23 show the pay-offs from the point of view of the option seller (short). In the case of a short call, as long as the underlying price remains below the strike price, the option will remain unexercised and he will simply receive his premium of 20 ¢/bu. If the price rises above the strike price, he will have to pay to the buyer of the call the difference between the market price and the strike price. The seller of a put has a pay-off schedule that is the mirror image of a short call, and the reader can work this out easily from panel D.

Although options can be used on their own simply to speculate, they are normally part of a hedging portfolio for market participants with a physical exposure in the underlying commodity. For example, a corn processor that is short on corn on the physical side may want to protect himself from paying an excessively high price for his corn input, but is happy to take advantage of the higher profitability when corn prices (i.e. his input costs) fall. To do this, the processor may wish to buy a call option that, in combination with his physical position, will help him form a *cap* on the price he pays for his corn. This combination is also called a *covered call*, and its pay-offs are shown in

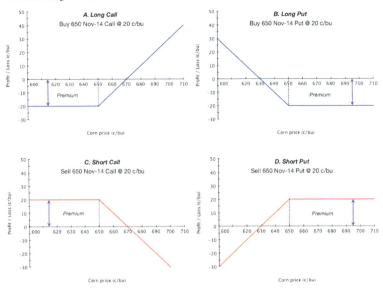

Exhibit 16.23 Basic option pay-offs

Source: Author

Exhibit 16.24. The processor's short physical position (-S) is depicted by the downward-sloping red line, while the pay-off of the long call option is shown by the now familiar green line, which implies that the strike price is 650 ¢/bu at a premium of 10 ¢/bu. If the market price of corn rises above the strike price, the option can be exercised. When the market price rises above 660 (the strike price plus the premium), any additional losses in the physical market (in the form of higher corn purchase costs) will be cancelled out by the payment that the processor will receive, which will equal the differential between the market price and the strike price. The combined pay-offs are depicted by the blue line, which sets a cap to the loss of profitability as the market price rises above 650 ¢/bu. This means that the effective purchase price for the corn cannot exceed (is capped at) 660 ¢/bu.

To help us understand how a cap works, consider the example given in Exhibit 16.25. Here, a processor has a commitment to supply corn starch and other products and will need to buy a certain quantity of corn at the end of a specified period. The processor decides to hedge the risk of rising corn prices by buying a call option at the specified price and premium. The exhibit provides the specific information on prices and data and then sets out two scenarios: one of falling and one of rising corn prices. Note how, in the second scenario, the effective purchase price for the processor (the cap) is set at 660 ¢/bu (i.e. the strike price plus the premium).

Just like a purchaser of the commodity is afraid that the market price will rise, a producer wants to hedge against prices going down, which will results in a loss of income from selling the commodity. In this case, the producer is

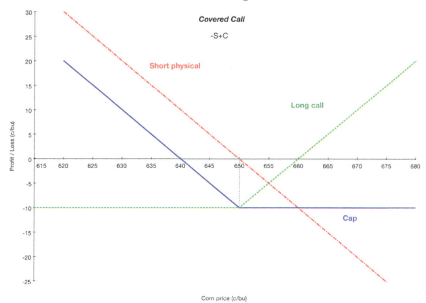

Exhibit 16.24 Covered call (cap)

Source: Author

On 01-Mar-14 a processor enters into a deal to supply corn starch and several other corn products to be delivered by end of May-14. To fulfill the order it will require to purchase 500,000 bushels of corn at the end of Apr-14

It decides to hedge the corn cost by buying a call option

Corn price at 01-Mar-14 = 645 c/bu

Corn required at the end of Apr, so expiry is 30-Apr-14

Amount required is 500,000 bu

Buy Apr 14 Call with strike price 650 c/bu @ premium 10 c/bu

Cap hedge for April 2014	
Physical market	**Options market**
Corn price on 01-Mar-14: 645 c/bu Current cost of oil: $3,225,000 (=500,000 x 645 ÷ 100)	Buy Apr-14 call, strike price 650 @ 10 c/bu Call cost: $50,000 (= 10 x 500,000 ÷ 100)
First scenario - Falling corn prices	
Corn price on 30-Apr-14: 630 c/bu Actual cost of oil: $3,150,000	Strike price (650) > Settlement price (630) Option NOT exercised
Total corn cost (incl. option premium) = 3,150,000 + 50,000 = $3,200,000 ***or 640 c/bu***	
Second scenario – Rising corn prices	
Corn price on 30-Apr-14: 680 c/bu Actual cost of oil: $3,400,000	Strike price (650) < Settlement price (680) Option IS exercised Payoff from options (680-650) x 500,000 ÷ 100 - 50,000 = $100,000
Total corn cost (incl. option payoff) = 3,400,000 - 100,000 = $3,300,000 ***or 660 c/bu***	

Exhibit 16.25 Cap hedge example

Source: Author

interested in fixing a minimum price (a *floor*) at which he can sell his production if prices fall, while still being able to take advantage of favourable price upswings. In this case, the producer may wish to enter a *protective put*, as described in Exhibit 16.26. Here, a farmer has a long physical exposure to corn, which is depicted by the upward-sloping red line. The more the market price falls, the more he stands to lose. He can therefore buy (long) a put option that will establish a floor for the price he gets for his corn. This is depicted by the now familiar green line, which implies that the put option has a strike price of 650 ¢/bu and a premium of 10 ¢/bu. If the market price of crude oil falls below the strike price, the option can be exercised. When the market price falls below 640 ¢/bu (the strike price minus the premium), any additional losses in the physical market (in the form of lower income from selling corn) will be cancelled out by the payment that the farmer will receive, which will equal the differential between the market price and the strike price. The combined pay-offs are depicted by the blue line, which sets a floor to the loss of income as the market price falls below 650 ¢/bu. This means that the effective sale price for the corn cannot fall below (has a floor of) 640 ¢/bu.

To help us understand how a floor works, consider the example given in Exibit 16.27. Here, a farmer is worried about the market price he will manage to get for his corn in the third quarter of the year. The farmer decides to hedge the risk of falling corn prices by buying a strip of put options at the specified prices and premiums. The exhibit provides the specific information on prices and data and then sets out two scenarios: one of rising and one of falling corn prices. Note how, in the second scenario, the effective sale price for the farmer (the floor) is set at 560 ¢/bu (i.e. the strike price minus the premium).

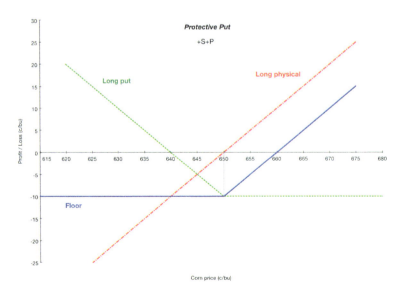

Exhibit 16.26 Protective put (floor)

Source: Author

In 01-May-14 a farmer is worried about the uncertainty of the corn market and would like to hedge its revenue from selling corn for the third quarter (Jul-Sep) of 2014. He decides to buy a strip of three put options as described below

Corn price at 01-May-14 = 580 c/bu

Production 300,000 bushels/month

Buy a strip of puts for Q3-14

Jul-14 put, strike 570 @ premium 10 c/bu; Aug-14 put, strike 570 c/bu @ premium 15 c/bu;

Sep-14 put, strike 570 c/bu @ premium 20 c/bu

Floor hedge for Q3 2014 - July payoffs	
Physical market	**Options market**
Corn price on 01-May-14: 580 c/bu Current expected revenue per month: $1,740,000 (=300,000 x 580 ÷ 100)	Buy Jul-14 put, strike price 570 c/bu @ 10 c/bu Put cost: $30,000 (= 10 x 300,000 ÷100) for the month
First scenario - Rising corn prices	
Corn price on 30-Jul-14: 620 c/bu Actual revenue per month: $1,860,000	Strike price (570) < Settlement price (620) Option NOT exercised
Total corn revenue (incl. option premium) = 1,860,000 - 30,000 = $1,830,000 or 610 c/bu	
Second scenario – Falling corn prices	
Corn price on 30-Jul-14: 530 c/bu Actual revenue per month: $1,590,000	Strike price (570) > Settlement price (530) Option IS exercised Payoff from options (570-530) x 300,000 ÷ 100 - 30,000 = $90,000
Total corn revenue (incl. option payoff) = 1,590,000 + 90,000 = $1,680,000 or 560 c/bu	
Repeat for Aug-14 and Sep-14, using the appropriate option premium	

Exhibit 16.27 Floor hedge example

Source: Author

The example only gives the results for the July-14 part of the strip, but the reader should be able to work out the remaining two months with little additional effort.

Useful though a protective put may be, it does create a substantial outflow of cash in the form of the upfront premium payment. In the previous example, the premium cost just for one month amounts to $30,000, whereas for the whole Q3 strip it is $135,000. It is not surprising, therefore, that option buyers are keen on constructing hedges that are less expensive.

A *collar* is a good example of such a hedge and works as follows. Imagine that the farmer in the previous example still wants to create a floor on the price that he receives for his corn, but he is willing to forego some of the profit opportunity he may have if corn prices rise. To do this in practice, he can sell (write) a call option, for which he will receive a premium, but which may require him to make payments to the buyer of the call if the corn price rises. Exhibit 16.28 shows this combination of a long put (green line) and a short call (blue line), with the farmer's natural long physical position (red line) on the commodity. As implied by the diagram, while the market price stands at 650 ¢/bu, the farmer has bought an out-of-the-money put at a strike price of 630 ¢/bu and sold an out-of-the-money call at a strike price of 670 ¢/bu. As long as the market price fluctuates between these two prices, the oil producer will simply get the market price and the premium of 20 ¢/bu he pays for the put will be covered by the 20 ¢/bu premium he receives for the call (zero cost). If the price drops below 630, his put option will become valuable and worth exercising. Let us say that the price drops to 610. This means that he will receive 610 ¢/bu from the market for his corn, as well as 20 ¢/bu from the option writer, a total of 630 ¢/bu, which is 20 ¢/bu below the original market price of 650 ¢/bu. Conversely, if the price rises above 670 ¢/bu, he will be making higher profits on the physical side, but he will have to make payments to the buyer of the call option. For example, if the price climbs to 690 ¢/bu, he will be receiving 690 ¢/bu, but he will have to pay 20 ¢/bu to the call buyer, leaving him a net income of 670 ¢/bu. In short, using a zero-cost collar, the farmer has created a collar between 630 and 670 ¢/bu, and hence protects himself from excess losses, but also foregoes excess profits.

In addition to plain-vanilla options and combinations thereof, several more complicated (or *exotic*) options have developed over time, in response to the needs of market participants and the peculiarities of certain commodities. One such type is an *average price* or *Asian* option. This is a European option with a settlement price calculated as an arithmetic average of underlying prices (e.g. spot or futures) over a period of time, typically one calendar month. More formally, the value of an Asian option is given as

$$V_{AP} = \max(A_T^t - K, 0) \ ,$$

where

$$A_T^t = \frac{\sum_{i=t}^{T} S_t}{T - \tau} .$$

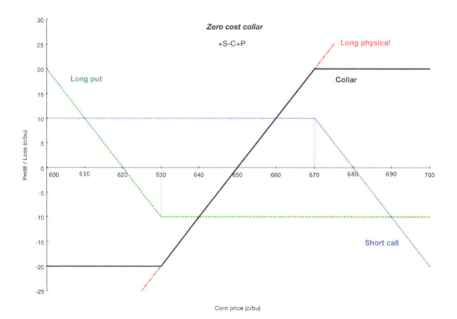

Exhibit 16.28 Zero-cost collar

Source: Author

This type of option is popular in all commodity groups, and in general for commodities or assets where the physical trade is done over a monthly or longer period, or where the underlying price is not easily identifiable or can be easily influenced.

Often the main risk is not found in the flat price of a commodity, but on the price differential between related commodity prices (i.e. the price spread). Spreads were discussed earlier, and one can simply envisage the purchase of options on the various types of spreads we encountered, such as calendar, inter-commodity and crush spreads.

A final type of option that is quite interesting is *quantos*. A quanto is a composite option, combining price risk hedging of the underlying commodity price in the currency in which the commodity is traded, as well as risk hedging of the exchange rate between the commodity currency and the user's base currency. For example, consider a European coffee roaster who buys arabica and robusta coffee from the international market in order to distribute it to its domestic customers. The coffee is bought at international prices, which are volatile and are denominated in US dollars. On the other hand, the coffee roaster is obliged to sell its ground coffee to its customers in euros and is only flexible to vary his sale prices at regular intervals (say quarterly). The risk faced by the utility is not only the commodity price risk from gas, but also the \$/€ currency risk. A quanto option allows the utility to hedge both risks at the same time with one instrument.

Basics of option pricing

As can be seen from the above discussion, options offer ample opportunities to hedge a variety of risks, both in terms of the price and the volume of the underlying commodity. Calculating the value and price of an option has been a challenging task, tackled by numerous authors, until the breakthrough by Black and Scholes (1973), who discussed pricing of European stock options. Their formula for pricing a European call option on a stock, $C_t^{K,T} = S_t N(d_1) - Ke^{-r(T-t)}N(d_2)$, is an elegant closed-form solution, whereby $C_t^{K,T}$ is the price at time t of a call option with strike price K and maturity T, $e^{-r(T-t)}$ is the discount factor until maturity and $N(x)$ is the cumulative normal distribution function. Once the price of a call is known, the put price can be calculated from the put-call parity: $P_t^{K,T} = S_t = C_t^{K,T} + Ke^{-r(T-t)}$, where $P_t^{K,T}$ is the price at time t of a put option and the other terms are as described earlier. This solution does come with a number of assumptions, however. These include continuous trading of the underlying stock, lack of tax and transaction costs, lack of dividend payments, knowledge and non-variability of the short-term interest rate, as well as the assumption that the price of the underlying stock is driven by a GBM process.

Merton (1973) extended the B-S pricing model by allowing interest rates to be stochastic, the option to be American-style and the stock to pay dividends. This latter property is quite relevant to commodities, as the convenience yield for a commodity works in a similar way as a dividend payment for the value of the stock. Hence, the formula for a European call option written on a spot commodity price can now be written as $C_t^{K,T} = S_t e^{-y(T-t)} N(d_1) - K e^{-r(T-t)} N(d_2)$, where y is the convenience yield. In a further breakthrough, Merton (1976) tackled the assumption of the price dynamics being described by a continuous-time diffusion process. He introduced the jump-diffusion process (mentioned earlier in this chapter), which allows the coexistence of both a continuous price motion and a jump stochastic process.

Black (1976) discussed the pricing of options written on futures contracts, which is particularly relevant to commodities, as many of the options written are of this type. The price for a call option with a strike price K and expiry time T, written on a futures contract F with expiry T_1, is given by the formula $C_t^{K,T} = F_t^T e^{-r(T-t)} N(d_1) - K e^{-r(T-t)} N(d_2)$. Finally, Cox *et al.* (1979) extended the option pricing literature by introducing their binomial option pricing methodology, which allows itself to generalisation and can be used to price more complex options.

A final note in this analysis is the brief mention of the sensitivity of an option value with respect to changes in the market parameters. These are commonly known as the *Greeks*. Starting with *delta* (Δ), this is the partial derivative of the call price C with respect to the price S of the underlying asset and it is positive (negative for a put option). *Gamma* (Γ) is the rate of change (i.e. the derivative) of Δ. *Theta* (θ) is the partial derivative of the option price with respect to time and is negative for both a put and a call option, representing the loss of the value of the option due to time decay. *Vega* is the rate of change of the option price with respect to the volatility σ and is positive for puts and calls – the higher the volatility, the higher the chance that the option will be exercised. Finally, *rho* (ρ) is the partial derivative of the option price with respect to the risk-free interest rate r.

The purpose of the preceding discussion was to only briefly expose the reader to some of the most important literature in the area of options and their pricing. For a more expansive discussion of option pricing methodologies for commodities, the reader is referred to Eydeland and Wolyniec (2003, Chapter 8), Geman (2005, Chapters 4–6), Burger *et al.* (2007, Chapter 2) and Edwards (2010, Chapters 3.4–3.6).

Conclusion

This chapter completes the review of agricultural markets undertaken in the previous three chapters. The focus was placed on the characteristics of the various agricultural commodity prices and the instruments available for hedging the price risk posed by the market. Although there is considerable overlap with respect to the range of derivative instruments available to the various commodity groups, we have geared the analysis primarily towards agricultural derivative contracts. It is now time to turn a close the journey through the key commodity groups – energy, metals and agriculture – in the hope that the reader has at least developed an appreciation of what is a long-running, fascinating, exciting and, hopefully, profitable industry.

References

Black, F. (1976) 'The pricing of commodity contracts', *Journal of Financial Economics*, 3: 167–179.

Black, F. and Scholes, M. (1973) 'The pricing of options and corporate liabilities', *Journal of Political Economy*, 81: 637–654.

Burger, M., Graeber, B. and Schindlmayr, G. (2007) *Managing Energy Risk: An Integrated View on Power and Other Energy Markets*, Chichester: Wiley.

Cox, J.C., Ross, S.A. and Rubinstein, M. (1979) 'Option pricing: a simplified approach', *Journal of Financial Economics*, 7: 229–263.

Edwards, D.W. (2010) *Energy Trading and Investing: Trading, Risk Management and Structuring Deals in the Energy Markets*, McGraw-Hill.

Eydeland, A. and Wolyniec, K. (2003) *Energy and Power Risk Management: New Developments in Modeling, Pricing and Hedging*, Hoboken, NJ: Wiley.

Geman, H. (2005) *Commodities and Commodity Derivatives: Modeling and Pricing for Agriculturals, Metals, and Energy*, Chichester: Wiley.

—— (2008) *Risk Management in Commodity Markets: From Shipping to Agricuturals and Energy*, Chichester: Wiley.

Gibson, R. and Schwartz, E. (1990) 'Stochastic convenience yield and the pricing of oil contingent claims', *The Journal of Finance*, 45: 959–976.

Merton, R.C. (1973) 'The theory of rational option pricing', *Bell Journal of Economics and Management Science*, 4: 141–183.

—— (1976) 'Option pricing when underlying stock returns are discontinuous', *Journal of Financial Economics*, 3: 125–144.

Pilipovic, D. (2007) *Energy Risk: Valuing and Managing Energy Derivatives*, 2nd edn, McGraw-Hill.

Pirrong, C. (2012) *Commodity Price Dynamics: A Structural Approach*, Cambridge: Cambridge University Press.

Working, H. (1949) 'The theory of price of storage', *American Economic Review*, 39: 1254–1262.

Index